THE
AGRARIAN HISTORY OF
ENGLAND AND WALES

THE
AGRARIAN HISTORY OF
ENGLAND AND WALES

GENERAL EDITOR

H. P. R. FINBERG

M.A., D.LITT., F.S.A., F.R.HIST.S.

Professor Emeritus of English Local History
University of Leicester

I·II

A.D. 43–1042

THE AGRARIAN HISTORY OF ENGLAND AND WALES

* Already published

iv

PREFACE

BY THE GENERAL EDITOR

THE FIRST volume of the *Agrarian History* is planned to begin in the New Stone Age and to end at A.D. 1042. It thus moves from a period in which archaeological evidence is all-important to one in which the written word claims more attention. Partly for this reason, partly because in the effort to complete their contributions the historians have left the archaeologists behind (but we hope not far behind), it has been decided to publish the volume in two parts, with the second part, covering the agrarian history of Roman Britain, post-Roman Wales, and Anglo-Saxon England, appearing first.

The first part will concern itself with the Stone Age, the Bronze Age, and the pre-Roman Iron Age. These chapters will be written by Professor Stuart Piggott, Professor Charles Thomas, and Mr P. J. Fowler. In addition the history of livestock from the beginning to 1042 is being written by Dr M. L. Ryder.

H. P. R. FINBERG

ADVISORY COMMITTEE
FOR THE AGRARIAN HISTORY OF
ENGLAND AND WALES

1956

THE
AGRARIAN HISTORY OF
ENGLAND AND WALES

VOLUME I

II. A.D. 43–1042

EDITED BY
H. P. R. FINBERG
M.A., D.LITT., F.S.A., F.R.HIST.S.
Professor Emeritus of English Local History
University of Leicester

CAMBRIDGE
AT THE UNIVERSITY PRESS
1972

Published by the Syndics of the Cambridge University Press
Bentley House, 200 Euston Road, London NW1 2DB
American Branch: 32 East 57th Street, New York, N.Y.10022

© Cambridge University Press 1972

Library of Congress Catalogue Card Number: 66-19763

ISBN: 0 521 08423 7

Printed in Great Britain
at the University Printing House, Cambridge
(Brooke Crutchley, University Printer)

CONTENTS

Roman Britain

By S. APPLEBAUM, B.Litt., D.Phil.
Professor of Classical Archaeology
University of Tel Aviv

Post-Roman Wales

By GLANVILLE R. J. JONES, M.A.
Reader in Historical Geography
University of Leeds

Anglo-Saxon England to 1042

By H.P.R. FINBERG, M.A., D.LITT., F.S.A., F.R.HIST.S.
Professor Emeritus of English Local History
University of Leicester

ILLUSTRATIONS

ACKNOWLEDGEMENTS

The editor, contributors, and publisher are grateful to the following for granting permission to reproduce copyright material: to the Ashmolean Museum, Oxford, for plates I and II; to the Council for British Archaeology for figs. 1, 3, and 40, and also to the Royal Commission on Historical Monuments for fig. 3; to the Land Utilization Survey of Britain for fig. 4; to Routledge and Kegan Paul Ltd. and to Praeger Publishers Inc. for fig. 7 (from A. L. F. Rivet: *Roman Villa in Britain*: 1969); to the *Journal of Roman Studies* and to Mr W. H. Manning for figs. 8 and 9; to the Society of Antiquaries of London for fig. 12; to Methuen and Co. Ltd. for fig. 28 and for fig. 33 (from Ward: *Romano-British Buildings and Earthworks*, 1911); to the Council of the Dorset Natural History and Archaeological Society for fig. 29; to the Ministry of Defence, Air-Force Department, for Plate III; and to Mrs Helen Smith for fig. 49 (from Gwyn Jones: *History of the Vikings*, 1968).

ABBREVIATIONS

A	*Archaeologia*
AA	*Archaeologia Aeliana*
AC	*Archaeologia Cambrensis*
A. Cant.	*Archaeologia Cantiana*
ACR	C. Fox, *The Archaeology of the Cambridge Region*, 1923
AHR	*Agricultural History Review*
ANL	*Archaeological Newsletter*
Ant.	*Antiquity*
Ant. J.	*Antiquaries Journal*
Arch. J.	*Archaeological Journal*
BBCS	*Bulletin* of the Board of Celtic Studies
BGAS	*Transactions* of the Bristol and Gloucestershire Archaeological Society
BJ	*Bonner Jahrbücher*
BkAJ	*Berkshire Archaeological Journal*
BM	British Museum
BRGK	*Bericht der römisch-germanischen Kommission*
BUS	*Proceedings* of the Bristol University Spelaeological Society
CAH	Cambridge Ancient History
CAS	*Proceedings* of the Cambridge Antiquarian Society
CBA.RR	Council for British Archaeology: *Research Reports*
CEH	*Cambridge Economic History*
CIL	*Corpus Inscriptionum Latinarum*
Corn. Arch.	*Cornish Archaeology*
CS	*Cartularium Saxonicum*, ed. W. de G. Birch
CW	*Transactions* of the Cumberland and Westmorland Antiquarian and Archaeological Society
DB	Domesday Book
DNHAS	*Proceedings* of the Dorset Natural History and Archaeological Society
EAS	*Transactions* of the Essex Archaeological Society
EE	*Ephemeris Epigraphica*, 1872–1913
EHAS	*Transactions* of the East Hertfordshire Archaeological Society
EHD	*English Historical Documents*
EHR	*English Historical Review*
ESAR	T. Frank, *An Economic Survey of Ancient Rome*, 1933–40
HFC	*Papers and Proceedings* of the Hampshire Field Club
It. Ant.	*Itinerarium Antonini*, ed. Wesseling, 1735

ILS	H. Dessau, *Inscriptiones Latinae Selectae*, 1892
JBAA	*Journal* of the British Archaeological Association
JRS	Journal of Roman Studies
K	Kemble, *Codex Diplomaticus Aevi Saxonici*
LAA	*Liverpool Annals of Archaeology and Anthropology*
LHA	*Lincolnshire History and Archaeology*
LMAS	*Transactions* of the London and Middlesex Archaeological Society
LUS	*The Land Utilization Survey of Britain*
MA	*Medieval Archaeology*
NA	*Norfolk Archaeology*
Not. Dig.	*Notitia Dignitatum Utriusque Imperii*, ed. O. Seeck, 1876
OM	*Oudheidskundige Mededeelingen*
Oxon.	*Oxoniensia*
PN	*Publications* of the English Place-Name Society
PPS	*Proceedings* of the Prehistoric Society
PPSEA	*Proceedings* of the Prehistoric Society of East Anglia
PRIA	*Proceedings* of the Royal Irish Academy
PRSAI	*Proceedings* of the Royal Society of Antiquaries of Ireland
PSA	*Proceedings* of the Society of Antiquaries
PSAS	*Proceedings* of the Society of Antiquaries of Scotland
PSIA	*Proceedings* of the Suffolk Institute of Archaeology
PWRE	Paully-Wissowa. *Realenzyklopädie der classischen Altertumswissenschaft*, 1894–
R	Robertson, *Anglo-Saxon Charters*
RBES	R. G. Collingwood, J. N. L. Myres, *Roman Britain and the English Settlements*, 1937
RCAHM	Royal Commission on Ancient and Historical Monuments (Wales): *Inventories*
RCHM	Royal Commission for Historical Monuments (England): *Inventories*
RIB	R. G. Collingwood, R. P. Wright, *Roman Inscriptions of Britain*, I, 1965
RNNB	I. A. Richmond (ed.), *Roman and Native in North Britain*, 1958
RVB	A. L. F. Rivet (ed.), *The Roman Villa in Britain*, 1969
RV Bel.	R. de Maeyer, *De Romeinsche Villa's in België*, 1937
SAC	*Sussex Archaeological Collections*
SANHS	*Transactions* of the Somerset Archaeological and Natural History Society
SARR	*Report of the Research Committee* of the London Society of Antiquaries

SHAAS   Saint Albans and Hertfordshire Architectural and
            Archaeological Society, *Transactions*
SyAC   *Surrey Archaeological Collections*
SxNQ   *Sussex Notes and Queries*
TRHS   *Transactions* of the Royal Historical Society
VCH   *Victoria County History*
W   Whitelock, *Anglo-Saxon Wills*
WAM   *Wiltshire Archaeological Magazine*
WHR   *Welsh History Review*
YAJ   *Yorkshire Archaeological Journal*

ROMAN BRITAIN

By S. APPLEBAUM, B.Litt., D.Phil.

Professor of Classical Archaeology,
University of Tel Aviv

FOREWORD

A WRITER ON the agrarian history of Roman Britain faces a situation in which the rapid progress of related research is only equalled by the relative slowness of publication, and by the growth of criticism of older published work which should furnish him with much of his raw material. Despite the labours of a few pioneers, it is only in the last few decades that students have become aware of the importance of the agricultural aspect of Roman Britain, and even today, although the techniques of archaeological investigation have been vastly expanded, an understanding of agriculture is not their inevitable accompaniment.

Faced with such a situation, the author might have found it easier to ignore the greater part of the work published down to 1950 and to avoid drawing conclusions based on researches conducted since that year. Clearly neither course was open to him; the risk had to be taken of finding a way between the unreliability of past data and generalizations based on unsummarized research. An endeavour has accordingly been made to distinguish the common, and, by inference, more reliable features emerging from past investigations of Roman villas and agricultural sites, and to reinterpret them in the light of new discoveries and of agricultural considerations.

It were well to observe that much that is fresh emerges from a new angle of approach, i.e. by taking into account the factors which a farmer would regard as important; such an approach lends the force of probability to many assumptions which may seem mere conjectures to those less familiar with the farmer's job. As the writer has been one of the few to apply this approach to Roman Britain, it has been necessary to describe in the present chapters much of his own unpublished research, the like of which it would not be necessary to reproduce in relation to later and better documented periods. However many conclusions may be modified as enquiry progresses, therefore, the present work will be justified if it directs readers to a new approach and to a new line of thinking.

The debts incurred, during the writing of these chapters, to various institutions, scholars, and workers in the field of Roman Britain, are so numerous that it is impossible to mention them all individually. Some of them are referred to in the footnotes, but I cannot refrain from naming a few colleagues whose aid and encouragement have been outstanding. I have been privileged to experience the friendship, inspiration, instruction, and hospitality of my teacher, C. E. Stevens, and my debt to him is immeasurable. The work also received the encouragement of Professor Sir Mortimer Wheeler, and has benefited from the criticisms of Professor Christopher Hawkes, Professor Stuart Piggott, and especially of P. J. Fowler, one of the younger workers who is tackling the essential problems of ancient agriculture in Britain systematically and squarely. Miss J. Liversidge placed at my disposal her thesis on *Roman Villas in Britain*, an inexhaustible mine of indispensable knowledge. G. C. Boon has for years furnished me tirelessly with all sorts of invaluable information. Among others who have assisted me are Professor H. Godwin, N. H. Field, Professor G. Clark, Dr E. W. Russell, Dr G. Webster, Humphrey Case, Professor A. E. van Giffen, G. Willis, R. S. R. Fitter, Miss E. Wightman, D. C. Brown, Mrs S. Hallam, Monsieur P. Fournier, and a host of museum authorities and excavators.

Among the institutions whose courtesies I have enjoyed are the Archaeological Division of the Ordnance Survey, in the persons of its former director, C. W. Phillips and of its present director, D. J. Stagg; the Land Utilization Survey of Britain; the Buro für Oedheidsbodenonderzoek of the Netherlands Government; the Ashmolean Museum, and last but not least, the Haverfield Library, Oxford, with its courteous and tireless staff.

The work has been generously assisted by the Sir Isaac Wolfson Research Fund and by my own college, the King's Hall and College of Brasenose. The University of Haifa, with true academic catholicity, has obtained for me books which hardly come within the purview of its normal fields of tuition.

I wish to record the patience and ready efficiency of the Cambridge University Press.

Lastly, I have enjoyed the encouragement, staunch support, and hospitality of the Editor of the *Agrarian History*, Professor H. P. R. Finberg.

Without the collaboration of all these, the work would have been impossible; but its errors are my own.

S.A.

CHAPTER I

THE CLIMATE

CLEARLY NO study of the agrarian life of Roman Britain can afford to neglect the character of the climate in the period under consideration. The opening of the British Early Iron Age coincided approximately with a deterioration of climate towards a greater humidity. The Roman period, indeed, as a whole falls within the Sub-Atlantic phase, whose characteristic European conditions were those of greater coolness and wetness as compared with the preceding Sub-Boreal phase. In the Somerset peats, Clapham and Godwin found that the infertile humus-free layer overlying the clear upper limit of a dry period corresponded with the Early Iron Age and with the onset of the wetter Sub-Atlantic climate, and that flooded areas between the Poldens and Wedmore had already then assumed the state of raised bog which had continued to grow to the end of Roman times. In the English Fenland a find of late Early Iron Age beads a few inches below the top of the upper peat suggested that peat-formation had continued down to the Roman conquest; this is confirmed at Blackstone Edge (Yorks), for instance, where a Roman road overlay twenty-two inches of peat, and was covered by a further peat-stratum. At Warcock Hill, Marsden, in the same district, Roman pottery was found three feet below the peat-surface, pointing in the same direction.[1]

In the Fenland the Roman period saw the covering of the seaward margin of the upper peat by calcareous marl silt owing to marine transgression; these silts extended into the peat in the form of roddons or silt levees which were formed in the course of the Roman period. While the silts were intensively inhabited from the last quarter of the first century A.D., it is important to note that only the silt areas and roddons exhibit Romano-British occupation; the peat remains practically uninhabited, thus showing a continuation of moist conditions.

In Somerset the evidence of climatic deterioration in the later Roman period is less definite. It is known that peat growth ceased in late Roman times at Shapwick Heath, but it is not clear if this was due to

[1] For ancient statements on the climate of Britain: Diodorus Siculus, v, 21, 6; Strabo, IV, 5, 2 (C. 200); Caesar, de Bell. Gall., v, 12, 7; Tacitus, Agric., 12, 3. They convey that the country was moist, misty, but temperate. Climatic deterioration: H. Godwin, The History of the British Flora, Cambridge, 1956, pp. 58, 339 sqq.; Somerset: Clapham and Godwin, Philosophical Trans., 233 B, 1947/9, 233 sqq.; Fenland, ibid., 229 B, 1939, p. 393; Blackstone Edge: Journ. of Ecology XVII, 1929, p. 14; Warcock Hill: ibid., p. 15. For the Fenland, see further p. 228.

marine transgression or to flooding by base-rich water from the uplands in a deteriorating climate. The laying down of silt over pits containing fourth-century pottery north of the Avon proved the late Roman marine transgression; and a similar phenomenon was observed on the Portishead-Clevedon ridge in 1956, where five Romano-British ditches were found to have been sealed by marine flooding, apparently before the fourth century. The discovery of a Roman building on King's Sedgemoor beneath a layer of peat nevertheless suggests, though it does not prove, that this transgression was accompanied by a climatic deterioration.[1]

Of a steady worsening of the British climate in the direction of increased precipitation, which reached a maximum somewhere towards A.D. 500, there is now ample evidence derived from the radiocarbon measurement of peat samples from a number of localities in England and Scotland. As an instance may be cited the results from Hatfield Moors (Yorks), where no less than six samples gave a consistent dating between A.D. 400–600.

How much wetter the climate became in the course of this deterioration, as compared with preceding or present conditions, cannot be ascertained; but suggestive evidence was obtained by General Pitt-Rivers at Rushmore (Dors), where he found that the Roman wells were much shallower than their modern counterparts, and remained dry when the latter filled up. Thus, unless some purely local geological factor was involved, the water-table was higher in Roman times and the climate possibly wetter than it is today. Against the validity of such a conclusion we should however set the influence of improved modern drainage. Evidence in the same direction is nevertheless to be seen in the location of Roman villas in central Hampshire on the upper courses of streams where they have long ceased to flow except in especially wet seasons.[2]

[1] Fenlands: Godwin, *Geological Journ.* xci, pp. 241 sqq.; cf. *Philosophical Trans.*, 233 B, p. 397; G. Fowler, CAS xliii, p. 12; the silts, *Ant. J.* xxix, 1949, p. 160; Fowler, CAS xliii, p. 9, and appendix, pp. 14 sqq. Shapwick Heath: *Philosophical Trans.*, 233 B, pp. 275 sqq. The Avon: information from G. C. Boon; Portishead-Clevedon: JRS: xlvii, 1957, p. 221; King's Sedgemoor: VCH *Som.*, I, p. 325, no. 6.

[2] *Radiocarbon* 4, 1962, 57–70, pp. 64–6, Q 483–6. Rushmore: Pitt-Rivers, *Excavations in Cranbourne Chase*, I, London, 1887, p. 27 and pl. v. Hampshire: Williams-Freeman, *An Introduction to Field Archaeology as illustrated in Hampshire*, London, 1915, p. 118, fig. 12. H. H. Lamb, *The Changing Climate: Selected Papers*, London, 1966, pp. 7, 162, 174, believes that the climate of Britain became dryer and probably warmer in the Roman period, and so similar to that at present. I cannot find that he cites evidence for this view, and the bulk of the known evidence on vineyards, which he believes to favour it, belongs to the Middle Ages. The evidence for such in Roman times (see above, pp. 117–19) might argue for higher temperatures but not necessarily for lower rainfall.

CHAPTER II

THE PRE-ROMAN HERITAGE

I T IS easier to trace the pre-Roman antecedents of Romano-British
agriculture than to isolate its specifically Roman characteristics. Ever
since the discovery and progressive exploration of the so-called
'Celtic' field system in the years between the two world wars, it has
become increasingly evident that a considerable part of the cultivable
land of lowland Britain continued to be tilled in the Roman period
much as it had been before it, and that over broad areas there was
a direct continuity between the Early Iron Age and Roman field
systems. Since this discovery, the problem has emerged, how far the
'Celtic', to be called from here on the 'native' field system, was
expanded in the Roman period, and what was the scale of its extent
before the conquest. It has also become evident that in the Roman
period at least, the native fields were not confined to the chalk downland areas where they had first been detected because the surviving
traces are there most responsive to the air-camera; air-reconnaissance
has now revealed their ramifications on the gravel terraces of the
river valleys in the west and east Midlands – the Trent, the Nene, the
Ouse, the Welland, and the Severn, and likewise in the Upper Thames
valley, where their presence was known before the development of
air-photography, though their full scope could not then be appreciated.
The investigation of the native field system has also revealed that only
in the lowland area of Britain, i.e. south of a line drawn from the
Dee south of the Peak District and north-eastward to Flamborough
Head, is this system pre-Roman in origin; in the highland zone,
apparently, agriculture remained at a Bronze-Age level till the Roman
conquest, and in so far as complexes of Early Iron Age type exist in north
Britain (chiefly in the Pennines), they originated under Roman rule.[1]

[1] The expression 'Celtic' field system has been abandoned as inaccurate. The
expression 'native' fields, though not as precise as could be wished, is at least not
historically misleading, although it is open to the criticism that it also seems to have
been used by romanized villa-owners in a number of cases. For the system generally:
O. G. S. Crawford, *Air Survey and Archaeology*, OS Professional Papers, N.S., 7,
Southampton, 1924; G. A. Holleyman, *Ant.* IX, 1935, pp. 443 sqq.; O. G. S. Craw-
ford, A. Keiller, *Wessex from the Air*, Oxford, 1928; E. Curwen, *Prehistoric Sussex*,
London, 1929; H. C. Bowen, *Ancient Fields*, London, 1961. Midland Surveys: *A
Matter of Time, an Archaeological Survey of the River Gravels of England*, RCHM,
London, 1960. The Highland Zone: S. Piggott, in I. A. Richmond (ed.), *Roman and
Native in North Britain* (RNNB), Edinburgh, 1958, pp. 11 sqq.

As has been abundantly revealed in the chapter on the agriculture of the Early Iron Age, the field complexes of that period do not represent a chronologically homogeneous phenomenon, and the unravelling of the chronological problem, if it can be achieved, is only at its beginning. But closer examination of the fields of the Fenland Area, which are *a priori* not earlier than the Roman period, shows that here too more than one type of system is represented and that in places one type superseded another. Hence the 'native' field system of the Roman period may not be itself of uniform character, and probably underwent certain modifications in the course of the occupation.

The difficult problem in the study of the native field areas is, as stated, to isolate the Roman from the pre-Roman features. On the other hand, it seems probable that far the greater part of these areas was cultivated in our period: in Berkshire, where the system covers an area of some 8,000 acres, P. Rhodes found pre-Roman pottery over only twenty per cent of the fields. In relation to the Sussex Downs, where the 'native' fields are virtually continuous, it has been stated that no Early Iron Age settlement has been found associated with a continuous tract of such; by inference, therefore, the system at its full uninterrupted extent was a feature of the Roman epoch. This evidence, naturally, is open to qualification; surface pottery is not always representative, and deeper finds may tell another story. Nevertheless, there is independent testimony of the expansion of the 'native' type of field under Roman rule; apart from the Fenland colonization, certain field forms are in all probability to be ascribed exclusively to the Roman period, and some Roman villas are associated with fields of pre-Roman appearance.

A degree of continuity between Early Iron Age and Romano-British rural sites may be demonstrated by citing a few examples from one or two districts. In the Basingstoke district four Early Iron Age sites without Belgic evidence continued their lives into the Roman period, and seven Belgic sites did the same. In the Letchworth region (Herts), whereas three Belgic settlement-points appear to have been abandoned with the Roman conquest, occupation went on at Wilbury, Baldock, and Weston. In Hertfordshire generally the main rural centres of the Roman period were all Belgic settlements (Welwyn, Braughing, Sandy, Baldock), hence the Roman roads between them may safely be assumed to represent routes in use before the conquest. Belgic pottery-sherds have been recorded on the sites of at least three Kentish villas, and pre-Roman coins at several Medway valley sites, as also at other villas in Hampshire and Somerset. Ample evidence for the occupation of native sites into the Roman era in Surrey has been forthcoming. Direct continuity of occupation and land-use cannot be postulated in all these cases, but instances are now to hand where excavations have revealed as clearly as could be hoped the native predecessors of Roman farmsteads. Beneath the carefully excavated villa at Park Street near St Albans a Belgic dwelling was found; likewise the native farms which preceded the villas of West Blatchington (Suss), Mansfield Woodhouse (Notts), and Norton Disney (Notts). Examples could be multiplied, but the point need not be laboured. On a slightly lower level of living may be cited the persistence of Romano-British farms on native sites at Casterley (Wilts) and Iwerne (Dors), both with degrees of romanization, and at the barely romanized steadings of Cranbourne Chase (Woodcuts, Rotherley). On some sites, on the other hand, change of proprietorship can be reasonably postulated, and an example is at Woodham's Farm near King's Worthy (Hants), where on an air-photograph a native farm of characteristically Early Iron Age type can be seen beneath the Roman villa, but no transitional phase is discernible, and the presence of a new, Roman, field system, is probable.[1]

The rudimentary features of the villa economy, indeed, are discernible before the Roman period and can be traced in the Belgic economy of south and south-eastern Britain. The construction of a fortified farm on a considerable scale is represented by Casterley, where an earthworked enclosure of sixty-eight acres surrounds a homestead made in the late Belgic period, and contains interior ditched enclosures which must have served as stock-yards and working areas, in a manner similar to those of the Cranbourne Chase farms. It is reasonable to suppose that the forty or so vacant acres inside the rampart were used for agriculture and constituted a considerable part (possibly all) of the farm's arable. But the farm itself clearly never housed or employed all the man-power necessary to construct a bank surrounding sixty-eight acres, much less defend it, and this must have come from the ranks of a population settled in the vicinity but owing some allegiance to the owner of the farm. The social pattern must therefore have corresponded to the noble with client peasantry of whom we hear in Caesar's Gaul, and the political setting must have been the comparatively recent conquest of Wessex by the Belgic invaders during the last few decades before the Roman invasion.[2]

[1] Berkshire: information from P. Rhodes. Sussex Downs: Holleyman, ANL 7, 1948, p. 16. The Basingstoke Region: HFC xviii, 1953–4, p. 122. Letchworth Region: survey conducted by the writer. Belgic pottery at Kentish villas: Otford, Faversham, Lullingstone etc.; cf. Philp, A. Cant. lxxviii, 1963, pp. 74 sqq.; VCH Kent, iii, p. 102. Hants and Som: Collingwood in Frank, ESAR iii, Baltimore, 1937, p. 83; J. Liversidge, Roman Villas in Britain, Cambridge M.Litt. thesis, 1949, p. 342.

[2] It has been questioned whether the Casterley earthwork was Belgic, and the farmhouse a farm rather than a temple (cf. Maiden Castle and Chanctonbury). I can

On a larger scale, some hill-forts of the later Early Iron Age in Britain had become centres of cultivation, and under the influence of a developing export trade in grain, cattle, and skins, a profitable agriculture was spreading onto the heavier loams, consonant with the ability of the Belgic plough to cut more deeply. The coincidence of Belgic with Romano-British centres in south-eastern England shows that the Belgae had also begun to develop communications, and the propensity of many Belgic settlements for the river valleys and for wooded sites (e.g. Camulodunum, Prae Wood, Welwyn, Braughing, Sandy; sites near Hertford) indicates a readiness to clear woodlands and to be near trade-routes, which implies surplus production – as indeed Belgic coinage and imports confirm. The Belgae developed the Kent lower tertiary zone along the line of the Watling Street and the Essex and Hertfordshire boulder-clays, where these soils were loam-covered – the 'intermediate' soils underlined by Wooldridge and Linton. Their northern frontier was where the loams ceased. Wooldridge and Linton explained the importance of the 'intermediate' loams as the soils which, off the chalk and oolites, were the most easily cleared and worked, and also the most productive. The soils of Hertfordshire and Essex developed by the Belgae were recognized by them as of this character, but have, they noted, a higher clay fraction; and Fox pointed out that they constituted zones not of primary but of secondary occupation. The exploitation of the richer soils was doubtless also bound up with the growth of a new class, the intermediate nobility or squirearchy emerging contemporaneously with the eccentric expansion onto new land caused by subdivision of the soil among coheirs, by the increase of trade and wealth with the introduction of coinage, and the growth of a client class attached to this group. Well-to-do Belgic burials indicate a command of imports, surplus production, and slave labour.

It is clear that at the time of the Roman invasion, the owners of such homesteads as Park Street already occupied enough land to be laying the foundations of flourishing farm-units in the succeeding decades, and Park Street already used slave labour, as the discovery of slave-irons showed. This agrees with the numerous *aedificia* which Caesar encountered in Belgic territory and which would have characterized lands held in severalty rather than in the open field, though perhaps in association with existent 'native' field complexes. The Belgic farmer buried at Welwyn chose a spot (there is no evidence here of pre-Belgic occupation) in the valley of the River Mimram

only refer critics to the details of Mrs Cunnington's report, where the evidence of date seems clear. The connection of the ditches within the enclosure with the internal structure's own ditch seems to me against identification as a temple.—WAM XXXVII, 1912, pp. 57 sqq.

a few hundred yards from a ford whose importance was growing with the advance of Cunobelinus from Verulamium to Camulodunum, and which served as the crossing-point of the route between the two towns via Braughing. There was certainly traffic along the dry gravels of the river valley, and another Belgic habitation existed at Digswell Water. The Belgic settler was therefore interested in trade, and he used some of the proceeds of his agriculture, apparently, to get wine, the amphorae containing it, and metal-ware from abroad; when he died, he was sufficient of a notable to be buried in a special vault adorned with these objects.[1]

The romanized farm of Lockleys which grew up about A.D. 60 not far away on a spot already marked by a brief Belgic occupation, was sited on a mixture of clay and gravel over chalk, described as the "finest barley-land in Hertfordshire;" a short distance to the south-west and north-west lay the gravel terrace of the Mimram; the chalk extended northward and eastward for a mile or so; but on the north-east a large patch of boulder-clay commences within a short distance, and this must have remained heavily wooded long after the chalk areas had been divested of timber, fuel, and charcoal, likewise pannage for swine and leaves for winter cattle-feed. This, indeed, may be regarded as the "brogillus" (coppice) of the estate.

In the early Roman period the farmer built near Lockleys an unpretentious timber dwelling and his home-field extended over something like four acres, as indicated by the ditched enclosure parts of which have been traced to the west of the house. The arable periphery is limited on the north-west by another Romano-British dwelling on the line of the by-pass, and to within half a mile on the south-east by the existence of another at Digswell Water; unless the estate extended southward over the river, some 120 acres of land were available. Here then we see the establishment of a romanized farm

---

[1] The present analysis, originally made on the assumption that the Lockleys villa possessed a Belgic predecessor, has had to be modified in the light of Dr G. Webster's revised interpretation of that site in RVB, pp. 243 sqq. But it is evident that a Belgic farm stood somewhere in the vicinity, to judge by the adjacent rich burial at Welwyn; in any case the observations on the Welwyn and Lockleys sites undoubtedly apply to numerous similarly situated farmsteads on the gravels of south-eastern Britain. The export trade: Strabo, IV, 5, 2; communications: cf. the wheel-ruts entering the stockade at Prae Wood, R. E. M. and T. V. Wheeler, *Verulamium*, SARR XI, Oxford, 1936, pl. lxxii and p. 43; at the crossing of the Oxfordshire Grim's Dyke by the Akeman Street, a Belgic predecessor of the Roman road was found – *Oxon.* II, 1937, p. 83. Belgic valley-settlements: Fox, *Personality of Britain*[4], Cardiff, 1943, p. 79; Hawkes, Dunning, *Arch. J.* LXXXVII, 1930, pp. 300 sqq.; Fox, PPSEA VII, 1932-4, pp. 159-60. Intermediate soils: Wooldridge, Linton, *Ant.* VII, 1933, pp. 297 sqq. Fox and gradational soils: *Ant.* VII, 1933, pp. 473-5. *Aedificia*: Caesar, *de Bello Gallico*, V, 12, 2.

on a virgin site selected both for its good barley soil and its position near a ford – a river valley site hemmed in by woods such as seldom tempted the men of the pre-Belgic Iron Age. Trade here plays a part, also cross-country communications of a type virtually unknown in the pre-Roman period, and both must have had their influence in determining the rise of the farm to villa status in the early fourth century.

More recently another clear picture has been obtained of the isolated Belgic *aedificium* by excavation of the farm-sites at Wyboston (Beds), and near St Ives, and to these we shall return. Both of these, it should be noted, remained occupied under Roman rule, though they did not, like Park Street, develop into 'villas.' The feminine plural form of the names Sulloniacae (Brockley Hill, M'sex), and Vagniacae (Springhead, Kent), both of which contain Celtic personal names and the Celtic proprietary suffix, imply the preceding word *villae* and suggest the possibility that Belgic landowners sometimes owned more than one farm in the same vicinity – a fact of importance for our understanding of the Romano-British rural pattern.[1]

The Belgic farm excavated at Wyboston (Beds) stood on the gravel close to the River Ouse and on its west bank; the river here flowed north-eastward. The site's maximum area seems to have been some eight acres under cultivation, and its importance is that it renewed its existence in the Roman period, evidently in the second century, when the occupants re-used and probably expanded the old farm. The complex consisted of eight plots of varying sizes enclosed by ditches. The boundaries were on the whole rectilinear, but the plots themselves were irregular. The Belgic enclosure lay at the east end, containing two elliptical huts surrounded by a ditch, probably filled with water from the Ouse. The Belgic holding embraced not less than three-quarters of the cultivation area and only the two smaller western fields remain undated, although their layout suggests that they were coeval with the rest; in the south-western enclosure a Roman installation, probably for corn-drying, was found, associated with coal-ash ascertained, on analysis, to be derived from Northumberland or Durham. The reoccupiers of the second century appear to have made no fundamental alteration to the old layout, although improved building techniques (wall-plaster, roof-tiles) were introduced; hence the excavator concluded that the new settlers were Belgae like the original occupants. The animal bones found were those of oxen, sheep, and pig. The general picture is that of a limited grain-production in both periods, but in the second, coal was got from as far north as the Wall area, implying export for commissariat purposes, and the presence of oyster shells suggests

[1] Sulloniacae: *It. Ant.*, 471.4 (Wesseling). Vagniacae: *ib.*, 472.2. On these names, JBAA³ xvii, 1954, pp. 77–8; AHR xi, 1963, p. 6, n.

I. Air-photograph of the Throckenholt area, Cambridgeshire, showing a cattle-enclosure and ditched droveways among 'native' fields.

a wider range of commercial contacts. But the relatively narrow basis of arable may be taken to mean that the livestock branch was important; the pigs show woodland grazing, and the cattle, use of the Ouse water-meadows, while the sheep would have needed dry pasture, preferably on gravels or limestone, to avoid the liver-fluke.

Another farmstead recently excavated a mile south-west of St Ives (Hunts) possesses fundamentally similar features. It lay on a small tributary of the Ouse. Its full area appears not to have been traced, but its occupation began, according to pottery, in the early first century A.D., i.e. in the Belgic period. Its main nucleus was a square enclosure with rounded corners, some twenty yards wide, which apparently surrounded the dwelling; this was superseded by a series of remarkably regular rectilineal field strips averaging 10 × 30 yards, whose boundary ditches contained pottery of the entire Roman period, beginning in the late first or early second century; they were evidently added to in the third and fourth centuries. Some of the plots, nevertheless, seem to have originated in the pre-Roman epoch. The cultivation area traced covered some two acres, but the unit was obviously larger. Economically, this would seem to be in much the same category as the Wyboston farmstead, but the difference in the manner of laying out the field boundaries at St Ives is significant .The plots of Wyboston and St Ives appear to correspond respectively to the two field types noticeable in the Fenland areas: Wyboston bears an affinity to the irregular and chaotic small native field complexes observable at such sites as Throckenholt (Cambs) (Pl. I); the St Ives plots resemble – at least in their rectilinearity – Romano-British fields, examples of which are to be seen in the same area east of Allen's Bridge, Throckenholt (Pl. II). (Tebbutt, the excavator of Wyboston, duly noted that this farm demonstrates the pre-Roman derivation of the type of farms seen in the Fenland area.) The chief difference between the two patterns is noteworthy; in the St Ives farm there is a striking absence of any fenced or ditched field ways approaching the farmhouses. A similar absence of such field ways is noticeable in the corresponding field pattern near Allen's Bridge. At Wyboston, on the other hand, the westermost enclosure (A–A) containing the two huts is open to the Ouse flood-plain on the south; the 'open-ended' ditches near the northerly hut Tebbutt suggested were "animal catching pens." The corresponding 'irregular' field pattern in the Fens – e.g. at Throcken-holt aforementioned, is characterized by the marked presence of ditched (? fenced) droveways communicating with isolated farmhouses standing in squarish double enclosures. Characteristic and instructive is one of these occupying the left centre of an air-photograph (Pl. I) of fields in the Throckenholt area; here the droveway is seen entering at the corner of the farm-enclosure so as to give continuous and uninterrupted access to the area between its double fences. The explanation is clear; in the space between the fences in the immediate vicinity of the homestead the livestock was enclosed at night, after it had returned from pasture. It should be remarked, however, that the limited accommodation between the fences implies a small herd, i.e. those cattle which it was necessary to winter. This implies that the summer accommodation was some distance away in distinct enclosures built where open pasture was available. If a further demonstration is needed of this point, we may turn to an analogy in north Britain. There, at Risehow near Maryport (Cumb), a fourth-century farmstead of native type was excavated by B. Blake. It consisted of two concentric walled enclosures, the inner of which contained a homestead; at the point where the two enclosing walls converged, a ditched entrance avenue led in, coming from the nearest water-supply outside. Clearly the cattle was driven from pasture to water in the evening and thence herded safely up the avenue to be held between the concentric enclosures during the night.[1]

Wyboston, then, and the double-fenced Fenland farms with droveways and 'irregular' fields, represented a livestock and arable economy. In the Fens the livestock may safely be assumed to have been cattle, for sheep-bones are scarce in the Romano-British sites of that region, which is too damp for successful flock-grazing. The St Ives farm-complex, on the other hand, and the corresponding field patterns in the Fens, would appear to represent continuous areas of arable devoted preponderantly to grain-growing. A development of the first stock-arable type of farm may perhaps be deduced from the site near Holbeach Drove Common, published by the late O. G. S. Crawford. Here two 'double enclosure' farmhouses in close mutual proximity stand near to a well-marked Romano-British droveway; the associated field system has the distinction of consisting of a series of strip fields, one group of which is certainly at least 200 yards long. There may well have been a connection between a mixed economy and the presence of ox-power sufficient to draw the long-furrow plough with which such strips are normally to be connected.

The pre-Roman pattern of farming and its subsequent development are equally clear in the farmsteads of Cranbourne Chase excavated by General Pitt-Rivers in the last century and restudied by Professor Hawkes; of these we shall speak when we come to consider the problem of farm layout.

---

[1] Throckenholt: Ashmolean Museum, photo M. 1201 (5), 65E3, the lower left hand of the photo. Allen's Bridge: Ashm. Mus., 1204 (161), 65E3, lower left hand. Throckenholt droveway: east of Malice Farm, Ashm. Mus., 1207 (10), 63F3.

II. Air-photograph of the Allen's Bridge area, Throckenholt, Cambridgeshire, showing 'native' fields unassociated with droveways.

In addition to the distinctive field systems traceable by air-photography and their associated farmsteads, which can be shown to represent, at their initial stages, and often later, the pre-Roman agricultural heritage – there are certain areas of the country which were, on historical evidence, the estates of British kings. They continued as recognizable entities in the Roman period, because they were taken over by the Roman government as successors of the British royal houses. One is the personal estate of Presutagus, king of the Iceni, which archaeology locates in the Suffolk Breckland. According to Tacitus (*Ann.*, XIV, 31), part of this domain was bequeathed by Presutagus on his decease to Nero, but the Roman administration seized the whole. It is a fairly safe assumption that the area remained *patrimonium* after the revolt of Boudicca. The view has been expressed that one of the centres of this estate was the villa of Stanton Chair, the size of which contrasts with the plainness of its appointments, and which is likely therefore to have housed a bailiff rather than a private owner.[1]

The other identifiable British royal estate is that of Cogidubnus, king of the Regnenses, whose capital from the time of the conquest was Chichester. Cogidubnus was a client sovereign granted the rank of legate by the emperor, and may be assumed to have owned his royal estates like other sovereigns. Moreover, we are told that the Roman government handed over to him additional territories which may be supposed to have lain among the less compliant Belgic tribes to his north and west. We have no specific evidence that Cogidubnus' property ultimately passed to the Fiscus, but virtually no client kingdoms survived within the empire after Trajan. That the addition to Cogidubnus' kingdom of further territories involved a growth of his personal appanages is probable enough, and evidence for such may exist. One of his coins, if rightly read, points to the absorption of the Atrebates, of north-east Hampshire and Berkshire, into his territory, and tiles found at Little London, near Silchester, the Atrebatan urban centre in the Roman period, bear the stamp of Nero, and suggest the presence of an imperial estate. The existence of a kiln turning out such tiles suggests a property of considerable extent; that this had been an appanage of Cogidubnus can be no more than conjectured; that the domain in question was derived in the first place from an estate of Commius the Atrebate or his sons, is an attractive notion.[2]

[1] The Iceni in the Breckland: Rivet, *Town and Country in Roman Britain*, London, 1958, p. 47; *Arch. J.* XCVI, 1939, pp. 1–113; PSIA XXV, 1939, p. 214; JRS XXIX, 1939, p. 214; XXX, 1940, p. 172.

[2] Cogidubnus as client: Tac., *Agric.*, 14, 2; legate, RIB, no. 91; additional territories: Tac. *Agric. loc. cit.*; Coins inscribed CRAB: Rivet, *op. cit.*, p. 159. Little London

As has been stated, there are sites which have been demonstrated archaeologically to have undergone a continuity of development from a purely native type of hutment to a romanized residence of the type generally referred to as a "villa."[1]

There is, however, evidence that some Romano-British farms, while their residences and outbuildings had assumed a more or less romanized form, retained a native field system, even though it is not always proved that that system is chronologically pre-Roman. Thus, the Little Milton farmhouse, in Oxfordshire, a modest but romanized establishment, was surrounded by a series of small plots of this type. Air-photography indicated that the basilical farmhouse of Eastfield near Thruxton (Hants) was also surrounded by fields of native type, and a Roman building is known to stand within such at Enscombe House near Kingston (Dors). Other Roman buildings within blocks of this type of cultivation have been noted at Stancombe Down (Berks) and at Shoddesden and Warren Hill in west Hampshire, also at Shroner Wood, Micheldever, in the centre of the county.

A number of other cases in which the association of relatively small plots akin to the 'native' type with farms of Roman date is being established by air-photography, could be mentioned, but in most of these the 'villa' status of the farmhouse is doubtful. An instance in which, however, such a status has been demonstrated by excavation, lies just east of Lechlade, where field boundaries of Early Iron Age character are associated with a house of romanizing type.[2]

Of some potential importance in our estimate of the pre-Roman element in the Romano-British rural system is the phenomenon of the so-called 'basilical' type of farmhouse. There is general agreement that this type of farmhouse, with its central nave divided from flanking aisles by rows of posts, originated in pre-Roman days on the continent of Europe. A rectangular dwelling with two internal rows of posts was excavated in 1969 at Chausseney (Aisne), France; it was dated to the early La Tène period. In timber form it has been found in Frisia in the third century B.C.; it existed in Scandinavia in the second century B.C. It is prominently represented in an urban context at Bibracte (Mont Beuvray) in Gaul in the middle of the last century before the current era. The Welsh legal codes also furnish a picture

tiles: *Ant. J.* VI, 1926, pp. 75–6; cf. EE IX, 1267. What relation, if any, the great Fishbourne residence bore to Cogidubnus' estates, is unclear, since it was preceded by what is thought to have been a Roman military supply depôt.

[1] By "villa" is meant a rural building complex embodying Roman building techniques, and including a residence and rooms or outbuildings devoted to the requirements of agriculture.

[2] I am grateful to Mrs M. U. Jones of the Ministry of Works for details and explanations of the site.

of it, and it figures in the *Mabinogion*. How far the Welsh documents can be taken as evidence of its pre-Roman origin in the British Isles, however, depends on the dating of the social system reflected in the law-texts. In romanized guise, the basilical farmhouse is distributed in northern Gaul (France, Belgium, Holland) and the Rhineland; the plan was at home as the Saxon farmhouse in northern Germany, where it survived into the Middle Ages, as it survives in Frisia today.[1]

In Britain, on the other hand, while the type is well represented in the Roman period, it has not so far been convincingly identified in a pre-Roman or even an early Roman context. It has not, to the best of my belief, appeared on any British Early Iron Age site; it is very difficult to see in the postholes discovered beneath the Roman villa at Park Street (Herts) a clear basilical plan. The small Roman building at Knowl Hill near Wargrave (Berks) contained postholes against the inner walls, but it was not clear if they had preceded the building or were contemporary with it. The intervals between the posts suggested a kinship with the basilical tradition and a La Tène sword was found, but actual pre-Roman occupation was not established. At Exeter, certain simple rectangular urban dwellings of the first century A.D. were regarded as belonging to the same family as the basilical plan. We may however note in passing that a Roman example at Eastfield (Hants) was associated with an Early Iron Age type of field system, and that another at Tidbury (Hants) occupied the centre of a hill-fort. A house of this type appears within the enclosed hut-group of Cefn Graeanog, Caernarvonshire (third-fourth century), and larger aisled buildings are believed to have stood within the hill-forts of Dinorben (third-fourth centuries) and Castle Dore (sixth-seventh centuries). Similar Dark-Age examples are now known in lowland Scottish hill-forts.[2] The presence of Dark-Age dwellings in Wales probably derived from the basilical type may, indeed, be regarded by some as affording a strong presumption of its pre-Roman origin. But all in all, there are still no well-established examples of such before the early second century, to which date belongs, in its first phase,

[1] European origin: I. A. Richmond, JRS xxII, 1932, pp. 96 sqq. Chausseney: *World Archaeology* I, June, 1969, pp. 106–41, fig. 28. Frisia: *Germania*, 1936, pp. 45 sqq.; 1958, pp. 45 sqq. Scandinavia: Richmond, *loc. cit.* Mont Beuvray: J. G. Bulliot, *Fouilles de Mont Beuvray*, Autun, 1899, II, pp. 225 sqq. *The Ancient Laws and Institutions of Wales*, H.M. Stationery Office, 1841, I, p. 293; Vened., III, 21; C. Guest, *The Mabinogion*, London, 1849, II, 393–5. Continental examples, Maulévrier: A. Grenier, *Manuel d'archéologie préhistorique, celtique et gallo-romaine*, VI, ii, Paris, 1934, p. 805; Olfermont (?): M. A. de Caumont, *Abécédaire d'archéologie*, Caen, 1870, p. 387; Heihof near Hulsberg, Holland: OM I, 1907, pp. 10–23; Bocholz: Leyden Museum of Antiquities (model). Modern survival in Friesland, Haubois near Sneek. General discussion: J. T. Smith, *Arch. J.* cxx, 1963, pp. 1 sqq.

[2] See now Laing in *Trans. of the Dumfriesshire Archaeological Society*, 1970.

a recently excavated farmhouse at Exning (Suff); and none of the rest known and dated precede the later second or third century, when a number of them appear, frequently not as independent dwellings, but as the outbuildings of corridor and courtyard villas. With the basilical building and its agricultural and sociological significance in the Romano-British rural system we shall deal at a later stage; in the meantime we may sum up by stating that while the plan is undoubtedly pre-Roman in north-western Europe, its pre-Roman origin in Britain itself is still unproven. Accordingly we cannot be sure that it does not represent an introduction from the continent during the Roman period rather than the local evolution of an indigenous form.

CHAPTER III

THE ROMAN BRITONS AND THEIR
AGRARIAN SOCIETY

THE DERIVATION and identity of the agricultural population of Roman Britain has not, perhaps, been discussed to the extent that the subject demands. Before the days of Haverfield there was a tendency to confine attention to the villas, and to assume that they were the homes of Roman officers and officials. Haverfield initiated a new view by emphasizing that the majority of the proprietors were more likely to have been romanized Britons. The greater degree of attention paid in the 1920's to the downland settlement of the Roman period created an awareness of the existence of two principal groups within the rural population: the villa-owners and the inhabitants of the 'native villages' of the type of Woodcuts and Rotherley.[1] Rostovtzeff, as early as 1926, expressed the opinion that the villa aristocracy would have included a proportion of owners derived from the other provinces of the empire, a view which drew little response or appreciation from British archaeologists. Collingwood wrote in 1939: "Sometimes no doubt a villa was the bailiff's residence on an imperial domain: sometimes it was built by a speculator on favourable terms; but these were exceptions. As a rule, villa-dwellers were British farmers, large or small..." This was, I think, his last statement on the subject *ex cathedra*. Frere, writing in 1967, hardly differs.[2] Study of the northern highland zone, however, chiefly from a military point of view, directed archaeologists to the problems of the settlement of veterans or returned soldiers upon the soil, and to the presence in Britain of Germanic military elements who might be potential agricultural settlers. The possibility was also envisaged of cultivation by border-forces in the fourth century, when the allotment of lands to such garrisons became a practice in some provinces.

To identify the origin of the proprietors and peasantry of the lowland areas of Britain is a much more difficult problem than it has been in such provinces as Gaul and Africa, because the lowland region

---

[1] Even as regards the composition of the 'native' villages, caution is necessary. Cf. the skull of negroid type among the Romano-British skeletons found at Benson near Wallingford in a native village area.—JRS xv, 1925, p. 231.

[2] Rostovtzeff, *Social and Economic History of the Roman Empire*, Oxford, 1926, p. 229; Collingwood, CAH xii, 1939, p. 284; Frere, *Britannia*, London, 1967, p. 265.

is singularly poor in inscriptions, and other written sources are few. Nevertheless, a tentative tabulation of such information as exists may prove not unprofitable.

1. *Sulloniacae*, the name of Brockley Hill (Msx), is recorded in the Antonine roadbook. The settlement contained a pottery-making industry originating at the beginning of the Roman period and turning out *mortaria* stamped by Sullonius; these were datable between 70 and 120 approximately. Square fields of native type are known to exist north-east of the occupied area. The place-name element –*acum* is a proprietary suffix widespread in the Celtic countries of the Roman Empire, meaning "property or place of," and originally before the name "Sulloniacae" evidently stood the word "villae." It may therefore be assumed that this settlement consisted of a pottery industry and several scattered farms owned, at least originally, by Sullonius, whose name is Celtic.[1]

2. *Vagniacae* is a similar case. It is recorded in the Antonine roadbook between London and Rochester (Durobrivae), and was certainly Springhead near Dartford, now known to have been an agricultural settlement superseded by a religious centre focused on a source-cult and adorned by five temples. The name of the proprietor of the lands, presumably, before the cult became important, was Vagnius, and he too, on the evidence, was owner of two or more adjacent farms.[2]

3. *Digesta*, 36, 1, 48, record a lawsuit involving the property of Seius Saturninus, a chief pilot (*archigubernus*) of the Classis Britannica or British fleet in the first century. As *bona* are involved, this included in all probability landed estate. One thinks of the Folkestone villa with its tiles stamped CL(assis) BR(itannica), which at least shows that villa estates in some way connected with the fleet existed from the later first to the fourth centuries. The Folkestone house is known to have been rebuilt about A.D. 100, and Iavolenus Priscus, who judged the case, was Iuridicus of Britain in the years before A.D. 90.[3]

4. A legionary soldier holding property in Britain is recorded by *Digesta*, 28, 3, 6, 7, referring to the years 118–22.

5. An inscription found one mile north of Lancaster was dedicated by Iulius Ianuarius, an ex-decurion of an *ala*, to the god Ialonus Contrebus in the third century A.D. The completion of the epithet

[1] Sulloniacae: *It. Ant.*, 471.4. The stamped mortaria: AA⁴ xv, 1938, p. 280, fig. 12; –*acum* names: A. Longnon, *Les noms de lieu de la France*, Paris, 1920–9, pp. 75–96; d'A. de Jubainville, *Recherches sur l'origine de la propriété foncière dans la France*, Paris, 1890, pp. 134 sqq.; N. D. Fustel de Coulanges, *L'alleu et la domaine rurale*, Paris, 1922, pp. 34 sqq. Native fields: LMAS ²x, 1950, p. 228.

[2] Vagniacae: *It. Ant.*, 472.2, The settlement: *A. Cant.* LXV, 1952 and subsequent volumes.

[3] Octavius Iavolenus Priscus: see PWRE XVII, 1937, col. 1830 sqq., sv. Octavius (59).

Contrebus by the late Sir Ian Richmond on the analogy of an inscription from Overborough, where "Contrebi" may mean "those dwelling together" (cf. Welsh *cantref*, a rural district), was interpreted by him to imply that Ianuarius was settled in a farm near Lancaster, and that the region where it was located was called Contrebia. A different interpretation of the name Ialonus, discussed by J. P. Alcock, would relate the name to a cultivated clearing, making Contrebis a spring deity.[1]

6. G. Indutius Felix dedicated an altar to the *numina Augg.* and to Silvanus at the Somerdale villa, Keynsham, in A.D. 155.[2]

7. Iventius Sabinus dedicated an altar to Mars Rigisamus at the villa of West Coker (Som) in the second or third century.[3]

8. Q. Pompeius Anicetus was buried at Bath in the second or third century A.D. It seems reasonable to connect him with the place-name *Anicetis* recorded by the *Ravenna Cosmography* in the south-west of the country, somewhere between the north Dorset border and Iwerne; Cranbourne Chase seems to be indicated. Anicetus was of oriental extraction, probably from Asia; men of this derivation are found contracting to work the mines in Britain; hence Anicetus might have been a lessor (*conductor*) of imperial domain in Cranbourne Chase. Richmond and Crawford suggested tentatively a connection with Tiberius Claudius Anicetus, a freedman of Claudius and prefect of the Classis Misenatis; this seems to me less likely.[4]

9. The *Ravenna Cosmography* also records the name *Coloneas* in south-western Britain. Richmond and Crawford note that this is a contracted form of Coloneacus, i.e. the property of Colon(eus); it is likely enough to represent Fundus Coloneacus, the estate of Coloneus. Colon is a well-known Celtic personal name; the place was apparently in Dorset, near Blackmore in the opinion of the above editors.[5]

10. *Villa Faustini* appears in the Antonine roadbook between Colchester and Caister-by-Norwich, located, according to the distances of the Itinerary, at Scole (Suff).[6]

11. Reburrus, a released cavalry-veteran, lost his discharge-certificate, dated A.D. 103, near Malpas (Ches), in Trajan's time. It has therefore been suggested that Reburrus had settled in the vicinity after his

---

[1] RIB, no. 600; CIL VII, 284; Overborough: RIB, no. 610. J. P. Alcock, *Arch. J.* CXXII, 1965, p. 5.

[2] Somerdale: RIB, no. 181.

[3] West Coker: RIB, no. 187.

[4] Anicetus: EE VII, 828; RIB, no. 148; *Ravenna Cosmography:* A XCIII, 1949, p. 23, no. 35. Cf. JBAA² XVII, 1954, p. 77.

[5] Coloneas: *Rav. Cosm.*, A XCIII, p. 29, no. 33.

[6] Villa Faustini: *It. Ant.*, 474.5; for a suggestion as to the identity of the Faustinus in question, see Stevens in CBA. RR VII, p. 122, n. 118.

release. Known Roman finds in the vicinity are somewhat doubtful, but another fragment of discharge diploma came from Middlewich and was dated to A.D. 105. Veteran settlement in the Cheshire plain therefore seems possible, but requires substantiation.[1]

12. Part of a Roman inscription has been found built into the structure of Godmanston church (Dors), five miles north of Dorchester. It is a dedication to Jupiter Optimus Maximus by Titinius Pines, a soldier of the Twentieth Legion Valeria Victrix, and presumably of second or third-century date. The nearest Roman building is the villa of Forston, one mile to the south, but no details are known of this structure. The inscription might have come from Dorchester, but even if it did, it has a value as suggesting the settlement of veterans in the southern *civitates*, and such men usually became landowners.[2]

13. Dedications by Roman citizens to the goddess Brigantia in Yorkshire have been interpreted as belonging to Brigantian veterans resettled in their native districts after discharge in the later second century. That they received land-grants is probable; they would certainly have lived by farming.[3]

14. The two portrait busts found in the villa of Lullingstone, Kent, eighteen miles east-south-east of London, have given rise to the opinion that this was the residence of a Roman official of importance. They are portraits of distinguished persons in official dress, apparently related, sculptured in the Mediterranean area in the mid-second century; they were thought by Professor J. C. Toynbee to belong to the proprietor of the villa who was represented by one of them.[4]

15. Sir Ian Richmond, having established from epigraphical evidence the existence about the fort of *Bremmetennacum* (Ribchester, Lancs) of a Regio Bremmetennacensis, i.e. an area allotted to the *numerus* or *cuneus* of Sarmatian cavalry who garrisoned the fort, concluded that these men were settled around the fort after their discharge. This is conveyed by the term *Bremmetennacum Veteranorum* applied to the fort in the fourth century. The peculiar reason for their *bloc*-settlement was probably their origin not as auxiliary troops but as prisoners of war transferred to Britain by M. Aurelius, who would not have received Roman citizenship on release.[5]

[1] Malpas diploma: CIL VII, 1193; T. Watkin, *Roman Cheshire*, Liverpool, 1886, p. 288; Middlewich diploma: F. H. Thompson, *Roman Cheshire*, Chester, 1965, pp. 93–4. Finds at Malpas: *ibid.*, p. 104.

[2] Godmanston inscription: DNHAS LXXXVI, 1964, p. 104.

[3] CIL VII, 200 = RIB, no. 627, Greetland; EE VII, 920, Longwood; *ib.*, IX, 1120, Castleford; cf. Jolliffe, *Arch. J.* XCVIII, 1940, pp. 36–41.

[4] The busts: G. W. Meates, *Lullingstone Roman Villa*, London, 1955, pp. 70–89; J. C. Toynbee, *Art in Roman Britain*,[2] London, 1963, p. 6; pp. 126–8.

[5] The Regio Bremmetenacensis: Richmond, JRS XXXV, 1945, pp. 15 sqq.;

16. In the fourth century a *clarissima mulier* who was *civis Dumnonia* is recorded as having died in Salona in Illyricum. Her title implies senatorial rank, hence she must have owned extensive property in her native Dumnonia, i.e. Devon or Cornwall. Stevens has pointed out that the only notable villa of the area is at Uplyme east of Exeter, occupied in the fourth century. Its bathhouse bears a remarkable resemblance to the bath of Lufton villa not very far away over the Somerset border, and perhaps this too was part of her family estate.[1]

17. Saint Melania the Younger, who lived 383–439, owned estates in Britain. The main body of her property was in Italy, Sicily, Africa, and Spain, and much of it consisted of farms held by slave-tenants.[2]

18. The father of Saint Patrick (Patricius), resident at the *vicus* of *Bannavem Taberniae*, was a *decurio*, and therefore may be regarded as a man of substance; he was the owner of a small estate (*villula*). There is no agreement on the location of *Bannavem Taberniae*; it is stated to have been "by the western sea," and in a late gloss to the *Life* it is called Nemet-tur, which has led to its identification with *Banna* (Bewcastle) north of Hadrian's Wall, and also with Banwen on the Severn estuary. But the recent find of a tile inscribed with the words *Civitatis Corielsoliliorum* at Caves Inn, the next road-station on Watling Street north of *Bannaventa* (Whilton Lodge) in the Antonine roadbook, shows that in that vicinity was a community with a municipal constitution and an *ordo decurionum*. The name suggests a *pagus* or tribal sub-unit promoted to municipal rank.[3]

19. A pewter vessel, part of a hoard of pewter dated to the fourth century, found in a Roman building one mile north of Weyhill, near Andover (Hants), was incised with the name VICTRICI, i.e. "of Victricius." Another of the vessels was inscribed with the Chi-Ro symbol, and presumably belonged to an estate-church. Victricius may well have been the owner; cf. Victricius, bishop of Rouen at this period (380–407), and founder of numerous churches in Gaul.[4]

20. A villa at Appleshaw (Eastfield), Hants, possessed a mosaic pavement figuring the god Dionysus. Around the central panel was

Bremmetennacum (Bresnetenaci) Veteranorum: *Rav. Cosm.*, A XCIII, p. 25, no. 124. Transfer of Sarmatae: Dio, LXXI, 16.

[1] Salona epitaph: Diehl, *Inscriptiones Christianae Veteres*, I, Berlin, 1924–31, no. 185; C. E. Stevens, *Tr. Devonshire Association* LXXXIV, 1954, pp. 172 sqq.

[2] Melania: *Vita*, 10; 18.

[3] Confessio S. Patricii: Whitley Stokes, *The Tripartite Life of Saint Patrick*, II, London, 1887, p. 357, lines 5–6; *decurio: ibid.*, Ep. S. Patr. ad Christ. Tyr. Corotoci, etc., p. 377, line 20. Civitas Corielsoliliorum: JRS LVI, 1966, p. 223.

[4] Weyhill pewter hoard: A LVI, 1898, pp. 1–20; Victricius, bishop of Rouen: Sulp. Severus, *Dial.*, III, 4; Paulinus of Nola, *Epp.*, 18; 37.

an inscription reading: "Q. Natalius Natalinus et Bodeni..." The date of the pavement is in the fourth century. The combination of the name of a Roman citizen with a Celtic name, whether of an individual or of a group, is notable.[1]

21. The Ambrosius Aurelianus recorded by Nennius as the enemy of Vortigern in the fourth decade of the fifth century, and who fought the battle of Guoloppum (Wallop, Hants ?) in 437, can hardly have been other than a romanized landowner of south-west Britain. His enemy at *Guoloppum*, Vitalinus (Guitolin), presumably Vortigern's kinsman, resident in Gloucester, would also have owned land. The estate of Ambrosius may have been Amesbury (Ambresbyrig, *c.* A.D. 880). *Guoloppum* may also be an estate-name; cf. the personal name Gulioepius recorded on a Roman inscription at Bisley (Glos).[2]

22. Firminus. This name was found inscribed on stone at the villa Barnsley Park (Glos), in a fourth-century context. The name is common in the first and second centuries, but is that of several high imperial officials in the fourth century, one being the *Comes rerum privatarum* of the west for 398–9, in charge of imperial property. The name might be interpreted to mean that the Barnsley Park site was imperial domain in the fourth century. The discovery at the site of a belt-buckle indicating the presence of troops, probably *comitatenses* (members of the field army – see p. 252) in that century, is suggestive but not decisive on this question.[3]

23. *Ariconium*, the Roman name of Weston-under-Penyard (Heref), an iron-mining centre, may be derived from a personal name, and therefore indicate the name of the original proprietor of an estate there; compare L. Aruconius Verecundus, who contracted for lead-

[1] The Eastfield pavement: CIL VII, 3.

[2] Ambrosius Aurelianus: Nennius, *Hist. Brit.*, 31; Guoloppum: Nennius, *ib.*, 66, also called Catguoloph. Gulioepius: RIB, no. 132, Customs Shrubs, near Bisley. Was the Bisley villa Guoloppum rather than Wallop, Hants, since Ambrosius' opponent Vitalinus was at Gloucester? Amesbury: *Ekwall, Oxford Concise Dictionary of English Place-names,*[2] Oxford, 1940, *ad voc.* Ambrosius' estates may have been considerable; cf. Amberley near Bignor and Ambersham, Suss, the first part of which names philologists seem to have difficulty in explaining as Anglo-Saxon because of the intrusive "b," which is either anachronistic or inappropriately Middle English. See Ekwall, *Studies in English Place-names*, Stockholm, 1936, pp. 84–5, *ad* Amberley (also existent in Gloucestershire); Mawer and Stenton, *Placenames of Sussex*, 1929, I, sv. Ambersham: R. G. Roberts, *The Placenames of Sussex*, 1914, p. 4, sv. Amberley. G. R. Jones has noted that medieval Amesbury possessed discrete manors at Lyndhurst and Bowcombe (Isle of Wight) (DB 52, 64b; VCH *Wilts*, II, pp. 60–1; *Hants*, I, p. 408). Bowcombe is the site of a Roman rural building (VCH *Hants*, I, p. 317), and the nearby Carisbrook villa has yielded a coin of Libius Severus (461–5)—*ibid.*

[3] Information on the inscription by kindness of Dr G. Webster. The *Comes: C. Theod.*, I, 11, 2; X, 2, 10, 22; XI, 19, 4.

mining in Derbyshire at a period not established. The place-name first appears in the later second century. As the name survived into the middle ages as Archenfield, the estate would have been of considerable area, and its bounds might be traceable.[1]

24. *Beroniacum* appears in a confirmation issued by Pope Adrian IV relating to estates in Shropshire and Herefordshire willed to the Church in the eleventh century. The form is Roman with the characteristically Celtic proprietary suffix, and should reflect a Romano-British place-name. Ekwall has suggested that it might be an old name for Ludlow.[2]

25. The name Eutherios appears on a platter forming part of the hoard of fourth-century vessels found at Mildenhall (Suff). This was perhaps the same Eutherios who performed the function of *praepositus sacri cubiculi* in Gaul (355–61) under Julian. There was a small Roman house in the vicinity, but there may have been a larger establishment as yet undiscovered.

26. B. Hartley has drawn attention to a stamped amphora handle found at Holywell Drove, Mildenhall (Suff), derived from an estate in Spain known to have been seized by Septimius Severus, and hence to have belonged to one of his political enemies. Hence an estate belonging to an absentee proprietor living abroad may be implied.[3]

The above list, short as it is, still has something to tell us. The names include those of seven (possibly eight) Roman citizens in the south of Britain, of nine ex-soldiers, of the *decurio* of a municipality, of a possible officer of the department of crown domain, of another probable high official, of four Celts, and of a contractor working for government. Not included are several important groups, such as the legionary veterans settled in and round the country's four colonies, and possibly *limitanei* enjoying land-grants on the frontier in the fourth century.[4] The list is a fair cross-section of the landed proprietors of the province; it includes veterans, officials, and some men obviously from outside the province; from the third century, two absentee landowners and several natives. Some of the Roman citizens (e.g. Q. Natalius Natalinus) were certainly of British descent.

[1] Ariconium: *It. Ant.* 485. 3. L. Aruconius Verecundus: VCH *Derb.*, I, p. 231, no. 2 (a lead pig from Hexgrave Park, Notts). Ariconium-Archenfeld: E. McClure, *British Placenames in their Historical Setting*, London, 1910, p. 139n.

[2] Beroniacum: JBAA² XVII, 1954, pp. 78–9. Ludlow: communication of Professor Ekwall to the late O. G. S. Crawford.

[3] Eutherios: Amm. Marc. XVI, XX. Ant. J. XXXVIII, pp. 91–9.

[4] *Limitanei* in agriculture: Richmond, RNNB, 1958, pp. 123–4, noting the settlement of barbarian *limitanei* with their families in the forts of Hadrian's Wall after 367, assumes that these held land by military service and farmed in the manner of the Tripolitan *limitanei* (Goodchild, JRS XXXIX, 1949, pp. 81 sqq.). I see no archaeological evidence in the vicinity of the forts for this supposition.

The restricted epigraphical evidence for the presence of landowners derived from other provinces is confirmed in some measure by other sources. G. C. Dunning observed that in south-east Britain a number of barrow-burials, some wealthy, appear from the Flavian period onward, dating from the late first and the middle of the second century. These landowners appear to be derived from central Belgium, where similar barrows occur. Somewhat similar evidence of immigrant capitalists appears in relation to the earlier third century in Suffolk, where after the abandonment of some farms occupation begins on new sites at that time. Among the cults prevailing in Cambridgeshire and Essex in the later second and third centuries, Belgic influence is strong, and much of it seems to have come from the Rhineland. The presence of continental settlers is also felt in Gloucestershire, where dedications show especially strong links with Belgica, southern Gaul, and the Rhineland. Our discussion of farmhouses (pp. 131, 140) will reveal the arrival of one type in an evolved state from across the Channel, and that the *Wirtschaftshalle* type, though not widely represented, is derived from the Rhineland. These conclusions would in the main support the belief that some at least of their inhabitants immigrated from abroad.[1]

What information have we of the social structure of the rural population of Roman Britain and of the forms of tenure whereby its components owned or cultivated their land? It is easy to rely on analogy from Gaul, where conditions are likely enough, *prima facie*, to have been similar. But assumptions based on analogy can only be accepted if they can be confirmed, wholly or in part, by independent evidence in this country.

It would be advisable to approach the problem by listing the types of tenure for which there is at least some evidence, direct or indirect in Britain.

1. Whether or not the *coloniae* founded in Britain with nuclei of veteran soldiers involved the allotment of land-grants to their members, such *coloniae*, and likewise other *municipia* possessing major or minor Latin rights, controlled *territoria*, i.e. lands subject to taxation by the city in question. These included the estates of their citizens and those natural resources – lands, mines, saltpans, quarries, fisheries, and the like – which contributed to the city's income. The land of the *territoria* of provincial *coloniae* was regarded juridically as *ager Romanus* and

[1] Barrow burials: G. C. Dunning, *Ant.* x, 1936, pp. 37–48. Suffolk immigrants: PSIA xxiv, 1949, pp. 170, 177; NA xxviii, 1945, p. 189. Cambridgeshire: F. Heichelheim, CAS xxxvii, 1935–6, pp. 52–67. Gloucestershire: RIB, nos. 110, 149, 151, 309; BGAS lx, 1938, pp. 301–2; JRS xxiv, 1934, p. 198; RIB, no. 126. Cf. CBA. RR vii, p. 104; Rivet, RVB, p. 209.

a citizen of a colony holding land within its *territorium* held it theoretically *ex iure Quiritium*, that is, in full Roman proprietorship. It appears, nevertheless, that unless *ius Italicum* was specifically granted, even holders of the land of colonies paid the land-tax (*vectigal soli*) to the state, in addition to such municipal taxation as their colony might impose.

2. We have seen that various discharged soldiers held land by grant from the authorities. As they were Roman citizens if legionaries, and received *civitas* on release if they had served in auxiliary units, their land would theoretically have been held *ex iure Quiritium*. Whether this was so in practice may be doubted.

3. Exceptions would have been the Sarmatian troopers settled round Ribchester, if, as has been suggested, they did not receive citizenship on discharge. In the fourth century, if not before, the *laeti*, or barbarians settled under obligation to military service and to cultivate the soil, would hardly have been freeholders in any sense; their practical position would have resembled that of *coloni*, who by the fourth century were tied to the soil. In Gaul by the Carolingian period documents show that they had been juridically assimilated to the colonate. There is no evidence that in the later fourth century the *limitanei* settled in the northern frontier forts of Britain practised agriculture.

4. The evidence already cited for immigrant capitalists, relating to the late first, the later second, and third centuries (p. 26), would show that there was in Britain vacant land to be taken up on favourable terms, either in complete proprietorship or by a favourable 'emphyteutic' lease, i.e. a lease which became permanent after a nominal payment and conscientious cultivation for a defined period (e.g. five years). Such a lease is referred to in African inscriptions as granted *conditione Manciana*, implying the existence of a "Mancian lease." The tablet from Chew Stoke (Som), dated to the first half or middle of the third century, records the conveyance of land *optimo maximoque iure*, probably though not certainly in Britain. E. G. Turner, who published this document, held that Caracalla's grant of Roman citizenship (A.D. 213) to all inhabitants of the empire except *dediticii* (a term of controversial meaning) did not affect the status of provincial land, and that legally such uninhibited proprietorship could only obtain on land granted the *ius Italicum*. Accordingly, if the land concerned was in Britain, it would have been (wrote Turner), on the territory, say, of Aquae Sulis (Bath), or Glevum (Gloucester), a colony; alternatively, the purchaser was not sure if the land was *fundus Italicus* and was trying to protect himself in case it was. Such a doubt might indeed have arisen precisely from Caracalla's grant of citizenship to owners

of provincial land. In any case, we know nothing of the status of
Bath in the third century, and as Turner himself admits, it is difficult
to see Chew Stoke as belonging to the *territorium* of Gloucester.
Stevens has pointed out that land acquired by "Mancian Lease" on
the outskirts of imperial domain could be transferred in a manner
valid in Roman law, and that this might well explain the presence
of the tablet where it was found, i.e. that Chew Stoke was on imperial
domain. The latter seems to be the more acceptable solution, but in
the absence of a final decision, we must recognize the value of the
Chew Stoke tablet in so far as it suggests that *ager Romanus* existed
in third-century Britain. The possession of Roman citizenship before
or after the Edict of Caracalla did not mean that the citizen could
ipso facto claim unrestricted possession of provincial land; such citizens,
owning land not enjoying *ius Italicum* (of which there is no evidence
in Britain), had to pay the *tributum soli*, even if they were of the senatorial
order – as was the *civis Dumnonia* recorded at Salona, who would
have paid on her estates the late imperial equivalents of *tributum –
capitatio* and *iugatio*. On the other hand Rivet has pointed out that
the Edict of Caracalla aimed, amongst other things, to increase liability
for the five per cent inheritance tax (Dio, LXXVIII, 9, 5), from which
new citizens would have continued exempt unless their land had
become fully Roman.[1]

5. In every province of the Empire there existed state domains;
in the provinces administered by the emperor's personal nominees, as
opposed to those of the Senate – according to arrangements nominally
valid till Diocletian's reign – these were the emperor's personal estates,
consisting of lands, forests, mines, and other economically productive
enterprises. The original nucleus of such properties was in nearly all
cases the crown-domains of previous rulers, but they were apt to be
enlarged by testamentary bequest, confiscation, and escheatment. They
frequently also included the lands of individuals and communities
which had actively resisted annexation.

We have noted above that the Chew Stoke document can be

---

[1] *Ager Romanus* in provinces: Marquardt, *Römische Staatsverwaltung*, Leipzig,
1884, II, p. 181; colonies paying land-tax: *C. Theod.*, I, 90–2. *Laeti*: Eum., *Paneg.*, V,
21; Amm. Marc., XX, 8, 13; XXI, 13, 16; Seeck, PWRE IV, 1900, s.v. Colonatus, cols.
495–6. *Conditio Manciana*: G. Courteois *et al.*, *Tablettes Albertini*, Paris, 1952, pp. 116–
41. Chew Stoke tablet: JRS XLVI, 1956, pp. 115–18. Uninhibited proprietorship:
V. Arangio-Ruiz, *Fontes iuris anteiustiniani*, Florence, 1941–3, III, Negotia, no. 90;
289; cf. Ulp. *Dig.*, XIX, I (A.D. 320). Transfer of land acquired by Mancian lease:
Stevens, CBA. RR VII, p. 109; cf. the *Lex Hadriani de rudibus agris*, CIL VIII, 25943.
Senators and land-taxes: Reid, CMH I, Cambridge, 1911, p. 50; Rostovtzeff, *Soc.
and Econ. Hist. Rom. Emp.*, p. 517. For Rivet on the question of *ager Romanus* in the
provinces after Caracalla, RVB, p. 185.

regarded as a strong, though not an incontrovertible, argument, in favour of imperial domain (*praedium Caesaris*) in Britain. In the fourth century the *Notitia Dignitatum, Occidens*, XI, 20, records the *Rationalis summarum Britanniarum* and the *Rationalis rei privatae per Britannias* (XII, 15). These two officials belonged to the establishment as it was reformed by Severus and reorganized by Diocletian; the first was responsible for imperial revenue, including mints and mines; the *Rationalis rei privatae* administered the remainder of the emperor's property, including what was down to the reign of Severus the *patrimonium Caesaris*, or emperor's personal fortune, and became under Severus two departments, the *patrimonium* and the *res privata*, the latter largely composed of the confiscated property of the emperor's opponents. In the fourth century, after Diocletian's reforms, the practical distinction between the departments of the two *rationales* disappeared, but their functions were perpetuated. Under the control of the *Comes sacrarum largitionum*, or chancellor of the exchequer, is further recorded (*Not. Dig. Occ.*, XI, 60) the procurator of the Venta weaving mill, which will be discussed elsewhere.[1]

Before the reign of Severus the imperial domains elsewhere were administered by procurators subordinate to a chief procurator of the province responsible directly to the emperor. Thus in 60 or 61 the royal domain of Presutagus, king of the Iceni, is taken over while the governor, Suetonius Paulinus, is away fighting in Anglesey, and the imperial procurator Catus Decianus is in charge of the civilian areas. In a similar manner (although not, probably, in the same violent fashion) the royal appanages of Cogidubnus of the Regnenses may be assumed to have passed to the *patrimonium* in the second half of the first century, perhaps including the tracts near Silchester, as hinted by the tiles stamped with Nero's name and titles from Little London and elsewhere.[2]

The probability of a cavalry remount depôt in the region of Irchester (N'hants) will be alluded to (p. 218), and seems to be strengthened by the inscribed stone from Thrapston marking the boundary between public and private property.

Further clear evidence of imperial domain is afforded by the inscription from Combe Down near Bath, dated in all probability to 212–17, and dedicated to the Augustus by an *adiutor* of the procurators who had rebuilt the *principia ruina oppressa* (a ruined headquarters building). There are various opinions on the whereabouts of the

---

[1] *Patrimonium* and *res privata*: A. H. M. Jones, *The Later Roman Empire*, I, Oxford, 1964, pp. 411–12.

[2] Presutagus' domains: Tac., *Ann.*, XIV, 31. Little London tiles: see Chapter II, p. 15.

property to which the *principia* related: Richmond thought the nearby quarries, Stevens has suggested the farms of unruly extraneous elements settled under government auspices; others have connected the offices with the Mendip lead-mines. In effect, as more than one procurator is mentioned, none of these possibilities excludes the others. It may be noted that the building where the inscription was found was ranged round three sides of an open yard, and this plan, resembling as it does that of the *principia* of a Roman fort, may furnish us, as Stevens suggests, with a clue to the existence of other administrative buildings relating to imperial domain.[1]

An inscription at Bath records the rededication to the emperor of a shrine which had been *insolentia dirutum*; the restorer is a centurion who signs himself *regionarius*, i.e. police officer of a *regio*, and the period is later second or third century. This admission of revolt is a rare occurrence in the empire; the term *regio* is used normally for the subdivision of an imperial estate, and in north Britain was applied to the settlement district of the Sarmatian troopers, administered by a centurion holding the title of *praepositus* and seconded from York. *Regionarii* are nearly always an indication of unromanized districts which lay outside city-territories and required firm handling. The officer who rebuilt the shrine at Bath may well have belonged to Salisbury Plain, which contained the largest block of native farmsteads and villages in the lowland zone unassociated with villas, and never seems to have been romanized with any thoroughness. Collingwood suggested that Salisbury Plain comprised an imperial domain; the Bath inscription would support his view.[2]

The name *Caesaromagus* (Moulsham, Ess) has been thought to imply that after the Roman conquest and the establishment of a colony at Colchester the Trinovantes received this place as their tribal capital. Richmond, however, has pointed out that room was left for *incolae* (non-citizens) within the walls of Colonia Victrix. It may also be observed that the name *Caesaromagus* might equally be interpreted to indicate an imperial estate; the place was connected by direct road with the two nearly parallel roads of central Essex discussed below (pp. 100, 59.), and suggestive of a state deforestation project. This seems to me more

[1] Combe Down: RIB, no. 179; the building: VCH *Som.*, I, pp. 309 sqq. Other possible analogies: Pitney, probably breeding pork for army-supply; (see pp. 179sq.). Southwick, Suss, closely connected with the downland 'native' field system; possibly Finkley Farm (Hants) with a *principia*-like plan; it is situated on what may have been imperial domain (see p. 32).
[2] The Bath inscription: RIB, no. 152; *Regio* as part of an imperial estate: A. Schulten, *Die Römischen Grundherrschaften*, Weimar, 1896, pp. 66, 68–9. Policing: cf. Dessau, ILS I, Berlin, 1892, 2,768–9. Salisbury Plain as imperial domain: Collingwood, Myres, RBES[2] Oxford, 1938, p. 224.

likely; *Caesaromagus* may have represented the confiscated estates of the kings of the Catuvellauni and the Trinovantes.[1]

In the areas of the Fens of East Anglia, Cambridgeshire, and south Lincolnshire, air-photography has revealed numerous traces of close settlement in the Roman period in the form of enclosures, field systems, droveways, and groups of habitations. The drainage of these areas, which perhaps began between 50 and 60 of the current era, and gained momentum in the second century, involved the cutting of several major waterways to drain the run-off from the uplands, and was clearly more than private enterprise was ready to undertake. Consequently it is a safe assumption that it was carried out by government initiative, and it would follow that the areas reclaimed for cultivation would have been regarded as state-domain, its settlers being state-tenants or *coloni*. Some confirmation of this status is to be seen in the boundary-stone found at Alconbury near Sawtry (Hunts), inscribed P[V]BL[I]C... and apparently marking the boundary between public and private land. The notable fact relating to the Fenland settlement area is that the field divisions belong preponderantly though not exclusively to the native field pattern, pre-Roman in origin, which is characteristic of the gravels of the Midland river valleys and of the chalk and limestone areas. The economic importance of the area to the authorities is emphasized by the Cardyke, a transport canal whose extensions put the Fens into communication with Lincoln, the Trent, and ultimately the Humber, so making possible the transport of agricultural produce – more particularly grain – to the northern military zone. Dug in the late first or early second century, it can hardly have been other than the work of the administration. Collingwood suggested that the settlement of the Fenland marls and silts was effected by state-leasing to capitalists on conditions of emphyteusis. It may be asked whether the practice of emphyteusis was developed so early in the Empire; nevertheless, leasing to *conductores* who sublet to native *coloni* is probable enough, though entirely hypothetical. But it should be noted that later enclosures of rectangular rectilinear character and considerable size, apparently for cattle, are seen to supersede earlier 'square field' complexes at various points, and this suggests that private enterprise may have taken over from crown tenants at some point in the development of these estates.[2] Hallam suggests that their

---

[1] *Caesaromagus*: It. Ant., 474.3. Cf. *Forum Claudii* (Tarantaise) in Gaul, an imperial estate (CIL XII, 103); *forum* is the Latin equivalent of Celtic *magus*.

[2] The Fens: S. Hallam, *Ant. J.* XLIV, 1964, pp. 19 sqq.; C. W. Phillips (ed.), *The Fenlands in Roman Times*, (FR), Royal Geographical Society, London, 1971; cf. CBA. RR VII, pp. 26–7. Sawtry inscription: RIB, no. 230; cf. analogous stones from Zabern, Vosges, CIL XIII, 11 645–6 and Stevens, *Rev. arch.* 110–11, 1937, pp. 26 sqq. Grain to the north: cf. the northern coal from the Romano-British farmstead of Wyboston

rectilinear character would connect them with settlement by soldier colonists, but they were early abandoned. Yet not all the Fenland may have been crown domain. Some years ago I pointed out that the *Salinae* marked by Ptolemy in the territory of the Catuvellauni would have been on the shore of the Wash, and that the salt industry there would have been the property of the *civitas*. As a parallel may be cited the evidence of inscriptions of Flavian date recording the *salinatores* of the Menapii and the Morini on the north French coast.[1]

The existence of an imperial estate is also a possibility in the Andover area of Hampshire: the reference is to the villa-group consisting of country houses known at Redenham, Clanville, Weyhill ("Vitrici"), Fyfield, Eastfield, Appleshaw, Thruxton, and several other points. The grounds for suspecting the existence of such an estate here are: (1) the discovery at Clanville of an inscription of the emperor Carinus (A.D. 283–4); (2) certain features of the components of the villa-group: (a) the wall decoration of the Clanville house resembled that at Fyfield; (b) the houses at Clanville and Eastfield were closely similar in plan and dimensions; (c) the dwellings at Appleshaw, Eastfield, Clanville, and Redenham used roof-slabs derived from a common source; (d) all were centred upon Weyhill, whose name (Anglo-Saxon *weo*, an idol) and tradition suggest was the market of the district.

The Carinus inscription may have been a milestone, but it was a considerable distance from the Portway, which lies to the south; if anything, it related to the road connecting Weyhill with Redenham. The emperor Carinus reigned only one year, in the course of which he was compelled to suppress the rebellion of the Gallic peasant insurgents known as the Bacaudae. He also took the title "Britannicus." It seems more than probable that he had to engage in similar operations in Britain, and the Andover district may have been a centre of trouble. Nevertheless, the imperial status of the land concerned must remain hypothetical.[2]

Finally, there remains the question, how far the less developed downlands and limestone uplands of Wessex and western England, generally unassociated with villas which normally reflect prosperous owners of private estates, were under direct imperial control. Possible evidence for such control has been discussed in relation to north Somerset (Great Chew) and Salisbury Plain. Professor Hawkes has

(see p. 12), evidently obtained by exports to the north (Tebbutt, CAS L, 1956, p. 83). Emphyteusis: Collingwood, *ap.* Frank, ESAR III, 1937, p. 86.

[1] Hallam, FR p. 75; *salinatores*: CIL XI, 390, 391.

[2] Clanville inscription: VCH *Hants*, I, 297; RIB, no. 98. Weyhill, derivation of name: Ekwall, *Concise Oxford Dictionary of English Place-names*, *ad voc.* Carinus and the Bacaudae: Eutropius, IX, 20; Britannicus Maximus: CIL XIV, 126.

expressed the opinion that the Cranbourne Chase area was imperial domain, since its population were initially recalcitrant and needed watching by a garrison at Hod Hill; in the fourth century the Bokerley Dyke, certainly no private undertaking, was erected to protect the area from the north. Stevens would see in the downland 'square field' area of Wessex and the Upper Thames (watched by a *beneficiarius* at Dorchester-on-Thames), imperial *saltus*, and he regards the existence of fragments of centuriation at Ripe and West Blatchington (below, p. 98) as pointing in the same direction. All this is possible, but in the absence of more definite proof, not certain.[1]

Much the same must be said of the status of the lands of the highland zone. The evidence for cattle-pasture outside the legionary fortresses of Chester and Caerleon suggests that both these legions possessed *prata* under their direct control and devoted to their supplies. In the light of the Chester-le-Street inscription, some if not all forts in the third century held *territoria* for the same purpose. What the position was round York, the third legionary depôt, is difficult to say, since we do not know where the *territorium* of the *colonia*, perhaps established in the third century, lay. The Regio Bremmetenacensis of Ribchester may be taken to indicate that the legion's control extended over a considerable area of the Pennines. The traces of Roman influence upon the Grassington fields (p. 195) suggest the possibility that these areas were under direct imperial administration, which would imply that the land was regarded as domain, but again, there is no absolute proof of this. Farther south, the very large corn-drying installation found near the fortress of Reculver (Kent) is

[1] Cranbourne Chase imperial domain: Hawkes, *Arch. J.* CIV, 1949, pp. 62 sqq. (Bokerley Dyke). Wessex: Stevens, CBA. RR VII, pp. 118–20. Ripe, West Blatchington: *ib.*, 121. Of some interest in this connection are the linear earthworks in west Berkshire known as the East Ditch, and the Grim's Ditch which commences four and a half miles to its north-east. The first earthwork closes off on the west an area of native fields clearly of Roman date, and associated with a Roman building, on Stancombe Down. It consists of a ditch with mounds both sides of it in the southern sector, and with one mound on its east side in the northern sector. Its characteristics are unmilitary and its right-angle turn at one point suggests a Roman date. The second earthwork, which follows the north escarpment of the Downs for eight miles, divides off the native field area from the land to the north. At various points its ditch is on the southern, i.e. uphill side, and it was not therefore defensive. The purpose of both earthworks would seem rather to have been to shut in the cultivators of the Berkshire Downs field systems. The double mound of the East Ditch reminds one of the Vallum behind Hadrian's Wall, the purpose of which was to prevent civilians from the south entering the military zone. The Berkshire earthworks, if their Roman date could be proved, would be one of the strongest pieces of evidence that the native population of the downland fields was subject to special administration and possibly to direct imperial control. For these earthworks, Peake, *Arch. of Berkshire*, London, 1931, p. 122.

certainly connected with the garrison, and could imply that the
garrison were cultivating the land in their vicinity for commissariat
purposes. But it might equally imply that local cultivators were
obliged by the *annona militaris* to deliver their unthreshed crops direct
to the fortress.[1]

It is a general assumption that the greater part of the landowning
class of Roman Britain was composed of the aristocracy of the self-
governing towns, the majority of which, till the third century, were
the centres of the tribal *civitates*. Here analogy from the other provinces
of the empire is in place, but the position can be demonstrated by
written and archaeological evidence. Tacitus states clearly that Agricola
encouraged and aided the Britons to build towns, and although the
Belgae were by no means unfamiliar with incipient town life, as
may be demonstrated by such sites as Camulodunum, Prae Wood,
and pre-Roman Canterbury, Agricola's work meant the transfer of
the British aristocracy to residence in newly built romanized cities.
As they were already cultivators, it may be assumed that they continued
to hold and to work their lands when the new urban centres were
founded. Many of them were doubtless younger sons who, to avoid
the over-parcellation of the family holding, had departed to acquire
new lands farther afield by the strength of their right arms, and had
risen to wealth thanks to the new money economy, by the export
of slaves and agricultural produce – grain, cattle, and hides. The same
surpluses freed man-power for the construction of hill-forts and the
building of bodies of dependent clients. The parallel process in Gaul is
alluded to by Caesar; large estates were being built up and an intermediate nobility was rising to power. In Britain Tacitus refers to
clientes, and if his statement "once they (the Britons) obeyed kings;
now they are being drawn by chiefs into parties and causes" refers
to the last decades of the first century A.D., this was the result of the
same economic processes.[2]

These new political figures had their centres, until the Roman
conquest, in the rudimentary Belgic towns and in the hill-forts; royal
predominance and Roman rule moved the foci to the towns. The
preconquest hill-forts doubtless served as refuges for the inhabitants
of the peripheral villages and farms; when the new Roman towns

[1] Reculver: *Kent Arch. Review* 13, 1968, p. 12.
[2] Agricola's encouragement: Tac., *Agric.*, 21. Belgic town life: Rivet, in *The
Civitas Capitals of Roman Britain*, ed. Wacher, Leicester, 1966, pp. 102–3. Parallel
social processes in Gaul: Caes., *de Bell. Gall.*, VI, 13, 2; 12, 2; 30, 3; intermediate
nobility: G. Dottin, *Manuel pour servir a l'étude de l'antiquité celtique*,[2] Paris, 1915,
pp. 227–32; cliency: H. Hubert, *Les celtes depuis l'époque de la Tène et la civilisation
celtique*, Paris, 1932, pp. 260–61; C. Jullian, *Histoire de la Gaule*, Paris, 1908–26,
v, pp. 174 sq.; II, p. 71 for sources. Clients, kings, and chiefs: Tac., *Agric.*, 12.

were established on the lower ground – in so far as the Belgae had not anticipated this – the chiefs were compelled to migrate to them. Such, at any rate, must be the explanation of the proximity of an important hill-fort to nearly every new tribal centre. Many of the peasants remained in their upland farmsteads, but others already inhabited *aedificia* on the gravels and loams of the lowlands (e.g. Welwyn, Park Street, Otford, Fawkham, etc.). But the hill-forts themselves, whether stormed and slighted or peacefully evacuated, gradually became empty, abandoned to herdsmen and deities. (Maiden Castle–Dorchester; the Trundle–Chichester; St Catherine's Hill–Winchester; Bigbury–Canterbury.) Nor is it insignificant that not a few of the hill-forts finally ceased to be occupied in the Flavian period, when the era of town-building began in earnest; examples are Maiden Castle, Ham Hill (Som), Edisbury (Ches), and Bury Hill (Hants). Their chiefs, once reconciled to submission, became the city aristocracy.[1]

Yet the direct connection between the chief men of the *civitas* centres and the villas that grew and multiplied in their territories is not easy to establish. It has been stated that the permanent inhabitants of the new towns cultivated the land in their immediate vicinity, and this would be the reason for the relative absence of villas from the immediate environs of some British tribal capitals; attention has been drawn to the tendency of villa-groups to develop round secondary centres instead. However, the generalization must be treated with reserve: Canterbury has one or two villas in its immediate vicinity (Wingham, Ickham); Verulamium more (Park Street, Gorhambury, Colney Street, Munden); Colchester has a number (Stanway, Alresford, St Osyth, Dovercourt, Felixstowe, Brightlingsea, West Mersea, Tolleshunt Knights, etc.). And if the immediate vicinity of Silchester is vacant, this is due to the heavy wooded clays surrounding the town; the villas begin to west and south of the clay belts. In Calleva itself only two buildings can be firmly identified as built for farming needs, and agricultural tools were found near them, although Boon points to large walled yards with attached outbuildings associated with five other houses, perhaps to be explained in agricultural terms. Small granaries and corn-driers elsewhere within the walls are probably to be explained by the emergencies of the fourth century.

Archaeology, nevertheless, can furnish some evidence otherwise lacking. The stamped tiles of the municipal tilery of Gloucester, distributed among the villas of the colony's territory, testify to the

---

[1] Maiden Castle: Wheeler, *Maiden Castle*, SARR XII, Oxford, 1943, pp. 66–7. Ham Hill: JRS XXXVIII, 1948, p. 108; SANHS XCV, 1950, p. 156. Edisbury: JRS XXIX, 1939, p. 206. Bury Hill: HFC XIV, 1938/40, p. 335.

link between the city and the surrounding estate-owners. Further
eloquent of the bond between the towns and their surrounding villas
is the superior growth of Cirencester, to be connected with the
flourishing north-Gloucestershire estates which were linked to it by
the Whiteway and other pre-Roman tracks. The relation between
Verulamium and its surrounding countryside can also be illustrated
by archaeological data. The most flourishing period of the city was
between 70 and the later second century: the Park Street villa is
rebuilt in the mid-second century; at Boxmoor the greater part of
the *sigillata* ware belongs to the same century. At Brockley Hill
occupation was strongest between 70 and 170, and weakened decidedly by the end of the same century. The mausoleum at Harpenden contained *sigillata* of the second half of the second century. The
numerous sites of the Letchworth and Baldock district reflected a
similar picture.[1]

If the new urban life of Roman Britain was built up initially round
the tribal aristocracies whose farms, often sited on the newly cleared
medium soils of the lowlands, grew steadily into modest but flourishing
Roman villas, what of the second and broader stratum of British
society, the small peasants? What was the social and economic relationship between the two classes and between them and the Roman
power?

In the first place, the tribal dignitaries did not work in a vacuum:
new elements from abroad penetrated to share in the new urban and
agricultural development. We must always remember that land was
regarded in the Roman world as the most reliable investment; veterans
came sooner or later to settle down in the lowlands; tracts were taken
over for direct imperial exploitation. All these needed man-power.
The problem was not new; slave-irons are known from Bigbury and
Park Street villa, and if slave-raiding and head-hunting were now
stopped by government action, prisoners of war were doubtless
available from over the border. How large a part they played in the
economy we have no means of knowing; the outstanding fact is that
while the bulk of the pre-Roman holdings were based on the labour
of the family, the Belgic aristocrat of Casterley, if it was a large fortified

---

[1] Villa-groups round secondary centres: Rivet *ap.* Corder, CBA. RR, I, London,
1955, *Romano-British Villas: Some Current Problems*, p. 32; in RVB, p. 178, he merely
emphasizes the grouping of villas about towns. Calleva farm-buildings: G. Boon,
Roman Silchester, London, 1957, pp. 178–9: Insulae XXIV, 2; XXIII, 1. Gloucester
tiles: Hucclecote, Ifold, Dryhill, Barnwood; BGAS LVII, 1930, pp. 350–2; JRS XLV,
1955, pp. 68 sqq. Verulamium and hinterland: Park Street, *Arch. J.* CII, 1945, p. 27;
Boxmoor, VCH *Herts*, IV, pp. 154–6; Brockley Hill: LMAS[2] X, 1950, p. 225;
Harpenden: VCH *Herts*, IV, p. 163; Baldock district, JBAA[2] XXXVIII, 1932, pp. 260–1;
Arch. J. LXXXVIII, 1931, p. 299.

farm, could not have fortified his homestead without the service of the surrounding population. Tacitus speaks of clients. The Gallic evidence records debtors and *ambacti*, but it is disputed if the latter were serfs or personal companions of the chief. There was, nevertheless, a basis for a dependent class which could furnish man-power, and the imposition of Roman tribute might well complete a social process by driving other free peasants into complete dependence on their notables. It may also be legitimate to consider the agricultural régime reflected by Figheldean and similar field complexes. In its developed phase this system entailed the regular seasonal movement of livestock from the outfield to the infield to graze the stubble in winter, in a period when the growing of winter crops was increasingly practised, so necessitating the fencing of the winter crops within the infield. The development of the interlocking of a summer-winter sequence with grazing took place *pari passu* with the fencing of the outfield from the infield, the formation of enclosures for flocks, and the linking of the field area by droveways with the nearby hill-fort, Sidbury, probably in the first century before the common era. This is, in other words, a communal agriculture "with established agricultural patterns and rhythms based on common customs," and "its structure implies both a controlling authority and cooperative practices."

The Figheldean Down pattern was almost certainly not uniformly repeated throughout the downlands; it can do no more than demonstrate the main lines of the agricultural and social pattern of the late Early Iron Age village in Wessex. But the upshot would seem to be that when the stronghold was evacuated and the chief settled in the *civitas* capital, either his authority remained or the agrarian pattern was apt to be in danger, especially under pressure of newly imposed taxation. Either the community would continue to look to its chief, now a potential villa-owner, therefore, or the Roman authority itself must ultimately step in.

The situation was not of course necessarily uniform throughout the lowlands. On the gravel areas, especially in the eastern Midlands, air-reconnaissance and exploration by the spade show a strong development of small farms, the successors of more primitive hut-groups. The former developed in the first century as Roman roads were laid out; with these they were linked by a close network of accommodation-roads made by the farmers themselves (Fig. 1). We shall later describe one such characteristic farmstead of the area – Tallington (p. 154). These steadings evince romanization in their enclosures and communications but in little else. Until the third century they remain fundamentally native, although some larger fields may indicate the influence of Roman methods. Their economy seems to have used

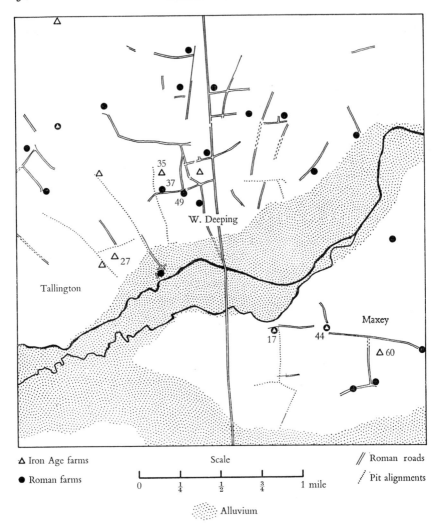

Fig. 1. Early Iron Age and Roman farms, Welland area, Lincolnshire.

little currency. It has nevertheless been noted that the Romano-British farms are more closely grouped than their Early Iron Age predecessors, and a twenty-two-acre village develops at Maxey in the first century. Villas are known in this area near Barnack, Barholm, and Helpstone, the first built in the third century.[1]

[1] Land the securest investment: Colum., I, 11–12; Varro, *de rust. re*, I, 2, 8. Slave-irons: Bigbury, *Arch. J.* LXXXIX, 1932, pp. 108–10; Park Street: *Arch. J.* CII, 1945, pp. 35, 66, fig. 9. Casterley: WAM XXXVIII, 1913, pp. 53 sqq. Ambacti: Caes., *de Bell. Gall.*, VI, 15; Dottin, *Manuel*, pp. 237–9. Figheldean Down: The enclosure

This comparatively early Roman rural settlement is essentially native, and possesses many of the features of the Wessex Early Iron Age Romano-British rural culture, but its traditions were less crystallized, and it may well have been more individualistic. One would not expect here, as one would envisage in Wessex, deeply rooted agrarian social patterns and practices. This did not apply, perhaps, to the more closely woven network of settlement in the Fenland, where palimpsests are not infrequent: here, two types of economy have been tentatively distinguished (above, pp. 13–14), without exhausting other possibilities. Here there appear to be no villas, though some larger conglomerations appear on the margins (Hockwold); the nearest villa estates are sites on the edges of the Fenland where dry land meets the low-lying areas.

There is no specific and incontrovertible written evidence of the colonate in Roman Britain. Even the well known reference in the Theodosian Code is not certainly referable to the province.[1] If the colonate can be proved to have existed, therefore, the proof must lie in archaeological evidence and its social analysis, in analogy from the continent and in the application of ancient Welsh sources. Rivet has said: "You can dig up a villa, but you cannot dig up its land-tenure." Like many wingèd sayings, this is only half true. Something of tenurial relationships can be deduced from a study of the plans of the of the area (the "Ellipse") interpreted by the present writer as for winter crops (PPS xx, 1954, pp. 107 sqq.), and thought by Messrs C. Bowen and P. J. Fowler to be non-existent (Bowen *ap.* Rivet, RVB, p. 22, n. 6), is clear on prints (kindly furnished to me by the Director of the Ordnance Survey Archaeological Division), taken from the air-photographs on which the late Dr Crawford worked. From them it is clear that the field system enclosed by the Ellipse extended west of it before the enclosure was made. Irrespective of this feature, the definition of infield and outfield remains here a later phase connected with cattle droveways and with the hill-fort of Sidbury Hill, while grain-finds of the period indicate an extension of winter-cropping. Fowler and Bowen have further established (see p. 106) that native field complexes included both open and enclosed fields. The Eastern Midlands: RCHM: *A Matter of Time*; CBA vii, pp. 15–25.

[1] C. *Theod.*, xi, 7, 2, was thought by Haverfield, *Romanization of Roman Britain*,[4] Oxford, 1923, p. 65; Collingwood, ESAR iii, p. 87, and originally by Stevens, JRS xxxvii, 1947, p. 132, to show the presence of the colonate in Britain. It should however be pointed out that in the last article, Stevens did not think that the case concerned necessarily involved *coloni* as such, but a point in ancient Welsh law. The enactment cited by C. *Theod.*, xi, 7, 2, he thinks (if I have understood rightly), would have been derived from the archives at Rome and had been cited by British lawyers in support of their case. In any event, Stevens is now of the view that the extract was part of C. *Iustin.*, viii, 52, 2 of 374, which relates to the claims of proprietors on exposed infants. (One thinks, nevertheless, of Hambleden, Bucks, with its numerous infant burials.) As the enactment in C. *Theod.* was addressed in 319 to the Vicar of Britain, I still find it difficult to understand how it could be interpreted to relate to other than Britain.

villas, and also from the topographical and chronological analysis of neighbouring sites. The chief considerations fall under three heads: (1) the tracing of shifts in rural population which can be interpreted as the result of the occupation of the soil by powerful proprietors, causing the creation of a reservoir of landless peasantry which must, if it remains, accept the status of tenant; (2) the presence in the proximity of villas of minor sites whose existence can best be explained in terms of tenurial subordination; (3) the analysis of the outbuildings of villas in order to determine the presence of working hands, their origin, and their vicissitudes in the history of the villa concerned.

Population shifts have been noted in two areas of Britain during the Roman occupation, namely, in Surrey and in East Anglia. The results of such a shift are evident in the Fenland settlement.

In Surrey, several villas are founded or enlarged in the course of the second century – Walton Heath, Farnham Six Bells, Compton, and Sandilands near Walton-upon-the-Hill. Titsey villa probably belongs to the same time. The industrial villa at Ashtead is dismantled about 150, and rebuilt in an inferior manner some years later, to be deserted during the century. Tileworks at Wykehurst Farm (Cranley) and Horton (Epsom) cease work in the later second century. At Farthing Down, Coulsden, native fields went out of cultivation at much the same date, while towards the end of that century native cemeteries at Haslemere and Charterhouse had ceased to be used. At Ewell occupation seems to have fallen off in the Antonine age, and at Purberry Shott nearby a gap intervened in the third century. Native sites at Crohamhurst (Croydon), Hooley near Cobham, Old Byfleet Rectory, and Street Cobham did not last beyond the second. On the other hand an extensive Romano-British site at Old Malden remained occupied from the first to the fourth century.

In Suffolk, changes were roughly contemporary: here evidences of external influences from the continent have been discussed above (p. 26); some five farmsteads now cease to be occupied and new sites begin at Burgh near Woodbridge, Whitton, Eye, Stonham, Stoke Ash, Ixworth, Mildenhall, and Stanton Chair. The potters' village at Needham (Norf) ends in the same period.[1]

---

[1] Rivet on tenure, CBA. RR VII, p. 108. Wykehurst Farm, Horton: SyAC XLV, pp. 75, 89, 90; Farthing Down, Coulsden: SyAC L, 1946–7, p. 47; Haslemere, Charterhouse: SyAC LI, 1949, pp. 27–8; Ewell: SyAC XLVIII, 1943, p. 59; Purberry Shot: SyAC L, pp. 12, 20; Crohamhurst, Old Byfleet Rectory, Street Cobham: SyAC L, p. xxiii; XLVI, 1938, p. 131; XLII, 1934, pp. 111–13; Old Malden: SyAC L, p. xxiii. The abandonment of most of the above sites has been redated after a fresh evaluation of the pottery; cf. Clark, Nichols, SyAC LVII, 1960, p. 70. The development of the Old Malden site may be comparable to that of the Maxey settlement in south Lincolnshire (see p. 38), and suggests a concentration of displaced peasants

The study of the relation of rural sites to villas has also something to tell us in terms of tenurial relationships, although here the conclusions are of necessity more tentative. This is illustrated by the Basingstoke district (Fig. 2), where at a number of sites which ceased to be occupied, according to the pottery, in the late Early Iron Age or in the Belgic period, habitation was renewed in the third or fourth century. These, with three other sites which were occupied before or during the third century and continued to be inhabited after it, form a periphery round the villa of Newtown, the appearance of which had apparently caused the abandonment of five sites in its vicinity in the first century A.D. The conclusion presents itself that in the late Roman period a series of satellite holdings sprang up round the larger estate or within its boundaries, and this suggests colonate tenure, especially as some of these are native sites rehabilitated after prolonged evacuation.

In this context we may note the occupation of the western half of the Bignor villa's cultivated area by Roman sites whose existence would indicate the presence of tenants. A similar conclusion may be derived from the evidence at Ditchley (p. 158), where the neglect of the house in the latter part of the fourth century and the absence of hands' quarters or livestock buildings, suggested the absence of the owner, despite the intensive continuation of farm activity. Radford interpreted these phenomena as the result of the settling out of slaves with livestock at this period, but it seems to me more probable that the estate had become absorbed in a larger property, while the absence of corn-driers, *de rigueur* in farms of the period, would mean that the grain was dried on the holdings of the *coloni* who brought it to the villa for threshing and storing. As possible farmhouses of such *coloni* earning their living by wage-labour or crafts. Compare, below, the evidence of Hockwold in the Fenland. Needham: NA xxvIII, 1947, p. 189. It should be mentioned here that R. G. Collingwood's belief that there was an extensive evacuation of native peasantry from the Salisbury Plain area in the fourth century, the result of "deliberate transplantation to serve capitalistic landlords or a socialistic state" (RBES, p. 223), does not seem to be warranted by a study of the archaeological evidence. Collingwood based his belief on the premise that coins at Woodcuts and other native sites die out in the Constantinian age. In effect, fifteen sites show coins later than that date, at four, coins end with Theodosius (392–5), and at five with Valentinian or Valens (364–78). As the currency of the latter two emperors was late in arriving in this country, sites with Constantinian coins may be assumed to have survived at least till 367, and those with coins of Valentinian or Valens after that date. Thus 29 sites survived till the Pict War of that year, and 15 were certainly occupied after it. Four additional sites can be shown to have existed after 367 by the presence of rosette-stamped pottery. Coinage shows that some villas around Salisbury Plain were hit by the disaster of 367, but six out of 13 survived. Hence it is clear that even if the chief cause of the evacuation of part of the native settlements of the area was not due to the Pict War, the event need have nothing to do with the economies of the villa estates in the proximity of the Plain.

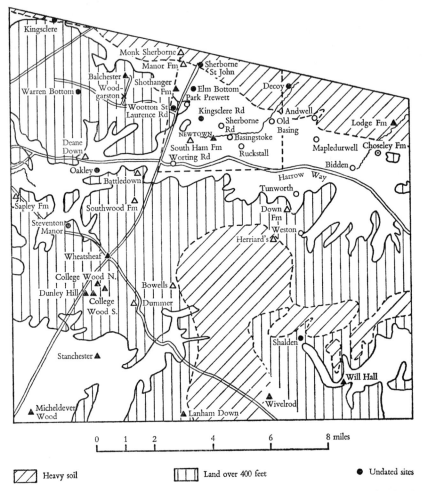

Fig. 2. The distribution of Roman settlement in the Basingstoke district in the third and fourth centuries A.D., showing the sites peripheral to the Newtown villa, Basingstoke.

may be mentioned Callow Hill, Lee's Rest, Hensington, a site near Kiddington, and perhaps Pump Copse.

The evident dependence of East Grimstead and Holbury on West Dean will be discussed below (p. 170). Attention may also be drawn to the Stroud villa (Hants), whose anatomy suggests that it formed the centre for a peasantry who cultivated the vicinity, and that Stroud itself was attached to a larger centre. (See p. 176.) Similar conclusions may be derived from North Wraxhall: here the reduction of accommodation for livestock and personnel in the fourth century and the appearance of a cemetery suggested the settling out of hands as *coloni* who looked to the villa as their centre (p. 179). We may also recall the villa of Great Wymondley and its adjacent village, both included in a 'grid' of centuriated fields of some 1,100 *iugera* (about 680 acres), implying the division of its tract among settlers who could hardly have been other than *coloni* (p. 90); how far the same applies to the Cliffe fields (p. 97), depends on whether we see the allotments as depending on the villa of Frindsbury or on the Roman town of Rochester. The West Blatchington field divisions also imply tenancies, but of a special character (see below, p. 98).

Generally speaking the ecology of the Roman villa, i.e., the detailed study of the estate centre in relation to its surroundings, with a view to casting further light on tenurial relations, is in its infancy, but some useful facts may be gleaned from one or two other recent studies. Thus, Rahtz's examination of the vicinity of the small villa at Downton (Wilts) established there the existence of minor buildings and drainage ditches north-west of the residence, and beyond them of peripheral roads, ovens, and hearths; Roman finds, in fact, were reported over an area of twelve acres, although the estate was thought to have been larger. On the peripheral remains, Rahtz wrote that they showed "domestic occupation on a small scale," but "no more than might be expected on the fringe of the villa, established in huts or hovels occupied by the estate dependents." Boon noted the proximity of smaller sites to the villa of Kingsweston (Glos), and thought they represented the homes of its *coloni*.

At Hockwold, on the chalk sloping north to the Fens from the Little Ouse (north-west Suff), Salway found two adjacent sites, the westerly characterized by masonry structures, the easterly a forty-acre hut-village intensively occupied in the mid-second century, when he believed it bore a relationship of social dependency (as of village to manor) on the site to its west. This he compared to a similar apparent relationship between two sites in the Brandon district (Fenhouse Farm and Hiss Farm); he has further recorded villa-village associations at Denver, Stonea, and Somersham-Colne. Stevens points to similar villa-village relationships in eastern Britain at Arbury Road (Cambridge), Scole, Ixworth, Icklingham, and Rivenhall. We also note the concentration of peripheral finds about the villa of Bisley (Glos), and the existence of at least three occupied sites close to the two villas at Shakenoake (Oxon), two of them with structural remains.[1]

[1] Basingstoke District: HFC xviii, 1953, pp. 126–7. The above conclusions have been criticized by Rivet because they are almost exclusively based on surface pottery finds. It must however be pointed out that they are based on several sites which yielded a fair quantity of such pottery, sufficient to justify the extension of the

There is little doubt that systematic examination would reveal minor sites in association with a considerable number of Roman villas in this country, and where the contemporaneity of the two elements can be established it would be reasonable to see in their association the reflection of a colonate.

The study of farm layout has also something to tell us of social and tenurial development. A general trend is elicited in the evolution of the average Romano-British farm: it may be defined briefly as centralization, decentralization, and devolution. The process of centralization is implied in the creation of the villa itself; this is a social as well as an economic development. The small self-contained farm-hut of the Romano-British proprietor gives way to a small bungalow, then to a masonry farmhouse, implying a concentration of means and population. A gradual change is seen at Lockleys, Mansfield Wood-house, or Park Street, a drastic one at King's Worthy. The concentration of hands no doubt often consisted of slaves, but the cases of West Blatchington and those villas which remain associated with an apparently native field system, are perhaps better explained as concentrations of free kinsmen beneath their chief's roof. A similar process is to be suspected at Northleigh, Clanville, Stroud, and North Warnborough. But romanization also commences a process of residential decentralization which has social implications. At such places as Ditchley, Clanville, Stroud, and Brading, no less at Norton Disney and Mansfield Woodhouse, probably at Northleigh, the agricultural functions of the self-contained farmhouse are devolved upon outbuildings round about or ranged each side of a yard; the process of the separation of the owner from his workers begins, and in some cases at least (e.g. Norton Disney in the third century) this probably meant the final degradation of kinsmen or freemen to the status of dependent labourers.

Of course, the proportion of slave to free labour is impossible to estimate; the status of the occupants of the basilical buildings will be discussed below.

Yet an understanding of the above process does not solve the problem of how the colonate related to the bulk of the native population, and whether owner and *colonus* cooperated in one form of cultivation or were divided by differences of agricultural régime. Neither the villas

conclusions concerning them to other sites with less pottery but a similar pattern. The pattern of first-century A.D. evacuation followed by late reoccupation has now been confirmed by excavation at Oakridge II Estate, Basingstoke—CBA *Archaeological Review*, 1966, I, p. 10. Downton: Rahtz, WAM LVIII, 1961/3, pp. 303 sq. Hockwold: Salway, CAS LX, 1967, pp. 39 sqq. Kingsweston: Boon, BGAS LXIX, 1950, pp. 5 sqq. Stevens on Arbury Road, Scole, Ixworth, Icklingham, and Rivenhall: CBA. RR VII, p. 126: fig. 1 and p. 122. Shakenoake: JRS LVIII, 1968, p. 193, fig. 15, C, D, G.

nor the native field system were necessarily homogeneous from an agricultural and social point of view, and the colonate was certainly not coincident with the totality of the native rural system. If the co-inhabitants of some villas were members of the same social structure with the owner, this suggests that such villas cultivated fields reflecting a native system, and there is some evidence showing this was the case.

The enquiry may find a point of departure by posing the question: who were the class which supplied the labour for the richer estate-owners represented by the villas? A key to the problem is perhaps to be seen in the aisled or basilical building. This type of building, whose origins have already been discussed (pp. 16 sqq.), appears both as an independent homestead and as an outbuilding in the yards of many of the larger villas. In recent years excavation has disclosed a very large number of new examples: at least twenty-nine have been found since 1952, not counting several doubtful cases, and geographically they range from Beadlam in Yorkshire to Cefn Graeanog in Caernarvon-shire and Gatcombe in Somerset; but they show a high percentage, namely, sixty per cent, in eastern England.

Where the aisled house appears as an independent homestead, there is very little doubt that the owner (or his bailiff) dwelt together there with his hands. Where it appears as an appendage to the residence it normally housed the labourers. But it fulfilled other functions as well; at Spoonley Wood, Ickleton, and elsewhere it was a byre, a stable, or both; at Rapsley Farm, Ewhurst (Surr), it was used for industrial purposes, as also at Huntsham (Heref). At Thistleton Dyer such a building was built in the mid-third century, as a temple of the god Veteris. There is no doubt therefore that this building was a maid-of-all-work, as befitted a very ancient form with deep roots, although the earliest certain cases known so far in Britain do not precede the second century of the current era. It may be said with a fair measure of assurance that many of the buildings which served to house hands subsidiarily to the residence belonged to the fourth century. As self-contained homesteads, on the other hand, they almost certainly existed earlier (Cherry Hinton), and some still performed that rôle in the fourth century (Denton, Lincs). But in essentials the type originated as the homestead where man and beast dwelt together, where all necessary indoor work was done, and produce stored, and this fact explains the subsequent ramification of its functions.

It seems on the whole likely that this was the house of the king and the chief, and at Exning (Suff) we see the owner residing, in the second rebuilding phase, in heated mosaic-paved rooms in his traditional quarters at the far end of the house. The appearance of the form from abroad comparatively late seems to be demonstrated at Thistleton Dyer, where the basilical temple was preceded by a circular shrine. Each structure in its turn represented the chief's dwelling, since the god was a chief, and dwelt in a chief's great circular hut – the same hut that appears at Little Woodbury, Hod Hill, and Dinorben. It seems evident, then, that in the third century too, when Veteris received a basilical temple at Thistleton, he was the peculiar god of the local landowner, and closely identified with him; he was the deity of the homestead. The rapid increase of basilical dwellings in the third century, therefore, represents more than a mere fashion or foible; it is a movement, the growth of a class. The Thistleton temple is the apotheosis of the chief's position in society, an 'etherialization' of his residence.

Is it possible to define this position more clearly? It may be useful to scrutinize the Caernarvonshire upland homestead of Cefn Graeanog; it is a replica, in miniature, of the villa of Stroud near Petersfield, already discussed. The similarity is almost complete, except for the bathhouse, and where Stroud has a polygonal temple (placed, it would seem, where the original villa gate was – in a position corresponding to the gate of Cefn Graeanog), the Welsh homestead has a large round hut which has moved to the other end of the aisled building. At Stroud, the chief or owner had gone elsewhere, and the polygonal hut-shrine had been built to perpetuate his *mana*. At Cefn Graeanog, apparently, he remained and dwelt.

Nothing could illustrate more plainly that Stroud, and no doubt many villas where matters are not so obvious, represent a profound fusion of Roman and Celtic social life. When J. T. Smith expressed the view that the basilical hall was *inter alia* a court of law he may not have been far wrong, because originally, at least, the chief administered justice. But the 'apotheosis' of the basilical house at Thistleton and the appearance of the circular temple to represent the chief *in absentia* at Stroud, take us further. This is a legitimization of the landowner in his society, a confirmation and reinforcement of his status vis-à-vis the people whom he heads.[1]

This conclusion may encourage us to risk a conjecture on the identity of the people who dwelt in the aisled buildings at Stroud, at Cefn Graeanog, and elsewhere. Cults are required to impose authority not upon slaves and helots, but upon potential equals. This potential equality, indeed, was grasped by Smith in his analysis of the plans of aisled houses, and more particularly on examination of Norton Disney (where owner and subordinates shared a common bathhouse) and

[1] Basilical temple at Thistleton Dyer: JRS LII, 1962, p. 171, fig. 19; pp. 172, 192. Cefn Graeanog: CBA. RR VII, p. 34, fig. 34; the bathhouse is provided for in Welsh law (*Anc. Laws and Institutes of Wales*, I, pp. 259, 447). Court of law: J. T. Smith, *Arch. J.* CXX, 1963, p. 13.

of the well-appointed aisled hall of Mansfield Woodhouse. If the dweller in the big Welsh hut corresponded in status to the man whose patron was the god of the Thistleton aisled temple and the divinity of the polygonal temple at Stroud, then Cefn Graeanog was not the dwelling of bondsmen or slaves but of his own kith and kin, who lived in the aisled house. This, indeed, is the testimony of the Welsh sources, which describe dwellings of the aisled type as the abode of the extended family, the kindred occupying the aisles and the chief the upper end. We therefore suggest that in the self-contained basilical villa (West Meon, Tidbury Ring, Denton) the labour-force consisted of the kinsmen of the proprietor. West Blatchington may make the matter clearer, for here the self-contained basilical house appears coevally with the squaring off of the arable by centuriation, at the end of the second or third century. In some instances, then, the new régime was the result of an administrative act, and if this new land-division was not actually the work of the government, a resettlement was taking place which combined Celtic forms with methods characteristic of the Roman administration. An official stamp was here placed upon the subdivision of the land among the members of the kinship.[1]

It is at the moment virtually impossible to know if the same conclusion should be applied to the inmates of the basilical outbuildings in the yards of large villas in the fourth century. What can be stated is that the growing gap between the proprietor and the dwellers in his hall is traceable before that: the aisled house is sometimes divided into rooms by the insertion of party walls, and economic functions, sometimes also hands' quarters, are relegated to buildings about the yard (Clanville, Brading, Stroud). But where the aisled buildings themselves occupy the yards separately from the residence, the social composition remains an enigma, nor can we ignore the fact that slaves too must have been an element in the rural economy of Roman Britain. Formal logic, nevertheless, would see these buildings as the final phase of the process of social degradation of the kinsmen from client to serf. This, however, is to assume that all the owners of the villas in question were Britons, which is improbable. If, however, we agree that the kinsmen of the Celtic kinship unit composed an important element among the labour of the country estates, the question arises: did a third element

[1] Relations of owners and subordinates: Smith, *ibid.*, pp. 12, 13. The aisled building as the abode of the kinship: *Anc. Laws and Institutes*, I, p. 293; Vened., III, 21; C. Guest, *The Mabinogion*, London, 1849, II, 394–5; cf. F. Seebohm, *The English Village Community*[4], London, 1890, pp. 239–42. J. Wacher, noting the drastic replacement of circular huts by rectangular buildings in the late second century at Winterton, Lincs, (paralleled at Mansfield Woodhouse and Norton Disney), suggests that government imposition was involved (*Ant. J.* XLIV, 1964, p. 84). In all three cases basilical houses are concerned.

exist, namely, the bondmen whose class is described in the Ancient
Laws of Wales?

It is controversial how far the Ancient Laws of Wales, and more
especially the oldest code, that of Hywel-Dda, may be legitimately
used to enlarge our understanding of life in Roman Britain. As far
back as 1905 Vindogradoff recorded his belief that "...in Britain
the rural arrangements of the Roman period seem to have been to
a great extent determined by Celtic antecedents," and with reference
to the growth of the power of landowners over their tenants and
neighbours, that "in the Celtic districts there was a special stimulus
for its development in the tenacious traditions of clientship;" the
powers of such prominent men "would merely appear as the continuation of a similar action on the part of clan-chieftains."

To emphasize the abiding Celtic undercurrent in Roman Britain
is a task beyond the scope of this chapter, but some of its aspects have
already been alluded to; cultic epigraphy tells the story, supplemented
by the ritual decapitation, the burial of the sheep under the threshold,
or of the teenage boy under the floor. At a higher level the Code of
Justinian enjoining the provincial governor to take cognizance of
long-standing custom in judging his cases (A.D. 224), envisages the
existence of local codes which persisted after the Edict of Caracalla.
Stevens has pleaded the case for such in Britain, and when Aggenus
Urbicus speaks of a veteran sharing his allotment among three or
four sons, he may have been thinking of Britain or Gaul. Archaeology,
moreover, speaks for the survival in Britain of Celtic law, at least in
the agrarian sphere; the Fenland field system, preponderantly native,
is known to have been under cultivation down to the fourth century,
indicating that native property rights enjoyed recognition and that
this aspect of the Celtic social system was acknowledged. The closely-
set system of native fields surrounding Thundersbarrow Hill (Suss)
was also under cultivation in that century, and other similar examples
could certainly be cited.[1]

It is another question, how far the oldest stratum of written Welsh
law can be applied to Roman Britain. The manuscripts, at least, have

---

[1] Vinogradoff and Celtic antecedents: *The Growth of the Manor*, London, 1905,
pp. 72, 87. Ritual decapitation: Great Casterton, JRS LVII, 1967, p. 183; but not all
are ritual – see p. 236 and CBA. RR VII, p. 103. Burial of sheep: Yatton, JRS LV,
1965, p. 216; of pony: *Bristol Arch. Research Group Bulletin* II, 1968, p. 62, Butcombe;
child decapitated: Springhead, Temple IV, *A. Cant.* LXXXII, 1967, p. 265; teenage boy:
Orton Longville, JRS LVIII, 1968, p. 189. *Codex Iustiniani*, VIII, 53, 1. Celtic law:
Stevens, JRS XXXVII, 1947, pp. 132 (perhaps no longer applicable); CBA. RR VII,
pp. 108–10. Aggenus Urbicus, *Gromatici veteres, de controversiis agrorum*, pp. 132 sqq.
(Thulin). Fens: cultivation to fourth century, *Ant. J.* XLIV, 1964, pp. 19 sqq., esp.
pp. 24–5. Thundersbarrow: *Ant. J.* XIII, 1933, pp. 109 sqq. and Fig. 12.

been edited to distinguish clearly between the original text and later commentaries, so that they are less prone to misapplication than the corresponding Irish records. Further, the laws contain certain obviously primitive features, and Alcock has pointed out that the law of the Pridolder implies occupation of land for at least thirteen generations, which takes it back to the sixth century; it may have been older still. On the other hand the same code indicates a fully settled society, with crystallized agricultural arrangements and practices, and archaeology bears out that in north and central Wales, where the Roman villa hardly penetrated, the British were living in huts and enclosed farm-groups as early as the second century. (Above, pp. 189.)[1]

G. R. J. Jones has emphasized in his studies that the bond-hamlets of Wales composed a not inconsiderable element of Welsh society in the eleventh century, and had probably been more important earlier. These were nucleated settlements of unprivileged inhabitants (*taeogs*), subordinated to the king or to a noble, and paying service in the form of produce. The king's *taeogs* were supervised by a royal steward (*maer*) who was responsible for a group of such villages. These bond-men cultivated common land (*tir cyfrif*) which, with its livestock, was redistributed whenever a member died or a youth attained his majority. This régime differed fundamentally from that of the free Welshman, who held his plot as part of the ancestral kinship holding, which was redivided among the sons for two generations and then reunited. Till then all lived in one homestead or *gwely*; when it occurred, each member founded his own kinship group or *gwely*. The land of the kinship was classified as *tir gwelyog*, and the settlement pattern composed of such kinship holdings took the form of isolated home-steads each in its ancestral tract, dispersed over the region, the more so as individual families might, if they chose, break away to bring new land under cultivation. But otherwise three generations of the *gwely* inhabited the same homestead or large house.[2]

Stevens has put forward the theory, that a considerable part of the rural population of Roman Britain was subject to one or other of these social régimes, i.e. that of freemen inhabiting dispersed homesteads and dividing their land unto the third generation, or of dependent bondmen inhabiting nucleated villages and cultivating common land periodically redistributed. The latter régime he saw as forming the basis for large and prosperous villa estates which rose to wealth by

---

[1] Irish laws: D. A. Binchy, *Proc. British Academy*, 1943, pp. 195 sqq., esp., p. 203 and n.; the law of Pridolder: L. Alcock, *Dinas Powys*, Cardiff, 1963, pp. 196–7; appealed to in Britain?—Stevens, p. 48, n. 1.

[2] Bond-villages: G. R. Jones, *Inst. of British Geographers, Trans. and Papers, 1953* (1954), pp. 65–9; *Geografiske Annaler* XLIII, 1961, pp. 175–6.

the exploitation of bond-hamlets; the former régime, in his view, formed the basis for the smaller and less prosperous villas, whose economics were permanently hampered by the necessity of redividing their lands. Using patterned mosaics as a criterion of economic status, he finds the main weight of the 'bond-village'-based villas in the west of Britain, and that of the 'kinship group' villas in the east.

In order to examine Stevens's hypothesis, let us ask: how would these respective régimes look to the archaeologist? The settlement of the proprietor with bond-villages at his disposal, in its Roman form, would have consisted of a well-to-do villa with one or more nucleated inhabited sites in its vicinity possessing open-field systems. The *tir gweliaug*, on the other hand, should have consisted of a more modest villa in which more than one family could live, and its fields should be such as to reveal, theoretically, subdivisions into smaller units. Hypothetically there would have been other villas in the vicinity which represented the hiving off of the fourth generation. The evidence to be derived from the place-names Vagniacae and Sulloniacae should be considered in this connection, perhaps also the inscribed pavement at Eastfield, Hants (see pp. 23–4).

If, moreover, there is to be a recognizable form of the kinship group's joint dwelling on *tir geweliog*, it should be the independent self-contained aisled farmhouse. A provisional distribution-map of such buildings throughout the country (unfortunately sufficient details are not forthcoming on all of them, and a number of uncertain cases occur, so that the analysis cannot be exact) shows how they are distributed between east and west. If the dividing line is drawn along the Jurassic Way, but leaving Nottinghamshire, Hampshire, and Berkshire in the east, then we find 16 basilical buildings of all types in the west, and 34 in the east. The west contains 6 independent aisled dwellings (without Wales) and the east 17. The west has 6 subsidiary aisled buildings, the east 12. This distribution, though provisional and certainly open to correction, is not entirely unfavourable to the Stevens hypothesis, but a majority of subsidiary aisled buildings in the east sector creates difficulties. Nor is it easy to find nucleated villages in the direct vicinity of villas, and most of the identifiable cases are in the eastern region. Future research may change the picture, but Stevens's suggested division, if it existed, is merely one of weight. Yet even for those who cannot accept the theory *in toto*, it contains valuable elements. It invites further prolonged study because it draws our attention to various unexamined possibilities, the more so because it is clear that much of Romano-British rural life had strong Celtic undertones beneath its external romanization.[1]

[1] Stevens, CBA. RR VII, pp. 108–28.

Four other aspects invite consideration in this context, namely: (1) the social significance of nucleated rural settlements; (2) the form of field pattern and its social implications; (3) the relation of bondmen to the tribal system of Roman Britain; (4) the relation of field patterns to villas.

Collingwood and Crawford wrote of "native villages" in reference to the upland areas generally associated with the 'native field' system. Bersu's renowned excavation of Little Woodbury created a reaction in favour of the view that native rural settlement upon the chalk and the oolites of the lowland zone consisted predominantly of isolated farmsteads. My own study of Figheldean Down (1954) suggested that the reality was more complex, and the work reported at the Council for British Archaeology's 1965 conference on Romano-British rural settlement restored the *status quo*, showing that in the south of England, at least, and also on the gravels of the eastern Midlands, nucleated villages associated with traditional native field systems were to be found. Almost at the same time Mrs Sylvia Hallam published her detailed analysis of Fenland settlement development, in which nucleations figured prominently. The work of Bowen and Fowler has made clear the existence of considerable nucleated villages at such places as Chisenbury, Knook Down, and Overton Down (Wilts), Town Hill near Frampton and Meriden Down north-west of Blandford (Dors). Overton Down covers some 10 acres; Chisenbury 14½ acres. Several of these sites reveal planned streets and numerous platform houses. Other nucleated settlements may now be quoted from Somerset (Gatcombe) and Northamptonshire (Maxey); smaller loose nucleations of farmhouses may be mentioned at Studland (Dors), Park Brow (Suss), and Wiggonholt (Suss).[1]

The possibility that nucleated bond-villages existed as part of the Romano-British rural system poses the question of field pattern. Common fields subject to periodical redistribution naturally suggest strips to the enquirer, and there is no doubt that strip fields are commoner among Romano-British fields both in the lowland and highland zones than previously thought. In the highland zone, however, they are seldom grouped, and at Grassington, where they are, they are enclosed. Nor is it always clear if fields of this form are open or closed in Wales, Cumberland, and Westmorland. At Chisenbury Warren near Enford (Wilts), however, we find a nucleated village associated with fields

---

[1] Little Woodbury: PPS² VI, 1940, pp. 30 sqq. Nucleated villages: CBA. RR VII, pp. 48–53 (Chisenbury, Frampton, Meriden Down, Knook Down, Overton Down south-east, etc.). The Fens: Hallam, *Ant. J.* XLIV, 1964, pp. 19 sqq. Gatcombe: SANHS CXI, 1967, p. 24; CXII, 1968, pp. 40 sqq.; BUS IX, 1965, pp. 173–5; XI, 1967, pp. 125–60. For a further list, Hallam, *loc. cit.*, pp. 23, 26, 28, 29–31.

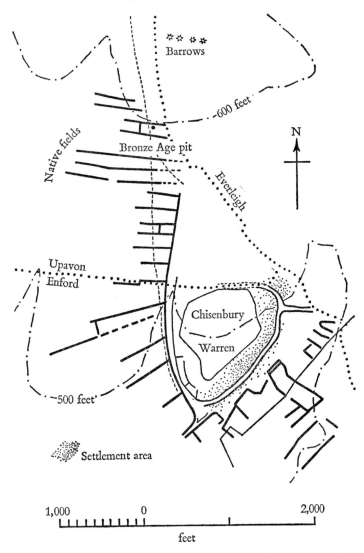

Fig. 3. The Chisenbury area, Wiltshire, with long fields of Roman date
near a Romano-British nucleated village.

of pronounced long-strip type, apparently up to 1,000 feet in length,
but information whether they were enclosed or not is awaited (Fig. 3).
Yet it is relevant to comment that in Ireland, at least, *rundale* (an
open-field system divided into very small strips), as the physical
expression of extreme partition among inferior tenancies, took place
within fields which resembled the normal 'native' plots of Early Iron

Age and Roman Britain, and this might have applied also in this country.

What is clear, none the less, thanks to the work of Fowler and Bowen, is that both enclosed and open fields occur in the Wessex field systems of the period. Sometimes they are enclosed by low walls or clearance banks, which would be no obstacle to livestock or to the carrying over of a plough; sometimes they are enclosed by fences which would have kept livestock both in and out, and would have been irreconcilable with common ploughing. How these variations are related to field-form and settlement-form we do not yet know.[1]

But we can say something more definite of the social significance of nucleation thanks to the work of Mrs Hallam in the Fens. Mrs Hallam showed that the hut-group of two or three huts in the first century became, in 21 per cent of the cases, a loose nucleation of 4–11 huts by the later third or fourth century, comprising 47 per cent of the sites *within* the groups in that period. This tells us that nucleation was in this area an organic natural growth, and not the result of conscious customary nucleation. If it reflects any pattern at all, it is that of the kinship group, and the process of subdivision of the kinship holding; huts multiply as the holding is divided, but remain in the same vicinity. In other words, loose nucleations associated with 'native' fields may represent the normal Celtic kinship system. How this relates to agrarian practices is another question, and we have already noted that two patterns are discernible among the Fenland fields, one of which was perhaps open; on this matter further observation is required. The provisional conclusion from Mrs Hallam's evidence then, is that the inhabitants of the Fenland *saltus* lived according to kinships on *tir gweliog*; in other words, if they were *coloni*, *colonus* is not apparently the equivalent of *taeog*.[2]

Were there then no bondmen of the early Welsh category in Roman Britain? In Ireland, at least, scholars have increasingly inclined to the view that two distinct agrarian patterns are discernible in the country's ancient economy, namely, the single farm (the *rath*), representing the free population, and the more ancient nucleated village (the *clachan*), to be associated with open fields. A reading of Irish historians and of the accounts of the Irish system in the time of Elizabeth, James I, and the Georges, makes it evident that the subdivision of land into minute

[1] Strip fields: Stevens, CBA. RR vII, pp. 113–17. Irish rundale: *ibid.*, p. 112, citing McCourt, *Journ. Donegal Historical Society* II, 1955, pp. 47–60; cf. also Seebohm, *English Village Community*, p. 226; Sir John Davies, *Primer Report des causes et matters en Ley* etc., London, 1628; H. Gray, *English Field Systems*, Cambridge, Mass., 1915, p. 154. Open and enclosed fields, see p. 106.

[2] Hallam, *loc. cit.*, p. 28, Table II.

strips jointly worked (*runrig*) was characteristic of the 'inferior' tenancies, and the result of the domination of chiefs. Such a process need not inevitably have occurred in Roman Britain, but taken with the evidence of the Welsh laws, it suggests the possibility of the existence of this pattern. Can historical evidence be used to deduce that an inferior class was to be found among the peasantry of lowland Britain?[1]

We may utilize for our purpose Rivet's account of developments in Britain before and soon after the conquest. A number of tribes referred to by Caesar have disappeared in Ptolemy's time (the mid-second century A.D.), and among them may have been the *civitates Cogidubno regi donatae* (Tac., *Agric.*, 14, 2) at the time of the conquest. The more limited number of tribes figuring in Ptolemy's account, which draws on first-century material, suggests that the weaker tribes had become, before the conquest, the clients of the stronger. When the Roman invasion took place, various subject tribes came to terms with the invaders, including one section of the Bodunni or Dobunni of Gloucestershire. What happened to the tribal section which did not? On Ptolemy's information, and on the evidence of coin-distribution, part of the Dobunni were attributed to the Belgae, just as part of the Atrebates were given to Cogidubnus' Regnenses, who were Roman allies. But the Belgae were an artificial creation occupying north Somerset, Salisbury Plain, and Hampshire. On their south, the Durotriges had also offered a stout resistance to the Romans, and for a period, at least, forces were stationed in their territory. Deeper into this situation we cannot go, but it emerges that there are two groups: the tribes who were clients of the expanding Belgae prior to the conquest, and those who, having offered a stern resistance to the conquest, might be expected to be penalized by inferior status after it. In strict logic the first group might now be thought to have assumed favoured status, while the second would have been degraded. The actual outcome was certainly not so simple, because the Romans, as political realists, often made it their policy to reconcile the stronger. Two facts emerge: Cogidubnus, non-Belgic and collaborationist, retains an enlarged kingdom; and part of the Belgae, with a section of the Dobunni, are concentrated in an area whose heartland is Salisbury Plain – Hampshire; the central part of this area, Salisbury Plain, remains permanently unurbanized, and villas are confined to its fringes. Here, if anywhere, we might expect a politically inferior

---

[1] Ireland, *rath* and *clachan*: *Advancement of Science* LX, 1959, E. E. Evans, p. 334; V. B. Proudfoot, p. 337. Subdivisions and inferior tenancies: A. Meitzen, *Siedlungsgeschichte und Agrarwesen der Westgermanen und Ostgermanen*, I Berlin, 1895, pp. 203–4; also Sir John Davies, Gray, and Seebohm as cited on p. 53, n. 1.

stratum, and here we find nucleated villages with strip fields, which may or may not be open and common. The colonists of the Fenlands were members of free kinships because the area was new and non-existent before the Roman administration stepped into the place of the Celtic kings, and created (or perpetuated) nucleations of cultivators paying direct to the crown, whose agents might have been the predecessors of the mayors of Welsh law. If the *taeogs* were also part of the villa economy, they may have been party to a parallel system. But how crown-bondmen can be reconciled with the information of Ptolemy that Salisbury Plain was, all or part, within the *civitas Belgarum*, is another question.

And here it would be wise to emphasize again that a number of villas were associated with fields of the native type (pp. 102 sqq.). Two farmsteads of this category whose fields have been surveyed by Fowler are Barnsley Park (Glos) and Lye Hole, Wrington (Som). Strips do not figure in the first of these patterns, so far as can be seen at present; in the second something like strips appears; but it still remains to be seen whether either of these is a normal villa or a nucleated settlement. Bowen has also planned similar plots in the immediate vicinity of Brading villa. But it may be tentatively concluded that a number of villas remained rooted in pre-Roman agriculture and agrarian social structure, and may be assumed, therefore, to have represented free kinship groups.[1]

[1] Rivet *ap.* Wacher, *The Civitas Capitals*, pp. 101 sqq. *Civitates Cogibudno regi donatae:* Tac., *Agric.*, 14, 2. Bodunni: Dio, LX, 20. Part of the Dobunni attributed to Belgae: Rivet, *loc. cit.*, p. 102. Imperial domain and the *civitas Belgarum*: cf. *American Journ. of Archaeology* II, 1886, p. 128, a Phrygian boundary stone marking the boundary between the Sagalassi and a κώμη Νέρωνος Κλαυδίου Καίσαρος. Brading: C. Bowen, in Rivet, RVB, fig. 1.8 and p. 44. For further evidence for the origin of some estates in the Celtic agrarian system, see p. 244.

CHAPTER IV

THE CHOICE OF SITE

IT HAS long been an axiom among students of Roman Britain that Roman settlement in the lowland zone and more particularly the wealthier rural economy represented by the villas, was restricted to the lighter well-drained soils of that region. If nothing has occurred to falsify this principle in the last decades of research, a more extensive and intimate knowledge of the Romano-British rural system has at least modified many of its details. First, extended archaeological research and the first utilization of soil-surveys have enabled us to qualify the generalization by pointing to over-emphases. Secondly, sub-classification of soil-types upon which Roman rural settlement flourished promises new possibilities of settlement classification. Thirdly, surveys have demonstrated that in many districts Roman occupation was considerably more intensive than hitherto supposed. Each of these actual or potential modifications may be illustrated. In respect of over-emphases recent study has shown that Roman settlement is also represented in certain areas of medium soils verging on the heavier categories, and that many farms and estates, although themselves situated on lighter soils, sought the margins of the heavier lands in a manner suggesting that their cultivation was not restricted to the lighter. In some districts we can also point to an invasion of the heavier soil-areas. With regard to sub-classification, it has become possible to point to the chalks, oolites, gravels, Jurassic limestones, and medium loams as those lighter soils peculiarly sought after by the population of the Roman province, and to recognize categories of settlers who tend to be associated with each of them. It has also become possible to identify the marl silts of the Fenlands of East Anglia, Cambridgeshire, and Lincolnshire as composing an area of agricultural settlement which was added to the available cultivable tracts of the Roman province by human labour and ingenuity. It has further become evident that certain coastal tracts in north Kent and in Somerset were in the later period of Roman rule lost to cultivation by marine transgression owing, in all probability, to a general rise in sea level; while inland tracts of the Fenlands were flooded by upland run-off. Thirdly, intensity of settlement: the more diligent recording of Roman finds in the last decades, and the technique of air-survey, have completely changed our notion of the degree of close settlement which existed in Roman Britain. A glance at the third edition of the Ordnance

Survey map of the province is sufficient to illustrate this advance. But an adequate notion of the intensity of occupation in given regions can only be acquired by an actual study of them. As examples of regions where such intensity is evidenced by the number of finds one may mention central Suffolk, the Letchworth region, west-central Somerset, and the north-east corner of Northamptonshire. Air-photography, on the other hand, has made it possible to establish, without the media of discovery or excavation, the pattern of settlement and even in some tracts the character of the ancient landscape. On the chalk downlands and the river-gravels, trackways, field complexes, accommodation roads, and farmsteads spring to life under the air-camera in a close-set mosaic which we might have suspected but might never otherwise have realized (cf. Fig. 1).[1]

Unfortunately not all aspects of these broadened potentialities have yet been adequately exploited. We still lack a thorough application to archaeological knowledge of available soil-surveys in order to analyse more closely the character of the different categories of Roman farming. Were the results of such analyses available, space would be inadequate to do more than summarize them; but they are not available, and much of the work remains to be done. Accordingly, we shall here restrict ourselves to a few brief general observations, and illustrate some of the characteristics of Roman settlement distribution by more detailed treatment of two selected districts, namely, Essex and Kent.

In the lowland zone of Britain which excludes the peninsula of Devon and Cornwall, Wales, and the Pennines with their flanking coastal plains, but not the East Riding, the villa economy is by and large restricted to the medium loams, the oolitic soils of Gloucestershire and Oxfordshire, and the limestone of the Jurassic ridge extending from Gloucestershire through Northamptonshire to Lincolnshire and the Humber. Villas are also present on the chalk soils of the Yorkshire Wolds of East Riding. Wooldridge and Linton pointed out the preference of Early Iron Age and Roman farming for the 'intermediate'

---

[1] General accounts of distribution: R. G. Collingwood, RBES[2], pp. 174–9; *OS Map of Roman Britain*, 3rd ed., Chessington, 1956. Medium or intermediate soils: *Ant.* VII, 1933, pp. 297 sqq.; pp. 473 sqq.; settlement on fringe of heavier soils: PSIA XXIV, 1946–8, p. 178; Fenlands: G. Fowler, CAS XLIII, 1950, p. 9; Clark, *Ant. J.* XXIX, 1949, pp. 145 sqq.; Collingwood *ap.* Frank, ESAR III, 1938, p. 86; Godwin, *Geological Journ.* XCI, pp. 241 sqq.; C. W. Phillips, *Philosophical Trans.*, 229B, p. 397; *Aspects of Archaeology in Britain and Beyond*, London, 1951, pp. 269 sqq.; S. Hallam, *Ant. J.* XLIV, 1964, pp. 19–32; P. Salway, CBA. RR VII, 1966, pp. 26–7; C. W. Phillips (ed.), *The Fenlands in Roman Times* (FR), 1971. Marine transgression: B. Cunliffe, CBA. RR VII, pp. 68–73; Air-photography and settlement intensity: e.g. RCHM: *A Matter of Time*, 1960; G. Webster, B. Hobley, 'Aerial Reconnaissance over the Warwickshire Avon', *Arch. J.* CXXI, 1965, pp. 1–22.

loams, which Sir Cyril Fox preferred to term 'gradational.' The main
character of these soils is that their equal mixture of clay and sand
and their lime status provide a structure favourable to moisture-reten-
tion, aeration, and nitrification; they combine relative ease of clearance
with a considerable productivity. These loam soils are found over
brickearth, calcareous boulder-clays, marls, lower chalk, upper greensand, and the Sandgate, Bargate, and Highgate beds. The broadest
areas lacking advanced exploitation were the Wealden clays, the damp
sandstones of the Midland Plain and Cheshire, the London Clays, and
the gaults.

In the highland zone the swampy valley floors and their wooded
sides were generally avoided; a few isolated homesteads attained to
villa-status in the Yorkshire dales (Gargrave, Castle Dykes, Well near
Middleham), but generally a poor peasant population, under the
pressure of Roman taxation and in some measure with Roman
technical aid, practised a pastoral economy eked out with the growing
of cereals upon the thin soils of the limestone plateaux, the millstone
grits, on the better drained boulder-clays and the drift-clay residues
of the Pennines, Northumberland, and Cumbria.

In the Fenlands of Norfolk, Cambridgeshire, and south Lincolnshire,
on the other hand, native immigrant settlers created a new agricultural
economy, based chiefly on the cultivation of cereals and the rearing
of cattle and pigs; this settlement was restricted to the areas of calcareous
marl silt, and was made possible by Roman engineering, which cut
canals to guide the upland run-off to the sea, and by the efforts of the
settlers themselves, who dug a network of ditches and minor waterways
to drain their cultivated areas.

In Sussex we may note the concentration of the villa estates upon
the brickearth loams extending from Havant eastward along the coast
to Brighton, and in the sandy loam belt north of the downland
escarpment. Some of these estates (Bramdean, West Meon, Stroud)
are sited on the border between the loams and the areas of heavy clay
and flints. A concentrated villa-group in north-east Hampshire coincides with the East Hampshire Chalk Arable Region, and is limited
on the east by the clay and flints area of the Nutley-Alton area, but
in the Andover region two interesting groups of villas occupy the
chalk, like another cluster in the extreme north-western corner of
Essex (the Hadstock-Ridgewell group). The majority of the Surrey
villas line the medium loam belt on the north of the North Downs;
the Romano-British villages on the Hog's Back occupy the loamy
beds and lower greensand, but avoid the clays.

In Buckinghamshire and Hertfordshire a series of villas exploited the
rich alluvial valley floors of the south-eastern slope of the Chilterns,

but also the clay with flints of the slopes, which included smaller patches of clayey chalk-marl, gravel, and pebbly glacial drift. In central Berkshire north of Newbury a group of estates was to be found on the clay residues of the Corallian beds, which were certainly wooded and must have been cleared to exploit the heavier soils.

In Oxfordshire, very marked is the concentration of an important villa-group (Northleigh, Ditchley, Great Tew, Stonesfield) in the region of Cotswold soils on the Great Oolite, consisting of brashy soils suitable for wheat, barley, and sheep; the Oxford Clay and the Chipping Norton region with their variable stony soils are generally avoided by the larger estates. The flourishing Gloucestershire villas are concentrated preponderantly on the calcareous sandstone brash of the Cotswolds, but one or two exploited the loamy clays north-west of Cheltenham (e.g. Spoonley Wood, Wadfield), and to the south of Cirencester some lesser farms are sited on the mixed loamy soils. But not a few estates on the western Cotswold scarp stood on the border between the sandstone and the loams. The imposition of Roman site-distribution over a map showing degrees and areas of soil-acidity in Worcestershire reveals, as we should expect, the concentration of the majority of sites on the soils of high lime status or moderate acidity.

On the eastern side of Britain, Sir Cyril Fox, studying the Cambridge region, found that while the greater part of the Roman rural population occupied the lighter chalk uplands, the valley gravels, and the Fenland marls, marginal deforestation had nevertheless taken place in the Roman era, extending settlement on to the heavier clay soils. It has further been noted that villas fringe the eastern and south-eastern limits of the Fens, though themselves built on the dryer chalk slopes. Beyond the damp clays of Bedfordshire, Roman farmsteads were numerous on the northern extension of the Jurassic Way, the Lincoln Edge, and sometimes rose to villa level; farms of humbler standing were not wanting farther east on the chalk of the Lincoln Wolds. Worthy of note in Nottinghamshire is the villa of Barton-in-Fabis, situated on heavy Keuper marl in the immediate vicinity of gypsum. Another villa-site on similar soils exists at Bunny, south of Nottingham.

In Suffolk on the other hand Moore noted that while the earlier Roman farms clung to the lighter soils, newly founded estates of the later second and third centuries were established on the edges of the heavy claylands, evidently with the intention of exploiting the corn-growing capacities of these soils. In this connection the work of A. Kosse on the siting of Roman villas in west central Somerset may be mentioned. In the Somerton-Ilchester district he found that of 28 villa-sites, 12 occupied calcareous silty clay or clay, 4 silty clay,

and 4 sandy loamy clay, the first two types being water-retentive
and in need of special management to prevent logging. In the Vale
of Glamorgan, among Roman civil sites at least three villas occupied
the fertile clayey residues overlying the Liassic uplands.[1]

The study of a restricted area of north-west Berkshire, which was
the subject of a detailed soil-survey by F. F. Kay – namely, the east
portion of the Vale of the White Horse – has something to tell us of
the distribution of Roman sites in relation to soils. Tabulation gives the
following picture:

Pebbly or fine sandy loam	14 sites
Medium loam, loamy sand to sandy loam	10 sites
Medium to heavy loam	4 sites
Coarse sandy brashy loam	3 sites
Light loam (Upton series)	3 + the native field area
Gravels	4 sites
Alluvium	2 sites
Clay with flints	2 sites

The light Upton loams should probably be placed at the head of the
column, since they include the 'square field' areas of the Berkshire
Downs, which are not expressible as individual sites. After these, the
highest incidence of occupation falls on the pebbly to fine sandy loamy
soils and the medium loams (66 per cent); the former includes the
native settlement areas in the Thames valley whose type site is Long
Wittenham. The gault and Kimmeridge clay are virtually empty of
occupation, but the medium to heavy loam was occupied, and there
was marginal settlement of the clayey loams through which the
Icknield Way runs. The way the economic basis of the villa at Cornhill
Farm near Challow becomes clear, when its siting is examined in
relation to its soils, is highly instructive. It is on the junction of the
Wantage belt and the Blewbury series (both medium loams), and
impinges on an 'island' of the Harwell series. The Blewbury soils
drain less rapidly than the Wantage group, but are deeper, and today

[1] Bramdean, West Meon, Stroud: Williams-Freedman, *Field Archaeology in Hamp-shire*, end map; North Downs: A. Clark, F. J. Nichols, SyAC LVII, 1960, pp. 42 sqq.; Buckinghamshire: Branigan, *Arch. J.* CXXIV, 1967, pp. 129–30; Berkshire: H. Peake, *Arch. of Berks*, p. 103; Oxfordshire: LUS no. 56, Oxfordshire, p. 204, fig. 3; Worcestershire: *ib.*, no. 68, Worcester, p. 435, fig. 5; Cambridgeshire region: Fox, ACR, p. 224; Fenlands, marginal villas: CAS LX, 1967, pp. 41–3; Barton-in-Fabis: *Trans. Thoroton Society* LV, 1952, pp. 3 sqq. Bunny: *ibid.*, LXXI, 1967, p. 5; Suffolk: PSIA XXIV, 1946–8, p. 178; Western Somerset: A. Kosse, *Soils and Agriculture in Roman Somerset*, University of Chicago M.A. Thesis, 1963. Glamorgan: BBCS XVII, 1958, pp. 293 sqq.

carry the only orchards in the downland region. The Wantage soils have a higher clay fraction. The Harwell soils are fine sandy loams, averaging six inches in depth, draining well and possessing layers of soft marl providing a slightly calcareous neutral character; they today carry orchards and are among the best wheatlands in Berkshire. It may therefore be supposed that the owner of this Roman farm attained to a villa standard of living by a mixed fruit and wheat economy, combined perhaps with some woodland clearance to southward. He had easy access to the Icknield Way, a quarter of a mile to the south, and lay less than two miles west of the north-south Roman road leading to Frilford, where he probably had a local market. Thus the results of the foregoing soil-settlement correlation confirm the observations of Wooldridge and Linton on the value of the medium or intermediate loams to the Romano-British economy. The siting of habitations at the junction of different types of soil is frequent, and in one case the exploitation of such a conjunction served as the basis of a profitable villa economy.[1]

The relation of Roman rural settlement to soils can further be studied by plotting the known sites on a soil map of Essex, as recorded by the British Land Utilization Survey (Fig. 4), the boulder-clays and loams being sub-classified into heavy clay soil, medium loam, and light sand and gravel. All sites with remains suggesting permanent occupation have been marked. Isolated finds such as coins and brooches have been omitted, but kilns and salterns have been regarded as indicative of permanent occupation. Churches embodying Roman materials in their structure have been included.[2]

The first feature of distribution that strikes the eye is the relative sparseness of occupation in the heavy southern London Clays, which must have remained almost entirely uncleared. There are nevertheless a few scattered sites, most of which are to be explained by the presence of streams on which they are sited (e.g. Chigwell, Theydon Bois). But very few of these sites are known to be villas – Chigwell probably was. Very prominent is the exploitation of a boulder-clay loam 'island' by a farmstead at Creekweeds Farm near Stock. In the London Clay area of the layer plateau between Colchester and the Blackwater estuary, two dwelling-sites appear at Tolleshunt Knights (a villa) and Varley; both are near the Salcott stream, the former close

[1] F. F. Kay, *Soil Survey of the Eastern Portion of the Vale of the White Horse*, University of Reading Faculty of Agriculture and Horticulture Bulletin, No. XLVIII, 1931.

[2] LUS no. 82, Ess., p. 411, figs. 4 and 5. Sources: RCHM *Ess.*, I–IV, London, 1916–23; A. H. Lyell, *Bibliographical List of Romano-British Architectural Remains in Britain*, Cambridge, 1912; EAS; JRS, annual reports on Roman Britain; the Ordnance Survey records, previously at Chessington.

62

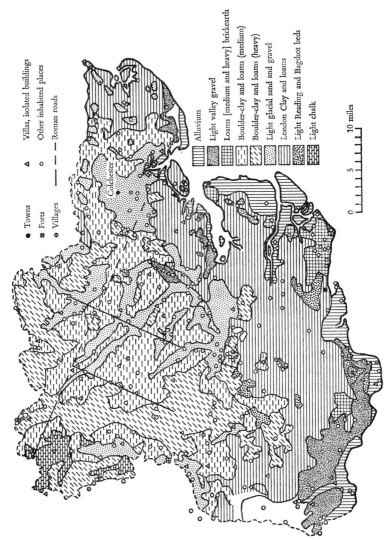

Towns ●   Villas, isolated buildings △

Forts ■   Other inhabited places ○

Villages ◉   Roman roads – – –

Alluvium

Light valley gravel

Loams [medium and heavy] brickearth

Boulder-clay and loams (medium)

Boulder-clay and loams (heavy)

Light glacial sand and gravel

London Clay and loams

Light Reading and Bagshot beds

Light chalk

Colchester

0   5   10 miles

Fig. 4. Essex: the distribution of Roman sites imposed on the various types of soils.

to its source. It is important to note on these stream sites that while the streams afforded water-supply, communications, and dry gravel on which to build (London Clay gives unstable foundations and sweating walls), the cultivated areas attached to these dwellings must have been forest clearings, involving working of the heavy clay soil, and probably much pasturage of swine, secondarily of cattle. A few sites at the junction of the London Clay and the Essex salt marshes must have been concerned with the summer pasturizing of sheep on the flats, where they would have been safe from foot-rot and the liver-fluke. The same perhaps applied to habitations indicated by Roman tiles in the churches at Asheldam, Dengie, and Southminster, which were situated on glacial sand and gravel islands in the clay, but were separated by only a mile or two from the salt-marshes to eastward.[1]

The brickearth medium loams of the Southend area were well inhabited, and it can almost be taken for granted that they were used for wheat; perhaps for market gardening, for the area is climatically early. Their proximity to salt-marshes on the east suggests summer grazing of sheep on the marsh, and winter feeding on the fallows of the brickearths. The brickearth 'island' in the Ockendens district, on the other hand, lacks recorded finds, and perhaps some ought to be expected in the future. The light gravels of the Becontree, Dagenham, and Rainham areas were inhabited, though not, apparently, densely, and more serious settlement commences between the Roding and the Lea. The Tilbury marsh had its native population, some of whose villages are now below the tide-mark, and granted that the sea level had changed (Roman finds in the peat 8–9 feet below the tidal mud of the Albert Dock, East Ham), it is possible that there were here Roman protective dykes, as early Norman occupation at West Thurrock suggests.[2]

In the Tendring and Clacton regions inland habitation is very conspicuously limited to the sand and gravel islands, with a couple of villas sharing one at Little Oakley and Dovercourt respectively and a third at Harwich with a clay hinterland, conceivably not a farm but a customs station for a ferry to Felixstowe over the Stour estuary. The first two mentioned are placed, significantly, at opposite ends of the gravel enclave on the edges of the clay, and some deforestation is therefore implied, or at least, exploitation of the woodland.[3]

With the exception of the chalk region in the north-west corner of the county and a London Clay area north of Colchester round

[1] LUS no. 82, Ess., p. 448; the liver-fluke: Fox, *Personality*, pp. 63, 94.

[2] RCHM *Ess.*, II (Central), p. 58; cf. Wheeler, *London Museum Guide, Roman London*, London, 1930, p. 35.

[3] Felixstowe: cf. the stamp figuring a stag and the letters PB from here, paralleled from the imperial *principia* at Combe Down, Som, VCH *Som.*, I, p. 310.

Wormingford, where, peculiarly, Roman tiles are known in the church, the rest of Essex is occupied on the one hand by boulder-clays, whose soils can be sub-classified into heavy clay and medium loams – and on the other by light sand or gravels. The three largest expanses of the sands and gravels centre respectively on Colchester, Chelmsford, and the Halstead–Castle Hedingham area round the upper waters of the River Colne. The Chelmsford tract also extends fingers north-westward up the valleys of the Brain and Pant, including Braintree and Coggeshall.

The Colchester area had a fair population, chiefly (in so far as it is recorded) to the south of the colony, with villas occupying the junctions with the alluvium on both sides of the Colne estuary, in a position that leaves little doubt that they combined arable with sheep-rearing and perhaps salt-making. Fishing may also have supplemented their income. One wonders if these villas were not the seat of the oyster industry, whose products had such an enormous and widespread consumption throughout the province. The occupation to the south-west of the city, in the direction of Stanway, must have been dense, to judge from the various roads found in the Sheppen Farm excavations and the important shrine of Gosbeck Farm with its associated theatre, but if we are to look for the bulk of the colony's lands, they would have lain westward and north-westward, probably occupying a heavy clay patch between Stanway and Marks Tey, which the finds suggest was cleared, and both sides of the Colne Valley, where the regular distribution of Roman tiles in the village churches and actual finds at some places (Colne Engaine, Mount Bures, Wormingford, Fordham, Great Tey, Alphamstone, Burton's Green, Countess Cross) indicate the possibility of a planned colonization.[1]

The second sand and gravel area, centred on Chelmsford, shows a dense occupation about the town (Caesaromagus), northward up the Chelmer, and westward up the Can, further on the gravel area of Rivenhall End and Kelvedon, and in the valleys of the Brain and Blackwater; but of the precise nature of most of these sites less appears to be known. Braintree must have been a local communication village at a crossroads. The third light-soil region, between Halstead and the Hedinghams, has seven or eight ill-defined habitation sites and a pottery industry; two building sites at Colne Engaine and Countess Cross lie at the junction of the light soil and heavy clays.

In addition, three light-soil areas may be noticed on the western

---

[1] Oysters: The villas of Southwick, Suss., and Hucclecote, Glos., were also suspected by their excavators of having engaged in oyster rearing. Stanway: Hawkes, Hull, *Camulodunum*, SARR xiv, Oxford, 1947, pl. i; the theatre: JRS xl, 1950, pp. 107–8.

confines of the county, viz. the gravel terraces of the Stort, one between Roydon and Sawbridgeworth, the other between Birchanger and Quendon; both have settlement, the one including a temple at Harlow, the other the villa at Stanstead Mountfitchet; the third area surrounding Chipping Ongar, where a building of some sort is recorded.

Outside the light-soil regions the county is divided between medium loams and heavy boulder-clays. While the light-soil regions already sketched present some of the thickest population, what has been said in anticipation of the medium-loam areas west and north-west of Colchester will show that they were by no means without occupation. The villa (?) of Moulsham and another similar house-site are to be found on such land, with three other habitations, south of Chelmsford; half a dozen habitations in the Dunmow area occupy this sort of soil; the same applies to the Finchingfield and Thaxted dwellings, to Rivenhall and Coggeshall. On the west border of the county a sprinkling of occupied sites lies along the boulder-clay medium loam belt between Little Hollingbury and Elsenham, and half a dozen are sited within the medium-loam enclave between White Roding and Latton. On the north Essex boundary, the settlement-group about the villas of Ridgewell and Steeple Bumpstead is explained by a stretch of the same soils, whose presence also accounts for the Alphamstone dwelling-site to south-eastward. On the watershed between the Blackwater-Pant and the Colne, north-west of Coggeshall, a scatter of minor sites is to be seen along soils of this type.

Not less interesting is the relationship between the medium loams and the heavy soils of the north-western Essex boulder-clay. The greater part of the heavy soils stretches in a belt from Ongar to the north-west corner of the county; along the north border, part of the Suffolk clays penetrate into Essex between Haverhill and Sudbury (the upper Stour basin), and south of Sudbury between the Stour and Colne (the Earl's Colne area). It is true that these heavy clays have proportionately fewer occupation-sites than the other soils (except the London Clay), and must have remained predominantly uncleared, but they were not quite deserted. Those in the north-west corner of the county (part of the east Hertfordshire heavy clay area) about the headwaters of the Stort have four or five sites along the Hertfordshire border (near Meesden and Berden). In the heavy-clay belt between High Roding and Bishop's Stortford there are settlement sites at Great Canfield and immediately to the west. Farther south in the same belt (north-east of Ongar) to the east of the River Roding, tiles in church-structures at Fyfield, Willingdale Spain, and Willingdale Doe, and burials at Shelley Bowells, indicate clearings in the forest. Detached

3

enclaves of heavy clay country centring on Havering-atte-Bower, and between Danbury and East Hanningfield, show settlement, in the latter region in the form of streamside sites. This slight though not completely insignificant penetration of the woodlands would give a false impression, were it not for an additional factor to be considered, namely, the large number of settlements clinging to the edge of the heavy clays, though themselves placed on medium loams or lighter soils. As other examples we may cite Chipping Ongar, Standon Hall, White Roding, Sheering, Tackley, Skreen's Park (Roxwell), Chagnall St James, High Easter, Pleshey, Gosfield, Thaxted and its companion-site at Boyton End, Radwinter, White Notley, Sporhams (near Danbury), and several sites on the south edge of Chelmsford. Of the above, Pleshey, Thaxted, possibly Ongar and White Roding, were villas. This siting may be compared to that enjoyed by the Little Oakley and Dovercourt villas, close to London Clay. The significance of the Essex sites is that the forest was being attacked, as Fox concluded in relation to the Cambridge region, but possibly on a slightly wider scale than in the area studied by him.[1] They further serve to demonstrate the importance of woodland to a considerable sector of the rural economy, for domestic fuel, building materials, industry, pannage, fruit, and winter fodder.

But if we survey the distribution of the settlement of Central Essex on the lighter sands and gravels on the one hand, and on the medium boulder-clay on the other, a new fact emerges. We gain a completely different picture from that presented by the second edition of the Ordnance Survey Map of Roman Britain (1928). Here the woodlands were hypothetically restored on the basis of the character of the parent soil-materials, and the result was to mark the area of central and western Essex, between the Romford-Kelvedon line and the Lea Valley, as a tract of unbroken forest alleviated only by the river-courses and by enclaves of light soil between Chelmsford and Brentwood. This may have been true in prehistoric times. In Roman days it was no longer true. Doubts as to the accuracy of the presentation would in any case have been aroused by Haverfield's famous parallel Roman roads which traverse this zone, one between Gosfield, Braintree, and Little Waltham, the other between Great Dunmow and Roundbush Green south of High Roding. The two roads fall almost entirely, in their nearly parallel sectors, within the medium loam region of central Essex, which is cut at four points by the equally workable gravels of the river valleys (the Pant, Brain, Ter, and Chelmer). At their southern ends these roads cease to be parallel approximately, but not precisely, where the heavy loam soils begin along the line High Roding-

[1] See p. 59.

Chelmsford. When they proceed from there, their courses have altered. The continuation of the near-parallel bearing for two miles into the heavy clay south-west of High Roding perhaps shows that the margin of the forest was here pushed back by clearance, and indeed not far to westward, near Great Canfield, are clayland sites already noted. We seem then to have here extensive deforestation, whose scope could only have been Roman. The connection between these roads and the medium loams is beyond doubt.

The results of the analysis of the distribution of Roman remains on the Essex soils may now be summarized.

1. The London Clays were thinly inhabited, but there were some isolated clearings, especially by streams, including at least one made by a villa; a number of sites are found on the margins of the damp clay forest.

2. The chalk, the valley gravels, the glacial gravels and sands, constituting light soil areas, represent some of the densest, probably primary, occupation.

3. In the area of boulder-clays, pre-Roman finds are more or less confined to the valley gravels. But there is a considerable expansion into the medium or intermediate loams in the Roman period. This expansion is interpretable in central and western Essex as the fruit of a concerted large-scale forest clearance, for the purpose of cultivation. It ceases on the south with the heavier boulder-clay soils. Sir Cyril Fox has observed that these soils are not easy to work; their character is such that they need ample aeration and hence a plough that can turn a slice.[1]

4. The considerable number of sites on the margins of the heavy boulder-clay soils, and the evidence of the south end of the western (Dunmow) alignment, indicate that these lands were marginally cleared; some occupation actually within the western heavy boulder-clay area and on such soils at other points, shows that these regions were penetrated. An example of the complete clearance of such a tract is seen west of Colchester (the Marks Tey area), probably to be connected with the veteran colony. This state of affairs contrasts with that in Suffolk, where the boulder-clay soils occupying the greater part of the county are distinctly heavier than in Essex, and possess a higher clay fraction; they were virtually unoccupied, and Roman sites were confined to the valley gravels and the lighter soils of the north-west of the county. The difference may also be partly attributable to lack of Belgic population. But the siting of many of the Suffolk settlements (including seven villas) on the edge of the clays emphasizes the marginal clearance observed in Essex.[2]

[1] *Ant.* VII, 1933, p. 473.
[2] Boulder-clays: *Ant.* VII, 1933, p. 308; marginal clearance: PSIA XXIV, 1946–8, pp. 177 sqq. and fig. 1.

5. The exploitation of the brickearths is well attested in south-eastern Essex; sites on the edge of or in the salt-marshes are to be explained chiefly by the profitable summer grazing immune from foot-rot and the liver-fluke. Settlement of farmers who become comfortable villa-owners on the edge of the alluvium and boulder-clay or sands on the Colne estuary is to be understood as the result of a prosperous mixed economy based on arable, sheep, and probably fishing.

The survey may be summed up statistically as follows.—

	Sites	Percentage
Light sands and gravels	80	29·41
Medium loams	65	23·89
Heavy boulder-clay loams	36	12·50
Valley gravels	28	10·28
London Clay	21	7·70
Alluvium	18	6·61
Brickearth	13	4·77
Chalk	11	4·44

On this list one may remark: (a) the low percentage of chalk sites corresponds with the very small chalk area in the county, and is therefore not significant in terms of the present question; (b) the brickearth provides a medium loam very similar to that of the medium boulder-clay soils. Taken with them, a percentage of 28·66 is arrived at, which nearly equals that of the light sands and gravels. The valley gravels, not more than 5 per cent of the county, have 10·28 per cent of the sites. The light sands and gravels are about 12 per cent of the county, but provide 29·41 per cent of the sites; the medium loams, about 15 per cent of the county, contain 23·89 per cent of them; the heavy boulder-clay loams, about 18 per cent of the county, have 12·5 per cent; the London Clays, which comprise 30 per cent, contain only 7·7 per cent of the sites.

We may compose a table of approximate intensity-ratios as follows, arrived at by the division of percentage-area into percentage-sites.—

Light sands and gravels	2·45
Valley gravels	2·05
Brickearth	1·90
Medium loams	1·59
Heavy boulder-clay loams	1·04
London Clay	0·25

In addition, we may note in particular the sitings of 14 known villas in Essex (these are not all the probable sites, but those where the finding of mosaic pavements proves a "villa" standard of living):

Alresford	margin of alluvium and sand/gravel
Bartlow	chalk
Brightlingsea	margin of alluvium and sand/gravel
Chigwell	streamside. London Clay
Hadstock	heavy boulder-clay loam
Linton	margin of chalk and heavy boulder-clay loam
Little Oakley	margin of gravel and London Clay
Lower Dovercourt	margin of gravel and London Clay
Pleshey	margin of medium loam and heavy-boulder clay
Ridgewell	medium loam
St Osyth	medium loam
Tolleshunt Knights	streamside. London Clay
Wanstead	sand/gravel
West Mersea	London Clay, near gravel 'island'

Eight out of fourteen sites are seen to prefer heavy soil or its proximity; the total number is small, but it gives grounds for suspecting that no inconsiderable part of the villa economy depended on a measure of forest clearance and the ampler crops yielded by heavier lands. Six of the villas listed are classed as marginal forest sites, again emphasizing the integral part played by woodland in Romano-British farming.

A second area adapted to a brief survey is Kent (Fig. 5). A detailed soil-survey mapped in convenient form has not been at the writer's disposal, but here the general soil-types coincide sufficiently closely with the parent materials to make some deductions possible.[1] The clays with flints capping the North Downs are negatively important in so far as they are nearly lacking in Roman finds. If such are to be found, they are in the deep brickearth of the valley floors penetrating the scarp from the north. An equal absence of habitation naturally characterizes the narrow gault belt (the Holmedale) that edges the scarp of the Downs on the south, likewise the Weald clays in the south of the county. The part played in permanent occupation by the medium loams which cover the chalk, and the Thanet beds to the north of the Downs, is prominent. The same applies to the belt of medium loams overlying the lower greensand between Folkestone and Westerham, forming the upper basins of the Darent, Medway, and Stour. It must nevertheless be admitted that considering the favourable conditions of this belt for ancient settlement, the recorded finds are not as numerous as might be expected.

A majority of the known sites are to be explained by the valley

[1] Compare Wooldridge and Linton's small-scale map, *Ant.* VII, p. 301, with the geological map, VCH *Kent*, I, between pp. xxviii and 1.

70

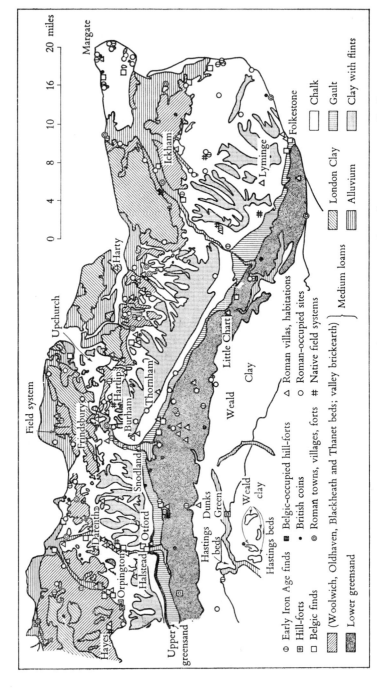

Fig. 5. Kent: the distribution of Early Iron Age and Roman sites imposed on the various types of soils.

gravels and alluvium of the upper Medway, but loam formed their arable hinterlands. These and the corresponding soils of the Cray and Darent attracted a very considerable number of settlers who were able to rise to a villa standard of living and some affluence. In the Darent valley villas are both numerous and wealthy. In the north-west the light soils of the Blackheath and Woolwich beds served as the arable of estates whose houses were built along the streams (Orpington, St Mary Cray, Bexley). The marshes along the north coast were by no means unoccupied; their inhabitants must have been principally potters, shepherds, and fishermen. The villa at Lower Halstow probably had some connection with the pottery industry, and another at Harty on the Isle of Sheppey may have had as its economic basis grazing in the salt-marshes combined with potting (a kiln was found to eastward) and marginal clearance of the London Clay which occupies the greater part of the island. To the north of Rochester the heavier loam of the Hoo district was largely deforested, to judge from the traces of a Roman field system there, very likely connected, in part, with the villa at Frindsbury, itself placed on medium loam soil. The Hoo area is still known for its high wheat-cropping. North of Canterbury the London Clay region eastwards was practically deserted, but the Thanet loams were occupied, and there was some sort of country house at Margate.[1]

Something specific can be said of the farming of one or two of the estates occupying the northern medium-loam belt. Sheep must have played a big part at Darenth in view of its fulling industry, and several pruning-hooks from Darenth and Hartlip indicate fruit-growing. Hartlip grew wheat and fruit, and reared cattle possibly with the help of green crops and roots. (Cf. p. 115.) Darenth quite possibly utilized the summer-grazing potentialities of the salt-marshes about Crayford, and grazed the flock in orchards during the winter much as is the practice in this district of Kent today. The villa of Ickham, also placed near the junction of alluvium and medium loam, perhaps engaged in a comparable economy. Weaving was carried on at Frindsbury (loomweights of two types are to be seen in Rochester Museum) and it is more than likely that the salt-marsh on the west of the Medway estuary here afforded pasture. The general coincidence of Roman occupation areas with the modern Kentish zone of highest barley production will be noted (see p. 111), and it may further be observed that nearly all the Romano-British settlements keep north of the 27·5 inch isohyet. This may well imply a special interest in cereal raising, as indeed Caesar

[1] Darent valley: *A. Cant.* LXI, 1949, pp. 180 sqq. – some ten sites between Horton Kirby and Shoreham. Hoo district (Cliffe), see p. 97. High wheat cropping: LUS no. 85, Kent, p. 596, fig. 3.

infers, and would agree with a drive to bring heavier soils into working.[1]

The siting of several other individual villas deserves some special comment. There is one site at Dunks Green south of Plaxtol, actually on Weald clay, though not far from its northern fringe; its tile industry may explain its choice of soil, both for clay and fuel. A more recently discovered villa at Little Chart must stand on the junction of the medium loams and the impermeable gault. The Folkestone villa is on impermeable gault with clay and flints to its north, yet the discovery there of a ploughshare is not favourable to Winbolt's belief that it was simply a naval headquarters. Otford occupies the meeting-point, near a stream, of clay with flints and gault, though there is medium loam a little further south; it may therefore imply woodland clearance in the Darent valley, but it is not surprising that after the villa had been burnt at the end of the second century, the farm went over principally to stock-rearing. To the north-west another site at Halstead occupied clay and flints over chalk. Two other habitations, Burham and Kit's Coity House, on the east edge of the Medway valley, also occupied the junction of chalk with clay of this kind. Snodland's streamside position was at the junction of chalk, alluvium, and a narrow gault belt. Hayes occupied the edge of the lighter sandy loams near the London Clay. All these examples point to a certain reduction of the edges of the woodlands, and to the exploitation of clay as well as the utilization of the woods themselves. The same phenomenon has already been noted in Essex.[2]

The concentration of the villas on the medium loams of Kent is striking. With the exception of the sites just quoted, most of the rest are on the light sandy loam. The Harty site, on London Clay surrounded by alluvium, is unique. The Kentish evidence, then, entirely favours the preference of the Romano-British farming economy for the medium loam soils, but it also emphasizes the liking of the ancient farmer for streamside sites, and a not entirely negligible attack upon the heavier clays. A partnership with saltmarsh grazing and industry (pottery, tiles, fishing) is also revealed; there are hints of coordination between flocks and grass-orchards. A very considerable project of deforestation appears in the Hundred of Hoo (Cliffe).

[1] Hartlip, pruning hooks: Maidstone Museum; cattle: see pp. 208 sqq.; green crops: tares found with wheat, VCH *Kent*, III, p. 118; cf. Plin., HN XVIII, 142; the isohyet, LUS no. 85, Kent, p. 566, fig. 3. Caesar, *de Bell. Gall.*, V, 20.

[2] Tile industry: VCH *Kent*, III, p. 123, no. 40; Little Chart: ANL, 1949, March, p. 12; Folkestone, the share: Winbolt, *Roman Folkestone*, London, 1925, p. 101.

CHAPTER V

TOOLS

A BRIEF SURVEY of the agricultural tools known to Roman Britain is essential to a knowledge of agricultural techniques and also to an appreciation of the degree to which Roman influence introduced improvements into British farming. The account that follows includes all the types of agricultural implement of the period known to me in Britain, except ploughs and their parts, which will be discussed below.

Sickles are not always clearly distinguishable from billhooks on the one hand or from pruning-hooks on the other. Most of the British Early Iron Age sickles are very small indeed, the blade sometimes measuring no more than 4 inches from butt to tip (Fig. 6; d, e, f). Curwen noted that the characteristic of the pre-Roman implement was that the blade continued the line of the handle or socket, curving from this line directly to the point; the effect was an ill-balanced blade which turned downward in the hand, a tendency that had to be checked by the grip of the user. In the majority of pre-Roman sickles the blade is folded over to enclose part but not the whole of the circumference of the handle, but towards the end of the Early Iron Age the tang appears. Only at the outset of the Roman conquest did the blade begin to bend away from the tang at a sharper angle, and the full-sized sickle developed (Fig. 7; m). The blade now curved well back and its upper end was lengthened and bent to bring the centre of gravity to the middle, so counterbalancing the downward pull. Nevertheless a very large number of sickles of the Roman period continued to follow the native principle, examples being found at Woodcuts, Alchester, and Caerwent. Even more or less romanized examples from Corbridge extend straight from the handle; one is socketed, and one rivet-hafted. Small native examples 2–4½ inches long are found at Caerwent, Hambleden villa (Bucks), and Silchester, showing that in such places the corn-stalk was cut very high, probably close to the ear. Larger fully-curved examples of developed Roman type come from Cowley (Oxford) and Woodyates.[1]

[1] *Sickles*. Balance: Curwen, ANL, 1948, no. 7, pp. 15 sq. Woodcuts: Pitt-Rivers, *Excavations* I, pl. xxix, 12; Alchester: Ashmolean Museum, Oxford; Caerwent: A LXII, 1910, pl. lxi, fig. 4, nos. 6, 7; Corbridge: ms. photo in Ashmolean Museum, Oxford; Hambleden: Yewden Museum; J. Ward, *Roman Era in Britain*, London, 1911, p. 197, fig. 56D; Cowley: Ashmolean Museum, Oxford; Woodyates: Pitt-Rivers, *op. cit.*, III, p. 109.

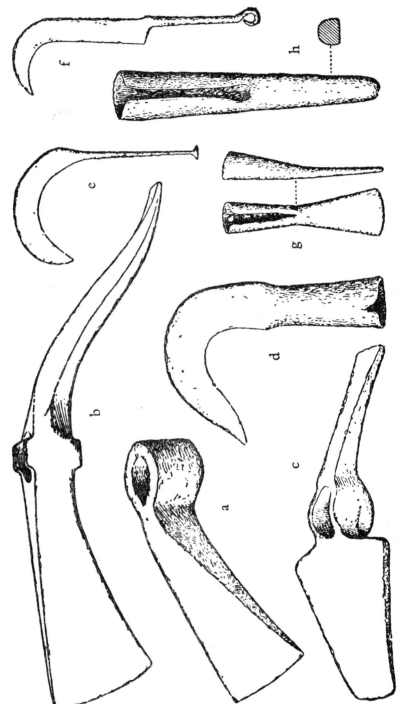

Fig. 6. Romano–British farm implements: picks, mattocks, hoes, sickles.

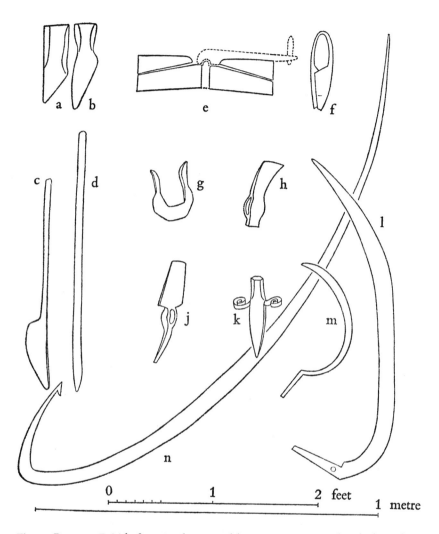

Fig. 7. Romano-British farm implements: (a) asymmetric iron plough-share from Brading (after Cleere, 1958); (b) asymmetric iron ploughshare from Folkestone (after Aberg, 1956); (c) coulter and (d) iron foreshare from probable coultered ard (after Manning, 1964); (e) quern (after Curwen); (f) cropping shears (after Boon, 1957); (g) iron spade-share (based on 111 a.4 in *Antiquities of Roman Britain*, BM, 1951); (h) iron axe-head of common form (after Collingwood, 1930); (j) iron 'Ascia-rastrum' (after Collingwood, 1930); (k) mower's anvil (after Collingwood, 1930); (l) scythe blade; (m) balanced sickle; (n) scythe blade from Great Chesterford (after Neville, 1856).

Scythes. Possibly the Belgae were experimenting with a larger harvesting implement, since two blades found at Bigbury, 16.9 inches and 20.5 inches long respectively, may have been hafted on handles turning through a right angle for use as true scythes. The invention of the two-hand scythe, a Roman device, made it possible to mow grass and corn close to the ground, but only on level fields which were without ridges and relatively free of stones. Pliny speaks of a longer two-hand *falx* in use on Gallic *latifundia*, which cut the grass in the middle; there is no doubt that long two-hand scythes were being used in Gaul and the Rhineland at least in the later Roman period, but whether Pliny was referring to such tools is not clear, as they would have cut short and low.

Finds of scythes (Fig. 7; l, n) have been made in Britain at Rushall Down, Corbridge, Newstead, Great Chesterford, Abington Piggotts, Bloxham, and Barnsley Park (near Cirencester). The examples from Newstead, which are probably Flavian, are between 35 and 45½ inches in length from tang to tip, and possess reinforced backs. The tangs, which possess rivet holes, are turned at right angles to the heel. The Great Chesterford and Abington Piggotts finds also compose a group; twelve were found at Great Chesterford and the Abington example certainly came from the same shop. The rear part of the blade of these scythes (5 feet 4 inches span) is curved through 160 degrees so that the heel looks to the point, the distance from the place of maximum curvature to the point being 62 inches. The heel possesses a 0·9 inch tang turned at right angles to the plane of the blade. Some examples from Germany (e.g. Cologne) whose blades are curved to return to the point above the heel are not so long as the Great Chesterford scythes, and were certainly hafted at right angles to, and in the same plane as, the blade, but this method would have made the British implements unusable, and their sneads must have been set obliquely to the blades. They are dated in the fourth century, and argue, with the accompanying tools, able and efficient farming.[1]

[1] *Scythes.* Ham Hill: SANHS LXII, 1926, p. 42, pl. xiv, 121; Bigbury: *Arch. J.* LIX, 1902, p. 214; Gaul: Pliny, HN XVIII, 261; Rushall Down: *Devizes Museum Catalogue* II, Devizes, 1934, pl. lxxx, 2; Corbridge: ms. photo, Ashmolean Museum, Oxford; Newstead: Curle, *A Roman Frontier Post and its People*, Glasgow, 1911, pl. lxii, pp. 284–5; Great Chesterford: *Arch. J.* XIII, 1856, p. 10, fig. 29; Abington Piggotts: Cambridge University Museum of Archaeology and Ethnology; Barnsley Park: inf. from Dr G. Webster; Bloxham, Oxon: Ashmolean Museum, Oxford. Germany: Schumacher, *Der Ackerbau in vorrömische und römische Zeit*, Mainz, 1922, p. 21, Abb. 10, 4. I owe a copy of the report by the Museum of English Rural Life on the Barnsley Park scythe to Dr G. Webster. Mr A. Jewell, Director of the Museum, kindly showed me the experimentally restored snead – massive but practical. The report expressed the view that this scythe was designed to cut corn.

The presence of *mowers' anvils* is to be connected with the use of scythes, the efficiency of which was increased by their use (Fig. 7; k). Examples are recorded from Newstead, Caerwent, Silchester, Great Chesterford, and Templeborough.[1]

Billhooks. The billhook or 'slasher', whether with long or short handle, is a woodland implement. Its chief original use was the lopping of twigs and branches, doubtless sometimes for firewood, but mainly for the sake of the leaves which were important as winter cattle-feed. The Celtic Esus, a woodland deity closely allied to Cernunnos, who is figured with the ox, is shown on occasion with an axe or billhook. In the Early Iron Age, bills are distinguishable from sickles by possessing a broader blade and a shorter curve to the point. Their length varied from 7 to 11 inches. Billhooks continued in use in the Roman period, when some of them assumed a more advanced form: two from Camulodunum are socketed and their blades tend to the rectangular, with a beak at the rear upper corner. An example from Corbridge possessed a curved blade like the native models and other Roman examples from Newstead. Lengths varied from $12\frac{3}{4}$ to 12 inches.[2]

Pruning-hooks, as stated, look very much like the smaller type of Early Iron Age–Roman sickle, and one tool may sometimes have performed the work of both. A knife of about $3\frac{3}{4}$ inches in length found at Roundaway Down near Marlborough, with a blade turned at right angles to the socket and a cut-off tip, was almost certainly for pruning; there is another from West Blatchington (Suss). Two examples are known from Hartlip (1·7 inches and 7·8 inches respectively). One had a lengthy socket and must have been fitted to a long shaft for use on fully-grown trees. Other examples which might be mentioned may equally have been reaping hooks. Lack of distinction makes it impossible to trace Roman fruit-growing by the incidence of finds.[3]

Turf-cutters are known from Newstead, London, Woodyates, and Shopfield near Little Waltham (Ess), in the shape of mushroom-shaped blades. A fifth from Great Chesterford is a stout vertical blade with

---

[1] *Mowers' anvils.* Newstead: Curle, *op. cit.*, pl. lxii, 1; pit xvi, Flavian; Caerwent: Ward, *op. cit.*, fig. 57c; Silchester: A LIV, 1893, p. 142, fig. 5; Great Chesterford: *Arch. J.* XIII, pl. i, 8; Templeborough: Rotherham Museum.

[2] *Billhooks.* Leaves as cattle-feed: Cato, *de rust. re*, 54; Varro, II, 5, 11; Colum., VI, 3, 5; Curwen, *Ant.* VIII, 1934, p. 238; E. Evans, *Irish Heritage*, pp. 95–8; Esus and Cernunnos: Rhys, *Lectures in the Origin and Growth of Religion as illustrated by Celtic Heathendom*, London, 1888, pp. 64, 65 n. Camulodunum: Hawkes and Hull, *op. cit.*, pl. cv, 31–2 and p. 343; Corbridge: ms. photograph, Ashmolean Museum, Oxford.

[3] *Pruning hooks.* Roundaway Down: WAM XXXVI, 1923, p. 483; West Blatchington: SAC XC, 1951–2, p. 239, pl. xii, 3.

socket, twisted like a modern mould board, with a projecting footrest. Its length is 1 foot 7 inches.[1]

Axes. Although axes were certainly in use in the British Early Iron Age, there is none among the ample tools of Hunsbury and Glastonbury, where billhooks must have taken their place; but split-hafted and eyeleted axes are known at Madmarston Camp (Oxon) in Early Iron Age B, at Maiden Castle, and Bigbury.[2] Axeheads appear in abundance in the Roman period, with considerable variety of size and shape, ranging from 4 to 8 inches in length, almost always eyeleted. A specimen from Box villa appears to have possessed a split haft. The commonest Romano-British type is wedge-shaped in plan with flat or slightly curved butt, the haft-hole being sometimes pierced through lugs in the upper and lower faces (Silchester, Woodcuts) (Fig. 7; h). Rather thicker blades, wedge-shaped and with flat end, resembling the American felling axe, are known from Great Chesterford and elsewhere. In a few cases the blade is made in one piece with a socketed haft, as at Richborough. In similar examples from Walthamstow and London the back of the head passes by a continuous downward curve into a long split socket. Here native influence may be suspected.[3]

The ascia-rastrum. The name is adopted by K. D. White, on the authority of Palladius' account of the tool, which is a combined hoe and two-pronged drag-hoe, but examples with one rear tine occur (Fig. 6; c and Fig. 7; j). The head was fitted by an eyelet. This is primarily an earth-moving tool, and would be especially useful in root-bound soil. Examples have both triangular and square blades (the latter for sandier soils); those from Rough Castle, Segontium, and Richborough were of triangular type; one from Thealby (Lincs) had a square end. There are others from London, Caerwent, and Lydney. The implement must have been used for entrenchment and fortification work to judge by its presence at the first three sites, but its distribution indicates that it was a handy tool in a variety of circumstances.[4]

[1] *Turf cutters.* Newstead: Curle, *op. cit.*, pl. lxi, 3; London: *Guildhall Museum Catalogue*, London, 1908, pl. xviii, 11; Woodyates: Pitt-Rivers, *Excavations*, III, pl. clxxxiv, 9; Shopfield, Ess: EAS³ II, 1966, p. 58; Great Chesterford: *Arch. J.* XIII, pl. i, 11.

[2] *Axes.* Iron imitations of Bronze-Age axes: *Arch. J.* LXXXV, pp. 170–5, chiefly from lowland Britain; Madmarston Camp, Oxon (Iron Age "B"), *Oxon.* XXV, 1960, fig. 18, 5; Maiden Castle: Wheeler, *Maiden Castle*, SARR III, Oxford, 1943, fig. 92, 8; Bigbury: *Arch. J.* LIX, 1902, p. 214, fig. 2c.

[3] Box: *Devizes Museum Catalogue*, II², pl. lxxx, 4; Silchester: Ward, *op. cit.*, fig. 55, G; Woodcuts: Pitt-Rivers, *Excavations*, I, pl. xxvi, 2; Great Chesterford: *Arch. J.* XIII, pl. i, 9; Richborough: Bushe-Fox, *Richborough*, II, SARR Oxford, 1928, pl. xxiv, 1; Walthamstow: *London Museum Guide, Roman London*, pl. xxxiv, 1, 2.

[4] *The ascia-rastrum.* Palladius, I, 43, 3; *axias in aversa parte referentes rastros*; K. D. White, *Agricultural Instruments of the Roman World*, Cambridge, 1967, p. 66; Rough Castle: G. Macdonald, *Roman Wall in Scotland*, Glasgow, 1934, p. 450, fig. 55;

Hoes and spuds are not very abundant among Romano-British finds (Fig. 6; g, h). The small split-socketed spud with flat end from Langton (Yorks) is fairly common and would have been used for hoeing close-set row-crops or perhaps for singling. The exclusively civil distribution of the type in Britain may be significant. It has been suggested that a V-shaped tool consisting of the bifurcating tines of a deer antler, pierced by a trapezoidal socket at the junction, and found in Roman contexts at various sites (e.g. Bartlow, Hadstock, Newstead), was a hoe or rake. Pitt-Rivers further published several socketed pointed iron tools which he found at Woodcuts, and another can be cited from the villa of East Grimstead. They were probably, as Pitt-Rivers suggested, the blades of single-tined picks. An excellent example of such an implement with eyelet and slightly expanded end, about 10 inches long, comes from Darenth (Kent).[1]

Rakes. A rake is illustrated on a mosaic pavement at Spoonley Wood (Glos). A nearly complete rake consisting of a wooden clog and iron teeth square in section was found at Newstead.[2]

Mattocks (Fig. 6; b). Implements possessing a vertical axe-like blade before the head and an adze-like pick-blade behind it, are recorded from Aldborough (Yorks), Worlington (Suff), and Newstead. These were probably for building and entrenchment rather than for tillage. The same applies to those found respectively in the early Roman coastal fortlet of Old Barrow (Som), and in the ditch of the camp on Ashley Heath (Hants). Both resembled the military *securis dolabrata*, six of which came from Newstead. That such implements were nevertheless sometimes used for agriculture is suggested by the presence of a model of one among miniature agricultural tools both at Cologne and Rodenkirchen, Germany. Columella indeed describes the *dolabra* as used by ploughmen for cutting roots, and sometimes instead of the *rastrum* for breaking clods and covering seed.[3]

Spades. Corder's study of Roman spades in Britain showed three

Segontium: Wheeler, *Segontium*, London, 1933, p. 144, fig. 66, no. 23; Richborough: Bushe-Fox, *op. cit.*, IV, 1947, pl. lxi, p. 338; Thealby: H. Dudley, *Early Days in North-West Lincolnshire*, Scunthorpe, 1939, p. 132, fig. 10; London: *Guildhall Museum Catalogue*, p. 54, no. 71; Lydney: Ward, *Roman Era*, p. 198.

[1] *Hoes.* Langton: Corder, Kirk, *op. cit.*, fig. 21, 14 and p. 73; V-shaped tool: T. W. Bagshawe, *Ant. J.* XXIX, 1949, pp. 86–7. *Spuds.* Woodcuts: Pitt-Rivers, *Excavations*, I, pl. xxv, 9, 12; pl. xxvi, 7; East Grimstead: H. Sumner, *Excavations at East Grimstead*, London, 1924, pl. xi, 21; Darenth: Rochester Museum.

[2] *Rakes.* Spoonley Wood: A LII, 1890, p. 658; Newstead: Curle, *op. cit.*, pl. lxi, 7.

[3] *Mattocks.* Aldborough: Ward, *op. cit.*, fig. 56c; Worlington, Suff: Cambridge Museum of Ethnology and Archaeology; Newstead: Curle, *op. cit.*, pl. lxi, 9, Pit xiv, Flavian; PSAS⁴ XLVII, 1913, p. 389; fig. 3, Pit lxxxix; Old Barrow: Taunton Museum; Ashley Heath: Williams-Freeman, *Field Archaeology*, pp. 229, 351; Cologne: Schumacher, *op. cit.*, p. 20; Rodenkirchen: BJ, 149, 1949, p. 98; Colum., II, 2 (fin.).

main methods of attachment of the spade-shoe to the wooden blade. (Complete iron blades are seldom found in Britain.) (1) By simple grooving (Fig. 7; g); (2) by clips or lugs projecting from the side of the shoe; (3) by nails or rivets attaching the side extensions of the shoe to the sides of the blade. Ends may be round, square, or with a round end splayed beyond the width of the blade. The pointed spade or shovel seen, for instance, in Gaul, has not yet been found in this country. Many spades were doubtless entirely of wood, as for instance those found at Shelve (Salop), Wookey Hole, and elsewhere. No iron spades, in fact, are known in the British Early Iron Age, and Curwen has noted that the Welsh word for shovel (*pal*) is derived from the Latin *pala*. At Camulodunum the scapulae of oxen were found chopped for use as spades in the Belgic period.

The variety in shape, size, and method of attachment seems to denote, as Corder thought, a variation of practice among smiths, coupled with adaptation to customers' wishes. It also indicates experiment and resourcefulness. It is interesting that the vast number of the quotable spade-shoes come from civilian sites in the lowland zone; in the military area the spade seems to have been replaced by the *ascia-rastrum* and the mattock as digging implements.[1]

Forks. Few iron forks seem to be known in Britain, although Collingwood calls them common. Two were among the hoard of iron tools found in Well 2 of Insula XXXII at Silchester; a two-tined implement with tines 4¾ inches long is recorded from Chesters, Northumberland. A tine was found at Alchester, 9 inches in length. Many hay-forks were doubtless of wood – one was found at Chew Stoke (Som) – but iron hay-forks were usual in Gaul.[2]

The absence in Britain of *harrows* or identifiable remains of them may be noted at this point. A harrow very like the modern type was certainly in use in the Roman Rhineland, as is clear from the Cologne and Rodenkirchen finds of miniature tools, which included models of them. But it is not evident from these models whether the originals were of timber with iron spikes or entirely of iron. In Britain, if clods were not broken solely by hand, the practice may have been to work down the soil with a bush, as is still done in the Middle East.[3]

[1] *Spades.* P. Corder, *Arch. J.* c, 1943, p. 224; Shelve: JBAA xiii, 1857, p. 174–5; Wookey Hole: H. E. Balch, *Wookey Hole*, London, 1914, pl. xxiv, 1; Welsh word from Latin: Curwen, SAC lxvii, 1936, p. 144; Camulodunum: Hawkes, Hull, *op. cit.*, p. 351.

[2] *Forks.* Silchester: A 57, 1900, p. 247; Chesters: E. A. W. Budge, *Chesters: An account of the Roman Antiquities preserved in the Museum of Chesters, Northumberland,*[2] London, 1907, p. 398, no. 1817; Alchester: *Ant. J.* ix, 1929, p. 135, no. 11; Chew Stoke: ANL v, 1954, p. 98; Gaul: *Rev. arch.*[5] iii, pl. viii, 29023 (Compiègne).

[3] *Harrows.* Cologne, Rodenkirchen: see p. 79, n. 3.

In this context the *threshing sled* (*tribulum*) may be mentioned. Flints belonging to this implement have been identified at Angmering (Suss), and Atworth (Wilts). We may note Columella's remark that the *tribulum* should be used in addition to cattle or horses for threshing if teams are few.[1]

Wheeled vehicles, presumably carts, are in evidence at Great Chesterford, represented by wheels, tire-bands, felloes, axles, axle-boxes, and other parts. At Silchester a clearly defined cart-shed was excavated in Insula XXXII (Block ii). This building showed that the vehicles housed did not exceed six feet in length, and presumably had two rather than four wheels. Linchpins are recorded from Langton, Engleton (Staffs), Hambleden (Bucks), and East Grimstead. Probably the list could be much extended.[2]

Ox goads are frequently encountered. They were already made of iron in the pre-Roman period (Glastonbury, Bigbury), and continued in the same form after the Roman conquest, viz. an iron ring twisted into a spike (e.g. Silchester). They seem frequently to have been dedicated at shrines, which explains their presence at Harlow (Ess), and probably also at Maiden Castle, Lowbury, and Cold Kitchen Hill.[3]

Carding combs with heavy iron teeth are on record from Castlefield (Andover, Hants), Baydon (Wilts), and Botley Copse, Ashdown Park (Berks); also from several places in East Anglia, and these are discussed on p. 217. The specimen from Castlefield has teeth 3 to 4 inches long fitted into a double iron cross-piece 5 inches long, but incomplete.[4]

Among the agricultural tools recorded, the following were Roman introductions: the balanced sickle, the two-hand scythe, the mower's anvil, the turf-cutter, the mattock, the iron spade, the iron fork, the rake, and the *ascia-rastrum*. The pruning-hook was in all probability a Roman introduction, as there is no evidence of the cultivation of fruit-trees in the British Early Iron Age. It seems probable that the *tribulum* was also a Roman innovation, and the axe with vertical eyelet also appears with any frequency first under Roman rule. The

[1] *Tribulum.* Angmering: *Ant.* XI, 1937, p. 93 sqq.; Atworth: WAM XLIX, 1942, p. 70.
[2] *Wheeled vehicles.* Great Chesterford: *Arch. J.* XIII, pl. i, 14, 15; pp. 4, 6, 7, 11; Silchester: A LIV, 1893, p. 145, fig. 7; LVIII, 1897, map p. 422; Langton: Corder, Kirk, *op. cit.*, fig. 21, 1; Engleton: *Staffordshire Record Society*, 1938, p. 282; Hambleden: A LXXI, 1921, p. 197; East Grimstead: Sumner, *op. cit.*, pl. xii, 8.
[3] *Ox goads.* Glastonbury: Bulleid, Gray, *The Glastonbury Lake Village*, Glastonbury, 1911, II, p. 391; I, p. 10; Bigbury: Roach-Smith, *Collectanea Antiqua*, London, 1848, VI, p. 262; Silchester: D. Atkinson, *A Romano-British Enclosure on Lowbury Hill*, Reading, 1917, pl. xv, 17; Harlow: *Ant. J.* VIII, 1928, p. 308, fig. 4, 6.
[4] *Carding combs.* Castlefield: VCH *Hants.* I, p. 302; Baydon: *Devizes Museum Catalogue*, II², no. 459, pl. lxii, 3; Botley Copse: WAM X, 1889, p. 105; East Anglia: see p. 217.

Romans also brought with them a considerably improved form of billhook.

The increase of iron tools in Britain takes its commencement from the last century B.C., but there is no doubt that the Roman conquest saw a further increase which brought well-made reliable tools within the reach of the common man. The variety of spade-forms suggests that there were enough of them to allow the growth of local craft-traditions, also that some free experimentation was going on, and the standard of the late tool-hoard from Great Chesterford may mean a certain progress in technique during the occupation – the scythes here differ considerably from the Flavian examples at Newstead. The Abington Piggotts scythe hints at the local marketing of tools from well-equipped workshops in the urban centres.

A more reliable axe meant greater facility in deforestation; a balanced sickle meant economy of labour in harvesting, and a two-hand scythe achieved an increase in the accumulation of hay stocks and straw; in a wet climate, it might save a threatened corn crop by its accelerated output. But the great improvement was almost certainly the iron spade, which must have halved the labour and doubled the output when ditches and channels had to be dug or banks thrown up. Rapid entrenchment was not the least of the Roman army's advantages over the native tribes in war; but the technical gain in peaceful agriculture can hardly have been less, and the impact on field drainage would have been important.

CHAPTER VI

PLOUGHS AND FIELDS

THE IMPORTANCE of a study of the ploughs used in Roman Britain lies in their influence upon agricultural techniques, upon field-form, and upon tenurial relationships.

In recent years the Romano-British plough has received several detailed studies. Finds in Scandinavian peat-bogs, Roman literary sources, and model ploughs derived from one or two Roman sites, show that the commoner north-western and more particularly British plough of the Roman period was derived from a type current in the Early Iron Age of the region, namely the 'ard' with curved stilt continuing into the share-beam and socketed through the plough-beam which was attached to the yoke. Upon the share-beam or main share lay a slender foreshare whose point projected in front of it and was the first to open the furrow. The essentials of the type are repeated in Roman bronze models from Cologne and Lewes (Fig. 8; a), but the Roman models are equipped with tanged arrow-shaped shares, and both possess twin ground-wrests. The Piercebridge Roman statuette (Fig. 8; b), complete with ploughman and team, though without ground-wrests, is also an 'ard'. These ploughs could be drawn by two oxen, and cut a shallow furrow.[1]

Other remains of ploughs in Britain consist of iron shares and coulters. There is no authentic evidence of coulters in pre-Roman Britain, but the probability that some Early Iron Age ploughs possessed mouldboards makes it possible that wooden coulters were also used. It is an accepted view that in the absence of mouldboards the plough was tilted sideways to turn the sod for purposes of drainage, but it must be clearly stated, contrary to an opinion sometimes expressed, that a coulter-plough, if tilted, will deviate from its course, and that therefore a coulter implies, in conditions requiring such drainage, the use of a mouldboard, or that the plough should possess a ground-wrest to clear the furrow. Pre-Roman shares in Britain are both flanged and tanged, as are Romano-British examples, but whereas pre-Roman examples are spatulate or shovel-shaped, Romano-British

---

[1] F. G. Payne, 'The Plough in Ancient Britain', *Arch. J.* CIV, 1948, pp. 82 sqq.; E. A. Aberg, *Gwerin*, I, 1956–7, pp. 171 sqq.; W. H. Manning, JRS LIV, 1964, pp. 54 sqq.; F. G. Payne, AHR v, 1957, pp. 74 sqq. Cologne plough: Schumacher, *Der Ackerbau*, pp. 20–1, Abb. 10. Lewes plough: *Arch. J.* CIV, p. 97, pl. 8. Piercebridge statuette: E. Wooler, *The Roman Fort at Piercebridge*, Frome and London, 1917, p. 148.

examples included additionally arrow-shares, bar-shares, and winged shares (Fig. 7; a, b and Fig. 9; a), and all four types include specimens whose length is greater than that of the known pre-Roman examples. All appear to have been part of 'ard' ploughs, and all, except the winged shares, threw the soil equally to the left and right side.[1]

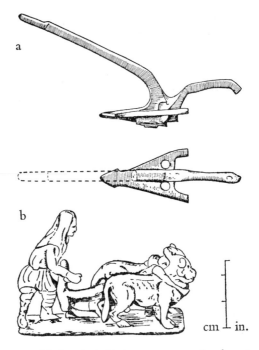

Fig. 8. (a) Bronze model plough (with beam cut away in plan view to show main share) from Sussex; (b) bronze model of a ploughman and his team, from Pierce-bridge, Co. Durham (both in BM).

The Romano-British coulter (Fig. 7; c), on the other hand, is a Roman innovation, and its considerable weight and length (sometimes as much as 16 pounds and 35 inches from tang to tip) indicate a biggish deep-cutting plough; the coulters themselves cut from 6¼ to 12 inches. Payne deduced from their existence that these ploughs had an elevated beam, were of varying sizes, possessed coulters consistently engaged to the left, could cut a strong furrow even by modern standards, could plough the stiffest soils, and turned the slice always to the right. Manning does not believe that the degree to which these coulters were set to turn the sod to left or to right can be reliably established, but what is clear is that with so deep a cut

[1] W. H. Manning, JRS LIV, pp. 54 sqq.

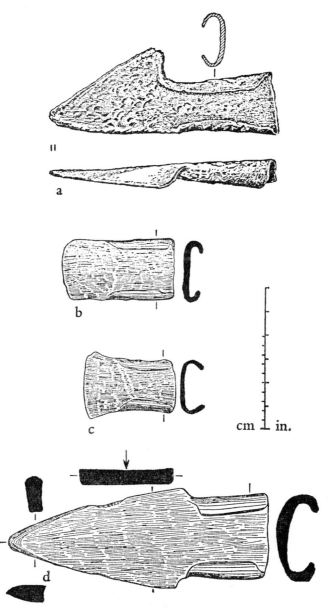

Fig. 9. Romano-British ploughshares: (a) asymmetrical share from Dinorben (National Museum of Wales); (b) short flanged share with broad edge from Silchester (Reading Museum); (c) short flanged share with broad edge from Wallingford (Reading Museum); (d) flanged share from Bucklersbury House, London (Guildhall Museum).

a mouldboard or ground-wrest would have been essential to clear the furrow, and the former would have raised a considerable ridge. Moreover, the model plough from Cologne has a share set to the left, like the winged share from Dinorben (Fig. 9; a,), suggesting that coulters with a right bias might have been used in Britain and the Rhineland, the more so in that the Cologne share has a parallel from the Roman villa at Hartlip (Kent). The German share was set on its side, and its extended socket seems to have acted as a mouldboard between the wrests. Consequently it looks as though alternating coulters were used in some Romano-British ploughs, so that permanently ridged fields would have been avoided. The Silchester coulters were associated with bar-points (Fig. 7; d) which Manning identifies as the shares of the ploughs to which the coulters belonged, implying that they were foreshares fixed to wooden main shares, that is, parts of 'ard' ploughs. This discovery may be important, since it has been suggested that the known coulters were used independently of the plough, being drawn ahead of it in a separate frame. But the corresponding main shares (improbably of wood) have not been identified. That the Romano-British coulters were an integral part of the ploughs is however made probable also by the discovery in the eastern Danube valley of Roman ploughshares in association with traces and a swivel coulter.[1]

The distribution of the large Romano-British coulter shows that its use, if not its introduction, was not exclusively related to highly romanized farms. Thus, examples have been found not only at romanized towns such as Great Chesterford and Silchester, and at the Roman villa of Great Witcombe (Glos), but also near the former hill-fort of Sandy in Bedfordshire, at the small settlement of Abington Piggotts (Cambs), which showed occupation from the Early Iron Age into the Saxon period, and near the village-site of Twyford Down (Hants).

Neither the big flanged ploughshares of the Belgic period as found, for instance, at Bigbury (Kent), nor the Roman coulters, and the mouldboards or ground-wrests that can be inferred from them, oblige us to believe that the fields worked by them stood in permanent ridges after the medieval fashion. The evidence from Cologne and Hartlip suggests reversible coulters and possibly mouldboards were used, while the associated shares turned the sod equally to right and left (exceptions will be discussed below), and if coulter and share turned the soil consistently to the right, the slice may well have been spread

---

[1] Dinorben share: Gardner, Savory, *Dinorben*, Cardiff, 1964, fig. 24, 11, and p. 158. Hartlip: Roach Smith, *op. cit.*, II, p. vi, fig. 8. Swivel coulter: Aberg, *Gwerin*, I, p. 180, fig. 8.

by the ground-wrests of which the models provide evidence. In any case, ploughing techniques exist whereby the non-reversible plough could have been used to lay the furrow slices on one side of the furrow in one half of the field and on the other side in the other half, the two sections being divided by a single ridge or by an unploughed land.

A different conclusion may however be drawn from the winged shares found at Brading, Folkestone, and Dinorben (Fig. 7; a, b; 9 a,), the first two villas and the third a north-Welsh hill-fort. These were clearly designed to turn the soil consistently to one side, and ploughing into permanent ridge and furrow is to be inferred. It is with these shares that Manning is disposed to connect the adoption of the mouldboard in Roman Britain. He points out that the introduction of the latter requires a reversible coulter, hence the use of the mould-board might thus have resulted in the production of a genuine frame-plough with brace and double stilt. It nevertheless seems probable that the normal known heavy Romano-British coulters needed mouldboards or wrests even when the shares were symmetrical. The use of the mouldboard plough between the sixth and the ninth centuries A.D. has indeed been proved by excavation of ancient fields near Gwithian (Corn), and one of the excavators, Professor Thomas, thought it probable that this novelty, i.e. the fixed mouldboard plough, was introduced in Roman rather than sub-Roman times.[1]

The question must now be considered, how far the evidence can be utilized to throw light on the problem of field-form in Roman Britain. It must be stated at the opening of the discussion that present enquirers have tended to reach the nihilistic view characteristically resulting from a prolonged and detailed examination of a vast quantity of evidence. It has been pointed out that there is in fact no stable corre-lation between plough-form or ploughing method and soil-type or field system. The heavy wheeled plough, for which there is no evidence in Roman Britain, has been used on the light chalk soils of the downlands, while the small swing-plough was commonly used on medieval acre-strips in between the communal ploughings of the eight-ox implement. There is no lack of cases in which the small scratch-plough has served to break wet and heavy soils, and in eighteenth-century Scotland tenants went over to the two-horse plough, abandoning the joint use of the large implement when *runrig* was given up. It should further be emphasized that open fields, long

---

[1] All plough parts discussed will be found under Payne, unless a reference is given. Sandy: Bedford Modern Schools Museum. Abington Piggotts: Cambridge University Museum of Archaeology and Ethnology. Brading, Folkestone: *Gwerin*, I, p. 180. fig. 7. Gwithian: P. J. Fowler, A. C. Thomas, *Corn. Arch.* I, 1962, pp. 61–84.

strips, communal working, and 'ridge-and-furrow' are not necessarily coincident with one another. While they were all part of one complex in the manorial system of medieval western Europe, both the first and the second have existed at various times independently of one another, and in Roman Britain if one case of ridge-and-furrow fields has been identified (Oakley Down), there is no proof that it represents any form of communal cultivation.[1]

When all this has been said, it is nevertheless desirable to recall certain generalities and to note certain facts. The soils of the chalk uplands, where a great deal of Early Iron Age and Roman agriculture was concentrated, are light, and shallow ploughing is essential there to avoid over-impregnation of the humus with chalk. Hence it is safe to assume a general association of the light scratch-plough with such areas. On the other hand, the growing damp of the British Early Iron Age would have led to increased humus. The same factor favours the slice-turning plough which secured better drainage and aeration, but need not have affected field-form. On the other hand the larger Belgic share and the appearance of the heavy iron coulter in the Roman period bear reliable witness to the spread of cultivation on to heavier lands, and it is hard to believe that ploughs of the size indicated could be usefully handled on the characteristically small plots of the chalk and gravel areas. Bloch noted that the adoption of a different plough in China caused a prolongation of the fields, and there was in France a rough correspondence between long-strip cultivation and the wheeled plough (*charrue*) on the one hand, and the "open irregular" (usually square) field system and the swing plough (*araire*) on the other. There may well have been a tendency in the Early Iron Age, as the climate deteriorated, to adopt a longer field, and while the division of holdings among agnates may not have produced strip fields, which are seldom traceable in the known Early Iron Age patterns of lowland Britain – though they may have been more frequent than thought – *runrig* or *rundale* (a minute subdivision into strips) has been a frequent product of this practice, albeit by no means certainly a very ancient one, in Ireland and Scotland, and it should not be forgotten that in the medieval open-field system such a process of partition among heirs played no inevitable part. Yet Stevens has argued, after carefully examining a number of records, that strips were commoner in association with farms cultivated in the Roman period in highland Britain than most archaeologists have been prepared to admit. In southern Britain,

[1] Light chalk soils: VCH *Suss.*, II, 1907, p. 281; medieval acre-strips: Lipson, *Economic History of England*, London, 1935, p. 63; C.S. and C.S. Orwin, *The Open Fields*[3], Oxford, 1967, p. 9; Scotland: H. Gray, *English Field Systems*, Cambridge, Mass., 1915, p. 162. Oakley Down: see p. 90.

too, one may observe cases of Romano-British villages (e.g. Chisenbury, Wilts) associated with strip fields which are certainly of the same period.[1]

When we turn to look for the archaeological evidence to convert theoretical inductions into facts, it is slender enough. We may note, in the first place, that the Cologne model plough already mentioned, whose reversed share is paralleled at Hartlip, possesses a low-pitched plough-beam best adapted to a form of trace-harnessing and a team working in line ahead rather than abreast. Further, we have some hint of the type of field cultivated by the Frindsbury ploughshare, which was symmetrical, turning the soil both to left and right. Frindsbury Roman villa was the base of the Cliffe area of Roman field divisions first traced by Nightingale north of Rochester. The Roman boundaries here contained within them, before enclosure in 1840, strips of an average area of three acres. The Frindsbury ploughshare resembled that of the old Kentish plough, and would therefore not have thrown up ridges in the heavy Cliffe loams. Moreover, ridge-and-furrow appears to have been non-existent in this region. More probably the Roman plough would have left periodical drainage furrows between the groups of ploughing. This may well have influenced the division of the Roman units into three-acre strips (five *iugera*). It is at any rate suggestive that the old French *bonnier* (*bunnarium*), a unit found in the Carolingian villas of Gaul, is thought to have been of this size, and was so till recently.[2]

While, therefore, the greater part of the chalk uplands of the south of England would appear in Roman times to have been cultivated within the pattern composed of what are loosely known as 'native' fields – although the presence among them of long strips must not be ignored – and more recent research has revealed considerable extensions of the form on the river gravels of the Thames valley, the Fens, and the east and west Midlands, the possibility exists that a different form was to be found on the heavier soils developed in the Belgic and more particularly in the Roman period. Such a possibility has been envisaged by scholars (Karslake, Hawkes, Collingwood) for a number of years, chiefly on the basis of the iron coulters whose size appears to indicate a plough of greater size, adapted to deep cutting in heavy lands and suggesting the existence of a longer and larger field. Karslake's belief

[1] China, France: M. Bloch, *Les caractères originaux de l'histoire rurale française*, Paris, 1931, pp. 55; 29–50. *Runrig*, Ireland: Sir John Davies etc. as cited in Chapter III, p. 53, n. 1. Strips: Stevens, CBA. RR VII, pp. 113–18.

[2] Frindsbury share: A. Cant. XVIII, pl. ii, p. 190, fig. 1. Cliffe field divisions: M. Nightingale, A. Cant. LXV, 1952, pp. 150 sqq. The *bunnarium*: A. Longnon, *La Polyptique d'Irminon*, Paris, 1886–95, pp. 20–1.

that such a plough possessed wheels has been shown to be without evidence, like Collingwood's statement that the big coulter derives from the Belgae. There is nevertheless some indication that the longer and larger field-form existed in Roman Britain. The evidence commences with the already cited interpretation of the shares from Frindsbury and Hartlip; very suggestive also is the case of Bury Lodge, Hambleden (Hants). Here a Roman farmhouse faced a slope falling to westward which possesses three broad strip-lynchets. The width of the easterly lynchet is 170 broadening to 330 feet, of the central, 250–350 feet, and of the westerly, 280 feet. The longest western lynchet measures 1,080–1,240 feet, the middle one about 730 feet. Strips of similar dimensions to the largest unit at Bury Lodge have also been recorded among fields of Early Iron Age or Roman date at Jevington and Wepham Down, both in Sussex, and Rhodes has further recorded fields of similar size (1,100 by 200 feet; 1,000 by 250 feet) at Stancombe Down (Berks), in association with a Roman building. Other strips here measured 900 by 200, 900 by 300, and 700 by 250/200 feet. A strip field at Oakley Down (Dors), earlier than a Roman road, measured 600 by 200 feet. In this context may be mentioned Early Iron Age fields also cultivated in the Roman period at Farthing Down, Coulsden (Surr), some of which measured 500/530 feet.[1]

In this connection the medieval field system surrounding Great Wymondley (Herts) is of considerable interest, since this complex appears to embody within it the fragments of a mathematically laid out "grid" division of Roman date (Fig. 10). (*Limitatio* or centuriation, for which see further below, p. 97.)

A Roman settlement existed immediately north-east of Great Wymondley church, and a Roman cemetery was found in the north-east corner of the attached area. In 1937 a habitation of poor character was excavated in the more northerly of the two earthworked enclosures north-east of the church. The east limit of the manor is bounded by the Roman road from Baldock to Stevenage, here running in a straight line NNE-SSW, and the manor boundary along the road covers the near-equivalent of 30 *actus*. The north-south boundaries of a number of strips in the medieval complex together form an axis (A-B) on a parallel bearing, which, produced southward, cuts the central crossroads of Great Wymondley. Their axis lies at a distance of precisely

[1] A different field-form: Karlslake, *Ant. J.* XIII, 1933, p. 455; Hawkes, *Ant.* IX, 1935, p. 339; Collingwood *ap.* Collingwood, Myres, RBES², pp. 211-12. Jevington strips: SAC LXIV, 1923, pp. 49, 50, n. 90; Stancombe Down, information from P. Rhodes; Oakley Down: O. G. S. Crawford, A. Keiller, *Wessex from the Air*, pl. xxxi, p. 74; Farthing Down: SyAC L, 1946/7, p. 54.

fifty *actus* from the Roman road. Boundary f between the two, gives a second north-south parallel precisely twenty *actus* east of A-B; g, a third, twenty *actus* to west of it; c, d, and e, together cut A-B at right angles, bearing on the north-east corner of the field area; i marks the next parallel to south at ten *actus'* distance.[1]

There seem, in addition, to be traces of subdivisions of the ten-*actus* squares. Thus h, fifteen *actus* from A-B, apparently bisected squares ε and ʒ; λ, two *actus* from A-B, cut square η from north to south, and k, four *actus* from i, subdivided it from east to west. Square θ was subdivided north-south by n, 3·35 *actus* from the parallel to west and 6·65 *actus* from the Roman road to east. In the nineteenth century Seebohm noticed a dark line (i.e. a ditch) running from north to south across the field immediately to east of the church area; this yielded many Roman potsherds, coins, and other objects, and falls parallel to axis A-B, about eight *actus* from it.[2]

On this reconstructed grid, the lines are frequently found to dissect the junction of lanes and headlands, and these, as well as the medieval field boundaries, frequently bisect the sides of the ten-*iugera* squares into equal halves where they cross. In the squares marked α to ʒ, the medieval shotts seem in an especially marked degree to retain the influence of Roman divisions in their grouping. They also provide evidence of the manner of subdivision of the quarter-*centuriae*. On the basis of the boundaries traceable, evidence is gained for nine squares of ten by ten *actus* (fifty *iugera*) each; their existence leads by inference to the reconstruction of five complete *centuriae* of 400 *actus*, or 200 *iugera*, each subdivided into quarters. *Centuriae* of this size are the normal and common unit of measurement in grids of this type throughout the Roman Empire.[3]

Three furlongs to west of Great Wymondley, but still within the Roman field system, is the Roman villa of Nine Springs or Purwell Mill.[4] The tenurial implications of these phenomena will be discussed elsewhere, as will the question of the extent to which they bear on the problems of continuity from the Roman to the post-Roman rural system. Here it is relevant to observe that the *centuriae* appear to have been subdivided into broad strips, the smallest of those recognizable being six *iugera* or 720 by 240 Roman feet. Strips in squares η and λ were 1,200 Roman feet, or 1,160 English feet, in length, comparable

[1] The 1821 enclosure map of Great Wymondley: F. Seebohm, *The English Village Community*, p. 432. The Roman cemetery: VCH *Herts*, IV, p. 169; 1937 excavations: Westell, EHAS 1937/9, pp. 11 sqq.

[2] The ditch, with coins from Vespasian to Julian: VCH *Herts*, IV, p. 169.

[3] Cf. J. P. S. Bradford, *Ant.* XXI, 1947, p. 200, where exceptions are noted.

[4] Purwell Mill (Nine Springs) villa: Fox, ACR, p. 186; VCH *Herts*, IV, p. 170.

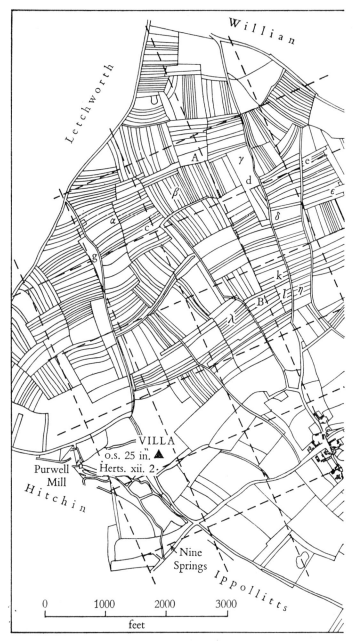

Fig. 10. The 1803 map of Much Wymondley, showing the medieval

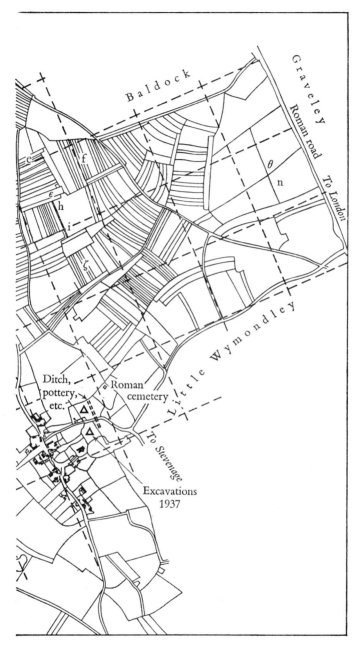

open-field boundaries retaining traces of Roman field divisions.

to that of the terrace at Bury Lodge and other instances cited below.
Assembling these and others, we find—

	Length (feet)	Width (feet)
Great Wymondley	754	232
Bury Lodge	730	250–350
Morton and Bourne "B"	60	120
Morton, Fenland no. 1423 (Hallam)	600	120
Jevington	600	120 × 3
Cliffe	580	232
Lye Hole	550	90/250
Great Wymondley	1,160	464
Eastfield (Thruxton)	1,100	270
Bury Lodge	1,080/1,240	265/330
Wepham Down	1,200	240
Lye Hole	1,100	90/250

It will be seen that these units fall into two classes, viz. (a) those
measuring 1,200 by 200/330 feet; (b) those measuring 600/700 by
230/350. Evidently the strip subdivisions represent much the same
agriculture as the fields not derived from mathematical parcellation,
and both classes are represented equally among measured fields, on un-
measured arable, and on terraced slopes. The evidence as a whole
agrees with what it is possible to deduce from the coulters, namely,
that a common type of Romano-British field, beside the 'square'
division of Early Iron Age economy, was a broad strip not necessarily
ridge-ploughed.

There is additional evidence near the villa of Woodham's Farm,
King's Worthy (Hants), to support the existence of strip fields in the
Roman period. The villa, as revealed by air-photography, was the
successor of an Early Iron Age farmstead (a 'spectacle' enclosure,
consisting of two linked circular enclosures); as Early Iron Age fields
are recorded less than half a mile to north of the site and about 1,000
yards to its north-west, the fields superseded by the villa were probably
of the same type. Between the north range of outbuildings lying at
right angles to the villa-residence, and the modern railway-embankment,
the air-photograph shows a series of north-south streaks which are
orientated with the Roman buildings; two more, parallel but on
a slightly different bearing, are to be discerned along the eastern side
of the villa-yard. None of these is a modern plough-line; the orientation
of the plough-lines in the photograph is quite different. The streaks
concerned seem to represent a set of field boundaries quite distinct
from the Early Iron Age complex, and must be of the Roman period.

This was confirmed by the publication in 1953 of crop-marks seen to the south of the site in 1948; these revealed a series of cultivation banks lying on an axis somewhat east of north-south.The strips so defined were some 35–40 feet wide and of a maximum length of 530 feet.[1]

In another case, that of Lye Hole villa near Wrington (Som), a field system associated with the villa, surveyed by P. J. Fowler, included strip fields but did not consist exclusively of such plots. There may have been some fifteen fields. The lengths vary in a ratio of 1, 2, and 4 (275, 550, and 1,100 feet) to the widths, but it will be seen that the lengths correspond to those already noted as characteristically Roman fields; widths vary between 90, 150, 200, 230, and 290 feet.

It is, indeed, possible to mention ancient strip fields elsewhere whose Roman origin is probable. Bowen states that in Dorset all strip fields in a 'native field' context have yielded Romano-British pottery; such at Muston Down have produced *terra sigillata*. Other cases may be cited between Baydon and Wanborough (Wilts), on Charlton Down in the same county, and at Gothic House Farm, Lincolnshire. Very notable is the case of Holbeach Drove Common, already referred to, where the fields occur in close-set 'shotts' scarcely distinguishable from the medieval pattern, being 200 to 300 yards in length. But not all the longer fields of Romano-British or Early Iron Age origin were so long as the cases just listed; Bowen cites proportions of 4/5:1, exceptionally of 6:1, up to an area of one and a half acres, sometimes replacing smaller squarish fields.[2]

In the Fenlands, where the Romano-British fields are preponderantly of the squarish 'native' type, normally from a quarter to 1¼ acres in area, Hallam notes that 48 per cent of the plots in "Block B" of the Morton and Bourne area were of the "long" type, their breadth constituting no more than 10 per cent of their length; breadths were in the neighbourhood of 60 feet, and lengths of 400–600 feet.

The Romano-British winged share, found in two cases at villas

[1] I am indebted to Commander W. H. C. Blake for permission to examine the air-photograph. Crop marks: HFC XVIII, 1953, pp. 63–4. "Ditched plots of long narrow form" at Gargrave villa, Yorks, and at Worthing, Suss, are alluded to in Rivet, RVB, p. 44.

[2] I am indebted to Mr P. J. Fowler for prior details of the field system at Lye Hole, Wrington, Som. See now also BUS XII, 1970, pp. 178–80, and fig. 27. An account of this and the Barnsley Park fields is promised in *Archaeology into History: Studies by Christopher Hawkes and his Pupils*, ed. S. Chadwick Hawkes and D. Britten, forthcoming; also in BGAS. Dorset: H. C. Bowen, CBA. RR I, Roman Villas, 1955, p. 35; Baydon-Wanborough: HFC XIII, 1933, p. 190, n. 6; Charlton Down: *Air Survey and Archaeology*, p. 22; pl. v; Gothic House Farm, information from C. W. Phillips; cf. *id.*, *Aspects of Archaeology in Britain and Beyond*, p. 267.

(Folkestone, Brading), may well support the existence, not only of strip fields, but of actual ridge-and-furrow cultivation in the Roman period. A survey by competent researchers, indeed, has failed to discover traces of such near Brading, where the traceable fields near the villa are of Early Iron Age type, but suggestive information comes from Great Witcombe villa, which has yielded a large coulter of the deep-cutting mouldboard or ground-wrest plough. "From the site of the villa an interesting group of long strips of agricultural ridges and furrows can be seen, extending only to the general lines of the villa, but their date is uncertain." It may also be relevant to note that this villa has yielded the bones of a larger variety of cattle than the common Romano-British *bos longifrons*, and similar bones occur in villas at Park Street (Herts), Hucclecote (Glos), and Nuthills (Wilts). Elsewhere, at Oakley Down (Wilts), a strip field earlier than a Roman road has been noted showing clear signs of ridge-and-furrow cultivation. Other cases of broadly ridged fields of ancient date, on the other hand (e.g. Combe Bissett, Knighton Hill), once suspected of Roman origin, are regarded with scepticism by recent investi-gators, who point to 'broad rig' as a characteristically medieval technique.[1]

The association of fields of Early Iron Age type with a number of minor farmsteads of Roman date and of what might be described as lesser romanization, is amply demonstrated by recent air-surveys of the gravel regions of the eastern and the western midlands. Much of this evidence awaits detailed analysis, but we may note as an example embodying a larger type of field a Romano-British farm east of the King Street at Northborough near Deeping (Lincs). The fields which can with certainty be connected with the farm cover not less than twenty-two acres; there may have been more, but the existence of an earlier phase, probably associated with a group of seven circular huts to be seen on the photographs, complicates the attempt to make a more precise estimate. The land immediately to the south of the dwelling is divided into closes, one a strip of about 300 by 60 feet, another 2·4 acres. But the southern part of the holding appears to be undivided, and composed a field of some 12–13 acres, an area far beyond the scale represented in the 'native' field system. The area just described is limited on its south and east sides by double ditched droveways, one of which bifurcates on the north-east to communicate with a double ditched 'rath'-like enclosure of the sort already alluded to (p. 13) in connection with the Fenland, and probably used to house

---

[1] Brading: Bowen, *ap.* Rivet, RVB, p. 43, fig. 1.8; Great Witcombe: E. M. Clifford, BGAS LXXIII, 1954, p. 34; Oakley Down: p. 90, n. 7. Broad rig (broadly-ridged fields): Bowen, CBA. RR I, Roman Villas, p. 38.

stock. Another example of larger fields of Roman date is to be seen at Grimstone Down, Stratton (Dors), where one enclosure measures some 7½ acres, another about 5 acres.[1]

In our discussion of field types under cultivation in the Roman period and not classifiable with the units of 'native' type, we must consider the mathematically surveyed field divisions, so characteristic of Roman methods and occurring in various provinces of the Roman Empire, to wit, the system termed centuriation or *limitatio*, which has already been referred to in connection with the field divisions at Cliffe and Great Wymondley. M. Nightingale was able to put up a good case for the survival of such a field pattern in the Cliffe district, north of Rochester. He noted that the Watling Street as it approaches Rochester from London is deflected three miles west of the Medway in such a manner as to fall at right angles to the Roman road leaving Rochester for Maidstone. A production northward of the latter he found to align with one of a north-south orientated series of lanes in the Cliffe region, and their intermediate measurements corresponded to Roman units, composing a grid divided into squares of 200 *iugera* in area. As we have recorded, these were subdivided down to 1840 into broad strip fields of some three acres in area (five *iugera*). Air-photographs showed the ancient ditches of some of the north-south roads surviving on their lines at several points where the modern lanes had deviated from their original course. The Watling Street turns south-eastward to enter Rochester, but a continuation of its line eastward to Frindsbury at the south-east angle of the grid-system corresponds with a fragment of Roman road found when the Roman house at Frindsbury was discovered in 1888.[2]

The authentic Roman character of the 'grid' discovered by Nightingale is to be accepted on the following grounds: (1) it is centred on a Roman town of local importance (Rochester); (2) the Roman ditches were detected where the modern successors of the boundary roads deviate; (3) the units measure 200 *iugera* in area, the normal unit among Roman centurial systems in the Empire; (4) the grid's alignments coincide at three points with known sections of Roman road; (5) the *cardo* or north-south base-line, of the system, if produced across the

---

[1] East and West Midlands: RCHM, *A Matter of Time*, 1960; cf. K. St Joseph, JRS LI, 1961, pp. 133 sqq. Northborough: *A Matter of Time*, p. 14, and fig. 6. Grimstone Down (Dors): RCHM *Dors*, I (West), 1952, p. 228, no. 11.

[2] Centuriation: PWRE, s.v. *Limitatio* (XIII, cols. 672 sqq. – Fabricius), 1927; J. P. S. Bradford, *Ant.* XXI, 1947, pp. 197 sqq. with numerous references to further literature; *id., Ancient Landscapes*, London, 1957, pp. 145 sqq.; C. E. Stevens, *Ant.* XXXII, 1958, pp. 25 sqq.; Ministère des Travaux publiques, Tunisie, *Atlas des centuriations romaines de Tunisie*, Paris, 1954; *Enciclopedia dell' Arte antica*, II, Rome, 1959, p. 476, s.v. *Centuriazione*; Cliffe fields: M. Nightingale, see p. 89, n. 2.

Thames estuary, hits Caesaromagus (Moulsham near Chelmsford), which was some sort of imperial administrative centre.

The case of *limitatio* at Great Wymondley has already been described. Another possible instance at West Blatchington (Suss) demands attention because it was detected both by air-photography and by excavation, and this is the first case in Britain supported by both types of evidence (Fig. 11).

A Roman villa was found there in 1818, and re-excavated in 1948. The farmhouse, of basilical type, was preceded by an Early Iron Age enclosure and by two Romano-British enclosures of the first and second to third centuries respectively; it was built in the third century. The area between it and the Romano-British enclosures was occupied in the late second and third centuries by eleven corn-drying furnaces, and to the east of these lay a long north-south ditch evidently a field boundary, dug in the same period. A northward extension of this field system was found on an air-photograph taken in 1950; it revealed a small area subdivided by rectilinear boundaries on a right-angle basis, and a precise east-west orientation. The westernmost visible boundary was accurately aligned with the aforementioned ditch to the east of the villa. Not enough of the divided area remained to indicate how far this was conventional centuriation, but it undoubtedly reflects a Roman survey executed on mathematical principles, sub-divided into various sizes, and including boundary roads, one of which is visible in the south-east corner of the area concerned. One interboundary interval measured 695 feet, the equivalent of the sides of 6 *actus*. Notable here are the relatively small sizes of the subdivisions, which may reflect native influence. The social and tenurial implications of this fragment will be considered later. Here suffice it to note that the survey almost certainly superseded a 'native field' pattern, since the villa was preceded by a farmstead of characteristically native type, and lay at a point where the soils of the coastal plain touch the chalk of the Sussex Downs.[1]

In the same context may be mentioned the small area of centuriation which I. D. Margary believed he had identified near Ripe (Suss), at the north-east end of the downs in the direction of Pevensey. Round this village exists a block of fields of regular rectangular form and layout, markedly different from the arrangements of the fields sur-rounding it. Its area is approximately two and a half square miles. Margary was able to show that the boundaries concerned went back to the Norman, and probably to the Saxon, period, that the main lines

---

[1] I am indebted to N. E. S. Norris, the excavator of the villa, for help and infor-mation concerning the villa and its surroundings. Cf. AHR VI, 1958, p. 72; XI, 1963, pp. 5 sq.; CBA. RR VII, p. 102.

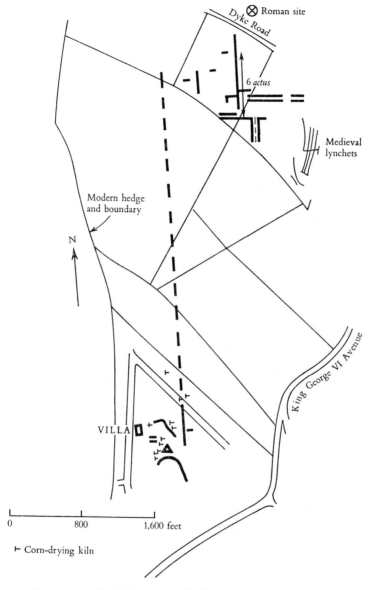

Fig. 11. The area north of the West Blatchington Roman villa, showing field divisions of Roman date according to excavations and to Air Ministry air-photograph 4110 of 1950.

and internal boundaries responded to Roman units of land-measurement, the *actus*, rather than to any English measure, and that the north-south roads limiting the area on east and west were the productions of probable Roman roads communicating with the downland to south.

The case of the Ripe land-divisions is a shade less convincing than the phenomena to be observed at West Blatchington and in the Cliffe region. The units that correspond to the Roman *actus* here result in *centuriae* consisting of both 210 and 240 *iugera*, and though such *centuriae* existed in Italy, the accepted norm throughout the provinces was 200 *iugera*, and the existence of two different norms side by side in one restricted area evokes doubts. Further, while the field divisions at Cliffe are associated with a Roman town and villa, and those of West Blatchington and Great Wymondley with villas, the Ripe fields are not situated in the direct vicinity of any known Roman settlement; Roman pottery has, however, been found within the boundaries concerned at three points.[1]

Lastly we may refer to the two well-known parallel Roman roads of central Essex, the one between Gosfield, Braintree, and Little Waltham, the other between Dunmow and Roundbush Green (Fig. 4). The first to draw attention to their possible origin in a centurial survey was Haverfield. More recently his suggestion has been opposed by the late Sir Ian Richmond, who, discussing the history of Colonia Victrix (Colchester), considered that the colony's territory was appropriated for settlement under the laws of war (i.e. as *agri captivi*) without an ordered assignment of plots; hence a systematic mathematical survey was not to be expected there. Far more important, Richmond pointed out that the roads were not precisely parallel; the easterly of the pair deviates from the necessary orientation by one degree.

It may be controversial how far the notion of *agri captivi* was operative in the first century of the Empire, but on the assumption that it was, and that the area concerned was connected with Colonia Victrix, an ordered readjustment after the Boudiccan revolt is eminently probable in the light of the policy of appeasement initiated by the Roman authorities. It may however be pointed out that the easterly of the two roads concerned turns south-eastward at its southern end to communicate directly with Caesaromagus, a name which implies an administrative centre; in Gaul instances occur of names embodying the element "Caesar" which were the centres of imperial domains. (Cf. pp. 30–1.) The area, then, may rather have been the confiscated property of the Belgic kings whose estate is likely to have been at Pleshey, a villa which has yielded Arretine pottery, and is

[1] The Ripe field divisions: SAC LXXX, 1939, p. 29; LXXXI, 1940, pp. 31 sqq.; I. Margary, *Roman Ways in the Weald*², London, 1965, pp. 205–7.

situated in an area still well-known for its high wheat-production. The hypothetical Essex *limitatio*, then, need have had no connection with the *territorium* of Colonia Victrix, but rather belonged to an imperial domain. Tracts of imperial property were sometimes squared off by survey in the Empire; cases may be cited in Apulia, Calabria, Numidia, and the Rhineland. The non-parallelism of the two roads is a far more damaging criticism; all that can be said on the point is that Roman surveyors might also have made mistakes, and before we dismiss entirely the possibility that these roads represent mathematical land divisions, one or two other aspects must be considered.

The roads concerned must be viewed in their geographical and political setting. The eastern alignment, deviating from the (approximate) parallel, continued northward (as the Peddar's Way) to Ixworth and the Wash, where a ferry joined it to the road to Lincoln. This was a political and strategical route *par excellence*, marking a stage in the conquest advance, and the late Rainbird Clarke believed that it was laid out after A.D. 61 as part of the suppression of the Boudiccan revolt. He wrote: "[The Peddar's Way] was probably constructed in the last third of the first century A.D." This would suggest a date for the origin of the central Essex roads, and they were part of a broader plan for the pacification of the region. At this point we may note, in favour of their centurial character, that the Roman road leaving Great Chesterford east-south-eastward falls at right angles to the two base roads, and that its production past Radwinter cuts the site of a Roman farm at Finchingfield, founded in the Flavian period.

Two other points may be made concerning the Essex roads under discussion. The first is that their straight, nearly parallel, sectors coincide precisely with the central medium loam region of the county (see pp. 66-7), and cease to be parallel where the heavy clay loam soils begin. It is therefore probable that they represent extensive deforestation, such as would have made a mathematical allotment feasible. Secondly, it is possible that these roads are part of a broader scheme with ramifications elsewhere; this is suggested by the coincidence of their bearing with that of the central sector of the Sussex Stane Street. That this is of significance is suggested by the fact that the line of the Roman road entering Rochester from the south, one of the base-lines of the Cliffe field divisions, if produced bears, as stated, upon Caesaromagus, which stands in direct communication with the eastern Essex highway.[1]

[1] Essex roads: F. Haverfield, EHR XXXIII, 1918, pp. 289 sqq.; RCHM *Ess*, I, 1916, p. xxv; I. A. Richmond, *Arch. J.* CIII, 1946, p. 61; *agri captivi*: Siculus Flaccus, de conditionibus agrorum, Bluhme, Lachmann, Rudorff, *Grom. Vet.*, I, p. 138; cf. Euseb., HE, IV, 6, 1. Pleshey: RCHM *Ess.*, II, p. xxix; F. Oswald, T. D. Pryce,

All these points taken together, therefore, should deter us from rejecting outright that the central Essex roads had something to do with a general land survey.

Although evidence has been assembled indicating that a form of strip field existed in Roman times, to be found in given cases in association with differing environments, by no means all villas seem to have worked fields distinguishable from the 'native' type of plots that originated in the pre-Roman period. The small subdivisions within the West Blatchington 'grid' have been noted. The fields on air-photographs of the area around the small Roman farmhouse at Little Milton (Oxon) are generally of the 'native' type, and some of the smallest measure no more than 70 by 20 feet. But two phases can be distinguished in this pattern, and in the second some rather larger fields were laid out, including several strips. Field boundaries are also visible on air-photographs of the Watt's Wells villa, Ditchley (Oxon), but here it is difficult to decide the character of the plots, and all that can be said is that they do not look strictly 'native', and they were probably larger than the normal enclosures of the Early Iron Age.[1]

Probably a number of Roman farms, including some villas, i.e. the centres of estates whose dwellings reveal evidence of cultural romanization, were set within a 'native' field pattern. One such is traceable in an air-photograph of the site of Eastfield villa near Thruxton (Hants), and the same is the case with Roman villas at Micheldever in the same county, and at Lechlade (Glos). Roman buildings surrounded by such fields are known at Stancombe Down (Berks), Kingston (Dors), Shoddesden, and Warren Hill (Hants). Others in the close vicinity of square fields have been observed in Hampshire at Lower Link Farm, Hurstbourne, and Lower Wyke near Andover. We may further note that Port's Road, in Sussex, which has 'native' fields laid out in reference to both sides of it, leads directly to the important villa of Southwick. It were further well to mention that the area south of Chichester, coinciding more or less with Selsea and in all probability constituting a considerable part of the territory

An Introduction to the Study of Terra Sigillata, London, 1920, p. 5; grain production: LUS no. 82, Ess., p. 426, fig. 13; Peddar's Way: Phillips, *Ant.* VI, 1932, pp. 342 sq.; Clarke, NA XXVI, pp. 155, 159 – cf. Moore, PSIA XXIV, 1935, p. 171; NA XXX, 1921, p. 143. Woodland clearance in central Essex: cf. Tac., *Agric.*, 31, where Calgacus is perhaps referring to this operation; in AHR VI, 1958, p. 79, n. 2, Vettius Bolanus is suggested as the governor (69–71) responsible for the scheme (cf. Statius, *Silvae*, V, 2, 43–4). Finchingfield: EAS XX, 1936, pp. 248 sqq.; XXI, 1937, pp. 249 sqq.; XXII, 1938, pp. 309 sqq. Central Essex medium loams: LUS no. 82, Ess., p. 411, fig. 4.

[1] Little Milton: JRS XL, 1950, pl. vi and p. 102. Ditchley: *Ant.* IX, 1935, p. 472, pl. v, vi.

of Roman Noviomagus Regnensium, was divided into small fields of the Early Iron Age type, but nothing seems to have been published to tell us if these plots were directly associated with some form of extramural farmstead.[1]

A recently authenticated case of a field system associated with a Romano-British establishment, apparently (though not certainly) a villa, may be cited from Barnsley Park (Glos). Its notable feature, as surveyed by P. J. Fowler, is that the area of the average plot does not exceed about 90 by 270 feet, the longest being 300 feet, so that none can be classified conspicuously as a strip field. The plots are defined by low banks, thought to mark the remains of stone walls. This is therefore an enclosed field system, and the area of the plots bears a marked resemblance to those of the normal 'native' field system.[2]

One other type of land-division must be mentioned here, namely, the vineyard. The vine had possibly been introduced into Britain before the Roman conquest, to judge from the popularity of wine among the Belgic nobility (see p. 117). Finds make it certain that it was cultivated in several districts in the Roman period. (Silchester, London – two sites, Gloucester; Stoke Newington, possibly Park Street, Hertfordshire and two or three sites in Kent.) It may be added that a network of ditches noted and tested near North Thoresby Lincolnshire, in 1959, covering some two acres, was regarded as connected with vine-growing. The contents of the trenches indicated intensive manuring, and the pottery appeared to cease in the seventies of the third century, a date appropriate to the reign of Probus, who allegedly removed the prohibition enacted by Domitian of vine-growing in the provinces. The excavators themselves nevertheless admitted certain objections to their hypothesis that these were vine-trenches; the intervals between them (25 feet) far exceeded those prescribed by modern practice (3–10 feet) or by Columella (15 feet), and the clay soil was not suitable for vines. It is possible to add a further damaging objection, namely, that the slope on which the trenches occur faces east, which is singularly unfavourable for vines; southern slopes have always been preferred because they receive a maximum of sunshine. Nor is it probable that Domitian's restriction of vines remained in force down to the late third century, and the information

---

[1] Eastfield, Thruxton: Air Ministry Photograph 2097, 30 Aug. 1946. Micheldever (Shroner Wood): information from Commander W. H. C. Blake; Stancombe Down: information from P. Rhodes; Lower Link Farm, Hurstbourne, Lower Wyke: O. G. S. Crawford, *The Andover District*, Oxford, 1922, p. 28; OS Records. Port's Road: *Brighton and Hove Archaeologist* III, 1926, pp. 35–7. Selsea: information from Dr A. E. Wilson.

[2] Barnsley Park: details prior to publication (see above, p. 95, n. 2) by the kindness of Mr P. J. Fowler and Dr G. Webster.

that Probus permitted vine-cultivation in the provinces is from an unreliable source (see p. 118, n. 1). The discoverers concluded that if this was a vineyard, it was an unsuccessful experiment; this is perhaps the most liberal interpretation of the evidence that one can admit.[1]

Vines, whether grown trellised for the table or ground-trailed for wine, imply carefully planned planting in parallel lines, and would therefore naturally, though not inevitably, have their place within a pattern of mathematically surveyed fields. The vine-production evidenced for Gloucester may well have been part and parcel of a centurial grid such as normally accompanied a veteran colony; but no such grid has yet been reliably identified round Gloucester.

While therefore the use of larger fields, both oblong and squarish, may be regarded as a development of the Roman period in Britain at various points, this was not a general phenomenon but one which occurred here and there on a local scale within a pattern which remained to a considerable extent as it had been in the pre-Roman epoch. Yet in some areas of this system certain features appear which may be attributed to Roman organization or influence. This is a tendency to a more regular layout and for the plots to hinge upon double ditched or bivallate ways which served as accommodation roads when improved transport and markets developed under the Pax Romana, and may also have marked divisions of property. Bivallate ways, indeed, sometimes precede the Roman period, as at Farthing Down, Coulsden (Surr), where some of the impinging fields appear to have been created in the Belgic phase, by throwing together plots, but a similar process on Martin Down (Hants) would appear to belong to the Roman period. Striking examples of the association of bivallate ways with regularized field systems occupied in the Roman era may be seen on Wylye Down west of Salisbury, at Thundersbarrow Hill (Suss) (Fig. 12) and at Stancombe Down (Berks). In the latter area, longish fields abut upon a well-marked Roman road whose extension northward has been traced to the vicinity of Oxford, and there is evidence of the modification of some of the field-boundaries in the course of Roman occupation.[2]

Of the effects of Roman influence on the agricultural régime of the 'native' field system something will be said later in the discussion of farm layout and agricultural techniques; and the problem of how far these fields, whether situated on the gravels of the river valleys or on the chalk and limestone uplands, represented an 'open' or

[1] North Thoresby, see p. 118.
[2] Farthing Down, Coulsden: SyAC L, p. 47; Martin Down, Wylie Down: Bowen, *Ancient Fields*, pp. 24, 26.

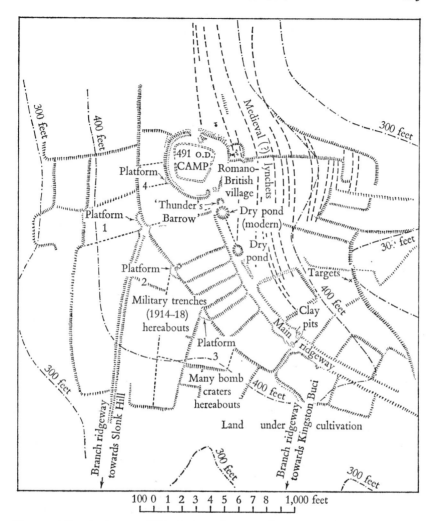

Fig. 12. Thundersbarrow Hill, Sussex, showing characteristic 'native' fields of Roman date ranged on bivallate ways and associated with a Romano-British village.

'enclosed' field pattern, is important for its bearing on the subject of land-tenure and its problems. Here, however, one or two remarks may be appropriate regarding the actual factors making for the formation of such field-forms.

Clearly both crop-divisions and subdivision of property among heirs may bring into being networks of relatively small parcels, but the predominance of comparatively small plots approximately square in form is a product of tradition and of limited man-power among a relatively poor population farming on the basis of the family unit. The persistence of such plots from the Bronze Age onward is a fact suggesting their origin in hand-working by digging-stick and spade. One other factor, however, is worth considering, namely, the need for drainage. In the gravel and silt areas, at least, the field boundaries were ditches which served to drain the plots, and this function automatically restricted the size of the unit cultivated in the absence of covered land-drains, a technique which was unknown till the advent of Rome. Yet the Fenland pattern, at least, and much of the field-plan of the gravel regions, does not differ fundamentally from that of the uplands in the same period. The development of larger fields in the Roman period depended, therefore, not only on a mouldboard or ground-wrest plough for the better drainage of the soil (a technique which in shallow chalk soils could be applied only on a restricted scale), but also on the introduction of the Roman iron spade as a more efficient digging tool (see above, p. 82). Further, the survival of the smaller field over large areas of lowland Britain in the Roman period implies not only the persistence of the family labour-unit, but also of an obstinate tradition, and it may be tentatively suggested that the Early Iron Age field pattern was originally evolved in conditions where the water-table lay at a higher level than is the case in the chalk downlands of southern Britain.

The factors making for the adoption of larger fields, nevertheless, extended beyond the operation of a larger deep-cutting plough. They arose with the multiplication of man-power not restricted to the family plot (slaves, wage-labourers, and tenants), with the availability of markets which led to the development of commercial farming; and in response to the demands of the armed forces and of taxation. From these factors was born the capitalist estate, with its exploitation of new imported techniques, such as controlled grazing, sown pasture, and the growing of fodder-crops; all these methods demanded controllable enclosed fields which needed to be larger in order to be profitable.

Recent work on the 'native' field system of southern England, more especially in Wiltshire, has begun to furnish an answer to the question, whether these fields were fenced or open, although much remains to be done before the picture is complete.

On Overton Down cases were found where broad tumbles of standing stones or orthostats suggested that the plots had been surrounded in the Early Iron Age by stone fences, and near South Street Long Barrow a line of stake-holes was found evidencing the use of a wooden fence as early as the Neolithic period. Traces of a fence were also noticed at the edge of a lynchet-field on Overton Down near Marlborough. This belonged to the Early Iron Age phase of cultivation, and the same line had been unfenced in the Roman period. But much of the evidence was against the enclosure of fields by more than a symbolic barrier which served rather as a mark and opposed no effective obstacle to the passage of livestock. Thus a lynchet eight feet high on Fyfield Down contained a dry-stone wall no more than a foot or a foot and a half in height, associated with a layer of soil cultivated in the Early Iron Age; the wall was non-existent in the Roman period, when, however, cultivation continued. Excavations at Streatley Warren (Berks), Berwick Down (Tollard Royal, Wilts), and Durrington Walls (Wilts), on the other hand, have failed to reveal any mark or barrier between such fields, and no case of the use of ditches as boundaries seems yet to have been recorded in Wessex; to westward, however, such appear in relation with Roman fields at Charterhouse-on-Mendip and at Gwithian, Cornwall, where their date was in the Early and Middle Bronze Ages. Ditches are, of course, of regular occurrence bounding Romano-British fields on the gravels, also occurring at West Blatchington on the medium soils, and in association with the Faversham villa. A flint bank served on Smacam Down (Dors), evidently accumulated by clearance-work on the fields, and at Grassington, where, however, part of the strips are walled. Such walling seems in general to be commoner in the highland area, especially in Devon and Cornwall, where it is known, for instance, at Kestor (Dev); field-walls occur also in Wales (Caerau), and have been referred to as probable at the farmstead at Barnsley Park (Glos).

Generally, then, it is not possible to define the 'native' field system, which reached its maximum development in the Roman period, as a wholly enclosed or wholly open field pattern, and much remains to be investigated before we shall understand the associated usages in relation to grazing, the protection of crops, and the management of fallow in Early Iron Age and Romano-British rural areas.[1]

[1] Overton Down: Fowler, WAM LVIII, 1961/3, p. 104; dry-stone walls: *ib.*, 105; Fyfield Down: *id.*, *Ant.* XLI, 1967, p. 296; Berwick Down, Durrington Walls: *ib.*, p. 298 n.; fences: *Ant.* XLI, 1967, p. 298; clearance banks: *ibid.*; Charterhouse-on-Mendip: BUS VI, 1949–50, pp. 201–4; cf. *ib.*, p. 82, fig. 20; Gwithian: *Corn. Arch.* I, 1962, pp. 77–8. Grassington: Raistrick, YAJ XXXIII, 1938, p. 168. Kestor and Caerau: *Ant.* XLI, 1967, p. 298. Ditched field boundaries attached to the Faversham villa: B. Philp, *Excavations at Faversham, 1965*, 1968, p. 72.

CHAPTER VII

CROPS AND PLANTS

THE EVIDENCE for the plants of economic value grown or utilized in this country in the Roman period is derived preponderantly from archaeological finds, and very rarely from written evidence. The recording of plant-finds from Roman sites began in this country at the end of the last century during the excavation of Silchester, but with isolated exceptions it has only been in the last twenty years that botanists have resumed the examination and definition of such evidence. Where the grain-finds are concerned, recent improvement of techniques has rendered a number of the identifications previous to 1952 of doubtful accuracy. Thus in previous literature, according to Helbaek, emmer, spelt, naked barley, and hulled barley have frequently been erroneously identified as bread wheat. As a result, Godwin in his summary of ancient grain-finds in Britain, written in 1956, expressly excludes older records of this grain. Consequently the present account will be based, where grains are concerned, on the work of Helbaek and Godwin, with the addition of some more recent finds and less defined information from the period prior to Helbaek's researches.[1]

The grains of the British Early Iron Age were spelt, emmer, and barley (naked and hulled). Oats appear, both wild and cultivated, but apparently as weeds exploited among host-crops. *Triticum vulgare* (bread wheat) or *Triticum compactum* (clubwheat), and rye, also occur. Hulled barley preponderates, and is the commonest crop of the period. During the Early Iron Age, under the impact of a moister climate, a trend set in to devoting larger areas to winter-sown crops (spelt, six-rowed barley), although summer crops still remained the majority.[2]

In the Roman period all the above crops are found, but rye and *Triticum compactum* (club wheat) now appear with greater frequency, spelt becomes a principal crop, and oats are established as a cultivated grain. While the latter appear to have been grown both in lowland and highland Britain (in the south they have been identified in Hertfordshire, Kent, Sussex, Essex, and Norfolk), their distribution

[1] Helbaek on previous literature: PPS xviii, 1952, p. 201; H. Godwin, *The History of the British Flora*, Cambridge, 1956, p. 272.

[2] The Early Iron Age: Helbaek, PPS xviii, pp. 207 sqq.; find-list A–B, pp. 228–9; Godwin, *op. cit.*, p. 262. Winter crops, PPS xx, 1954, p. 104.

in the northern zone may be significant. Of ten sites where they have
been identified, five are those of Roman forts or their immediate
vicinity, one (Castle Cary) on the Scottish Wall, four elsewhere
(Malton, Birrens, Cockermouth – not quite certainly of Roman date –
Caerleon). Three more are from the vicinity of the Scottish Wall.
It is natural to suppose that at least part of this cereal was grown
locally, presumably by the natives, and evidently the history of the
oat as a hardy northern crop well adapted to the wetter conditions and
greater cold of the highland zone, goes back to the Roman period.
At York Hill, Glasgow, the grains were found with a coin of Trajan
and second-century pottery, and the fact that a number of the north-
of-England native villages and their field systems develop in the same
period, makes it reasonable to suppose that the cultivation of oats as
a summer crop was introduced under the influence, if not the pressure,
of the Roman corn levy. This supposition gains some confirmation
from the discovery in the area to the south-west of the legionary
fortress of Caerleon of a deposit of burnt grain dating between
A.D. 90–130, and including hulled barley (*Hordeum distichum*), wheat,
rye, oats (cultivated and wild), spelt, horse beans, and lentils. Helbaek
concluded from the last two elements that the grain was imported,
and it therefore follows that the increase of oats in the period of
Trajan and Hadrian was being aided by the import of grains from
the continent for purposes of army supply. How far government
initiative was directly responsible for the spread of oats in the north
of Britain, or how far it was the result of astute adaptation to new
conditions on the part of native farmers, we cannot say; it should
nevertheless be noted that while Pliny regarded the oat as a mere
weed, his contemporary Columella, writing not later than A.D. 65,
recommends it as a fodder crop, so that in the period of Nero there
may have been a change of attitude to this cereal. Oats, as prime
horse-fodder, must indeed have been in demand by the military. The
establishment of cavalry garrisons in fixed stations would have raised
the demand for it, and under Roman occupation there were doubtless
more horses in north Britain than at any previous time. Both Birrens
and Castle Cary, where oats have been found, were held by *cohortes
miliariae equitatae* in the second half of the second century. The
connection between the presence of cavalry and the spread of oat
cultivation must therefore have been a close one. In the lowland zone,
at Verulamium too, the oats found with other cereals belonged to
a stratum of the first quarter of the second century.[1]

[1] Roman cereals: Helbaek, *loc. cit.*, p. 229; find-list B; Godwin, *op. cit.*, pp. 262 sqq.
Oats: Verulamium, PPS XVIII, 1952/3, p. 229; SHAAS, 1953, p. 89; Park Street:
PPS XVIII, p. 229; Halstead, Ess., *ibid.*; Caistor-by-Norwich, information from the

Before the work of Helbaek it was possible to gain the impression that bread wheat was grown in Roman times over the greater part of southern and south-eastern Britain. The records of *Triticum vulgare* or of unclassified wheats extend from Langton in the East Riding to Ilchester in Somerset, and as far as the Welsh marches (Wroxeter, Leintwardine, Weston-under-Penyard). In the light of Helbaek's finding, we are forced to assume that many of these samples represented emmer, spelt, hulled, and more especially naked, barley. In the very south-east of the country (Kent), ancient sources confirm the ample raising of grain, and from Essex Caesar got in a few days enough corn to support four legions and 1,700 cavalry for a fortnight. During his first campaign Caesar in Kent was feeding his two legions daily by cutting corn in the immediate vicinity of his camp. It may be estimated that he would have needed 300–400 acres for a fortnight's supplies. It is nevertheless by no means clear what the grain was that Caesar collected or harvested. The grain ears on the coins of Tasciovanus, Epaticcus, and Cunobelinus have been identified by experts as wide-eared barley (*Hordeum distichum*). Indeed, if the areas of most intensive wheat production in the counties of Kent, Surrey, and Sussex, as mapped by Russell and Hall, are compared with the distribution of known permanent Roman sites (Fig. 13), the results are significant. The year 1911 fell within a period of depressed prices, therefore it may be assumed that, as wheat had been reduced to a minimum, the areas of high wheat cultivation represented in the 1911 map coincide with the soil best adapted to that crop. The result is to show that while the belt of wheat sowings, which covers the Thanet beds and extends from Dover north-west to Canterbury and along the coastal loams and alluviums to the Cray, coincides very closely with the route followed by Caesar, and so suggests that wheat was the crop he fed to his forces, it includes but is not identical with the area of permanent Roman occupation. If on the other hand known Roman villas and sites of permanent habitation are plotted on the areas of heaviest barley sowings for the same year, a much closer identity between the scope of one and the scope of the other may be observed. In the case of both crops, the common factor shared by them with the Roman distribution is the preference for the 'gradational' loams and

late R. R. Clarke; East Dean, Suss, *Agriculture* 64, 1957–8, pp. 35 sqq.; Little Chart, Kent, *A. Cant.* LXXI, 1957, p. 143; Lullingstone, *Agric., ibid.*, p. 38; Stonesfield, Northleigh, *Oxon.* XXIV, 1959, p. 13 sqq. Malton, Birrens, Castle Cary: Godwin, *op. cit.*, p. 265; Caerleon, information from G. C. Boon; York Hill; Queen's Park (Glasgow); Forth and Clyde Canal: Godwin, *op. cit.*, pp. 265–6; north-of-England villages: J. G. D. Clark, *Prehistoric England*, London, 1940, p. 34; Raistrick, YAJ XXXIV, pp. 143–4; corn-levy, cf. Tacitus, *Agric.*, 19, 4–6; 20; attitude to oats: Columella, II, 10, 32; Pliny, HN, XVIII, 149.

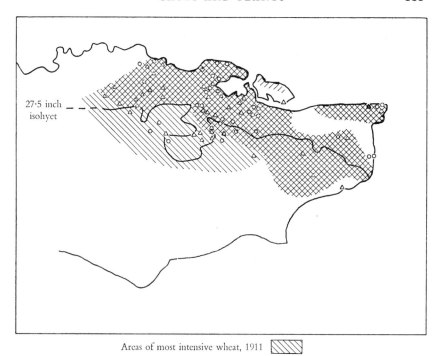

27·5 inch
isohyet

Areas of most intensive wheat, 1911
Areas of most intensive barley, 1911
Roman villas and occupied sites   △ ○

Fig. 13. Kent: areas of highest wheat and barley production in 1911,
according to Hall and Russell.

alluvial tracts of north Kent. But the coincidence of the Roman
distribution with the barley soils is striking, and suggests that barley
was then, as in the Early Iron Age, grown in excess of wheat.[1]

An examination of the distribution of the Hampshire Roman villas
shows that of some 45 recorded on the Ordnance Survey Map of
Roman Britain (second edition), 24 occur within the agricultural
region called by the Land Utilization Survey the Central Chalk Arable

[1] Grain in Kent: Strabo, IV, 5, 20; Caesar, *de Bello Gallico*, IV, 31. Wide-eared
barley: E. S. Beaven, J. M. Munro *ap*. Beaven, *Barley*, 1947, p. 12, and fig. 5 a–b;
the coins: J. Evans, *Coins of the Ancient Britons*, London, 1864, pl. viii, 12; ix,
3–14; xiii, 3–4. But for the explanation that the barley-ear is derived from the
wreath of Apollo on Greek coins: Rivet, RVB, p. 188, n. 4, citing D. F. Allen,
A XC, 1944, p. 25, n. The acceptance of this opinion, however, need not imply the
peculiar view that the Belgic artist did not know what he was representing. Wheat
and barley in 1911: A. D. Hall, E. J. Russell, *Agriculture and Soils of Kent, Surrey and
Sussex*, London, 1911, maps 44, 45.

Region.[1] This is traditionally a sheep and barley country. The areas of most intensive barley sowings in 1937 fall entirely within this region, and coincided on the one hand with the villa-group centred on Woodmancott, Preston Candover, Wivelrod, Brighton, and on the other hand with the Weyhill villa-group west of Andover. Further, if our suggestion is correct that brewing was carried out at the large villa of Woodchester (Glos) (see p. 165 and p. 167 n. 1), this implies that barley figured as an important crop in that part of the province. This supposition perhaps gains support from the evidence that beer was drunk at the large Belgic *oppidum* of Bagendon in the same region.[2]

The heaviest wheat cultivation of 1911 in Kent and Sussex was confined to Kent, with the exception of one area, the Sussex brick-earths extending from Havant west of Chichester along the coast to Shoreham and Brighton. This coastal belt possesses the largest percentage of the known Sussex villas; additionally the *territorium* of Chichester, apparently laid out native-wise in small irregular square fields, must have included much of the brickearths, and wheat production would have formed an important source of the city's income. Similarly, the two areas of most intensive wheat-growing in Surrey in 1937 coincide precisely with the Titsey villa on the east, and the group of Roman villas and villages to the east of Farnham on the west (Puttenham, Compton, Guildford, Tongham). In Essex there is a certain coincidence between areas of modern intensive wheat production and the country houses of the Ashdon, Bartlow, Hadstock group, also of the Ridgewell group. The Rodings region, known as the richest agricultural area in the county, with one of the highest wheat intensities in 1937, and with a very considerable barley production, is served by the Roman road from Chelmsford (Caesaromagus) to Dunmow. The point of most intensive wheat and barley culture here was Pleshey, where a Roman house is known to have existed. The Thaxted villa is also the centre of a modern area of high wheat cropping.[3]

In general it is evident from the finds that the main Romano-British wheat-grain in the lowland area was spelt, but it is conspicuously absent from the highland zone. *Triticum monococcum* (eincorn) vanishes in the Roman period, and emmer suffers a steep decline. But if wheat had begun to spread in the Early Iron Age, barley still maintained

[1] The third edition of the *Ordnance Map of Roman Britain*, Chessington, 1956, re-emphasizes the concentration of villas in the Central Chalk Arable Region (LUS, no. 89, Hants, Land use region no. 14, pp. 336, 357).

[2] Bagendon: E. M. Clifford, *Bagendon, a Belgic Oppidum*, Cambridge, 1961, p. 154.

[3] Wheat in Surrey, 1937: LUS, no. 81, Surrey, p. 371, fig. 9. Essex: LUS, no. 82, Essex, p. 426, fig. 13.

itself and may even have been grown in excess of it. Rye, improbably a cultivated crop in the Early Iron Age, is found in Roman Britain in both the highland and lowland zones, but not with great frequency, and its spread in the Roman Empire was a late phenomenon. Emmer was not a common grain in Roman Britain. It has been found, nevertheless, at Stonesfield and Northleigh villas (Oxon), and the possibility should be considered that it figured with barley among the commonly grown summer grains.[1]

In relation to the 'cleanness' of Roman cereal crops in this country, Reid found as many as twenty sorts of corn weeds among Silchester deposits. The increase of crop-weeds in the Roman period is demonstrated, indeed, by comparison of the Glastonbury and Silchester finds. Godwin found that pollen-analysis revealed a great increase of cultivation weeds between 350 B.C. and A.D. 150 in the Somerset peats, the last fifty years showing the highest agricultural intensity. He has listed fifty weeds which appeared in this country in post-glacial times and have been found in a Romano-British context. It may be supposed that this phenomenon faced the native cultivator, who went on cultivating his plot coterminously with the newly developed Roman holdings, with a problem that must have been quantitatively, at least, new to him.[2]

It is notable that the grain-find at Verulamium, made in a context of the period A.D. 125–50, lacked crop-weeds. The grains appeared to have been thoroughly threshed; they included wheat (chiefly spelt and club-wheat, and a little emmer), possibly also some rye and bread-wheat. Helbaek noted that the grains were unusually large and had evidently enjoyed good cultivation, and thought therefore that they were imported. The presence of spelt, on the other hand, is in favour of a local origin, since in ancient Europe this cereal was confined to southern Germany and Switzerland, occurring only on one Roman site so far. It is absent from early deposits in the Mediterranean area; on the other hand it occurs in Britain in the Early Iron Age, is alleged from Belgian villas, and appears in Diocletian's Edict of Prices. It will be noted with regard to the Verulamium find that while spelt and rye are winter crops, club-wheat and emmer belong to the summer-sown grains, suggesting a three-course rotation. If we assume that the grains came from the same field, their proportions would mean that

[1] Rye: Castle Cary, Forth and Clyde Canal: Helbaek, Jessen, *Cereals in Great Britain and Ireland in Prehistoric and Early Historic Times*, Copenhagen, 1944, p. 25; Stonesfield, Northleigh: *Oxon*. XXIV, 1959, p. 19; Verulamium: SHAAS, 1953, p. 91 – not quite certain according to Helbaek.

[2] Silchester crop-weeds: A LVII, 1900, p. 254; Somerset peats: *Philosophical Trans.*, 233B, 1948, pp. 276 sq.; fifty weeds: Godwin, *History of the British Flora*, p. 342.

the harvesting of club-wheat, emmer, and rye, had preceded that of
the spelt, but had this been so, it would imply a summer-winter
sequence, which would necessitate the immediate ploughing and
sowing of the summer field after harvest – a not very convincing
arrangement. It is more probable that the remnants of the spring-sown
harvest were already in the barn when the winter grains were brought
in after drying or maturing in the rick. In this case, a sequence of
winter crop, summer crop, fallow may be assumed. This is indeed
supported by the finds from Little Chart (Kent) consisting of undefined
wheat, containing also oats, barley, and chess (*Bromus secalinus*); and
by those from East Dean (Suss), which consisted of undefined wheat,
spelt, four-rowed barley (*Hordeum tetrastichum*), oats, and rye-brome.
A fairly equal division between summer and winter crops is also
suggested by the grains recorded from the Belgian villas, to wit,
wheat, spelt, rye, barley, millet, and oats.[1]

It may be noted that five farms yielding grain-finds (Park Street,
Rivenhall, Halstead, Stonesfield, Rockbourne Down) were growing
spelt as their main crop, and that four villas (Park Street, Halstead,
Northleigh, Stonesfield) are known also to have been growing summer
grains, among which oats figured.

If we examine the grain finds from Malton, in the East Riding of
Yorkshire, we find the following composition:

Various wheats	300	Clubwheat	11
Naked barley	14	*Avena sativa* (oats)	5
Emmer	12		

It is probable that the "various wheats" included a proportion of
spelt, and even if this was not the case, the small proportion of summer
crops is notable in an area today known for its high production of
oats. Clearly this find has little to do with the traditional north-of-
England Celtic pattern, in which cereal crops were largely confined
to the summer due to the restrictedness of valley soils available for
winter-grazing; hence the consignment concerned, which had been
delivered as military supply, had probably not come from the Pennines.
If the Malton finds were of local derivation, therefore, the adequacy

[1] Verulamium: SHAAS, 1953, pp. 89 sqq.; spelt in Europe: Helbaek, Jessen,
op. cit., p. 41; Belgian villas: De Maeyer, *op. cit.*, p. 42; in Diocletian's Edict of
Prices (Mommsen), cap. I, 7, 8. For the new view on the origin of spelt, see now
H. Jahnkuhn, *Vor- und Frühgeschichte vom Neolithikum bis zur Volkerswanderungszeit
(Deutsche Agrargeschichte)*, Stuttgart, 1969, pp. 217–18. Little Chart: *A. Cant.*, LXXI,
1957, p. 143; East Dean, Suss: *Agric.*, 64, 1957/8, pp. 35 sqq.; De Maeyer, *loc. cit.*;
Rockbourne Down: H. Sumner, *A Romano-British Enclosure on Rockbourne Down*,
London, 1914, p. 18.

of winter grazing on the Wolds enabled the ample sowing of winter cereals, even at the expense of summer crops.[1]

Professor Godwin is able to list sixteen plants of economic value, excluding cereals, which have been found in Roman deposits in this country. But his list does not include all the agricultural plants found in Britain in Roman times. We can abstract from Godwin's full inventory, as probable field-crops, broad beans, peas, vetch, turnip, flax, and corn-spurry. A small bean was known in Britain in the Early Iron Age, and the Roman cultivator knew the use of winter beans and tares as cleaning crops following corn or on fallow. In northern countries the tendency would have been to sow them on fallow land in the spring, and the technique of ploughing in the crop was also understood. The straw, however, might well have been used as winter fodder. In addition tares may be referred to: those from Hartlip villa were found with wheat, and may have been no more than a weed, but the sowing of legumes with corn was a Roman practice. Vetch found at the Forth and Clyde Canal accompanied oats – here the main crop – but there were also spelt and summer grains. At Betzingen, Germany, vetch was found in association with *Triticum sativum*, emmer, and barley, very suggestive of a winter-summer sequence in which vetch occupied part of the spring field or the fallow. At Colliton Park, Dorchester, seeds from deposits of the third or fourth century were wheat accompanied by the broad bean and vetch; this is suggestive of an alternation of 'green fallow' with corn. A find at Downton villa (Wilts) comprised spelt, *Trit. aestivum*, rivet, and barley, vetch composing fifteen per cent of the seed; this led the excavators to believe that it had been sown as a crop, perhaps with cereals, a Roman practice. Both at Wickbourne Estate and East Dean (Suss), vetch was found with summer cereals.[2]

Turnip and rape were used in Gaul as cleaning crops and cattlefeed. A single doubtful turnip seed is known from Silchester, but a well-established find occurred at Pevensey. The adoption of its cultivation from Gaul is a high probability, in view of its uses and the strong Gallic influence to be detected in the ground-plans of Romano-British farms. The main obstacle to the extensive cultivation of roots that faced the ancient farmer was shortage of manure (roots require at least twelve tons of farmyard manure per acre in northern countries).

[1] Malton: Helbaek, Jessen, *op. cit.*, p. 25; oats in East Riding: R. Ede, *Principles of Agriculture*, 1946, p. 32.
[2] Economic plants: Godwin, *History*, p. 343; beans and vetch: *ibid.*, p. 108; Dorchester: DNHAS LXXXIV, 1962, p. 101; Betzingen: *Korrespondenzblatt für Anthropologie*, 1908, pp. 33 sq. Vetch: Downton, WAM LVIII, 1963, p. 328; Wickbourne Estate, East Dean, Suss.: *Agric.*, 64, p. 39.

Columella knew this requirement quite well. Winter maintenance of stock, in the absence of mangolds and clover, was therefore difficult, and we do not know how far Gallic use of turnips and rape solved the problem. It is also difficult to say how far the autumn grazing of livestock on the stubbles (a practice suggested on a number of sites in Roman Britain by the use of the small harvesting sickle, which implies a high cut to leave the stalk) interfered with the sowing of roots; the required fencing would have been peculiar to private estates free of communal and open-field customs. But there is little doubt that some of the larger villas wintered a considerable number of cattle and sheep (e.g. Bignor, Hartlip – see p. 147), and a tentative calculation of the livestock of the Bignor villa suggested that the owner could accumulate sufficient farmyard manure to grow roots.[1]

A single flax capsule occurred at Silchester, and the plant was further identified at Pevensey and Meare West in Somerset. It was widely grown in Gaul, two of the peoples mentioned in this connection being the Caletes and the Morini of the Channel coast, whose strong British connections can hardly be doubted. Corn-spurry was found at Silchester, and has not been certainly identified in Britain before the Roman period; it is common as a corn weed, but was also cultivated in north-western Europe, and was a utility plant in Jutland in the Roman Iron Age.[2]

We know too little of the Romano-British kitchen garden. Godwin lists the radish among the known plants of economic value brought by Rome, but himself defines the find as that of wild radish. The parsnip and pea are known; cabbage appears at two sites. Mustard, recorded at Silchester, is regarded by Columella as a garden culture. It may also be permissible to cite Professor Estyn Evans's observation, that as onions, leeks, and cabbages were the only common Irish vegetables before the introduction of the potato, they were perhaps the result of Roman influence.[3]

To the vegetables may be added the potherbs, doubtless sometimes cultivated: coriander, horse-parsley, dill, and fennel. Poppies may have been grown for their seed, and are first recorded in the Roman period. If the commoner vegetables and herbs listed in the Carolingian

[1] *Turnips.* Gaul: Colum., II, 10; Silchester: Reading Museum; Pevensey: SAC LII, 1907–8, p. 94. *Manure.* Colum., II, 10; Pliny, HN, XVIII, 192; *Standard Cyclopedia of Agriculture,* ed. R. Wright, London, 1908–11, s.v. Farmyard Manure.

[2] *Flax.* Silchester: A LVII, p. 253; Pevensey: SAC LII, p. 94; Gaul: Pliny, HN, XIX, 7–8. *Corn-spurry.* Godwin, *op. cit.,* p. 95.

[3] *Radish.* Godwin, *op. cit.,* p. 86. *Pea. Ibid.,* p. 292; add Goathill, Sherborne, DNHAS LXXX, 1958, p. 97. *Parsnip.* A LIX, 1891, p. 368. *Cabbage.* Great Casterton: Corder, *The Roman Town and Villa at Great Casterton,* Nottingham, 1951, p. 19. *Onions, leeks, cabbages in Ireland.* E. Evans, *Irish Heritage,* p. 34.

Capitulare de Villis and the fifth-century Anthimus, as cited by Parain, are compared with known Romano-British finds, we may note that Britain had at least nine out of the eighteen vegetables or roots listed for Gaul, and of the latter, the province had most of the common market garden products. Of the potherbs, Britain had five of the ten listed for Gaul that can also grow over the Channel. It may be noted that among them horse-parsley, corn salad, and dill are natives of the Mediterranean. While the restrictedness of the evidence prohibits a final conclusion, the impression is that the British market garden and herbarium lacked little, if the truth were known, that the continent possessed, within the limits set by climate.[1]

Pliny states specifically that the cherry was first imported into Britain under Roman rule in the year 47, but a pre-Roman find is known, hence Pliny was probably referring to the introduction of an improved or domesticated variety; cherry-wood is said to have been found at Pevensey, but there is no evidence of the earlier occurrence of the cultivated cherry. In addition there are records from Roman strata of the sloe, bullace, and plum or damson (*Prunus domestica L.*), all found earlier in prehistoric contexts. At Silchester, Reid identified one specimen of plum stone as allied to the 'Orleans' which resembles the ancient 'black plum' grown in Cornwall. The bullace from the same town corresponded to a form still cultivated in Wales.[2]

The medlar was found at Silchester, and its name suggests that it was a Roman introduction. The apple and pear are both found on Roman sites, but had existed in wild form in pre-Roman times; it is not clear how far the Romans introduced cultivated varieties. The mulberry was among the Silchester seeds, and its existence here is hard to conceive prior to the Roman period. The raspberry occurs in both pre-Roman and Roman contexts; the blackberry, though not a cultivated plant, is so well represented among the finds of our period as to leave no doubt that it was used for food.[3]

It is possible that the Belgae were already engaged in acclimatizing

[1] *Coriander* (horse-parsley): Godwin, *op. cit.*, pp. 131, 343; *fennel*: p. 132; *dill* (Silchester): A LX, 1892, p. 164; *Capitulare de villis*, Parain, CEH I, 1942, pp. 154–5.

[2] *The cherry.* Pliny, HN, XV, 102; Pevensey: Godwin, *op. cit.*, p. 110. *Sloe, bullace, plum*: *ib.*, pp. 109–10. *The 'Orleans'*: A LIX, p. 368. Cherry stones or cherry wood are nevertheless recorded, rightly or wrongly, in Roman contexts at Holt (Haverfield, *Roman Britain in 1914*, British Academy, 1915, p. 16), Silchester (A LXI, 1893, p. 213); Westgate-on-Sea (VCH *Kent*, III, p. 174), and Langton (Corder, Kirk, *Roman Villa at Langton*, York, 1932, p. 55). A more recent find (cherry and plum): Chew Stoke, (Som), ANL V, 1954, p. 98.

[3] *Medlar.* Godwin, *op. cit.*, p. 119; *apple, pear*: *ib.*; *mulberry*: *ib.*, p. 292; *raspberry*: *ib.*, p. 111; *blackberry*: *ib.*, p. 112.

the vine in Britain, since the vineleaf is seen on coins of Verica, and they were already importing wine with some enthusiasm. Bede states that vines grew in Britain, and grapeseeds are known from Roman strata at Silchester, London (Tooley Street, Bermondsey), Gloucester, and Stoke Newington. Some of the Silchester finds came from a pit (XVII) with other cultivated plant remains, and a house in the immediate vicinity possessed at its north-east corner a two-roomed building of the type identifiable as housing stock and hands in rural villas. (See p. 123.) Close to this house was found a collection of iron tools, including plough-coulters, forks, and mowers' anvils. The dwelling itself stood close to the north gate of the town, with easy access to the land outside; hence there is little doubt that the grapeseeds from Pit XVII represented viticulture on the spot as part of general farming. At Gloucester the presence of ex-soldier colonists, some doubtless of Mediterranean extraction, and the foundation of the colony immediately after the demise of Domitian, who had attempted to restrict vine-growing in the provinces, may have encouraged experimentation. It should be added that the tithes of wine in medieval Gloucestershire were considerable. The presence of cellars at the villas of Hartlip (Kent), at Burham and Chalk in the same county, and at Park Street (Herts), may perhaps be interpreted as evidence of Roman vine-cultivation. Recently, too, a ditch-system has been recorded near North Thoresby (Lincs), and interpreted as a complex of trenches in which vines had been planted. The investigators, nevertheless, offered their conclusion with justifiable reservations, to which we may here add another, namely, that the said trenches did not occupy a southern-facing slope, which would be a *sine qua non* for vine-growing in a country where sunshine is so restricted. (See p. 103.) If this was a vineyard, it was, as the investigators justly observed, an unsuccessful experiment.[1]

[1] Verica's coins: Evans, *Ancient British Coins*, p. 173; pl. ii, 9; Belgic imported amphorae: Fox, PPSEA VII, p. 160 and map, pl. v, 6c; Hawkes, Hull, *Camulodunum*, p. 251, types 181–4. Bede, *Hist. Eccl.*, I, i, suggesting that vine-growing was transmitted to Saxon England from Roman Britain. Silchester: Godwin, *op. cit.*, p. 290; London: *ib.*, Bermondsey: *ib.*; Gloucester: *ib.*; Stoke Newington: C. Reid, *Origin of the British Flora*, London, 1899, p. 112. Domitian's decree against vine-planting in the provinces: Suet., *Domit.*, 7, 2; Silchester agriculture: Boon, *Roman Silchester*, pp. 178–9. North Thoresby: H. Webster, D. Petch, LHA 2, 1967, pp. 55 sqq. What seems to be the strongest point in the case for this being a vineyard may actually be the weakest; the cessation of pottery in A.D. 275–80 may have no significance, since Probus' alleged permission to plant vines in Britain, Gaul, and Spain (SHA, Vopiscus, *Vit. Probi*, 18) is a mere inflation of Aurelius Victor, *de Caes.*, 37, a point I owe to C. E. Stevens. For medieval vineyards in this country, H. H. Lamb, *The Changing Climate*, pp. 174, 190. Their location corresponds more or less with the area of Roman civilian settlement.

The Silchester grapeseeds were accompanied by fig-seeds, also found at Tooley Street and Finsbury Circus, London, with weeds of cultivation. The fig may therefore be regarded as a Roman introduction, and the tree is said to do reasonably well in the south of England in a sheltered southward-facing situation. Wiggonholt villa (Suss) has yielded an almond, presumably imported, but the walnut came with the Roman conquest, like the Spanish chestnut, found at Langton and Magor villas, and possibly the horse-chestnut, which is somewhat unreliably recorded for pre-Roman times, but has been identified in the Roman village of Needham (Norf) and at the villa of Great Witcombe (Glos). The holm oak too seems to have been a Roman introduction, but has been found in an Early Iron Age context at All Cannings Cross. There seems on the other hand to be no evidence that the plane tree and the lime tree were Roman innovations in Britain; plane has been tentatively identified in the Early Iron Age, and the lime tree (*tilia*) is widely recorded here in the prehistoric periods. The box, used in at least five cases in Roman Britain as a burial adjunct, is generally regarded as a native. The sycamore, noted by Godwin as absent from this country till the sixteenth century, is nevertheless said to have been identified at the Langton villa.[1]

In summarizing the evidence at our disposal on the crops and plants of Roman Britain, we must note the considerable implications of the wide diffusion of oats as a crop in its own right. Parain has pointed out that the increased use of the horse and the consequent need of oats may have contributed to the growth of a three-course agriculture. Horses would indeed seem to have been one of the factors encouraging oat production in the north of the country. Besides their fodder-value, oats are easier to cut than wheat or barley and climatically sturdier. Further, oat-straw absorbs 15–20 per cent more liquid than wheat-straw, and is accordingly superior both as cattle-bedding and as a basis for farmyard manure.[2] As the greatest deficiency in the value of manure occurs owing to the loss of the urine, the increased productivity to be obtained from the growing of oats was considerable. Further, intensification and growing markets would have encouraged the partial suppression of fallow, and pressure of taxation would have favoured equal autumn and spring cropping to diminish risks of failure. A reduction of pasture by the growth of livestock breeding

---

[1] *Figs.* Godwin, *op. cit.*, p. 292; *almond.* Wiggonholt: SAC LXXXI, 1940, p. 65. *Holm oak*: All Cannings Cross: Cunnington, *All Cannings Cross*, Devizes, 1923, p. 52. *Plane tree*: Godwin, *op. cit.*, p. 292. *Lime tree*: *ib.*, p. 97. *Box*: *ib.*, p. 181. *Sycamore*: *ib.*, p. 106; Langton: Corder, Kirk, *op. cit.*, pp. 17, 55.

[2] Parain, CEH I, p. 130. *Barley straw*: C. H. Eckles, *Dairy Cattle and Milk Production*[3], 1948, p. 487.

would have worked in the same direction, since under a three-course system two-thirds of the arable can be grazed from harvest to spring, as against half under a simple crop-fallow pattern. The climatic factor may also have favoured changes: oats do best in an increasingly moist climate, such as had begun in Britain in the middle of the last millennium B.C. and was being decidedly felt in the second century of the current era. Barley, which requires dryer conditions than wheat, may well have ceased to be more popular than oats. Our examination of the cereals from such sites as Verulamium, East Dean, Little Chart, and Park Street has shown a fairly equal division between winter and summer grains, and that four villas which revealed this division were growing oats. This evidence for a three-course agriculture agrees with what is recorded in the north of France in Carolingian times on estates which inherited their technique from Roman practice.

Apart from transforming the internal relations and balance of crops in the cereal branch, Roman influence introduced the cultivated cherry, the medlar, the mulberry, and the fig. If the vine was not a Roman innovation dating from the conquest, it was certainly Roman rule that propagated its expansion. The turnip, cabbage, pea, parsnip, mustard, and several potherbs also first appear under Rome. Among other trees owed to Roman initiative we can list the walnut, the Spanish chestnut, the horse-chestnut, the holm oak, and perhaps the sycamore. What one farm in Britain owed to such imports we may judge from the finds at Langton (Yorks), which present the picture of a windbreak composed of oak, ash, elder, willow, alder, walnut, sweet chestnut, sycamore, and cherry. Of these ten trees, three if not four were Roman introductions.

Finally, we may refer to the Roman plant-finds from Pevensey, which are sufficiently striking in combination to suggest a specifically romanized agriculture in that neighbourhood. The specimens identified were unclassified wheat, barley, turnip, *vicia* (perhaps pea), flax, the cultivated cherry (*Prunus cerasus*), the Spanish chestnut, and the holm oak. We may add the violet, which philology suggests was a Roman introduction. The presence of wheat and barley would imply a winter-summer crop sequence, and flax, a spring crop, does well when sown with legumes (cf. the find of *vicia*). These might have been used to feed to stock, and Pevensey yielded remains, not only of *Bos longifrons*, the common indigenous shorthorn cow, but also of a larger breed of cattle (see p. 96), which is at least in harmony with the evidence for the growing of turnips and with the manure requirements of that crop. It remains to add that the cultivated cherry, like the Spanish chestnut, the holm oak, the turnip, and the violet, were

Roman introductions. Further extraneous contacts are suggested by the rope of tamarisk bark found in the same well which yielded the above plant-remains. All this suggests an intensive mixed farming in southern Sussex, in which rich loamy soils played their part, and which owed much to specific continental techniques.[1]

[1] Pevensey: SAC LI, 1906, p. 114; LII, 1907, p. 94.

CHAPTER VIII

HOUSES

THE AIM of the study of Romano-British rural dwellings of the 'villa' type within the present section is to detect extraneous and indigenous derivations and to throw light on function.

It has long been held that the three main forms found among Romano-British farmhouses (the basilical, the corridor and courtyard villas) are north-west European – possibly Celtic, rather than Roman-Mediterranean. In point of fact the types are two: the basilical or barn house, described above; and the corridor house. The latter is a row of rooms fronted by a corridor and frequently flanked or backed by additional rooms; the development of its wings gave rise to the 'courtyard' house. It may be stated in advance that whereas there is evidence abroad that some of these residences included, in their initial stages and sometimes later, rooms or wings devoted to agricultural purposes, most recognizable corridor villas in this country appear to be predominantly residential, agricultural functions being relegated to nearby outbuildings. If evidence of evolution of the corridor house from pre-Roman types can be found, we may be in a better position to ascertain whether it was indigenous or imported, and this would aid our estimate of the continuity of agricultural technique from pre-Roman times. It may also illuminate certain aspects of function and social structure. The function and significance of the basilical farmhouse will be studied below; let us first examine the antecedents and development of the 'corridor' dwelling.

As a point of departure we may take two plans found in Britain, viz. those of Iwerne A and B (Dors). It has been noticed that these two houses, consisting of a single long apartment with a small room or rooms at one end, may represent a long-standing indigenous form, whose derivatives are found surviving in Irish, Welsh, and Scottish farmhouses to the present day. The plan is found in the Jutland houses of the pre-Roman and Roman Iron Ages excavated by Hatt and others; these usually consisted of an oblong hut on the west and, attached to its east end, a covered extension with mud floor where the livestock was kept. The long west room of Iwerne A, indeed, had housed animals, and in Iwerne B there were indications that the long eastern room of the cottage had been used for a similar purpose; here Houses A and B date from the third and fourth centuries respectively, but they stand on a site continuously occupied from the Belgic period.

Parallels to this sort of native dwelling are to be seen in Gaul; it appears at Mont Beuvray (Fig. 14) and also in the Vosges at Wasserwald-sur-Saverne (Fig. 15), associated with half-romanized enclosed upland steadings.[1]

The two-room design had a long history, and is found in various

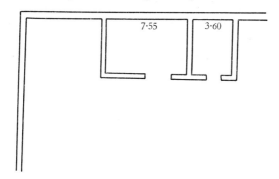

Fig. 14. Gallo-Roman house at Mont Beuvray, France.

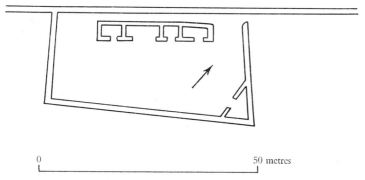

0   50 metres

Fig. 15. Wasserwald-sur-Saverne, France: native farm of Roman date.

associations throughout the Roman period. At Arches (Maillen, Belgium) it is seen constituting the main hall of a small farm with an *Eckrisalit* or small square projecting wing-room, attached to the south-east angle of the front, and a bath-house abutting on the south-

[1] Iwerne: *Arch. J.* CIV, 1947, p. 55; Wales: I. Peate, *The Welsh House*,[2] Liverpool, 1944, ch. iv, pp. 51–84; Scandinavia: *Ant.* XI, 1937, pp. 162 sqq.; G. Hatt, *Société royale des antiquaires du nord*, 1928, p. 189 (Soljberg). Mont Beuvray: Grenier, *Manuel d'archéologie préhistorique, celtique et gallo-romaine* VI, ii, 1934, p. 750. The Vosges: R. Forrer, *L'Alsace romaine*, Paris, 1935, fig. 43. Comparable with Iwerne may be the dwelling at Cwmbrwyn, a half-romanized farm in Carmarthenshire (AC 1907, pp. 175 sqq.). Though fortified, it is not regarded as a fort by the editor of Nash-Williams, *The Roman Frontier in Wales*, 2nd edn. M. G. Jarrett, Cardiff, 1969.

west angle (Fig. 16). Precisely such a hall was found to have been the
original nucleus of the Mayen farm (near Coblenz), in the early
Roman period, having replaced a timber and pisé dwelling of roughly
similar orientation dating from pre-Roman days. The Roman hall
was two-roomed, with one aisle divided off by posts along its north
side.[1] The two-roomed cottage is seen in enlarged form as the largest
economic (as opposed to purely residential) building at Al Sauvenière
(Maillen, Belgium) (Fig. 17), where it was the quarters of the farmhands, and probably at Ronchinnes (Belgium); at Betsveld-Landen

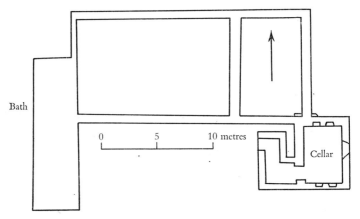

Fig. 16. Arches te Maillen, Belgium.

(Belgium), it is a detached outbuilding. At Le Roux le Fosse (Belgium),
it plays the part of a granary with a smaller room at the end. A building
of the two-room plan at Wankenheim, near the Roman villa of Flur
Krautland, Württemburg, stood in the centre of a quadrangular
cattle-enclosure. A structure of this type also served as a workshop
in the yard of the Roman farm at Garsdorf near Erfurt. In Britain, at
Hartlip (Kent), there is a large two-room building which, on the
assumption that Building K was the granary, is likely to have housed
farmhands; the same applies to Building XXIX–XXX at Woolaston
Pill (Glos). At Stroud near Petersfield (Hants) we may perhaps
discern the same plan in the eastern outbuilding, the longer room

---

[1] Other examples of farmhouses with halls thus divided may be noted in Germany
at Stahl (*Germania* v, 1921, p. 65); Neckeremms (*ib.*); Stockbronnerhof (A.D. 90–160;
E. Wagner, *Fundstätte und Funde in Baden*, II, 1911, p. 397, fig. 311; BRGK VI,
1910/12, p. 58); Bollendorf (*Trierer Jahresberichte*, 1918–19, pp. 1 sqq.). While
rejecting the relation of such buildings with the basilical type, J. T. Smith finds it
advisable to be cautious in rejecting the affiliations of West Dean north-east (*loc. cit.*,
p. 9) with its single row of internal posts.

being here used for livestock, the shorter beoming a tower-granary
(Fig. 36; 26, 25). At Northleigh (Oxon), the form is found as a large
building of Period I (rooms 4 and 10, late second century?) attached
directly to the west end of the dwelling house. Two-roomed outbuildings appear attached to two dwellings near the north gate of
Silchester; agricultural tools and plant remains found in their vicinity
showed that their owners farmed land outside the town walls.[1] Two
similar outhouses enclosed the north side of the yard of the Great
Weldon villa (N'hants), but the smaller room of one was a later

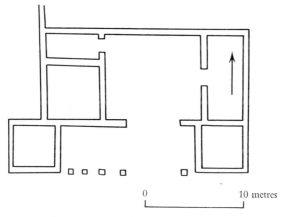

0   10 metres

Fig. 17. Al Sauvenière, Belgium: Roman villa-residence.

addition. In the other building grain was found. The original second-
century dwelling at Cox Green, Maidenhead (Berks), was likewise
a two-roomed structure, later subdivided and added to. In other
words, this plan, originally a simple combination of stall and dwelling
house, evolved under the Empire, and grew enormously in given
cases, but its more usual function became that of housing hands, stock,

[1] Insula XXIII, house 1; XXIV, house 2, rooms 36–7 – A LVII, 1889, p. 247;
G. Boon, *Roman Silchester*, pp. 178–82. Other examples of the plan serving as
outbuildings of villas: Olfermont, Haute Rhin (Section II, n. 11); Thuit, Eure-et-
Loire (de Caumont, *Abécédaire*, p. 389); Oberentfelden, Switzerland (F. Staelin,
Die Schweiz in römische Zeit,[3] Basel, 1948, p. 396, Abb. 84); Merklingen (Paret *et al.*,
Die Römer in Württemburg, III, Stuttgart, 1928–32, p. 117, Abb. 74): Kirchheim am
Neckar (*ib.*, p. 118, Abb. 76); Wössingen: (A.D. 90–160; Wagner, *op. cit.*, II, p. 114).
Cf. the two-roomed farmhouse at Besigheim (*ib.*, p. 283, Abb. 125). More recently
excavated two-roomed structures of Roman date in this country include Hemel
Hempstead (outbuilding – JRS LVI, 1966, p. 209); Dicket Mead near Welwyn
(JRS LVIII, 1968, p. 194 – third century); Rapsley Farm, Ewhurst, Building 3 –
c. A.D. 120–200 (SyAC LXV, 1968, pp. 8 sqq.); Studland, Dors (H): (DNHAS LXXXVII,
1966, p. 25); Overton Down, Site OD XII, Building 2, (fourth century, WAM 62,
1967, pp. 27–9).

and perhaps crops. We may here recall the outbuilding of Houdeng-Goegnis (Belgium), a 'hall' building with attached projecting wing-rooms, a third of whose hall was used as a granary.[1] The two-room building, indeed, seems to have evolved from combined residential and agricultural to purely domestic and agricultural uses; but in a few cases cited above, it remained a dwelling house to which various modifications were made.

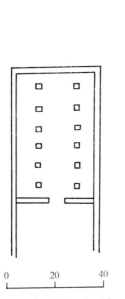

0　　　　20　　　　40

0　　　　　　　　　5 metres

Fig. 18. Spoonley Wood, Gloucester-shire: outbuilding.

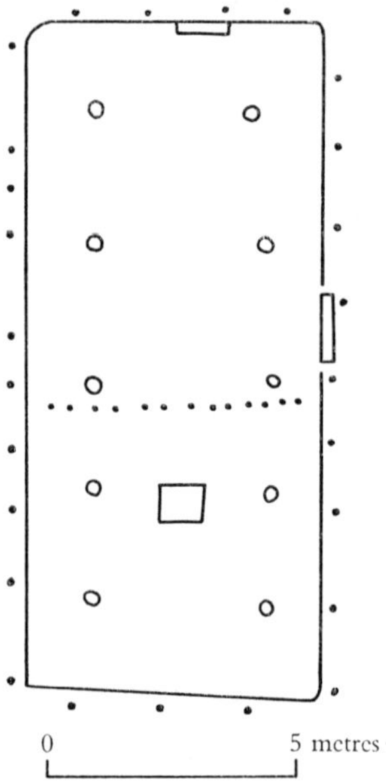

Fig. 19. Ezinge Warf, Groningen, Holland: Stratum VI, House "G" of the early La Tène period.

Now one or two instances occur where features derived both from the two-roomed cottage and the basilical house appear together; thus in the basilical building at Ickleton (Cambs), the west end is cut off from the hall as a distinct room across the width of the building. At Spoonley Wood (Glos), the basilical outbuilding to north-west of the residence was similarly subdivided across the north end (Fig. 18).

[1] It may have been in such buildings that threshing was carried out in the winter. Fremersdorf (BJ 135, 1930, p. 115) thought he had found traces of this activity in the hall of the Köln-Braunsfeld farmhouse. A large number of the smaller buildings in the great yard attached to the villa of Chiragan in south-west Gaul (L. Joulin, *Les établissements gallo-romains de Martres-Tolosanes: memoires...de l'académie des inscriptions et belles lettres*, XI, 1901) were of the two-roomed type; three were thought to have accommodated livestock, but many were considered to have housed craftsmen practising their trades.

The same applied to the north-western aisled stock-building at West
Dean (Wilts), subdivided at its east end. At Maulévrier near Caudebec,
Normandy, we have a house whose front two-thirds constitute a hall
with nave and aisles divided by posts; the rear third is a room across
the full width of the house. It was clear that Iwerne A, with its division
into two parts, was nevertheless influenced by the aisled plan, since
the eastern section consisted of three rooms, reminiscent of the nave
and aisles. All this suggests that the two-roomed and basilical plans
have a common origin, or that one may on occasion have evolved
from the other. This indeed would seem to have been the case, since
we find, for instance, at the Ezinge Warf near Groningen, Holland, in
the earliest La Tène stratum, an aisled house one end of which had
been divided off by an internal transverse partition – whether or not
it was built subsequently is unknown (Fig. 19). Peate ascribes the
two-room dwelling to western Europe and Scandinavia,[1] but it is
difficult to agree that there is no connection between it and the
'basilical' plan; if their origins were distinct, there was certainly
interaction between them, and Lady Fox regards the early Roman
two-roomed house with posts at Exeter as "a member of the same
family" as the basilican plan.[2]

As already hinted, a number of the Roman farm-dwellings in
Germany consist of a large hall, sometimes subsequently subdivided,
to which wing-rooms were often added at the flanks of the frontage.
These 'hall' villas show traces of both two-room and basilical
influences. At the villa of Stockbronner Hof (A.D. 74–90) the main
hall was not only subdivided so that it had a short room at the south
end, but a row of posts ran along the west (long) and returned along
the north (short) side – suggesting an aisle-like internal subdivision
(Fig. 20). At Mayen also a row of posts occurred along the north
(long) and east (short) interior sides of the hall. Other cases of this
are to be seen at Ruit (Fig. 21) and Stammhamm, both in Württemburg.
A single row of posts is a feature in the 'Hall-*Eckrisalit*' house at
Schlossellackern near Mundelsheim, Neckar.[3]

Thus in Germany, at least, the two-roomed house might develop
into the 'hall' of a farmhouse with the addition at the corners of
wing-rooms joined by a verandah, with subsequent internal subdivisions and the accretion on its flanks and rear of baths and other
rooms. In various instances the hall seems to be structurally influenced

[1] Peate, *op. cit.*, p. 54.
[2] A. Fox, *Roman Exeter*, Manchester, 1952, pp. 10–14. For Groningen etc.,
E. Van Giffen, *Germania* XXXVI, 1958, pp. 45 sqq.; *Prähistorische Hausforme auf
Sandböden in den Niederlanden.*
[3] For the affinities of the Mayen hall, cf. p. 124.

by the basilical form. In other cases, seen in Germany, Belgium, Switzerland, France, and Britain, the two-roomed building became an outbuilding with economic functions.

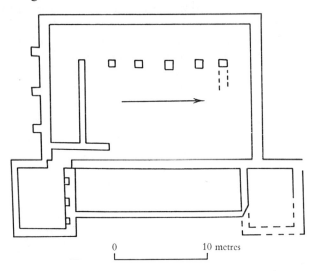

Fig. 20. Stockbronner Hof, Baden: Roman villa-residence.

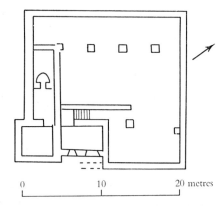

Fig. 21. Ruit, Württemburg: Roman villa-residence.

We must now examine how far these developments apply to Britain. It must be said at once that we still know too little of early Romano-British house-plans to draw final conclusions on their origin. The first house at Folkestone, which Winbolt believed to have preceded the Roman conquest, was a simple strip-building divided into several rooms. What was the plan of the early Roman hut preceding the

Roman villa at Park Street (Herts) is not clear. The supposed Belgic farmhouse at Casterley (Wilts) was surrounded by a rectangular ditch, but its plan is otherwise unknown. Radford regarded the timber building preceding the Ditchley villa as having had a "hipped" roof, implying a central row of posts, but not all its plan was recoverable. The early Roman houses at Park Street (Period VI) and Lockleys near Welwyn (Herts) were both simple strip-plans subdivided internally; to the latter a wing-room, verandah, and other rooms appeared in the third century. The earlier Knowl Hill house, already mentioned (p. 17), was a simple rectangle; we cannot be certain that the posts did not strengthen the walls rather than constitute internal aisles. The first structure at Norton Disney (Notts) appears to have been a small

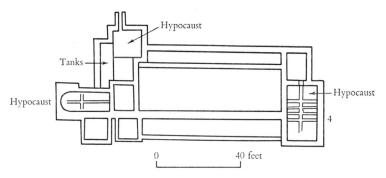

Fig. 22. Titsey, Surrey: Roman villa.

square timber hut. It is possible that the simple undivided plans at Ditchley and Knowl Hill should be regarded as the equivalent of the German-Belgian 'hall', but the evidence is inadequate. None of the examples cited appears to have developed from a two-roomed cottage. At both Catsgore (Som) and Mansfield Woodhouse (Notts) the dwellings prior to the erection of the first romanized buildings were circular huts.

There do occur in Britain, nevertheless, certain examples of plans closely analogous to the Rhenish and Belgian 'hall' farmhouses. Such is Titsey (Surr), where the main hall remains undivided, and the south-eastern wing-room appears in unmodified form; here baths were added on the north-west side much in the manner of German examples (Fig. 22). Finds showed occupation from the second century. House I at Camerton (Som) had a large central hall as its nucleus with corridor and exedral room to north, and rudimentary wing-projections. Coins found belonged to the period A.D. 270–350. The hall here had traces of a lesser partitioned subdivision at its east end.

5

The small farmhouse at Colerne (Wilts), a tripartite house with wing-rooms embodied in the corridor, had a central range composed of a large flagged hall, and a smaller room to east (Fig. 23). At Engleton (Staffs) a corridor house built at the end of the second century and modified in the fourth, the central and largest room had no mosaic, but remains of an oven, suggesting that it perpetuated the place, and in part the function, of the continental 'hall'. At Gayton Thorpe (Norf)

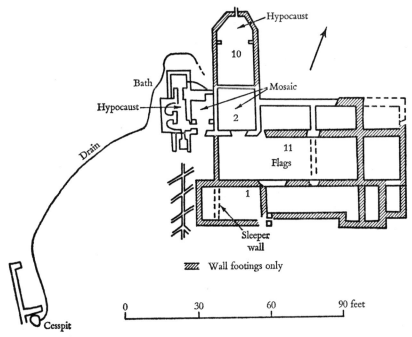

Fig. 23. Colerne, Wiltshire: Roman villa.

(second-third century A.D.), the hall had shrunk to be the central living room in a range of six between corridors, having lost any economic function, and this is so in the majority of known Romano-British farmhouses of this type. But the later outbuilding to south was divided into two rooms, a larger and a smaller, the former reminiscent of the old 'hall' and doubtless housing the farmhands and some of their work (Fig. 24). Such a hall, without doubt the farmhands' quarters, is seen in the east wing of Spoonley Wood villa (Glos), flanked by smaller rooms. Notable too is a farmhouse at Great Staughton (Hunts), apparently of fourth-century date; it was a corridor block with large flanking wing-rooms, but the main nucleus behind the corridor consisted of a long central kitchen with hearth, and smaller rooms to east and west. It may be noted that in the tripartite corridor residence at Penn Mead, High Wycombe (Bucks), built in the later second century (A.D. 150/70), the main central space between the corridors was occupied by a large room with mosaic pavement; the large central room-flanked court behind the corridor of the Kingsweston Park villa (Glos) (third century) might also be regarded as a de-functionalized reminiscence of the central *Wirtschaftshalle*.

We may therefore conclude that the two-roomed cottage and the basilical dwelling had a pre-Roman origin in the north-west of

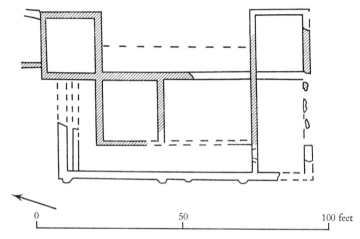

Fig. 24. Gayton Thorpe, Norfolk: south building.

Europe, but we have no certain pre-Roman antecedents of either in Britain as yet. Whether or not they have a common prototype, the two-roomed hut is found in Scandinavia and Jutland in the Early Iron Age and seems to be 'crossed' with the aisled type at Groningen and at various other sites of the La Tène and Roman periods in Friesland. In Flanders and Germany it was common for the two-room cottage to become the 'hall' of the Roman farmhouse, with the addition of wing-rooms, verandah, and other rooms; this happened in the Roman period, and continued almost throughout it. It must however be stressed that while the two-roomed hut is impeccably pre-Roman, it has not been found as a pre-Roman antecedent of the romanized two-roomed 'hall' on one and the same site. In Britain, at a comparatively early date, houses were being built in which wing-rooms were an integral part of a corridor plan (Ditchley, Hartlip – both late first or early second century), and the hall had shrunk and been merged into a continuous range; in short, the *Eckrisalit* house arrived in Britain in a developed state, and was still being adopted in the third and fourth centuries. But there are a few known cases in this country – and their number is growing – of the 'hall' farmhouse of the Belgian-Rhenish type, and at Spoonley Wood and Gayton Thorpe such a plan appears in association with the quarters of the farmhands. Where the two-roomed cottage survives, it is chiefly as an outbuilding for farmhands and other agricultural purposes, but occasionally as an independent farmhouse (Iwerne).

In short, the British corridor house seems to be an importation from across the Channel, and at the moment the weight of evidence suggests that it came more particularly from Belgium, to a lesser extent from Germany. It should further be noted that in Britain the dwelling-house of the farm in most cases became early purely residential, and the agricultural functions were relegated to outbuildings. The basilical house, on the other hand, does not always follow this rule; nor apparently do those examples of farm-dwellings in which the 'hall' figures in its pristine form. But in the farms characterized by the corridor dwelling, a sharp separation took place between the owner's quarters on the one hand, and the staff and farm activities on the other, in contrast to the numerous prosperous farmsteads of the Rhineland and Germany, where the hall frequently remained the centre of economic activity. The British situation spells a less patriarchal and more divided society such as might appear initially if new immigrants were exploiting a native population. It also implies that in a number of cases Roman villas in Britain were founded by immigrants from Gaul, or built by architects influenced by Gallic traditions.[1]

Although the basilical or aisled barn farmhouse probably formed, as indicated, one of the elements from which the corridor villa developed, this type of building, when it appears in Britain, nevertheless represents a distinct current, whether local or continental is still difficult to decide. The problem of its origin has been outlined above. Here we may re-emphasize that no example in Britain has yet been reliably dated before the early second century A.D. It may however be added that an example is known associated with 'native' fields at Eastfield (Hants), where an inscription on one of the house's mosaic pavements suggested that some of the occupants bore a Celtic name or names. Further must be considered the case already mentioned, in which a basilical house was observed from the air to lie within the small hillfort of Tidbury Rings (Hants). Finds had already been noted here,

[1] Very striking is the resemblance between the plan of the fourth-century phase of Ditchley and the Belgian corridor house at Houdeng-Goegnis, whose date appears to be unknown (de Maeyer, RV *Bel.*, p. 83, fig. 19a). For the evidence of migration of capitalists and others from abroad, see above p. 126. Cf. Rivet, RVB, pp. 208–9.

and in 1927 digging produced signs of a Romano-British building and two coins of Constantine I. In 1929 the main building was detected from the air. This is a basilical building 140 × 35 feet, lying north-south, with square rooms inside the south angles. To the west lies a small oblong outbuilding (discovered in 1927), orientated east-west, containing what may be a grain-drying furnace at the west end.[1]

The main point to be noted is that this aisled building is a nearly self-contained establishment (apart from the outbuilding, whose existence may have been due to the necessity of obviating fire-risks in the main dwelling), and that there are no other subordinate installations near it; the main house must therefore have contained within it, apart from the quarters for owner or bailiff and hands, storage space for fodder and crops, accommodation for livestock, and probably the threshing floor. The basilical house at Lippen Wood, West Meon (Hants), also seems to have been, and remained, an entirely self-contained building. How far Tidbury is a parallel to Casterley (p. 36), perpetuating the relation of a Celtic landlord to the peasantry around him, cannot be stated till the site is excavated. It is, however, relevant to mention the presence of a bath-building, apparently attached to a villa, within the hill-fort of Borough Walls near Daventry, and the alleged remains of aisled halls of Dark Age date found within hill-forts at Dinorben, Denbighshire, and Castle Dore, Cornwall.[2]

The basilical house, however, was not always an independent farm-dwelling. In a number of cases, having begun as such, it is internally adapted as a residence, the agricultural functions being relegated to outbuildings (Clanville and Stroud, Hants). There are also various instances where it was a subsidiary building to a more highly romanized residence, presumably having been built to house hands, livestock, and crops (e.g. North Wraxhall (Wilts), Brading (IOW), and Mansfield Woodhouse (Notts)).

The three forms of the basilical house therefore are:

1. The independent self-contained farm-residence.

---

[1] No exception to the statement concerning the earliest date of known basilical buildings is furnished by the structure at Wingham, Kent (JRS LVIII, 1968, p. 206), built, apparently, in the late first century A.D. The internal peristyle was inserted later, and would not in any case qualify the house to be classed as an aisled farmhouse of the type under discussion. I am indebted to Mr F. Jenkins, the excavator, for details. As regards the Knowl Hill building, Berks (BkAJ xxxvi, p. 28; xxxviii, p. 75), it was not established if the two parallel lines of posts preceded or were contemporary with the second-century building; they did not necessarily belong to an aisled dwelling. Tidbury Rings: the air-photograph was kindly shown to me by Mr F. C. Cottrel.

[2] Other self-contained aisled buildings are North Warnborough, Hants (see below), Denton, Lincs, and West Blatchington, Suss.

2. The same, wholly or partly re-adapted for residence, with agricultural functions decentralized to other buildings.

3. The purely economic building (for hands, livestock, and crops) subsidiary to the residence.

In the twelfth-century "Dream of Rhonabwy" we have a picture of the livestock housed in the body of the house, the floor littered with branches, and the occupants sleeping in cells each side.[1] In the Ancient Laws of Wales a similar dwelling is described with aisles divided into compartments for families, the upper part being occupied by the chief and his immediate retainers.[2] In the earliest dated example so far known in Britain – at Exning (Suff), we see that in the second phase (later second century) the upper end, where the chief would have dwelt according to the Welsh account, was rebuilt as a three-room suite; two of these rooms were floored with mosaics and the third was heated. The houses at Ezinge Warf and their Frisian descendants show plainly that the plan originated among a stock-rearing people and that its aisles were used for the stalling of cattle, though it does not follow that this continued to be so everywhere unmodified. If we wish to see a self-contained farmhouse of this plan combining beneath its roof all the functions of residence and agriculture, we shall find it in some of the old German and Frisian farmsteads illustrated, for instance, by Henning.[3] He figures and describes examples in Hanover, Westphalia, and Holstein, which differ very little in principle, and even in detail, from some excavated 'barn' houses of the Romano-British period. All these have in common the accommodation of both cattle and horses in compartments flanking the large central hall, which serves as a threshing floor; and the placing of the quarters of the hands (men and women separately) in a similar position. In three out of the cases illustrated, the hearth occupied one end of the hall; in a fourth, it was at one side. In two cases the quarters of the owning family occupied the end behind the hearth; in two others they were on one side towards the hearth end. In one or other of these west-German houses additional rooms occupying the sides of the hall were the dairy, pantry, tool-store, wood-store, and in one case, kitchen and bakery. In Hanover the pigsty and goose-pen were within the building, each side of the main door. In all cases, it seems, the wall-height to the eaves did not exceed 10–12 feet, having ample space for the storage of hay and grain in a loft beneath the roof. Unfortunately Henning seldom gives scales and dimensions, but those of the West-phalian house – 80 by 40 feet – compare fairly closely with some

[1] Guest, *The Mabinogion*, II, 393–5.
[2] Vened., III, 21; *Ancient Laws and Institutes of Wales*, I, p. 293.
[3] R. Henning, *Das Deutsche Haus*, Strassburg, 1882.

examples of British basilical houses (Eastfield, 85 × 50 feet; Clanville, 96 × 52 feet).[1]

A satisfactorily excavated basilical house of the self-contained type is that at North Warnborough (Fig. 25). Here absence of post-holes raises a major problem of how the hall (55 feet broad) was roofed, but of the resemblance of the general plan to the basilical, there is no doubt. The width of the room-ranges corresponding to the aisles was 12 feet both on the north and the south; this exceeds most known parallels in this country, but aisles at West Meon and

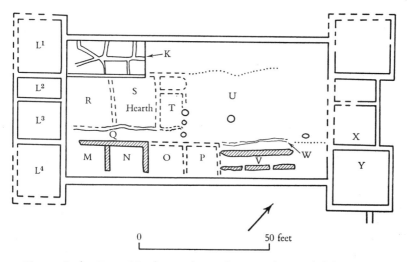

Fig. 25. Lodge Farm, North Warnborough, Hampshire: aisled farmhouse.

Tockington Park (south building) were 11 feet wide; 12 feet at Whittlebury (N'hants). The south aisle was formed by lath and plaster partitions and subdivided into rooms; on the north, sub-divisions were confined to the north-west angle, consisting of one walled chamber, equipped with a channelled hypocaust; but the chalk floor of the central floor or nave stopped on the north in line with this room. The west end of the central space was divided into dwelling rooms by lath and plaster partitions, and across the west end of the building a distinct wing lay T-wise, containing five rooms with stamped earth and cobble floors, thought by the excavator to have been byres or stables. These had no direct communication with the interior of the house. The corresponding wing at the other end of the hall consisted of four rooms, those of the corners being larger and

[1] Hanover: Henning, *op. cit.*, p. 31, fig. 15; Westphalia; *ibid.*, p. 33, fig. 16.

projecting in the manner of *Eckrisaliten*; traces of mosaics in this wing showed that they had been the owner's quarters.

The excavator noted that finds connected with the presence of women (combs, shuttles, spindlewhorls, etc.) were limited to rooms O, P, S, T, K, whereas objects characteristic of the other sex (spearheads, keys, padlocks, knives, etc.) came from rooms L, Q, T, U, V, W. This means that the women lived in the 'aisles' at the west end of the house, and used one of the main rooms at the west end of the hall, i.e. S – which contained a hearth; T, immediately east of this, was common to both sexes. The men were associated with the stalls and byres at the west end of the farmhouse, with the passage between the west-central rooms and the south 'aisle', with the more easterly part of the south 'aisle', and with the main hall, where, one may suppose, threshing was carried out.

The west wing was 15 feet across from east to west, in which it resembles the width of the cowhouse at Iwerne B and the depth of stock accommodation at Titsey. In the extreme north and south rooms together (each 20 × 15 feet) there is room to house four pairs of oxen.[1]

The walls of the farmhouse were 2 feet thick, and Miss Liddell calculated them to have been 10 feet high, but it is doubtful whether they could have supported a loft beneath the roof at eaves-level, and produce must have been stored either in one of the end rooms in the west wing or in the main central area of the hall. In room V were two wall foundations parallel with the axis of the building, which Miss Liddell interpreted as a corridor; what was the function of a corridor here is hard to see, and it is more probable that these were dwarf-walls carrying a raised storage floor for grain.[2]

When we come to consider those basilical houses which were wholly or partly converted to more romanized residences, it becomes possible to show that they had in their original unconverted form fulfilled similar functions to the self-contained peasant-dwelling.

To demonstrate this, we may first mention the earlier house at Iwerne (A – third century), which, though without aisles, showed by the tripartite division of its east end a clear affinity to the basilical

[1] Columella (*de re rust.*, I, 6) prescribes between 8 feet 7 inches and 9 feet 8 inches stall-width per pair; Vitruvius (VI, 6) between 9 feet 8 inches and 14 feet 6 inches: 10 feet is therefore average accommodation. This leaves the third room from the north, which may have been a stable (12 by 15 feet), since loose boxes at Carzield were 12 by 10 feet; at Benwell 12 by 30 feet (AA[4] XIX, pp. 27–8; 31–3).

[2] Its area, 28 by 12 feet, multiplied by a height of 10 feet, gives a capacity of 2,584 bushels. Taking 100 *iugera* or 62 acres as the area workable by one ox-team (with fallow), four teams would have ploughed 125 acres per year, giving a yield per acre of 13·8 bushels and a total arable of 250 acres.

plan; as stated, its main hall had housed livestock. At West Meon, an apartment in the east part of the house, divided from the west dwelling quarters by a passage across the body of the building, measured 21 feet in breadth, and may well have served as a byre. (For the significance of this width, see below.) Next we may notice the basilical building at Spoonley Wood (Glos) (Fig. 18). The hands' quarters in this villa are clearly distinguishable in the south-east wing, where they take the form of a complete hall with projecting wing-rooms, without any communication with the central residential block on the south-west, and closely resemble structures of this type to be found next to the owner's residence in various French and Belgian villas. Evidently then the basilical building lying to the north of the yard cannot be for hands, and must have been a livestock house. Its aisles are 8 feet 9 inches in depth and the compartments 8 feet 2 inches wide between the posts. The stall-width thus approximates to allowances found in some old Welsh farmhouses.[1] The depth corresponds to Vitruvius' minimum depth with the addition of 2 feet for the manger.[2]

At West Dean (Wilts), besides the main house, there were at least two basilical outbuildings, which differed from one another in so far as the first, on the south-west, was of the 'converted' type, with nave and aisles, and contained a bath, hypocausts, and mosaics in the second stage; but the other, to north-east, was never anything but a livestock building, having a pillared aisle on the north side only, 9 feet 6 inches wide (= depth of stall) and distances of 9 feet 6 inches between the pillars. The last stall to west had been walled off as a square room for the cowman or for fodder, in a manner characteristic of many Roman stables or stalls. Here the stall-width approximated to Columella's maximum prescription (9 feet 8 inches).

At Ickleton (Cambs) a barn-building was probably built for stock, in view of the fact that the accommodation for hands was provided by a three-roomed cottage immediately to the north-west of the dwelling-house. In the 'barn', the widths of the aisles on the north

---

[1] E.g. Landeilo (Carmarthenshire), where stalls are 4 feet 2 inches wide; at Blainwaun, Llansadwrn (Carmarthenshire), 3 feet 2½ inches. See Peate, *Ant.* x, 1936, p. 451, figs. 5, 6.

[2] At Ezinge Warf, Groningen, the La Tène accommodation for two beasts was as little as 5 feet 8–6 feet 4 (Huts IVE and VA – *Germania*, 1936, p. 44, Abb. 6; 6a). The average per beast at Soljberg (pre-Roman Iron Age – see Chapter IX, p. 145), three cows and one horse – was 4 feet 2 inches. Stroud (stalls for ox-teams): 8 feet; Graux, Belgium: 8 feet 4 inches (de Maeyer, *op. cit.*, p. 57, fig. 6); Gerpinnes, single stalls: 4 feet 5 inches (*ib.*, p. 85, fig. 20a, Building B'–B). Modern allowances vary from 3 feet 6 inches to 4 feet 6 inches: 4 feet 2 inches appears to have been the allowance in Buildings VII and X at Köln-Müngersdorf (Fremersdorf, *Köln-Müngersdorf*, p. 117 sqq.).

and south were 9 feet 7 inches and 7 feet 6 inches respectively, the average distance between the columns 7 feet, which is a low allowance for two beasts, though not impossible. Two walled-off compartments on the north side, on the other hand, 7 feet 6 inches and 8 feet wide respectively, are best explained as stalls for two pairs of oxen. It may here be noted that in two cases (Denton Phase III, and Winterton IIB) byres were found in the northern aisles of the lower end in the fourth and third centuries respectively.[1]

If the three groups of basilical houses of which the dimensions are known are compared (i.e. the self-contained, re-adapted, and subsidiary), it is seen that, with a few exceptions, the average measurements of aisles, nave, and post-intervals vary only within narrow limits. The aisles measure from 8 to 12 feet, 8–10 feet being the commonest dimensions; exceptional only are Wellow (east aisle, 15 feet), West Dean south-west (north aisle, 14 feet 4 inches), Norton Disney III (4 feet), Bignor (14 feet 6 inches), Winterton IIB north (14 feet), and Hartlip (14 feet south). The Norton Disney building clearly never housed livestock; Bignor and Hartlip are not strictly basilical buildings in the sense of the present discussion, but are barns whose aisles are defined by continuous walls instead of posts; the dimensions of their aisles are explicable as being self-contained cattle-stalls; the same suggestion offers itself in relation to Wellow and West Dean (see pp. 137, 147). Most naves fall between 19–22 feet in width, and of those far the majority are in the neighbourhood of 20 feet. Exceptionally narrow are Ickleton (13 feet 6 inches), Spoonley Wood (17 feet 2 inches), North Wraxhall (probably 15 feet), and Norton Disney (6 feet 11 inches). This is explicable for the first three cases by the fact that they were stock-buildings only. Exceptionally wide are North Warnborough (25 feet), Holbury (29 feet), and Bignor (28 feet). The central part of the last probably served as a granary. The post-intervals listed vary between 6 and 13 feet, far the commonest distances being 8–10 feet. The only cases where the intervals could hardly have admitted of use as stalls for pairs were Norton Disney (6 feet) and some of the intervals at Brading north, which varied from 6 to 6 feet 10 inches.

Generally, therefore, we may sum up that the measurements of the main divisions of the basilical buildings are relatively standard, and the dimensions of the side-compartments constituted by the posts or pillars correspond to those necessary for the housing of cattle. From this use they may have originated, and some of the known cases

[1] As a continental parallel of Roman 'basilical' stock-buildings may be cited the east building of Heihof near Hulsberg (Limburg), which had two stalls on one side and a dung-pit in one corner (OM, I, 1907, p. 13), and the east building at Bocholst (Limburg – model in Leyden Museum).

certainly retained this function in part at least of their space, as demon-strated by Spoonley Wood, Ickleton, and West Dean (north-east). We may conclude that nearly all the examples classified as 'self-contained' and 're-adapted' must, in their original form, have divided the accommodation in their aisles between livestock, living quarters, and storage space. The exception is Norton Disney, and there were doubtless others. Those classified as 'subsidiary' must also have been divided between living space and the housing of stock and produce, but some were later re-adapted, at least in part, as more tolerably equipped residences (e.g. Mansfield Woodhouse, Brading north). North Wraxhall appears to have been afterwards divided up into cross-rooms and its function as stock-building transferred elsewhere. Of all these buildings, concerning only two are we in a position to say that they possessed second storeys (Stroud (Hants) – walls 3–3 feet 6 inches wide; West Meon – walls 3–4 feet); at the latter the probability is very great that the upper floor served as a loft for storage below the roof, as the dwelling seems to have been quite self-contained, and there would seem to have been no other accommodation.

With the problem of the second storey and storage-space generally is connected the type of agriculture to which the basilical farmsteads of the self-contained type belonged in Britain. Relevant here are the observations of Professor E. van Giffen resulting from his excavation of Early Iron Age-Roman aisled houses in Frisia, and the comparative study of their Frisian and Lower Saxon successors. The Frisian aisled farmstead of the prehistoric period evolved in the Middle Ages into a steading in which the part devoted to agricultural purposes, i.e. the aisled hall contained cattle stalled in the aisles with heads facing outward; hay was stored in the nave, and crops were laid up in a special storeroom in one aisle. In the Lower Saxon farmhouse, on the other hand, while the aisled stock-building resembled the Frisian in its general lines, the hay was stored over the stalls, the harvest laid on planks over the nave (these ultimately became a second storey or loft), and the threshing was carried out in the nave; hence the cattle were stalled with head inward to prevent them fouling the crop.

Of the two above types, the Frisian aisled building was much the narrower, possessing a width of some 25 feet; if 8 feet are allowed for the depth of the stalls each side, less than 9 feet are left for the width of the nave. The Lower Saxon aisled building, by contrast, is over 53 feet wide, which means a nave of some 35–37 feet. While we have noted some British aisled buildings with nave-widths of 13 feet 6 inches (Ickleton), 15 feet (North Wraxhall), and 17 feet 2 inches (Spoonley Wood), these are exceptional and explicable by the fact that they were outbuildings exclusively devoted to cattle; the naves of most

British examples vary from 19–25 feet in width, widths of 28 feet (Bignor), 29 feet (Holbury), and 30 feet (Finkley), being exceptional. The Frisian farmstead represents a preponderantly stock-raising economy where the cattle are wintered indoors and fed on hay cut from the polders; the Lower Saxon farm, on the other hand, practised a mixed agriculture in which cereal-growing was no less important than cattle; it was this difference which determined the greater width of the aisled building associated with the latter form of farming. There is accordingly little doubt that most of the British basilical farmsteads belonged to a mixed farming economy. Yet, as noted, only two of these buildings can confidently be stated to have possessed lofts, and at North Warnborough, where a granary probably existed in one aisle as in the Frisian type, the evidence was against the wintering of much stock within the building, and the finds suggested rather a pre-occupation with grain-production and wool. Be that as it may, the evidence of analogy is in favour of a mixed economy in the British examples, whose origin would be traceable rather to the mixed farming districts of Belgium and Gaul than to the polders of the Netherlands.

J. T. Smith in his important critical discussion of the aisled house in Roman Britain comes to the conclusion that the predominating and decisive feature of the Romano-British aisled dwelling is its division into the private residential quarters, which he sees as constant and traditional, and the remainder of the house, which represents a process of modification and social development, in so far as it is partly devoted to farmwork and partly to the life of a distinct social element. He suggests that this section served, not as the permanent residence of the second social element, but for particular purposes and occasions, e.g. as a court-leet. The only valid analogies to the Romano-British aisled house Smith sees in the Frisian Iron Age aisled dwellings of the Groningen type (e.g. those excavated at Ezinge Warf); but he regards these as differing fundamentally from the British type in so far as the non-residential half of the Dutch dwelling was devoted solely to agricultural purposes (the housing of cattle, the storage of fodder and grain in the ear; threshing). But, as we have shown, most of the aisled houses in Britain seem to have taken their origin – even if only indirectly – in buildings made to hold cattle, and not only can cases be cited in which some livestock continued to be housed in the 'working' end, but there are others in which the aisled structure was used purely for agricultural needs, i.e. for cattle and crops; Winterton IIB and North Warnborough contained what were probably granaries; Winterton IIB a threshing floor. In several cases aisled houses were used as workshops in which handicrafts were carried on (see p. 45).

This being the case, Smith's definition of the aisled dwelling to exclude any plan which does not contain the distinctive "upper and lower" ends, seems to be too arbitrary and to rest on an assumption that such a subdivision had always been present. But evidently it was not invariable either earlier or later, and it follows that some of the continental analogies (e.g. Mont Beuvray) and British instances (e.g. Cherry Hinton B) excluded by Smith must nevertheless be regarded as belonging to the same pattern.[1]

[1] Frisia: *Germania*, 1936, pp. 68–70; general discussion, J. T. Smith, see p. 46, n. 1.

CHAPTER IX

BYRES AND STABLES

IT IS not an easy task to define the use of the constituent agricultural buildings of the Roman villa in this country; the material is still slight, and little attention has been paid to what there is. Even abroad, where the remains are considerably richer, no comprehensive study appears to have been made, and in only two cases known to the writer (Chiragan, France, and Köln-Müngersdorf, Germany) has any sort of analysis been carried out.

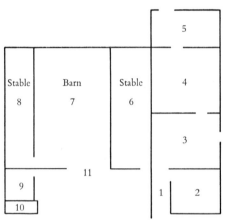

Fig. 26. Limerle, Luxemburg: eighteenth-century farmhouse.

The farmhouse consisting of hall with projecting wing-rooms (the 'Hall-*Eckrisalit*' dwelling) may serve as the point of departure for our investigation, as it constitutes the simplest form of romanized farmstead and a pre-phase of the corridor house, and has itself been found in this country. De Maeyer drew an analogy between this plan and the eighteenth-century farmhouse at Limerle, Luxemburg (Fig. 26), and was able to indicate an especially close correspondence between Limerle and the Roman 'Hall-*Eckrisalit*' farmhouse at Al Sauvenière (Belgium) (Fig. 17). On these lines, the residential wing at Al Sauvenière was confined to the west end, including the west wing-room and the cellar beneath it, three rooms behind (flanking the hall), and the bath-range (X, XI, XIII, II and III). The hall was here subdivided into a main room (XIV), two flanking rooms to west (VII, VIII) and one to the east (IX). XIV would have served, on analogy to Limerle, as the barn; the other rooms as stables, and XII, the eastern wing-room, also. That IX discharged this function is supported by independent evidence at other sites; an apartment in a precisely parallel position at Gerpinnes contained internal masonry counterforts for dividing stalls from one another. A correspondingly-placed room at Betzingen, Württemburg, was identified by the excavators as a stable. The stable in the plan of the *villa rustica* as described by Vitruvius, in spite of the vital differences of design, occupies a very similar position at the north-east end of the building.[1] British parallels will be referred to later.

There is also some confirmatory evidence that part of the hall was used, in given instances, for the storage of crops; thus, in the 'Hall-*Eckrisalit*' Building II at Houdeng-Goegnis, Belgium, lying by the main residence, the eastern third of the hall had been converted to a granary, as indicated by the presence of parallel dwarf-walls to carry the floor. At Köln-Braunsfeld in Period I the hall contained two timber-lined storage basements and a paved threshing floor, as well as hearths and various small postholes for arrangements in connection with cooking and other domestic activities.

At the Limerle farmhouse the space between the projecting wings of the house, i.e. in front of the barn, was occupied by the dungheap, and here the heavier agricultural implements were kept under the shelter of the verandah. How far this was so in the 'Hall-*Eckrisalit*' farm is doubtful, for the verandah was usually closed by a low wall, and sometimes there was an entrance porch.

At Colerne (Wilts), on the other hand (Fig. 23), a drain from the baths at the north-west angle of the building led south to a rock-cut cesspit near an outbuilding which was probably an open cowhouse or stable.[2] The bath-range was probably an addition, and the east part of the house, which showed traces of later modification, had been, on the analogy of Limerle, Gerpinnes, and Betzingen, a stable or byre later subdivided by the insertion of walls; the south-west out-building may have been built to replace it. Colerne is not the only Romano-British farm where stables or a byre can be distinguished in an analogous position to that at Limerle and its Roman prototypes. At Rodmarton and Cherington (Glos) (Fig. 27), at both of which the hall figures undivided in the main range, a long compartment lies across the end of the house (the north end at Rodmarton, the west

[1] Vitruvius, *de archit.*, VI, 6; cf. Daremberg-Saglio, *Dictionnaire des antiquités grecques et romaines*, Paris, V, 1912, s.v. Villa, p. 878, fig. 7486.

[2] The surviving compartment is 16 feet long, closed by a southern cross-wall 8 feet in length. The accommodation would have been for four beasts. In the following discussion the word "breadth" is used to denote the internal measurements of buildings across the long axis; "width" denotes the side-to-side measurement of the accommodation of each animal or pair of animals.

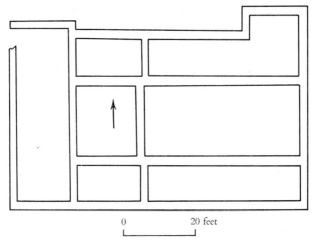

Fig. 27. Cherington, Gloucestershire: Roman farmhouse.

end at Cherington); their dimensions as well as their positions correspond so closely to the examples at Gerpinnes and Betzingen that
their identity as accommodation for livestock can hardly be doubted.
Another case can be seen at Titsey (Surr) (above, Fig. 22 and p. 129),
where room 4, later converted to other uses, occupies a similar
position. The use of the south-west wing of the North Warnborough
house has been referred to. The dimensions of the structures so far
discussed were:

	Breadth		Length	
	feet	inches	feet	inches
Al Sauvenière	11	8	28	4
Betzingen	13	4	59	2
Gerpinnes	13	4	40	0
Rodmarton	14	0	35	6
Cherington	14	0	45	3
Colerne	13/14	0	42	0
Titsey	15	0	27	0
N. Warnborough	15	0	60	0

Can the more precise use of this accommodation be defined?
Vitruvius requires that ox-stalls (*bubilia*) be between 14 feet 6 inches
(15 *pedes*) and 9 feet 8 inches (10 *pedes*) in width, and 6 feet 8 inches
in depth. It is to be assumed that these dimensions provide for a team
of two, i.e. that the width allowed per beast was between 7 feet 3 inches
and 4 feet 10 inches. If some 2 feet are allowed for the manger and

6 feet for the gangway behind the stalls, the whole byre would have been some 14 feet 8 inches in internal breadth; a building containing stalls along each side would have measured 23–4 feet.

Columella (I, 6) prescribes that the ox-stall be between 8 feet 8 inches (9 *pedes*) and 9 feet 8 inches (10 *pedes*) in width; the allowance per beast is therefore 4 feet 8 inches to 4 feet 10 inches. At Ezinge Warf near Groningen, Holland, in the proto-Frisian settlement, Hut Va, the accommodation was: Width of stall (2 cows) 6 feet 4 inches, depth 5 feet, plus mat on the inner side 2 feet 4 inches. The total width of the structure, which had stalls down both sides, was 15 feet 6 inches. The width of the stalls may here be compared with the span of the yoke found at the same site – 1·5 metres (5 feet). To the Ezinge dimensions may be added the information yielded by the Early Iron Age hut at Soljberg, Denmark, in whose annexed outhouse were found the skeletons of one horse and three oxen which perished when the byre was destroyed by fire. The byre was trapezoidal, and slightly broader at its east than its west end; the measurements were 5½ × 4·75 × 5 × 4·3 metres, i.e. 16 feet 8 × 18 feet 4 on the long axis and 14 feet 5 and 15 feet 10 on the ends. Thus the average accommodation per beast was approximately 4 feet 7 inches.

At Gerpinnes the stable or byre previously referred to had stalls measuring approximately 4 feet 5 inches and 5 feet 10 inches in width (cf. the dimensions of Columella); the total internal breadth of the building was 13 feet 4 inches. At Graux, Belgium, the outbuildings included a long trapezoidal structure (H) 28 feet 4 inches broad internally at the wider end, 26 feet 8 inches at the narrower; the internal buttress in its north wall was 5 metres (16 feet 8 inches) from the north-west corner, leaving room for precisely two ox-teams (8 feet 4 × 2) to its west. The breadth of 28 feet 4 inches here bears a clear relationship to that of 14 feet seen at the sites above.

At Stroud, near Petersfield (Hants), in room 25, three counterforts on the west wall stood 8 feet from one another, and obviously provided for three or four teams of oxen. The internal breadth of the building was 18 feet.

The Phase II aisled house "B" at Winterton (Lincs) was characterized by a northern aisle of 14 feet breadth, containing a trench to support a feeding trough parallel with and four feet from the wall, thus leaving 10 feet for stall accommodation.

Building "A" at the same farm was a two-roomed building: the longer room was a byre 21 feet in breadth, and contained a channel four feet from and parallel with the south wall, apparently to support a feeding trough; a depth of 15 feet thus remained for the cattle. A line of postholes belonging to Phase IIIA in the aisled barnhouse at Denton

(Lincs) was interpreted to indicate the addition of a cattle stall; it stood 13 feet from the north wall of the dwelling.

In the croft of Blaen-Nedduchaf near Ystradfellte, Brecknockshire, described by Sir Cyril Fox, and typologically descended from the Roman two-roomed cottage, the cowhouse was internally 13 feet in breadth; the old Irish 'long house', sheltering cattle and family under one roof, was usually 12 to 15 feet in breadth. The byres of the old Welsh farms described by Peate varied in internal breadth from $17\frac{1}{2}$ to 26 feet 10 inches; but in some (Llanerchy Cawr, Pantydrain) the normal depth of stall-accommodation and feeding walk within the building measured 13 feet 10–14 feet. The stall-width was sometimes as little as 2 feet 10 inches (Blaenwaun near Llansadwrn, Carmarthenshire), but more often 3 feet 9 inches to 4 feet 6 inches. In the seventeenth-century Frisian 'long house' farm at Haubois near Sneeck, Holland, the depth of stalls and mangers was 7 feet $3\frac{1}{2}$ inches, or 8 feet 4 inches, the total internal breadth of the building (with two ranges of stalls) being 17 feet $8\frac{1}{2}$ inches. The stalls had two widths, viz. 6 feet 11 inches and 7 feet 3 inches.[1]

We may therefore summarize as follows:

	Width of stall per head				Internal breadth of byre			
	feet	inches	feet	inches	feet	inches	feet	inches
Ezinge Warf	3	2	—		15	6	—	
Soljberg	4	7	—		14	5 to 15	10	
Vitruvius	4	10	7	3	14 (double)	8	23–4	
Columella	4	4	4	10	—		—	
Gerpinnes	4	5	5	10	13	4	—	
Graux	4	2	—		26	8 to 28	4	
Stroud	4	0	—		18	0	—	
Blaen-Nedduchaf	—		—		13	0	—	
Irish long houses	—		—		12–15		—	
Welsh farms (byres only, 2 cases)	2	10	4	6	$17\frac{1}{2}$–26 10			
Sneeck	3	$5\frac{1}{2}$	3	$7\frac{1}{2}$	17	$8\frac{1}{2}$ (2 rows)		
R. W. Dickson, *Practical Agriculture*, 1805	3	0	3	2	—		—	
Studland Cottage B	4	3	3	4 (approx.)	11 (approx.)	0	11	9
Cottage H, Phase I	4	3	3	4 (approx.)	12	8 to 13	0	
Winterton B	—		—		14		—	
A	—		—		15		—	
Denton (IIIa)	—		—		13		—	

[1] Blaen-Nedduchaf, *Ant.* xiv, 1940, pp. 363 sqq.; the Irish long house, E. Evans, *Irish Heritage*, p. 57; Llanerchy Cawr, Pantydrain, Blaenwaun; Peate, *Ant.* x, 1936, pp. 448 sqq.; *The Welsh House*,[2] ch. iv, pp. 51 sqq.; Haubois: personal observation.

From these figures it will be seen that 13–15 feet are the commonest internal breadths of the ancient byres; 4–4 feet 6 inches seem to have been the commonest average allowances per head. It is therefore clear that the compartments at Rodmarton, Cherington, Titsey, Colerne, and probably North Warnborough, were ox-byres. With 13–14 feet as the basic average breadth, we may make a similar identification at Brading (Fig. 32), where room xxxii on the south of the yard measured 28 feet in breadth. Rooms xxxiii and xxxiv, occupying the east end of the building, were for fodder and the oxherds, or else a dairy, and a barn with roof supported on posts, and (it seems) with open sides (xxxv), continued the range eastward, possessing the same breadth (28 feet). It would have been conveniently placed to house the hay-rick. The eastern part of the east long room at Iwerne B was subdivided by a drain down its length; the room's total breadth was 15 feet and the space south of the drain was 9 feet from north to south; here oxen would have been housed. The length of the drain, 33 feet, suggests 7 or 8 animals. The breadth of Langton building L (Yorks) – 26 feet – suggests a multiple of 13 feet and that it was a byre (Fig. 35). This is confirmed by its position to leeward of the dwelling-house and the small room for fodder or the cowherd in the north-west corner, resembling that at Müngersdorf VII. Considerations of proportion also make it likely that the inner north-south outbuilding at the north-east angle of the courtyard of Pitney villa (Som) was a byre; its dimensions were 13 × 45 feet.

Building 71–4 at Bignor, an aisled barnlike structure in the farmyard to east of the dwelling, possessed a nave 28 feet in breadth, and aisles 14 feet broad. The central room (70) would have been for grain or fodder, and the aisles housed cattle, being 122 and 102 feet in length respectively. In the same way the south aisle of Building K at Hartlip (Kent) – an outhouse of similar plan – measured 14 feet in breadth, and would therefore seem to have housed cattle. The north aisle (11 feet) was perhaps for horses, and the nave (20 feet broad) would have served for storage.[1] In the Wellow villa (Som) the eastern aisle of the basilical building on the south-east of the yard was 15 feet in breadth and may well have been a byre. Three basilical buildings at Spoonley Wood, Ickleton, and West Dean, probably devoted to livestock, have already been described (p. 137). In the light of the afore-mentioned figures, it is reasonable to identify as byres also an isolated building, no. 19 (20 × 14·15), of Period III (between the second and fourth centuries A.D.) to the west of the Cox Green villa,

[1] For a close parallel, Marburg near Pommern, on the Mosel, outbuilding I; the aisles measured 14 feet and 13 feet 4 inches in breadth respectively (BJ 101, 1897, p. 80).

Maidenhead (Berks); the later long corridor-like block (no. 11) 13 feet in breadth, to the east of the dwelling-house of the Thistleton Dyer villa (Rut); a small isolated building of third-century date, internally 25 feet 6 inches by 14 feet, with a corridor on its north side, at Thurnham (Kent); an outbuilding attached to Insula IV, House 2, at Verulamium, lying along the garden wall, with a small room divided off at the west end, the internal dimensions of the long compartment being 40 × 14 feet; and possibly an outbuilding lying along and outside the boundary wall of the villa of Penn Mead, High Wycombe; only its northern end was excavated, but it possessed a minimal length of 22 feet 6 inches and an internal breadth of 28 feet; it was built in the second half of the second century A.D.

While, therefore, we may with some confidence see outbuildings with breadths of 13–15 feet as byres, we cannot be sure that some buildings of greater width did not fulfil the same function, since internal arrangements would vary, and the animals might be accommodated in stalls placed across the building instead of along its greatest length. A consideration of the dimensions of the old Welsh cowhouses figuring as part of the Welsh version of the long-house shows how various the measurements could be according to the varying arrangements inside them, which involved the inclusion of one or two horse-boxes and of calf-boxes.

With stalls lengthwise			With stalls crosswise		
	feet	inches		feet	inches
Pantydrain	14	1	Ciloerwynt	18	5
Llanerchy Cawr	14	10	Blaenwaun	19	6
Cwmeilath	17	5	Nantyffyn	19	8
Eagair	17	6	Lan	21	3

In the first two cases, not the total breadths of the cowhouses are given, but the total breadth of the cow-stalls plus feeding walks without a loose-box and calf-box arranged beside them in the respective farms named. The byres of these Welsh farms varied from 17 feet 9 inches to 26 feet 10 inches internally in breadth, and this makes the distinction from stables very difficult.

A fourth-century building at Great Casterton (Rut) contained sleeper beams clearly defining stall accommodation. The internal dimensions of the building were 20 × 18 feet (it had not been originally built as a stock-building); a stall across the north end was 7 feet 6 inches in depth; another down the east side 12 feet 6 inches in depth. Here it seems probable that the northern stalls housed cattle, while the easterly were for horses. An alleged stable in the west wing at Northleigh

(Oxon) consisted of two stalls 12 feet deep and 8 feet and 7 feet wide respectively.

At Boscoreale, Italy, the stable was 3·1 metres (10 feet 4 inches) in breadth; here the skeletons of three horses were found; but at Gregnano, 19 feet 2 inches broad, the remains of both horses and oxen came to light, and the stabling of both together must have been a common practice in Roman farms. The stable-building attached to the Roman posting-station on the Little St Bernard Pass was 20 feet in breadth, and the boxes inside were 10 feet in depth; the side-to-side measurements did not appear. Here a small compartment, for groom or fodder, occupied the end of the building. A stable in the Roman farm at Stammheim, Württemburg, occupied the end of the dwelling; it measured 10 feet 8 inches in breadth.

Additional information has to be derived from military sources. At Gellygaer, Caerhyn, Cadder, and Balmuildy, buildings thought to have been stable-blocks varied from 16 feet 8 inches to 32 feet in external breadth, but not in all cases were the dimensions closely ascertained. The most satisfactory information was obtained at Halton Chesters, Carzield (Dumfriesshire), and Benwell:

	Breadth feet	Length feet	Dimensions of boxes feet
Halton	60 (30 × 2)	130	11 × 25
Benwell	70 (35 × 2)	154	12 × 25/30
Carzield	?	?	11 × 12
Hod Hill	—	—	10 × 12/16/20

The allowance for a light horse is 60 square feet,[1] but Sir Ian Richmond, pointing out that the Roman cavalry horse was a much smaller animal than that in use today, regarded 10/12 by 25/30 feet as sufficient for seven horses, allowing 3 feet 6 inches width per beast.[2] While, therefore, we may expect a more liberal allowance of width in the stall for each horse on civilian sites, where it was unnecessary to conform to "King's Regulations" or to crowd men and mounts into the confined area of a fort, the Little Saint Bernard, the Italian, and the military figures alike suggest that the average depth of stall amounted to 10–11 feet, and that buildings of 10–20 feet in breadth are to be looked for when stables are to be identified. Taking into consideration the Welsh byres, then, we shall have difficulty in distinguishing between stables and cowhouses where breadths in the neighbourhood

[1] R. G. Linton, *Veterinary Hygiene*, 1934, p. 145.
[2] AA⁴ xix, 1941, p. 32; Hod Hill: information from the late Sir Ian Richmond.

of 20 feet are concerned, and a similar ambiguity may apply to buildings with a breadth of 30 feet or so.

As some confirmation of our conclusion we may quote the barn-building at Neerharen-Rekem, Belgium, where the presence of horses was evidenced by the finds (horse-bones, horse-furniture, a bit). Here the side-compartments inside the aisles were 10 feet (3 metres) in depth on the west side, and 9 feet 2 inches on the east. On the basis of these data, we may plausibly identify the north aisle of Building K at Hartlip as a stable (depth 11 feet).

CHAPTER X

FARMS AND THEIR USES

I. THE VILLA

THE STUDY of such evidence as survives of Romano-British farm layout can contribute both to our knowledge of agricultural techniques and to our reconstruction of the tenurial system of the province.

For a full account of the Early Iron Age farmstead of Little Woodbury near Salisbury, one of the few examples of its type of which a considerable part has been excavated, the reader is referred to the chapters on that period: its importance for us is that its agricultural techniques differ little in essence from those of similar isolated farmsteads of southern Britain in the Roman period. It may be briefly noted that at Little Woodbury the installations showed traces of a rough practical planning: the working hollows used for threshing and winnowing were confined to the areas west, north, and south of the dwelling, to avail themselves of the west wind, and the same applied to the known seed-granaries, so securing them from ignition by sparks from the domestic hearth and exposing them to the prevailing wind. The drying racks for hay or grain seem to have been concentrated near the house, and for that reason it may be regarded as certain that livestock was not allowed within the enclosure. In Little Woodbury, then, there is no division between residential and agricultural quarters; there is a close identification between normal farming processes and everyday life. But there is consideration for wind and probably precaution against fire.

The study of Pitt-Rivers's excavation of the Romano-British farmstead of Woodcuts in Cranbourne Chase, as interpreted by Professor Hawkes, enables us to see what was apt to happen to such a farmstead in the Roman period (Fig. 28).[1]

Here in Period I (A.D. 10/15–c. 150/75) the steading was a simple circular kraal with approach-roads entering from the north-west and south-east; it was of much the same type as Little Woodbury, and probably contained a timber hut which remained undetected. Storage pits were found, 32 or 39 out of 78 yielding Early Iron Age material, and the remainder Roman finds. It was noted that the number of pits in proportion to the comparatively short period of pre-Roman

[1] Little Woodbury: PPS² VI, 1940, pp. 30 sqq. Woodcuts, Rotherley: Pitt-Rivers, *Excavations*, I, II; Hawkes, *Arch. J.* CIV, 1947, pp. 42 sqq.

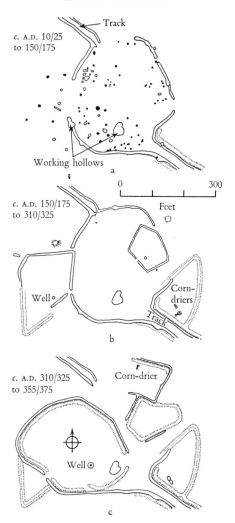

Fig. 28. Successive phases of the native homestead at Woodcuts,
Dorset. (After Hawkes, *Arch. J.* CIV, 45, fig. 6.)

occupation was large compared with the number used over the first
hundred years of Roman rule, and this contrast was interpreted to
mean Roman requisitioning of three-fifths of the grain.[1] Working
hollows of the Little Woodbury type were also found, which yielded
Roman pottery, and generally the pre-Roman methods of farming
continued here unchanged till the end of the second century. Finds

[1] This theory can be accepted so long as it is not held that pit-storage was at this
date giving place to above-ground storage.

included *terra sigillata*, showing that the inhabitants had some spare cash for external purchases; the farmstead enjoyed, in the words of Professor Hawkes, "a modest prosperity" in Phase I, in spite of the supposed heavy impositions of the corn tribute.

In Phase II (A.D. 150/75–310/25) a considerable change took place: the habitation remained in the same spot, but a kite-shaped enclosure (the "north-west quarter") was added to the yard on the west, evidently for stock, as it was entered from the outside; it contained a well dug at this time. Two more enclosures, the East Quarter and the South-East Quarter, were also appended to the east of the kraal, the former entered from inside the yard, and apparently for work, but exactly for what is unclear; the other containing two corn-drying furnaces. Pit-storage was now probably becoming obsolete, as only three pits were identified as belonging to this phase. Finds showed that the kraal continued in occupation to the end of the third century. The changes represented by the three new enclosures signify a minor revolution in farming technique. The wintering of at least part of the stock beside the kraal is now possible, owing to the Roman introduction of well-sinking, and if Hawkes's suggestion that Cranbourne Chase was imperial domain is correct, this may be seen as the result of government initiative. It almost certainly indicates the presence of cattle rather than sheep, as sheep do not drink much during the winter. At Woodcuts ox-bones constituted 39 per cent of the total, as compared with 29 per cent of sheep. The result of this winter stalling would have meant an increased conservation of manure and the possibility of improved yields. The introduction of corn-drying furnaces of the pit and flue type, in place of the primitive clay ovens which may be assumed to have existed, meant a rise in storage efficiency and a greater ease of grinding, as well as the ability to dry larger quantities more speedily. Apparently the storage was also improved, though we do not know how, as pits ceased to be used to any extent for this purpose. Above-ground structures must be assumed. While grain-production was greatly improved, it seems improbable that there was a surplus with which to feed the stock during the winter, as the government took much of the harvest. On the other hand, the introduction of the Roman two-hand scythe may well have made possible an increase of hay-stocks (see p. 82). It should be noted that the nearest woodland from which some winter fodder (e.g. leaves) could have been derived must have been reasonably near; bones of swine, insignificant at Rotherley and Woodyates, were 13 per cent at Woodcuts, so that access to the woodland is evident.[1]

The Roman improvements in Phase II reveal a degree of planning.

[1] Cranbourne Chase as imperial domain: Hawkes, *loc. cit.*, pp. 33, 41, 71–2, 79.

While the cattle-yard is to windward, showing the inhabitants to have been inured to wind-borne odours (but when the cattle was there during the winter, the wind may frequently have blown from the east), the corn-drying furnaces were carefully placed to leeward to keep sparks from the dwelling and the ricks.

In Phase III, beginning between 310 and 325, and lasting till 355/70, a radical replanning took place. The kraal, now lightly fortified, was moved farther westward so as to overlie the west periphery of the former Central Quarter, and only a small part of the North-west Quarter or stock enclosure was left in use, now entered from inside the new kraal, and therefore possibly no longer used for animals. Its well was blocked, and another dug in the new kraal. The South-east Quarter no longer contained corn-drying furnaces, but a fresh one was made in the new enclosure to the north-east; the East Quarter was enlarged.

The interpretation of these changes is none too clear. A reduction of both stock and corn-growing is a possibility, if we could be sure that the corn-drying furnaces were really reduced from two to one. The use of the enlarged East Quarter is however unknown (a sheep-fold or garden?). The obsolescence of the North-west Quarter as a cattle-pound probably led to the use of the South-east Quarter in its place (though there are burials here), a new "Corn Yard" being laid out to the north-east of the site. In general a reduction of arable and the maintenance of the stockrearing branch seem to be indicated, but it is doubtful whether on available evidence an actual expansion of pastoral economy can be postulated as Professor Hawkes has suggested. Notable is the shifting of all the farming installations to leeward – probably the fruit of a century of Roman influence.

The rather different Belgic-Roman farm at Wyboston (Beds) has already been described (p. 12). It may merely be noted that the Roman period here witnesses a multiplication of enclosed areas for the handling of stock and the drying of corn. The alleged stock-enclosure is situated to the east of the dwelling, so avoiding odours, but the placing of the corn-drier to the west of it was not so happy an expedient.

Characteristic of native farming in the early Roman period was Site 37 at Tallington on the Welland gravels of south Lincolnshire. It may have been the successor of an earlier farmstead to its north, which consisted of a circular hut contained in an enclosure. Site 37 was enclosed by an oblong palisade 250 by 150 feet. "Three-quarters of the area," says W. G. Simpson, "were excavated and postholes of a square granary and of racks for drying straw, and two working hollows for threshing, milling, or cooking, were identified. Fragments of fired clay found in the rubbish pits probably came from clay ovens for drying grain, and clay loomweights indicate that weaving was practised. No living hut was found, but there are faint indications on air-photographs that this occupied the north-west quarter of the enclosure which was destroyed by a modern gravel quarry. . .Potsherds found in the larger of the two working hollows were mostly handmade, scratchmarked vessels of the Trent Valley type, but included a few fragments from wheelmade Romano-British vessels. Samian sherds from the fill of the ditches suggested that the farm was abandoned about A.D. 80/90. The first occupation of the farm was therefore A.D. c. 50/60." Simpson concluded that the farming was essentially of the Little Woodbury type, carried on by a single family, all the Little Woodbury installations being represented except the grain storage pits. The absence of the latter he explained by the high water level in winter; he thought that the grain was likely to have been stored in large jars. Analysis of the pollens from the soil of the site showed that cereals and weeds of cultivation constituted 47 per cent, while animal bones indicated that stock-breeding was important. The concentration of installations to the south and east of the dwelling shows precaution against fire and avoidance of odours. The farm's direct association with a ditched accommodation road connected with the King Street also reflects the need to get produce to market and probably to move livestock in a controlled fashion. This and the multiplication of native farms in the direct vicinity of the Roman main road, as well as the network of branch roads tying them to the highway, illustrate graphically the close link between the Roman development of communications and the growth of farming and agricultural production in the province.

It is possible to classify the general layout of the more developed romanized farms in Britain under the following heads:

(1) Self-contained farmhouses (two-room and basilical).

(2) Houses within enclosures containing outbuildings scattered about them and arranged in no strict plan.

(3) Houses set in one line with their outbuildings.

(4) Houses with additional wings or outbuildings set at right angles to them to form an L.

(5) Houses whose outbuildings are laid out in two lines at right angles to them.

(6) Houses whose outbuildings are set round one or more courtyards.

(7) Houses whose outbuildings conform to none of the foregoing types.

The basilical or aisled farmhouse originally constituted a self-contained establishment with few or no dependent outbuildings. Self-contained examples continued to exist and are found in Britain as late as in the fourth century; the type has been discussed elsewhere. Well-known as a self-contained farmstead is that at Iwerne (Dors), which was a two-roomed 'long house' combining dwelling and byre in two successive periods. Less well-known or recognized as belonging to the type are Rodmarton and Cherington in Gloucestershire. Both were 'tripartite corridor' dwellings, but Rodmarton was better

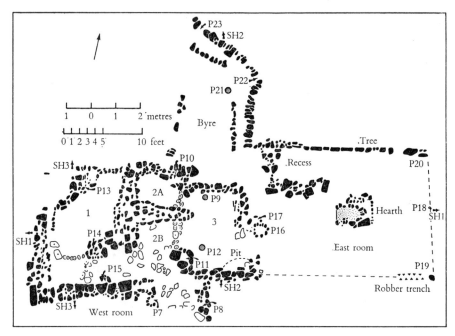

Fig. 29. Studland, Dorset: Romano-British farm-cottage "H" (third or fourth century).

appointed, with a bath-suite crossing one end and a cowhouse the other. Two rooms adjacent to the byre were also devoted to agricultural uses, judging by the fact that they were stone-paved.

Cherington (Fig. 27), not far away on the same ancient route, was of very similar size and roughly of the same plan, with a byre across the west end. Each of its three remaining parallel parts was divided into a shorter and a longer room, reminiscent of the two-roomed 'longhouse'. A similar plan, i.e. a two-roomed subdivision of two parallel ranges, is to be seen in the outbuildings of the Roman villa at Noyers-sur-Serein.

The Titsey house (Fig. 22), on the other hand, also fundamentally a self-contained farmhouse in its first phase, originated as a 'hall' type of building of Belgian-Rhenish affinity, with large undivided

Wirtschafthalle, baths to west, and a byre on the east flank. It was later fundamentally modified.

On a much more primitive level, the self-contained farmhouse is represented by the three cottages excavated near Studland (Dors). Cottage B of this group consisted of three rooms, the westerly a living room, divided from the easterly, apparently a forge and store, by

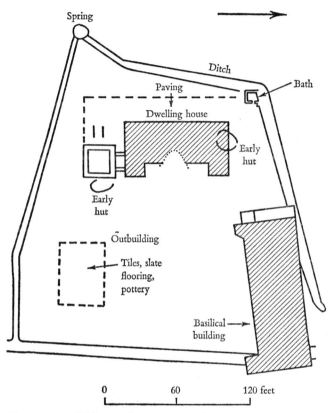

Fig. 30. Mansfield Woodhouse, Nottinghamshire: Roman villa.

a byre running across the building with entrances both to north and south. Cottage H (Fig. 29), on the other hand, was divided between a dwelling room on the west, a byre subdivided by a partition, and another room on the east.

If the villa at Mansfield Woodhouse (Notts) belongs only approximately to our Type 2 (enclosed, with buildings distributed about the dwelling), it may nevertheless be described at this point because it is one of the clearest examples of an unromanized farmstead which developed into a villa (Fig. 30). A pit-dwelling and circular hut of

timber, wattle, and daub, with associated pits and ovens, made about
A.D. 80 within a rectilinear enclosure, were supplemented by another
circular hut in about 110, and replaced by two or more rectangular
timber cottages in 130 or so. These were replaced by a corridor house
in the late second century, and in the earlier third century a rectangular
building was added to east, probably for stock and crops. In the early
fourth century a large aisled building was built to north-east of the
dwelling-house and at right angles to its north end. This must have
served mostly for personnel, since the other outbuilding continued
in use in the fourth century, and the basilical building received mosaics
and heating apparatus, though precisely when is unknown. Both the
replacement of two cottages by a corridor house in the late second
century and the addition of the basilical building in the early fourth
indicate a step forward in economy, and the latter shows an expansion
of staff, either by the purchase of slaves or by absorption into the estate
of kindred or neighbours; alternatively it meant absorption into
another, larger, property.

A well-studied example of the enclosed farm residence surrounded
by outbuildings not systematically arranged is Langton (Yorks), but
we shall postpone the account of this site because its analysis is such
as to contribute to our knowledge of agricultural methods. (See p. 171.)

In much the same class, but a little more regular in arrangement is
the Watt's Wells villa, Ditchley (Oxon) (Fig. 31). Of its outbuildings
a good deal (though not perhaps enough) was learnt. The dwelling-
house, replacing a timber building of uncertain character in the Flavian
period, faced south; to its south-west a series of timber barracks,
possibly but not certainly of aisled plan, lay along the west side of
the enclosure, for the housing of farmhands or slaves. A circular
threshing floor was situated between them and the house. To the
north-west and west of the house, cobble pavements suggested to
the excavator timber huts for domestic staff. A gap in occupation
intervened during the second century, but at the commencement of
the fourth the house was repaired on an enhanced scale, although the
latter part of the occupation was thought to have continued well into
the fifth century in an intensified but barbarized fashion suggestive
of the absence of the owner. At the beginning of the reoccupation
the threshing floor was renewed, the hands' quarters were demolished,
and a large granary was built in the south-east quarter of the yard;
Radford calculated its capacity (minus a third) at 5,600 bushels,
representing 540 acres sown, with a yield of 1·3 quarters (rather over
ten bushels) the acre. Adding seed-corn and tenants' maintenance,
this would have represented over a thousand acres of arable, without
woodland and pasture. (For further discussion see p. 267.)

The two striking features emerging from the Ditchley excavation were, as the excavator pointed out, the intensification of corn-production in the fourth century, accompanied by tenurial devolution, i.e. the non-renewal of the hands' quarters, which he took to imply

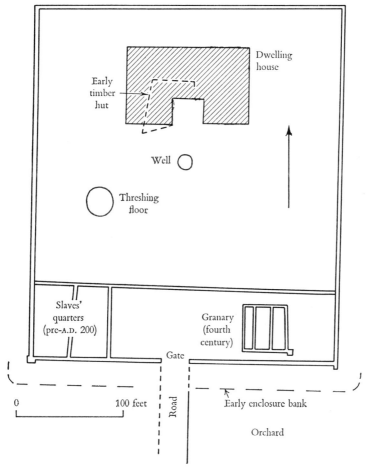

Fig. 31. Watt's Wells, Ditchley, Oxfordshire: Roman villa.

that they had been settled out on the estate in their own farms. Nevertheless, this interpretation raises some problems, which will be discussed later. In the second period there was no accommodation within the yard for livestock, unless they were kept in the timber barracks and shared them with the hands. The absence of byres in the last phase, on the other hand, is accountable by distribution of livestock to the *coloni*, and something similar is suggested at North Wraxhall and Hartlip. The two enclosures attached to the outside of the farmyard on the south and east were apparently not corrals but orchards, covering about four acres, since tree-pits were found within them.

For the rest, Ditchley shows a simple practical symmetry. The placing of the farm buildings to the south of the house avoided odours; the building of the barns to leeward in Period III carries with it no particular difficulty, as there is no evidence of any corn-drying installations, which may well have been located in the tenant farms, so that the grain was brought for threshing ready-parched. Notable is the circular threshing floor, suggesting the use of oxen for treading out the corn – an improvement, for instance, on the method at Langton, where apparently the grain was beaten out by hand.

Type 3 has not generally been recognized as a distinctive arrangement in this country, but its clear existence abroad serves to draw attention to its presence in Britain also. Continental examples may be quoted from Ronchinnes-te-Maillen and Al Sauvenière-Maillen, both in Belgium. At Ronchinnes a very large dwelling-house, planned as an east-west corridor block, forms one line with a malting house and a combined hands' quarters and iron workshop, in the form of a corridor building with wing-rooms (*Eckrisaliten*). To the south of the residence lay a solitary structure, a corn-drying building. No enclosures seem to have been detected in association with this complex. Al Sauvenière took the form of a tripartite corridor building (which had evolved from a single square hall) ranged east-west and joined by a corridor with an agricultural building in the same line eastward; the latter consisted of a large buttressed 'two-roomed' hall flanked by the linking corridor, and was evidently for crops and hands. A bath-block lay at right angles to both to northward.

It is possible that the original nucleus of the Northleigh villa (Oxon) resembled Al Sauvenière in general principle. Here the "Period I" structure (as known till 1943) consisted of two blocks, a 'two-room' *Wirtschafthalle* to south (4–10) like that at Al Sauvenière, and a corridor wing to north (11–17) in the same line, which conceivably but not certainly originated as a basilical building. But until the chronological relationship between the above and the vast extensions to southward detected from the air in 1943 are clarified, this can remain no more than a conjecture.

Another British parallel on a modest scale is Gayton Thorpe (Norf) (Fig. 24), where a staff and work building with wing-rooms and two-room internal division lay end to end, and nearly in line with the dwelling immediately to north. The two buildings were later joined by an intermediate room or lobby, in a manner recalling the linking corridor at Al Sauvenière. The farm was occupied from the mid-second century to the end of the third; what heating arrangements there were in the dwelling-house were dismantled before the occupation ended, and their slightness suggested to the excavator that the house had been a summer residence only. Gayton thus reveals hints of absentee landlordism and later cultural decline.

A house between Paulton and Camerton (Som) was classifiable with the same type of plan; here the dwelling faced east, and a farm-building containing nine rooms and a corridor lay in line to west of it, but very little is known beyond its mere plan. Its westernmost room, sixty by twenty feet, was probably for livestock.

The buildings at Bedmore Barn, Ham Hill (Som) presented a crude version of the same arrangement; a tripartite corridor house faced eastward, and two further buildings were aligned with it to north, all being joined by sections of wall on the east side. One building hinted at corn-grinding, the making of tesserae and pottery; but that this was also a farm seems to be indicated by the isolated paved patch to the east of the house, which was a threshing floor. Analogous may well be the two adjacent buildings at Six Bells near Farnham (Surr), consisting of a dwelling-house and bath-range, both apparently built in connection with a pottery industry.

An alternative to the linear arrangements is that in which the house and its outbuildings lie at right angles to one another, so forming an L-pattern. Perhaps the most interesting example of this plan is the villa at Woodham's Farm near King's Worthy as revealed by air-photography. The problem of this estate's field-form has already been discussed. The dwelling-house lay north-south, facing east. At the north end of the main block is a circular structure, possibly a threshing floor but more probably a circular pavilion or a shrine. A wall, likely to be associated with outbuildings, runs south-south-westward from the house, to close the west side of the yard, and a detached line of smaller structures, of domestic or industrial appearance, extends from the north-east corner of the main house along the north side of the yard.

At Atworth (Wilts) the main building faced south and the 'economic' wing took off at right angles from the east end; probably a ditch joined the far ends of each, forming a yard in a manner resembling that at King's Worthy. In Period I the subordinate wing was separate from the residence, but the two were joined in Period II; the climax in the development of the house came in Period III (probably third century) with considerable rebuilding and enlargement. Very little light was thrown on agricultural functions by the excavations, however, and

6

down to the third century the subordinate wing seems to have composed hands' quarters rather than outbuildings. In Period IV (second half of the fourth century) corn-driers were installed in the hands' quarters and the bath, to the accompaniment of slovenly repairs and lowered standards in the residence; the story is the same at Brading and King's Worthy, but we learn little of farm layout.

Not entirely classifiable with the "L" group, but showing some affinity, is Cromhall (Glos). Here the residence, a tripartite corridor house, formed an L, its main wing looking east, and the other arm, the eastern half of which may have been for staff, looking south. The latter was distinguished by the fact that it consisted of two very large rooms between the corridors. A wall ran south from its east end and enclosed the yard on the east side, joining a large rectangular outbuilding which helped to complete the enclosure on the south-east. This building, internally 74 feet 6 inches by 47 feet 6 inches, had a massive east wall 3 feet 1 inch broad, and there remained against the inner sides of this and the northern wall an offset indicating the former existence of a raised floor. The other walls were 2 feet 10 inches in width. It may be concluded that the building was a granary of very considerable capacity. The chronology is obscure, but *terra sigillata* indicated that occupation began not later than the middle of the third century.

Instead of extending one line of buildings at right angles to the dwelling-house, the villa-owner might lay out two such parallel lines each side of his yard. Typical of such a plan is Brading in the Isle of Wight (Fig. 32). Its layout stands intermediate between the farmhouse arranged with outbuildings on each side of the yard on to which it faces, and the fully developed courtyard villa. In this case, a tripartite house faced eastward on to a yard enclosed by a wall; a large basilical building for hands lay along the north side of the court, and opposite along the south side was a three-roomed building (xxxii–xxxiv) with attached pillared barn. The east side of the yard was closed by another wall, and it seems that a second outer yard lay to east, of which one building only on the south was dug out. A road ran round the north and north-east side of the inner yard, entering by a gate in the east enclosing wall. The basilical building had evidently been modified more than once, for the west half had been completely rebuilt at a time when the dwelling-house was constructed, a bath had been inserted in the east end of the south aisle and a corn-drier in the east end of the north aisle. The building appears to have possessed a large entrance with verandah in the middle of the south side and another at the east end, which was virtually open. This and the subsequent insertion of the corn-drier both indicate that in the

later period, if not before, agricultural work was carried on in the
eastern half of the building.

Other corn-driers were later inserted into building xxxvi to east
of the southern barn (xxxv), also between xxxv and xxxvi and into
the northern end of the east corridor of the dwelling-house. An
isolated square structure to the west of the residence (room xxxi)

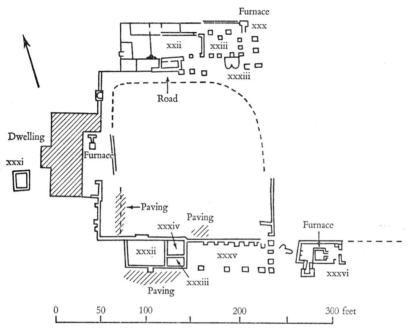

Fig. 32. Brading, Isle of Wight: Roman villa.

corresponded in position to the granaries at various continental villas
in Belgium and Germany;[1] it may have corresponded in function, for
there seems to have been a tendency to place the granary under the
master's eye for reasons of security and perhaps to be out of reach of
fire; room xxxi, however, had walls of normal thickness. We note
concerning Brading:

1. That the basilical building appears to have preceded the residence
as we know it; there may have been an earlier dwelling a little farther
to the east.

[1] Isolated granaries in Belgium and Germany: Aiseau (de Maeyer, RV Bel., p. 63);
Altstatt bei Messkirch (BJ 74, 1879, p. 54; Building C) Pforzheim (BRGK VI, 1910,
p. 61, Abb. 6), Building D; Bierlingen (Paret et al., Die Römer in Württemburg, III,
Stuttgart, 1928–32, p. 120, Abb. 77).

2. There is very generous accommodation for hay (building xxxv) indicating the maintenance of a fair number of stock; building xxxii–xxxiv next to it was probably for cattle, and this is confirmed by its dimensions. Between twenty and twenty-two head could have been housed. On the other hand xxxii is close to the residence, with which it was contemporary and it would be natural to expect stock to have been accommodated in the eastern outer yard.

3. The later period shows a development of corn-growing, as is indicated by the addition of four corn-driers.

4. The insertion of one of these into the front corridor of the main house, and of another into building xxxvi, previously containing a hypocaust and coloured wall-plaster, points to a decline of standards and an adaptation of residential amenities to workaday needs of intensified production, perhaps when the proprietor had removed elsewhere.

The Bignor villa is in a certain sense a development of this type of plan, and will be described in detail below. It is on the way to the fully developed courtyard type, in which the outbuildings are distributed with greater or lesser continuity about one or more courtyards, either forming an enclosed court with the residence or enclosing one or more separate additional yards. The completest and perhaps simplest example is Pitney (Som), which will be described later in connection with the subject of farming technique.

Llantwit Major (Glamorgan) may be classified as a double courtyard farm. Its residence faces east; it was a winged corridor dwelling surrounded by an earthwork, probably to exclude livestock or to secure drainage. The winged house defined the inner yard, which was not, however, shut off from the east. A basilical building yielding evidence of corn-grinding, corn-drying, and also of habitation, closed the south side of the outer area, being clearly the hands' quarters. This area was closed on the east by two end-to-end barnlike structures, the southerly (21 feet wide) divided into three rooms, the northerly (25 feet wide) undivided. These may be classified respectively as byres and a fodder store.

The north wing of the dwelling-house threw off to its east end another range at right angles to northwards; this was devoted to smithery and metal-work. Nash-Williams noted that Llantwit represents a transitional stage from the single to the double-yarded plan; the farm was occupied from the late second century, but the dwelling-house was abandoned in the mid-fourth when the basilical building continued to be lived in. At a later stage, an iron-smelting furnace was inserted into the baths of the former. Thus in the later fourth century the landlord was absent and the character of the establishment became entirely agricultural and industrial, probably under a bailiff, suffering the cultural decline and adaptation to more exclusively economic purposes common in villas at that time.

Woodchester (Glos) was one of the largest and the most fully developed of the double courtyard villas (Fig. 33); its outer third court is largely unexcavated, hence much of the agricultural aspect of the estate remains a closed book to us. The house faced south-east; the south-west and north-east sides of the outer yard were flanked by oblong blocks of approximately similar size; the wall dividing the inner from the outer court was pierced by a monumental entrance consisting of a gatehouse and two flanking rooms or subsidiary doors. The south-west block, in which no mosaics east found, contained a long room (59) divided by a corridor and court from a further range of smaller rooms along the north-east side facing on to the main court (51–4). A possible explanation of this building is that it was a combined byre and farmhands' quarters; this is suggested by the breadth of the long room 49, across the north-west end of the building, 13 feet. Its length was 78 feet. Rooms 56 and 59 were 20 feet 9 inches and 23 feet in breadth respectively, and may well have been stalls, while the hands would have lived in rooms 51–4. The general plan is not unlike that of the large stable-block at Bauselenne-te-Mettet, Belgium. It would seem anomalous to have the stock on the south-west side of the yard, but the site is sheltered against wind on both the west and east sides; there may, moreover, be a further explanation, arising out of the use of the opposite north-eastern block. This consisted of a series of rooms ranged about an internal court or hall; in general plan and character it resembles the two oblong buildings (B and C) flanking the residence at Darenth; of these the westerly (B) must originally have accommodated hands, but was later (Period II) converted to a fullery; the easterly (C) was probably built in Period II as a dyeing plant in connection with the same industry. All the features of the north-east block at Woodchester support its use for agricultural or industrial purposes. The width of the walls (3 feet) shows a second storey or at least a considerable height, and the east wall, which faced downhill, was strengthened by six buttresses. A room on the north-west side (39) possessed a furnace with a long flue to develop a strong draught, heating a horizontal tubular hypocaust under a cement floor. In room 38, immediately to north-east, was a basin drained by a lead pipe. The long south-west room (43) was entered by a broad door 8 feet 8 inches in width, evidencing the bringing in or out of bulk produce, and the long north-east chamber (42) had a floor raised on two dwarf walls along its greatest length to conserve the stored contents from damp. The wider interval between two buttresses on

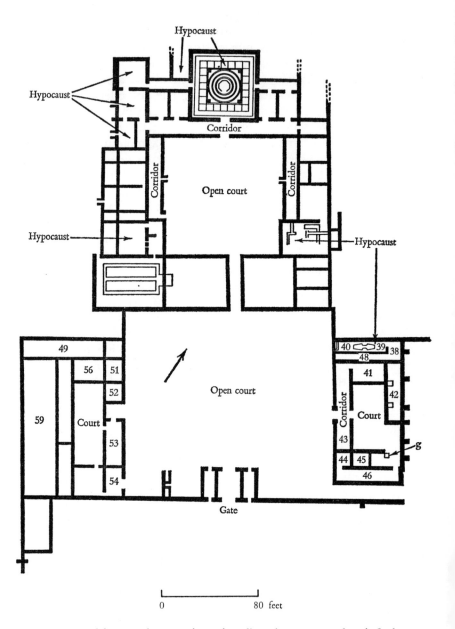

Fig. 33. Woodchester, Gloucestershire: the villa and its inner yard with flanking
outbuildings, probably a byre (west) and malting house (east).

the outer side of this room points to the existence of a broad entrance for bulk deliveries (not necessarily at ground level), and a granary with a capacity of some 3,000 bushels is indicated.

The planned order of an industrial process is here discernible – perhaps a malting establishment.[1]

There were, however, villas whose residences occupied their own enclosure, their outbuildings being confined to an outer court in which they might be ranged along the sides or more freely distributed. Typical of such a plan is Apethorpe (N'hants). The house faced roughly south, and a basilical building on the west side of the yard lay half in the inner, half in the outer enclosure, but a peculiar inner curved wall and another wall-length leaving its west side at an acute angle make one suspect two periods or more in this quarter. The east part of the south side of the inner yard was closed by a bath-range, and the east side by undefined buildings. A pitched road entered the inner enclosure by a gate between the baths and the basilical block. Other unexcavated buildings extended along the east edge of the outer court. The west wall of the basilical building was extended north into a curve to reach the corner of the dwelling-house, a feature also found in an exactly analogous position at Southwick (Suss). At Apethorpe, abutting on this wall from the outside, was an irregularly laid out long building, broader in the south than the north, and the north wall 'raked' to the southern. It recalls the cowhouses at Graux, Burgweinting, and Mangravets Wood. The internal dimensions were 19 feet at the north end and 22 feet at the south; the length, 55 feet. In old Welsh farms, cowhouses in which stalls were arranged across the building varied from 18 feet 5 inches to 21 feet 1 inch in breadth. The accommodation at Apethorpe would have been sufficient for some twelve or sixteen head. The position of this byre is exceptional, for it lay between the wind and the dwelling, but its shape and dimensions speak plainly for its identity.

Another instance of the type is North Wraxhall (Wilts), an account of which will be deferred because of the evidence it embodies on tenurial and agricultural development.

In addition to the above types of farm layout, there are a number of instances whose arrangement corresponds to none of them.

[1] There is a superficial resemblance to the east drying plant at Darenth, but this is not a fullery, for there are no beating platforms. It may be suggested that the grain was brought into the granary by the eastern entrance; sacks could have been weighed at ''g,'' where a stout pedestal may have been a support for a heavy pair of scales. Sorted and sifted in 44 and 45, the grain returned by passage 46. Steeping went on in 38, drying in 39, cooling in 40 and 43. From there the malt was taken to a boiler for brewing. Cooling and bottling were perhaps done in the outermost yard.

East Grimstead, well but incompletely excavated, consisted of an east-west block facing south upon a walled yard. An unexcavated building seems to have lain south-west of the house, probably at the south-west corner of the yard. The construction of the dwelling-house itself was not clear; six rooms were concentrated at the west end, and the rest appeared to form a broad rectangle containing three rooms at the north-east corner (these yielded a sickle and pruning-hook), and a bath-block in the south-east corner. A gate or wide door entered the block between these two groups of rooms. It was not entirely evident whether the vacant intervening area between the walls was a yard, or had been roofed. The tripartite arrangement of both the western and eastern ends suggested that the whole had originally composed a basilical plan, but the dimensions (140 by 50 feet internally) were so considerable as to make this questionable. Abutting on the south side of the house, south of the narrower west block, a detached cottage served as a store, yielding iron tools. Outside the enclosure to east was a square walled curtilage for stock or heavy agricultural implements (36 by 33 feet). In the habitation block, a corn-drier had later been inserted into one of the three north-eastern rooms; two more into the vacant intervening area. The establishment possessed two bath-houses additional to that already mentioned, one immediately to south of room 4, the other outside the enclosure to east and south of the curtilage.

Several points may be noted about this farm. (1) The layout is accurate and all buildings have a uniform bearing, but there is little luxury. (2) Corn, sheep, cattle-raising, and possibly fruit-growing are indicated (the second and third by animal bones). (3) Evidence showed that all three baths were in use together, even if they were not installed contemporarily. (Coin of Constantine I near 1; of Constantine II from 2, of Valentinian from 3.) But 3 fell into partial disuse at a later date and was readapted for living in. (4) The later insertion of corn-driers indicates the agricultural intensification and brutal utilitarianism of the later period; one of the three furnaces yielded New Forest pottery, i.e. it was in use in the third or fourth century; and the same may be safely assumed for the others. Occupation in the farm seems to have begun before the later second century.

It is abundantly clear that East Grimstead, like Stroud which will be discussed below, possessed bathing accommodation in excess of the needs of the hands resident on the site itself. East Grimstead must therefore have served as a centre for neighbouring inhabitants who dwelt and farmed farther afield. But the house is not luxurious and was not the seat of a proprietor, but of a bailiff, and the accurate mathematical planning of the buildings reinforces this impression.

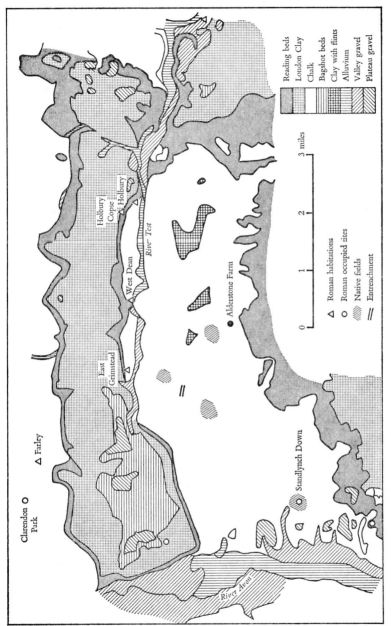

Reading beds
London Clay
Chalk
Bagshot beds
Clay with flints
Alluvium
Valley gravel
Plateau gravel

△ Roman habitations
○ Roman occupied sites
 Native fields
═ Entrenchment

0   1   2   3 miles

Clarendon Park ○

△ Farley

Holbury [Copse] [Holbury]

West Dean

River Test

East Grimstead

River Avon

Alderstone Farm

Standlynch Down

Fig. 34. The surroundings of the villas of West Dean and East Grimstead, with their soils.

The area of land to whose exploitation East Grimstead was party can be defined with some accuracy on the basis of geology (Fig. 34). It consisted of a long strip of chalk country sandwiched between the impermeable wooded London Clay to north and the alluvium or gravels of the River Test to south. Between the London Clay and the chalk lay a further narrow belt of Reading beds (upper greensand) whose junction with the former created a fertile loam productive in corn. Three further sites are known in this zone, viz. West Dean, at its centre near the Wiltshire-Hampshire border; Holbury, at its east end; and a third/ fourth-century occupation site at Holbury Copse, a quarter of a mile from the last. In addition, various coins (Antoninus Pius, Faustina) are recorded from West Dean parish. It is notable that all were on the north side of the stream, and the well-defined chalk strip on that side would have constituted the main nucleus of their arable. The West Dean villa was an establishment of importance, with a residence of some pretensions; to its north at right angles lay a bath-block, and in line with it to east, a basilical building for hands and bailiff, with an additional bath. To north-east again was a well-constructed basilical building combining hands' quarters and accommodation for seven pairs of cows or oxen. Holbury, on the other hand, was a small basilical building 60 by 54 feet, well fitted to be a tenant farm or the quarters of labourers. It is notable that here were found no fewer than three belt-buckles of the type studied by Sonia Hawkes and G. C. Dunning and established by them as being associated with the presence of barbarian troops in Britain in the later fourth and the first half of the fifth century. Finds suggest their presence also in other villas of the south and east of Britain at this period. It would therefore seem probable that East Grimstead, West Dean, and Holbury formed part of one estate; their mutual relationship, taken with the plan of East Grimstead and the finds at Holbury, suggest a strictly controlled colonate and a body of troops concerned with protection against external aggressors or internal unrest, or both.

A development of the single residence with farm-buildings scattered about it, seems to be the originally self-contained farm residence which later acquires outhouses arranged around an enclosed farmyard. A case is Clanville (Hants). Here the farm may have evolved from a steading of the Early Iron Age type as known at Woodcuts, for earlier ditches were found to the west of the house. The house, of basilical type, faced east and showed two periods at least, the latter involving the insertion of further rooms in the aisles, and also an extension of the north end. The explanation is the relegation of hands, stock, and crops to outbuildings around the farmyard at whose south-west corner the dwelling lay. Not much is known of the outbuildings at

Clanville; building 2 had no rooftiles or pavements, and its upper parts were evidently of timber; it was therefore a farm-building. The building along the east side, on the other hand, had at least one hypo-caust, and would have housed farmhands. A wall leaving the south side of the yard at right angles in a southerly direction showed that at least one other enclosure lay on that side; in view of the fact that the east or leeward side of yard I was closed by the hands' quarters, which occupied a position where normally livestock would have been expected, it is very probable that yard II was a stockyard, but certainty is impossible. Clanville presents, in short, a case of decentralization: a once self-contained basilical house, housing master, hands, stock, and produce, is decentralized so that the last three found their accommodation round the yard or yards outside.

Another incomplete and less orthodox plan is that of Thistleton Dyer (Rut). A small corridor residence with short flanking wings built in the early fourth century to face south, stood at the centre of farm-buildings which surrounded it on all sides. An important group lay south of the dwelling, but could not be wholly investigated; a long straight wing also extended eastward from the main house, beginning behind it. It took the form of a long barn about 26 feet in internal width, with what appears to be a byre (internal width 14 feet) across its east end. Two attached rooms on the north look very like granaries, but cannot be defined with certainty. After the middle of the fourth century the entire barn was subdivided equally down its entire length, undoubtedly to house cattle, and a narrow structure was attached to the old byre on the east; its internal breadth, hardly more than eight feet, suggests a pigsty. It is evident that this period beheld a considerable expansion of the cattle-breeding branch.

We must now devote some attention to several villas the layout details of which are sufficiently known to afford us some information on both agricultural and tenurial development.

Langton (East Riding, Yorks) is an example of the enclosed farm surrounded by scattered farm-buildings; this type is common in the Rhineland and Württemburg. At Köln-Müngersdorf, a well-developed example thoroughly excavated, in the ultimate development a big residence with many outbuildings, evidenced large-scale grain farming; here all outbuildings, including granaries, byres, stables, pigsty, sheep-fold, cart-shed, and rick-yard, were placed to east of the dwelling-house; the sheep-fold was tucked away in the north-east angle of the yard well out of the wind, and the pigsty lay in the same quarter, to leeward of the main body of buildings. Stables and cart-shed were on the south.

Langton (Fig. 35) was not comparable in wealth or scale to Köln-

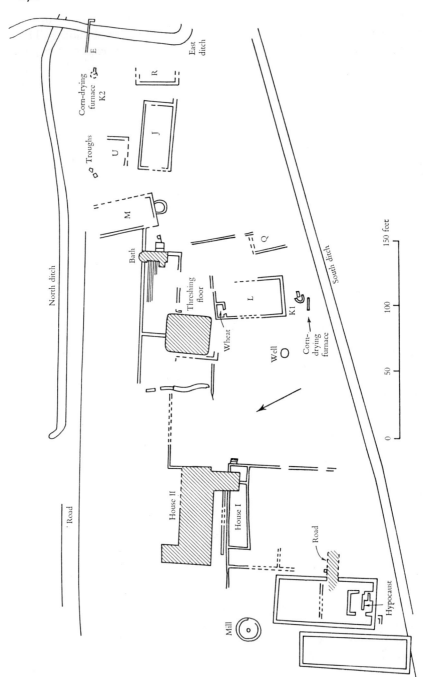

Fig. 35. Langton, East Riding, Yorkshire: the Roman farm and its outbuildings.

Müngersdorf, but a considerable part of it was laid bare by the spade. It was not proved that the farm was surrounded by a bank on all sides, but such banks certainly enclosed it on the north and south. Here a comprehensive farm-complex did not emerge until the fourth century. The buildings prior to that period were somewhat confused and difficult of interpretation, incomplete, and probably not all excavated. All that can be said is that most of them belonged to the third century, and the succession of erections or modifications within that century suggests an intensive development, when one dwelling-house seems first to have received a bath, then perhaps to have been supplemented by another simpler dwelling-house farther to westward (House I). In the early fourth century the obscurity clears. A new dwelling was built to the north of House I (House II); two large barns appeared to the south-west of House II, also a circular mill-house that would have required a beast or several slaves to work it. To east a threshing floor was laid out, to the south of which was a long outhouse (L) with a small internal room at the north-west corner and a part of the east wall open to the yard. To the south and east respectively were two corn-driers. The farm as a whole had shifted westward from the previous site. The more easterly of the two barns was divided into two by a cross-wall, the southern room being partly used as a bath and entered by a large doorway from the east. It is difficult to define the use of these barns more precisely, except to say that they are unlikely to have been for stock since they lay to windward of the farm; the large door and approach road of the easterly building show it was meant to be entered by carts, and hay or corn in the ear are implied. The mill lay immediately to north-west of it; it is therefore natural to see the north room of this barn as the granary.

Building L, with its small north-west room for fodder or cowman, and its width of 26 feet (13×2) was almost certainly a byre, the more so in the light of its wide entrance towards the north-east corner. The accommodation would have been for between ten and thirteen head on the west side (the total interior length was 53 feet), and eight along the east side, and this suggests that the easterly stall housed four pairs of oxen. The ox-bones found during excavation represented at least three, probably five or six individuals, perhaps the farm's draft-stock at the moment of abandonment.

Although the fourth-century farm at Langton was not symmetrically laid out, its arrangements nevertheless show some care. The drying furnaces were placed to leeward, to obviate risk of fire, and the stock-buildings likewise, to avoid odours. The threshing floor was located close to the cattle-byre (corn was actually found in the small north-west room of the latter), suggesting that grain was also fed to the stock. It looks as though the dungyard lay to the east of the cow-shed, in view of the eastern entrance of the latter, and of the finding of cattle-troughs in the same direction. The easterly ditch perhaps helped to drain off excess moisture from that area. The barns, on the other hand, were relegated to windward, not only to be out of the way of the sparks from the corn-driers, but also to be under the eye of the master or bailiff in the dwelling-house. They may have been placed where they were partly as windbreaks; Corder noted the extremely exposed nature of the site, and flora from the well were interpreted as indicating trees planted as a windbreak on one side of the farmyard. The barns were nevertheless easily accessible from the threshing floor and close to the mill. But if hay was kept, they were not well placed to afford fodder for the animals. Somewhat paradoxically, the easterly barn housed a bath in its south end, which may explain why it was abolished in the reconstruction of the later fourth century.

To the fourth century belongs a well-paved road along the north side of the enclosure, indicating the need of improved communication with the outer world, presumably for the transport of produce to the local markets. The effect of the fourth-century plan was to form two yards, the westerly south of the dwelling, and limited by the house, barns, and byre, and on the north by a wall; the easterly between the byre and the easternmost ditch. Thus Langton exhibits what is dis-cernible elsewhere in the later stage in different form, namely, the development of double yards. But here both were economic in function, and there is no sharp separation of the agricultural and residential. In this sense Langton is a working farm pure and simple, and as such may well have been the home of a bailiff or tenant rather than of an independent farmer. Two additional features lend colour to such a supposition, namely: (a) that in the fourth century a larger residence (House I) gave place to a smaller one, although production expanded, and (b) there are no identifiable separate quarters for farmhands; the farm staff must have lived together with the bailiff or tenant in the dwelling-house. If he was a tenant, he perhaps leased his land from the owner of the house known to have existed a quarter of a mile to the west.

The villa of Stroud near Petersfield was extensively excavated, and most of its buildings would seem to have been found (Fig. 36). The large basilical house faced south, composing most of the north side of a nearly square farmyard. As at Clanville, rooms had later been inserted into it in the western half (Period 3), but the original (Period 2) walls themselves contained reused material, and a Period 1, anterior to the basilical house, must be inferred. The Period 2 building possessed projecting wing-rooms (*Eckrisaliten*) at the south-west and south-east angles, the south-westerly being later extended westward – probably for an upper storey. At the south-east corner of the house lay an octagonal structure (of Period 3 date) the problem of whose function has elicited various suggestions; that it was religious is indicated by the finding of a pit in its interior, best explained as of sacrificial nature, and paralleled at the temples at Frilford (Berks) and Jordon

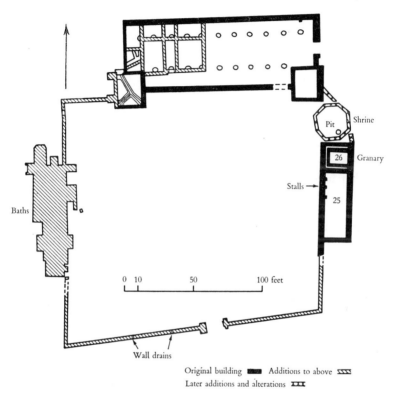

Fig. 36. Stroud, Hampshire: the aisled farmhouse and its yard.

Hill (Dors), where such pits contained dedicatory deposits. In a villa, the building would seem to find an analogy at Great Witcombe (Glos).

Immediately to the south of the octagonal shrine a long rectangular outbuilding lay along the east side of the yard; it was divided into a smaller northern compartment 18 by 17 feet internally, and a long room on the south (25), 52 by 18 feet internally. The northern room (the excavator's 26) possessed an internal masonry offset all round, whose function was to support a timber floor over a void, and to maintain the contents in a dry condition; there can be little doubt that this was a granary, parallels to which can be cited, for instance, at Iwerne II and at Mayen in the Eiffel. If its height is taken at ten feet, the capacity would have been 1,569 bushels. In the long room (25) to the south, the northern part of the west wall possessed on the inner side three buttresses or counterforts that clearly divided stalls, whose width of eight feet leaves no doubt that each accommodated a pair of oxen. Three such teams, on Columella's figures (*De rust. re*, XII, 13), were sufficient to work 300 *iugera* (187·5 acres) of arable, including fallow. The rest of the outhouse (25) may have been used for other stock, or alternatively for hay and other produce. In addition a timber outbuilding seems to have existed, probably in the form of a lean-to shed along the west part of the south wall of the yard to the west of the gateway. It was not found, but its existence was inferred by the finding of two drains piercing the yard wall in this sector. It is also possible that the dungheap occupied this area, conveniently near the gate to be carted to the fields during the winter.

Along the west wall of the yard lay a large bath-building embodying two distinct ranges both of Period 3, and the excavators correctly noted that its scale far exceeded the needs of the farm-staff alone. It obviously served a broader area, whether on a commercial basis, or because there was a surrounding population connected with the farm but living on its own tenant holdings. Our knowledge neither of the villa nor of the district is such as to enable us to say which explanation is correct; the Ridgehanger farmstead not far to the west may have represented the type of peasant who used this bath-building, and the steading seems to have been essentially for the rearing of pigs and cattle in a woodland milieu, suggesting a dependent tenant character. Its occupation extended into the fourth century, as at Stroud. On the other hand, the small granary of Stroud does not suggest that it was ever the centre of a colonate estate. Yet if the octagonal building was a shrine, it was a large one, and like the baths, it may well have served more than the farm's immediate occupants. The aisled house too is very large. Whether or not Stroud was the focus of a colonate, therefore, it was something in the nature of a local centre. On the other hand, there seems no way of explaining its small granary as contrasted with its bath and shrine, except by supposing that the villa and its surrounding peasant population formed part of a larger whole – i.e. a very large estate, and that the produce from the surrounding holdings went, not to Stroud, but to some more important centre. It is possible that the local name of Liss, which lies about four miles to the north-east, and is a Celtic word meaning 'palace', preserves a memory of the still undiscovered centre of that estate.[1] In this case,

---

[1] Liss: Ekwall, *Concise Oxford Dictionary of English Place-names*, p. 286, ad voc. Cf. R. Lennard in *Wirtschaft und Kultur; Festschrift zum 70. Geburtstag von Alfons Dopsch*, Baden-bei-Wien, 1938, p. 62.

it seems possible to see in the evolution of Stroud two stages, in the first of which it constituted the home of a British owner whose family was in some way associated with a cult of local importance; in the second his estate was absorbed into a still larger unit. The social and tenurial implications of these phases will be discussed later.

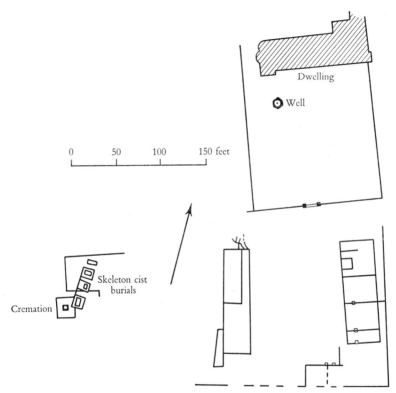

Fig. 37. North Wraxhall, Wiltshire: the Roman villa.

On the plan of Stroud we may summarize that in Period 3 there was a partial decentralization of economic functions, the owner or bailiff adopting separate quarters in the west of the basilical house, while the hands continued to be housed in the eastern half of the same building. Stock and grain were transferred to buildings round the farmyard. It is this decentralization, complete agriculturally but incomplete socially, which favours the view that the house in Period 3 was the seat of a bailiff rather than of an independent owner.

North Wraxhall (Wilts) presents an interesting plan excavated by an antiquary, Poulett Scrope, in some respects ahead of his age (Fig. 37).

A corridor house faced southward over an internal yard containing a well; from this a gate gave southward into a larger yard stretching farther westward, also walled, and containing farm-buildings. Along the east of this lay a long block 112 by 35 feet, whose internal arrangements were not completely elucidated, but of which enough remained (including three pillars or post-bases) to show that it had been a basilical building later divided off into rooms by cross-walls. Other buildings, incompletely known, also embodying pillars or post-bases, were attached to its south end in the south-east corner of the enclosure. To the west of this building, another long building lay north-south, measuring internally 112 by 30 feet; within its northern part another long compartment or building, 50 by 20 feet, was divided off against the west wall. To the south-west of the whole was attached a long irregular structure 43 feet from north to south, its north end 7 feet 5 inches in width, its southern end ten feet. On these latter buildings we may observe: (1) the dimensions of the inner division are those of a stall or stable; (2) the building as a whole is exactly the same length as the basilical block; (3) the axis of the former is at a slight angle to the perpendicular of the house, whereas the latter lies at a strict right angle to it; (4) the outer attached irregular structure can only be a pigsty.

The early excavation of the site does not enable us to say whether the inner subdivision of the west long building was a later addition, or superseded the latter. But there is some auxiliary evidence. The west building is orientated with a fourth building to westward, incompletely known, which appears to have been coeval with a cremation burial in a square enclosure to south of it, but to have been superseded by an inhumation cist cemetery in the third or fourth century. It has been noted that the basilical building is at right angles to the dwelling-house, while the west long building lies slightly out of perpendicular to it. The urn found in the bath of the dwelling-house is second century in date, indicating a *terminus ante quem* for its occupation; the well in the inner yard yielded coins of the Lower Empire "low down." The coins from the site as a whole began with Trajan, but nearly all were of the third and fourth centuries. *Terra sigillata*, however, showed occupation before the middle of the third century and some (the stamp of PVGN on Dragendorff 44; AMM(o) of Rheinzabern) was Antonine. The sequence would therefore seem to have been: (1) the building of the main house not later than the later second century, and with it the basilical outbuilding, to house hands and stock; (2) the construction of the long building as a stable or byre to west, and of the structure to the west of it again, not earlier than the later second century or later than the third. (Such a dating is supported by Steinhausen's attribution of square cist-burials to the second century in the Rhineland.) When this occurred it is possible that the eastern basilical building was reconstructed to hold an increasing number of hands, and the livestock previously housed there was moved into the new byre, which was exactly the same length. In the same period the pigsty was built against the south-west of the byre, indicating a grain-surplus used for fattening, i.e. an increase of corn-growing contemporary with an expansion of staff; (3) the westernmost buildings were superseded by an inhumation cemetery in the later third or fourth century, and the plentiful Constantinian coinage of the villa might be taken to push this event to the middle of the fourth century. The falling out of use of these quarters suggests a devolution of activity, in harmony with the construction inside the long building of new reduced accommodation; the ox-teams were reduced by half, and perhaps some were distributed to tenants, i.e. the hands who had previously occupied the western outbuilding. It was to this time that belonged, apparently, the "Type II" buckle associated by Sonia Hawkes and Dunning with the presence of elements of the later fourth and fifth-century British garrison, and the crescentic horse ornament made of boars' tusks, to be ascribed to the same source.

Thus, in the second century the villa seems to have been engaged in mixed farming including both arable and stock. In the later second or third century there was an expansion of staff, perhaps of teams, and of corn-production, and fattening of pigs with surplus grain was introduced. In the later third or fourth century, however, hands and stock were reduced, and we may suppose that hands were settled out as *coloni*. But when this took place, the villa probably remained their centre, if we may so interpret the presence of the inhumation cemetery which superseded the westernmost building of the southern yard.

Pitney (Som) exhibits a very large courtyard (325 by 210 feet) with interesting outbuildings of which we would gladly know much more than we do (Fig. 38). A handsome residence faced eastward onto a courtyard completely enclosed by walls; the whole of the east side was blocked by a continuous range of outbuildings, and others lay along the north and south limits of the yard. The southern buildings, consisting of a single range of rooms of varying length and a uniform interior width of 12 feet, ended in a bath-block to east. This suggests that they were living quarters for hands, a notion supported by the presence of three plaster floors and a flag pavement laid one over the other, showing long use and continuous occupation. The width of the walls (about $2\frac{1}{2}$ and three feet) suggests a second storey. The use of the northern range, impinging at its west end on the north-east corner of the dwelling-house, is more problematic. It consisted of

a long room 75 feet in length with a small compartment attached at
the east end 12–13 feet long; the internal width was no more than
a uniform 8 feet, and the walls were notably thick – about 3 feet.
There are two possible explanations for its use: an *ergastulum* where
slaves were confined at night, or a pigsty, with an end compartment
for the swineherd or for farrowing sows. A structure interpreted as
a sty at Köln-Müngersdorf was similarly without apparent access or
internal subdivisions, and possessed a hearth at one end. Eight feet is

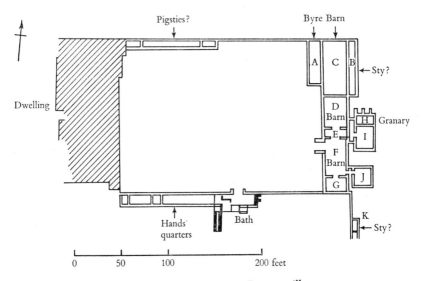

Fig. 38. Pitney, Somerset: Roman villa.

indeed a common depth of sties in modern farming practice. The
walls of the Müngersdorf sty were 60 cm. thick, i.e. 24 inches. Pigs
need strong enclosures, but the 3-feet walls at Pitney indicate an
upper storey for a loft, perhaps for pig-food, and the storage of pig-food
in a storey above the sties is a modern practice in Scandinavia. If this
was a sty, however, though down-wind, it was unpleasantly near the
house.[1]

   The northern block of the eastern range was a tripartite basilica-like
building with nave and long side-rooms (not, I think, aisles). The
compartment composing the eastern room (B) measured 8 feet
internally and possessed a stone floor; its walls were 3 feet thick and
its dimensions convey that it was another pigsty. The western room
of the same building (A) with earth floor measured 45 by 13 feet

---

   [1] Sty at Köln-Müngersdorf: Fremersdorf, *Römische Gutshof Köln-Müngersdorf*,
Berlin, 1938, pp. 38–9, 120.

internally, suggesting a cowhouse with accommodation for ten to
thirteen head. The central long room (C), 57 by 22 feet, also with
earth floor, would have served as a barn for fodder. The whole plan
recalls the quadruple range of Building J at Marburg near Pommern
on the Mosel, Hartlip Building K, and Bignor Building 71–4.

The two rooms (D, F) to south were divided from one another by
a passage (E) running east into a mosaic-paved lobby which connected
the range with a detached block outside (H-I). This block was a
two-roomed building, with east wall 2 feet 6 inches thick and the
north (outer) wall of the northern smaller room (H) strongly reinforced
with three external buttresses. The west wall of this room was also
2 feet 6 inches thick, as opposed to that of the southerly room (I),
which was thinner. The northern room, then, was carried up to a
second storey level or more, and its walls had to take an outward
stress; its floor was of *opus signinum*, and the whole building is analogous
to that of the granary at Stroud. Indeed, it probably is a granary,
placed next to a room for the staff responsible for its care and supervision. The southernmost part of the eastern range south of the
passage consisted of a large stone-paved room 39 by 22 feet (F), and
a narrow compartment to south (G) paved with tesserae. The first
gave access eastward by another lobby with mosaic, to a detached
outer chamber (J), apparently also quarters for staff. It was entered
from the farmyard by a large door covered with a projecting porch,
nine feet wide, clearly for bulk deliveries. This must therefore have
been a barn, and the whole series A-M can be defined as a range of
store-rooms for fodder, grain, and produce, closely associated with
quarters for the supervisory staff and with cowhouse and pigsty.

The granary, H, internally ten by eleven feet, possessed, on a
presumed height of twelve feet, a capacity of 2,000 bushels. (Two-thirds
would be 1,334 bushels.) If the stock housed in room A was five teams of
oxen, an arable of some 500 *iugera* or 312 acres is implied, and a yield
of eight bushels the acre if half were fallowed. But we may suspect
further storage of grain, for instance, above the pigsties along the north
of the yard, and probably the harvest was considerably larger.

Another yard, not excavated, lay to the south of that just described;
the north end of its eastern wall was discovered, with the end of
a narrow outbuilding (K) abutting along its outer side. This had an
internal width of six–seven feet, and was perhaps another pigsty.

The Pitney establishment has the marks of a carefully planned
farm-complex. The layout, in so far as we know it, looks like the
result of a single coordinated design, and recalls that of Southwick in
Sussex, which also enclosed an inner yard on all four sides. At Pitney
there is careful attention to storage of crops and to their supervision,

and the main granary is placed outside the yard to be away from the bathhouse. Pig-keeping seems to have been important here, and the pigs would seem to have been fattened – this is the significance and function of penning pigs in the yard as opposed to running them freely in the woods – implying a comfortable surplus of grain and a ready market in ham and lard – perhaps the army. The villa is not far from the Roman road connecting Ilchester with the mouth of the Parrett, whence an easy ferry could take produce direct to Caerleon or to the fortress of Cardiff, and the placing of the Welsh forts to command sea-borne connections has been noted by Nash-Williams.[1] Possibly a similar economic rôle was filled by Woolaston Pill villa, where pig-bones and large millstones showed a preoccupation with pig-rearing and corn-growing, in close proximity to Caerleon. It may further be noted that Pitney occupies the calcareous silty clay of the Somerton series, which is poor pasture, but is today rotated between wheat, beans, and oats. Thus while the villa's herd would find excellent summer grazing on the marshes of Somerton Moor to the north, they would have to be stall-fed in winter.

The outbuildings of the large Sussex villa of Bignor were excavated with reasonable completeness (Fig. 39). They lie in a well-defined area enclosed by a wall to the east of the residence, and to its leeward. The plan belongs to that group of villas, generally of the fourth century, where agricultural buildings are separated from the residence in one or more distinct yards. But it also resembles in a certain sense those continental establishments (e.g. Odrang, Blankenheim, Chiragan) where the residence was confined to one end, and was walled off from the agricultural and industrial buildings, which were arranged in rows down the long axis of an outer yard and at right angles to the dwelling. Bignor, though it did not attain to this scale, may have been influenced by them.

At Bignor there are four known structures, the first being an unroofed square enclosure (65), either a stock pound or a curtilage for carts and agricultural equipment. The fact that its southern wall was accurately aligned with a building to its east (66) which can be shown to be a sheepfold makes it probable that it too was for livestock. The easterly structure measured 120 feet in length and 24 feet in internal width. The easterly of its three divisions was a small room such as is often found at the end of Roman stock buildings; this and similarity of depth to a fold at the Roman villa of Köln-Müngersdorf make it probable that this was a sheepfold holding about 197 head. The third building, in the north-east angle of the yard, is 77 by 21 feet internally. This depth resembles that of some old Welsh byres in which stalls

[1] *The Congress of Roman Frontier Studies, 1949*, ed. Birley, Durham, 1952, p. 70.

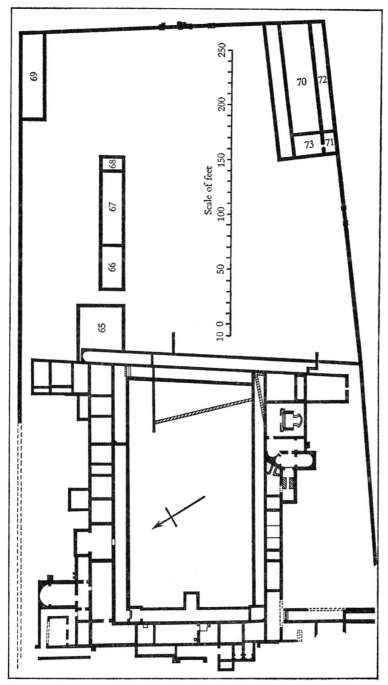

Fig. 39. Bignor, Sussex: the Roman villa and its farmyard.

are arranged across the long axis of the building; the Bignor structure
would have accommodated six rows of stalls, allowing 12–13 feet for
the depth of each stall including manger and feeding walk, each row
holding at least four beasts at four feet a head, with room for a gangway
down the side of the byre. This byre therefore housed some twenty-four
animals, and the even number suggests that here were stalled the
plough-teams of the villa, twelve in number. This supposition is
strengthened by the fact that there was additional accommodation for
cattle (fifty-five head) in the building occupying the south-east angle
of the yard.

This was a barn, divided into a nave and flanking aisles, the nave
and southern aisle having small rooms at their western ends for the
stockmen. The width of the aisles, 14 feet 6 inches, has a close affinity
to that of the buildings noted as byres in various ancient farmsteads
and also in Roman villas (see above, p. 148). At Bignor the central
nave would have served for storage, i.e. for grain and fodder, while
the aisles constituted self-contained byres with enough space both for
stalls and feeding walks. Allowing for four feet per head, there would
have been room for thirty head in the building's northern aisle and
for twenty-five in the southern. This knowledge of the villa's approximate barn capacity, and of the minimal number of stock which it was
able to winter, combined with a study of the farm's immediate
environment, will enable us to gain something like a comprehensive
notion of its extent and economy.[1] (See p. 212.)

We may now sum up, provisionally, the evidence on farm layout.
Only two Romano-British house plans can be regarded as having their
roots directly in the pre-Roman; these are the basilical or aisled house
and, apparently, the 'two-roomed' building. In the present state of
knowledge we know of only a few of the latter type which survived
as independent farmhouses (Iwerne "A" and "B"; Studland, Dors).
The former represents a self-contained farm and in origin, at least,
had an especially strong connection with stock rearing. Its social
significance must be considered elsewhere. The building recently
found at Wingham, Kent, basilical at first sight, is in reality a peristyle
building, and while the outer structure belonged to the first century
of our era, the peristyle was added later. The known certain houses

---

[1] Rooms at ends of Roman stock-buildings: e.g. Köln-Müngersdorf, Building
VII: Fremersdorf, op. cit., pp. 37, 119; Langton, Building L: Corder, Kirk, Langton,
p. 55; Bignor ox-byre; cf. Neufchâtel de Jemelle villa, Building C, where 4 feet
per head were allowed on de Maeyer's calculation, RV Bel., p. 92, and fig. 21 b;
at Köln-Müngersdorf, Fremersdorf, op. cit., p. 119, 4 feet are allowed per head, 10 feet
for depth of manger and stall; Stroud has similar accommodation.

of this type do not appear in Britain until the second century of the present era (possibly North Wraxhall; Landwade near Exning, Suff), and it often becomes functionally decentralized, most of its agricultural duties being relegated to outbuildings. It also begins to be built as the staff-quarters dependent on a landowner's residence. It becomes, in some cases, exclusively a stock-building (Spoonley Wood, Ickleton, West Dean).

The earliest known Romano-British farmhouses are circular huts, replaced directly, in the first stage of romanization, by strip-buildings or square huts. The few known parallels to the self-contained continental 'hall-*Eckrisalit*' house with *Wirtschafthalle* are such as to suggest that they were usually the seats of tenants or slave-gangs under the charge of a bailiff. (Titsey, Surrey; possibly Colerne, Wilts, in its first phase.) It was usually with the adoption of masonry dwellings (e.g. at Mansfield Woodhouse) that agricultural functions began to be separated from living quarters, but in the Cranbourne Chase farms separate stock and work-enclosures followed with varying rapidity – once fairly early in the Roman period, once only in the middle of the third century – without such a change taking place. The immediate adoption of fully-developed corridor houses, for example at Ditchley, in the later first or early second century, indicates a rapid economic development and the import of the design from outside the country. This is associated, at Ditchley, with the introduction of outbuildings for staff and, in all likelihood, for livestock. Yet while the well-planned farmyard could be laid out so early, as late as the early fourth century Langton could represent the small farmhouse with outbuildings scattered about it, not, it is true, without system, but with a certain asymmetry resulting from native tradition. At the other end of the scale stands East Grimstead, planned with a mathematical regularity, and we should recollect the basilical villa of West Blatchington (Suss), set close to a mathematically surveyed 'grid' of land-divisions. The native tradition could persist into the fourth century not only in the basilical building, and in the self-contained farmstead of Iwerne II, but in the 'linear' layout of such villas as Gayton Thorpe, representing a simplified version of the arrangement seen at Ronchinnes, Belgium, in which it is possible to perceive the final development of the combined stall and dwelling appearing in the two-roomed building.

In the Early Iron Age farmstead there was no distinction between agricultural and residential quarters, but some attention was paid to direction of wind and avoidance of fire, and animals were kept under control by the enclosure of working areas. Roman innovations in such settlements are the improvement of grain-drying plant, well-sinking as a means of water-supply, and the consequent ability to winter cattle near the upland farm, and so conserve manure.

A general feature of the romanized farm, indeed, is the attention to water-supply and to the planning of buildings with consideration for the prevailing wind: in the vast majority of cases villas have wells or are placed near streams, and water-supply is sometimes preferred to a dry site (e.g. Ely near Cardiff). Similarly there are only a few villa-residences that do not face south or east, to catch the sun or to turn their backs to the west wind, and outbuildings are either placed to leeward or out of line with the dwelling. In some cases the granary was placed near or abutting on the dwelling for reasons of security.

The technical implications of certain elementary improvements of the Roman period are considerable. The development of a farmyard distinct from the residential area, and usually supplied with water, meant the possibility of keeping stock at hand and using their manure for a longer period of the year. This meant the increase of farmyard manure which stood at the free disposal of the farmer, enabling him to plan his crops to a greater extent and to increase his yields. A planned stock yard also meant increased security against theft or wild animals. The pounds at Bignor, Otford, and probably East Grimstead, indicate systematic collection of dung, and the same seems to be the aim of guiding waste from the bath-house at Colerne into a rock-cut cesspit in the vicinity of an outhouse for livestock. Manure-collection was also aided by the erection of livestock buildings – stables, byres, folds or sties – and by the installation of latrines (e.g. at Southwick; perhaps at Woolaston Pill). Livestock buildings improved the health of the animals, reducing rheumatism, colds, hoof injuries, and other ailments. In some cases we see a very close association between the barns where grain and hay were stored (Brading, Pitney, Hartlip, Bignor) and the stalls, which speaks clearly for the wintering of considerable herds – especially at Hartlip and Bignor. The same interpretation is to be set upon the special stock-buildings seen at Ickleton, Spoonley Wood, West Dean, Thistleton Dyer, and probably Woodchester. Evidently the problem of winter fodder had been solved by the presence of a grain surplus, by the more efficient cutting of hay (see p. 82), and probably by the cultivation of legumes and roots. (See pp. 115–16.) In summer most of the stock would have gone to pasture, and here we may note the favourable position of some villas, including especially West Dean and Bignor, to utilize water-meadows for summer fattening. An example of the extensive grazing of herds seems to be furnished by the large cattle-enclosure of Mangravets Wood, near the Roman road running south from Maidstone. There is less evidence for the wintering of sheep in villas, but this seems to have been done with at least part of the flock at Bignor, where the fold was carefully placed to be out of the wind. Generally sheep-running must have retained its semi-transhumatory character in so far as the folds tended to remain apart from the farmsteads; at Bignor a kite-shaped enclosure on the scarp to the south of the villa certainly served the flock.[1]

The evidence of Pitney shows a close connection between pigsties and grain-storage. The usual method in ancient times and in the Middle Ages was to run swine freely in the woods to pick up their own living for most of the year, and doubtless their winter shelters were in pens removed from the farms. But the construction of solid sties in the farmyard implies fattening for pork and the presence of ample feed. This is likely to have included grain; at Köln-Müngersdorf Schmitz's analysis showed that the pigsty was introduced at a time when the farm went over from a preponderantly stock-raising economy to extensive grain-growing; one cattle-stall was demolished in the course of the third century and not replaced, while two granaries and the sty were erected in this century or later. A number of sources point to the increase of pork consumption in the Empire in the third century; the intensified grain-production of Köln-Müngersdorf could also be brought into connection with the increased demands of the Lower Rhine army under Albinus and Severus, and the fact that this region, unlike south and central Gaul, escaped the damage wrought by the civil wars of the period. At North Wraxhall too a pigsty indicated systematic fattening, and the same may have been practised at Hambleden (Bucks), where Cocks noted that the numerous pig-bones were chiefly those of stores and sucklers, meaning that the majority of the males and grown females were sent to market. At Hambleden intensive corn-production was marked. Woolaston Pill too showed a preoccupation both with pig-rearing and grain-growing. The same presence of a grain surplus over subsistence needs is evidenced at Woodchester, whether or not we are right in interpreting the north-east out-building of the outer yard as a malting establishment, since the granary is unmistakable. Periodical grain surplus is demonstrated by granaries here and elsewhere, and by the attention paid to dry storage. Such cases as the development of the farms at Catsgore, Mansfield Woodhouse, Park Street, and Ditchley, demonstrate a steady rise in productive capacity throughout the first, second, and (in the north)

[1] Dung-accumulation in Roman times: cf. Roman dung pit at Marburg (BJ., 101, p. 69, R); at Hulsberg, Holland – OM, I, 1907, pp. 13–14. Water-meadows: e.g. the alluvial banks of the Test between West Dean and Holbury, excellent for the spring forcing of lambs and the summer-grazing of cattle; cf. Colum. II, 17; Pliny, HN, XVIII, 67 (254, 258, 263). Present practices in Wiltshire: LUS, no. 87, Wilts, pp. 180–4; Brentnall, Carter, *The Marlborough Country*, London, 1932, p. 64. Bignor kiteshaped enclosure: Egg Bottom.

third centuries. The growth of Bignor from a lesser early farm of unestablished date to a winged corridor house in the third century and the systematic laying out of its second farmyard in the fourth, require an explanation in terms of considerable investment, successful production and enterprise, and a remarkable rise in the standard of living.[1]

There is, indeed, indication of a greater agricultural specialization among some of the farms: Pitney and Woolaston Pill paid attention to fat pork, Woodchester to grain-production, perhaps, *inter alia*, for malting, perhaps to cattle-rearing; Cromhall seems to have engaged in extensive corn-growing; Hambleden (Bucks) shows an almost unparalleled devotion to corn-production by the large number of its corn-driers, combining this branch, it seems, with piggeries and cattle reared for meat (see p. 182). If the preoccupation of Chedworth (Glos) with fulling was shown by the late Sir Ian Richmond to be illusory, Darenth's fulling industry may yet stand up to critical examination. At Appleton (Norf) horse and cattle bones showed a free-range herd reared for meat and probably for hides. A cattle yard may be noted at Otford (Kent) coming into use at the end of the second century, while Spoonley Wood, Ickleton, and Hartlip all possessed buildings for cattle-rearing on a respectable scale. At Ely near Cardiff an industrial economy was superseded in the later third century by agriculture, in which cattle-rearing played a part. The byre accommodation of Thistleton Dyer, occupied during the fourth century, indicated the organization of this branch on a very considerable scale.

On the other hand, it is a distinct question, how far the livestock branches became more important in the Romano-British rural economy during the later centuries of the province, and to what extent sheep-farming and the production of wool exceeded the cattle-raising branch in the later period. There may have been areas where stock-farming predominated. These problems will be discussed when an attempt is made to summarize the character of Roman agriculture in this country. (See pp. 208 sqq.)

Livestock apart, there is abundant evidence of intensified grain-production everywhere, more especially in the later period, in the form of corn-driers, as R. G. Goodchild has demonstrated. It is sometimes forgotten that if Darenth was adapted as a *fullonica* or fulling-mill, it was later re-adapted and the function reduced or abandoned. The insertion of corn-driers is nearly everywhere secondary or late, and carried out with a brutal indifference to other amenities in a fashion suggesting the semi-abandonment of the houses concerned to a lower

[1] Schmitz's analysis of Köln-Müngersdorf, BJ 139, 1934, pp. 80 sqq. Professor Frere's excavations: JRS XLVII, 1957, p. 223; XLIX, 1959, p. 131; LIII, 1963, p. 155.

standard of living and to exclusively utilitarian purposes. Some of the early cases (Woodcuts, West Blatchington) tend to confirm the hypothesis of state initiative, if Woodcuts was on state domain, and if the inclusion of West Blatchington, with its eleven corn-driers, in a mathematical field division suggestive of state action is similarly interpreted; at both places the first installations belonged to the period of the Severi. It is further to be observed that the finding of no fewer than seventy *stili* at Hambleden means a large clerical staff and checking of the produce, and if the farm was not a state concern, that its economy was probably geared to supplying the government. To such evidence may be added the conversion at Angmering (Suss) of a tower-like edifice, apparently a mausoleum, to use as a granary in the third or fourth century.[1]

II. THE HIGHLAND FARM

The highland zone of Britain is taken by historical geographers as the area north of a line drawn from the Dee round the south of the Peak District and northward of the East Riding. The line is, in effect, the northern limit of uninterrupted plainland, but Piggott has shown that until the Romans overran the Pennines and penetrated Scotland, agriculture remained largely in its Bronze Age phase in most of the region north and west of the 'Jurassic Way' that links the Cotswolds with the Humber, and throughout Yorkshire if the Yorkshire Wolds are excluded. The position in Wales was more complex, since Early Iron Age settlers of southern origin had certainly penetrated parts of the country, chiefly its southern part, about 400 B.C., and by about 300 B.C. a broader penetration of iron-users had taken place. In Scotland, too, iron-users of relatively advanced culture had settled in restricted groups by the first century B.C. and introduced the rotary quern; but by and large in the north British and Welsh regions of the highland zone, Bronze Age agriculture remained unmodified. In Cornwall and Devon too, which belong geographically in many senses to highland Britain, agriculture was fundamentally Bronze Age in origin and character, and if newcomers from Brittany during the last century before the common era had done much to expand the cultivated areas, it was in the Roman period that the most important agricultural development took place. The Early Iron Age agriculture characteristic of England south of the Jurassic Way and east of the Severn – whose main features were the 'native' field pattern, the pit-storage of grain, covered cattleways, rotary querns, and a relatively adequate equipment with iron tools – ceases west of the Exe in this

[1] R. G. Goodchild on corn-driers: *Ant. J.* xxiii, 1943, pp. 151 sqq.

period (except for those field complexes which go back to the Bronze
Age) as it ceases at the Trent. No field systems have been proved
pre-Roman in Yorkshire, Northumberland, or the lowlands, nor is the
evidence for the pre-Roman date of terrace-fields in northern and
central Wales adequate or convincing. It is agreed by prehistorians
that before Roman penetration the economy of northern Britain was
based preponderantly on the raising of cattle, horses, and sheep, and
that cereals, in so far as they were grown, depended not on the plough
but on the caschrom and the hoe. In this sense, the accounts of Strabo
and Caesar appear to have been accurate.[1]

The highland zone, for all its variety, imposes a certain uniformity
upon agriculture which distinguishes it from the lowland area of
Britain. The mountain massif dominates, the plains are restricted to the
coasts and to limited intramontane tracts. The country is more austerely
subdivided into defined and secluded districts, and communications
are more severely determined by the restrictions of hill and moor.
The swampy valleys and heavily wooded slopes limit the more sheltered
cultivable tracts, while the rocky formations, whether of limestone
or of older igneous and crystalline rocks, are exposed by their height
to longer winters, heavier precipitation, and lower temperatures.
Without iron tools man cannot master the heavier and damper soils
of the coastal plains, and on the high plateaux which he seeks for the
sake of security, the soils are thin when they are not eroded, acid,
waterlogged, or converted to permanent peat-bog.

The Romano-British agriculture of the northern areas, therefore –
in so far as we know it – is based overwhelmingly on animal husbandry
and the cultivation of summer crops, and the occurrence of winter
grains in the zone in the Roman period may with reasonable certainty
be attributed to Roman influence. Thus, for instance, rye is recorded
from Castle Cary and the Forth and Clyde Canal. Yet it has already
been noted that the promotion of oats in the area was almost certainly
the result of the Roman military interest in supplying the army, more
especially the cavalry.[2]

---

[1] The division between highland and lowland Britain, as defined by Sir Cyril Fox
(*The Personality of Britain*,[4] 1943) is generally held to be archaeologically out-of-date.
It is here retained because broadly speaking it does apply to the division between the
military and civilian zones of Roman Britain, and villas are, with a few exceptions,
confined to the lowland zone. Pre-Roman agriculture at a Bronze-Age level: Piggott
ap. Richmond, RNNB, p. 11. Wales, Early Iron Age penetration: A. H. A. Hogg
ap. I. Foster, G. Daniel, *Prehistoric and Early Wales*, London, 1965, pp. 115–30. Pre-
Roman stock-raising: Piggott, *loc. cit.* Roman descriptions: Caesar, *de Bello Gallico*,
v, 14; Strabo, IV, 5, 2. But for suspected pre-Roman fields at Staple Howe, Yorks:
Bowen in RVB, p. 28.

[2] Rye at Castle Cary and the Forth and Clyde Canal: Godwin, *History*, p. 273.

The prominent feature which strikes the observer of the highland settlements of our period is the confinement of the vast majority of known sites to the high plateaux and the hill slopes above the 400-foot contour. A few are indeed to be found on the southern and western coastal plain of Cumberland, and it is therefore possible that heavy cultivation of the lower areas has destroyed traces of others. The group of semi-romanized native farms on the north-west maritime plain of the same region, on the other hand, is to be explained by specific logistic factors relating to the Roman military occupation. Generally, however, it remains true that the bulk of the characteristic native homesteads and hamlets of the period occupy the the mountainous areas.[1]

The description of native agriculture in southern Scotland and Northumberland, i.e. in the northernmost area which was subject for longer or shorter periods to Roman administration and influence, faces a peculiar problem, produced by the present stage of research.[2] Till recently, as a result of field surveys and some excavation, a number of palisaded settlements in those areas were regarded by archaeologists as belonging, at least in a given phase of their occupation, to the Roman period, and this view had been widely published and accepted. Recent carbon-14 testing of finds, however, has indicated a date in the sixth or fifth centuries B.C. for some of these sites. How far these results are definitive cannot yet be judged, owing to absence of publication at the time of writing; moreover, pottery defined as Roman has been found in some of these settlements. Whether views on the period of this material will change in consequence of the new dating remains to be seen.

Accordingly the only course seems to be to devote a brief account to the southern Scottish and Northumbrian settlements, mentioning specifically those of them where alleged Roman material has been recovered, and leaving the final verdict on date to the publishers of present and future research.

The settlements of Roxburghshire may be taken as representative of lowland Scotland. Two main types of site have been distinguished: those consisting of one or two round huts, usually surrounded by a compound, and larger groups of circular huts, numbering from five to twenty, also usually enclosed by a stockade or wall. None is fortified

[1] Heights above sea-level: AA⁴ xxxvIII, 1959, pp. 217–22 (Huckhoe); RCHM *Roxburghshire*, Edinburgh, II, 1956, p. 426 (Tamshiel Rig); CW² LXIII, 1963, p. 83 (Ellerbeck); PSAS LXXXI, 1946/7, p. 139 (Crock Cleugh); AA⁴ xxxvIII, 1960, pp. 19–22 (Northumberland); YAJ xxxIV, 1939, p. 145; RCHM *Westmorland*, 1936, p. xxxii; CBA. RR VII, p. 32 (North Wales); RCAHM *Caernarvonshire*, III, 1964, pp. lxxxviii sqq.
[2] For a brief report on the new situation, I am indebted to Professor S. Piggott.

in the full sense of the word. Some of the palisaded sites are occupied by timber buildings, and solitary timber homesteads within enclosures are commoner in the western area between the Solway and the Clyde. Notable among the larger groups is Hayhope Knowe, with eleven huts, some 30 feet in diameter, contained by a palisade later replaced by an unfinished defensive bank. Further eastward, between the Tyne and Forth, circular timber hut-groups are found, within a ring-ditch, as at Sundhope Kipp. Some of these hamlets were certainly pre-Roman, as shown by two such palisaded enclosures beneath the hill-fort of Hownam Rings, but some have yielded material of the first century A.D. The stone-walled settlements are distinct. Compact groups of this type exist, and among them stone huts overlay the hill-fort of Hownam Rings and third-century pottery was found in them.[1]

Two Roxburgh sites furnish rather more information as they have been investigated with the spade. Tamshiel Rig, in Southdean parish, was a hamlet superimposed upon an obsolete circular hill-fort lying between the 800 and 900-foot contours. Closely associated with a field system, it consisted of a circular enclosure formed by an earth and boulder rampart 5–6 feet thick with entrance to the east. The interior was divided into two by a wall, the southern area being excavated to obtain a level floor. The north court contained three circular stone-walled huts and two more existed to south of the enclosure. The finds included beehive querns, previously dated in the Roman period. The other site, Crock Cleugh in the same county, on the lower Cheviot slopes, comprised two among the fifteen settlements strung out along the valley-sides of the local streams below the 1,000-foot contour. These included both single-hut enclosures and hamlets of over an acre. The Crock Cleugh homesteads stand on glacial gravel overlying boulder-clay, each consisting of an ovoid walled court occupied by a large circular hut. Connected with both are fields defined by three parallel lynchets subdivided by dry-stone walls. The pottery found in these homesteads was not closely datable.

The early farmsteads of Northumberland have been the object of systematic study in recent years. They fall into two broad types, namely, rectilinear enclosed steadings, which preponderate in the south of the county, occupying chiefly the basin of the North Tyne and its tributaries, but also spreading eastward between the valleys of the Wansbeck and the Blyth; and irregular enclosed stone-built hamlets focused in the area between the River Coquet and the southern Cheviot slope. The first group consists of rectilinear banked enclosures of a third to half an acre, generally square, but sometimes polygonal

---

[1] Sundhope Kipp: RCHM *Roxburghshire*, I, no. 303; Hayhope Knowe, *ib.*, no. 665; Hownam Rings: PSAS LXXXIII, 1948–9, pp. 63 sqq.

in shape. The interior is almost invariably divided into two; the first part consists of two depressed areas each side of a causeway entering from the east, and giving access to circular stone huts situated in the other half of the compound. The huts vary from two to five in number; at Riding Wood they contained storage pits; sometimes other huts appear, clearly added later. Most sites of this type lie between 400 and 600 feet above sea level, but in the Upper Wansbeck valley they occupy lower ground. Whatever the date of these settlements, some of the finds have been dated in the middle of the second century A.D. and nothing yet suggests an occupation after the end of the same century.

The second type of homestead, which lies farther north, consists of oval enclosures or irregularly shaped agglomerations of circular stone huts and courtyards. Single stone huts enclosed by a wall may face into a hollowed forecourt, but oval enclosures with four or five huts are also frequent facing a forecourt. Larger groups evolved by the concentration or accumulation of units about a primary nucleus; the largest example of this process is Greaves Ash with twenty-seven stone huts. These farms lie at 600 to 1,100 feet above sea level, generally near a stream, and often at the entrance to a confined valley. Some of the huts of this type overlie known hill-forts; very occasionally rectangular buildings appear at these settlements, but are certainly of later date. The scanty finds from the series were originally thought to point to their occupation from the second to the fourth century of the current era, and there was a tendency to connect them with the Votadini who inhabited this region.

An enclosure of oval form, Huckhoe, which lies in the Wansbeck valley to east of the area of rectilinear settlements, has been carefully excavated. It occupies a limestone bluff at 500 feet above sea level, and encloses about half an acre. Its oval enclosure revealed two phases, the first protected by a triple stockade, and evidence suggested that live-stock was housed between the two outer stockades in the east quadrant. This is one of the enclosures now dated on radio-carbon evidence to the sixth or fifth century B.C.; in the second phase, formerly attributed to the Roman period, the stockades were replaced by stone walls. In the interior, circular stone huts also belonged to the second period (*terra sigillata* was found in association with one of them) being in one case superseded by rectangular stone buildings, whose occupation was certainly prolonged.[1]

[1] Tamshiel Rig: RCHM *Roxb.*, II, p. 426, no. 943; Crock Cleugh, PSAS LXXXI, 1946-7, pp. 63 sqq. Northumberland: AA⁴ xxxvIII, pp. 1 sq.; XLII, 1964, pp. 41 sqq.; CBA. RR VII, pp. 1-14 (with comprehensive bibliography); Huckhoe: AA⁴ xxxvIII, pp. 217 sqq.; Greaves Ash, AA⁴ XLII, 1964, p. 44.

Numerous hill-farms and hamlets are known in Cumberland and Westmorland. In Westmorland they belong to a single type, situated on upland ledges and plateaux always near streams, not far below the 1,000-foot contour. Most of them consist of circular stone huts or rectangular buildings grouped round a yard in an irregular manner, but some hut-groups occur within rectilinear compounds (Ewe Close) and one enclosure may be added to another. While the best explored hamlet, Ewe Close, consisted of three closely adjacent enclosures, two clearly subsequent to the original yard, at Crosby Garrett three distinct settlements stood within a system of fields. Only occasionally are such hamlets in any sense fortified, as at Castle Hill, Dufton. In many of them two phases, one characterized by irregularly arranged round huts, the other by the addition of a more regular rectilinear enclosure, are visible. In the Crosby Ravensworth area, where at least eight sites are identifiable, existent dykes appear to bear a close relationship to property boundaries. No pre-Roman finds are recorded in any of the Cumbrian settlements.[1]

An exceptional group of native farmsteads is to be found on the north Cumberland coastal plain in the vicinity of the Roman road from Papcastle through Old Carlisle to Carlisle. Here the farm-units occupy the well-drained gravel and sand ridges of the coastal belt. Some of them stand in oval or circular dry-stone enclosures. In one case, Wolsty Hall, a pre-Roman oval structure stood in the direct vicinity of a circular neighbour first occupied in the later reign of Hadrian. A rectangular enclosure to eastward contained an interior palisade and a complex of habitations yielding pottery of the third and fourth centuries. The farmstead of Risehow in this area has already been referred to (p. 14); it was certainly held during the fourth century. Only Wolsty, near the Solway, was strongly defended. Although some of these farmsteads evince pre-Roman phases, their late period is the product of Roman colonization, and they were clearly related to the Roman forts in the vicinity of which they were sited.[2]

The area of the Pennines in which native farming of the Roman period is best known lies between the valleys of the Lune and the Wharfe, roughly within a triangle between the Lune-Wenning watershed at Ingleborough, the sources of the Skirfare near Arncliffe, and the neighbourhood of Grassington on the Upper Wharfe. But there is little doubt that traces are to be found at least as far south as Derbyshire.

[1] Cumberland: CW² XXXIII, 1933, p. 186, map 5; CW² LIX, 1959, pp. 7 sqq. Westmorland: RCHM *Westm.* 1936, pp. xxxii sqq. *et passim*; Ewe Close, *ibid.*, p. 83, no. 25; Crosby Garrett, *ibid.*, p. 74, no. 8; Castle Hill, Dufton, *ibid.*, p. xxxii.
[2] Cumberland coastal plain: CW² LIX, 1959, pp. 1 sqq.; P. Salway, *The Frontier People of Roman Britain*, Cambridge, 1965, pp. 112 sqq.

The areas of settlement are the limestone pastures between the valleys and the limestone terraces beside the river valleys. Nearly all the sites are above the 1,000-foot contour, since these areas carry a fine quality of well-drained limestone pasture. The main known concentrations of these farmsteads are to be found in Upper Wenningdale, on the watershed between the Wenning and the Ribble, between the Ribble and the Aire, and along the valleys of the Skirfare and Wharfe, but recent surveys have revealed that the field systems extend over considerably wider areas than hitherto suspected. Further homesteads are known in the lower country to the west, in the Lune valley.

Some account can be given of the Grassington fields, which fall into three types lying parallel to one another on a roughly north–south axis. The central strip consists of roughly square fields of irregular character, among which six hut-sites can be traced. To its east the fields are long and narrow, measuring some 350–400 by 75 feet; as in the first group, the plots are here divided by banks, but these are much higher than those of the first, rising to as much as five feet. In the third sector, to west of the central strip, the fields are larger, taking the form of broad rectangles averaging 200–300 by 500 feet, and their boundary baulks are much slighter than those of the more easterly group. The evidence is that all these fields were in use between the second and third centuries of the present era, but third- or fourth-century pottery is also known at similar settlements at Linton, Kettlewell, and Hawkeswick in Wharfedale. At Grassington the topographical arrangement is such that the two outer strips of larger fields may fairly be regarded as later; it is notable that the area of the largest plots was associated with two large nucleated groups of round huts, one enclosed by a dry-stone wall.

Notable among the homesteads of the Yorkshire highland settlements is the very regular stone building found at Arncliffe in the dale of the Skirfare. This may be conceived as a rectilinear version of the hut-groups assembled about courtyards known at various highland hamlets of the period. It consists of an oblong southern court surrounded on all sides by rectangular rooms, with two round huts embodied in the western wing; the court communicates with a second enclosure to north, the structure as a whole being connected by a sunk road with a group of fields. The entire complex is clearly influenced by Roman planning, as if the owner wished to imitate the rectilinear layout of a Roman villa.[1]

The Lune valley homesteads have been referred to; these lie along the river bank above the 500-foot contour, on glacial boulder-clay,

[1] Yorkshire: *Ant.* III, 1929, pp. 165 sqq.; YAJ XXXIII, 1938, pp. 166 sqq.; XXXIV, 1939, pp. 115 sqq.; extensions of the area, JRS XLIII, 1953, p. 96.

and one group in the vicinity of the Ellerbeck has been tested with the spade. The entire field system covers some 150 acres, including six farmsteads comprising stone hut-groups associated with walled enclosures, but isolated huts may also exist among the fields. The Ellerbeck farmsteads gave evidence of occupation from the end of the second to the middle of the fourth century A.D.[1]

In Roman Wales settlements of the type which we have described seem at the moment to be restricted to the north-west of the country, west of the Conway valley, in Caernarvonshire, Anglesey, and northern Merioneth. No research appears to have been made in central Wales, in south Merioneth, Cardiganshire, Montgomery, and northern Brecknockshire, and further complexes may yet be discovered. We may however note four small areas of very small square fields recently recorded by C. B. Crompton at Waun Gunllwch, Mynydd Illtyd, Llandefalle, and Garth – all in Brecknockshire – and probably associated with small nucleated settlements, from which, at the time of writing, no dating material has been published. In the north-western area the extant huts and enclosed hamlets have been elaborately classified (1964), but it seems better to follow the simpler classification adopted by Hogg in his survey of 1965 (Fig. 40).

We may list (1) isolated huts, enclosed or unenclosed; (2) enclosed hut-groups, which can be subdivided into the polygonal and the oval. Among the latter, some are sub-classified as 'thick-walled', others as 'thin-walled'; (3) unenclosed hut-groups. Many of the isolated huts, which are commonest between 600 and 1,000 feet above sea level, are not associated with known field systems, but others are found scattered over the terraced fields which are the general accompaniment of the enclosed groups. One or two of those not associated with fields have produced Roman finds of the first and second centuries. A distinct class is constituted by those unenclosed huts associated, when grouped, with paddocks for livestock, and generally occupying the higher mountain sides between 800 and 1,000 feet above sea level. The enclosed groups, on the other hand, which comprise stone huts varying in number from three or four to as many as fifty in a rare case (Ty-Mawr, Anglesey), are generally associated with square or strip fields of no great size, laid out along hillside terraces and some- times lyncheted. While individual huts associated with fields appear to have cultivated from as little as a quarter of an acre to as much as sixteen, the grouped enclosed homesteads worked areas from two to nineteen acres. The polygonal enclosures contain both round stone huts and rectangular buildings (Din Lligwy; Cefn Graeanog); those

[1] Lune Valley: Lowndes, CW² XLV, 1945, p. 192; LXIII, 1963, pp. 77 sqq.; LXIV, 1964, pp. 6 sqq.

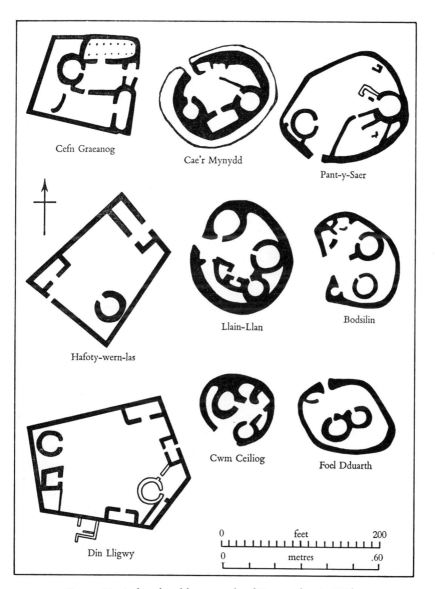

Cefn Graeanog

Cae'r Mynydd

Pant-y-Saer

Hafoty-wern-las

Llain-Llan

Bodsilin

Din Lligwy

Cwm Ceiliog

Foel Dduarth

Fig. 40. Typical enclosed homesteads of Roman date in Wales.

excavated have yielded material from the second to the fourth centuries A.D. In the oval thick-walled homesteads, on the other hand, the huts are embodied in the perimeter walls, and date, apparently, between the third and fifth centuries A.D. In the thin-walled oval enclosures, by contrast, the huts tend to be freestanding; at the only excavated site of this type, Pant-y-Saer, "pottery" (if it is really such), previously regarded as Dark-Age, has now been shown to be of Early Iron Age date.

It has been noted by students of the Welsh mountain settlements that their distribution coincides with that of hill-forts (e.g. Tr'er Ceiri) which also contain stone-built circular huts of the type featured in the homesteads; Tr'er Ceiri, like several other north-Welsh strong-holds, was occupied in the Early Iron Age and reoccupied in the second century of the present era. This would suggest a common pre-Roman origin of forts and homesteads, but Pant-y-Saer is so far the only farmstead known to have originated in the pre-Roman period; as a thin-walled oval type it was perhaps among the progenitors of the thick-walled homestead, but unfortunately the distribution of the two types, although they overlap, is largely distinct. Three other sites, however, established in the third century A.D. (Din Lligwy, Graeanog, and probably Hafoty-wern-las), all polygonal, superseded earlier settlements of unknown character.[1]

There is a general resemblance between the oval class of homestead in Wales and those of similar plan in Northumberland, but only in a general fashion; affinities to examples in Spain and Cornwall are perhaps to be more seriously considered. The polygonal enclosures suggest Roman influence, and even Roman 'inner colonization' of extraneous elements. Such planned settlement may indeed be demonstrated by nine contingent sites at Llandwrog near Nantlle, Caernarvon-shire, where they are distributed with some regularity along a leat which was their common water-supply, and stand in a fairly well-defined pattern of 'native' fields. Hogg considers that the general evidence is in favour of a governmental transplantation of settlers in the early third century. He has estimated the total population of the hamlets described in north-western Wales as some 2,000 in all, excluding the inhabitants of the hill-forts.[2]

Outside the north-western region, little can be said of the forms of

[1] Wales: *Ant.* XVIII, 1944, pp. 183–6; RCAHM *Caern.*, III, pp. lxx sqq. CBA. RR VII, pp. 28–38 (comprehensive bibliography); Brecknockshire: AC CXVI, 1967, pp. 57 sqq. Pant-y-Saer "pottery": *Trans. and Proc. Birmingham Archaeological Society* LXXXII, 1965, pp. 77–91; CBA. RR VII, p. 33 sq.

[2] Discussion of origins and affinities: CBA. RR VII, pp. 35–6; Llandwrog, Nantlle: RCAHM *Caern.*, II, nos. 1216–1227; population estimate: CBA. RR VII, p. 31.

Welsh rural settlement in the Roman period. Villas are represented in the Vale of Gwent and even in the vales of northern Glamorgan; a few alleged farmhouses, two fortified, are known in Pembrokeshire (Ford, Cwmbrwyn, Trelissey), and there are other less defined rural sites. In the north-east (Denbighshire, Flintshire), on the other hand, some light has been thrown on rural economy by the excavation of the hill-fort of Dinorben not far from the north coast. Here the hill-fort was reoccupied in the third and fourth centuries by a large circular hut, which was superseded, apparently at the end of the fourth century, by an aisled house. The economy of both phases was based on agriculture involving the use of a winged ploughshare apt to produce a ridged field, and stockbreeding which included the rearing of cattle and more especially of sheep for the production of wool; the opinion has been expressed that a villa-owner had transferred his residence to a fortified place in the second phase because of the insecurity resulting from the withdrawal of Roman garrisons in the later fourth century. The aisled building at Dinorben finds an analogy not only at Castle Dore in Cornwall, and at Tidbury in Hampshire, but also in Wales itself, on a miniature scale, at the homestead of Cefn Graeanog, an interpretation of which has been attempted.[1]

In Cornwall and most of Devon, rural settlement clung initially to the coastal areas because easy communication was primarily by sea and here were to be found the better-drained soils. From the Bronze Age onward, nevertheless, the more difficult granite and sandstone uplands were settled, and the agriculture of this poor and isolated region remained largely Bronze Age down to the Roman advent and even later, its economy based chiefly on barter. Iron-users from abroad penetrated the area from the second century B.C., followed by Venetic intruders. Iron Age culture introduced the *souterrain* or *fogou*, an underground storeroom in the form of a covered masonry-revetted trench, likewise the "courtyard" house, which consisted of living and store-rooms terraced into the hillside or embodied within massive peripheral masonry, and ranged about a paved central court-yard. These habitations, which occur both isolated and in groups, are confined to the uplands, sometimes also incorporating round huts, and always in association with field systems. Their minimal components include, beside the courtyard, a circular main living room and a long room for work or industry. A house of this type at Chysauster included

[1] Central and South Wales: CBA. RR VII, pp. 28–31; Dinorben: Gardner, Savory, *Dinorben*, 1964, especially pp. 107 sqq. and pp. 222 sqq. Castle Dore: Radford, *Jour. Royal Institute of Cornwall*,[2] I, 1951, pp. 60 sqq.; Tidbury Rings: HFC XVI, 1944, p. 38; Cefn Graeanog: RCAHM *Caern.*, III, A 852, p. 113; CBA. RR VII, p. 34, fig. 3.

a stable, and various other rooms may be found. In the first century B.C. also appears the 'round' or *ker*, a farmstead enclosed by a circular or elliptical enceinte containing one or two circular huts. The fields, continuing the Bronze Age tradition, were divided by clearance banks and lynchets, and show signs of terracing and manuring. Investigation at Gwithian indicated that probably during the Roman period the mouldboard plough was introduced into Dumnonian territory.

The Rounds are the predominant form of Cornish farmstead in the Roman period; they are often sited at altitudes between 200 and 400 feet, on the upper edges of the valleys, but seldom primarily for defence, and often occur in association with fields, though avoiding the granite moorlands. Open hut-groups are also found, suggesting a different social category of occupier. Thomas has estimated the number of rounds in Devon and Cornwall as between 750 and 1,000, with a population, including the inhabitants of the other forms of settlement, of some 10,000 in the Roman period. This would provide an average of ten acres of land for hut-groups, and of 40 acres for each round or courtyard house.[1]

What information can be extracted from our brief survey of the highland hamlets of northern and western Britain in the Roman period? It is at once evident that if north Britain had remained at a Bronze Age level till the Roman conquest, it moved into a more advanced phase under Roman influence. The direct evidence is meagre enough, since few tools have been preserved, owing to the acidity of the highland soils. Nevertheless, the finding of iron sickles at Grassington and Settle and of an iron adze and axe-hammer at other sites is significant, and if the large Roman ploughshares from Traprain Law, Blackburn Mill, and Eckford are almost certainly imports from the south, they would nevertheless suggest active Roman encouragement and precept for the improvement of cultivation. In Cornwall, at least, the evidence for the introduction of a mouldboard plough in this period, if indirect, is acceptable (Gwithian).

Further improvements are the prevalence of the rotary quern, now generally superseding the saddle quern, and the adoption, in Wales, Yorkshire, and Cumbria, less certainly in the lowlands and Northumberland, of defined and terraced fields, implying more persistent if not deeper ploughing. In Devon and Cornwall fields tend in the Roman period to increase in size; the same process is visible at Grassington, and individual fields of an area far in excess of the contemporary

[1] Cornwall and Devon: C. Thomas, CBA. RR VII, pp. 74–98; A. Fox, *South-West England*, London, 1964; Gwithian: *Cornish Archaeology*, I, 1962, pp. 61–84.

norm are discernible, for instance, at Crosby Garrett (Westm), and at Moel Faban, Caernarvonshire. How far fields were enclosed is not evident; but the case is clear at Grassington, where the easterly strip fields were surrounded by banks five feet high, as at Crock Cleugh, and this implies that livestock was to be kept in or out – possibly both, signifying in one case the intention to manure by grazing, in the other the necessity of protecting a winter crop. Another symptom of progress would appear to have been the introduction, on occasion, of the long-strip field, which may be taken to indicate an increase of traction power in the form of plough-oxen. This advance is plain at Grassington as a secondary phase, and strips are a commoner phenomenon in the highland field pattern of the period than some archaeologists have been prepared to admit (e.g. Ellerbeck, Crosby Garrett, possibly Nantlle, and other sites noted by Stevens). Strips are also perceptible among some of the Cornish field complexes. Terracing and lyncheting certainly progressed in the Roman period in Wales and the south-west.[1]

We know next to nothing of the cereal crops of the highland farms. In Wales it has been noticed that numerous unenclosed hut-groups seek the upper mountain slopes, evidently because their concern was primarily pasture, and at Ellerbeck the higher plots were too steep for ploughing, and may therefore have served to fold the livestock. It follows that a proportion of the defined field systems connected with the highland farmsteads may not have been sown at all. The presence of oats and rye, already noted, would imply both summer and winter crops, and barley (*Hordeum polystichum*) found at Old Kilpatrick, if local, and at Grassington, would have multiplied the summer-sown cereals. The presence of pestles at some of the Yorkshire settlements may well imply the growing of husked grains such as spelt. Lowndes has very sensibly suggested that the "non-arable" enclosures already referred to may well have been used for the wintering of stock when the arable, or part of it, was under a winter crop. Nevertheless the known arable areas attached to the hill-farms of the period are so restricted that one wonders how far their owners could permit themselves winter sowings in the climatically severe conditions which affected the high altitudes and thin cold soils, more especially as the Sub-Atlantic phase drew to its climax. In Northumberland, nevertheless, far the majority of the early farmsteads occupied the glacial clays and boulder-clays, which would have given good straw, and the latter soils are less prone to acidity, but both would

---

[1] Highland tool-finds: AA[4] xxxviii, 1960, p. 30; YAJ xxxiv, 1938–9, p. 129; large fields, Crosby Garrett: RCHM *Westm.*, p. 74, no. 8 and map p. 75; Moel Faban: RCAHM *Caern.*, I, East, p. 146, fig. 143. Strip fields: CBA. RR vii, pp. 114–17.

have been slow-drying 'late' soils better adapted, perhaps, to winter wheats.[1]

In this situation it is not surprising that the mainstay of most of the highland farms should have been, in the view of archaeologists, stock-rearing. This is indeed evident from the approximate acreages of field associated with some of the Welsh steadings; the largest estimated tract attached to an enclosed hut-group is 19 acres, which might with difficulty support six adults with grain for a year on modern rations, assuming half the land was fallowed and the yield amounted to five bushels per acre, one-third being deducted for seed and wastage. Clearly the arable could be no more than a minor aspect of such an economy. Naturally, there are variations, and the Cornish rounds could have supported themselves at a higher standard on 40 acres. But evidently Dio wrote with knowledge when he mentioned the herds of the Caledonians. Chariotry reached eastern Yorkshire perhaps in the second century B.C. The size of Stanwick hill-fort and the travelling dykes of the East Riding have been adduced as evidence in support of stock-rearing in general and horse-rearing in particular. The archaeological evidence for horse-rearing in the hill-settlements is nevertheless scant, and the nave-band of a cart found at the homestead of West Gunnar Park – if it belongs to our period – is a proof rather of the presence of oxen. A stable is thought to have been identified in one of the courtyard houses at Chysauster.[2]

The rearing of livestock in the hill-farms is nevertheless shown by the presence in some field systems of fenced droveways whose purpose is to prevent the herds straying on to the fields when they were under crop; examples may be cited from Crosby Garrett (two instances) and Grassington. The droveway at Rise How (Cumb) has already been referred to. Corrals near unenclosed hut-groups on the higher mountain slopes of north-western Wales have been alluded to, and many of the yards in the larger enclosed hut-groups of Wales and Cumbria must have sheltered animals during the winter. Byres are perhaps to be identified at Ewe Close, Crosby Garrett, and Cefn Graeanog.

The paucity of animal bones is nevertheless such, that it is extremely difficult at the moment to state whether cattle or sheep constituted the more important branch of stock-raising in north and west Britain. Sheep or goat composed 68 per cent of meat-bones at the prehistoric Cornish promontory fort known as the Rumps; this need not reflect

[1] Barley at Old Kilpatrick: Godwin, *History*, p. 266; Grassington: YAJ XXXIV, p. 129; Lowndes, "non-arable" fields: CW² LXIII, 1963, p. 90. Pestles: YAJ, *loc. cit.*, p. 130.
[2] Chariotry: *British Museum Guide to the Early Iron Age*, London, 1925, pp. 113, 119; Frere, *Britannia*, pp. 13–14. Stanwick: Wheeler, *The Stanwick Fortifications*, pp. 27–30. Carts: West Gunnar Park, AA⁴ XXXVIII, p. 26.

north Britain or Wales in the Roman period, and where those areas are concerned, some general considerations may be entertained. The presence of loomweights and spindlewhorls for instance at Grassington, shows that flocks were not unimportant in that district. Piggott and others have stressed the logistic aspect of native settlement in the highland zone under Roman rule: in other words, the importance of agriculture for the provisioning of the Roman forces. The bone-finds from the legionary fortresses and some of the auxiliary forts leave very little doubt that the British forces received beef as their normal ration; pork only secondarily, and mutton, apparently, *faute de mieux*. Two legionary fortresses, namely Chester and Caerleon, may have had their own cattle-ranches, on the evidence provided by inscriptions of the *pecuarii* of legion XX in the Rhineland (CIL XIII, 8287), and by the name Bovium which occurs in the vicinity of both legionary bases. The IX legion at York, on the other hand, and after it the VI Victrix, would have had some corresponding 'indent depôt' in the York area, but it may well have drawn also upon the Yorkshire dales. The number of young cattle slaughtered at Newstead in the Flavian and Antonine periods suggests that they were purchased from neighbouring tribes for the garrison, since their origin must have been among people unable to maintain them in winter. At Mumrills in the Antonine period, on the other hand, all the bones were of adult animals, and presumably the fort received its meat from a locality where winter fodder was forthcoming. This last information accords with what is known from Stanwick, where in the third quarter of the first century of our era a large proportion of the cattle was sufficiently mature at death to suggest winter feeding. This agrees also with the conclusions of several recent specialist studies of animal bones of the Early Iron and Roman ages, that by no means all stock-farmers of those periods were obliged to kill off the greater part of their animals as winter set in. Most of these studies, indeed, relate to sites of the lowland zone, but if we accept the Stanwick data as applicable, we must ask how the problem of adequate winter fodder was solved.[1]

---

[1] The Rumps: *Corn. Arch.* 3, 1964. Grassington, loomweights: YAJ XXXIV, p. 136. Legionary meat-diet in Britain: Caerleon, F. Nash-Williams, AC, 1931, Prysg Field (III), pp. 80 sqq.; Chester: LAA XI, 1925, p. 85; XVIII, 1931, p. 146; Corbridge: AA[3] VII, 1911, p. 230; Castle Lyons: Acton, Grimes, *Castle Lyons* (*Y Cymmrodor* XLI), 1930, p. 186. Auxiliary units Benwell: AA[4] V, 1928, p. 74; Mumrills: PSAS LXIII, 1930, p. 569; Newstead: J. Curle, *A Roman Frontier Fort*, pp. 371, 374; Pevensey: SAC LI, 1906-7, p. 113; LII, 1907-8, p. 63; Bar Hill: Macdonald, Park, *The Roman Fort on Bar Hill*, Glasgow, 1906, p. 126; *pecuarii*: CIL XIII, 8287; Bovium: *It. Ant.* 469.4; in south Wales: JRS LVI, 1966, p. 220; *It. Ant.* 484.3 (Bomium). Newstead, slaughter of young cattle: Macdonald, Curle, PSAS LXIII, 1930, p. 572; Mumrills: *ibid.* Stanwick: Wheeler, *op. cit.*, p. 27.

Both sheep and cattle in their original wild condition wintered
without artificial shelter or feed; in any case in many of the highland
farms of the Roman period the actual observable accommodation for
stock is limited, suggesting at best the wintering of the breeding and
working stock. The availability of roots, legumes, and surplus grain,
probable in the lowland villa agriculture, may largely be discounted
for the highland region. But it may be pointed out that the physical
condition of animals that had wintered out would not be such as to
furnish good meat on the hoof to the army commissariat. It might
be tentatively proposed that the army took over the saleable stock
in the autumn. This would find support in the inscription which
records the Venatores of Banna (probably Bewcastle) whose business,
it seems, was not hunting, but the care of the regimental cattle. This
may also have been a function of the *territoria* of the auxiliary forts,
one of which is recorded in A.D. 216 in connection with the fort
of Chester-le-Street. The cattle-rearing of the northern villages, then,
may well have been partly transhumant in character, and it is likely
enough that on the approach of winter the requisitioned stock departed
on the hoof for the clement plains where deficiencies of pasture were
made up by regimental fodder. The finding of scythes at Newstead
and of a mower's anvil at the auxiliary fort of Templeborough (Yorks),
further of vetch in the Forth and Clyde Canal, is suggestive in this
connection. That the bulk of the consignments was tribute is probable,
but whether such a factor had any connection with the Brigantian
revolt of the mid-second century, it is for northern archaeologists
to decide.[1]

The presence of sheep in the northern hill-farms is evidenced by
spindle-whorls, which are not numerous. Sheep-bones, however, are
recorded from the forts of Newstead, Bar Hill, and Mumrills, at the
depôt-town of Corbridge, and at the Scottish hill-fort of Traprain Law.
In north Wales, the economy of the hill-fort of Dinorben was in the
third and fourth centuries partly based, in Cowley's view, on a flock
run for wool; the existence of this branch was deduced from the
rapid decrease of sheep-bones used for food at the hill-fort in the
later Roman period.

The picture of the hill-peasantry under Roman rule is, indeed, a
poverty-stricken one. Something was done to raise the technical level
of their agriculture, but the scarcity of imported objects and coins in
their hamlets tells a plain tale; not merely were they not paid for their

---

[1] Venatores of Banna: RIB, no. 1905; *territorium* of Chester-le-Street: RIB,
no. 1049; EE vii, 986; JRS xxxiv, 1944, p. 88. Scythes: Curle, *Roman Frontier Fort*,
pl. lxii; pp. 284–5; mower's anvil: Rotherham Museum, from Templeborough.
Vetch: Chapter vii, p. 115.

products in cash; apparently they received (if there is any truth at all in their function as army-suppliers) little by way of payment in kind; whatever their output, their tribute was heavy.

This belief can only be in agreement with the conclusions of researchers who have observed in the polygonal homesteads of north-west Wales signs of Roman influence, and interpreted these phenomena as well as the development of native farms in the vicinity of Roman forts in north-west Cumbria, as the results of Roman planning and possibly even of the deliberate colonization of certain areas by extraneous elements transferred by the authorities.[1]

[1] Spindle-whorls: AA⁴ xx, 1942, pp. 172–3; RCAHM *Caern.*, III, p. lxxix. Sheep-bones: Newstead, Corbridge, Bar Hill, Mumrills: see p. 203, n. 1. Traprain Law: PSAS L, 1915–16, pp. 142 sq.; Dinorben: Gardner, Savory, *op. cit.*, pp. 107, 222. Roman colonization of highland areas: RCAHM *Caern.*, II, p. 194, nos. 216–27; CBA. RR VII, p. 35; CW² LIX, 1959, pp. 1 sqq.

CHAPTER XI

THE BRANCHES OF THE ECONOMY

Grain. Strabo refers (IV, 4, 3) to the export of grain from Britain across the Channel in the reign of Augustus. We have already cited Caesar's exploitation of the Cantian grain-crops and may add the prompt supply of corn by Mandubracius to Caesar's army. Strabo also refers (IV, 5, 5) to British wheat-beer, while Dioscorides, in the first century of our era, writes both of the barley-beer (κοῦρμι) and of the wheat-beer brewed in Britain (*de mat. med.*, 1, 88). The fourth-century Latin panegyrist (*Pan. Lat.*, Baehrens, VI (VII), 9.207) speaks of Britain as possessing "a fertility of crops as suffices for the gifts both of Ceres and Bacchus," which means either abundant wheat, or abundant wheat and barley together. A survey has already been attempted of the finds of grain in Britain datable to the Roman period, and this showed that they are sufficiently numerous and widely enough distributed to demonstrate that cereal production was a well-developed branch of the Romano-British economy. The increase of cultivation under Roman rule is graphically indicated in the palaeobotanical record by the great increase of weeds of cultivation noted, for example, in the Somerset peats, at Tallington (south Lincs), and at Cottenham (Camb). The evidence can be reinforced by the presence of numerous millstones at almost every Romano-British site, whether villa, isolated farm, or village community. Some of these are large, suggesting the need of animal propulsion to meet a high rate of production (Langton, Hamworthy, Corfe Mullen); the romanized millstone becomes larger and flatter in the later Roman period, evidently to deal with increased yields. The presence of water-mills at Wherwell (Hants) and elsewhere, in the third or fourth century of the present era, points in the same direction. Valuable in this respect is the presence of well-built granaries at various country houses where the perspicacity of the excavator has identified them; among these were Bignor, Cromhall, Woodchester, Ditchley, Stroud, Iwerne II, Lodge Farm (North Warnborough), Pitney, Shakenoake Farm (Oxon), possibly Eccles (Kent), Whitton Crossroads (Glamorgan), Brickhills Farm (Chilgrove, Suss), Churchie Bushes (Bawdrip, Som) and Denton (Lincs). No less eloquent of corn-production are the numerous grain-drying furnaces first recognized at the Hambleden villa (Bucks), and since identified on dozens of sites ranging from humble homesteads in Cranbourne Chase, through medium romanized farms like that at West Blatchington and large villas such as Brading, to the impressive installation connected with the Saxon Shore fort at Reculver. They are also found in urban centres such as Winchester and Verulamium. Britain was certainly under pressure to supply the continental Roman armies in Julian's time; there is no reason to doubt that the military demand existed also in the first century, and the probable effect of the partial transfer of burdens from south Britain to the north can be envisaged (cf. below, p. 224). The Cardyke canal which connects the Fens with the Trent is normally explained as designed to serve the transfer of grain to the armies of the north, but Salway thinks that cereal production in the Fenlands was a secondary branch, and that the transport of cattle, sheep, and salt meat is likely to have been its chief function. The consistent presence in every permanent Roman fort of a granary capable of holding a two years' supply is evidence for what the province had to furnish.[1]

The existence of a surplus in grain production in at least some lowland areas is further indicated by the evidence for the grain-feeding of pigs at Pitney, Woolaston Pill, and Hambleden (Bucks) (see p. 182). We also have found reason to observe the coincidence of the Kent villas with the areas of highest wheat and barley croppings – particularly with barley – and of other villa-groups with wheat-areas in Essex, Sussex, and Surrey, also with barley-soils in east Hampshire. The analysis of the Figheldean Down field complex (even without the "ellipse" enclosure, whose existence has been questioned but now confirmed), indicated that the so-called 'native field' agriculture of the chalk downland country cultivated preponderantly summer cereals (presumably barley) but had begun also to grow winter grains (i.e. wheats) in the Early Iron Age – as the grain-finds show – and doubtless continued to do so in the Roman period. It is accordingly fair to conclude that Romano-British agriculture stood squarely on a corn-growing basis.[2]

[1] Mandubracius: Caesar, de Bello Gallico, v, 20; the Somerset peats: *Philosophical Trans.*, 233B, pp. 275 sqq. Cottenham: *Ant. J.* xxix, 1949, p. 160; Tallington: CBA. RR vii, p. 18 and fig. 4. Power mills: Langton (?): Corder, Kirk, *Langton*, p. 39; Hamworthy, Dors.: H. P. Smith, *History of Poole*, Poole, 1948, i, p. 63, fig. 31; Corfe Mullen: information from R. A. H. Farrar. Water-mills: W. H. Manning, *Ant. J.* xliv, 1964, pp. 38–40. On the evolution of Romano-British querns: Curwen, *Ant.* xi, 1937, p. 140. Corn-driers: R. G. Goodchild – see p. 231, n. 1; Sir Lindsay Scott, *Ant.* xxv, 1951, pp. 196 sqq. Reculver: *Kent Archaeological Review* xiii, 1968, p. 12; Winchester: HFC xviii, 1954, pp. 315–24; Verulamium: JRS l, 1960, p. 227. Julian: Amm. Marc., xviii, 2, 3; corn-levy in the first century: Tac., *Agric.*, 19, 4. The Cardyke: *Ant. J.* xxix, p. 160. Cattle etc.: Salway, FR p. 14. Granaries in forts: CW² xx, 1920, pp. 127 sqq.; Anderson in Furneaux, Tac., *Agric.*, Oxford, 1922, pp. 182–7.

[2] Figheldean Down: PPS xx, 1954, pp. 107 sqq.

Cattle raising was well-developed before the Roman conquest. The Early Iron Age agriculture of Wessex combined, if we may generalize from the anatomy of the Figheldean Down pattern, cereal production with livestock, in which cattle and sheep played an essential part. In fact, wherever we find square-field complexes in association with banked or ditched droveways, we may be certain that the moving of livestock from the homesteads to the outfield pasture and back, or from the outfield pasture on to the stubble after harvest, was practised, and the shortness of the pre-Roman reaping-hook means that the stubble was left long for the livestock to feed on in the autumn. As such implements continued in use in some Roman villas – e.g. at Hambleden (Bucks) and High Wycombe in the same county, this practice must have persisted under Roman rule. What precisely was the change that took place in those farms where the balanced curved sickle and the two-hand scythe were introduced, may be tentatively envisaged; the implication is that the winter feeding of stock passed to the farmyard and the stall, and was supplemented by legumes and hay. We cannot hope for precise information on the relative importance of the cattle and sheep branches on the chalk and limestone uplands. Generally, sheep increased in the Early Iron Age as deforestation progressed; in the Roman period sheep were 33 per cent of the bones at Woodyates, 40 per cent at Rotherley, and 29 per cent at Woodcuts, and cattle normally decreased in proportion as the site was more distant from woodland and water. While these bones represent diet, and might therefore be taken not to reflect the relative importance of the branches, the above evidence shows that there is nevertheless a relation between the finds and the topographical situation of the settlement concerned.[1] At Hockwold (Norf) a considerable quantity of animal remains from the Neolithic to the Roman period revealed a great increase of both cattle and sheep under Roman occupation in comparison with that present in the Early Iron Age.

Amongst the Celtic tribes cattle-owning was a status symbol and one of the principal criteria of wealth. The aisled house, which originally at least was the chief's or the noble's, was initially a combined dwelling and cattle-byre, and the importance of cattle in the conceptions of the class is also reflected in the various escutcheons and bucrania representing the heads of oxen or cows, found in both the Belgic and the Roman periods in this country. Cattle were being exported by the Belgae in Strabo's time and Caesar says explicitly that the British *oppida* were cattle-enclosures. Air-surveys of the valley gravels in the east Midlands make it plain that livestock enclosures figure prominently

[1] i.e. cattle-bones were more numerous in proportion to the farm's proximity to woodland.

in the settlement pattern both of the late pre-Roman and Roman periods. This emerges clearly from a scrutiny of the south Lincolnshire survey of the Royal Commission for Historical Monuments, and no less of the reports of K. St Joseph on the air-reconnaissance of Nottinghamshire, the Yorkshire Wolds, the Doncaster area, the Godmanchester district, the Vale of Evesham, the Nene, Ouse, Trent, and Thames valleys. How far the enclosures served for cattle, and how far for sheep or horses, is a question only research can answer. The plan of the Thistleton Dyer villa's outbuildings is in favour of the preponderance of cattle, but we hear also of the bones of sheep and pigs, and must await a statistical report. The same applies to the very large quantity of cattle-bones from Chesterton (Durobrivae). It is nevertheless clear that cattle dominated the Fenland settlements, for here sheep would have fallen victim to the liver-fluke. This is borne out both by the existence of cattledroves and enclosures among the field patterns (see p. 13), and by the bone-finds, among which sheep barely figure. There are, moreover, several Roman villas where the animal remains tell a clear story of the maintenance of free-ranging cattle herds for the production of meat and hides. Such was Appleton (Norf), where the association of cattle-bones and horse-bones made it plain that the herds were grazed, rounded up, and driven by mounted herdsmen. The same association was evident at Hambleden (Bucks), where, however, sheep and pigs were also in evidence, and it would be attractive to understand the Buckinghamshire Grim's Dyke (if Roman) as defining a large ranch producing meat, hides, and pork for the forces and shipping its produce down the Thames to London for further distribution. The third site where horse- and cattle-bones in association point to free-range herding is the Rockbourne Down enclosure. Its rôle as a cattle-kraal has recently been challenged, but the Roman date is not in doubt, its 'kite' shape is connected with the function of rounding up herds, and despite the corn-driers, the bone-finds tell of a preponderantly pastoral economy. Similar was the kite-enclosure of Mangravet's Wood, near Maidstone, coeval with the Roman road and close to several Roman homesteads. The combined cattle and sheep-rearing activities of Bignor have been referred to and among other villas exhibiting accommodation for the wintering of cattle may be mentioned West Dean, Brading, Apethorpe, Hartlip, Spoonley Wood, Thistleton Dyer, Ickleton (Camb), North Wraxhall, Pitney, Iwerne II, and probably Woodchester. Finally the cattle-stations of legions II Augusta and XX Valeria Victrix must be taken into account. It has already been stated that the evidence is in favour of beef having been the meat which the British legions preferred or received. The name Bovium occurs in the *Itinerary of Antoninus* in the immediate vicinity of Chester; it has been identified with Heronbridge on the south bank of the Dee, or alternatively with Holt, Denbighshire, and explained as the cattle-depôt of the legion, the more plausibly since the XXth is known to have had its own cowboys (*pecuarii*) when stationed on the Rhine. The matter becomes more probable in the light of the recent discovery of very small tiles stamped BOV–– at St Lytham near the Roman villa of Whitton Cross Roads, Glamorgan. This is clearly the correct form of Bomium, the road-station recorded by the *Itinerary of Antoninus* west of Caerleon, and is to be placed, on Wright's suggested emendation of the mileage, to west of Bonvilston not far away. The villa is known to have had an elaborate constructional history beginning in pre-Roman times, and a timber granary of military appearance, not yet dated. The Goldcliff boundary stone, found to the east of Caerleon, and recording the construction of some work (dyke or ditch?) by Roman troops, may have marked, on G. Boon's suggestion, the east boundary of the legionary ranches or *prata*, which supplied the legion with fresh beef, just as Woolaston Pill seems to have supplied it with pork.[1]

The evidence adduced for the winter maintenance of cattle and sheep in the farms of the period takes two forms: the testimony of animal bones found at various sites, and the identification of byres and sheepfolds. Both indicate that at some sites animals were wintered successfully and reached their third or fourth year before being slaughtered for food. The remains of oxen were predominantly of adult animals at Bitterne and Mumrills; at Great Witcombe villa the sheep eaten included also adult animals. As these three sites are respectively a seaport town, a fort on the Scottish wall, and a prosperous Gloucestershire villa, the above finds have considerable significance. The practice of winter maintenance, however, preceded the Roman period. This was first shown and stated by Higgs and White, who wrote: "there is no evidence in any period for killing of livestock in

---

[1] Status symbol: *Ancient Laws of Ireland*, H.M. Stationery Office, 1865, III, p. 42; IV, pp. 299–341; P. W. Joyce, *Social History of Ireland*, London, 1903, I, p. 158; E. O. Curry, *On the Manners and Customs of the Ancient Irish*, London, 1873, p. xcvi and III, p. 26. Escutcheons and bucrania: C. F. C. Hawkes, *Aspects of Archaeology in Britain and Beyond* (ed. Grimes), pp. 191–9. Oppida: Caes., *de Bello Gallico*, V, 19. Livestock enclosures: *A Matter of Time*, passim; K. St Joseph, JRS XLIII, 1953, pp. 95–6; XLVIII, 1958, pp. 99, 101; LI, 1961, p. 134 etc. The liver-fluke: Fox, *Personality*, pp. 63, 94. Criticism of Wessex stock-enclosures: Fowler, Musty, Taylor, WAM LX, 1965, pp. 52 sqq.; C. C. Taylor, *Ant.* XLI, 1967, pp. 304–6. Bovium: *It. Ant.* 469.4; Heronbridge: *Jour. Chester Archaeological Society*, XXX, 1939, p. 119; other authorities identify Bovium with Holt, Denbighshire – V. E. Nash-Williams, *The Roman Frontier in Wales*, ed. Jarrett, Cardiff, 1969, p. 43; F. H. Thompson, *Roman Cheshire*, Chester, 1965, p. 21. St Lytham: JRS LVI, 1966, p. 220; Bomium: *It. Ant.* 484.3. Goldcliffe inscription: Boon, *Monmouthshire Antiquary*, II, Pontypool, pp. 125–6.

autumn because of lack of winter-fodder" – a situation most clearly demonstrated at the Early Iron Age site of Hawkeshill in Surrey. C. L. Cram, reporting on the animal bones recovered from Hockwold (Norf), stated that there was "no evidence for cattle having been killed before four years of age between the Bronze Age and Iron Age;" in the latter period cattle here lived over one year, and in the Roman period the majority were killed at 30–51 months. There must nevertheless be some reservations. The position may have differed from place to place or from year to year; the sites where the bones have been most thoroughly studied and in largest quantities are in lowland Britain; younger animals (oxen, sheep, pigs) were killed off at Boscombe Down West in the Early Iron Age, and more young sheep and pigs were slaughtered than old ones at Braughing in the Roman period. At Newstead in the Flavian period young cattle were eaten. But in general it is clear that the problem of winter maintenance had been solved at least up to a point in given conditions.[1]

We are not yet in a position to say how this was done by the Early Iron Age farmer, and a solution may come in the course of further investigation. But the question can be answered without an undue measure of conjecture where the romanized cultivator is concerned. The evidence for the wintering of cattle in various villas has been cited. The problem of fodder encountered by the north-European farmer in the winter faced the Mediterranean farmer in the summer, and he solved it by feeding leaves, hay, vetch, peas, beans, grape-residues, wine-lees, and every possible form of consumable vegetable waste. In Gaul, however, the use of root-crops – rape and turnip – was known, and the turnip occurs in Roman deposits at Pevensey and probably at Silchester. From the finds recorded above (p. 115) it is clear that the farmer of the Roman period in Britain was well acquainted with the tare, vetch, broad bean, and the smaller bean, and such leguminous crops would have been sown in the spring on the fallow or have followed cereals in the autumn. At Downton villa (Wilts) vetch and clover were found with spelt, *triticum aestivum*, rivet, and barley, and vetch composed 15 per cent of the seed, suggesting to the excavators that it had been sown as a crop, perhaps with the cereals, a common Roman practice. At Wickbourne Estate (Suss) vetch was also found with winter and summer cereals, and the same

[1] Animal bones at Bitterne: *Ministry of Works Archaeological Report no. 2: Excavations at Clausentum, Bitterne, Southampton* (Cotton, Gathercole), London, 1958, pp. 141–2; Mumrills: Macdonald, Curle, *Mumrills*, p. 572; Great Witcombe: BGAS LXXIII, 1954, p. 64. Higgs, White, *Ant.* XXXVII, 1963, pp. 282–9; Hawkeshill: Carter, Phillipson, Higgs, SyAC, LXII, 1965, pp. 41–2; Boscombe Down West: WAM LIV, 1951-2, pp. 165–6; Braughing: EHAS XIII, 1952/4, p. 124. On the problem of autumn killing, see further Dr Ryder's remarks in Part I of this volume.

occurred at the villa of East Dean, not far west of Bignor. In this connection the find of vetch together with other cereals (p. 115) at the Forth and Clyde Canal is of particular interest, since it may well mean that this crop was grown on the native fields of the Scottish lowlands, and thus have helped to solve the winter fodder problem in the highland zone. Hay was also important for winter maintenance, and the short Early Iron Age reaping hook would have made a close cut difficult. The Roman scythe, developed in Gaul and Germany, remedied this shortcoming.

It has been remarked that the growing of roots would have depended on freedom from autumn stubble-grazing, and therefore it is likely to have been initially a characteristic of developed Roman farming, i.e. of the villas, which could enclose their fields. We have already noted that the turnip was identified at Pevensey, where the plant-finds reflect a mode of farming strongly influenced by a continental pattern.[1]

A case can be made for the growing of root-crops at the villa of Bignor, which attained to its highest agricultural development in the fourth century. The villa wintered, on the evidence of its buildings, twelve pairs of plough-oxen, 55 head of other cattle, and about 200 sheep. The maximum extent of the arable within its natural boundaries was some 2,000 acres (see Fig. 41), but if twelve plough-teams were available, and account is taken of the division of the arable into roughly equal parts composed respectively of the more tractable greensand and the stiffer lower chalk, on a two-field system and three ploughings a year, some 800 acres would have been cultivated. (The calculation is based on a year's work of 292 days and a biennial fallow; 40 per cent has been subtracted to cover other work performed by the ox-teams. Both Roman and medieval English rates of ploughing have been taken into consideration.) If a three-field system was employed, calculation makes the arable some 730 acres.

Columella provides figures on the dung output per month of larger and lesser livestock, and also of human beings. His unit is the *vehes* or load, which he does not define. 800 acres would have received from the Bignor livestock and human community some 19,000 loads, or 24 loads per acre (14·8 loads per *iugerum*). If however the seasonal movement of the stock is taken into account, there would be about

[1] Mediterranean summer fallow: Colum., II, 2, 14; VI, 2, 3; Pliny, HN, XVIII, 175. Forth and Clyde Canal: Helbaek, Jessen, *Cereals in Great Britain and Ireland*, p. 59. Pevensey: C. E. Stevens has suggested to me that the Abulci who furnished the garrison of Pevensey (*Not. Dig., Occ.*, VII, 109; XXVIII, 20 – Seeck) may have borne the original Celtic name of the Regnenses of Chichester. If so, these were the province's earliest romanizers, and their agriculture would be expected to elicit strong romanizing traits.

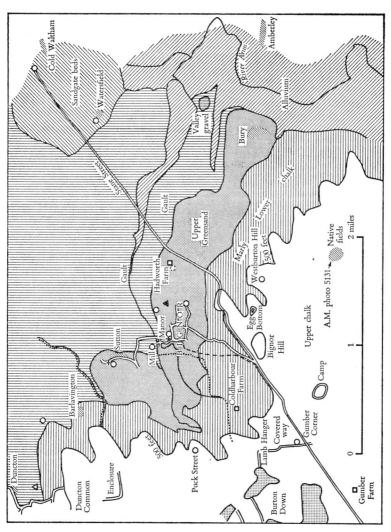

Fig. 41. Bignor, Sussex: the surroundings of the Roman villa.

17,100 loads of farmyard manure available to the owner, which would
dung, on Columella's requirements, 446·5 acres, a figure near enough
to the cultivated area we postulate minus the fallow half. If the Romano-
British cow gave half the amount of manure of her modern successor
(nine tons per annum) the *vehes* would have been in the neighbourhood
of 83 lb. In that case, 24 loads per *iugerum* meant 17·7 cwt or 28·3 cwt
the acre, but the owner disposed of 17,000 loads of farmyard manure
to concentrate as he saw fit.

It would therefore seem that the number of livestock maintained
at Bignor and the area of sown arable bear some relationship to one
another in terms of Roman manuring scales. The manure yield is
also slightly more in favour of a two-crop system than of a three-crop
course. This point, however, should not be pressed, and it may be
noted that both at Wickbourne Estate and at the villa of East Dean
not far east of Bignor, winter and summer grains were being cultivated.
Precisely the apparent affinity between the farmyard manure yielded
and the total calculated arable (without fallow) would appear to
militate against the growing of roots at Bignor. However, the distribution of Roman finds strongly suggests that the western third of the
estate, between the villa and Sutton, was in the hands of tenants of
the villa, who would have possessed their own livestock, and if
this was the case, additional manure would have been available for a
smaller area of arable. On balance, we may believe that Bignor grew
roots.[1]

Only at Bignor is the *sheep* economy evidenced by a recognizable
fold. The main evidence consists of the bone-finds, and of the testimony
of the ancient sources, which report the products of British wool and

[1] Bignor, livestock. The correctness of this estimate of the villa's flock seems to
be confirmed by the size of the dyked grazing area on Burton Down to the south
of Bignor, which according to modern grazing scales would have been appropriate
to 200 head. The enclosure (SAC LIX, 1918, p. 58) originated in the Early Iron Age,
but was also used in the Roman period. Columella's year of 292 work-days – II, 12,
and Dickson, *The Husbandry of the Ancients*, Edinburgh, 1798, I, p. 62, n. Average
manure output – Colum., II, 14, 8. Human manure: Colum., *ib.*; Varro, I, 13.
Dung per *iugerum*, Colum., II, 5. Cow's manure output: Eckles, Palmer, *Dairy Cattle
and Milk Production*[3], 1948, p. 481, Table 68, halved for the Romano-British cow.
Dickson's estimate of the Roman *vehes* is hopelessly wrong, and would have worked
out at 66 tons per year (!). My own estimate is about one tenth of this (one *vehes* =
83 lb.); cf. that a load was carried on a stretcher by two workers, as seen on the
mosaic at St Romain-en-Gal (Rostovtzeff, *Social and Economic History of the Roman
Empire*, pl. XXXVI, cf. the model from Rodenkirchen, BJ 149, p. 98, Abb. 2:2 and
30). Roman finds to the west of the villa: S. E. Winbolt, cited G. Herbert, *MS.
Notes on the Roman Villa at Bignor*, 1929, Haverfield Library, Oxford, pp. 9–10; the
Manor House and the Church at Bignor village; Bignor Mill; Sutton (M. A. Lower,
History of Sussex, II, 1870, p. 193); Barlavington (*Suss. Notes and Queries* XIII, 1950,
p. 87).

the flocks which yielded it. Eumenius in the time of Constantine spoke in his panegyric of Britain's *pecorum innumerabilis multitudo...onusta velleribus*; an early third-century inscription records that a British governor made to one Sennius Sollemnis the present of a *tossia Britannica* (rug); Diocletian's Edict of Prices lists the British horse-rug (*tapete*), which commands the highest prices in its group of wares, and the *Birrus Britannicus*, or British cape, which shares the lowest price among six products with wares from Meditomagus. Finally in its westerly sector the *Notitia Dignitatum* records in the fourth century a *gynaeceum* or weaving mill at Venta, in Britain, under the supervision of a procurator. This no doubt turned out woollen garments for the imperial civil service and armed forces.[1]

Sheep-rearing grew steadily in the Early Iron Age economy as the clearing of woodlands progressed in the light-soil areas of Wessex. As the predominant type of British prehistoric sheep (*Ovis aries studeri*) does not apparently evince signs of physical improvement from the prehistoric to the Roman epoch, it has been concluded that it was successfully reared mainly for wool-production. More recently, however, it has been demonstrated that British wool was produced by an improved white breed. At Hockwold (Norf) bone-finds showed a steep rise in the number of sheep maintained in the second century of the present era, and here they constituted 40 per cent of the livestock as against cattle, which constituted 41 per cent. It has already been remarked that generally mutton figured third in the menu of the Roman forces in Britain, and was relatively unimportant in this respect; this confirms that the sheep's function was to produce wool, possibly milk and cheese, and certainly manure. At Hockwold the flock supplied only 10 per cent of the meat consumed, despite their ample representation in the bone record.[2]

Fox pointed out that the grazing of sheep in the damp Fenland area and in areas of corresponding conditions was prevented by the presence of the liver-fluke. On the other hand, summer grazing of sheep is still the main occupation on the alluvium of the Essex salt-marshes, where the salt water immunizes the feet of the sheep from foot-rot, and is free from the liver-fluke, which is carried by a freshwater

<hr>

[1] Eumenius, *Paneg. Const. Aug.*, 9; third-century inscription, CIL XIII, 3162; *Tapete Britannicum*: Diocletian's Edict of Prices (Mommsen) XIX, 35 (28) (= 17); *Birrus Britannicus*: ib., XIX, 47 (M-B. 36); cf. JRS XLV 1955, p. 114. *Gynaeceum*: Not. Dig. Occ., XI, 60.

[2] Growth of sheep-rearing: G. D. G. Clark, *Ant.* XXI, 1947, p. 134; rearing for wool: *ibid.*, p. 135. On the white wool breed, see Dr Ryder's observations in Part 1 of this volume. Army rations: as will be seen from Dr Ryder's chapter, sheep-bones attested the bulk of the meat eaten by the troops guarding the turrets of Hadrian's Wall.

snail. Hence there can be little doubt that some of the Roman sites in the Foulness and Shoebury areas of Essex are to be explained by the presence of a peasant population engaged in sheep-rearing. Although the wool-dyeing plant at Chedworth has been shown to be an illusion, Gloucestershire is not *ipso facto* eliminated as a possible centre of the Roman wool industry, even if the evidence for a similar industry at Hucclecote seems less convincing. The Darenth villa, however, holds its place as a centre of cloth-dyeing, and the finding of loomweights at the villa of Frindsbury near Rochester, at the base of the Cliffe centurial grid, suggests that the salt-marshes of the north Kent coast may have afforded grazing for flocks that migrated to the inland farms in the winter.[1]

The matter of loomweights invites consideration of the whereabouts of the weaving centres in Roman Britain. The fourth-century *Notitia Dignitatum* records the *procurator gynaecei Ventensis*, i.e. the super-intendent of a government weaving-mill at Venta. The existence of such an establishment, of course, does not in any way prove that the manufacture of textiles was a government monopoly in that period. The purpose of the mill at Venta was to turn out garments and uniforms for the civil service and the armed forces. Two factors, however, deserve consideration when we are seeking to estimate the importance of the Venta weaving-mill – namely, the tendency of the later imperial system to organize the vital technical trades within a corporate framework controlled by the state; and the peculiar dis-tribution in Britain of finds connected with the occupations of spinning and weaving.

In Britain, published finds show that while spindle-whorls, an essential of spinning, are found in nearly every occupied site, some-times in numbers, finds of loomweights are relatively rare. The picture may alter as the result of a prolonged search among the collections, yet it is difficult to see how the rarity of loomweights could reflect anything but a reality in the course of a century and a half of archae-ological recording. The circumstances of the finding of loomweights on four sites in particular call for remark; these are Westbury (Wilts), Botley Copse, Ashdown Park (Berks), Thealby (Lincs), and Bagwood near Beer Regis (Dors). In all these cases they were associated with iron-working, at Westbury on a large scale, at Thealby with the working of ironstone. At this site there were buildings; the Ashdown Park remains came from an earthworked downland enclosure. The area at Thealby seems to have been divided out systematically for

---

[1] Grazing of Essex marshes: LUS, no. 82, Essex, p. 452; Roman sites: RCHM *Ess.*, South-east, pp. xxvii sqq. Chedworth, supposed wool-dyeing BGAS LXVIII, 1960, pp. 5–23; 162–5.

exploitation – Professor Hawkes thought for *coloni* – and it is to be recalled that in the estates of St Germain-des-Prés in the Carolingian era, in villas the essential lines of whose economy and social structure were derived from the late Roman period, ironworking was characteristic of servile tenures; and that under the same régimes the wives of *lidiles*, i.e. tenants whose status was derived from that of *laeti* (see p. 257), paid dues in woven stuffs to the *mansi dominicati*. The disproportion between spindle-whorls and loomweights, therefore, may well mean that while spinning of the raw material was the practice in every household, weaving was limited to established mills associated with industrial centres, located on large estates private or governmental.[1]

How does this fit in with the distribution of the iron carding-combs which have in recent years attracted the notice of archaeologists? A group of four is found concentrated in the north-west corner of Suffolk, and a loomweight at Lakenheath belongs to the same region. The first area is that of the lighter loams known as the Breckland, and Manning saw in this group, coupled with the cropping shears from Great Chesterford, and a carding-comb from Caister-by-Norwich (the Venta Icenorum of Roman sources) evidence that the Venta of the *Notitia* where the *gynaeceum* was located was at Caister, rather than at Venta Belgarum (Winchester) where it has been customary to place it. J. P. Wild, taking up the discussion, cites authority for a state guild of weavers, each of whom lived and worked *en famille* in the town of Cyzicus (Asia Minor) in Julian's time, and furnished fixed quotas to the government, but these, he admits, had no necessary connection with the *gynaeceum*, which was operated by slaves and convicts in conditions of confinement. In any case, carding-combs are evidence, not of weaving *in situ*, but of spinning; these instruments were used to comb out the raw fleece prior to spinning, and must be distinguished from the bone combs used to pack the woof after it had been passed among the warp. Nor did the sheep-rearing area of this region necessarily extend in Roman times far into Norfolk, which then contained large areas of woodland. The carding-combs prove wool-production in the area in the primary stage – only the loomweight from Lakenheath proves weaving. The Breckland is archaeologically the heartland of the Iceni, and the very large house at Stanton Chair (near Ixworth) may well have marked the estate of King Presutagus, converted to imperial domain. Wild, arguing that the name Venta was no longer

[1] Thealby, possible colonate divisions: H. Dudley, *Early Days in North-West Lincolnshire*, Scunthorpe, 1939, p. 193. Iron-working and servile tenures; payments in woven stuffs: A. Longnon, Guérard, *La Polyptique d'Irminon*, Paris, 1886/95, pp. 68, 109.

in current use in the fourth century, rejects Caister as the site of the *gynaeceum*, but comes to no final decision, concluding that Winchester is still the best candidate.

The evidence for Winchester, indeed, is little worse than that for Caister. Hampshire is well-known sheep-country, wider in extent than the Breckland. Carding-combs have been found at three points: at Ashdown Park, at Baydon (Wilts), and at Castlefield near Andover. The last site is of interest since the comb appears to have been associated with an aisled house resembling in principle Building II excavated by Atkinson at Caister-by-Norwich in 1929, and found to have been a glass-factory. It must nevertheless be again emphasized that carding-combs represent a pre-weaving stage of the industry. The order of production was generally dyeing of the fell, combing, spinning, weaving, napping, and fulling. In the simpler ancient economy doubtless the tendency would be to concentrate as many processes as possible in one place, but the British evidence indicates a general division between spinning and weaving.[1]

The horse was not prominently employed in agriculture in antiquity; it was not used for ploughing, and the nature of the harness used, which reduced the animal's pulling-power by constricting the wind-pipe, explains why the ox and mule were preferred for drawing carts. Sumner nevertheless believed that the New Forest potters used ponies to convey their wares, as horseshoes were found near their kilns. Horses were also used for threshing and, one may assume, for harrowing. They further served to round up free-ranging and transhumant herds, as has been noted above. They were eaten as meat.

The Roman army certainly imported its own breeds of horse for military and transport purposes, but it would seem equally reasonable that they should have established their own local studs to furnish remounts. The epitaph of a *strator consularis* at Irchester (N'hants) may well be evidence of governmental horse-rearing ranches in the vicinity, as cavalry remounts in the second century were attended

---

[1] W. M. Manning, *Ant.* XL, 1966, pp. 60–2; J. P. Wild, *Latomus* XXVI, 1967, pp. 663–7. The Cyzicus weaving guild: Sozomenos, H.E., v, 15, 6. Norfolk wood-land: of five Roman sites in Norfolk from which animal bones had been recorded in 1951, four had yielded no sheep-bones (information from the late R. R. Clarke). Wool from imperial domains: cf. *C. Theod.*, XI, 16, 1–23. Cf. two fourth-century military belt-buckles at Icklingham and two more from Ixworth; on the significance of these finds, see below p. 257. Ashdown Park and Baydon: possibly one find. Building II, Caistor-by-Norwich: NA XXIV, 1930, pp. 105 sqq. For the industrial use of aisled buildings, cf. Birch Abbey, Alcester: JRS LVI, 1966, p. 206. Loomweights and spindle-whorls have been found at Kensworth, Herts, on the same site: *Arch. J.* CXXIV, 1967, p. 153; Irchester, probably on imperial domain (see p. 29), has yielded a loomweight (*Arch. J.* CCIV, 1967, p. 91, fig. 16, 16).

to by *stratores* or governors under the charge of an *archistrator*. In favour of the location of such a depôt at Irchester may be cited the discovery at Thrapston, where the road from Durobrivae to Irchester crosses the Gartree Road, of an inscribed boundary-stone marking the separation between public and private property. There is some reason to suspect selective horse-breeding also in Cranbourne Chase. The average height of the horses whose bones were recovered at Rotherley was 11–12 hands, with a minimum of 10·49 and a maximum of 13·3 hands; at Woodcuts they stood 11·2–13 hands, but at Woodyates they averaged 13 hands, suggesting uniformly better care and fodder. Richmond also believed that the Sarmatian cavalry veterans settled in the Regio Bremmetenacensis round Ribchester practised the rearing of horses in the Lancashire Fylde. This is an eminently reasonable conjecture, but proof is lacking.[1]

Pigs are woodland animals and can winter in the woods for most of the colder months. Their representation at Woodyates, Rotherley, and Woodcuts respectively was 2, 3, and 13 per cent, and as the last farmstead had the lowest proportion of sheep, its economy was obviously more closely connected with the woodland. In general the situation of many villas close to the heavy wooded clays may have been for the purpose *inter alia*, of pig-rearing. On the other hand pig-bones are absent from some excavated villas, among which Newport (IOW), Wiggonholt (Suss), Gayton Thorpe, and Appleton (Norf) may be mentioned. Reference has been made to the grain-fattening of pork on several estates (Pitney, Woolaston Pill, Hambleden, Bucks; North Wraxhall etc.).

The domestic fowl, goose, and pigeon all figure among the livestock of Roman villas in this country. Only the domestic fowl, however, is represented by fairly ample bone-finds; it was certainly not present at every farmstead. Langton had ten geese when it was abandoned, and Pliny refers to a specific British breed, the *Cheneros*.[2]

---

[1] Constriction of windpipe: Lefèbvre des Noëttes, *L'Attelage, le cheval, et la selle à travers les âges*, Paris, 1931. Ponies: H. Sumner, *Sloden and Linwood*, 1927, p. 82 and n. Threshing: Colum., II, 20. Rounding up cattle: cf. *Paneg.*, II (x), 4, 3 (in relation to Gaul): . . . *cum arator peditem, cum pastor equitem . . . imitatus est.* Army breeds: Ewart ap. Curle, *A Roman Frontier Post*, pp. 363–71. Strator consularis: RIB, no. 233; duties: Schehl, *Oesterreiche Jahrbuch* XXIV, 1928, Beiblatt, pp. 97 sqq. Boundary-stone: JRS LVI, 1966, p. 217. And see further Dr Ryder in Part I of this volume. Other names suggesting localities where horses were reared in Roman Britain are Epeiacum (Co. Durham) and Eposessa (Heref.), but they may refer to such activity rather in the pre-Roman period. Regio Bremmetenacensis: JRS XXXV, 1945, pp. 22–3. Rotherley, Woodcuts, Woodyates: Pitt-Rivers, *Excavations*, I, p. 172; II, p. 217; III, p. 234.

[2] Woodyates, Rotherley, Woodcuts: Clark, *Ant.* XXI, 1948, pp. 126–7. Geese: Langton: Corder, Kirk, *Langton*, p. 68. The Cheneros: Pliny, HN, x, 56.

The *cultivated fruits* known to us in the Roman period in this country have been listed; the introduction of the vine, fig, and mulberry constitute sufficient evidence that there was some activity in the planting of fruit-trees, a supposition confirmed by Pliny's information on the introduction of an improved or cultivated cherry. The evidence for the Roman acclimatization of several new trees also speaks in favour of the laying out of orchards. The Ditchley villa seems to have had enclosed plantations attached to its yard, but otherwise the archaeological evidence is meagre. Probably some enclosures thought to be for livestock served to fence fruit-trees, but to prove such cases the identification of tree-pits is desirable.[1]

In summing up Roman farm structure in the province of Britain, we may cite the composite picture figured in another source:

"The dwelling is placed near light calcareous soil or medium loamy soils, but not far from the heavier loams or clays, whose wooded margin has been pushed back to clear part of them for arable. A stream flows not far away. The dwelling house is sheltered on three sides by slopes, itself standing on a southward-facing swell to catch the maximum sunlight, and facing eastward away from the prevailing west wind. It is joined by a dirt track to the main road a few miles away; this track is older than the villa, but has in sectors been straightened and improved by the owner to facilitate getting his produce to market. The residence is closed off by a wall from the farmyard. In the close is a garden planted with vine, fig, and box; on the west side sycamore, walnut, sweet chestnut, and holm oak have been set to form a windbreak. In the garden are beds of flowers, amongst which are seen the pansy, rose, poppy, and lily, and various useful potherbs. Part is devoted to market-gardening, and here are planted the cabbage, carrot, parsnip, and celery.

"On the south side of the yard is an aisled building for the farmhands and bailiff; the latter lives in a heated room at the west end. In the same part the women of the household live and work at spinning and weaving. The hands inhabit the aisles and the nave. Originally livestock was housed in the aisles, but these have been shifted elsewhere and the aisles divided off into rooms. Threshing also was originally done here in wet weather, but now a circular threshing floor has been made in the yard, and a roomy barn has been built near it where the unthreshed grain can be stored if rain comes. In the yard poultry and geese are kept, the latter both for their plumage and for their meat.

[1] Tree-pits, Cromwell, Notts: JRS LI, 1961, pl. xi, 3, on the right of the photograph.

"On the east side of the yard is a composite block in which byre and pigsty are ranged each side of a central barn where fodder and grain are stored for food. The pigs are grain-fed for fattening, and the oxen get oats and barley in seasons of heavy labour, but also beanstraw, vetch, turnips, hay, and leaves. Besides the working oxen, twenty or so cows and heifers are wintered on turnips, vetch, and hay scythed from the meadow. Some of the farms in the neighbourhood run large herds of cattle in the woodland and on the downs, driving them from pasture to pasture under charge of mounted herdsmen. In the winter the breeding stock picks up a living in the forest-rides, and is confined in enclosures next to water, sometimes near to a highway along which those to be sold are driven to market.

"The pigs graze the forest, but the sows are brought into the sty for farrowing and selected young pigs are housed for fattening. The dung is cleared into a pit, and taken to the fields in autumn and winter on stretchers for manuring. This is light by modern standards (not much over a ton an acre), but the heavy land is chalked periodically and the lighter loams are marled to improve the texture. A good deal of the farmyard manure, and the clearings from the latrines also, are kept for the roots. The farm is first and foremost a corn farm; wheat, spelt, emmer, and barley are the main crops, but the owner is experimenting with oats, which he finds stand up well to the series of cold wet years which seem to be becoming increasingly common. He finds that oat-straw gives better bedding and manure than bracken, and the beasts relish the grain. He would generally prefer to expand his summer crops on the chalk soils above his main estate, in spite of their distance, which hampers working – but these are more favourable to autumn-sown grains in wet seasons. Further, rainy autumns have been spoiling his wheats on the heavy lands and making it hard to get the autumn seed in. But the government presses him for wheat, which it wants in easily ground grist. To meet the situation he reduces his fallow to a third, and adopts a three-course scheme, in order to have equal summer and winter grains, and constructs several grain-drying furnaces to leeward of the farm."

In addition to agriculture, a number of villas, and perhaps some villages and homesteads that did not attain to a villa standard of living, developed branches of industry as a means of supplementing income (e.g. tile-making, quarrying, fulling, the working of ironstone, glass manufacture). There is no need to enter into further detail on this subject, but the fact is important for an appreciation of Roman rural economy in Britain, since it is to some degree a measure of the proprietor's resource and organizational ability, of his awareness of the need to buttress his economy against the vicissitudes of nature and society, and of his general initiative and adaptability.[1]

[1] From CBA. RR vii, pp. 104–6. Accommodation roads: Great Wymondley, Balchester (Hants), Bignor; villas on the Harroway and Whiteway (Glos). For flowers, etc. Godwin, *History*, *ad voc.* Geese and plumage: Fremersdorf, *Köln-Müngersdorf*, p. 130; Pliny, HN, x, 53. Marling: Pliny, HN, xvii, 42. Straw to bed horses: AA[4] xiv, 1937, p. 164. Field-walls, Holmstreet (Pulborough), Suss.: PSA[2] xxiii, pp. 377 sq.; in Gaul: Varro, i, 14. Division of undeveloped land among tenants: Vened. Code, ii, 12, 6; 18, 7. Industry in villas: e.g. iron-stone: Dudley, *op. cit.*, p. 193, etc.; fulling: Darenth; glass-making: Liversidge, *Roman Villas in Britain*, p. 324; stone quarrying: Liversidge, *op. cit.*, p. 326.

CHAPTER XII

THE PATTERN OF AGRARIAN CHANGE

P RE-ROMAN POTTERY and first-century A.D. coins are not infrequent on south-of-England Roman sites, and it would not have been difficult for a number of Belgic farmsteads to evolve into something like Roman villas soon after the first pacification of those areas, particularly as the export of grain and livestock had begun before the conquest. Evidence of Claudian occupation comes from sites as far apart as Park Street (Herts), Casterley (Wilts), Stanton Chair (Suff), and Ashtead (Surr). In Somerset and the north it took longer for native hutments to become romanized farms, but at such sites the process had begun before the end of the first century. We know from Dio that British notables received credits from the emperor Claudius, also from Seneca, and the premature foreclosures on these debts was one of the causes of the revolt of Boudicca. The inference is that Roman capitalists during the first years of the conquest were investing in British development, and as the main urban colonization was still to come, this must have meant chiefly agriculture. In Suffolk and Norfolk the effect of the Boudiccan revolt was felt mainly in cultural stagnation which lasted till the second century. The cooperative attitude of the Coritani evinced by pottery evidence, and the peaceful agricultural development of the south Lincolnshire gravels, may account also for the beginning of prosperous native farmsteads such as Mansfield Woodhouse and Rudston in the late first century. Round Winchester and Basingstoke, on the other hand, the evacuation of various native sites occurs during the first half-century of Roman rule, and the first Roman villas appear between 60 and 70. In Surrey the population grew and expanded into hitherto untilled areas immediately after the conquest.

It was the Flavian period that supplied the strongest impulse to the growth of the capitalist farmstead. In the Basingstoke area at least six villas seem to have originated during that period. In 1948 Liversidge knew of no fewer than ninety villas which had yielded material from the end of the first century. The active aid and encouragement of Agricola is well known. Minor rural centres also manifest growth at this time, examples being Brough-on-Humber, Dorchester-on-Thames, Alchester, and Baldock. In Surrey there was an intensification of movement and trade, and at this time throughout the country a number of hill-forts are finally abandoned. (Above, p 35.)

Agricola, according to Tacitus, stopped the oppressive practice of forcing natives who could not deliver the corn-levy to purchase it at local granaries, or of compelling its delivery at distant stations; he appears to have equalized the burden over various districts. We are told that the delivery of grain was the duty of the *civitates*, and Flavian urbanization was no doubt not unconnected with the administrative arrangements involved. The formation of rural divisions for fiscal purposes is implied, and this probably went hand in hand with the setting up of the *ordines* of the *civitates*, composed of romanizing upper-class natives, and the definition of the districts for which they held responsibility. This reorganization may have been facilitated by the cadaster of landed property, which evidence at Sulloniacae (Brockley Hill, M'sx) suggests was completed by about 70. The *mortaria* dated to 70–120 and stamped with the name of Sullonius were made at Sulloniacae; if the French archaeologists are right that Gallic place-names with this proprietary suffix *-ac* originated with the state survey of properties, the survey of southern Britain may well have been completed when Vespasian succeeded.[1]

Another aspect of the Flavian organization was the beginning of the settlement of the Fenlands and the deforestation of central Essex. The two nearly parallel roads of central Essex, whether or not they reflect centuriation (pp. 100–2), coincide accurately with the Essex medium loam area, and appear to date from this period; the words put into the mouth of Calgacus with reference to the draining of swamps and the felling of forests may well refer to this and to the Fenland project. The latter may have begun as early as between 50 and 60, but the main colonization of the Fenland marls took place in the second century, more particularly in its first half. Where the new population came from we do not know; Hallam, noting that *Salinae* was attributed by Ptolemy to the Catuvellauni, suggests that the first settlers came from that *civitas*. That they came from the Iceni, on the other hand, seems improbable, because just in this period the Icenian tribal capital was founded at Caister-by-Norwich. A population thus free for transfer nevertheless implies overpopulation or displacement by newcomers, who might have been men of capital from abroad or of their own people, for the Flavian period is the time of

[1] Credits of Claudius and Seneca: Dio, LXII, 2. First-century sites in Kent: B. J. Philp, *A. Cant.* LXXVIII, 1963, pp. 74 sqq. Norfolk stagnation: Moore, PSIA XXIV, 1938, pp. 169 sq. Basingstoke, first villas: HFC XVIII, 1953, p. 123; first-century villas: Liversidge, *Roman Villas*, p. 343. Brough-on-Humber: JRS XXVII, 1937, p. 230; Dorchester, Oxon.: *ib.*, p. 238; Alchester: Kendrick, Hawkes, *Archaeology of England and Wales, 1914–1931*, London, 1932, p. 257; Baldock: JBAA² XXXVIII, 1932, p. 259. Agricola and the grain tribute: Tac., *Agric.*, 19, 4–5. Compilation of cadaster: LMAS² X, 1950, p. 226.

the emergence of the first villas, and the contemporary immigration into East Anglia from abroad has been mentioned (p. 26). Additionally, a surplus population might have been created by the taking up of areas previously used by the village communities for transhumatory grazing. The imposition of taxation alone may well have thrown onto the labour market a section of the population previously semi-nomadic or engaged in stock-rearing.

The reigns of Hadrian and the Antonine emperors were the high-water mark of British urban prosperity, and the close connection between the development of the towns' rural territories and of the towns themselves has been outlined. Among the country houses founded in the middle years of the second century may be mentioned examples in Buckinghamshire, Sussex, Berkshire, Gloucestershire, Cambridge-shire, Norfolk, and the Isle of Wight. Some of them, e.g. Tockington Park (Glos), Litlington (Camb), Northleigh (Oxon), and Keynsham (Som), already in existence by that date, were the centres of considerable estates, to judge by their size. Such estates, however, do not seem invariably to have disturbed the existent peasant population, so far as we know. There is little evidence for displacement at this period in the Basingstoke district, and in Surrey and Suffolk it did not occur till later. In Norfolk the first farm-buildings appear in the course of this century. The beginnings of the village of Nordelph in the Fenlands in 125/50, its intensive life in the second century, and the expan-sion of Runcton Holme in the same period, suggest a prosperous period, confirmed by the contemporary progress of Fenland settle-ment as established by Salway, Hallam, Bromwich, and others. In this area, the number of farms was doubled in the course of the second century.[1]

In the middle or later years of the second century a small series of villas sprang up in the Yorkshire dales and East Riding (Castle Dykes, Collingham, Gargrave, Hovingham, North Newbold) and several others in Nottimghamshire (Norton Disney, Mansfield Woodhouse) made decided advances. During the second century the native villages of the Pennines also developed, apparently under the spur of the growing of grain required for the army. The Brigantian ex-soldiers whose dedications are known in the Pennines in the second half of the century may have been party to the same process.

Agricultural production in this period may, indeed, have been intensified; Clapham and Godwin found evidence of this in the north-Somerset peats between 100 and 150 approximately; the Park Street

[1] Calgacus: Tac., *Agric.*, 31. Caister-by-Norwich: G. Macdonald, Roman Britain 1914–1928, in BRGK 1929, pp. 64–6; Kendrick, Hawkes, *op. cit.*, p. 257. First villas in Norfolk: PSIA xxiv, 1938, pp. 177–8. Fenland: Phillips, FR p. 9.

villa receives a large corn-drier between 150 and 200; and at West Blatchington no fewer than eleven such installations were made in the late second or early third century. These developments find their background in the general situation: in the second half of the period the state, driven by the crushing weight of the defence estimates, increased fiscal pressure on the towns, shifting financial responsibility to the richest citizens, and many of the cities were already in financial difficulties. Intensive production in the rural estates in the later second century, therefore, is the symptom of the early phase of that trend which was to threaten urban prosperity in the succeeding century.[1]

The Severan age involved political disturbance, the breakdown of the northern frontier, administrative reorganization, and the intensified economic exploitation of the province. It also meant the confiscation of the property of those who had supported the imperial candidature of Albinus, and the resultant growth of Severus' newly established *Res Privata* (pp. 29–30). Direct evidence there is none, although a holding near Mildenhall (Suff) might have belonged to an absentee proprietor known to have suffered confiscation of his Spanish estates at this time (see p. 25). But Otford, burnt about 200, is not rehabilitated in its previous form; Boxted and Lullingstone cease to be occupied; Knowl Hill (Berks), Kingston Buci (Suss) and Ditchley are in like case. Various other rural sites indicate interruption or cessation of occupation, examples being Brockley Hill, Lea Cross villa (Salop), Great Oakley (N'hants), and Ashley in the same county, but it is not easy to know whether these cases are to be interpreted as the result of confiscation or of absorption into new estates. Other villas show reconstruction at this time, examples being Walton-on-the-Hill, Norton Disney, Mansfield Woodhouse, Wiggonholt, Chedworth, and Langton. A number of new villas take their origin in the Severan epoch: instances are Westland near Yeovil, Nuthill near Calne, Iwerne I, Atworth, Low Ham, West Coker, Great Staughton (Hunts), Cawood and Hovingham in Yorkshire, Huntsham (Heref), and Hinton St Mary (Dors). In addition, there are some signs of efforts to strengthen the life of the rural elements: roads are laid out tapping the Berkshire Downs in the late second or early third century; new temples are built at Frilford and Yatton, and the material at the Farley Heath temple in Surrey includes a preponderance of third-century pottery, in this resembling the probable sacred site of Lowbury Hill (Berks).

Two facts however stand out in relation to the later second and early third century in Britain. The first is the evidence, already cited, for the displacement of peasants in Surrey and East Anglia, concomitantly with the appearance of new estate centres, and for the

[1] North Somerset peats: Clapham, Godwin, *Philosophical Trans.*, 233B, pp. 275 sqq.

immigration into Gloucestershire of new elements from abroad. The second is the considerable increase of large aisled houses as the main buildings of their establishments. Only a part of the known basilical buildings, unfortunately, can be dated, and the necessary information on several, recently excavated, is not forthcoming. But the statistics appear to show that out of 43 examples dated, sometimes with a margin of uncertainty, 15 can be ascribed to the second century, only 2 being prior to the middle of the century, and 6 to late in that century; 16 belong to the third, 2 to the third or fourth, and 11 to the fourth century. In other words, 13 belong to the period 150–200 approximately and 16 to the third. This development is surely to be interpreted as the rise of a class of prosperous and consciously Celtic landed proprietors representing and reflecting in the plans of the houses they built the characteristic social structure of their nation.[1]

The Severan age was the age of the crystallization of new tendencies; while it witnessed a strengthening of centralization and of the military despotism, and the elevation of the imperial domains to one of the major factors in the economy of the Empire, it also beheld the intensification of the influence of oriental religion, great activity in the codification of the law, the levelling down of distinctions by the grant of citizenship to the majority of the provincial populations, and a greater toleration towards the customs, languages, and cultures of the provincial peoples. In this period new expressions of local provincial art emerge – in Britain, for instance, Castor pottery and new styles of bronze work – an awakening to be connected, no doubt, with the new latitude exercised by the rulers.

But there was also a determined effort to meet the liabilities of the Empire by an increase and reorganization of production. The process, perhaps, was only to reach its peak later in the third century; it was in the middle of the century that Veteris received his basilical shrine at Thistleton Dyer, an apotheosis of the chieftain-proprietor of the basilical house, which implies an official approval of his position. Yet fifty years before, the residents of a basilical villa had been allotted land by an official Roman method of land-division (West Blatchington). We might tentatively suggest that at some point in this period, recognition was accorded by the state to Celtic law in such a way as to legalize the chief or head of the kinship-group as seigneur of its members through the medium of the villa. The notion has something in common with J. T. Smith's attribution to the aisled house of the function of a manor hall or court-leet, at least in so far as it ascribes certain powers to the owner.[2]

[1] Roads to Berkshire Downs: *Newbury and District Field Club Trans.*, 1948, pp. 23–4.
[2] J. T. Smith, *Arch. J.* cxx, 1963, p. 13.

The third century was characterized in Britain by an expansion of urbanization (Chesterton-on-the-Nene; Corbridge), and also of rural production. The native villages of the Pennines and Cumbria evince a certain development from the mid-second century, continued into the third, and during the latter, the emperor Probus placed Germanic military settlers in the north of the country. North Wraxhall evinces expansion of staff, West Blatchington engages in intensive corn-growing; round the Charterhouse-on-Mendip mining village fields are laid out apparently to make the population equally productive in minerals and food. Rockbourne Down begins its grain-growing and free-range cattle-rearing. The third century can probably show more new villa foundations and more rebuilding activity in villas than any other century, and this is the beginning of an era of prosperity in the Somerset area around Ilchester. New foundations have been ascertained in the civilian zone at 26 sites since 1952; in at least eleven more, rebuilding or the addition of rooms or buildings has been established.

In the late second century, on the other hand, extensive flooding by run-off from the higher area to the south, evidently to be connected with increased rainfall, caused extensive disruption of the settlement of the southern Fenland silts, and a new concentration of farmsteads on the higher sites fringing the shores of the Wash. This episode was followed by rehabilitation work in the southern fringe areas, expressed, at least in part, by the emergence of some small but wealthy villas (e.g. Mildenhall), perhaps later held, thinks Salway, by proprietors who received their land on terms of emphyteusis.

In the course of the century other signs of adversity appear. There is neglect of public buildings at Verulamium and Wroxeter, probably owing to the impact of overtaxation and inflation. Odd symptoms also show disturbance to the life of the estates: Ditchley lacks signs of occupation; Saunderton is in decay; Magor (Corn), built in this century, is deserted by its owner; Park Street falls into disrepair; at Hambleden (Bucks) finds suggest alarm and disorder. Ashtead is abandoned about 250 and Lullingstone in the first half of the century. Eccles (Kent) is gradually allowed to fall out of use; at Faversham occupation ends late in the century. Economic oppression or the pressure of big landowners may have played their part; the coast of Kent was evidently under threat of barbarian sea-raiding. But the discontent of slaves and tenants may also have begun to make itself felt. This had begun in Gaul as early as in the reign of M. Aurelius among the Sequani, and under Commodus bands of Gallic malcontents had been organized by one Maternus. In the third century the name Bacaudae is heard of for the first time. We have already spoken of the fate of an imperial shrine at Bath, *insolentia dirutum*, in the second or third century (p. 30), and of the possibility of trouble in central Hampshire under Carinus (A.D. 283). At the end of the century the barbarian raiding of the coast had become more dangerous, extending also to the western shore. Among the seaboard villas which fell victim to their depredations were Fingringhoe (Ess), Ely near Cardiff, probably Woolaston Pill (Glos), and Havant (Hants); the occupation of Gayton Thorpe did not survive the beginning of the fourth century.[1]

The turn of the third and fourth centuries was preceded, as was that of the second and third, by civil war, invasion from the north, and social administrative changes. The accessions of Carausius and Allectus meant disorder, reconquest, and probably expropriation by Constantius Chlorus of the property of their supporters. On the other hand Constantius restored movable property to landowners who had lost it at the hands of plunderers, and the new government made a determined effort to reinject life into the towns.

On the countryside, Liversidge counted 200 sites of villas that have yielded fourth-century material, but only twenty of these have yielded no earlier finds. Today the number of new foundations known in this period could doubtless be increased. In other words, the villa system remained stable, with a measure of growth. Rebuilding or rehabilitation can be noted at a number of villas around the year 300 as far apart as Langton and Wiggonholt (Suss). The villas of western Somerset exhibit remarkable prosperity in the fourth century, and the division of the Durotriges into two, the new second capital being

---

[1] New *civitates*; Chesterton-on-Nene: RIB, no. 2235; Corbridge: RIB, no. 2299. Northern villages: YAJ XXXIV, 1939, p. 145; Charterhouse-on-Mendip: BUS VI (1949–50), pp. 201–4; cf. *ib.*, p. 82, fig. 20. German military settlers: see Professor Finberg, below, p. 385. Prosperity west of Ilchester: JRS XXXIX, 1949, p. 109; SANHS XCVI, 1952, p. 77. Fenland flooding: FR pp. 114 sqq.; rehabilitation (late 3rd–4th century): *ib.* p. 16. Barbarian raids: cf. the building of Reculver *c.* A.D. 200–25: *Ant. J.* XLI, 1961, pp. 224–8. The Sequani: Julius Capitolinus, *M. Aur. Phil.*, XXII, 10; Maternus: Herodian, I, 10; Bacaudae: Eutrop., IX, 20; Victor, *de Caes.*, 39, 17. Third-century building and abandonment of villas: Rivet, RVB, pp. 201–2, puts the process of abandonment first and an increase of new establishments later, evidently towards the end of the century. Rivet proposes as causes for the abandonment, economic depression, civil war, and barbarian attacks. Only the early building of Reculver obviously supports the last factor; but was the earlier third century a time of economic depression? I am not sure how far the archaeological evidence for the dates of abandonment and new foundations has been satisfactorily studied; on the first there should be enough third-century *terra sigillata* and colour-coated ware to furnish an answer. Rivet's suggestion of abandonment by owners but not by staff seems to require archaeological demonstration. As regards the Irish threat, it should be noted that Llantwit Major, according to Dr Webster's revision of Nash-Williams's dating (RVB, pp. 238–43), was built about 180 and much enlarged about 300.

Lendiniae (Ilchester), suggests that liabilities could be concentrated over smaller areas which had increased their populations in the meantime, despite the burdensome corvées which the Durotriges, as well as the Catuvellauni and Dumnonii, had to perform in the repair of the northern frontier. The rural stability of the province is further demonstrated by the Basingstoke district, where most sites continue occupied, and several abandoned in the first century are resettled. But some coastal villas damaged by sea-raiders remain deserted.

The literary evidence is in favour of considerable surplus agricultural production in fourth-century Britain. Julian used the province to feed the starving cities of the Rhine in 360, but Ammianus Marcellinus makes it clear that the British grain was a regular export – *a Britanniis sueta transferri*. Intensive production is confirmed by the ubiquity of corn-drying furnaces in the British lowland zone. Many of them are of the fourth century, although some are dated as early as the second (Park Street) and the late second century (West Blatchington). They are found uniformly over the civilian areas of the province; one very large installation just outside Reculver was certainly military. Goodchild drew attention to the ruthless insertion of these furnaces into dwellings, both urban and rural, in the later period; he suspected state action, and the evidence at West Blatchington and in Cranbourne Chase favours the idea. The impression is gained of a situation in which the niceties of life had declined and production was regarded as all-important.

One aim of the drying process was to make the grain easier to grind; light parching also prolongs its power of germination. Later Scottish and Irish parallels make it highly probable that the object was chiefly to facilitate the grinding of a wet-cut crop, but also to make possible the husking of husked crops such as spelt, emmer, millet, and pannic. There can be little doubt, however, that other crops too had to be so dried in a period when the climate of Britain was becoming steadily wetter (pp. 5–6).

The ubiquitous corn-driers leave us with the impression that the province was being pressed to produce in conditions where amenities receded before necessities and the standard of life was being lowered. The life of some towns was in decay; a few owners may have abandoned their estates for the protection of their walls, but it is more probable, at least till the Pict War of 367, that government stewards had taken over individual estates and that others had been absorbed into larger entities. We have discussed this probability at Ditchley, and the same seems to have applied to Stroud. The fourth century in general is the era of the big estate in Britain; it is in this century that the villa with external yard – sometimes with two yards – appears; Woodchester, with two or more, can hardly precede this time. In all probability the Weyhill area of Hampshire had become a large estate in the third century; Langton seems now to be a tenant holding. Mansfield Woodhouse builds a big aisled house for farmhands, as though it had expanded its farm-area, and Bignor reaches its maximum development with spacious farm-buildings arranged in an outer yard. It is now that the Newton villa near Basingstoke acquires its peripheral tenures, and there is a general increase of rural sites in the region which is probably paralleled throughout the lowland zone. Furthermore, although such may have existed before, it is to the third and fourth centuries that belongs the little information that we possess on absentee proprietors owning estates in Britain – Melania, and probably the woman-citizen of Dumnonia.[1]

The entire process of landed accumulation, moreover, seems to have taken place *pari passu* with the steady social degradation of the free Celtic members of kinships, if we have rightly interpreted the development of the aisled house and the gradual separation of the labouring residents from the proprietor's family. In the fourth century, if not before, the aisled building takes its place in the outer yard and either the kinship has broken up and its members have become simple labourers, or they have become *coloni* on peripheral holdings within the estate. In either case, we begin to discern the faint lines of a social revolution.

Whether it was the members of these disintegrated groups who paved the way for the growth of the colonate in Britain it is hard to say. The interpretation of the evidence from the Fenlands would suggest that the earliest colonate existed in the later first century, and Hawkes's interpretation of the storage pits in the Cranbourne Chase farmsteads – that their sudden decrease in the Roman period implies a heavy drain of tribute and rent – also points to tied tenantry on imperial domain. The symptoms of a landless proletariat in formation more especially in the later second century have been outlined. The economic needs of the fourth century, with its shortage of man-power and constant drain of production to military expenditure, may have thrown these people into the arms of the big estate-owners or made them available for emphyteutic settlement on more favourable terms. Whatever occurred, archaeology makes it clear that cultivation did

[1] Constantius restores property: *Paneg. Const.*, 17. 200 villas: Liversidge, *Roman Villas*, p. 345. Division of Durotriges: Lendiniae, Stevens, SANHS xcvi, 1951, pp. 188 sqq. Corvées of tribes: RIB, 1672; 1843; 1844; 1962; cf. JRS xiv, 1924, pp. 244–5. West Somerset: SANHS xcvi, 1952, pp. 77, 191, n. 2. Basingstoke: HFC xviii, pp. 126–7. Corn-export: Amm. Marc., xviii, 2. Reculver: p. 34, n. 1. Corn-driers: Goodchild, *Ant. J.* xxiii, 1943, p. 151; corn-drying: *Ant.* xii, 1938, pp. 151, 239; husking: Pliny, HN xviii, 10.

not lapse in Britain, as in some provinces, but expanded in the fourth century. An additional factor certainly caused a major displacement of population and may have turned numbers of people into landless labourers and candidates for the colonate. This was the rise of the sea-level and the resultant inundation of the coasts of north Somerset and north Kent. The Somerset inundation, which probably also affected the south coast of Wales, resulted in the flooding of some hundred square miles of coast till then well inhabited by a population in part engaged in pottery-making and salt-manufacture. This appears to have taken place progressively or repeatedly from the beginning of the third till the beginning of the fourth century. For the same reasons the Upchurch pottery industry of the north Kent coast had come to an end by the early third century. Stevens has suggested in relation to north Somerset that these conditions may have provided the inland villas of the region with a reservoir of cheap labour which materially increased their prosperity in the fourth century; Cunliffe believes that the situation also caused a shift to industrial activity (lead-working, the manufacture of pewter) in northern Somerset. Inland run-off flooding in the southern Fenland basin, already mentioned, led to the abandonment of the Hockwold village shortly after 200, and the situation was repeated in the Fenland settlement area in the later third century. Mrs Hallam has suggested that the subsequent recolonization of the north Fenland coastal silts was carried out by Probus or Carausius, and that the new settlers were elements from the Low Countries who understood the local conditions; she reminds us that Carausius is once described as a Batavian. For Britain, at any rate, the century was one of more intensive settlement and agricultural output, and superficially at least, of prosperity. Numerous humbler farmsteads in stone or timber dotted the countryside. A high proportion of these originated in the third century, but continued their lives into, and often throughout, the fourth.[1]

At this point a comment is required on the till recently accepted view that much arable in the south of England gave place in the later Roman era to ranches and sheep-walks as a result of the expansion of cattle-rearing and probably of the British wool trade. The theory originated with some of the leading authorities on Roman Britain (Collingwood, Hawkes, Crawford, Richmond) and rested on the identification as livestock kraals of several Wessex enclosures, which appeared to replace 'native' fields of the period; on the fourth-century evacuation of the Wiltshire and Cranbourne Chase villages, on the location of the Venta weaving-mill at Winchester; on the definition

[1] Decrease of pits in Cranbourne Chase farms: Hawkes, *Arch. J.* CIV, 1947, p. 41. Marine transgression: p. 57, n. 1. Recolonization: FR p. 75.

of the Bokerley Dyke, which closes off Cranbourne Chase from the
north, as the boundary of a pastoral area, and of a similar attribution
to the travelling dykes of west Hampshire, Dorset, and Wiltshire.

This theory has been criticized by C. C. Taylor and others; Taylor
has pointed out that most of the pastoral enclosures cited are not
Romano-British, and that the fields overlain by some of them have
been shown to be post-Roman. Doubt has been cast on the identification of the Venta weaving-mill with Winchester (p. 215), and the
travelling dykes of Hampshire, Wiltshire, and Dorset are challenged
as localized and undated. Here we may add that the abandonment
of the Romano-British sites of Wiltshire and Dorset takes place, in
most cases, not early in the fourth century but very much later
(see p. 41, n. 1.).[1]

Most of these criticisms are valid. It may however be remarked that
if the travelling dykes of Hampshire, Wiltshire, and Dorset are
undated, their function as pasture-boundaries and droveways is
hardly in question and they are intimately bound up with the Early
Iron Age and Romano-British economy. If a dozen alleged Roman
stock-enclosures have to be removed from the map, Grinsell has three
others to add. There is also no doubt that the livestock branch gained
a great impulse with the Roman conquest; so much is proved by the
Hockwold animal bones, which record a steep local rise in the rearing
of sheep and cattle; at War Ditches, Cherry Hinton (near Cambridge),
cattle increased greatly in the Roman period while sheep decreased
in comparison with their part in the Early Iron Age economy. At
Dinorben, Cowley explained the fall in mutton consumed by the
growing importance of British wool-production. Further details of
the importance of these branches in Roman Britain have been discussed
above (p. 215), but the question is, can we trace any actual increase
in the scope of these branches in the later centuries of the Roman
occupation? It is generally agreed that meat-eating increased in the
later Roman Empire, whether by reason of climatic factors or the
influence of barbarian penetration. The provision for the wintering
of sheep and cattle belongs to the fourth century at Bignor and
Thistleton Dyer, probably at Woodchester, Brading, Apethorpe,

[1] Expansion of livestock branches: Hawkes, *Arch. J.* CIV, p. 71; Collingwood,
Myres, RBES[2] pp. 223–4; Crawford, Keiller, *Wessex from the Air*, pp. 254–5;
Richmond, *Roman Britain*,[2] Harmondsworth, 1963, p. 131. Bokerley Dyke: *Arch. J.*
CIV, p. 71. Enclosures formerly defined as for livestock and wrongly dated Roman:
Soldiers' Ring (Damersham), "Wuduburh" (Knighton Hill), Broad Chalk, and
others. Travelling dykes as pasture boundaries: *OS Map of Celtic Earthworks on
Salisbury Plain*, Southampton, 1934, Introd.; HFC XIV, 1938, p. 143; PPS XX, 1954,
p. 111. Criticism: Fowler, Musty, Taylor in WAM LX, 1965, pp. 52 sqq.; C. C. Taylor,
Ant. XLI, 1967, pp. 304–6. The Wiltshire and Dorset villages: see p. 41, n. 1.

Spoonley Wood, and Pitney. The free-range cattle-grazing of the Appleton villa (Norf) took place between about 150 and the fourth century, but the farmyard there belonged to the third and fourth. Ely near Cardiff appears to have passed to a predominantly stock-rearing economy in the third century. Extensive activity in these branches at Chesterton-Durobrivae is of the fourth century, of the third and fourth at Rockbourne Down. This evidence cannot be said to be decisive, but it at least leaves the question open; it will be reverted to when we discuss the fate of the native downland economy. Nor can the evidence on wool-production be taken as decisive: the fact that all our extant written evidence for the British wool industry belongs to the third and fourth centuries is highly suggestive, but need not indicate that only then was the industry of importance.[1]

While therefore the increase of grazing land at the expense of the native upland cultivation cannot be proved, there were nevertheless certain circumstances common to the period in the Empire as a whole that led to the spread of colonate tenure. The contemporary inflation, well evidenced in Britain in the third century, increased the importance of agriculture, since payments began to be made increasingly in kind. Urban indebtedness also caused the loss of municipal lands sold up to cover deficits. Both these phenomena increased the importance of the landowning class. Secondly, there were certainly crown domains in the province (pp. 28 sqq.) to serve as models for colonate tenure. Thirdly, displacement of peasantry had taken place in East Anglia and Surrey in the late second and third centuries. Large estates existed by the second, and must have been considerable by the fourth. We hear of absentee owners of estates at this period. Evidence of the conversion of villas to tenancies and their absorption into larger estates, against a background of forced intensification and lowered living standards, has been cited. Taxation paid in kind under inflationary conditions and the transfer of the responsibility of exacting it increasingly to the landowner – a situation legalized by Valens and Valentinian – led inevitably to the colonate wherever it had not previously existed. How far this was offset in the latter half of the fourth century by the fact that Britain was better supplied with silver than other provinces, is hard to estimate. But the disaster of 367 may have influenced the government to compel surviving owners to take responsibility for

[1] L. Grinsell, *The Archaeology of Wessex*, London, 1958, p. 227; cf. Hawkes, *Arch. J.* CIV, p. 33: Brown's Barn; another west of Yarnbury Castle; a third south of Bratton Castle – all "kite" enclosures of characteristic Roman type. War Ditches at Cherry Hinton: CAS LVI–LVII, 1963–4, p. 29. Increase of meat-eating: O. Seeck, *Geschichte des Untergangs des antiken Welts*,[4] Stuttgart, 1921–2, I, pp. 262 sqq. Pork consumption: Apicius, VII; *Scriptores Hist. Aug.*, *Vopiscus, Aurelian*, 35; Seeck, *op. cit.*, I, i, pp. 381, 383, 422. Chesterton-Durobrivae: JRS XLVIII, 1958, p. 139.

vacant tracts. If Salvian's Gallic picture applies also to Britain, the bigger proprietors did not need much encouragement to do so, but this would have meant the conversion of floating labour to *coloni* and would have encouraged the settling of barbarian prisoners as *laeti* bound to military service and their holdings equally. How far the latter category of settler is traceable archaeologically will be discussed in our final section (below, pp. 258 sq.).[1]

The great barbarian confederate attack on Britain in 367 dealt a grave blow to the rural economy of Britain. But how grave is not entirely clear. In 1929 Collingwood wrote that the coins "ordinarily found" in villas went down "at furthest" to Valentinian I and Valens, i.e. to the great invasion, and then stopped. The exceptions were in Somerset and Kent, where, he thought, they continued to Arcadius and Honorius because the arrival of Theodosius had saved them. But otherwise "the villa system had vanished." This is certainly an exaggeration. It has been remarked that the presence of coins of Valentinian and Valens is apt to be evidence for occupation after 367. On this assumption, seven Wiltshire villas may have ended in the invasion of that year, but five survived. Moreover, coin-evidence can be deceptive unless weighed together with datable finds. Thus, at the Westlecott Road villa, Swindon, the only known coin was of Constans, but rosette-stamped pottery showed occupation after 360 and probably after 367. In 1931 Hawkes and Kendrick were able to write of coins continuing to Valens at Somerdale, Ipswich, and Newport villas; coin-stops at Nuthills (Wilts), Folkestone, and Longstock (Hants) suggested destruction in 367, but Keynsham, Twyford (Hants), North Warnborough, and Hambleden survived. Since 1952 no less than 23 rural sites, most of them villas or farmhouses, have been excavated which have revealed evidence of survival after 367, most of them to the last years of the fourth century; these include such houses as Great Weldon (N'hants), Thistleton Dyer, Walls Coppice (Charminster, Dors), Arbury Road, Shakenoake Farm (Oxon), and Great Tey (Ess). In the Chilterns at least five villas were held till the last decade of the fourth century if not for longer.[2]

Frere says "in the south of Britain the damage...is hard to detect." He sums up: "it is only possible to say that a number of villas appear to have gone out of occupation about this time to judge from their coin-lists, though the great majority continued to exist." In general,

[1] Landowner's responsibility for taxation: *C. Theod.*, XI, 1, 4. The Gallic picture: Salvian, *de gubernatione Dei*, IV, 74–5; V *passim*.

[2] The barbarian attack of 367: Amm. Marc., XXVII, 8, 1–9. Collingwood and the coins in villas: *Ant.* III, 1929, p. 272; cf. Hawkes, Kendrick, *op. cit.*, p. 294. Coins of Valentinian and Valens: p. 41, n. 1.

even if 367 was, in the words of Wheeler, the beginning of "the unromanization of Roman Britain," it was a catastrophe that can be overestimated.

It has also been suggested that many owners now abandoned their estates, the meaning of the thinning off of the coin-finds in the villas after 367 being that only the *coloni* remained behind, or that they had revolted or fled. It is very difficult to establish a social movement of peasants at this date in Roman Britain on the analogy of the Gallic Bacaudae in the late third and fifth centuries. The rising which expelled the government immediately after the rescript of Honorius in 410 was not, apparently, an insurrection of the poor. The best evidence – the Bath inscription and the Carinus inscription from Clanville – is controversial, and belongs to the previous century. Only an accumulation of suggestive finds may ultimately bring an answer – under-nourished skeletons, sometimes buried decapitated, may not all be explicable in terms of primitive ritual, and most belong to the late period (e.g. at the Mount, Rushton (N'hants), where 24 men, women, and children had been inserted as secondary inhumations into a second-century barrow). When, as at Arbury Road, Cambridge, a robbed fourth-century house is converted to a simple aisled barn, and the well near by yields the cornice fragment of a polygonal monument and three human skulls, something has happened to the established order that may have come from without or may have come from within. If the steady degradation of the Celtic kinship group took the form suggested here, against the background of crushing fourth-century taxation, and the tying of the *colonus* to the soil which was made law by Constantine, the basis for a movement of agrarian discontent certainly existed.[1]

How productive and viable was the Roman villa-system in this country? We have traced a process of centralization, technical devolution, and geographical decentralization, as a general trend in the history of villas. A number of capitalistic estates, it is true, must have been established down to the third century, whether by expropriation or on unbroken land – as integrated areas worked centrally from the beginning, presumably by slave labour. But not a few, we believe, grew out of kinship groups whose land ultimately came under the control of one man and whose occupants became his clients or tenants, as the patriarchal farmhouse evolved into residence, outbuildings,

---

[1] Frere, *Britannia*, pp. 356–7. Revolt of *coloni*: Hawkes, Kendrick, *op. cit.*, with suggestions of Stevens, p. 294; CBA. RR VII, p. 103. Rising in 410: *de vit. Christ.*, 3 (Migne, *Patrologia Latina*, 40, 1034); cf. J. Morris, in *Britain and Rome: Essays presented to Eric Birley*, ed. Jarrett and Dobson, Kendal, 1965, p. 147. Rushton: JRS LV, 1965, p. 210. Tying of *coloni* to soil: C. *Theod.*, V, 17, 1.

and hands' quarters. This stage was the technical peak of production. But estates were in process of expansion just at a time when inflation and taxation were becoming oppressive, and when, on the consolidated estate, slaves were becoming more difficult to obtain. The larger a farm, the less profitable it was to work with slave-gangs, and the less efficient it became to use wage or client labour living centrally. The solution was the colonate, a structure that became more natural as land fell out of working and vacant tracts came under the control of the proprietors; but it clashed with the growing insecurity of conditions, which demanded geographical concentration. In a time of growing discontent concentration of personnel encouraged sedition, yet their dispersion made them less amenable to surveillance. Increased absenteeism meant that control fell into the hands of bailiffs, while decentralization and the removal of the master's eye caused technical decline. Precisely those estates that were immune from burdensome exactions, namely those of the senatorial order, were the possession of absentee owners; thus, what they gained by immunity from *munera*, they were apt to lose by mismanagement.

The villa attained, so long as its farm was integrated, a considerable technical level of agriculture such as was not seen again till the agricultural revolution of the eighteenth century. The romanized temperate-zone farmer knew the use of green crops as winter fodder and the value of enclosed crop-fields. In the Mediterranean, at least, the three-course rotation was known, and evidence in north-west Europe suggests that it existed there in the Roman period. Field-drainage was practised, but we have little evidence for it in Britain outside the Fens and south Lincolnshire. The advantage of nitrogenous crops as a refresher on corn land was recognized, and vetches and lucern were used as cattle-feed. Columella prescribes a scheme of reseeding irrigated meadows, which shows that grass was understood as part of a rotation with turnips or beans, corn, and vetches mixed with hay. This was also known in simpler form to Pliny. In the north-west, liming to improve the base-exchange, and marling to secure better soil texture, were familiar.[1]

Whatever was known of these practices in Roman Britain, we may be certain that the repository and exponent of most of them was the villa of the highly romanized type. The study of Bignor and other sites favours the wintering of considerable stock by means of roots; yet at Bignor the probability is that the manure sufficed only for a low average of dung per acre, the more so if part was concentrated

---

[1] Three-course rotation: see p. 119. Field-drainage: Cato, *de agric.*, 145; Colum., II, 2, 9; Pliny, HN XVIII, 47. Nitrogenous crops: Cato, *ib.*, 37; Varro, *ib.*, I, 23; Colum., II, 13. Vetches and lucern: Cato, *ib.*, 27; Colum., II, 10; Pliny, HN XVIII, 137 sq. Reseeding of meadows: Colum., II, 17; Pliny, HN XVIII, 258.

for turnips or rape. It is problematic if the north-western Roman world broke the vicious circle of deficient dunging and absence of root-crops, and this serves to emphasize the problem of how winter killing was avoided. The growing of roots was a feature of Gallic agriculture, and there is enough evidence for immigration from Gaul and Belgica to Britain to justify a belief that these practices were transmitted from there. Yet there remains the question: How far did Mediterranean practice influence the husbandry of Roman Britain? A complete reply will probably never be possible, but there are some hints.

Pliny's recommendation that the farm should face south in cold climates is frequently followed in Britain, though this may have been mere plain common sense. Columella's peculiar provision that in cloudy climates the residence should look north is obeyed in one case (Spoonley Wood). Palladius' warning that the threshing floor should not be sited near gardens or orchards, to which the chaff is destructive, is ignored at Ditchley, where the floor lay to windward of the orchards. On the other hand the threshing floors here and at Old Durham were circular like Varro's recommended model, and that at Ditchley was, like Varro's, surrounded by a wall. Columella's advice to place the floor where the owner or bailiff could keep it in view, is taken at Ditchley, Langton, and Bedmore Barn. The *tribulum*, described by Varro, was used at Angmering and Atworth. Varro's instruction that granaries should face east and north was followed at Stroud, Woodchester, and Pitney; that at Iwerne was exposed to the north; those at Ditchley and Cromhall looked to the east. Columella proposes that access to the granaries be by ladder, and this probably applied to the granaries at Iwerne, Stroud, and Woodchester. Pliny's prescription that barns should have walls 3 feet thick reflects the actuality at Pitney and Stroud; at Cromhall they were 2 feet 10 inches; at Iwerne 2 and 3 feet; at Ditchley 2 feet 6 inches. Vitruvius' view that barns for hay-storage should be built *extra villam* seems to hold at Brading and Hartlip; perhaps at Spoonley Wood and Ickleton. It may be observed that the shift of working areas and furnaces to leeward of the dwelling in the third century at Woodcuts was almost certainly the result of Roman education.[1]

These observations suggest that Roman Mediterranean practice was being imitated in Britain, and Mediterranean farmers may in their turn have been learning something from the north-west. Pliny's

[1] Facing south: Pliny, HN xviii, 33; north: Colum., i, 5. Vineyards: Colum., i, 9. Threshing floors: Pallad., i, 36; Varro, i, 51. The bailiff: Colum., i, 6. *Tribulum*: Varro, i, 52. Granaries: Varro, i, 57. Ladder: Colum., i, 6. Walls: Pliny, HN xviii, 301. *Extra villam*: Vitruv., de archit., vi, 6.

remarks on British and Gallic marls, *plura nuper exerceri coepta profici-entibus ingeniis*, shows that the Celtic technique was being tried out intelligently in the south, and the differing opinions to be found in Pliny and Columella on oats indicate that Romans were then learning to know this cereal, certainly from Gaul, Britain, and the Rhineland. Columella and Pliny discuss summer cropping and ploughing in northern climes; both knew of the turnip's use as a cattle-fodder in Gaul. Pliny refers to flax-growing among Gallic peoples and describes the Gallic two-hand scythe, also the Gallic reaping machine. The brick field-walls of Gaul recorded by Varro perhaps find a parallel at Holmstreet (Suss). It is a legitimate inference that reciprocal influences were at work, and that Roman elements were not wanting in British agriculture.

This is confirmed in a measure by our survey of the agricultural tools of the period, which showed that no less than nine tools, in the form they are found in this period, were Roman introductions. Querns also underwent a considerable evolution; methods of corn-drying were improved, and the iron coulter plough, likewise a Roman innovation, was diffused by Roman civilization as far as the lowlands of Scotland and the green fields of Ireland. Threshing technique advanced; the donkey-mill and water-mill reached Britain contemporarily. Hygienic housing of animals, farm-planning, and well-sinking were all innovations of the Roman period, combined with improvement of communications, efficient means of storage, and the provision of more amenable markets. Fruit cultivation, certain useful and ornamental trees, and a number of vegetables seem to have come in simultaneously. The occupation saw the appearance of larger fields and of systematic surveying; Roman law and a reliable judiciary secured property rights and provided an incentive to investment.[1]

Under these circumstances, it is difficult to hold that Roman agriculture was not an improvement on what preceded it, even if Belgic husbandry was by no means negligible. In the sphere of livestock, the province owed to Rome the domestic use of the hen and the goose,

[1] Marls: Pliny, HN xvii, 43. Oats: Pliny, HN xviii, 149; Colum., ii, 10. Summer cropping: Colum., ii, 4; 9; Pliny, HN xviii, 182. Turnips: Colum., ii, 10; Pliny, HN xviii, 127–8. Flax: Pliny, HN xix, 7–8. Scythes: Pliny, HN xviii, 261. Reaping machine: Pliny, HN xviii, 296; Pallad., vii, 2. Brick field-walls: Varro, i, 14. In Britain: PSA² xxiii, pp. 377 sqq. Querns: *Ant.* xi, 1937, pp. 140 sqq. Donkey-mills: *London Museum Guide, London in Roman Times*, pp. 109, 110. Water-mills: J. Collingwood Bruce,¹¹ ed., Richmond, *Handbook to the Roman Wall*, Newcastle-on-Tyne, 1957, pp. 85, 152, 172; Richmond, *Roman Britain*,² p. 171 (Lincoln, Woolaston Pill, Chedworth, Great Chesterford); Wherwell, Hants: ANL vii, 1965, p. 261; Silchester: *Ant. J.* xliv, 1964, pp. 38–40. Judiciary and property rights: cf. p. 20, nos. 3, 4; also Tac. *Ann.*, xiv, 31: Presutagus' will, clearly drawn up in Roman form.

but this is where we encounter the negative aspect. On the whole, the evidence that the Romans improved the livestock of the country is still limited, and if they introduced new breeds of horse, we do not know how far these affected the local stock. The native sheep, the most successful earner of dividends in the Romano-British farm economy, shows no signs of change of physique from the prehistoric period; there is nevertheless evidence that breeding achieved a true wool-producing animal. Various Roman innovations in the crops of the country have been noted, but we shall also have occasion to record the possible adverse results of the insistence on winter cereals in the downland native farming areas.

The Roman attitude to soils was necessarily deficient: lacking chemical knowledge, the Roman farmer was apt to classify soils statically. Columella knew that legumes made soil "grow fat" (*gliscere*), and this evidently means "become rich in nitrogen" in our terminology. Virgil apparently recognized as causes of barrenness want of juices, i.e. acidity; solidity that hindered the roots from getting food, i.e. poor crumb and perhaps pan; and sponginess. But the ancient world seems to have had no great faith in active soil amelioration as we understand it; the tendency was to regard one sort of soil as particularly suitable for one sort of crop or rotation.[1]

The limited Romano-British success (if we may so interpret the available evidence) in improving domestic animals shows that if the growing of roots and green fodder and the more efficient harvesting of hay and management of meadows were practised, they were of limited application. They were dependent on enclosed fields held in severalty, i.e. the villa of centralized type, and on a careful regulation of plough and pasture free of communal custom. But it is becoming increasingly evident that a proportion of the villas were associated with the old type of field of native origin and restricted area.

At this point it is relevant to ask, how productive were the normal categories of farm-unit in Roman Britain, and what was their average size? We may consider (1) large villas; (2) middlingly prosperous romanized farmhouses; (3) native villages and farmsteads. It may be pointed out in preface that there is no necessary connection between the area of an estate and a unit, since the former may include a number of tenancies or farmsteads run by bailiffs with slave- or wage-labour. Naturally, no estimate can be more than tentative, and must nearly always be an estimate of the arable land, without much prospect of

---

[1] For the wool-producing sheep, see Ryder in this volume. "Grow fat": Colum., II, 13. Dryness: Virg., *Geor.*, I, 84, interpreted by Dickson, *Husbandry of the Ancients*, pp. 324–6. Soils: cf. Cato, 6; Varro, I, 23; Colum., II, 9.

arriving at the areas of meadow, woodland, and pasture which stood at the farmer's disposal.

Very little can be said as yet of the area cultivated by the very wealthy villas. Woodchester's known granary, apparently connected with a brewery, could have contained 3,000 bushels, representing something like 600 acres down to barley with the addition of fallow, but the total arable can hardly have been less than three times that area and was probably larger. Bignor, as we have seen, appears to have cultivated some 800 acres for corn, but the natural boundaries of the area enclose about 1,900 acres. Its barn, at two-thirds' capacity, could have stored over 14,000 bushels. Cromhall (Glos) possessed a very large granary capable of storing, at two-thirds' capacity, nearly 25,000 bushels of grain, which might represent an arable of 2,500 acres on a yield of 20 bushels per acre. Ditchley (Oxon) was thought, on the strength of its fourth-century granary, to have cultivated close on 1,000 acres (but see p. 267).

Stroud, on the other hand, clearly produced much more than was needed to fill its small granary, which could have held not more than 1,570 bushels; nevertheless its three pairs of plough oxen, whose stalls can be clearly distinguished, could have worked some 300 *iugera* or 187 acres including fallow. If a third is added for seed and waste, the yield was about 22 bushels per acre.

A topographical study of the central Hampshire Roman sites to the east of Andover, consisting of nine farm-sites, suggested an approximate computation of the areas of these units, the distances between them and some natural boundaries (the Port Way, streams, etc.) being taken into account. The farmhouses of only two of them are known (Finkley Farm, Castlefield); both were small aisled buildings. Another building lay close to Castlefield, but it seems improbable that either represented more than a minor farmhouse.

The approximate areas belonging to the above units were (in acres):

Lower Wyke	960	Finkley Down Farm	597
Lower Link	268	Castlefield	340
Upper Wyke	704	Hurstbourne Priors	768
Finkley Farm	597		

These farms are situated on the Hampshire Chalk Arable Region, traditionally a sheep and barley country. A wool-stapler's comb was found at Castlefield, and evidently the above supposed areas contain sufficient tracts for extensive farming, combining barley-growing with the grazing of flocks. To the north-west of Andover, on the other hand, the six villas of Lambourne's Hill (Redenham), Great Copse, "Vitrici," Fyfield, and Eastfield are compactly enclosed by definable

natural boundaries and together shared an area of approximately
4·39 square miles. The last three occupy an area which can be defined
in a secondary manner, and may have possessed each 0·6 square miles
or approximately 384 acres. Little is known of these sites, but Eastfield
in the fourth century possessed a patterned mosaic pavement and one
of its proprietors was a Roman citizen; "Vitrici" probably had an
estate church, and Lambourne's Hill was a building of 141 feet in
length with wing-rooms at the corners of the façade. The details of
the North Warnborough farmhouse in the same county suggested
an arable of some 250 acres and a yield of 13·8 bushels per acre (see
p. 136, n. 2.).[1]

An attempt has also been made to estimate the sizes of the villa
estates of the Chiltern river valleys. K. Branigan found these situated
at an average of one to 2½ miles apart, and calculating that each held
half a mile up the flanking slope of the valley, thought that the average
estate covered 450–600 acres. Among the more prominent villas to
which this calculation related were Latimer, Sarratt, Boxmoor,
Gadebridge Park, Park Street, Saunderton, and High Wycombe. On
these estates it is possible that livestock-rearing may have figured more
prominently than cereal-growing, but not enough is known of their
economies as yet.[2]

In the Yeo valley of north-west Dorset, J. Leach has noted six sites
strung out between Pinford Lane and Bradford Abbas at intervals
of a mile approximately, implying areas of some 300–600 acres. Of
these, Lenthay is a villa of pretensions, Thornford is a modest establishment of five rooms or more, but without mosaics.

It may be noted that the important villa of West Dean (Wilts)
disposed of some 580 acres, East Grimstead (Wilts) of some 230 acres.
The field area of the Faversham villa (Kent) was estimated at some
300 acres.[3]

Solid data can be obtained from the villas of medium or minor
importance whose field pattern is at least partly known. These are
Great Wymondley, Barnsley Park (Glos), and Lye Hole, Wrington
(north Som).

Owing to the identification of part of the centurial "grid" about
the Purwell Mill villa, Great Wymondley, it is possible to ascribe
to the estate not less than 1,100 *iugera*, the equivalent of 680 acres.

[1] Lower Wyke: OS Records. Lower Link: Crawford, *The Andover District*, p. 28;
JBAA xxiii, 1867, p. 280. Upper Wyke: Crawford, *op. cit.*, pp. 59–60. Finkley
Down Farm: VCH *Hants*, I, 303. Hurstbourne: HFC xvi, p. 192; VCH *Hants*, I,
p. 304. Hampshire Central Chalk Arable Region: LUS, no. 90, Hants, p. 357.

[2] Chiltern valleys: K. Branigan, *Arch. J.* cxxiv, 1967, p. 139.

[3] Yeo Valley (Dors): DNHAS lxxxvii, 1966, p. 107. West Dean, East Grimstead:
see pp. 168–70. J. Philp, *Excavations at Faversham, 1965*, p. 72.

An area of about 50 acres bounded on the north, south, and west by marshy ground, and east by the Lye Hole villa, Wrington (Som), contains a field system of some 15 fields, covering over 30 acres. Additional arable land may have lain to east of the homestead. A field system of some 200 acres surrounds the farm at Barnsley Park. The fields are bounded on the west by a ditch, on the north by a shallow valley with a stream, to east and south by presumed medieval ridge-and-furrow. The east-west banks are orientated with the buildings. Of the Lye Hole villa very little is known; only part of the working buildings has so far been detected at Barnsley Park, and it is still problematic where the villa-residence was, if it existed.[1]

Among the lesser farmsteads, it is possible to attribute to Cherington and Rodmarton (Glos) 300 and 340 acres of arable respectively, on the evidence of the accommodation furnished in their ox-stalls.

House II at Iwerne (Dors) possessed a tower-granary holding about 820 bushels, and accommodation for four teams of oxen. If 240 acres were held and 120 sown, the yield (adding one-third for seed and waste) would have amounted to ten bushels per acre.

The modest earthworked farm of Callow Hill (Oxon) according to an area defined by woodlands on the north and south, contemporary dykes on the east, and the Roman way communicating between Watt's Wells (Ditchley) and Northleigh villas on the west, cultivated an area of approximately 300 acres (Fig. 42).

Hallam, observing that five-sixths of the Romano-British village field blocks in the Fenlands covered between 70 and 150 acres in area, half between 80 and 130 acres, and a quarter between 100 and 110 acres, considered that an approximation to the 200 *iugera* unit (125 acres) might have been involved.

We also have some evidence on the minimal areas cultivated by farmsteads and nucleated settlements in Wiltshire, which do not appear to have reached the villa level of agricultural technique, but here the doubtful factor is the difficulty of estimating precise areas owing to the obliteration of ancient fields by later cultivation.

Two nucleated villages of Roman date at Town Hill, Frampton (Dors) disposed together of some 900 acres. Chisenbury Warren, a Romano-British village in Wiltshire, had an area approaching 200 acres, but an incalculable additional area of fields lay to the south and south-east of the village. A field complex near Ashley, west of Winchester, occupies a minimal area of 320 acres, centring on a large fortified farm at Farley Mount; on the edge of the area are three other sites occupied in the Roman period, viz., Ashley Camp, Somborne

[1] Great Wymondley: see pp. 90-4. Lye Hole and Barnsley Park, see pp. 95, 103; and further Fowler, BUS XII, 1970, pp. 178-80.

Wood, and Cow Down Copse. Two farms in the Welland valley were definable by pit-alignments and natural features as covering respectively some 55 and 140 acres. In the Fenlands as observed, Mrs Hallam reports that the original allocation of most of the hut-groups recorded may have been about 110 acres.

In Sussex on Holleyman's map of the 'native field' system between the Rivers Ouse and Adur may be noted three distinct blocks in each of which the number and distribution of the settlements suggest that all or nearly all of them are known. These are:

1. Slonk Hill. Area 600 acres. Two settlements.
2. Tegdown Hill. Area 1,260 acres. Five settlements.
3. Falmer Hill. Area 600 acres. Two settlements.

The average areas per settlement, then, are respectively 300, 252, and 300 acres. While not all these settlements were necessarily occupied at one and the same time, the figures are suggestive, and it is known that in Sussex continuous blocks of this type of cultivation belong to the Roman period, when the local 'native field' system reached its maximum expansion. The three average figures find approximate correspondences to the areas attributed to some of the lesser villa sites, such as Faversham, Cherington, Rodmarton, Castlefield, Andover Down, "Vitrici," Fyfield, Eastfield, Callow Hill, and the field-area of Ashley. The common average of the 'quarter', the ancient Irish agrarian unit, ranges through 200, 300, and 400 acres; Professor Estyn Evans gives its average as 325 acres. Such a unit normally contained four or six homesteads. It is therefore possible that some of the lesser villas and farm-units of the Roman period in southern Britain held lands originally derived from the British equivalent of the Irish quarter or 'townland', corresponding to the north Welsh *trev*, which contained 256 *erws* (acres) according to the Venedotian Code, or in south Wales to the *randir*, containing 312 *erws*.[1]

We turn to the problem, why did the agricultural system of Roman Britain break up? We have seen reason to doubt Collingwood's "great depopulation of the Wiltshire downs" in the fourth century; the fact remains that by the tenth century the downlands were relatively empty, the shift had taken place to the lowland soils, and agriculture was largely an exploitation of the heavier lands. It is now certain that in Britain a climatic deterioration had begun in the middle of

[1] Wiltshire nucleated villages: Fowler, Bowen, CBA. RR VII, pp. 48–53. Ashley: Crawford, *Air Survey and Archaeology*, end map II. Welland Valley (Sites 17, 27): W. G. Simpson, CBA. RR VII, p. 18. Fenland: Hallam, *Ant. J.* XLIV, 1964, p. 30, n. 1. FR. pp. 67–7. Sussex: *Ant.* IX, 1935, pp. 443 sqq. and fig. 84. The Irish quarter: Seebohm, *The English Village Community*, pp. 221 sqq.; Meitzen, *Siedlung und Agrarwesen*, Berlin, 1895, pp. 174 sq.; E. Evans, *Irish Heritage*, p. 12; the *erw*: *Ancient Laws and Institutes of Wales*, pp. 90–1, 375, 829.

the second century, which reached its peak in the fifth. The effect on light chalk soils is an increase of humus; an increase of rain in late summer and autumn has an adverse effect on wheats, causing slow ripening and mildews; it also renders more difficult the sowing of winter crops in heavier soils. The main effect of such a change, therefore, falls on the heavier lands the margins of which it had been the achievement of the Belgae, and to a greater extent of the Romans, to cultivate. It would have encouraged the concentration on the lighter rapid-drying soils of the uplands, and may well have given a considerable impulse to the raising of sheep and cattle. The evidence from the Early Iron Age villages of Wessex was in favour of a pre-ponderance of summer grains; here these do well if sown early before the rapid drying out under spring winds, and if springs become later, the tendency to grow spring crops on the chalk would be accentuated. In the dry Sub-Boreal conditions of the British Bronze Age the chalk was relatively empty; but with the return of damper climate in the Late Bronze Age (the Sub-Atlantic phase) settlement recommenced. Why then, in an increasingly damp climate, did population thin off on the chalk downs in the fifth century? The pagan Saxons did in fact settle those regions; the shift of emphasis is later, with the climatic improvement that had become pronounced by the year 1000, and by the date of Domesday the valleyward movement was complete. The pagan Saxon settlement is nevertheless thin, and hardly comparable with the Romano-British. As Fox puts it: "the sites represent a change in agricultural outlook." But there must have been some factor additional to the innate habits of the invaders or their impact upon the Romano-Britons for the decline of the downland population, the more so since Roman occupation of the chalk was far from negligible down to the end of the fourth century.[1]

It has been noted that Romano-British agriculture in the fourth century (and probably before) was being subjected to considerable pressure to produce wheat, a not negligible part of which was sent abroad. The climatic position was increasingly unfavourable to the sowing of autumn crops on the heavier soils, but the chalk, with its quickly drying well-drained soils, was in a better position to produce both winter and summer crops in these conditions. Extended spring rain facilitated the success of spring sowings in rapidly draining soil; the windy open downs gave quick-drying days between the earlier autumn rains for the autumn ploughing, and better drainage enabled the ripening wheat to overcome tendencies to mildews and murrains.

[1] Exploitation of heavier lowland soils: Fox, *Personality*, pp. 82–3. Saxon settlement on chalk: cf. e.g. Collingwood, Myres, RBES², map vi. Valleyward movement: Fox, *op. cit.*, figs. 35–6.

Both soil and climate, indeed, were more favourable to summer grains, the classic downland crops, and the wheat was probably far from first-class; but we may believe (and the corn-drying kilns confirm) that increased pressure was put on the upland areas to sow it. But the climatic deterioration also encouraged the livestock branch, which certainly increased in the Roman period, and the wool industry was certainly flourishing in the later Roman age. The encroachment of Bignor on the Sussex Downs for the purpose of cattle- and sheep-rearing was probably no isolated phenomenon, and we see in Berkshire the closing off of downland village areas by dykes (the East Ditch on Stancombe Down and the Grims Ditch to east of it) from the pastures and lowland soils, probably by administrative action. The native downland economy relied preponderantly on summer crops and winter grazing of the stubbles; winter grains needed to be enclosed. With the government pressure to sow more winter grain (easily enforceable by the dictated quotas common to fourth-century Roman fiscal practice), the winter stubbles would have been considerably reduced at a time when common pasture was being increasingly invaded by the estate-owners. In an economy to which common outfield grazing and pasturing on winter stubbles were indispensable, the enforced emphasis on winter crops and the limitation of external pastures would have meant overgrazing of the remaining areas, and the reduction of available manure and food. If cattle were regarded as the main index of income and status, dictating a traditional reluctance to reduce the herd – and the evidence from Ireland, as well as the various representations of bulls and cows in Celtic and Romano-British art, suggest that this was the case – then the situation would be further accentuated. Production would begin to fall when pressure was strongest to produce. It seems probable that Roman fiscal pressure ultimately destroyed the traditional native rural economy and thus caused the ultimate abandonment of the southern uplands as soon as the government that held the peasantry to its soil by coercion was removed.[1]

The villas, on the other hand, were the repository of the more advanced capitalist agriculture. Their economy, which was to some extent bound up with the exploitation of the medium and heavier loams, may have suffered a decline with the climatic deterioration. On the other hand, our discussion of the invasion of 367 has shown that it was less serious in its effects than Collingwood and others have thought. Nor can the diminution of coins in a proportion of the villas

---

[1] Fourth-century government quotas: Rostovtzeff, *Social and Economic History of the Roman Empire*, p. 517. Cattle cult: see p. 210, n. 1. For modern parallels in South Africa: E. Hellmann, L. Abrahams, *Handbook of Race Relations in South Africa*, Oxford, 1949, p. 182.

after 367 be confidently explained by social revolutionary disturbances until more solid evidence is available.[1]

We may therefore put forward as possible factors in the decay of the villa: (1) overtaxation; (2) insecurity; (3) climatic deterioration; (4) absentee landlordism.

Before we turn to a final evaluation of the causes of break-up, it may be wise to discuss one other problem, viz. the degree of economic autarky of the average villa. It is sometimes suggested that in the latter part of the Roman period the villas became almost economically self-contained, and that there was an increase of both economic and administrative regionalism, encouraged by inflation. There is no doubt that many villas were capable of supplying some of their own needs; this is clear from the evidence of industrial branches in some of them, and the smelting and working of iron is an extremely common feature of the excavated sites occupied in the late Roman period.[2] But there is little doubt that, at least in the earlier period, the average estate had a wide range of exchange contacts. East Grimstead got building material from the New Forest, tesserae from Cirencester, pottery from Gaul and the New Forest, shale from Kimmeridge, oysters and mussels from the south coast. Bignor received stone from the Boulonnaise, Southwick wine from the Narbonnaise. The wide distribution of New Forest ware in the third and fourth centuries needs no emphasis. And on evidence referred to above, while spinning was carried on in many country houses, very few apparently engaged in weaving. The wide distribution of coal in villas between Gloucestershire and the Isle of Wight, and the ubiquitous oyster shells of most Roman sites in this country, represent a wide traffic of itinerant vendors.[3] The recognizable by-roads linking various villas with the main highways (e.g. Great Wymondley, Wiggonholt, Bignor) alone witness the economic relationships of these estates with the main centres.[4]

[1] Collingwood on the year 367: *Ant.* III, 1929, pp. 271–2. Sudden diminution of coins: Hawkes, Kendrick, *op. cit.*, p. 293; conclusion, *ib.*, p. 294.

[2] Industry: see pp. 221–2.

[3] New Forest ware: H. Sumner, *Excavations in New Forest Pottery Sites*, London, 1927, pp. 83–5. Coal: WAM XLV, 1930, pp. 170–1; Collingwood *ap.* Frank, ESAR III, p. 37; Webster, *Ant. J.* XXXV, 1955, pp. 199–217; Liversidge, *Roman Villas*, p. 123. Wine: among the rural sites yielding amphorae that have come under my notice, those in eastern Britain appear to preponderate; clearly a thorough survey is desirable.

[4] By-roads. Pulborough: VCH *Suss.* III, p. 63; Harroway and Pilgrim's Way: HFC XVIII, pp. 129–30; Great Wymondley: JBAA² 1933, p. 262; *Arch. J.* CVI, 1951, p. 13; Bignor: SAC LVII, 1916, p. 146; Balchester: HFC XVIII, pp. 129–30. (Westheath-Woodgarston: GR. 4592/1582 to 4584/1550 with extensions in both directions. This line invites investigation.) Cf. generally Haverfield, *Arch. J.* LXXV, 1918, p. 15; The Viatores, *Roman Roads in the South-East Midlands*, 1964, *passim.*

Granted, then, the essentially interlinked character of the rural economy of the villa, did this also hold good in the later period of insecurity? There is not yet a full answer to this question, and a few observations must suffice. Currency shortage may have encouraged barter, but barter does not abolish trade. New Forest pottery seems to have been paid for chiefly in kind, but its diffusion is very wide. Minims were extensively used at Chedworth after 367, also at Woodeaton, showing that if currency was short, trade was lively. Pottery used at Great Casterton in the later fourth century combined both northern and southern influences, which therefore were moving freely along Ermine Street at that time. Rosette-stamped ware, manufactured in the second half of the fourth century, had a wide distribution. Examples could be multiplied, but it is clear that the roads were still open, and local road-centres such as Baldock, Mildenhall (Wilts), Canklow near Templeborough (Yorks), and Catterick, were far from moribund.[1] On the other hand, Dunning has shown that the products of the Purbeck marble industry were distributed in the earlier period up to a radius of 200 miles, its customers including seven villas, whereas in the later fourth century their radius was 50 miles only. Despite liveliness of trade, some industries were tending to revolve in smaller regional circles; one of the reasons may have been that in some areas the population was concentrating in more compact blocks for reasons of security. But the villa economy was not naturally autarkic, and there were some indispensable products which no villa could obtain except from abroad or from limited centres, viz. oil, essential for lighting, and salt, necessary to man and beast. Clearly the villas fought a game fight to keep trade moving, and had they been more self-contained, they might have survived longer; their rapid decay is itself sufficient to show that they were not so.[2]

If the villa was the guardian of a relatively advanced agricultural technique, how are we to reconcile this with the restrictedness of such a technique which it seems necessary to posit in order to explain the general failure to improve stock, fodders, and manure? The answer would seem to be that only part of the villas can have worked at a high level; a large number would appear to have been associated with unchanged native field systems, and the techniques that they imply,

[1] New Forest pottery: Sumner, *op. cit.*, p. 82. Inflation: Hawkes, *Ant. J.* XVIII, 1938, p. 128. Minims, Chedworth: Kendrick, Hawkes, *op. cit.*, p. 397; Woodeaton: JRS XXI, 1931, pp. 105–6. Great Casterton: Corder, *Roman Villa...Great Casterton,* I, 1951, p. 39. Rosette-stamped ware: Bushe-Fox, *Richborough,* I, pp. 89–90.

[2] Purbeck marble: ANL VIII, 1949, p. 15. Compact blocks: e.g. Great Chesterford, Alchester, Richborough, Bitterne (Sutherland, *Coinage and Currency in Roman Britain,* Oxford, 1936, pp. 95–6); Chichester (ANL VII, 1948, p. 17); Thundersbarrow (*ibid.*).

only partly modified, or to have cultivated large tracts extensively after the manner seen east of Andover and south of Basingstoke. The later villa seems, in various instances, to have suffered a devolution by being split up into colonate holdings whose tenants were probably unable to enclose a root-crop or maintain more than a few head of cattle. As the new system advanced, it became diluted with barbarian newcomers who had no part in the Roman agricultural tradition. The smallholder rooted in his soil, the backbone of every healthy peasantry, was absorbed into the estates as a client-labourer, remained the over-taxed tenant of the state-domain, or became the overburdened tied *colonus* of the large estate. It is doubtful whether, by the late Roman period, an appreciable class of progressive farmers remained, and if they did, they were probably estate-owners of Gloucestershire and the south-west, who in their ultimate flight imported their large plough coulters into Ireland. (See p. 256.) But the devolutionary process which produced the colonate could also mean that after the villa had been abandoned, its tenantry survived peripherally and that hence the estate boundaries might in some cases survive with them.

CHAPTER XIII

CONTINUITY?

OUR FINAL task, then, is to discuss the problem, how far, if at all, did the Romano-British rural system survive the break-up of the Roman administration, and whether it contributed something to the Anglo-Saxon rural life which took its place.

In the last thirty years the views of many scholars have been moving steadily away from the assessment which had till then held the field, that Roman civilization collapsed precipitately and utterly with the removal of the imperial administration in 410, and that the following century beheld the nearly complete annihilation of the Romano-British population in so far as it had not withdrawn to the highland zone or to Brittany.[1]

Alternative opinion may perhaps be divided into two schools: the first sees direct continuity between Roman and Saxon society as minimal or negligible, but nevertheless, on the basis of a critical reassessment of the historical sources, recognizes that the period of transition was more prolonged than scholars previously thought, and that Roman Britain offered a strenuous and for some time a successful resistance to the barbarian attack. The other school, composed chiefly of students of agrarian history, tends to believe that the legacy of Romano-British civilization to the succeeding rural system was not inconsiderable, and that accordingly a degree of continuity is to be expected from one to the other.

In the purely archaeological sphere, without reference to the claims of either school, the climate has begun to change because a new generation of investigators, keenly alive to the archaeological hiatus relating to the period of transition from Roman Britain to Saxon England, has been alert to all evidence bearing on that period, and with the improved techniques of research and excavation, evidence is beginning to appear which bids fair to close the gap.

The new orientation takes its origin from several factors: (1) a reassessment of late Romano-British coinage; (2) the identification of types of pottery ascribable, however controversially, to the age of transition, and reflecting both Roman and Saxon cultural elements;

[1] For a previous summary of the problem relating to the age of transition from Roman Britain to Saxon England, resulting on the whole in a retention of the more conservative view, see R. Lennard, in the Dopsch Festschrift, *Kultur und Wirtschaft*, Baden-bei-Wien, 1938, pp. 71 sqq.

(3) a new estimate of settlement distribution in the period concerned; (4) a more accurate estimate of the length of survival of the Roman towns and rural settlements, gained from new excavation and from reassessments referred to under clauses 1–3; (5) the identification of culture-objects – more particularly belt-buckles and the associated accoutrements – whose character and distribution have thrown light on the deployment of Roman troops or veteran settlers in this country in the late fourth and earlier fifth centuries; (6) the excavation of sites in Wales and the west of England, which has revealed continued trade and cultural contacts with the Mediterranean during the fifth and sixth centuries; (7) a growing awareness that the continental evidence does not favour the exclusively external origin of the Anglo-Saxon rural system as it emerges on the eve of the Norman conquest. It has become more and more difficult to discover in the countries where the invaders originated those elements prior to the fifth century that constitute the English rural system in the tenth or eleventh, viz., the open fields, strip-cultivation, and the two- or three-field system.

These preponderantly archaeological considerations have been assisted by two other branches of research, to wit, place-name study and the scrutiny of documents bearing upon early English and Welsh agricultural society.

None of the problems posed by the above developments, however, can be intelligibly discussed unless we endeavour to gain a general understanding of the political situation prevailing in Britain during the fifth century of the present era.[1]

When the main body of the Roman forces was withdrawn from Britain in 410, Honorius wrote to the British *civitates* to look to their own defence. There is no reason to suppose that the imperial governors, commanders, and civil service did not remain, but they seem to have been removed almost immediately by a *coup d'état*, conducted, apparently, by the municipal aristocracy, which was composed chiefly of the landowning class, who would have constituted the *seniores* and *concilium* with whom Vortigern, according to Gildas, ruled. That this was so is suggested by the fact that Vortigern, who gathered power into his hands, was kin to a resident of Gloucester, Vitalinus, and one of his chief political rivals was Ambrosius Aurelianus, a romanized landowner of the west.

We are told that 410 was followed by a period of prosperity, which may well have been created by Britain's release from the taxation

---

[1] For the following brief historical account I have adopted the general lines of Dr J. Morris's brilliant interpretation 'Dark Age Dates' in *Britain and Rome: Essays presented to Eric Birley*, 1965, pp. 145 sqq. I have also accepted Dr Morris's revised chronology.

imposed to support the occupying forces and to supply the continent with corn. But towards 429 the new ruler faced an invasion of Irish from the north-west and of Picts from the north. The province was not defenceless; it had liberated itself from the earlier barbarian threat, says Zosimus; and the forces that remained appear to have included, on the evidence of the military accoutrements studied by Mrs Hawkes and G. C. Dunning, *comitatenses*, i.e. troops of the field-army, of Germanic origin, manning the Saxon Shore forts and distributed in garrison in the towns and even, perhaps, in some estates and centres of crown domain. There also may have been, in Kent and elsewhere, bodies of *laeti*, barbarian captives settled on the land under obligation to cultivate and to serve in emergency.

With the aid of Saint Germanus, then in the country, the western attack was repelled. To meet the northern danger, Vortigern resorted to the employment of Saxon mercenaries under Hengist and Horsa. These troops, led by their own leaders, served under treaty and come under the category of the *foederati* who feature in the fifth century as an important component of the Roman forces in Europe and the east. Their burials, whose furniture distinguishes them sharply from that of the *comitatenses*, indicate a deployment in eastern Britain and along the Iknield Way to the Upper Thames. The defence plan appears to have been successful, but two subsequent events conspired to threaten Vortigern's government. The first was a collision with Ambrosius, whose estate may have lain near Amesbury – for the name may be derived from his – and who commanded "Roman" support. The other was the refusal of the estate-owners to furnish further support to the Saxon *foederati* of Hengist and Horsa. The clash with Ambrosius took place in 437 near Guoloppum, possibly Wallop (Hants); the results of the battle are unknown, but as a result of the second episode the Saxon *foederati*, deprived of their pay, flung themselves upon the province, and in the words of Gildas, literally destroyed it. This took place (on Morris's chronology) between 442 and 457. The British fought an ultimately successful series of battles in Kent, but the outcome was the cession to the Saxons of Norfolk and east Kent. The famous British appeal to Aegitius (Aetius), *magister militum* in Gaul under the emperor Majorian, was made in 446, but in 457 the enemy took Pevensey from a Romano-British garrison and so won eastern Sussex.[1]

[1] Honorius' rescript: Zosimus, VI, 10. *Coup d'état: ib.*, VI, 5. *Seniores* and *consilium*, Gildas, *de excid. Brit.*, 22; Nennius, *Hist. Brit.*, 22; Vortigern in power: Nennius, *Hist. Brit.*, 31. Vitalinus, *ib.*, 49. Prosperity: Gildas, 21. Barbarians repelled: Zos., VI, 5. *Comitatenses*: S. Hawkes, G. C. Dunning, *Medieval Archaeology*, V, 1965, pp. 1 sqq. Western attack repelled: Constantius, *Vita S. Germani*, 17, 18; Hengist and Horsa: Nennius, 31; Gildas, 23. Deployment of Saxon *foederati*: Morris, *loc. cit.*, p. 160. Dismissal of *foederati*: Nennius, 36. Collision with Ambrosius: Nennius, 31. Battle of

The crucial points in this escalation are constituted by the battle of Guoloppum, the dismissal of the *foederati*, and their catastrophic retaliation. The conflict between Ambrosius and Vortigern implies a split in the ranks of the landowning class. If Ambrosius held estates from Wiltshire to Oxfordshire and Sussex (see p. 24, n. 2), and had Roman support, he may have represented the old colonate régime from which Vortigern had perhaps freed the eastern districts of Britain. In such a conflict, in which the Saxon *foederati* could only be indirectly involved, Ambrosius would have drawn for his forces either on the ranks of the *coloni* or on other sections of the Romano-British peasantry. The refusal of the notables ruled by Vortigern to pay the *foederati*, on the other hand, meant essentially the denial of provisions or the cash to purchase them. The *foederati* replied by taking these supplies by force – and presumably by sacking the villas and farms of the province as they did so. This means several things. First of all, that to that date the food-producing sector of the British economy was in working order. Secondly, that there was still present peasant man-power to be mobilized either from the villas, from independent peasant farms, or from imperial estates. How far does archaeology support these assumptions?

The villa system may have been seriously weakened by the "barbarian conspiracy" of 367, but numerous estates remained, as well as many medium farms romanized to the extent of possessing masonry buildings. In a number of them coins stop with the house of Theodosius; at some with Arcadius. But Theodosian issues are known to be common on sites occupied long after 395, as the Gallic mints closed down in that year. The coins tend to dwindle in the last decades before 400, but Sutherland believes that the many known coin-hoards ending with Theodosian issues were not buried till well after 410, as Britain was relatively peaceful between 410 and 430. Since 1952 a number of villa sites have been investigated where the occupation continued into the fourth century but concerning the precise date of their abandonment evidence is not yet published. Nevertheless, among instances of villas and rural buildings showing signs of occupation well down to the end of the fourth century, if not later, may be mentioned Lullingstone, Totternhoe (Bucks), East and West Coker (Som), Locking (Som), Stanton Low (Bucks), Whittington Court (Glos), Arbury Road (Camb), Tickhill, Langton (Yorks), and Great Tey (Ess). In some villas, at least, this period was one of great activity if not of prosperity. Building, reconditioning, or intensive activity can be cited from Great

Guoloppum: Nennius, 66. Destruction of the province: Gildas, 24. Battles in Kent: Nennius, 44, cf. Anglo-Saxon Chronicle, *ad ann.* 457–65 (Whitelock, p. 10). Appeal to Aegitius: Gildas, 20.

Casterton, Ditchley, Barnsley Park, Denton, Hemel Hempstead, and Colney Street. At Hucclecote (Glos) a mosaic was laid down at the very end of the fourth century. Six sites in the Basingstoke district present finds continuing till its last decades. The list could be extended; as will be seen, the known evidence tends to concentrate in the south, but extends to Tickhill and to Langton in south-eastern Yorkshire. At Barnsley Park and Great Witcombe villas, on the other hand, the coin-evidence is unusually high between 365 and 388, but virtually disappears between 388 and 400, when coinage is abundant at neighbouring Cirencester.

The evidence which will add details to our picture of the first half of the fifth century is not yet extensive, at least in published form, but the first lines are beginning to be discernible. At the small country town of Dorchester in the Upper Thames Valley, Anglo-Frisian pottery of the mid-to-late fifth century is found with Romano-British, and in the sixth a Saxon hut is built to be entered from a Roman street. The inhabitants of Building "A" at Shakenoake (Oxon) were reduced by the year 430 or so to living in the north-eastern room, which alone retained its roof. After the abandonment of the villa buildings at Latimer (Bucks) not later than 380, a timber building was built, later covered by another building in turn superseded by a rubble floor. A robbed fourth-century building at Arbury Road, Cambridge, was converted to a simple aisled barn. The latest occupation supervening on the destruction in the fourth century of the Star villa, Shipham (Som), was marked by handmade pottery indicative of the breakdown of the commercial pottery industry. The Whittington Court villa revealed within its ruins squalid habitation associated with coins of Arcadius, safely to be attributed to the fifth century. The same phenomenon was encountered in the west wing of Great Witcombe, associated with the postholes of timber huts and a corn-drier. Such huts also characterized the last occupation at Stanton Chair and Whitton (Suff). Ultimate "barbaric" or "squatter" phases at Great Wymondley, West Coker, Woodchester, Wiggonholt, and Low Ham, are probably to be interpreted in the same sense. A small building was erected at Gadebridge Park at the very end of the fourth century; Boxmoor, in the same county, was occupied well into the fifth century. Denton villa in Lincolnshire was somehow maintained, though not apparently lived in, for nearly a century before it was used for a Saxon burial and destroyed. In Hertfordshire these phenomena corresponded to what has been archaeologically established in Verulamium and is confirmed by the account of the second visit of Saint Germanus to the town, still existent in organized form in 445. In describing this visit, indeed, the saint's biographer appears to make an all too little noticed reference to two of the country's administrative divisions, Maxima and Prima, which suggests that Britain was then still in administrative shape.

The general picture is less of destruction than of decay, an inability to maintain the amenities of life, and ultimate abandonment due to insecurity, which prevented normal agricultural work, and above all due to the breakdown of communications which made the obtaining of non-agricultural materials and commodities impossible. This agrees with Gildas's account of the disastrous Saxon retaliation of 442–57 which is rather that of the destruction of cities than of the countryside. Moreover, in most of the villas that survived into the fifth century signs of catastrophic destruction are frequent about 400 – but not later, and are often followed by rehabilitation. But Gildas also writes of Britain in the forties of the fifth century that *vacuaretur omnis regio totius cibi baculo excepto venatoriae artis solacio*. The reference is clearly to the collapse of British agriculture at this time, and Myres read into it the death of the Romano-British rural economy, more especially of the villa estates, as an organized entity with a technical level. This may not perhaps have applied so drastically to the west of the country, but elsewhere it must have meant the demise, sooner or later, of the Romano-British towns, which may however have continued to support themselves for a period by cultivating the land in their immediate vicinity. Verulamium survived most of the century, Canterbury was transformed imperceptibly into a Saxon city; Caerwent persisted for most of the fifth century, and Silchester during the fifth, perhaps into the sixth, her cultivated area defended, in all probability, by her travelling dykes. Catterick endured, perhaps, into the sixth century. Probably in the fifth century, the west gate of Kenchester was modified, and still later the defensive ditch was recut.[1]

The situation in the west of Britain, indeed, may not have been quite so desperate. Here archaeological work during the last decade has identified some six post-Roman cemeteries, i.e. cemeteries used by the descendants of Romano-Britons after the separation of Britain

---

[1] Theodosian coins: Sutherland, *Coinage and Currency*, p. 93. Theodosian hoards: *ibid.*, p. 94; cf. J. P. C. Kent *ap.* R. H. M. Dolley, *Anglo-Saxon Coins*, London, 1961, p. 2. Barnsley Park and Great Witcombe coins: Webster, BGAS LXXXVI, 1967, pp. 78–80. Germanus' second visit: Constantius, *Vita S. Germ.*, 25–7. Devastation of British agriculture: Gildas, 19; cf. J. N. L. Myres, CBA. RR I, p. 42. Continued settlement: Verulamium: Frere, *Britannia*, p. 367; Canterbury: Frere, *ap.* Wacher, *Civitas Capitals*, pp. 91–4; Caerwent, Silchester: O'Neill, *Ant.* XVIII, 1944, pp. 113 sqq.; cf. Frere, *Civitas Capitals*, p. 96. Catterick, *ibid.*, p. 97. Kenchester: *Trans. Woolhope Field Club* XXXVII, 1961–3, pp. 166–7. For villas, we must add a Roman building at the Swan Inn, Bosham, with a coin of Honorius embedded in its wall (VCH *Suss.*, III, p. 50).

from the empire. Another is known at Llantwit Major in south Wales, and a recent view holds that it belonged to people who still inhabited part of the same villa. Here the burials were cut through the floor, as they were at the Banwell villa; one cemetery is associated with a Roman townlet, Camerton; three are associated with hill-forts (Blaize Castle, North Cadbury, Bream Down), presaging the return of Early Iron Age conditions. In this region Romano-British life must have survived, in however attenuated a form, till the later sixth century (577), for not till then did the Saxons capture Gloucester, Cirencester, and Bath. At several points evidence of continued occupation is provided by finds imported in the course of trade from the Mediterranean area, and trade implies local production, almost certainly preponderantly agricultural. Among the sites yielding such finds are Ilchester – where they include coins of Anastasius I and Justinian – South Cadbury, Glastonbury Tor, and Cannington. The Roman villa at Star, Shipham, and the Butcombe settlement have yielded sub-Roman wares, which are also known at Whitecliff Down on Salisbury Plain. Continued research will certainly multiply such sites.

In south Wales, Llantwit is one aspect of a continuing civilization more fully reflected in the Dark Age culture of Dinas Powys, furnished with pottery and glass imported from the Mediterranean area, and supplied with grain and meat not produced, it would seem, from the immediate vicinity of the hill-fort. It was from western Britain that the last representative of Roman Britain, Arthur, emerged to bear arms against the Saxon invaders. The economic background of his warriors is fitfully illuminated by the epic account of the death of Geraint at Porchester: they drank wine from glass vessels and fed their steeds with wheat. More advanced Roman agricultural techniques may, indeed, have survived in some estates. This at least may be tentatively suggested on the strength of the iron plough-coulters found in Ireland, which are clearly of Romano-British derivation; these come from Drumaroad, Co. Down, Lagore Crannog, Meath, and Ballinderry II Crannog, and it is notable that the second and third of these sites have also yielded evidence of the presence of Romano-British refugees. A link between Ireland and Gloucestershire is indeed suggested by the nut-shaped ploughshares from Randalstown Crannog and Lochnabuaile fort, Co. Kerry, since these have a parallel from Chedworth villa.[1]

---

[1] Somerset and the west in the post-Roman period: P. A. Rahtz, *Bristol Archaeological Research Group Bulletin*, II, 1967, pp. 103 sqq.; P. A. Rahtz, P. J. Fowler, *ibid.*, III, 1968, pp. 57 sqq. Saxon capture of Cirencester and Bath: Anglo-Saxon Chronicle, *ad ann.* 577 (Whitelock, p. 14). Ilchester coins: Grinsell, *Archaeology of Wessex*,

If we exclude the highland zones of the west and north, was the Saxon conquest of Bath, Gloucester, and Cirencester the end of Roman agriculture in Britain?

Discussion of this question carries with it the danger of becoming involved with the entire problem of Roman-Saxon continuity. Some brief points must therefore suffice. One primary fact interpretable in favour of a certain merging between Romano-Briton and Saxon is what may be termed the "prior Saxonization" of Roman Britain. Germanic elements had been present in the province since the third century, settled by the emperor Probus and by Constantius. The *laets* of Kent found in Ethelbert's time further evoke from students of the Roman Empire the question whether they may not be regarded as the descendants of Germanic captives (*laeti*) settled in Kent by the later Roman authorities under the obligation to till the land and serve in the forces when called upon to do so. In Britain they would have been distinct from the element represented by the military buckles analysed by Mrs Hawkes and G. C. Dunning, since the latter can be identified in Gaul and the Rhineland as the equipment of regular troops of Germanic origin serving in the Roman army, and this is what they must represent in Britain. The *laeti*, on the other hand, were tied cultivators liable to militia service only, and as such their distribution would be dictated primarily by agricultural considerations. The *comitatenses* or field-army troops represented by the buckles may nevertheless be regarded as a third Germanic element likely to have contributed to the "prior Saxonization" of Britain, more especially if we are prepared to accept their presence at rural sites where the appropriate equipment has been found. The earlier continental types, dated in the later fourth and early fifth century, occur at rural sites which include Holbury, Icklingham, Snodland, Ixworth, Barnsley Park, and Shakenoake, all at or near villas. The sites where examples of the later British types, dated to the first half of the fifth century, are recorded include Holbury, Shakenoake, Clipsham (Rut), Gesting-

---

1958, p. 194. Sub-Roman pottery, Whitecliffe Down: Devizes Museum; Dinas Powys: L. Alcock, *Dinas Powys*, Cardiff, 1963. Death of Geraint: The Lament of Geraint (*The Black Book of Carmarthen*, 22), cited by Morris, *Britain and Rome*, p. 169. Irish coulters: Drumaroad, *Ulster Journ. Archaeology*[3] XIX, 1956, p. 85, fig. 9; Lagore: PRIA LI, 1946, p. 67; Ballinderry II: PRSAI LXXIV, 1944, p. 133. Romano-British refugees: R. A. S. Macalister, *Archaeology of Ireland*, London, 1949, p. 350. Ploughshares: Randalstown Crannog: W. G. Wood-Martin, *Lake-Dwellings of Ireland*, 1886, p. 141, pl. xxxiii, 8; Lochnabuaile fort: PRSAI LXXIV, 1944, p. 137, fig. 5, 3; Chedworth: Aberg, *Gwerin*, I, 1956-7, p. 177. fig. 5, 6. As possible evidence of continuity of agricultural technique may be mentioned the existence of vineyards in the early Saxon period (Lamb, *op. cit.*, p. 188; Bede, *HE*, I, I). It is hard to believe that these were a Saxon introduction in the conditions of the time.

9

thorpe (Ess), Popham, Chedworth, Lullingstone, North Wraxhall, Spoonley Wood, and West Dean.[1]

The *foederati* of Hengist and Horsa are represented by their own Jutish or Anglo-Frisian material. What element is represented by the 'Romano-Saxon' pottery isolated by J. N. L. Myres? This pottery Myres believes to represent the first process of fusion, being distributed preponderantly over eastern Britain. His view, however, has been strongly criticized: the main distinguishing feature of the pottery, circular bosses or sinkings, though Germanic, thinks Frere, had been assimilated into the general repertoire of Romano-British pottery before the Saxon advent. J. Morris, while he accepts that this type of pottery does reflect the presence of Saxons, does not think that it marks Saxon garrisons in eastern Britain in the period prior to 410. How far does this ware contribute to the problem of continuity? Much of it is dated to the fourth century, but at Baldock it occurred with Saxon pottery, at Burgh Castle in a mixed Roman-Saxon cemetery, at Highsted near Sittingbourne on a site whose position accords well with the presence of early Saxon settlers.

There is in addition other pottery not of the above class, which may be defined as Saxon ware exhibiting certain Roman characteristics. Examples have been found, for instance, at Hartlip and Wingham in Kent, both villas, where *laeti* or *foederati* might be expected. At Wingham there were no more than two vessels, but early Anglo-Frisian pottery *over* the villa showed that the site continued to be occupied without an appreciable gap between the late Roman and Saxon inhabitants. It might therefore be tentatively suggested that both the Roman wares with Saxon features and the Saxon wares with Roman influences represent *laeti*, and that in this case the *laeti* too constitute a potential element of continuity. Outside Kent, very significant is the occurrence of such pottery at Abington Piggotts (Camb), on a site where the occupation was continuous from the Early Iron Age through the Roman to the Saxon period.

It is worth citing some other cases suggesting a degree of continuity of occupation. The cemetery at Burgh Castle contained, as stated, both Roman and Saxon interments. At Linford (Ess) a sherd combining Roman and Saxon features was found in a Saxon weaving hut; while most of the pottery was Saxon, several sherds of fourth-century Romano-British ware also occurred. Grass-tempered ware at Frocester villa of fifth-century Saxon type would seem to indicate continuous occupation. The presence of similar pottery at two Romano-British sites in Wiltshire, Ogbourne St George and Wellhead near

[1] For Germanic settlers, see Professor Finberg in the present volume. *Comitatenses at* villas; see p. 282, n. 1.

Westbury, has been published by P. J. Fowler. Saxon huts discovered at Mucking (Ess) were built in silted Romano-British ditches and at their intersections, and finds included Roman pottery and quern fragments, also a saucer-brooch and grass-tempered wares. Hallam inclines to see in the finds of 'Roman-Saxon' pottery in or near the Fens (Old Sleaford, Coldham, Threckingham), and in the "puzzling continuity of layout" of Romano-British and Saxon sites in the same region (e.g., Spalding, Crowland, Aswick, Gedney Hill) indications that Romano-British occupation there did not end with the English settlement. Suggestive too was the position at Upton (Glos), where Roman pottery, coins, and other objects were found during excavation in the deserted medieval village. The coins included issues of the house of Theodosius indicating Roman occupation till the end of the fourth century at least; the internal width of the medieval western byre of Site A, where these finds were made, was 13 feet, a dimension very common in Romano-British cattle buildings. An early Saxon settlement also existed, apparently, immediately to the north of the Shakenoake villa (Oxon).[1]

At various sites, of course, the evidence tells graphically against continuity, as when pagan Saxon burials are found in or near a deserted villa. Instances of this sort may be cited at Denton (Lincs), Worlaby (Lincs), Southwell Minster (Notts), and Great Tew (Oxon). But several considerations favour a greater degree of rural continuity than has been accepted hitherto.

First, a glance at the distribution-maps of the earlier Saxon settlement areas in the south of England reproduced by Collingwood and Myres will reveal that these largely coincided with the Romano-British occupation areas. The penetration of the forested heavy soils came later. Secondly, close studies of the Romano-British field systems of the south of England, especially of Wessex, conducted over the last few years, have seriously called in question O. G. S. Crawford's dichotomy of pre-Saxon and Saxon settlement-areas. Bowen and Fowler have found that Romano-British settlement extended into the valleys in Wessex no less than did the Saxon, which, after all, it is

---

[1] 'Roman-Saxon' pottery: J. N. L. Myres *ap.* Harden, *Dark Age Britain*, London, 1956, pp. 16 sqq.; ANL III, pp. 103–4; *Arch. J.* CVI, 1949, pp. 69–71. Frere's criticism: MA VI/VII, 1962–3, pp. 351–2; Morris, *Britain and Rome*, p. 176, n. 15. Baldock: Letchworth Museum; Burgh Castle: PSIA XXIV, 1949, p. 117, Fig. 7, 5. Highsted: *Ant. J.* XV, 1941, p. 211; fig. 3, 1, 2; Abington Piggotts: PPSEA IV, 1924, p. 221; MA III, 1959, p. 110; Wingham: *Ant.* XVII, 1943, p. 210; XVIII, 1944, p. 52; Anglian pottery: JRS LVI, 1966, p. 217. Great Casterton: JRS LVII, 1967, p. 183; Linford: EAS I, 1961/5, p. 89; Frocester: CBA, *Archaeological Review*, III, 1968, p. 17; Ogbourne St George, Westbury: Fowler, WAM LXI, 1966, pp. 31 sqq. Mucking: MA XI, 1967, pp. 264–5; Fens: Hallam, FR pp. 75, 87; Upton: R. H. Hilton, P. A. Rahtz, BGAS LXXXV, 1966, pp. 99–100.

natural to expect after the results of the aerial surveys of the Thames Valley and Midland river-gravels. Thus, near Barford St Martin, between the Rivers Nadder and Wylie, the Romano-British and later field systems overlap, and precisely in the Nadder valley some seven Celtic names have survived in the modern toponymy. Strip-lynchets are also stated to overlie 'native' fields at Poxwell (Dors), and 'native' fields stand in close relation to medieval settlement and fields at Tyneham and Plush in the same county. A "fairly dense scatter" of Romano-British pottery is reported over the site of the abandoned medieval village of Sturthill, Burton Bradstock (Dors).

Attention may further be drawn to the very large number of village churches in whose immediate proximity Roman finds have been made. A random survey of such cases reveals instances from Leicestershire through Norfolk to Surrey, Kent, Sussex, Hampshire, Berkshire, Dorset, Gloucestershire, and Herefordshire. Naturally in a percentage of cases the churches may not occupy the sites of the original places of worship, but where they do, they may indicate a degree of coincidence between the type of site chosen by Roman and by English settlement that may modify the previous impression of a geographical hiatus between the two societies. There are other hints that indicate neglected lines of investigation in this field. Such is the circumstance that the very ancient fair of Weyhill, which bears a clear relation to a group of villa-sites to north of it (see p. 32), was originally held in part at Clanville Lodge, and in part at Ramridge Manor, Penton, both the sites of Romano-British farms belonging to the group concerned.[1]

The pre-conquest penetration of Kent by Germanic elements has been emphasized, and in general Kent possesses special significance for the problem of the legacy of Romano-British agriculture to later

---

[1] Earlier Saxon settlement areas: Collingwood, Myres, RBES,[2] plates vi–ix. Romano-British valley settlement: CBA. RR vii, pp. 55, 62. Overlapping field systems: *ibid.*, p. 55. Celtic names: *ibid.* Poxwell: DNHAS lxxxix, 1967, p. 135; Tyneham, Plush: *ib.*, p. 138; Sturthill: DNHAS xc, 1968, p. 167. Weyhill fair, Clanville, and Penton: VCH *Hants*, iv, pp. 396–7. It may be noted here that a Saxon *sceat* was found in the foundations of the Romano-British temple at Weycock Hill, Berks. I owe this information to Mr G. Boon. Traces of probable cult-continuity were noticed by me in this area some time ago; one is the name of Waltham St Lawrence, one mile south-east of Weycock; in Germany churches of this dedication are of Roman origin (A. Dopsch, *The Economic and Social Foundation of European Civilization*, London, 1937, p. 63, citing *Oberbayrische Archiv*, i, 1897, pp. 339 sqq. and *Beitrage zu Anthropologie und Urgeschichte*, xiv, p. 178). Cf. also the tradition of Herne the Hunter located in Windsor Forest to eastward – clearly an echo of the Celtic Cernunnos, and St Leonard's Hill in the same district – St Leonard possessing similar attributes to Cernunnos. For the suggestive evidence furnished by the place-name Wīchām, see M. Gelling, MA xi, 1967, pp. 87–104, and Professor Finberg's remarks in the present volume (p. 424).

England. Here the centres of local administration were perpetuated (Canterbury, Rochester, Sittingbourne); the unit of Lyminge retained a Romano-British name. The fact that Canterbury is the only British *civitas* centre which retained its tribal appellation could be interpreted to the disadvantage of continuity, since Cantaware was after all the name adopted by the Jutes of eastern Kent. In the city, nevertheless, Jutish strata overlie Roman with no intervening gap. Jutish *foederati* settled in Kent while a Romano-British political entity was still in control, and were probably preceded by *laeti*. The Kentish field system, as is well known, was unlike that of the greater part of medieval England, being characterized by compact blocks of fields lacking the nucleated settlements and two- or three-field groupings common to much of the rest of the country. The customs associated with these Kentish fields, moreover, included inheritance by gavelkind, a practice universal among the Celtic peoples.

Gray believed that the Kentish field system was a survival from Roman Britain, not less because its chief unit of division was the *iugum*. Jolliffe, on the other hand, relying on the work of Leeds, drew attention to the community of Frankish culture in the Rhineland and Jutish culture in Kent, and regarded Roman-seeming features in the latter as derived from the former. However, there is no longer unanimity of opinion on the Frankish-Rhenish derivation of the relevant culture-objects. On the contrary, it is now stressed that most of the so-called Jutish objects of Kent in the fifth century are quite distinct from those of the Franks (whose crafts resemble those of the *comitatenses* and other Germanic military elements found in north Gaul and the Rhineland); the fifth-century material is derived from north-west Germany over the Rhine.[1]

Hence it is today no longer so plausible to derive the custom of Kent and the Kentish field system from the continent. Nor is belief in a purely extraneous origin strengthened by the survival of Roman field-divisions in the Cliffe district near Rochester. The strips into which both these and other tenements in Kent were divided also require an explanation. Jolliffe himself stated that parallels were not to be found in the Düsseldorf-Frankfurt-Trier triangle whence the Jutish culture-objects were allegedly derived – but they have since been found in a Roman context precisely here (see below).

[1] Kentish field system: H. L. Gray, *English Field Systems*, pp. 272 sqq.; J. Jolliffe, *Pre-Feudal England: the Jutes*, Oxford, 1933, pp. 98–120; Collingwood, Myres, RBES, pp. 425, 443–4; R. Lennard in *Kultur und Wirtschaft*, pp. 71 sqq.; Hawkes *ap.* Harden, *Dark Age Britain*, pp. 108–9; J. N. L. Myres, *Arch. J.* xc, 1933, pp. 156 sqq. Origins of Jutish style: E. T. Leeds, *Archaeology of the Anglo-Saxon Settlements*, Oxford, 1913, pp. 126, 128; S. Hawkes, A xcviii, 1961, pp. 29 sqq.

The matter of the strip fields is common to the problem as it affects entire lowland England. Not only does it appear that Kentish strips within consolidated land-blocks need not inevitably be ascribed to the Jutes, but historians are experiencing increasing difficulty in attributing the open-field strip system with its two or three large fields and its three-course rotation, which is found evolved in lowland England on the eve of the Norman Conquest, to the Saxon invaders.[1] The view of the majority of German scholars has been for some years that this system in Germany was a relatively late introduction superimposed by seignorial interests, and Dopsch stated that there was absolutely no evidence of common holdings among the Franks. Archaeological investigation in Germany, moreover, has shown that while the Saxons in their original homes along the north German coast and in Denmark sometimes inhabited small nucleated hamlets, their usual field systems bore a remarkable resemblance to the mosaics of small 'native' fields cultivated in Britain in the Early Iron Age and Roman periods. On the other hand, recent research has discovered that strip fields existed in association with some Roman villas in the Mayener Stadtwald, west of Coblenz, precisely in the so-called "Frankish" triangle, a result corresponding to some of our own findings in Britain (cf. especially the villa at Woodham's Farm near King's Worthy (Hants), pp. 94–5).

This would seem to mean, not that the Franks brought such strips from Germany, but that the type having been introduced into Britain and the Rhineland in the Roman period – in Britain as a development of a field type found dispersed in some localities among the Early Iron Age pattern – the Franks found it easy to adopt it on their arrival in eastern Britain. Professor Hawkes writes: "In Kent...since the main body of settlers were Franks, the [field] system set up was of the west German or Istaevonian type, to which the Franks adhered. Its affinity to Celtic custom due to the old Celtic element in western Germany made it all the easier to establish in this other older Celtic land." But perhaps, where strips are concerned, the Roman element in Kent was the decisive factor in this fusion. It may be asked, whether, in some localities where the very ancient nuclei of open-field systems can be traced in this country, the boundaries enclosing the shotts of the medieval system do not represent pre-Saxon plots in certain cases.

Seebohm viewed the manor as "the compound product of barbarian and Roman institutions," but Gray, ascribing a Roman origin to the

[1] Cf. J. Thirsk, *Past and Present*, no. 29, 1964, pp. 3 sqq. and especially p. 11: "In these circumstances, it is no longer possible for English scholars to argue that the Anglo-Saxons brought from Germany in the sixth century a fully-fledged common-field system."

Kentish system and likewise to usages in East Anglia, saw the manorial unit elsewhere as Saxon. D. C. Douglas proved that the *tenementum* on which Gray based his view had never existed in eastern England. The possibility nevertheless remains that strip fields were found by the English settlers when they reached Britain, and the case of Great Wymondley with its Roman villa standing amid a Roman centuriated field pattern surviving vestigially as part and parcel of the medieval open fields, raises the question whether further instances of such transmission may not be discovered in the future. Continuity of settlement here is suggested not only by the survival of the Roman pattern, but also by the coincidence of the village of Great Wymondley with the Romano-British village attached to the villa.[1]

Two other cases have something to contribute to the question. Professor Finberg demonstrated that no discernible factor need have prevented the area cultivated by the Roman villa of Withington (Glos) from persisting intact through the Saxon and medieval periods in recognizable fashion. The assumption here would be that the *coloni* of the villa survived the Roman establishment and continued to work the estate, and one would welcome archaeological finds to strengthen this eminently probable thesis, whose statement has done more than any other to create a new approach to the problem. The survival of the *coloni* of another Roman villa can also be postulated by the name Woodgarston – Wealgaerstone (= Welsh grazing-ground) in 945 – just south of the late-occupied villa of Balchester (near Monk Sherborne) in north-eastern Hampshire.

A further contribution is that of Ditchley villa (Oxon). Here a combination of archaeological and topographical evidence shows that woodland had surrounded the estate of Watt's Wells villa on the north, east, and south sides in Roman times, so constituting its boundaries, and all the known nearby Romano-British farm-sites outside this area were occupied contemporarily with the villa in the first or second centuries. The same area is additionally defined by the present parish boundaries on three sides and part of the fourth. The evidence is set out in greater detail in an appendix to this chapter; here it is only

---

[1] Seignorial imposition: Dopsch, *Economic and Social Foundation*, pp. 39 sqq.; p. 112. No common holdings among the Franks: *ibid.*, p. 106. German nucleated hamlets: J. Brønsted, *Danmarks Oldtid*, III, 1960, pp. 125–8; W. Haarnnagel, *Neue Ausgraben in Deutschland*, 1958, pp. 215–38; cf. Thirsk, *loc. cit.*, p. 8, that in the sixth century German settlements consisted of three or four families. See further Professor Finberg in his contribution, where the field systems of contemporary Germany are discussed. Mayener Stadtwald: BJ 163, 1963, pp. 316–41. I owe this reference to Miss Edith Wightman. Istaevonian field type: Hawkes, *Dark Age Britain*, pp. 108–9. The manor: Seebohm, *English Village Community*, p. 422; D. C. Douglas, *The Social Structure of Mediaeval East Anglia*, Oxford, 1927.

necessary to emphasize that future research may disclose similar phenomena in relation to other villa estates. The case of Ditchley does not, of course, prove continuity of occupation at the villa from the Roman to the Saxon period; but it does show that the Saxon settlers encountered the estate in visible and defined form, and something occurred in their rural society which perpetuated the estate as a recognized unit. A possible correlation between Anglo-Saxon estates and Roman villas is also now being noticed in the Butcombe area of north Somerset.[1]

The continuity problem is not restricted to the lowland zone. Various groups of Celtic place-names, or to a greater extent of English names alluding to Britons, Welshmen, or Cumbrians, occur in the north of England outside Cumbria, and indicate enclaves of surviving British population. The investigation of such settlements from an agrarian point of view is only at its beginning. G. R. Jones has however shown that about half the villages of this type in south-western Yorkshire, where they represent the Dark Age Celtic kingdom of Elmet, constituted in the Middle Ages discontinuous estates of federal manors. This structure he traces to a Celtic pattern already discussed here (pp. 49 sqq.), that of bond-villages cultivating open fields under the supervision of a mayor's hamlet or *maerdref*. Such bond-villages Jones believes to have figured more prominently in ancient Welsh society than they did in the Middle Ages, and some bore the names of adjoining hill-forts. A prominent case is Dinorben (Denbighshire), once a manor, associated with five bond-hamlets and occupied by a large homestead in the late Roman period. Accordingly Jones has extended his deductions to lowland England, and tentatively connected various villages known to have constituted discontinuous estates in the Middle Ages, through their manors with nearby hill-forts, more particularly those of the Sussex Downs. "As the widespread distribution of hill-forts in Britain implies," he writes, "discrete estates comprising a number of hamlets were once to be found in every district of England and Wales," and "together with the elaboration of the Romano-British villa economy this led perhaps to the cultivation of enlarged areas." Elsewhere he emphasizes that "on or near the site of almost every Roman settlement

---

[1] Withington: H. P. R. Finberg, *Roman and Saxon Withington*, Leicester, 1955 (= *Lucerna*, London, 1964, pp. 21–65). Woodgarston: R. E. Zachrisson, *Romans, Kelts and Saxons in Ancient Britain*, 1927, pp. 45, 69. G. R. Jones, *Geog. Annaler* XLIII, 1961, p. 180, believes that the name Comberton (Camb), the site of a Roman villa, embodies the *cumbran* place-name element; but Ekwall, *Concise Oxford Dictionary of English Place-names*, ad voc., derives from Cumbra, "a well evidenced personal name." For the remarkable correlation between villas and the medieval parishes of Banwell, Wrington, Butcombe, and Sutton (Som), in so far as each parish has one villa, see F. A. Neale, BUS XII, 1970, p. 170, fig. 25, cf. p. 173.

in Yorkshire, civil or military, there was a *mansio* or capital of a discrete estate in 1086."[1]

Jones nevertheless has emphatically rejected the inference which might be drawn by students of the agrarian system of Roman Britain, that the bond-hamlet with its open fields would, if he is right, have constituted an essential component of Roman rural structure.[2] It is difficult to understand exactly how the numerous discrete estates of Sussex and Wiltshire which, on his view, existed contemporarily with the Early Iron Age hill-forts of the South Downs and Salisbury Plain, "came through" to the Middle Ages without appearing on the Roman scene. His hypothesis would in any case require the discovery of Early Iron Age settlements at each of his medieval discrete estates; theoretically, it would work well for the Early Iron Age, and could with relevance be applied, for instance, to Casterley (cf. p. 36–7), or to Sidbury Hill in its dependence on Figheldean Down. In the later period it seems to be proved for Dinorben, could be relevant to Tidbury, and might apply to Castle Dore, South Cadbury, and Dinas Powys in an age when the hill-fort and fortified house of the chieftain were resuming their importance. Difficulties arise, however, for the Roman period, when the hill-forts were no longer seats of authority and were abandoned to gods and herdsmen. Such relationships are more likely to have been then transferred to the villa-hamlet axis, but, as we have seen, we still have no clear notion what proportion of the 'native' field complex was an open-field system, and the social status of the Romano-British nucleated villages of Wiltshire is still a matter of conjecture. But Jones's theory may be applied, perhaps, to western Britain (Somerset, Gloucestershire, and maybe elsewhere) in the post-Roman period, and should not be lost sight of in relation to Roman Britain as a whole.

---

[1] Settlements with names alluding to Britons: G. R. Jones, *Advancement of Science*, 1961, pp. 192 sqq.; *Geog. Annaler* XLIII, pp. 178–81. Bond-villages: G. R. Jones, *Advancement of Science*, 1961, p. 193; Elmet: Jones, *Trans. Caernarvonshire Historical Society*, 1963, p. 19. Dinorben; Jones, *Ant.* XXXV, 1961, p. 223; AHR VIII, 1960, pp. 66–81. Sussex Downs: *Ant.* XXXV, pp. 224–6. Distribution of hill-forts: *ibid.*, p. 231. Elaboration of villas: *ibid.*, p. 232. Yorkshire: *Advancement of Science*, 1961, p. 199.

[2] In a personal communication to the writer.

APPENDIX: THE BOUNDARIES OF
THE DITCHLEY VILLA ESTATE, OXFORDSHIRE

Grim's Dyke encloses the area round Watt's Wells (Ditchley) villa on the north and east sides (Fig. 42). It was thrown up shortly before the middle of the first century A.D. (*Oxon.* II, p. 92). It is not a continuous work, but has gaps, across which the discovery of butt-ends of the

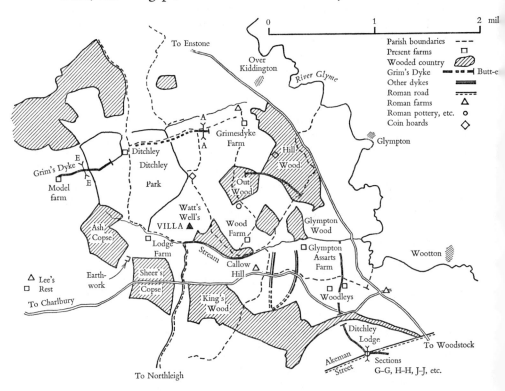

Fig. 42. Watt's Wells, Ditchley, Oxfordshire: the surroundings of the Roman villa.

ditch showed that it had not continued; these gaps must originally have been blocked by woodland. Such gaps, then, prove the existence of wooded tracts immediately north-west and north of Ditchley itself, north-east in the direction of Over Kiddington and Hill Wood, and eastward where it is still present in the form of Glympton Wood.

Another woodland belt crossed its line at Ditchley Lodge and still survives. The former existence of Glympton Wood on a larger scale is indicated by the name Glympton Assarts, showing clearance during the sixteenth century. Woodland probably existed outside the Dyke, for the ditch-filling of sections cut near Model Farm, Ditchley (*Oxon.* II, 70) and Grimsdyke Farm (*Oxon.* II, 78, Section A-A) suggested that the land to north was wooded in Roman times. Thirteenth-century records speak of wood clearance at the Dyke in Ditchley Park.

Ancient woodland can therefore be proved to have been continuous along the north edge of the Dyke from Model Farm to Hill Wood and round to Glympton Assarts, where the westerly of the two dykes near the Callow Hill Roman farm (thrown up in the first century A.D.) shows that woods existed as far as Wood Farm and probably as far west as Lodge Farm. On the other hand the gap immediately south of Watt's Wells, repeated farther southward by the modern ride between King's Wood and Sheer's Copse, down which runs the lane followed by a parish boundary to Stonesfield, may well be ancient. It is orientated upon the entrance to the Roman enclosure of Watt's Wells villa, and its south continuation points to a ford over the River Glym whence a path reached Northleigh villa. If the gap is ancient, then Sheer's Copse also represents ancient woodland bordering Watt's Wells on the south-west.

A nearly complete periphery of ancient woodland can therefore be traced round the villa through Ditchley Farm, Grims' Dyke Farm, Glympton Assarts Farm, and Lodge Farm. The area enclosed is about 875 acres; Radford (*Oxon.* I, p. 54) calculated the arable of the villa as approximating to 1,000 acres on the basis of the granary, two-thirds of which had a capacity of 5,400 bushels. The assumed yield was 10 bushels per acre. But if the grain came mainly from outside the domain, this calculation ceases to be relevant, and the yield of the estate itself would have been somewhat less.

The case for the correctness of the identified estate boundary is strengthened by the fact that it is marked on the whole of the south, west, and east sides of the area, and in the western half of the north side, by parish boundaries, which show that there was here some unit already recognizable in Saxon times. Other known neighbouring Roman farmsteads (Over Kiddington, Lee's Rest, Callow Hill, Woodleys-New Inn) all lie outside this periphery.

BIBLIOGRAPHICAL LIST OF SITES MENTIONED
IN THE FOREGOING CHAPTERS

Abington Piggots, Camb. PPSEA 3, p. 211; MA 3, p. 110.
Alchester, Oxon. VCH *Oxon.*, I, p. 281.
Allington, Kent. VCH *Kent*, III, p. 103.
Alresford, Ess. RCHM *Ess.*, III, p. 5; pp. 136–9.
Al Sauvenière, Maillen, Belgium. RV *Bel.*, p. 56.
Angmering, Suss. SAC 79, p. 3; 80, p. 88; 84, p. 82; 86, p. 1.
Apethorpe, N'hants. VCH *N'hants*, I, p. 199.
Appleshaw, Hants. VCH *Hants*, I, p. 297.
Appleton, Norf. JRS 38, p. 90.
Arbury Road, Cambridge. JRS 57, p. 189; 58, p. 195; CAS 48, p. 10.
Arches, Maillen, Belgium. RV *Bel.*, p. 54.
Arncliffe, W. Riding, Yorks. ANT III, p. 121.
Ashdown Park, Berks. WAM 10, p. 105; Peake, *Arch. of Berks*, 1930, p. 102.
Ashley, N'hants. JRS 54, p. 164; 58, p. 191.
Ashley Heath, Hants. Freeman, *Field Arch. in Hants*, 1915, pp. 229, 259.
Ashtead, Surr. SyAC 37, p. 144; 38, pp. 1, 132.
Atworth, Wilts, WAM 49, p. 46.

Bagwood, Beer Regis, Dors. JRS 57, p. 196.
Balchester, Hants. HFC 18, pp. 129–30.
Ballinderry Crannog, Ireland. PRSAI 74, p. 133.
Banwell, Som. VCH *Som.*, I, p. 307.
Barford St Martin, Wilts. CBA. RR VII, p. 55.
Bar Hill, Dunbartonshire. G. Macdonald, A. Park, *The Roman Forts on BH.*, 1906.
Barholm, Lincs. CBA. RR VII, p. 23.
Barnack, N'hants. CBA. RR VII, p. 22.
Barnsley Park, Glos. BGAS 86, p. 74.
Bartlow, Ess. RCHM *Ess.*, NW, p. xxiv.
Barton-in-Fabis, Notts. *Trans. Thoroton Soc.* 55, p. 3.
Bauselenne-te-Mettet, Belgium. RV *Bel.*, p. 99.
Baydon, Wilts. *Devizes Mus. Cat.*, II, no. 459.
Beadlam, N. Riding, Yorks. JRS 57, p. 179.
Bedmore Barn, Ham Hill, Som. JRS 3, p. 127.
Benson, Oxon. JRS 15, p. 231.
Benwell, N'umb. AA[4], p. 19.
Betzfeld-Landen, Belgium. RV *Bel.*, fig. 13.
Betzingen, Germany. Paret, *Die Römer in Württemburg*, 1928–32, III, p. 34.
Bewcastle, Cumb. RBES, p. 272, Map IV.
Bigbury, Kent. *Arch. J.*, p. 59.
Bignor, Suss. Herbert, *Notes on the Roman Villa at Bignor, Sussex*, 1929 (MS); VCH *Suss.*, III, p. 20; JRS 49, p. 131; 50, p. 234; 52, p. 189.
Birtley, N'umb. AA[4] 41, p. 215.
Bisley, Glos. JBAA I, p. 44; *Arch. J.* 2, p. 42; JBAA 2, p. 234.
Bitterne, Hants. Cotton, Gathercole, *Min. of Works Arch. Report, no. 2: Excavations at Clausentum*, 1958.
Blaize Castle, Glos. *Bristol Arch. Research Group Bull.* 2, p. 104.

Blankenheim, Germany. BJ 123.
Borough Walls, Daventry, N'hants. VCH *N'hants*, I, p. 195.
Boscombe Down West, Wilts. WAM 54, p. 165.
Boscoreale, Italy. *Monumenti Antichi* 7, p. 446.
Bosham, Suss. VCH *Suss.*, III, p. 50.
Bowcombe, IOW. VCH *Hants*, I, p. 317.
Box, Wilts. WAM 33, p. 236; VCH *Wilts*, I, p. 44.
Boxmoor, Herts. VCH *Herts*, IV, p. 154; JRS 57, p. 188.
Boxted, Kent. VCH *Kent*, III, p. 103.
Brading, IOW. Price, Price, *Description of the Roman Buildings at Morton near Brading*, 1881; RVB, p. 44.
Bramdean, Hants. VCH *Hants*, I, p. 307.
Braughing, Herts. VCH *Herts*, IV, p. 150; EHAS 13.
Bream Down, Som. *Bristol Arch. Research Bull.* 2, p. 104.
Brickkiln Farm, Chilgrove, Suss. JRS 54, p. 177; 55, p. 218; 57, p. 198; 58, p. 202.
Brislington, Som. VCH *Som.*, I, p. 304.
Brockley Hill, Msx. LMAS 9; 10 et sqq.
Bunny, Notts. *Trans. Thoroton Soc.* 71, p. 5.
Burgh near Woodbridge, Suff. VCH *Suff.*, I, p. 301.
Burgweinting, Germany. *Germania Romana* II, Taf. xxvi; Wagner, *Die Römer in Bayern*, p. 73.
Burham, Kent. VCH *Kent*, III, p. 109.
Bury Lodge, Hambleden, Hants. JRS 34, p. 83.
Butcombe, Som. JRS 57, p. 195; 58, p. 198; *Bristol Arch. Research Group Bull.* 2, pp. 62, 129; 3, p. 62.

Callow Hill, Oxon. *Oxon.* 22, p. 11.
Camulodunum (Lexden, Ess.). Hawkes and Hull, *Camulodunum*, SARR XIV.
Canklow, W. Riding, Yorks. YAJ 37, p. 239.
Cannington, Som. *Bristol Arch. Research Group Bull.* 2, p. 105.
Carisbrook, IOW. VCH *Hants*, I, p. 316.
Carzield, Dumfriesshire. AA⁴ 19, p. 27.
Casterley, Wilts. WAM 37, pp. 57 sqq.
Castle Dore, Corn. *Jour. Royal Instit. Corn.*² I, p. 60.
Castle Dykes, N. Stainley, Yorks. *Arch. J.* 32, p. 135.
Castlefield, Andover, Hants. VCH *Hants*, I, p. 302.
Castle Hill, Dufton, Westm. RCHM *Westm.*, p. xxxii.
Catsgore, Som. SANHS 46, p. 41.
Cawood, W. Riding, Yorks. YAJ 32, p. 333.
Cefn Graeanog, Caernarvonshire. RCAHM *Caern.*, III, A852, p. 115.
Chalk, Kent. JRS 52, p. 190.
Charminster, Dors (Walls Coppice). JRS 51, p. 188.
Charterhouse, Surr. SyAC 51, p. 27.
Charterhouse-on-Mendip, Som. VCH *Som.*, I, p. 334; BUS 6, p. 201.
Chedworth, Glos. BGAS 78, pp. 5, 162; JRS 55, p. 215; 56, p. 212.
Cherington, Glos. A 18, p. 112.
Cherry Hinton, Camb. CAS 56/7, p. 30.
Chesterton-Durobrivae (Water Newton), Hunts. JRS 48, p. 139.
Chew Stoke, Som. VCH *Som.*, I, p. 309; JRS 45, p. 139; 46, p. 115; *Archaeology* 9, p. 110.
Chiragan, France. L. Joulin, *Les établissements gallo-romains de Martres-Tolosannes: Mem. Acad. Inscrs. et Belles Lettres*, XI, 1901.

Chisenbury, Wilts. CBA. RR VII, pp. 50, 51.
Churchey Bushes, Bawdrip, Som. *Som. & Dors. Notes & Queries* 27, no. 80.
Chysauster, Corn. A 83.
Clanville, Hants. VCH *Hants*, I, p. 296.
Clipsham, Rut. JRS 30, p. 169.
Cold Kitchen Hill, Wilts. WAM 43, p. 330.
Colerne, Wilts. *Arch. J.* 13, p. 328; WAM 45, p. 184.
Collingham, W. Riding, Yorks. YAJ 37, p. 237.
Colney Street, Herts. *Arch. J.* 124, pp. 132, 151.
Combe Down, Som. VCH *Som.*, I, p. 309.
Corbridge, N'umb. AA[3] 3–11; [4]15; 17; ms. Haverfield Library, Oxford.
Corfe Mullen, Dors. Inf. R. A. H. Farrar.
Cornhill Farm, Challow, Berks. *OS Map of Rom. Brit.*,[3] p. 32.
Cow Down, Westwood, Hants. VCH *Hants*, I, p. 313; HFC 3, p. 201.
Cowley, Oxon. Ashmolean Museum, Oxford.
Cox Green, Maidenhead, Berks. BkAJ 60, p. 62.
Crock Cleugh, Roxburghshire. PSAS 81, p. 138.
Crohamhurst, Surr. SyAC 50, p. xxiii; 46, p. 131; 42, p. 111.
Cromhall, Glos. PSA[2] 23, p. 20; Witts, *Arch. Handbook of Glos.*, 1883, I, p. 59.
Cromwell, Notts. JRS 51, p. 133.
Crosby Garrett, Westm. RCHM *Westm.*, no. 8, p. 74.
Crosby Ravensworth, Westm. RCHM *Westm.*, p. 82.
Cwmbrwyn, Carm. RCAHM *Carm.*, I, p. 58.

Darenth, Kent. VCH *Kent*, III, p. 111.
Denton, Lincs. *Lincs. Archit. and Arch. Soc. Reports and Papers* 10, p. 75.
Dicket Mead, Welwyn, Herts. *Ant. J.* 44, p. 143.
Digswell Water, Herts. EHAS 10, p. 145.
Dinas Powys, Glam. L. Alcock, *Dinas Powys*, 1963.
Din Llygwy, Anglesey. RCHM *Anglesey*, p. 133, no. 6; CBA. RR VII, pp. 35, 37.
Dinorben, Denbighshire. Gardiner, Savory, *Dinorben*, 1964.
Ditchley, Oxon. *Oxon.* I, p. 24; *Ant.* 9, p. 472.
Downton, Wilts. WAM 58, p. 303.
Drumaroad, N. Ireland. *Ulster Arch. Jour.* [3]19, p. 85.
Dryhill, Glos. Witts, *Arch. Handbook of Glos.*, p. 60.

East Coker, Som. VCH *Som.*, I, p. 329.
East Dean, Wilts. JRS 45, p. 143.
Eastfield, Thruxton, Hants. VCH *Hants.*, I, p. 299.
East Grimstead, Wilts. H. Sumner, *Excavations at E. Grimstead*, 1924.
Eccles, Kent. *A. Cant.* 78, p. 125; 79, p. 121; 80, p. 69.
Ellerbeck, Westm. CW[2] 63, p. 77; 64, p. 6.
Ely, Glam. JRS 11, p. 67.
Engleton, Staffs. *Staffordshire Historical Collections*, 1938, p. 267.
Ewe Close, Westm. RCHM *Westm.*, no. 25, p. 83.
Ewell, Surr. SyAC 48, p. 59.
Ewhurst (Rapsley Farm), Surr. SyAC 65, p. 1.
Exning (Landwade), Suff. JRS 50, p. 28.
Ezinge Warf, Groningen, Holland. *Germania*, 1936, p. 41.

Falmer Hill, Suss. *Ant.* 10, p. 443 and fig. 84.

Farley Heath, Surr. SyAC 42, p. 18.
Farnham, Surr. SyAC 54, p. 47.
Faversham, Kent. J. Philp, *Excavations at Faversham, 1965,* 1968, pp. 67–74.
Farthing Down, Coulsden, Surr. SyAC 50, p. 47.
Fawkham, Kent. *A. Cant.* 78, p. 55.
Figheldean Down, Wilts. PPS 20, p. 103.
Finchingfield, Ess. EAS 20, p. 248; 21, p. 219; 22, p. 309.
Fingringhoe, Ess. JRS 28, p. 184.
Finkley Down Farm, Hants. VCH *Hants,* I, p. 303.
Finkley Farm, Hants. VCH *Hants,* I, p. 303.
Fishbourne, Suss. *Ant. J.* 42, 1962 onwards.
Flur Krautland, Württemburg. Paret, *Die Römer in Württemburg,* III, p. 132.
Folkestone, Kent. S. E. Winbolt, *Roman Folkestone,* 1925.
Frilford, Berks. *Oxon.* 4, p. 1.
Frindsbury, Kent. *A. Cant.* 18, p. 189.
Frocester Court, Glos. BGAS 77, p. 23; 50, p. 230; 52, p. 182; 53, p. 143; pp. 54, 171.
    183; 55, p. 216; 56, p. 212; CBA *Arch. Review* 3, p. 17.
Fullerton, Hants. JRS 12, p. 250; 54, p. 174; 55, p. 217.
Fyfield, Hants. VCH *Hants,* I, p. 295.

Gadebridge Park, Hemel Hempstead, Herts. JRS 55, p. 211; 56, p. 208; 57, p. 187;
    58, p. 194.
Gargrave (Kirk Sink), W. Riding, Yorks. *Bradford Antiquary,* n.s. 3, p. 353.
Garsdorf, Germany. *Germania,* 1959, p. 296.
Garth, Pembrokeshire. AC 116, p. 67.
Gatcombe, Som. SANHS III, p. 24; 112, p. 40; BUS 9, p. 173; 11, p. 125; JRS 56,
    p. 212; 57, p. 195; 58, p. 198.
Gellygaer, Glam. J. Ward, *The Rom. Fort at Gellygaer;* Nash-Williams, *The Rom.
    Frontier in Wales* (ed. 2, M. G. Jarrett).
Gerpinnes, Belgium. RV *Bel.,* p. 85.
Gestingthorpe, Ess. VCH *Ess.,* III, p. 133.
Glastonbury, Som. Bulleid, Gray, *The Glastonbury Lake Village,* 1911.
Glastonbury Tor, Som. *Bristol Arch. Research Group Bull.* 3, p. 59.
Gothic House Farm, Holbeach, Lincs. *Aspects of Arch. in Britain and Beyond* (ed.
    Grimes), p. 267.
Grassington, W. Riding, Yorks. YAJ 33, p. 166.
Graux, Belgium. RV *Bel.,* p. 57.
Great Casterton, N'hants. Corder, *The Rom. Town and Villa at Gt Cast.,* 1st, 2nd,
    and 3rd Interim Reports.
Great Chesterford, Ess. *Arch. J.* 13.
Great Oakley, N'hants. JRS 56, p. 207; 57, p. 186.
Great Staughton, Hunts. JRS 59, p. 118; 50, p. 224.
Great Tew, Oxon. VCH *Oxon.,* I, p. 310; *Oxon.* 26/7, p. 153.
Great Tey, Ess. JRS 57, p. 189; 58, p. 197.
Great Weldon, N'hants. VCH *N'hants,* I, p. 193; JRS 44, p. 135; 46, p. 131.
Great Witcombe, Glos. BGAS 73, p.5; JRS 51, p. 186; 53, p. 141; 56, p. 212.
Great Wymondley (Nine Springs, Purwell Mill), Herts. VCH *Herts,* IV, p. 170;
    EHAS 10, p. 11.
Greaves Ash, N'umb. AA⁴ 42, p. 44.
Gregnano, Italy. *Notizie degli Scavi,* 1923, p. 275.
Grimstone Down, Dors. RCHM *Dors.,* I, p. 228, no. 11.
Gwithian, Corn. *Corn. Arch.* I, p. 61.

Hadstock, Ess. RCHM *Ess.*, I, p. xxi.
Hafoty Wern Las, Caernarvonshire. RCAHM *Caern.*, II, no. 1340; AC 1923, p. 87.
Halstead, Ess. JRS 15, p. 230.
Hambleden, Bucks. A 71, p. 141.
Ham Hill, Som (Bedmore Barn). JRS 3, p. 127.
Harlow, Ess. *Ant. J.* 8, p. 308.
Harpenden, Herts. VCH *Herts*, IV, p. 163.
Harpham, E. Riding, Yorks. YAJ 38, p. 117; 39, p. 55.
Hartlip, Kent. VCH *Kent*, III, p. 117.
Haslemere, Surr. SyAC 51, p. 27.
Havant, Hants. HFC 10, p. 286.
Hawkeswick, W. Riding, Yorks. *Ant.*₃ p. 170.
Hayhope Knowe, Roxburghshire. RCHM *Roxburghshire*, I, no. 665.
Helpstone, N'hants. VCH *N'hants*, I, p. 189.
Hemel Hempstead, *see* Gadebridge Park.
Hensington, Oxon. VCH *Oxon.*, I, p. 310.
Heronbridge, Ches. *Jour. Chester Arch. Soc.* 30; 39; 41.
High Wycombe, Bucks. *Records of Bucks*, 16, p. 227.
Hinton St Mary, Dors. DNHAS 85, p. 116; 86, p. 150.
Hockwold, Camb. CAS 60, p. 39.
Hod Hill, Dors. J. W. Brailsford, I. A. Richmond, *Hod Hill*, I, II.
Holbeach Drove, Lincs. Crawford, *Archaeology in the Field*, p. 206.
Holbury, Hants. WAM 13, pp. 33, 276; VCH *Hants*, I, p. 312.
Holmstreet, Suss. PSA² 33, p. 377.
Hooley, Surr. SyAC 50, p. xxiii.
Horton, Epsom, Surr. SyAC 45, pp. 75, 89, 90.
Horton Kirby, Kent. *A. Cant.* 61, p. 180; JRS 51, p. 189.
Houdeng-Goegnis, Belgium. RV *Bel.*, p. 83.
Hovingham, E. Riding, Yorks. M. K. Clark, *An Arch. Gazetteer of Rom. Remains in E. Yorks.*, p. 88.
Hownham Rings, Roxburghshire. RCHM *Roxburghshire*, I, p. 20; PSAS 83, p. 63.
Hucclecote, Glos. BGAS 55, p. 323; 79, p. 159; 80, p. 42.
Huckhoe, N'umb. AA⁴ 38, p. 217.
Hulsberg, Holland. OM 1907, pp. 13–14.
Huntsham, Heref. JRS 52, p. 169; 55, p. 208; 66, p. 206.
Hurstbourne Priors, Hants. VCH *Hants*, I, p. 304; HFC 16, p. 192.

Ickham, Kent. VCH *Kent*, III, p. 119.
Ickleton, Camb. JBAA 4, p. 356; *Arch. J.* 6, p. 14.
Icklingham, Suff. VCH *Suff.*, I, p. 309; PSIA 28, p. 92.
Ipswich (Castle Hill, Whitton), Suff. PSIA 21, p. 240.
Irchester, N'hants. *Arch. J.* 124, p. 91.
Iwerne, Dors. *Arch. J.* 104, p. 48.
Ixworth, Suff. JRS 28, p. 189; *Ant.* 40, p. 60.

Jordon Hill, Dors. DNHAS 52.

Kemsing, Kent. *A. Cant.* 63, p. xliv.
Kensworth, Herts. *Arch. J.* 124, p. 153.
Kettlewell, W. Rid., Yorks. *Ant.* 3, p. 170.
Keynsham, Som. A 75, p. 109.
Kiddington, Oxon. VCH *Oxon.* I, p. 329; xix.

Kiddington, Over, Oxon. *Oxon.* II, p. 79.
Kingston, Dors. DNHAS 75, p. 54; JRS 45, p. 141.
Kingston Buci, Suss. SAC 72, p. 185; 94, p. 1.
Kingsweston, Glos. BGAS 69, p. 5.
King's Worthy, Hants (Woodham's Farm). JRS 15, p. 243; HFC 18, p. 63.
Kirk Sink, *see* Gargrave.
Knook Down, Wilts. CBA. RR VII, p. 53.
Knowl Hill, Wargrave, Berks. BkAJ 26, p. 28; 38, p. 75.
Köln-Braunfeld, Germany. BJ 135, p. 115.
Köln-Müngersdorf, Germany. Fremersdorf, *Die Römische Gutshof K-M.*, 1933.

Lagore Crannog, Ireland. PRIA 51, p. 67.
Lambourne's Hill, Redenham, Hants. VCH *Hants*, I, p. 294.
Landwade, *see* Exning.
Langton, E. Riding, Yorks. Corder, Kirk, *The Roman Villa at Langton near Malton, E. Yorks*, 1932; RVB, p. 246.
Latimer, Bucks. *Arch. J.* 124; p. 133; VCH *Bucks*, II, p. 8; *Rec. of Bucks* 18, p. 138.
Lea Cross, Staffs. *Tr. Shropshire Arch. Soc.* 56.
Lechlade, Glos. JRS 52, p. 179; inf. Mrs M. U. Jones.
Lee's Rest, Oxon. VCH *Oxon.*, I, p. 313.
Lenthay Green, Sherborne, Dors. JBAA I, p. 57; *Arch. J.* 22, p. 360; RCHM *Dors.*, I, p. 199.
Le Roux lez Fosse, Belgium. RV *Bel.*, p. 52.
Limerle, Belgium. RV *Bel.*, p. 130.
Linford, Ess. EAS² I, p. 88.
Linton, Wharfedale, W. Riding, Yorks. *Ant.* 3, p. 170.
Litlington, Camb. CAS 19, p. 4; Fox, ACR, p. 184.
Little Chart, Kent. *A. Cant.* 71, p. 130.
Little Milton, Oxon. JRS 40, p. 102.
Llandefalle Common, Brecknockshire. AC 116, p. 57.
Llandwrog, Caernarvonshire. RCAHM *Caern.*, II, nos. 1223–7.
Llantwit Major, Glam. AC 55, p. 106; 102, p. 89; RVB p. 238.
Lochnabuaile, Ireland. PRSAI 74, p. 137.
Locking, Kent. JRS 48, p. 156.
Lockley's, Welwyn, Herts. *Ant. J.* 18, p. 339; RVB p. 243.
Longstock, Hants. JRS 12, p. 271; Crawford, Keiller, *Wessex from the Air*, 1928, p. 29.
Lowbury Hill, Berks. Atkinson, *The Romano-British Site on Lowbury Hill in Berks*, 1917.
Lower Link, Hurstbourne, Hants. VCH *Hants*, I, p. 304.
Lower Wyke, Hurstbourne, Hants. VCH *Hants*, I, p. 304.
Low Ham, Som. SANHS 92, p. 25; JRS 36, p. 142; 37, p. 173; 39, p. 109; 44, p. 99.
Lufton, Som. SANHS, 97, p. 91; JRS 52, p. 82; p. 146.
Lullingstone, Kent. G. W. Meates, *Lullingstone Roman Villa*, 1955.
Lydney, Glos. R.E.M., T. V. Wheeler, *Lydney Park*, SARR XII.
Lye Hole, Wrington, Som. VCH *Som.*, I, p. 308; P. J. Fowler: see p. 95, n. 2.

Madmarston, Oxon. *Oxon.* 25.
Magor, Camborne, Corn. *Ant. J.* 12, p. 71; JBAA 39, p. 117.
Maiden Castle, Dors. R. E. M. Wheeler, *Maiden Castle*, SAAR III.
Malpas, Ches. T. Watkin, *Roman Cheshire*, p. 288.
Mangravets Wood, Maidstone, Kent. Crawford, Keiller, *Wessex from the Air*, p. 255.
Mansfield Woodhouse, Notts. *Trans. Thoroton Soc.* 53, p. 1.

Marburg near Pommern, Germany. BJ 101, p. 80.
Maulévrier, France. Grenier, *Manuel des antiquités préhistoriques, celtiques et gallo-romaines* VI, ii, 1934, pp. 800, 802, 805.
Maxey, Lincs. CBA. RR VII, p. 21.
Mayen, Germany. BJ 133, p. 51.
Mayener Stadtwald, Germany. BJ 163, p. 316.
Meriden Down, Dors. CBA. RR VII, p. 49.
Mersea Island, Ess. VCH *Ess.*, III, p. 158.
Micheldever, Hants. HFC 15, p. 240; VCH *Hants*, I, p. 307.
Mildenhall, Suff. *The Times*, 11 July 1946.
Moel Faban, Caernarvonshire. RCAHM *Caern.*, I, p. 146, fig. 143.
Moulsham, Ess. JRS 38, p. 92.
Mucking, Ess. MA 11, p. 264.
Mumrills, Stirlingshire. PSAS 63, p. 104.
Munden, Bucks. *Arch. J.* 124, p. 135.
Mynydd Ultyd, Brecknockshire. AC 116, p. 57.

Nantlle, Caernarvonshire. RCAHM *Caern.*, II, nos. 1223–7.
Needham, Norf. NA 28, p. 187.
Neerharen-Rekem, Belgium. RV *Bel.*, p. 113.
Newport, IOW. *Ant. J.* 4, pp. 141–354; JBBA[2] 36, p. 81.
Newstead, Roxburghshire. J. Curle, *A Roman Frontier Fort and its People*, 1911.
Newtown, Hants. JBAA 23, p. 280.
Nordelph, Norf. JRS 23, p. 197; *Geog. Jour.* 82, p. 440.
Northborough, Lincs. RCHM: *A Matter of Time*, p. 33 and fig. 6.
North Cadbury, Som. *Bristol Arch. Research Group Bull.* 2, p. 104.
Northleigh, Oxon. VCH *Oxon.*, I, p. 316; JRS 34, p. 81.
North Newbald, E. Riding, Yorks. *Pr. Leeds Philosophical Soc.* 5, p. 231.
North Thoresby, Lincs. LHA I, p. 55.
North Waltham (Wheatsheaf), Hants. HFC 15, p. 240, no. 14.
North Warnborough, Hants. JRS 19, p. 205; 21, p. 242; HFC 10, p. 235.
North Wraxhall, Wilts. WAM 7, p. 59.
Norton Disney, Notts. *Ant. J.* 17, p. 138.
Noyers-sur-Serein, France. *Gallia* 16, p. 320.
Nuthills, Wilts. Lansdowne, *A Roman Villa at N. near Bowood.*

Oakridge II Estate, Basingstoke, Hants. CBA *Arch. Review* 1966, p. 10.
Odrang, Germany. *Germania Romana*, 1924, II, pl. xx, 2; Steinhausen, *Archäologische Siedlungsgeschichte des Triere Landes*, 1936, p. 335.
Ogbourne St George, Wilts. WAM 61, p. 99.
Old Byfleet Rectory, Surr. SyAC 50, p. xxiii; 46, p. 131; 42, p. 111.
Old Durham, Co. Durham. AA[4] 22, p. 1; 29, p. 203.
Old Malden, Surr. SyAC 50, p. xxii.
Olfermont, France. De Caumont, *Abécédaire d'archéologie*, 1870, p. 387.
Orpington, Kent. VCH *Kent*, III, p. 122; *Kent Arch. Review* 7, p. 9.
Otford, Kent. *A. Cant.* 39, p. 153; 42, p. 157.
Overton Down, Wilts. WAM 58, p. 98.

Pant-y-Saer, Anglesey. AC 89, p. 1; *Trans. Birmingham Arch. Soc.* 62, p. 77.
Park Brow, Suss. A 76.
Park Street, Herts. *Arch. J.* 102, p. 21.
Paulton, Som. VCH *Som.*, I, p. 315.

Pevensey, Suss. SAC 51; 52.
Pitney, Som. R. Colt Hoare, *The Pitney Pavement*, 1832; VCH *Som.*, I, p. 326; CBA. RR VII, p. 102.
Pleshey, Ess. RCHM *Ess.*, II, p. xxix.
Popham, Hants. HFC 15, p. 239 sq., nos. 9, 10.
Poxwell, Dors. DNHAS, 89, p. 135.
Prae Wood, St Albans, Herts. R. E. M., T. V. Wheeler, *Verulamium*, SARR IX.
Pump Copse, Kiddington, Oxon. VCH *Oxon.*, I, p. 311.
Purberry Shott, Surr. SyAC 50, pp. 12, 20.
Purwell Mill, *see* Great Wymondley.

Ramridge Manor, Andover, Hants. VCH *Hants*, I, p. 295.
Randalstown Crannog, Ireland. Wood-Martin, *Lake Dwellings of Ireland*, p. 141.
Redenham, *see* Lambourne's Hill.
Reedham, Norf. VCH *Norf.*, II, p. 298.
Ridgehanger, Hants. JRS 38, p. 196; ms. C. E. Stevens.
Ripe, Suss. I. Margary, *Rom. Ways in the Weald*, p. 204.
Risehow, Cumb. CW² 59, p. 10.
Rivenhall, Ess. VCH *Ess.*, III, p. 171.
Rockbourne Down (Soldiers' Ring), Hants. H. Sumner, *Excavations on Rockbourne Down*, 1914.
Rockbourne Down, Hants (villa). Morely-Hewett, *The Roman Villa at West Park... Interim Report*, 1960; *2nd Interim Report*, 1962; JRS 53, pp. 150, 162; 55, pp. 217, 228; 56, pp. 214, 219, 225.
Rodmarton, Glos. A 18, p. 113.
Ronchinnes, Belgium. RV *Bel.*, p. 94.
Rotherley, Dors. *Arch. J.* 104, p. 27.
Rudge Farm, Froxfield, Wilts. WAM 46, p. 108; 53, p. 332; VCH *Wilts*, I, p. 71.
Rudston, E. Riding, Yorks. YAJ 31, p. 366; 32, p. 214; 33, p. 81; 222, 320; JRS 53, p. 130.
Ruit, Württemburg. Paret, *Die Römer in Württemburg*, III, p. 36.
Runcton Holme, Norf. PPSEA 7, p. 231.

Saint Bernard Pass, Switzerland. *Notizie degli Scavi*, 1924, p. 386.
Saint Ives, Hunts. JRS 49, p. 118; CAS 52, p. 15.
Sandilands, Walton-on-the-Hill, Surr. SyAC 51, p. 65.
Sandy, Beds. VCH *Beds.*, II, p. 9.
Sarratt, Herts. *Arch. J.* 124, p. 131.
Saunderton, Bucks. *Records of Bucks*, 13, p. 398.
Schlösselackern, Mündlesheim, Germany. *Fundbericht aus Schwaben* IX, p. 101.
Scole, Suff. NA 30, p. 151.
Shakenoake, Wilcote, Oxon. JRS 54, p. 166; 55, p. 210; 57, p. 188; 58, p. 193.
Shoddesden, Hants. HFC 9, p. 214.
Shopfield, Ess. EAS³, p. 58.
Slonk Hill, Suss. *Ant.* 9, fig. 84.
Snodland, Kent. VCH *Kent*, III, p. 124.
Soljberg, Denmark. *Mem. de la Soc. des antiquaires du nord*, 1928, p. 230.
Somborne, Hants. Crawford, *Air Survey and Archaeology*, 1924, end map II.
Somerdale, Som. D. P. Dobson, *The Arch. of Som.*, 1930, p. 135.
Southwell Minster, Notts. VCH *Notts.*, II, p. 34; *Tr. Thoroton Soc.* 70, p. 13.
Southwick, Suss. SAC 73, p. 13; JRS 56, p. 214.
Spoonley Wood, Glos. JBAA 38, p. 215; A 52, p. 651.

Stammheim, Württemburg. Paret, *Die Römer in Württemburg*, III, p. 29.
Stancombe Down, Berks. VCH *Berks*, I, p. 211.
Stanton Chair, Suff. PSIA 22, p. 339; Rivet, *Town and Country in Rom. Brit.*, 1958, p. 157.
Stanton Low, Bucks. JRS 49, p. 119.
Stanwick, N. Riding, Yorks. R.E.M. Wheeler, *The Stanwick Earthworks*, SARR VII.
Star, Shipham, Som. SANHS 108, p. 45.
Stockbronner Hof, Germany. BRGK 6, p. 58.
Stoke Ash, Suff. VCH *Suff.*, I, p. 316; PSIA, 22, p. 177.
Stonesfield, Oxon. VCH *Oxon.*, I, p. 315; *Oxon.* 6, p. 1.
Stonham, Suff. VCH *Suff.*, I, p. 315; PSIA 22, p. 174.
Street Cobham, Surr. SyAC 50, p. xxiii; 46, p. 131; 42, p. 111.
Stroud, Petersfield, Hants. *Arch. J.* 65, p. 66; 66, p. 33; CBA. RR VII, p. 103.
Studland, Dors. DNHAS 87, p. 142.
Sturthill, Dors. DNHAS 90, p. 167.
Sundhope Kipps, Roxburghshire. RCHM *Roxburgh*, I, no. 303.

Tallington, Lincs. CBA. RR VII, p. 15.
Tamshiel Rig, Roxburghshire. RCHM *Roxburgh*, II, no. 943, p. 426.
Tarrant Hinton, Dors. J. Hutchins, *Hist. of Dorset*, p. 318.
Teg Down, Suss. *Ant.* 9, fig. 84.
Thealby, Lincs. Dudley, *Early Days in North-West Lincolnshire*, 1939.
Thistleton, Rut. JRS 47, p. 212; 48, p. 98; 49, 112; 51, p. 174; 52, p. 172; 55, p. 207.
Thornford, Dors. JRS 54, p. 171; DNHAS 87, p. 104.
Thruxton, Hants (Eastfield). VCH *Hants*, I, p. 299.
Thuit, France. De Caumont, *Abécédaire d'archéologie*, p. 389.
Thundersbarrow Hill, Suss. *Ant. J.* 13, p. 109.
Thurnham, Kent. *A. Cant.* 76, p. 165.
Tickhill (Stancil), W. Riding, Yorks. YAJ 52, p. 261.
Tidbury Rings, Hants. HFC 16, p. 38.
Titsey, Surr. SyAC 4, p. 214.
Tockington Park, Glos. BGAS 12, p. 159; 13, p. 196.
Totternhoe, Beds. JRS 47, p. 214.
Town Hill, Frampton. CBA. RR VII, p. 49.
Traprain Law, Haddingtonshire. PSAS 58.
Tr'er Ceiri, Caernarvonshire. RCAHM *Caern.*, III, p. civ.
Twyford, Hants. JRS 14, p. 238; 15, p. 243.
Tyneham, Dors. DNHAS 89, p. 138.

Uplyme, Dev. *Arch. J.* 2, p. 49; A 45, p. 462.
Upper Wyke, Andover, Hants. Crawford, *The Andover District*, p. 59.
Upton, Glos. BGAS 85, p. 31.

Verulamium, Herts. R.E.M., T.V. Wheeler, *Verulamium*, SARR XXI; JRS 50, p. 227.

Walls Coppice, Charminster, Dev. JRS 51, p. 188.
Walton Heath, Surr. VCH *Surr.*, IV, p. 369.
Walton-on-the-Hill, Surr. (Sandilands). SyAC 51, p. 65.
Warren Hill, Hants. VCH *Hants*, I, p. 304.
Wasserwald-sur-Saverne, Vosges. Grenier, *Manuel d'arch...gallo-romaine*, VI, ii, p. 749.

Waun Gunllwch, Brecknockshire. AC 116, p. 57.
Well, W. Riding, Yorks. R. Gilyard Beer, *The Romano-British Baths at Well*, 1951.
Wellhead, Westbury, Wilts. WAM 61, p. 99.
Wellow, Som. VCH *Som*, I, p. 312.
Welwyn, Herts. A 63, p. 1; *Arch. J.* 87, pp. 247, 260.
West Blatchington, Suss. SAC 89, p. 1; AHR 6, p. 72.
Westbury, Wilts. *Devizes Museum Cat.*, II, p. 180.
West Coker, Som. VCH *Som.*, I, p. 312.
West Dean, Wilts. WAM 22, p. 243; VCH *Wilts*, I, p. 119.
West Gunnar Peak, N'umb. AA⁴ 38, p. 26.
Westlecott Road, Swindon, Wilts. WAM 41, p. 349.
West Meon (Lippen Wood), Hants. *Arch. J.* 64, p. 1.
Weycock Hill, Berks. VCH *Berks*, I, p. 216.
Weyhill, Hants ("Vitrici"). VCH *Hants*, I, p. 297.
Wherwell, Hants, *see* Fullerton.
Whitecliffe Down, Wilts. Devizes Museum.
Whittington Court, Glos. BGAS 71, p. 13.
Whittlebury, N'hants. VCH *N'hants*, I, p. 199.
Whitton, Suff., *see* Ipswich.
Whitton Crossroads, Glam. JRS 48, p. 131; 49, p. 102; BBCS 17, p. 293.
Wickbourne Estate, Suss. SAC 92, p. 43.
Wiggonholt, Suss. SAC 78, p. 13; 80, p. 54; SxNQ, 3, p. 37.
Wingham, Kent. VCH *Kent*, III, p. 125; *Ant.* 17, p. 210; 18, p. 52; JRS 58, p. 206;
    57, p. 202; inf. from the excavator, Mr F. Jenkins.
Winterton, Lincs. *Ant. J.* 46, p. 72.
Witcombe, *see* Great Witcombe.
Withington, Glos. A 18, p. 118; Finberg, *Roman and Saxon W.*, 1955.
Wolsty Hall, Cumb. P. Salway, *Frontier People of Rom. Brit.*, p. 113; CW² 59, p. 360.
Woodchester, Glos. Lysons, *An Account of Roman Antiquities discovered at W.*, 1797;
    BGAS 48, p. 75; 74, p. 177.
Woodcuts, Dors. *Arch. J.* 104, p. 27.
Woodeaton, Oxon. JRS 7, p. 98; 21, p. 105; *Oxon.* 19.
Woodleys, Oxon (New Inn). VCH *Oxon.*, I, p. 310.
Woolaston Pill, Glos. AC 93, p. 93.
Wookey Hole, Som. Balch, *Wookey Hole*, 1914.
Worlaby, Lincs. LHA I, p. 45.
Worlington, Suff. JRS 36, p. 137; PSIA 27, p. 45.
Wrington (Lye Hole), *see* Lye Hole.
Wyboston, Beds. CAS 50, p. 75.
Wylie Down, Wilts. Bowen, *Ancient Fields*, p. 26.
Wykehurst Farm, Cranley. SyAC, 45, p. 75.

Yatton, Som. SANHS 31, pp. 1, 64; JRS 55, p. 216.
Yeovil, Som. SANHS 74, p. 122.

POST-ROMAN WALES

By GLANVILLE R. J. JONES, M.A.

Reader in Historical Geography
University of Leeds

POST-ROMAN WALES[1]

WITH THE waning of the Roman Empire in the West, some elements of an older pattern of life emerged almost unchanged in the area that came to be known as Wales. The British monk, Gildas, writing towards the middle of the sixth century, could state that the Britons had abandoned the customs and laws of Rome.[2] The precise meaning of Gildas in this particular context is none too clear. Nevertheless his observation, which echoes a statement made by the Greek, Zosimus, a century or so earlier, must refer in part at least to Wales; indeed it has been plausibly suggested that Gildas lived and wrote at a monastery in South Wales.[3] Thus it would appear that during the dark centuries which intervened between the withdrawal of the Romans and the coming of the Normans the economy of Wales was largely of Celtic inspiration. Our purpose in this essay is to portray as fully as possible the overwhelmingly agrarian aspects of that essentially native economy.

To historians of an earlier and confident generation this objective was one readily attained. Influenced, if only indirectly, by Darwinian theories of unilinear evolution, they assumed that pastoral farming invariably preceded cultivation, and Wales, regarded as a remote and backward upland fastness, was deemed to have remained the preserve of nomadic pastoralists. On the basis of an analysis of written records and an equally theoretical elaboration of legal concepts, early Wales was envisaged as an area where Welsh patriarchs and their tribes roamed at will with their flocks and herds. Given the modern rural landscape of Wales, with its great expanses of rough pasture and enclosed grazings, but, at present, only fugitive patches of cultivation, it was not difficult for pioneer investigators to believe that the traditional way of life was almost exclusively pastoral.[4] Large expanses of upland

---

[1] I am particularly indebted to the following for their comments on this chapter: Professors W. H. Davies, H. P. R. Finberg, M. Richards, and A. C. Thomas. The responsibility for the views expressed, however, rests with me.

[2] Gildas, *De Excidio Britanniae*, ed. H. Williams, Cymmrodorion Record Series III, London, 1899, pp. 30–1.

[3] Zosimus. *Historia Nova*, VI, cited by C. E. Stevens in *Rural Settlement in Roman Britain*, ed. C. Thomas, London, 1966, pp. 109–10; W. H. Davies in *Christianity in Britain, 300–700*, ed. M. W. Barley and R. P. C. Hanson, Leicester, 1968, pp. 138–9.

[4] See for example F. Seebohm, *The English Village Community*, 2nd ed., London, 1905, pp. 8, 126, 224–5, 228–9, 437; id., *Customary Acres and their Historical Importance*, London, 1914, pp. 18, 76, 261; T. P. Ellis, *Welsh Tribal Law and Custom in the Middle Ages*, I, Oxford, 1926, p. 203.

with an unpleasant ecological temper marked by bleakness, heavy rainfall, and scant sunshine – all unfavourable to cultivation – reinforced this impression. Nevertheless, closer examination should have generated second thoughts.[1]

The uplands of Wales obtrude, yet some 42 per cent of the country lies below 500 feet. Much of this lowland, it is true, is ill drained and unsuitable for cultivation but there were opportunities for tillage, above all on the coastal lowlands and peninsulas.[2] Even now cultivation is not entirely absent from the moorland core of Wales when the need arises. Such a need probably existed during the Dark Ages.

No coins have been recorded with certainty for Wales from the end of the fourth century to the middle of the ninth century, so that early Welsh society was essentially rural. Such trade as there was must surely have been carried on by barter.[3] Under these circumstances of near self-sufficiency recourse is likely to have been made to all available resources. Hence the use made of upland grazings in the summer months so as to preserve lowland pastures for the lean months of Lent; hence too the cultivation of at least some grain for use as a filling food.

In the heroic verse of our period a constant emphasis on war and cattle-reaving by free warriors, proud of their lineage, provides evidence of pastoral farming. But the poets also remind us that the warrior who was valiant earned his mead.[4] This mead was produced from honey, some of which was presumably provided by the substrate population. Such lesser folk, mentioned in verse only in passing, also supported the poets who, like the war-bands they praised, were part of a hierarchical structure attached to the households of kings. In this hierarchical society the very presence of these lesser folk, like that of their small patches of cultivation, implies a greater stability of settlement and hence a greater continuity of social organization than hitherto envisaged for early Wales.

[1] G. R. J. Jones, 'The Tribal System in Wales: A Re-assessment in the Light of Settlement Studies', WHR I, 1961, pp. 111–14; id., 'Die Entwicklung der ländlichen Besiedlung in Wales', *Zeitschrift für Agrargeschichte und Agrarsoziologie* x, 1962, pp. 174–6.
[2] F. Emery in *Agrarian History of England and Wales*, IV, ed. J. Thirsk, Cambridge, 1967, pp. 133 sqq.
[3] L. Alcock in *Celtic Studies in Wales*, ed. E. Davies, Cardiff, 1963, pp. 38–9; id., 'Some reflections on Early Welsh Society and Economy', WHR II, 1964, p. 3; but see also below p. 378.
[4] I. Williams, *Lectures on Early Welsh Poetry*, Dublin, 1944, pp. 28–9, 62; K. Jackson, *The Gododdin*, Edinburgh, 1969, pp. 34–7.

THE PAUCITY OF CONTEMPORARY EVIDENCE

The pointers, though clear, are few, for the total body of evidence dating directly from our period is meagre. The fragmentary picture which is the best that can be obtained from written sources of the Dark Ages must be supplemented not only by that of contemporary material remains but also by the fuller evidence of later medieval sources including the extents and surveys of the thirteenth and four-teenth centuries.[1] Some account of these contemporary and retro-spective sources is necessary as a preface to our discussion of agrarian conditions in early Wales.

The primary source for the opening of our period is the *De Excidio et Conquestu Britanniae c.* A.D. 540 by the British monk, Gildas.[2] This was largely a work of moral exhortation to the kings and the clergy of the Britons, calling attention to the evils of British society as Gildas saw them. Like the few other written sources dating from our period, it provides but little insight into agrarian organization. Thereafter until the *Historia Brittonum* was finally compiled by Nennius, probably in Gwynedd between 787 and 829, we have virtually no written evidence whatsoever. Fortunately the History by Nennius incorporates older material perhaps deriving from the seventh century.[3] This can be supplemented by fragments of information derived from the *Annales Cambriae* and the royal genealogies whose originals were probably brought together in the tenth century. The mid-ninth century had been a phase of intense literary activity when it was royal policy in North Wales to foster among the Cymric peoples a pride in their past.[4] Hence the cultural achievement of the court of Rhodri Mawr in collecting, and committing to writing, traditional bardic poetry which provides a tenuous yet informative strand of our evidence. The impetus of this literary revival probably persisted into the tenth

[1] These extents and surveys of the thirteenth and fourteenth centuries include among numerous others: SC 11/769 printed as Appendix Aa in F. Seebohm, *The Tribal System in Wales*, London, 1895; *The Black Book of St Davids*, ed. J. W. Willis-Bund, Cymmrodorion Record Series v, London, 1902, but on this edition see also J. Conway Davies, 'The Black Book of St Davids', *National Library of Wales Jnl* iv, 1945–6, pp. 158–76; *Survey of the Honour of Denbigh, 1334*, ed. P. Vinogradoff and F. Morgan, B. Acad. Records of Social and Economic History i, London, 1914; *The Record of Caernarvon*, ed. H. Ellis, Record Commission, London, 1838.

[2] Gildas, *op. cit.*; D. P. Kirby, 'Vortigern', BBCS XXIII, 1968–9, pp. 39–40.

[3] Nennius, *Historia Brittonum*, ed. T. Mommsen, *Chronica Minora Saeculi IV–VIII*, *Monumenta Germaniae Historica, Auct. Antiquiss.*, iii, Berlin, 1898, pp. 111 sqq.; K. Jackson, in *Celt and Saxon*, ed. N. K. Chadwick, Cambridge, 1963, pp. 20–62.

[4] N. K. Chadwick in *Studies in the Early British Church*, ed. N. K. Chadwick, Cambridge, 1958, pp. 47–8, 74, 79.

century when the greatest of all Welsh patriotic poems, *Armes Prydein*, was composed *c.* A.D. 930 in South Wales.[1] But save for a few stanzas, fortunately preserved in a ninth-century manuscript, almost all our early Welsh poetry is preserved in manuscripts dating from *c.* 1150–1350. The survival in these manuscripts of ninth-century linguistic forms makes credible the view that the poems of Aneirin and Taliesin were first converted from an oral to a written form in the ninth century. In their oral form, moreover, twelve poems of Taliesin have been plausibly back-dated to the sixth century and the *Gododdin* of Aneirin to *c.* A.D. 600.[2] The latter is more Cumbric than Welsh in tradition, but, like some of the poems of Taliesin which relate directly to Wales, it belongs to the same general culture. The agrarian allusions of this literature, though few, are almost identical with those of verse of Welsh origin like *Canu Llywarch Hen* which deals with the Powys border and is tentatively dated *c.* A.D. 850.[3]

These contemporary sources notwithstanding, the best evidence for the agrarian economy of early Wales comes from the so-called laws of Hywel Dda. To the social historian the importance of early Welsh verse lies in the confirmation it can provide that certain aspects of the agrarian economy described in the Welsh lawbooks are much older than the earliest extant legal texts. Of these, the text known as Redaction A of the Latin versions is dated no earlier than the end of the twelfth century and all other texts are later in date.[4] Moreover, the whole body of Welsh law as recorded can hardly have been in force at any one time, for the texts were the handbooks of the lawyers who arranged the contents for their own convenience, so that archaic edicts jostle with later glosses and whole new sections. Even the oldest text in its surviving form is a product of a period later than the reign of Hywel Dda (*ob. c.* 950) to whom a codification of the laws is attributed. But already when this oldest redaction was composed and up-to-date sections introduced, there existed a body of law which was regarded as authoritative. Pre-existing copies were probably transmitted in the vernacular, partly in oral triadic form and partly in writing. Consequently there is general agreement that the well-established medieval tradition of legal activity on the part of Hywel Dda is unlikely to be a completely false one. His achievement was probably that of clarifying and introducing some degree of consistency and order into existing

[1] *Armes Prydein*, ed. I. Williams, Cardiff, 1964, pp. ix–xvii.

[2] *Canu Taliesin*, ed. I. Williams, Cardiff, 1960, pp. xvii, xlii–xlv; see also the English version of the Introduction and Notes by J. E. Caerwyn Williams in *The Poems of Taliesin*, Dublin, 1968, pp. xxviii, lxviii; Jackson, *The Gododdin*, pp. 56–67, 86–91.

[3] *Canu Llywarch Hen*, ed. I. Williams, Cardiff, 1955, pp. xxxvii, lxxii–lxxxi.

[4] H. D. Emanuel, *The Latin Texts of the Welsh Laws*, Cardiff, 1967, pp. 1 sqq., 84–5.

customary law, an undertaking certainly consonant with the intense cultural activity of tenth-century Wales. Nevertheless it is probable that the range of topics covered in our extant texts was wider than that with which Hywel concerned himself.[1] The problem before us therefore is to determine which of the older strata of Welsh law can be attributed to the period before 1042 and also, if possible, to the period before 950. Fortunately, as we shall see, this can be determined in part from the contents of the lawbooks themselves.

For Wales there are no contemporary charters of the kind which illuminate agrarian conditions in early England and buttress the agrarian evidence of the English laws. The nearest equivalents are six records of grants written in the margins of *Llyfr Teilo*. The insular majuscule of this gospel-book suggests a date in the early eighth century and the records of grants were probably inserted in the eighth, ninth, and tenth centuries, perhaps when the book was at Llandeilo Fawr (Carm). Certainly, however, they were inserted before the gospel-book, now known as the Book of St Chad, was transferred to Lichfield and there inscribed with the name of Bishop Wynsi (974–92).[2] These records of grants provide evidence of unimpeachable authority, though the information they yield becomes meaningful only in the light of the law-texts. Much less satisfactory as a source of information is the *Liber Landavensis*, compiled it seems in the second half of the twelfth century to support the claims of an old Celtic church which at that time was busily transforming itself into an Anglo-Norman diocesan see.[3] This compilation contains a large number of so-called charters which no scholar nowadays accepts at face value. Nevertheless, as a recent study suggests, the forger appears to have used for his purpose various sources including an authentic

[1] T. Jones Pierce, 'The Laws of Wales: the Kindred and the Blood Feud', *University of Birmingham Historical Jnl* II, 1952, pp. 119–37; id., 'Social and Historical Aspects of the Welsh Laws', in WHR, *Special Number, The Welsh Laws*, 1963, pp. 33–49; J. G. Edwards, 'The Historical Study of the Welsh Law Books', TRHS, 5th series, XII, 1962, pp. 141–55; R. R. Davies, 'The Twilight of Welsh Law, 1284–1536', *History* LI, 1966, pp. 143 sqq.; D. Jenkins, *Cyfraith Hywel*, Llandysul, 1970, pp. 1–12.

[2] The *marginalia* of the Book of St Chad are given in facsimile in *The Text of the Book of Llan Dav (Llyvyr Teilo vel Liber Landavensis)*, ed. J. Gwenogfryn Evans and J. Rhys, Oxford, 1893, preface xlii–xlvii and the accompanying plates; I. Williams, 'Meddyfnych', BBCS VII, 1933–5, pp. 369–70; K. Jackson, *Language and History in Early Britain*, Edinburgh, 1953, pp. 42–7.

[3] E. D. Jones, 'The Book of Llandaff', *National Library of Wales Jnl* IV, 1945–6, pp. 123–57; M. Watkin, 'The Chronology of the *Annales Cambriae* and the *Liber Landavensis* on the basis of their Old French Graphical Phenomena', *National Library of Wales Jnl* XI, 1959–60, pp. 182–226; C. W. Lewis, 'Agweddau ar Hanes Cynnar yr Eglwys yng Nghymru', *Llên Cymru* VII, 1963, pp. 162–71; H. P. R. Finberg, *Early Charters of the West Midlands*, Leicester, 1961, pp. 19–20.

royal genealogy of the kings of Archenfield, memoranda of donations entered informally in gospel-books like *Llyfr Teilo*, lists of churches and ordinations, Welsh annals, and genuine local traditions. The grants purport to range from the sixth century onwards and their chronology remains very doubtful, but this need not necessarily apply to their substance.[1] Indeed, since the compiler was presumably anxious to convince his contemporaries about the superiority of Llandaf claims over those of Hereford and St David's, he is likely to have recorded features of the agrarian landscape accurately. The details of topography and agrarian organization are therefore likely to have been valid for the period when the compiler was at work, save that the claims to commonage were probably exaggerated. The topographic detail of the Book of Llandaf may therefore be used to supplement and refine the necessarily idealized picture of agrarian organization presented in the handbooks of the lawyers. Even more confidence, it appears, can be reposed in the memoranda of grants incorporated in the roughly contemporary *Vita Sancti Cadoci*, whose compiler, Lifris, belonged to the same tradition as the author of the Book of Llandaf.[2] To the same milieu belongs a document written about the mid-thirteenth century and incorporated in the *Liber Ruber Asaphensis*.[3] This fortunately gives some pointers to early donations in North Wales.

Nevertheless the contemporary archaeological evidence remains our surest guide since it enables us not only to test this written evidence but also to view it clearly in its territorial setting. More of the history of Wales lies in the earth than is recorded in our libraries, but as yet the archaeological evidence for our period is slight. Unfortunately not many sites have been excavated and these have yielded but few finds. Dating is dependent on imported Mediterranean pottery, but this appears to have been used only up to about A.D. 650.[4] There were no coins until the mid-ninth century and the number of hoards increases only gradually as the money economy developed.[5] Building was in earth, wood, or rough stone which cannot be dated readily. Even the dry-stone fortifications used by prominent figures in society

[1] C. Brooke in *Studies in the Early British Church*, pp. 201–42, and the review by J. Morris in WHR I, 1961, pp. 229–30.

[2] A. W. Wade-Evans, 'The Llancarfan Charters', AC LXXXVII, 1932, pp. 151–65; *Vitae Sanctorum Britanniae et Genealogiae*, ed. A. W. Wade-Evans, Cardiff, 1944, pp. 24–141.

[3] I. Ll. Foster, 'Wales and North Britain', AC CXVIII, 1969, pp. 13–14; National Library of Wales: Peniarth MS. 231 B; St Asaph MS. B/22.

[4] It is now considered that some of this pottery of continental (i.e. French) origin may have been produced after A.D. 700.

[5] A. H. M. Dolley, *The Hiberno-Norse Coins in the British Museum*, London, 1966, pp. 14, 23, 26, 33.

appear to have changed little over the half millennium before the twelfth century. Thus it is only a chance reference by Gerald of Wales to the recent building of the castle sited in the Iron-Age hill-fort on Carn Fadrun (Caern) which permits this castle to be ascribed to the twelfth century rather than to the seventh.[1] Given these deficiencies of the archaeological record, it is especially fortunate that Early Christian inscribed and sculptured stone monuments are sufficiently numerous to give, at least for the western half of Wales, a broad impression of the main areas of permanent settlement.[2] Although these monuments cannot be dated to the nearest half century their inscriptions supplement Gildas in providing strictly contemporary documentation.[3] Their utility as sources of evidence is enhanced by the fact that they continued to be erected until the close of our period. The most numerous of our remains, they provide a sound distributional framework against which more fragmentary categories of evidence can be viewed.

Our written sources reveal that in the fifth century the country was divided into a number of petty kingdoms at war with each other as much as with the English. The south-west, and to a lesser degree the north-west, were inhabited by Irish, many of aristocratic status. If Nennius is to be believed, it was to evict the Irish that Cunedda and eight of his nine sons were transferred to Wales from the southern fringe of the Forth and in due course founded many a local dynasty.[4] The inhabitants of these warring kingdoms were nominally Christian, though, according to Gildas, of no great devotion. Besides the new monasteries there are hints also of surviving episcopal dioceses and the Church certainly appears to have been sustained by royal endowments.[5] In Dyfed, the ancient territory of the Demetae was ruled by an Irish king named in Latin as Voteporix and in Ogam as Votecorix,

[1] RCAHM, *Caernarvonshire*, III, 1964, pp. cxvi–cxviii.
[2] V. E. Nash-Williams, *The Early Christian Monuments of Wales*, Cardiff, 1950, pp. 1–47. The almost complete absence of these monuments from most parts of eastern Wales may be due to the use of timber rather than stone in these areas.
[3] L. Alcock in *Prehistoric and Early Wales*, ed. I. Ll. Foster and G. E. Daniel, London, 1965, pp. 200–7. Mr Leslie Alcock has argued that "a very large proportion of stones in the fifth to seventh centuries were set up away from religious sites" and only subsequently moved into the protection of churches and churchyards. Professor A. C. Thomas in a personal communication writes that, at this period, the majority of inscribed stones were originally erected in cemeteries and not at settlements. Thus the transfer of a stone to some other nearby cemetery or church would hardly affect its significance as a pointer to the location of the subject's homestead.
[4] M. Richards, 'The Irish Settlements in South-West Wales', *Jnl Royal Soc. Antiquaries of Ireland* XC, 1960, pp. 133–62; Nennius, *Historia Brittonum*, pp. 156, 205–6; Chadwick, *op. cit.*, pp. 32–6.
[5] W. H. Davies in *Christianity in Britain*, pp. 140–2; cf. K. Hughes, *The Church in Early Irish Society*, London, 1966, pp. 70–90.

on an inscribed stone found at Castelldwyran (Carm). The inscription refers to Voteporix as 'Protector', a title possibly dating from Roman times and perhaps hereditary in his family. Nevertheless Gildas castigated Voteporix as a *tyrannus*, the wicked son of a generous father. This earlier generosity probably involved giving to the Church, for the father may be identified from later genealogies as the appropriately named Aergol *Lawhir* (Agricola of the Long Hand).[1] In North Wales Cadwallon *Lawhir*, grandson of Cunedda, had won Anglesey, for in the next generation Gildas addresses his son Maelgwn Gwynedd as the island dragon. Whatever the significance of the epithet open-hand as applied to Cadwallon, his son, unlike Voteporix, was praised by Gildas for his liberality in giving. This, too, was perhaps land given to the Church, for at a much later date a claim was made by the clergy of St Asaph that Maelgwn gave Kentigern much territory in North Wales (*villas et quamplures alias villulas*).[2]

The more direct references to land-use which Gildas makes concern Britain as a whole rather than Wales, hence his observation about hills suitable for fine tillage. None the less we may legitimately see in his statement about the "mountains of the greatest convenience for alternate pasturage of stock" (*montibus alternandis animalium pastibus maxime convenientibus*), a reference to the practice of seasonal trans-humance later so characteristic of Wales and other parts of the Highland Zone of Britain.[3] Appropriately, the metaphors of Gildas are often those of the animal world. Sheep and shepherd loom large, as do crafty foxes and timid fowl.

THE ARCHAEOLOGICAL EVIDENCE

According to Gildas the high precipitous hills were fortified. Yet until recently some archaeologists viewed with scepticism the suggestion that pre-Roman hill-forts were re-used in the post-Roman period. Now, however, in keeping with new discoveries and the ensuing dialectic of archaeological scholarship, it is deemed quite reasonable to suggest that not only small fortified sites with relatively feeble defences, but also some hill-forts of pre-Roman origin, or even perhaps first created in the late-Roman period, were still being used in the sixth century.[4]

[1] Nash-Williams, *op. cit.*, pp. 107–8; Jackson, *op. cit.*, p. 169; the stone actually reads 'Protictor'. See also: Gildas, *op. cit.*, pp. 72–3; J. E. Lloyd, *A History of Wales*, I, 3rd ed., London, 1948, pp. 261–2; RCAHM, *Carmarthen*, 1917, p. 11.

[2] Gildas, *op. cit.*, pp. 77–83; National Library of Wales: Peniarth MS. 231B; St Asaph MS. B/22.   [3] Gildas, *op. cit.*, pp. 16–17.

[4] Gildas, *op. cit.*, pp. 58–61. Compare Mr Leslie Alcock's review of the Ordnance Survey Map of Britain in the Dark Ages, AC cxv, 1966, pp. 185–6, with his earlier

The fortified coastal hill top of Degannwy in North Wales provides a good example. This was customarily accepted as a principal seat of the dynasty of Maelgwn and in Wales such traditions generally have a strong factual basis. As recent excavation has shown, the hill, which rises to about 350 feet, was fortified by a dry-stone wall and used alike in Roman and post-Roman times though it is not possible to say whether the post-Roman occupation grew out of that of the third and fourth centuries. Occupation at the later phase is firmly attested by eastern Mediterranean *amphorae* in the range A.D. 470–600. There is also a little pottery that might belong to the period between 600 and 1080 but none that certainly must. Thereafter, until the early thirteenth century, archaeological evidence is lacking. Yet the *Annales Cambriae* record that Degannwy (*Arx Decantorum*) was burnt by lightning in A.D. 812 and destroyed by the Saxons in A.D. 822. Consequently it is being increasingly recognized that the apparent absence of archaeological evidence from a site may simply be due to the hazards of discovery and need not necessarily imply that ancient hill-forts were not re-used in our period.[1]

Dinas Emrys, a fort occupying a small hill rising to 400 feet near the southern end of Nant Gwynant, provides an instance where archaeology has confirmed the validity of some elements of traditional stories. Its name, established at least as early as the twelfth century, purports to commemorate the Ambrosius Aurelianus of Gildas whose encounter with Vortigern at a citadel in Snowdonia is described in the *Historia Brittonum*. Nennius refers to a pool on the summit and describes how Vortigern attempted to build a palace above a spring there. Recent excavation, appropriately, has revealed a massive stone platform built partly on the peat-filling of a silted-up cistern. The site had been occupied in the Iron Age and in the early Romano-British period. There was also evidence, notably in the form of late-Roman glassware and a sherd decorated with a Chi-Rho monogram, of a late-Roman and Dark-Age occupation. This may well have embraced the fifth century, the time of Vortigern and Ambrosius Aurelianus. To this phase belong the hut-circles on the lower slopes of the hill where all suitable areas had been revetted to form small terraced plots for cultivation. Rotary querns were found at Dinas Emrys; attributed to the fifth century, they were no doubt used for

arguments in: 'Settlement Patterns in Celtic Britain', *Ant.* xxxvi, 1962, p. 52, *Dinas Powys: An Iron Age, Dark Age and Early Medieval Settlement in Glamorgan*, Cardiff, 1963, pp. 64–7, 197–8, and 'Hill Forts in Wales and the Marches', *Ant.* xxxix, 1965, pp. 188–9.

[1] L. Alcock, 'Excavations at Degannwy Castle, Caernarvonshire, 1961–6, *Arch. J.* cxxiv, 1967, pp. 190–201; E. Phillimore, 'The *Annales Cambriae* and Old-Welsh Genealogies from *Harleian MS. 3859*', *Y Cymmrodor* ix, 1888, p. 164.

milling the grain yielded by these plots. During this occupation the defences were elaborated and the cistern constructed near the pool, presumably for the watering of cattle and sheep. Since the feeding on the hill is very limited the construction of the cistern implies that animals had to be watered, at least temporarily, near the summit and not at the streams near its foot. But lowland grazing was probably the normal procedure, for pollen analysis of the peat and mud stratified in the pool has shown that already in the Dark Ages the natural woodland of Nant Gwynant had been cleared fairly extensively. In all probability this cistern is bound up with the fortification of Dinas Emrys and its conversion into a ruler's stronghold. There then followed a long phase of reduced activity on the site, marked by the reassertion of natural vegetation, before the stone platform was built during the later Dark Ages.[1]

From the viewpoint of the agrarian historian, the most important of the excavated sites in North Wales is the hill-fort named Parc-y-Meirch which occupies about 5½ acres on a summit of 500 feet at Dinorben (Den). The hill-fort, initiated, it now appears, in the late Bronze Age and refortified, possibly as a refuge, a number of times between the first century B.C. and the third century A.D., became the scene of intense activity from the end of the third century to c. A.D. 360. During this period an important Romano-Celtic household occupied a large hut, of Little Woodbury type, at the northern end of the fortified enclosure. To judge from the numerous Roman coins on the site the household was affluent, perhaps deriving its wealth from the large-scale production of hides. But Dinorben was also a place where up-to-date techniques of cultivation had been introduced, probably before the opening of our period, for the recent excavations revealed, in a layer containing numerous late-Roman and sub-Roman objects, an iron plough-share with a wing on its left side. Since the outcome of the use of such a plough-share would have been the formation of 'lands' in 'rig-and-furrow', it seems likely that Dinorben was already a place of more than local importance, where advanced ploughing techniques had made possible the exploitation of lowland soils. Parallel rows of postholes within the hill-fort were at first interpreted as an aisled house of the kind postulated for the Dark Ages in the Celtic West, but this has been disputed.[2] In the absence of imported Mediterranean wares a significant occupation of the hill-fort by an important family after

[1] H. N. Savory, 'Excavations at Dinas Emrys, Beddgelert (Caern), 1954–6', AC CIX, 1960, pp. 13–72; B. Seddon, 'Report on the Organic Deposits in the Pool at Dinas Emrys', AC CIX, 1960, pp. 72–7; RCAHM, *Caernarvonshire*, II, 1960, p. 25; Nennius, p. 199.

[2] H. N. Savory, 'Excavations at Dinorben Hill Fort, Abergele (Denbs.), 1956–7', BBCS XVII, 1958, pp. 296–309; L. Alcock in *Culture and Environment*, ed. I. Ll. Foster and L. Alcock, 1963, pp. 299–300.

the early fifth century is regarded as non-proven. Analogy with Degannwy suggests, however, that this may be a hasty judgement. In any case only parts of the hill-fort have been excavated and even these have yielded two Dark-Age objects, one of which is a buckle-plate fragment probably of the late sixth century.[1] Moreover in the *Englynion y Beddau* (Stanzas of the Graves), which were probably composed in the ninth or tenth century, reference is made to the hearth of Dinorben where the grave of one Hennin Hen-ben (Hennin Old-head) was located. This name was probably given to the cromlech whose ruin survives near the present farm of Dinorben.[2] In the fourteenth century this farm was the site of the lord's court (*llys*) for the commote (neighbourhood) of Rhos Is Dulas. Use of the term hearth for this locality in the later Dark Ages therefore adds force to the suggestion that an estate of some importance, focused on a court at one time within Parc-y-Meirch hill-fort and at other times in its immediate vicinity within the small township of Dinorben, is likely to have remained in being throughout our period.[3]

At Dinas Powys (Glam), on a low whale-back hill at a height of some 200 feet, recent excavation has yielded evidence of what appears to have been the court of some important ruler during the fifth and sixth centuries A.D. Around two sub-rectangular dry-stone houses enclosed within feeble earthworks there accumulated middens containing kitchen refuse, Mediterranean table wares and *amphorae*, together with the débris of Celtic metalwork and other crafts, including those of the jeweller working in bronze, gold, and Teutonic glass. Despite the discovery of a sizeable collection of iron objects there was not one that can be connected with the tilling of the soil, but then implements diagnostic of arable farming are rarely found on settlements of this period, even where such farming is known to have been practised. Their absence therefore is no evidence that cultivation did not occur near by, and, in any event, fragments of three rotary querns show clearly that corn was ground at Dinas Powys. Strikingly large quantities of whole and fragmentary bones, especially of young animals, were also found almost everywhere on the site. To judge at least from the larger of the bones, the main basis of the Dinas Powys economy was stock-raising. Analysis of a small sample of these bones has provided some indication of the order of frequency of stock raised and also of

[1] W. Gardner and H. N. Savory, *Dinorben. A hill fort occupied in the Early Iron Age and Roman times*, Cardiff, 1964, pp. 14, 98–9, 162–3, 205.

[2] T. Jones, 'The Black Book of Carmarthen: "Stanzas of the Graves"', *B. Acad.* LIII, 1967, pp. 100, 133.

[3] G. R. J. Jones, 'The Pattern of Settlement on the Welsh Border', AHR VIII, 1960, pp. 73–4, 76–8; id., 'Settlement Patterns in Celtic Britain', *Ant.* XXXVI, 1962, pp. 54–5.

the kinds of meat which were chiefly favoured. The percentages, to the nearest integer, are as follows: cattle 20, sheep 13, pig 61, horse very rare, deer 1, and birds 4. The meat available from one ox would of course be several times that from a pig or a sheep. Thus it would seem that pork, whether from wild or half-domesticated swine, made approximately the same contribution to the table as beef; that horse-flesh was avoided, and that wildfowl or venison made only an insigni-ficant addition to the diet. Mutton or lamb was little eaten, but although sheep would have provided wool, spinning and weaving do not seem to have been major activities at Dinas Powys. The relative insignificance of sheep need not therefore be construed as justifying the suggestion that the range of the Dinas Powys stockmen, at least as cattle-keepers, did not extend to the moors of Blaenau Morgannwg, less than ten miles to the north. The numbers of pig on the other hand imply the existence not far from Dinas Powys of widespread woodland providing pannage in autumn and winter as well as opportunities for hunting. The evidence for Dinas Powys suggests that this naturally strong and secluded hill-top site formed an ideal location for a ruler's household in the troubled times of the post-Roman period. But as the political system regained stability in the seventh century a more accessible site, and perhaps one already used seasonally, was preferred. Conse-quently the hill-top was abandoned until the military exigencies of the eleventh and twelfth centuries once more called attention to its advantages.[1]

Households of a lower social standing are less well represented in the archaeological record of our period. One example which was certainly occupied in the fifth century is the homestead of Pant-y-Saer (Ang) which stands a little below 300 feet on the summit of a small plateau of limestone. This is one of the homesteads known to archaeologists as 'enclosed homesteads' which are common in north-west Wales. The discovery of Romano-British pottery reveals that most of the excavated homesteads were occupied in the second to fourth centuries A.D. At Pant-y-Saer, however, most of the sherds found were crude hand-modelled material of the type generally regarded as post-Roman, and Roman pottery was represented only by meagre scraps. Estimates for the date of a silvered-bronze penannular brooch found on the site vary from c. A.D. 400 to after A.D. 700, but the settlement plan, consisting of two round huts and two later rectangular huts within an enclosure wall, suggests that the building of Pant-y-Saer cannot be far removed

---

[1] L. Alcock, *Dinas Powys*, pp. 26–55, 71–3, 191–3. The presence of imported *mortaria* points to the continuance of romanized culinary practices and suggests that vegetable foods played some part in the diet of the times. Similarly *amphorae* imply the survival of a romanized taste for wine drinking.

from the Roman period. The brooch indicates that probably it was occupied by a household of only moderate wealth, well down the social scale as compared with Dinas Powys. This household kept domestic animals – ox, sheep, pig, horse, and dog – but the contents of the middens were not rich enough to reveal their relative frequency. Corn was ground by means of both old-fashioned saddle querns and more up-to-date rotary querns. Appropriately, there are slight traces of cultivation terraces with a dividing wall to the north-west of the homestead.[1]

The remaining archaeological evidence for our period gives only an indirect insight into agrarian conditions. There are some material remains to show that Celtic saints had effected settlement not only in their eremitical retreats but also on or near fertile well-drained soils capable of sustaining monastic communities in their missionary activities. The primitive structure below the sixteenth-century chapel at Clynnog (Caern) may well be the seventh-century oratory of St Beuno.[2] On the other hand, sherds of imported Mediterranean pottery found at Longbury Bank near Penalun (Pem) may be tentatively interpreted as pointing to the existence in this locality of a hitherto unlocated monastery, perhaps one associated with St Teilo in the sixth century.[3] Presumably because pottery was not in general use, even in noble households, between the seventh and eleventh centuries, very few sites can be attributed to the latter part of our period. Of these, Dinas near Cadnant (Ang) with its rectangular huts and pottery of Pant-y-Saer type may be the *Castle of Dindaethue* (Dindaethwy) mentioned in connection with Cynan ap Rhodri (*ob.* 816) in a twelfth-century source. The site, overlooking the Menai Strait, is adjoined by irregular terraces probably used for cultivation; while between it and the Strait there are some small parallel strip-like terraces, each about 150 feet wide.[4] On the site of the Roman fort of *Segontium* (Caernarvon), where some rough post-Roman structures were erected, a Northumbrian coin of the ninth century was found.[5] Along the coasts elsewhere, as at Penard in Gower or at Bangor in Arfon, rare coin hoards of the

[1] C. W. Phillips, 'The Excavation of a Hut-Group at Pant-y-Saer in the Parish of Llanfair-Mathafarn-Eithaf, Anglesey', AC LXXXIX, 1934, pp. 1–36; L. Alcock in *Culture and Environment*, pp. 282–4, and in *Prehistoric and Early Wales*, pp. 194–7.

[2] B. Stallybrass, 'Recent Discoveries at Clynnogfawr', AC, 6th series, XIV, 1914, pp. 271–96; RCAHM, *Caernarvonshire*, II, 1960, pp. 36–7.

[3] L. Alcock, 'Post-Roman sherds from Longbury Bank Cave, Penally (Pemb.)', BBCS XVIII, 1958–60, pp. 77–8.

[4] RCAHM, *Anglesey*, London, 1937, pp. xcii–xciii, 52–4; *The History of Gruffydd ap Cynan*, ed. A. Jones, Manchester, 1910, p. 102.

[5] R. E. M. Wheeler, 'Segontium and the Roman occupation of Wales', *Y Cymmrodor* XXXIII, 1923, pp. 93–4; RCAHM, *Caernarvonshire*, II, 1960, p. 162.

ninth and tenth century point to the rôle of Viking maritime traders in fostering a money economy.[1]

In the interior, material evidence for the Welsh is slight. Along the eastern border the linear earthworks by which "the boundary line of Cymru" was ultimately defined are all Saxon works with their ditches facing west. In the struggles of the Welsh with the growing kingdoms of Deira and Mercia these were at first designed locally as cross-ridge dykes to control upland lines of communication, or as cross-valley dykes to protect English lowland settlements. In a later phase, represented by Wat's Dyke and especially Offa's Dyke, which is attributed to the late eighth century, these earthworks were designed nationally to define, with the aid of natural features, an agreed frontier. As Sir Cyril Fox has stressed, Offa's Dyke in certain places bears witness to the power of Welsh interests. Thus on the lower Wye the Mercian frontier was set back from the river so as to leave the control of the tidal water in Welsh hands. Even more significantly from our standpoint, the alignment of Offa's Dyke so as to exclude the commanding spur on which stands the Iron-Age fort of Pen-y-Gardden suggests that in the north too the designer of the linear earthwork did not have an entirely free hand. Despite the lack of positive evidence for the use of the hill-fort at this date, as Sir Cyril Fox observed the simplest explanation for this exclusion is that the Welsh still held Pen-y-Gardden and, presumably, they did so for a purpose.[2] On the March there is no indication that the Welsh deliberately constructed counter-works, but in South Wales there are short dykes which clearly imitate Mercian technique. Aligned across the narrowest parts of ridges or plateaux and with their ends on springheads or natural obstacles, they traverse, and thus control, upland routes followed by ridgeways or Roman roads. In the uplands of Glamorgan a series of such works, all facing northwards, was designed to control movement from the interior towards the coast. Interpreted as marking a fluctuating dividing line between Morgannwg and Brycheiniog in the eighth and ninth centuries, they demonstrate that the ancient territorial components of Morgannwg were sound economic units consisting of coastal lowland or plateau (*bro*) suitable for cultivation and of upland plateau (*blaenau*) suitable for pasture.[3]

The suggestion that economic activity was focused on the lowlands

[1] Dolley, *op. cit.*, pp. 14, 23, 26, 33; B. G. Charles, *Old Norse relations with Wales*, Cardiff, 1934, pp. 156–63.

[2] C. Fox; 'Offa's Dyke: A Field Survey', AC LXXXIII, 1928, pp. 102–7, and *ibid.* LXXXVI, 1931, pp. 63–7; id., *Offa's Dyke*, London, 1955, pp. 81–3.

[3] A. Fox in *A Hundred Years of Welsh Archaeology, Centenary Volume 1846–1946*, ed. V. E. Nash-Williams, Gloucester, n.d., pp. 117–18.

but extended in the summer months into the uplands is reinforced by the distributional pattern of our most numerous remains, the Early Christian sculptured stone monuments. Throughout the period they occur mainly in the lowlands. A general impression of the main areas of settlement is the best that these monuments can provide, for we cannot be sure how many have remained on their original sites or how many were removed to churches and churchyards for safe preservation. Nevertheless there appears to be a sound economic basis for their characteristic avoidance of the central moorlands except where these are penetrated by wide valleys or traversed by Roman roads.[1]

The occasional occurrence of these sculptured stone monuments in the vicinity of Roman roads suggests that this economic basis may have been Roman, if not earlier, in origin. Especially is this true of north-west Wales where the dynasty of Cunedda certainly appears to have been established by an act of Roman military policy, or at least romanized authority. The Early Christian memorial stones in Gwynedd include most of those in Wales whose inscriptions bear witness to settled political arrangements. Moreover, horizontal inscriptions in the Roman manner are very common on the stones of Gwynedd as compared, elsewhere, with vertical inscriptions in the Celtic fashion. A stone of the fifth or sixth century at Penmachno church in an interior Snowdonian strath bears a horizontal inscription which reads "Cantiorix lies here. He was a citizen of Venedos (and) cousin of Maglos the Magistrate" (*Cantiori hic iacit [V]enedotis cive fuit [c]onsobrino Ma[g]li Magistrat*). This suggests an ordered system of government, and possibly an administrative district, focused on *Segontium*, or perhaps even Degannwy. If so, this district possibly derived its name *Veneda*, whence Gwynedd, from the tribal name Venia meaning "country of the Venii."[2] Significantly another Venedotian stone, again at Penmachno, provides a unique Welsh example of the consular system of dating and suggests the existence of contacts between Wales and Burgundy in the sixth century.[3] There are hints too that smaller administrative units had also been constituted, as for example in the district which included the early Roman fortlet of Pen Llystyn (Caern). In this vicinity there are several farms bearing the name *llysdin* which is derived from *llys*, court, and *dyn(n)*, height or fort. Here too a Latin and Ogam memorial probably of the later sixth century was erected

[1] *Ibid.*, p. 109; Nash-Williams, *op. cit.*, 1950, p. 4.

[2] Nash-Williams, *op. cit.*, pp. 14, 92–4; Jackson, *op. cit.*, p. 188; Jackson in *Celt and Saxon*, p. 30; M. Richards, 'Early Welsh Territorial Suffixes', *Jnl Royal Soc. Antiquaries of Ireland* xcv, 1965, p. 205.

[3] Nash-Williams, *op. cit.*, pp. 93–4.

less than a quarter of a mile from the fortlet, itself a scene of unmilitary and unromanized settlement at the very end of the Roman period.[1]

The word *sacerdos* inscribed on a stone at Bodafon (Caern) and Llantrisant (Ang) – like *episcopus* and possibly *diaconus* elsewhere in Britain – points to the survival of an episcopal and diocesan church in the sixth century alongside the emergence of monastic *paruchiae*.[2] Bodafon was only some two miles distant from Degannwy. Llantrisant on the other hand was in western Anglesey but on the eastern side of the island another inscribed stone, attributed to the sixth century, points to the existence of a centre of authority. Commemorating an Irish aristocrat of the Deccheti lineage, this stone was preserved at the church of Penrhosllugwy in the township which contained the medieval court (*llys*) of Twrcelyn commote. Within a mile or so was Din Llugwy, the most sophisticated Romano-British homestead yet discovered in north-west Wales. Some four miles distant, but within the area of Twrcelyn commote as later defined, was Parys Mountain with its long famous copper-bearing lodes. Under Roman rule copper obtained from these lodes continued to be smelted on native hearths widely dispersed over the island. As Sir Ian Richmond has suggested, this primitive organization was probably the customary working arrangement of a temple estate, found in existence by the Roman procurators but confiscated and treated as an imperial *saltus*.[3]

Near the south coast of Anglesey a roadside stone of the fifth or early sixth century commemorates, by means of a vertical inscription, an Irishman of importance named Cunogusos. This name survives in its Welsh form *Conws*, together with the territorial suffix *-iog*, in *Conysiog*; and since the latter was used to designate both a court (*llys*) township and a church (*llan*) township in this locality during the Middle Ages, we may well have here an instance of a Dark-Age estate of some importance.[4] The same is true of the nearby estate of Aberffraw, deemed to be the traditional capital of Gwynedd. Within two miles of Aberffraw, in the church named Eglwys Ail at Llangadwaladr, a stone of the seventh century with the horizontal inscription "King Catamanus, wisest (and) most renowned of all kings (lies here)" (*Catamanus rex sapientisimus opinatisimus omnium regum*) com-

---

[1] Nash-Williams, *op. cit.*, pp. 86–7; M. Richards, 'The Irish Settlements in South-West Wales', *op. cit.*, pp. 145–6; A. H. A. Hogg, 'Excavations at Pen Llystyn', *Arch. J.* cxxv, 1968, pp. 101–7.

[2] Nash-Williams, *op. cit.*, pp. 63–4, 84–7; cf. also Hughes, *op. cit.*, pp. 70–90.

[3] Nash-Williams, *op. cit.*, p. 67; RCAHM, *Anglesey*, 1937, pp. lxxxvii, cix, 132; Jackson, *op. cit.*, p. 140; *Record of Caernarvon*, pp. 70–2; I. A. Richmond in *Prehistoric and Early Wales*, pp. 155–6.

[4] Jackson, *op. cit.*, p. 531; Richards, *op. cit.*, p. 141; *Record of Caernarvon*, p. 234; National Library of Wales: Welsh Church Commission MS. 1.

memorates in grandiloquent terms a member of Cunedda's dynasty; this was Cadfan, the great-great-grandson of the island dragon, Maelgwn Gwynedd. Cadfan died *c*. 625 and the stone was probably erected by his grandson, the celebrated royal warrior and subsequently monk, Cadwaladr ap Cadwallon; for, at a later date, the township of Eglwys Ail was held of St Cadwaladr *Rege* save that certain dues were reserved to the ruler of Gwynedd. Eglwys Ail, it would appear, was the burial place of the dynasty, so that already by the sixth century its chief court was probably at Aberffraw, the *large* township which in later centuries emerged as a royal Venedotian vill where the court buildings were enclosed within a stone wall. In the sixth century there was probably in this vicinity a multiple royal estate comprising at least two units, the court (*llys*) at Aberffraw and the church (*llan*) at Eglwys Ail. Royal control no doubt explains the echo of Byzantine court formulae in the inscription, and royal wealth the familiarity of the craftsmen with the latest fashion in continental book script.[1] Anglesey, later to be known as the granary of Wales, was already a productive unit. Before Cadwaladr's accession Edwin of Northumbria had besieged Cadwallon on the island sanctuary of Priestholm and for a brief interlude brought the Mevanian islands, that is Anglesey and the Isle of Man, under English rule. Hence the application to these areas of English units of assessment which, as cited by Bede, show that the island of Anglesey was the larger and more fertile of the two, having, by English reckoning, land for 960 households. The Isle of Man, we are told, had land for "over 300" but since it is only slightly smaller than Anglesey the latter was clearly deemed to be either actually or potentially the more productive.[2]

In less closely settled country a similar, though more wide-ranging, territorial organization is suggested by an inscribed stone of the fifth century found on a farm at Llanaber on the coast of Ardudwy (Mer). Deemed to be among the earliest of Welsh Christian memorials, this bears the horizontal inscription *Caelexti monedo rigi*. Professor Kenneth Jackson has suggested that *monedo* contains the late British *monido* meaning mountain, so that Caelestis (i.e. Caelexti) was probably "the mountain king."[3] If this is a memorial which has remained *in situ* there is surely a suggestion here that the royal authority of Caelestis extended from Dyffryn Ardudwy (The Plain of Ardudwy) to the mountains, thus making possible the kind of seasonal transhumance

[1] Nash-Williams, *op. cit.*, pp. 55–7; RCAHM, *Anglesey*, 1937, pp. civ–cv, 87; *Record of Caernarvon*, pp. 48–50, 70–2; N. K. Chadwick, *Celtic Britain*, 1964, pp. 70–1.
[2] Bede, *Hist. Eccl.*, ed. Plummer, I, pp. 89, 97.
[3] Nash-Williams, *op. cit.*, pp. 164, 167; Jackson, *op. cit.*, p. 355.

which was recorded by Gildas. The *maenol,* or minor administrative district, of Llanaber certainly extended to the interior mountains in the medieval period and, appropriately, a clansman residing in Llanaber was fined in 1336 for keeping his animals "in the common pasture of the old settlement" (*in communi pastura del hendreve*) after the community of the township (*communitas villate*) had moved, early in May of that year, with its animals to the mountains. The medieval commote of Ardudwy extended still further inland and north to embrace the township of Trawsfynydd which, as its name reveals, was beyond the mountains of the Harlech dome.[1] In the southern part of the township, near a north-south Roman road, was a memorial stone of the late fifth or early sixth century with a horizontal inscription commemorating one Porius. Further north in the adjoining township of Maentwrog there was formerly, in the immediate neighbourhood of the Roman fort at Tomen-y-Mur, a stone of about the same date. Between the two, near a point where the north-south Roman road crossed the River Prysor, was a third stone with a horizontal inscription ascribed to the sixth or seventh century. It is perhaps significant that in the medieval period, matching the lowland bond settlement of the Llanaber district, there was in Trawsfynydd and Maentwrog one of the most important upland concentrations of bondage in north-west Wales.[2]

Elsewhere in Wales the inscriptions on the early memorial stones are generally less informative. Among the exceptions are a Latin and Ogam inscribed stone of the fifth to early sixth century at Llandeilo (Pem) and another Latin inscribed stone of roughly the same period at Maenclochog (Pem) which between them appear to commemorate three successive generations of the same family.[3] By so doing they give a hint of social stability in early Dyfed.

The inscriptions on the memorial monuments of later periods are in general too formal and stereotyped to yield much in the way of relevant data. The stone found near Llanllyr House (Card) and attributed to the period between the seventh and the ninth century is an exception which suggests that the Church was still acquiring land. This inscription records that Occon son of Asailgen gave to Madomnauc, possibly a saint of that name, "the small waste plot of Ditoc."[4] The wording is particularly significant, for it is less a pointer

[1] PRO SC2/225/28; *Record of Caernarvon,* pp. 284–6.

[2] Nash-Williams, *op. cit.,* pp. 171–2; W. J. Hemp and C. A. Gresham, 'A New Early Inscribed Stone from Trawsfynydd, Merioneth', AC cx, 1961, pp. 154–5; G. R. J. Jones, 'The Distribution of Bond Settlements in North-west Wales', WHR II, 1964, pp. 22, 26–7.

[3] Nash-Williams, *op. cit.,* pp. 186–8, 193.

[4] *Ibid.,* pp. 26, 100–1.

to incipient parsimony in Ceredigion than a salutary reminder that in the middle of our period even the poorest land is unlikely to have been regarded as a free commodity.

THE EVIDENCE OF THE LAWBOOKS

A deeper insight into the conditions of land holding can be obtained from written sources compiled after the close of our period, notably the Welsh lawbooks. In the group of texts known as *Llyfr Iorwerth* (the Book of Iorwerth) the earliest extant manuscript, which is also the oldest of the surviving Welsh texts, dates only from the thirteenth century. Perhaps for reasons bound up with population growth these relatively late texts, which reflect the viewpoint of Gwynedd, convey an impression that the lawyers of North Wales regarded territorial resources as finite. They record, with an affectation of numerical exactness, that there were four townships in every *maenol* (plural *maenolau*) and twelve of these territorial units plus two other townships in every commote. Thus the *cantref* (hundred) of two commotes contained in theory a hundred townships. The two townships in the commote which were not ascribed to any *maenol* were for the use of the king. One was to be his demesne land (*tir maerdref* – literally the land of the reeve's township), and the other, significantly, was the king's waste (*diffaith*) and summer pasture.[1]

Every *maenol* of the twelve attributed to the commote was apportioned: four were assigned to the king's bondmen (*eilltion*); one was for the support of the chancellor, and another for the reeve (*maer*); thus six were left for free 'notables' (*uchelwyr, optimes*), the kind of men described by Gerald of Wales *c.* 1190 as noble chiefs or men of superior rank.[2] The laws are primarily concerned with royal rights but nevertheless reveal that the notables, no less than the chancellor and reeve, were supported by bond under-tenants and, at an earlier date were served, for good or ill, by slaves (*gweission caeth*).[3] This bond sub-structure of the eight free *maenolau*, when taken into account alongside the servile population of the four bond *maenolau* and the two royal townships, reveals that under the idealized arrangements of the Book of Iorwerth a bond majority was to be expected in the typical commote. Confirmation of this view is provided by the

[1] *Llyfr Iorwerth*, ed. A. R. Wiliam, Cardiff, 1960, p. 60.
[2] *Giraldi Cambrensis Opera*, ed. J. F. Dimock, Rolls ser. 21, 1868, VI, p. 166.
[3] *Facsimile of the Chirk Codex of the Welsh Laws*, ed. J. Gwenogfryn Evans, Llanbedrog, 1909, p. 41; 'Copy of *The Black Book of Chirk, Peniarth MS. 29*, National Library of Wales, Aberystwyth', ed. T. Lewis, *Zeitschrift für Celtische Philologie* xx, 1936, p. 75.

Domesday evidence for the easternmost districts of North Wales. Thus in Tegeingl, the only *cantref* to be surveyed in detail, we learn that, of the population recorded for 1086, no less than 17 per cent were slaves (*servi*) and oxmen (*bovarii*), and a further 34 per cent were cottagers (*bordarii*) probably of servile origin.[1]

From each of the eight free *maenolau* in the commote the king was to have a food-rent (*gwestfa*) worth a *twnc* pound (240d.) yearly. Originally the *gwestfa* had been a payment in kind, but in due course this had become a payment in cash. By the thirteenth century lawyers could therefore envisage a theoretical scheme whereby 60d. were charged on each township of the four in a free *maenol* and these 60d. in turn were further subdivided into quarters in succession until every 'acre' (*erw*) of every 'homestead' (*tyddyn*) was assessed at a farthing.[2] Late case-law claims that there were no farthings when the law of Hywel was made. Nevertheless a surviving coin minted at Chester for Hywel Dda suggests that during his reign Welsh money was at least beginning to circulate. Certainly coins were in circulation in Wales by A.D. 989, for in that year, according to *Brut y Tywysogion* (the Chronicle of the Princes), Maredudd ab Owain of Deheubarth, grandson of Hywel Dda, levied a penny from every person as tribute for payment to the Black Host or Vikings.[3] The food-rent, as indeed its primitive nature would suggest, was therefore much older than the late tenth century. As recorded in the Book of Iorwerth, this food-rent comprised a horse-load of the best flour from the land; the carcase of a cow or an ox; a full vat of mead, nine hand-breadths in length diagonally and as much again in breadth; seven 'thraves' of oats for provender; a three-year-old swine, a salted flitch of three finger-breadths in thickness; and a vessel of butter, three hand-breadths in depth, not heaped, and three in breadth.[4]

---

[1] DB I, 268b–269a; J. Tait, 'Flintshire in Domesday Book', *Flint Hist. Soc.* XI, 1925, pp. 1–8; Jones, *op. cit.*, p. 31.

[2] *Llyfr Iorwerth*, pp. 23, 62. To make this even theoretically feasible it was probably necessary to envisage a charge of 64d rather than 60d. per township. Significantly assessments of 64d., based on 4 ores of 16d. each, were recorded in Domesday Book for the lands between the Ribble and the Mersey. For a similar assessment in Archenfield (Her) see p. 307.

[3] *Ancient Laws and Institutes of Wales*, ed. A. Owen, II, 1841, pp. 596–7; *Brut y Tywysogion* (Peniarth MS. 20 Version), ed. T. Jones, Cardiff, 1952, p. 10; *Brut y Tywysogion* (Red Book of Hergest Version), ed. T. Jones, Cardiff, 1952, pp. 16–17. Cf. however *Annales Cambriae*, ed J. Williams ab Ithel, Rolls ser. 20, 1860, p. 21, which records that Maredudd redeemed the captives of the "black gentiles" by the payment of a penny a head. See also Charles, *op. cit.*, pp. 35, 158. Merchants from Wales, presumably of Norse origin, went to Dublin Bay for the battle of Clontarf in A.D 1013.

[4] *Llyfr Iorwerth*, p. 64; a *gwestfa* was recorded in verse of the ninth century (*Canu Llywarch Hen*, pp. 25, 168).

Half the value of the pound in lieu of *gwestfa* was deemed to be for 'bread' and a further quarter for 'drink'. Thus only a quarter of the pound was for 'relish' obtained principally from pastoral produce. In addition the great progress of the household was imposed on each *maenol* in winter. The notables also owed military service, and, at least in the thirteenth-century texts, we are told that all were to work on the castles (*cestyll*) whenever the king willed, except the men of the *maerdref* (reeve's township).[1]

The bondmen of this demesne vill of the king performed more onerous services. Under the guiding hand of the lesser reeve, known contemptuously perhaps as the dung reeve (*maer biswail*) so as to distinguish him from the greater or superior reeve, they harrowed the mensal land (*tir bwrdd*), used for the supply of the king's table. They reaped, threshed, and kiln-dried the corn and, besides, they mowed the king's hay. They produced straw and fuel for the fire whenever the king visited the court and on these occasions presented him, according to their ability, with sheep, or lambs, or kids, or cheese, or butter, or milk. They also had to make a kiln and barn for the king. Their *gwestfa* however was rendered to the lesser reeve. It was the latter, we are told, who regulated the king's palace and what pertained to it, such as ploughing, sowing, as well as tending the king's cattle and therefore his summer pasture.[2]

The remaining bondmen of the king were subject to the superior or commote reeve, and to the chancellor who together regulated the bondmen on their lands and, significantly, were also said to "keep the king's waste." Twice a year these two superior officers made a progress among the king's bondmen. Once a year too these bondmen supported various groups of retainers on circuit (*cylch*) and provided them with quarters (*dofraeth*); they also supported the huntsmen, the dogs, the falconers, and young freemen on military training. They presented the queen once a year with food and drink but they were not to support the king and the royal bodyguard. For this reason they were not to retain their honey or their fish but were to send them to the court.[3] The bondmen also furnished pack-horses to the king for the hosts, and to make the encampments for these hosts they provided one man with an axe from every bond township. Nor did this exhaust their obligations, for, in addition, they were to erect the seven buildings of the king's court. These differed slightly in different texts but were specified in the Book of Iorwerth as the hall, the buttery, the kitchen, the dormitory, the privy, the stable, and the porch-house

---

[1] *Llyfr Iorwerth*, pp. 29, 60–1.
[2] *Ibid.*, pp. 18–19, 62–3; *The Black Book of Chirk*, pp. 46–7.
[3] *Llyfr Iorwerth*, pp. 23, 29, 54, 60–2.

(*kynorty*).[1] Finally the bondmen contributed two foodgifts to the
king every year. The winter foodgift included a three-year-old
sow, a vessel of butter, a 'thrave' of oats for provender, twenty-
six loaves of the "best bread that shall grow on the land," and a vat
of bragget. That of the summer included a three-year-old wether, a
dish of butter, twenty-six loaves, and the cheese made from one milking
in the day, of the cows possessed by all within the township (*tref*).[2]

By the thirteenth century the commote was the territorial unit
within which the townships of the king, the notables, and the bondmen
were envisaged. This unit had come to supersede the larger *cantref*
(hundred) which itself was the historical successor of the *gwlad* (country),
the larger countries being divided into a number of hundreds and the
smaller countries like Dyffryn Clwyd (the Vale of Clwyd) becoming
hundreds themselves. Likewise the theoretically small *maenol* of the
thirteenth century, as envisaged by the lawyers, could have resulted
from the progressive fission of the larger *maenol* apparently characteristic
of an earlier period. According to the theoretical provisions of the
thirteenth-century texts the two commotes in the ancient *cantref* of
Arfon should have contained twenty-four *maenolau* as well as the four
townships belonging to the king. A tractate incorporated into the oldest
extant vernacular text of the laws reveals, however, that there were
only nine *maenolau* in Arfon. This section purports to deal with the
privileges granted to the men of Arfon by Rhun son of Maelgwn
Gwynedd. On account of the length of time they had remained at war
in northern England, their wives had allegedly slept with their slave
servants, and for this reason the men of Arfon were recompensed.[3]

[1] Redaction B, a Latin text of the mid-thirteenth century (*The Latin Texts of the
Welsh Laws*, pp. 204–5) lists among these buildings a 'domus canum, id est *kynordy*';
Llyfr Blegywryd (ed. S. J. Williams and J. E. Powell, Cardiff, 1961, p. 47) refers to
a *kynhorty*, and *Llyfr Colan* (ed. D. Jenkins, Cardiff, 1963, p. 40) to a *kyuordy*. These
variant forms show that the lawyers of the thirteenth century did not know which
building of the court complex was meant. If the original word was *kyuordy* then
a drinking chamber is implied. But if it was *kynhorty* then what was meant was
a small building or lodge before the gateway in the enclosure surrounding the court
buildings, and such a lodge could well have been the precursor of a gatehouse (cf.
B. K. Davison, 'The Origins of the Castle in England', *Arch. J.* CXXIV, 1967, pp. 202–
11, and R. Allen Brown, 'An Historian's Approach to the Origins of the Castle in
England', *Arch. J.* CXXVI, 1969, pp. 131–48). This uncertainty in itself suggests
that the court as an institution was old-established and, appropriately, some manuscripts of *Llyfr Blegywryd* refer to the disuse of the customs of the court.—D. Jenkins
in WHR, *Special Number, The Welsh Laws*, p. 54.

[2] *Llyfr Iorwerth, op. cit.*, p. 64. According to a triad in *Llyfr Blegywryd*, p. 110, there
were three worthless milks, those of a cat, of a bitch, and of a mare. See also *The Laws
of Hywel Dda (The Book of Blegywryd)* translated by M. Richards, Liverpool, 1954, p. 103.

[3] *The Black Book of Chirk*, p. 29. Among the privileges accorded to the men of
Arfon was that of not being restricted over the number of querns they owned.

Traces of this seemingly ancient division of Arfon into a relatively small number of *maenolau* survived into later centuries when an estate of the bishop of Bangor was known as Maenol Bangor. Focused on the ancient settlement of the *clas* (church community) at Bangor, this was a multiple estate flanking the Menai Strait. During the fourteenth century it contained, in an area of about ten square miles, no less than thirteen contiguous townships, some inhabited by freemen but most occupied solely by bondmen.[1] Pennardd, to the west of Caernarvon, was in all probability another ancient *maenol* in Arfon although by the fourteenth century it had come to be described as a township (*tref*). Designated in a legal trial as the seat of a chancellor, it was, according to the Privileges of Arfon, the abode of the lord (*pendefig*) of Pennardd, the judicious Maeldaf the Elder. He apparently lived in the sixth century so that his seat, like Maenol Bangor, was probably ancient.[2] From *Math vab Mathonwy*, one of the *Mabinogion* tales which were no doubt related orally for centuries before being committed to writing in the eleventh or twelfth centuries, we learn that Pennardd was a *maenor*.[3] This, as the lawbooks reveal, is none other than the word for *maenol* in the dialect of South Wales. The etymology of this word *maenor*, or *mainaur* as it appears in its oldest recorded form, may well be significant for early social organization. A derivative of *maen* (stone), it was perhaps first applied to the stone-girt residence of the chief so as to distinguish it from ordinary settlements usually built of timber.[4] There is here an obvious link with the word *llys* (court) which was originally used to denote an enclosure and subsequently the building, or buildings within. Similarly *llan* appears to have been applied successively to cleared land, marked out land, enclosed land, then to an enclosed cemetery, and after a stage when a church or monastic cells were established within, to a church in its churchyard. The meaning of the word *bangor*, as in the specific place-name for the *chef lieu* of the Venedotian *maenol* of Bangor, may not have been unrelated for

Presumably therefore they had sufficient slaves or servants to mill by hand the grain they required.

[1] *Record of Caernarvon*, pp. 90–2; National Library of Wales: Welsh Church Commission MS. 1; G. R. J. Jones, 'Early Settlement in Arfon; the setting of Tre'r Ceiri', *Caernarvon Hist. Soc.* 1963, pp. 16–17. Similarly there was a township named *Faenol* (Vaynol) associated with the ancient *clas* and later diocesan seat of Llanelwy (St Asaph). To judge from *Liber Ruber Asaphensis* this was a multiple estate, but, at least by the fourteenth century, it contained far fewer component settlements than Maenol Bangor.

[2] *Ancient Laws and Institutes of Wales* II, pp. 584–5; R. Bromwich, *Trioedd Ynys Prydein*, Cardiff, 1961, pp. 3, 440.

[3] *The Mabinogion*, ed. G. Jones and T. Jones, London, 1949, pp. xi, 59; a comprehensive list of place-names in *maenol* and *maenor* is given in M. Richards, *Welsh Administrative and Territorial Units*, Cardiff, 1969, pp. 68, 149–51.

[4] J. E. Lloyd, 'Welsh Place Names', *Y Cymmrodor* XII, 1890, pp. 32–4, 57–8.

it has been interpreted as a cross bar in a wattled fence, or a strong plaited rod in a fence. It thus referred to either the wattled construction of an original monastic cell, or to the fence which surrounded it.[1]

According to the oldest extant text of the laws, a twelfth-century Latin redaction, "There are seven shares of land, that is, *rhandir*, in a full *maenor*" (*Maynaur vero plenarie est que septem particulas, id est, rantyr, continet*). Though probably compiled in South Wales and reflecting a Demetian and even Menevian viewpoint in its content, this redaction resembled the other law-texts in that its contents were not applicable solely to that part of Wales. In *Llyfr Blegywryd* (the Book of Blegywryd) which again reflects a South Welsh viewpoint, we are told that there are seven townships (*trefi*) in a lowland *maenor* and thirteen townships in an upland *maenor*. *Llyfr Cyfnerth* (the Book of Cyfnerth), which was compiled before 1220, presents a further slight variation, so that, although there are said to be thirteen townships in every *maenor*, we are also told that there are seven townships in the *maenol*, or, in some texts the *maenor*, of the bond townships.[2] Arrangements such as these certainly existed at an earlier date, for, as Domesday Book shows, they are quite compatible with the territorial dispositions recorded for Gwent in 1086. Despite the Norman conquest, Welsh law was still in force in parts of the ancient *cantref* of Gwent Is Coed which extended along the coastal plain of south-east Wales. Thus, according to the Domesday survey there were in the jurisdiction of Caerleon Castle "three Welshmen living under Welsh law" (*lege Walensi viventes*) and these were apparently men of some substance for each of them had one plough-team. Yet, unlike the notables of the laws, they, together with two cottagers (*bordarii*), rendered four sesters of honey. In another section of Domesday Book which likewise deals with Gwent we are told that "Alured has in Wales 7 vills which were in the demesne of Earl William and Roger his son. These render 6 sesters of honey and 6 pigs and 10s." This group of seven demesne townships, which recalls the group of seven bond townships in the Book of Cyfnerth, certainly antedates 1075 for in that year Roger rebelled and so forfeited his lands to the king.[3]

---

[1] M. Richards in *The Names of Towns and Cities in Britain*, ed. W. F. M. Nicolaisen, London, 1970, p. 46; cf. *Geiriadur Prifysgol Cymru* IV, Cardiff, 1954, p. 254; I. Williams, *Enwau Lleoedd*, 1969, pp. 76–7. I am particularly indebted to Professor A. C. Thomas for the suggestion that this interpretation of *bangor* is at variance with the known archaeology of the post-Roman church. The latter would accord more readily with the interpretation of *maenor* as a stone-girt residence of a dignitary.

[2] *The Latin Texts of the Welsh Laws*, pp. 135–6; J. G. Edwards in WHR, *Special Number, The Welsh Laws*, pp. 3–9; *Llyfr Blegywryd*, p. 68; *Welsh Medieval Law*, ed. A.W. Wade-Evans, Oxford, 1909, pp. 55, 344.

[3] DB I, 185b; *ibid.*, 162a; G. R. J. Jones, 'Rural Settlement: Wales', *Advancement*

To judge from the value of the mills at Domesday, Gwent was quite well cultivated but nevertheless the Welsh inhabitants had been allowed to retain their lands on the same easy terms conceded to them by Gruffydd ap Llywelyn (*ob.* 1063), and their reeves (*prepositi*) were left undisturbed in office. The survey records that in 1086 there were thirteen vills under Wasuuic the *prepositus*, otherwise known from *Liber Landavensis* as the Guassuith, who witnessed a grant made by Caradog ap Gruffydd of Llangwm in Gwent Uwch Coed. In 1086 there were also fourteen vills under Idhel, the Ithail filius Teudus who, again according to *Liber Landavensis*, witnessed a grant made by Llywelyn ap Gruffydd. In that same year there were another fourteen vills under Elmui, the Elinui filius Idnerth of *Liber Landavensis*, and also a further group of thirteen vills under Blei. Each of these groups bears a superficial resemblance not only to the larger *maenor*, the so-called upland *maenor* of the South Welsh law-texts, but also to the late surviving Maenol Bangor on the coastal lowlands of Gwynedd. Confirmation of this identification is provided by the characteristically Welsh nature of the renders which the Gwent groups contributed in 1086; thus the four groups together made a joint contribution of "47 sesters of honey, 40 pigs, 41 cows and 28s. for hawks."[1]

In the case of one further group we can, moreover, discern that process of fissioning of the larger *maenol* (or *maenor*) which the compilers of *Llyfr Iorwerth* had in mind when they framed their theoretical picture of the small *maenol* of four townships in the much divided commote. This was a group of 14 vills, apparently in Gwent Is Coed. Of the 14 vills, four had been wasted by King Caradog, probably during the Welsh raid on Portskewett in 1065. One vill in 1086 is said to be in the alms of the king and renders to the church "2 pigs, 100 loaves, and beer." Berdic joculator (Berddig, the king's poet) has three vills, but though these are worked by five plough-teams, he pays no rent. Likewise the remaining six vills are worked by six plough-teams but

of Science xv, 1959, p. 342. Compare also the seven 'clanlands' (*gwelyau*) in the ancient *clas* township of Llanelwy (Flint) during the fourteenth century, and the seven 'clanlands' in the ancient *clas* township of Llangyfelach (Glam) in the thirteenth century. For Llandysul (Card), a place of importance in the sixth century, a similar grouping was recorded in later centuries; this comprised a reeve's township (*maerdref*) and seven hamlets. To judge from the inscribed stone in the churchyard Llandysul was a settlement of some importance in the sixth century. Significantly it stands on the north bank of the Teifi opposite the Iron-Age hill-fort of Craig Gwrtheyrn, traditionally identified with the *arx* or stronghold in "Demetia on the banks of the Teifi" which is mentioned in the *Historia Brittonum* as the last refuge of Vortigern (Gwrtheyrn) in the fifth century A.D.—Nennius, *op. cit.*, p. 191.

[1] DB I, 162a; *Liber Landavensis*, pp. 270, 273, 274; A. Ballard, *The Domesday Inquest*, London, 1906, pp. 197–200.

render nothing. Of these six vills we learn that Morinus has one vill, Chenesis a second, Sessibert a third, and Abraham the priest (the archdeacon of Gwent) has two vills.[1] The remaining vill is held by the sons of Wasuuic, probably the reeve of the same name, and thus presumably in shares.

Similar arrangements can be discerned in the Domesday account of Archenfield in western Hereford, west of the Wye, an area under the spiritual care of the bishops of Llandaf until about 1130. The opening sections of the Domesday survey of Hereford give details of certain customs which were observed among the Welsh of Archenfield during the reign of Edward the Confessor (1042–66). The nucleus of the customs described for Archenfield constitutes virtually a statement of Welsh practice in relation to theft, homicide, and arson, as given in the Welsh law-texts.[2] This, moreover, was an area where Welsh lawmen were in being in the tenth century if, as Sir Frank Stenton believed, the "Ordinance concerning the Dunsaete" of *c.* 926 relates to the Anglo-Welsh border between Hereford and Monmouth rather than to a greater length of the frontier. This Ordinance records an agreement reached between the English Witan and the counsellors of the Welsh people about such matters as homicide and theft, especially that of cattle, horses, pigs, and sheep. Twelve lawmen, six of them English and six of them Welsh, were to declare what was just to both sides.[3] Significantly the Ordinance refers to Welshmen, no less than Englishmen, who could be either thane-born or churl-born. This is certainly in keeping with the statement in Domesday Book that there were in Archenfield not only freemen but also villeins.

Archenfield had been laid waste by King Gruffydd and Bleddyn in the time of King Edward. Accordingly the Domesday account reports that "it is not known what it was like in that time." Nevertheless Welsh arrangements appear to have been characteristic in 1086. From Domesday Book we learn that "in Archenfield the King has 100 men less 4, and they have 73 ploughs *with their own men* [my italics] and give as customary due 41 sesters of honey, and 20s. for the sheep which they were wont to give, and 10s. for smoke-silver. Nor do they pay geld or any other customary due except that they go forth in the king's army if commanded." In a twelfth-century transcript of Domesday Book this entry is immediately preceded by an explanatory statement to the effect that here begin the customs of the manor of

[1] DB I, 162a.

[2] B. G. Charles in *Angles and Britons: O'Donnell Lectures*, Cardiff, 1963, pp. 87–96; DB I, 179a; *The Latin Texts of the Welsh Laws*, pp. 92–3.

[3] RCHM, *Herefordshire*, III, 1934, pp. lviii–lix; F. Liebermann, *Die Gesetze der Angelsachsen*, Halle, 1903–16, I, pp. 374–9; II, pp. 355–6; III, pp. 214–19.

Wormelow in Archenfield (*manerium de Wormelowe in Irchynffeld*).[1] In Domesday Book proper the entry about the king's men is followed by an account of "a manor (*manerium*) there in which are 4 freemen with 4 ploughs. It renders 4 sesters of honey and 16d. as customary due." In the twelfth-century text there is added here the name Ballingham, which is that of a settlement located a few miles to the east within a great bend of the river Wye; and opposite the end of this same entry the name *Meiner Reau* is also added.[2] The latter, it may be suggested very tentatively, is a late, corrupt, form of Maenor Fro meaning lowland *maenor*, a suggestion reinforced perhaps by the use of typically Welsh multiples of four in the assessment of Ballingham.

Wormelow was specified in Domesday Book as the moot of the hundred of the same name. The moot, it appears, was at Wormelow Tump, a prominent burial mound recorded by Nennius and sited near a north-south Roman road at the western boundary of the township of Much Birch. Under the rubric "Wormelow Hundred" the Domesday survey refers to a Westwood which can be identified as lying, in part at least, within Llanwarne, a parish which marches with Much Birch near the Tump. Immediately afterwards we are told that the *caput* of this manor (*caput huius manerii*) was held by King Edward and that "here there are 6 hides 1 of which has Welsh custom (*waliscam consuetudinem*) and the others English."[3] Elsewhere in Domesday Book, in a section entitled "the border of Archenfield," there is recorded a *Mainaure* where Roger de Lacy in 1086 had one Welshman who rendered 5s. and a sester of honey. At Mainaure, which was also said to be held of Roger by the son of Costelin, there were, in addition, four plough-teams and the render was six sesters of honey and 10s. A marginal entry in the twelfth-century transcript of Domesday Book identifies this *Mainaure* as the Birches, presumably the two townships known as Little Birch and Much Birch, below Caer Rein, otherwise Aconbury hill-fort, which dominates upland Archenfield.[4] This small multiple estate named *Mainaure* in 1086 was probably a late surviving vestige of a once wider *maenor* fissioned by the alienation of its component townships. Nevertheless the hundredal framework of Wormelow suggests that besides its *caput* at, or near, Much Birch this wider entity had formerly included a *maenor wrthtir* (an upland *maenor*) embracing Aconbury hill-fort, and also a *maenor fro* (a lowland *maenor*), adjoining the banks of the Wye near Ballingham.

---

[1] DB 1, 181a; *Herefordshire Domesday c. 1160–1170*, ed. V. H. Galbraith and J. Tait, London, 1950, p. 19.

[2] Cf. DB 1, 181a; *Herefordshire Domesday*, p. 19.   [3] DB 1, 181a.

[4] Cf. *ibid.*; *Herefordshire Domesday*, p. 20; see also *Liber Landavensis*, pp. 8, 43, 135, 363; RCHM, *Herefordshire*, 1, 1931, pp. 13–14.

Nowhere else in the Domesday folios is a *maenor* recorded by name but some of the attributes of both the upland *maenor* of thirteen townships and the lowland *maenor* of seven townships are portrayed in the Domesday account of the manor of Bistre in Moldsdale (Flint). When surveyed in 1086 Bistre manor itself extended into five distinct settlements and also eight outlying berewicks, among them Gwysaney where a priest resided.[1] If Gwysaney was the *llan* (church) of the complex, Bistre itself was the *llys* (court), for we are told that King Gruffydd ap Llywelyn had one manor here. In this manor he "had 1 plough in demesne and his men 6 ploughs." Even more significantly, we are informed that "when the said king came thither, every plough rendered him 200 *hesthas* [*sic*], and one vat full of beer, and one vessel of butter." This ambulatory feeding within an estate having seven plough-teams must be attributed to the period before 1063 when King Gruffydd died. Nevertheless, the definition of the *maenor* in the earliest Latin law-text as a territorial unit containing seven shares of land is still regarded by legal historians as a late meaning adopted under the influence of the Norman *manerium*.[2] Heptads, no less than triads or enneads, are mnemonic devices, appropriate to an oral tradition and therefore likely to be ancient. The use of these multiples in Wales for agrarian institutions implies that the latter are rooted in ancient fact.

THE MARGINAL ENTRIES IN THE BOOK OF ST CHAD

Fortunately for the student of early Welsh institutions there is even more positive evidence in the Book of St Chad to suggest that the *maenor* of seven townships was not unknown in Wales centuries before the Norman conquest. The sixth marginal entry in this gospel-book refers, partly in Latin and partly in Welsh, to a *maenor*, known as *mainaur med diminih*, and gives its measure (*mensuram eius*). As we have seen, the Book of St Chad must be dated before 974 but on the bases of palaeography and philology this particular entry, known for convenience as Chad 6, can be attributed to the period *c.* 800.[3] The words *med diminih* have been equated with Meddyfnych, which, in the form *Myddynfych*, is now borne by a substantial farm in the parish of Llandybïe (Carm). The measure of the *maenor* is given by means of a series of place-names. Many of these names have been identified as referring to features which occur near the boundary of Llandybïe parish (Fig. 43). Moving in a clockwise direction these are:

[1] DB I, 269a.   [2] *The Latin Texts of the Welsh Laws*, p. 6.
[3] *Liber Landavensis*, p. xlvii; I. Williams, 'Meddyfnych', BBCS VII, 1933–5, pp. 369–70; Jackson, *op. cit.*, pp. 42–7.

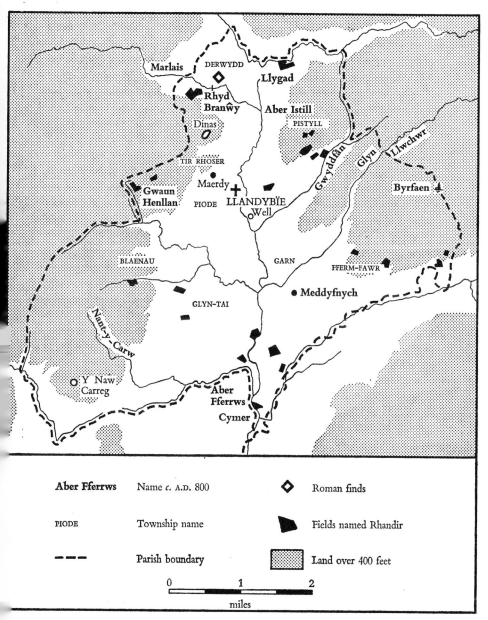

Aber Fferrws	Name *c.* A.D. 800	◆	Roman finds
PIODE	Township name	◢	Fields named Rhandir
---	Parish boundary	▨	Land over 400 feet

0   1   2

miles

Fig. 43. The measure of Maenor Meddyfnych, Carmarthen, according to
a marginal entry of *c.* A.D. 800 in the Book of St Chad.

Gwyddfân, a stream entering the parish from the north-east; the Llwchwr entering from the same direction; Cymer, the confluence of the Llwchwr with the Amman; Aber Fferrws, the mouth of the Fferrws where it joins the Llwchwr; Pen Nant-y-Carw, the Head of the Stream of the Stag, a tributary of the Fferrws; Gwaun Henllan, the upland meadow of the old church settlement; Marlais, the stream entering the parish in the north-west; and Aber Istill the mouth of the Istill, a small stream running through Cors Astell (Astell Bog) near Derwydd, where it joins the Marlais. On the strength of these identifications it has been suggested that Maenor Meddyfnych was probably co-extensive with the parish of Llandybïe.[1]

When recently beating these bounds the present writer was able to add a few more identifications, some tentative, others certain. Hytir Melyn (the Yellow Cornland) named in the perambulation immediately before Marlais is possibly the cultivable slope, a former shareland, to the south of the Marlais near the parish boundary. Rhyd Branŵy, named in the perambulation between Marlais and Aber Istill, is probably the ford across the Marlais near Derwydd. Llygad is almost certainly used in the sense of the eye of the spring, as was *Oculus Amr* by Nennius, of the source of the Gamber near Wormelow Tump, for in the Llandybïe district Llygad Llwchwr is the source of the River Llwchwr; moreover the Istill has a well-defined source in a number of closely-juxtaposed springs at the head of Cors Astell. These additional identifications show that Meddyfnych did not include the township of Derwydd, with its later mansion of the same name on a site where were found Roman remains including pottery, mosaic *tesserae*, glass, and a copper cup.[2] The other firm new identification is Byrfaen, "the short stone" named in the perambulation after the Llwchwr and therefore placed to its south. This is almost certainly the stone standing near the summit on the south-eastern boundary of the parish. Leaning against a low natural outcrop, this stone now attains a height of only about eight feet. Significantly, however, in this position it is just visible from a medieval trackway and transhumance route. The inclusion of this stone in the measure of Meddyfnych but the omission of any reference to Y Naw Carreg (The Nine Stones), the remains of a stone circle on former common pasture near the western boundary of the parish, suggests that here too the *maenor* of Meddyfnych and the later parish of Llandybïe were not coterminous. Nevertheless the *maenor*, though defined so as to exclude both Derwydd

---

[1] J. Fisher, 'Meddynfych, Llandebie', *Carmarthen Antiq. Soc.* xx, 1926–7, pp. 14–15; G. M. Roberts, *Hanes Plwyf Llandybïe*, Cardiff, 1939, pp. 33–6; PRO, D.L./42/120.

[2] Nennius, pp. 217–18; 'Meeting at Llandeilo Fawr: Report of Proceedings', AC x, 5th series, 1893, p. 158.

and the south-western corner of the parish, remained a quite substantial area of some twelve square miles. To judge from later records it contained seven townships.[1] In each of these there are field names which indicate the presence at some time of sharelands alike of arable and meadow. A number of these still contained unfenced quillets of meadow, and one even contained unfenced quillets of arable as late as 1839.[2] When these elements of the agrarian landscape were introduced, we cannot tell. It is likely, however, that some degree of communal organization was already present in Meddyfnych by *c.* 800, for the perambulation refers to a Gwaun Henllan.[3] A productive upland meadow, this lay at an altitude of about 500 feet, a mile or so west of the lowland settlement which clearly was already known by the name Henllan (*Old* Church). That a distant upland meadow should be thus attributed to the Old Church in itself hints at the possibility that there was a hamlet community here even by this date. Its site, near the lowland farm later known as Maerdy (Reeve's house) and below the elevated strongpoint of Dinas, was advantageous. With its church and holy well dedicated to Tybïe, one of the numerous progeny of Brychan, the semi-legendary and half-Irish founder of Brycheiniog, this settlement perhaps was already some centuries old. But be that as it may, there can be no doubt that there was an old *llan* within the *maenor* of Meddyfnych by *c.* 800. The name of the *maenor*, as we have seen, is preserved only in that of one large farm, but this forms part of the township which, significantly, is named Fferm Fawr (Large Farm).[4] Since Myddynfych farm, like the *llan*, occupies a sheltered and favoured lowland site it too was no doubt the site of an early settlement, Meddyfnych, which probably served as the *llys* (court) of the *maenor*. As at early Aberffraw and eleventh-century Bistre, the *llys* was some distance from the *llan*. Already in A.D. 800, the *maenor* in the interior of South Wales was, it appears, a multiple estate containing more than one significant settlement.

Viewed in terms of this composite structure of the *maenor*, the statements made in the marginal entries known as Chad 3 and Chad 4 become more readily intelligible than they were to Seebohm in his great pioneer study, *The Tribal System in Wales*.[5] Both entries, which

[1] M. Richards, *Welsh Administrative and Territorial Units*, Cardiff, 1969, p. 109.

[2] National Library of Wales, Tithe Apportionment and Map, Llandybïe, 1839.

[3] *Liber Landavensis*, p. xlvii.

[4] By *c.* A.D. 800 Henllan was almost certainly being used of a church in its churchyard, rather than in the older senses of the word *llan* cited above (p. 303). But, even if this were not the case, the implication of a multiple estate consisting of scattered components would still hold good.—RCAHM, *Carmarthen*, pp. 104–5.

[5] *Liber Landavensis*, p. xlv; F. Seebohm, *The Tribal System in Wales*, 1st ed., London, 1895, pp. 85–6.

again are in Latin and Welsh, are attributed to the mid-ninth century, and since they are our only other early evidences of unimpeachable authority giving topographic detail, they merit close consideration. Chad 3 records that "Rhys and the kindred of Grethi" (*ris et luith grethi*) have given Trefwyddog (*treb guidauc*) to God and St Eliud (i.e. Teilo). We are told that "its render (*census eius*) is forty loaves and a ram in summer, and forty loaves in winter, and a sow and forty *mannuclenn*." The meaning of the last item is not known, but, this apart, the render is reminiscent of the bondmen's foodgift (*dawnbwyd*) in North Wales and even more reminiscent of the bondmen's foodgift in South Wales. For this reason Sir John Lloyd suggested that *mannuclenn* should be interpreted as 'sheaf' or 'handful' and thus equated with the sheaves of oats of the South Wales foodgift. Unlike the *gwestfa*, which was contributed only once a year, foodgifts were made in summer and winter.[1] This is a further reason for suggesting that Trefwyddog, whence a *census* was rendered in summer and winter, was a bond township. The reference to Rhys and the kindred in this context of a donation to the Church would appear to suggest two possibilities. The first, and less acceptable, alternative is that it was Rhys who donated the land but, in keeping with the kind of customary law, as later recorded, that a proprietor was a custodian on behalf of his descendants, he did so with the consent of his kinsmen, who, moreover, may be envisaged as perhaps having rights here without necessarily exercising them. The second alternative is that Trefwyddog was a part of the joint holding of Rhys and his kinsmen but that Rhys acted as the spokesman. But, in any event, Trefwyddog was evidently not the only landed possession of the donor or donors. Rhys, either as an individual or in concert with his kinsmen, held an estate which comprised a number of townships with already defined boundaries and within which there were settled communities of bondmen. The donation of Trefwyddog justifies the suggestion that early Welsh society *c.* 850 was organized on an aristocratic basis, an interpretation which is buttressed alike by the evidence of contemporary verse and that of later sources. Freemen, men of pedigree privileged by noble birth, or elevated by virtue of their ministerial functions, were maintained, it would appear, by a substrate bond population. Supporting testimony is provided by the entry known as Chad 5, again dated to the mid-ninth century. This reveals that family stocks of bondmen were owned by groups of kinsmen, for the entry records that the four sons of Bledri gave liberty (*dederunt libertatem*) to Bleiddud son of Sulien and his heirs (*Bleidiud filio Sul(gen) et semini suo*) for

---

[1] Lloyd, *op. cit.*, I, p. 214; *Llyfr Iorwerth*, p. 64; *Llyfr Blegywryd*, p. 69; *The Laws of Hywel Dda*, p. 73.

ever, in return for a payment which cannot be deciphered in its entirety but which certainly included eight ounces, presumably of silver.[1]

That the bondmen owned by such seemingly prosperous kinsmen were *adscripti glebae* and thus tied to the soil of their townships is implied by the wording of Chad 3 and its companion Chad 4. It is appropriate therefore to view these entries against their territorial setting. Seebohm, although he cited Chad 3 and Chad 4, failed to do this; hence his continued adhesion, even in the second edition of *The Tribal System in Wales*, to the belief that the Welsh remained, well into our period, at the "pastoral stage of tribal life" when the grazing of cattle was "the main subject of agrarian rights."[2] A topographic assessment of these entries enables us to modify this belief by showing that in the ninth century the notables and their bondmen held land within a well organized and old-established territorial framework. Chad 4 records that Rhys and other named individuals made a donation of some territory. Although the name of this territory cannot be deciphered it appears to have extended from a battlefield as far as Hirfaen Gwyddog (*hirmain guidauc*) and from the wood of Gelli Irlath as far as Camddwr (*Cam dubr*).[3] The entry then gives details of a render, namely sixty loaves, a ram, and butter. The witnesses are almost identical with those of Chad 3. Since the name Gwyddog (*guidauc*) together with that of Rhys as a donor appears in both Chad 3 and Chad 4, it is likely that both grants refer to the same area, with the latter providing a clarification or, more probably, an amplification of the former. From the inclusion of a ram and butter, as in the summer foodgift of South Welsh bondmen, and the exclusion of a sow given as part of the winter foodgift, we may infer that the grant in Chad 4 was especially concerned with summer rights like those over upland pasture. The near contemporaneity of the two entries as implied by almost identical lists of witnesses, it is true, could be construed as pointing to the grant by Rhys and others of two bond townships. Such generosity in itself is not unlikely, but in this case the first interpretation is the more probable. Acceptance of the second interpretation however would only serve to reinforce further our argument that early Welsh society contained a wealthy and privileged upper stratum.

The names Hirfaen Gwyddog and Camddwr enable us to identify the area whose donation is recorded in Chad 4. Hirfaen Gwyddog (The Long Stone of Gwyddog) is the very appropriate name of an erect stone standing to a height of fifteen feet on the northern boundary

[1] *Liber Landavensis*, p. xlvi.
[2] Seebohm, *The Tribal System in Wales*, 2nd ed., London, 1904, pp. xi–xii.
[3] *Liber Landavensis*, p. xlv.

of Llan-y-crwys (the Church of the Crosses) which coincides with
the northern boundary of Cantref Mawr, and now therefore of
Carmarthenshire (Fig. 44). It is recorded under the name *Hyrvayn-gudauc* in a charter of 1324 confirming a grant to Talley Abbey of the
grange of Llan-y-crwys then known as Llanddewicrwys (St David's
of the Crosses). The named limits of the grange coincide with points
near to, or within, the boundaries of the small triangular parish of
Llan-y-crwys. Hirfaen Gwyddog, which later figures in a presentment
of the manorial boundary of Llan-y-crwys in 1633, was also noted
by the topographer Edward Llwyd in 1698 and its position was
indicated alike on the first edition of the Ordnance Survey map of
1834 and on the tithe map of Llan-y-crwys in 1839. That Llwyd
should name as Byrfaen Gwyddog (The Short Stone of Gwyddog)
a short stone shown on these maps at a point three-quarters of a mile
to the north-east adds strength to the identification.[1] The other fairly
certain identification is that of Camddwr, literally 'the crooked water',
a name probably applied to the rivulet, now known as Camnant
(Crooked stream), which flows southwards from the vicinity of
Hirfaen Gwyddog. Meandering has long been characteristic of the
lower reaches of this stream where its numerous small bends deviate
frequently from the parish boundary. The bounds of the territory
donated by Rhys would thus appear to have run from Hirfaen Gwyddog
downslope towards the wood named Gelli Irlath (probably the Gelli
[Wood] on the bounds of the medieval forest of Pennant), thence
to the Camddwr, and thence northwards up the course of the River
Twrch. Certainly the grange of Llanddewicrwys was described in 1324
as lying between two rivers. Moreover the battlefield which comes
earlier in the Chad 4 perambulation may be tentatively located at the
north-eastern corner of Llan-y-crwys where a sepulchral mound on
a mountain summit near a north-south Roman road bears the traditional
name Bedd y Milwr (The Soldier's Grave). At its upper limits the
territory granted by Rhys and his fellow donors included common
pastures which survived down to the nineteenth century in a band,
over 1,000 feet high, near the parish boundary. Below, there were
favoured south-east facing slopes which, though exceeding 500 feet in
altitude, must have been cultivated in the ninth century if only to
provide the loaves in the render.[2]

[1] W. Dugdale, *Monasticon Anglicanum* IV, p. 162; National Library of Wales: Tithe
Apportionment and Map, Llan-y-crwys, 1839; E. Owen, 'A Contribution to the
History of the Praemonstratensian Abbey of Talley', AC x, 5th series, 1893,
pp. 39–40; RCAHM, *Carmarthen*, pp. 208–9; W. Rees, *Historical Map of South Wales
and the Border in the Fourteenth Century*, Cardiff, 1932.

[2] By Welsh upland standards an unusually large proportion of the land in Llan-y-crwys was cultivated during the inter-war period of the twentieth century.

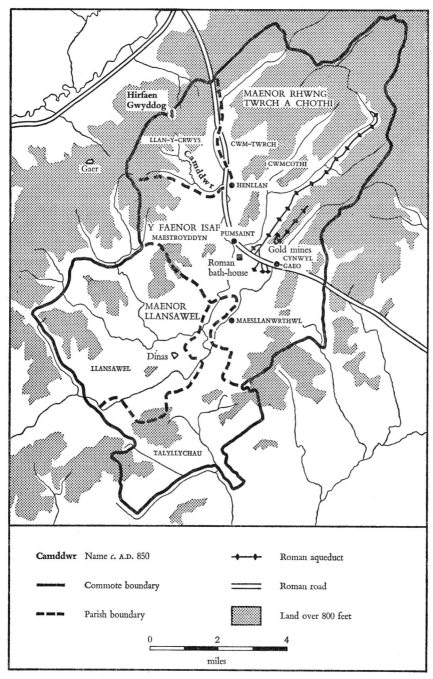

Fig. 44. The territorial framework of Trefwyddog, Carmarthen, a bond township donated to the Church c. A.D. 850.

The wording of Chad 3 and 4 implies that the lands so granted formed part of a larger estate. Precisely the same kind of impression is given by the shape of Llan-y-crwys parish. The latter, as a triangular segment, appears to have been carved out of a larger entity, almost a natural unit of relief and drainage, which coincided at a later date with the commote of Caeo, a subdivision of Cantref Mawr. Presumably the other territories retained by Rhys and his kindred for their own maintenance were within this commote of Caeo. During the later Middle Ages the commote was certainly inhabited by freemen, "ancient tenants in *westfa*;" indeed, it was divided into nine *gwestfa* districts each paying a uniform rent of 53s. 4d. per annum, so that the commote total was precisely that current in the days of Welsh lords. There were also bond tenants who paid, for every 4d. of one-fourth of the total *gwestfa* payment, one bushel of oats as *dofraeth*, the ancient render for the billeting of the lord's retainers on the unfree community of the commote.[1] At some stage in the history of the commote the territorial unit known as the *maenor* had been adopted as a larger subdivision. On the hills to the north-east was Maenor Rhwng Twrch a Chothi (Maenor between Twrch and Cothi) which, as its name implies, had well-defined river boundaries. Towards the south, Maenor Llansawel was dominated by Dinas, an elevated strongpoint where fortifications survived into the nineteenth century, but at the core of the commote was Y Faenor Isaf (The Lowest Maenor) also known as the township of Maestroyddyn (The Open Field of the Fortified *Tref*).[2]

Early in our period the lowlands of the commote were of importance. At Maesllanwrthwl one Paulinus was commemorated in Latin on a horizontally inscribed stone as a "Preserver of the Faith, constant lover of his country...the devoted champion of righteousness." It is often suggested that the Paulinus commemorated was St David's reputed teacher who allegedly as an old man attended a Church synod held at Llanddewibrefi perhaps in A.D. 545. Paulinus was eminent enough a saint for his life to have been written by a Breton monk in the ninth century and, appropriately, the laudatory terms of the inscription seem to imply no ordinary person. On the other hand, it has been argued that the phrasing, with its echoes of classical authors, rather suggests a secular ruler and the epigraphy a date in the fifth century.[3] But in any case, a second inscribed stone of the sixth century

[1] W. Rees, *South Wales and the March 1284–1415*, London, 1934, pp. 226–7, 238; *History of Carmarthen*, ed. J. E. Lloyd, Cardiff, 1935, p. 225.

[2] RCAHM, *Carmarthen*, pp. 190–1; Richards, *op. cit.*, p. 25.

[3] Nash-Williams, *op. cit.*, pp. 107–9; E. G. Bowen, *The Settlements of the Celtic Saints in Wales*, Cardiff, 1955, pp. 129–30; Ralegh Radford in *The Land of Dyfed in Early Times*, p. 20.

commemorating in a vertical inscription one Talorius Adventus, son of Maquerigius, has been found at Maesllanwrthwl. Moreover, at Cynwyl Gaeo, which later emerged as the main bond settlement of the commote, there was found a stone with a vertical inscription of the sixth century commemorating one Reginus, son of Nudintus.[1]

The district has a still earlier claim to fame because of the exploitation of gold near Dolau Cothi. Very soon after the Roman conquest *c.* A.D. 75 the Romans mined gold at Dolau Cothi so that gold was probably being worked here by pre-existing Celtic communities.[2] The Roman activity helps to explain the presence of the hoard of gold ornaments of the second and third centuries A.D. found during the early nineteenth century in "The Common Field," which formed part of the Dolau Cothi estate near the mines. Numerous other finds have been made in the area, among them the 3,000 Roman coins dug up "at Cynwyl Gaeo" in 1762 and the 682 radiates of the third century found about three miles to the north on the farm of Erw Hen (Old Acre) in 1965. A Roman hypocaust and other remains, including *tesserae*, interpreted as belonging to a bath-house, have been found on a gravel spur overlooking the Cothi half a mile from the main mining area. Military tile stamps from the bath-house suggest that there was a fort close at hand, either at the bath-house itself or at Pumsaint, half a mile distant beyond the Cothi, where the remains of a substantial Roman settlement underlie the present hamlet. The existence of a fort is likely, given the overall context of state control in Roman mining. Certainly the exploitation of gold near Dolau Cothi was on a large enough scale to justify the construction of two carefully engineered aqueduct systems. The recently discovered Annell aqueduct was four miles long; and the Cothi aqueduct was no less than seven miles long and served a series of sluices, tanks, and reservoirs, among them that known as Melin y Milwyr (The Mill of the Soldiers). This longer aqueduct alone was capable of delivering three million gallons of water a day to the workings.[3] Significantly this aqueduct tapped its water supplies from the River Cothi at a point near to, but within, the north-eastern extremity of the commote of Caeo as delimited in later centuries.

The overall development of such a tremendous undertaking must have required not only a considerable supply of labour for mining as

[1] Nash-Williams, *op. cit.*, p. 109; Rees, *op. cit.*, p. 222.

[2] G. D. B. Jones, 'The Dolaucothi Gold Mines. I: The Surface Evidence', *Ant. J.* XLIX, 1964, pp. 244–67.

[3] RCAHM, *Carmarthen*, pp. 25–32; S. S. Frere, *Britannia*, London, 1967, p. 285; G. D. B. Jones, I. J. Blakey, E. C. F. MacPherson, 'Dolaucothi: The Roman Aqueduct', BBCS XIX, 1960–2, pp. 71–9; D. R. Wilson, 'Roman Britain in 1968', JRS, 1969, pp. 198–9.

well as subsidiary industries, but also raw materials and, not least, food
supplies. The mines were worked mainly in the first and second
centuries, but Roman occupation of the area must have continued at
least into the third century and the inscribed stones of the district
point to the existence of at least some local settlement in the fifth and
sixth centuries. Of post-Roman working at the mines nothing certain
is known, however, until exploitation was resumed in the nineteenth
century, though it may be significant that there was a medieval motte
near the entrance to the main workings. Silver and lead were exploited
near Talley Abbey in the southern part of the commote, possibly in
the Middle Ages. In any case an area like this, where precious metals
were available, is likely to have commanded the continuous attention
of rulers, though not necessarily only local ones, for besides the
onomastic evidence there are early literary allusions to military activity
in the district. From the Stanzas of the Graves, first composed perhaps
in the latter part of our period, we learn not only of a warrior's burial
in the upper reaches of Pennant Twrch but also that:

> "The grave of Dywel son of Erbin is in the plain of Caeo;
>   he would not be vassal to a king,
>   a faultless man who would not shun conflict."[1]

The so-called charters in *Liber Landavensis*, while showing that
cattle were used for payments in the eighth century, also reveal that
gold and silver were used in the ninth, and this in a compilation which
emphasizes the links between Llandaf and the *patria* of St Teilo.
William of Malmesbury reported that Athelstan in A.D. 926 imposed
on the Welsh an annual tribute which included not only dogs and
birds of prey, but also 25,000 oxen, 300 pounds of silver, and 20 pounds
of gold.[2] Since those who submitted to Athelstan included Hywel
Dda, then ruler, among other areas, of Cantref Mawr, it is not unlikely
that some exploitation of gold occurred in Caeo in our period.

In the light of such evidence it may be tentatively suggested that
here on the moorland fringe of Central Wales if anywhere in the
country one might expect a degree of administrative continuity from
the Roman period onwards. Nor is this suggestion without a possible
bearing on the *marginalia* in the Book of St Chad, and least of all
Chad 3 with its evidence of the donation of Trefwyddog to the
church of St Teilo. Adjoining Maesllanwrthwl, where Paulinus and
Talorius were commemorated, is the site of the medieval chapel of

---

[1] T. Jones, 'The Black Book of Carmarthen: "Stanzas of the Graves"', *B. Acad.*
LIII, 1967, p. 123.
[2] William of Malmesbury, *Gesta Regum*, ed. W. Stubbs, Rolls ser. 70, 1887, I,
p. 148.

Llandeilo Garth Tefyr. Attributed in *Liber Landavensis* to the time of St Teilo in the sixth century, it was also described in this work as "Llandeilo Garth Tefir a vill only above the bank of the Cothi" (*Lann Teliau garth tevir villa tantum super ripam cothi*).[1] The same compilation includes a Bull of Pope Innocent II (*c.* 1130) which refers to the claim of Llandaf to various possessions including Llandeilo Fawr and Llandeilo *Mainaur* with their appurtenances, as well as *lannteliau pimseint caircaiau* (Llandeilo of the Five Saints of the Fort of Caeo).[2] The latter, recorded in a context which includes a reference to some associated fortification, is none other than the chapel which once stood in the hamlet of Pumsaint, itself the site of a substantial Roman settlement. The dedication to the five saints may also be meaningful. One of these was Gwynio, whose name is also preserved in that of Ffynnon Gwenno, a cave in the Roman workings where the waters were reputed to possess curative properties. Moreover the five saints are associated in local legend with the four or five hollows on Carreg Pumsaint (The Stone of the Five Saints), a block of diorite imported to the locality for use in the crushing of gold-bearing quartz.[3] That these two chapels, one of which was certainly on the site of a known early settlement at the core of Caeo, should be dedicated to the Teilo whose foundations were later supported by the donation of the outlying Trefwyddog, may well reflect a long-abiding awareness of an ancient administrative circumscription.

Whatever the precise significance we attach to the four Chad entries already considered, they clearly point towards the existence of a social organization much more stable than that until recently envisaged. A similar impression is conveyed by the two remaining entries. Chad 1, an entry ascribed to the early ninth century, states that "Gelhi the son of Arihtiud bought this Gospel from Cingal, and gave him for it a 'best horse', and gave for his soul's sake this Gospel to God and St Teliau upon the altar." Chad 2, better known as the *Surexit* Memorandum, was written into this gospel-book in the eighth century and besides Latin also contains the oldest known piece of Old Welsh. Consequently this entry, which is couched in obscure phraseology, has been interpreted only tentatively.[4] Nevertheless it appears to give details of a lawsuit in which Tutbulc, son of Liuit and son-in-law of Tutri, claimed *tir telih* which was in the hand of Elcu son of Gelhig

---

[1] *Liber Landavensis*, pp. 124, 254.

[2] *Ibid.*, pp. 56, 62, 287.

[3] RCAHM, *Carmarthen*, p. 33.

[4] *Liber Landavensis*, p. xliii; J. Morris Jones, 'The *Surexit* Memorandum', *Y Cymmrodor* XXVIII, 1918, pp. 268–80; Jackson, *op. cit.*, p. 42; see also I. Ll. Foster in WHR, *Special Number, The Welsh Laws*, pp. 64–5.

and the kindred of Iuguret (*haluidt iuguret*). As a result Elcu was dispossessed of his right, but they made peace; afterwards Elcu gave
a horse, three cows, and three newly-calved cows so that henceforward
till the day of doom there should be no hostility between them. Finally
we are told that Tutbulc and his people (*cenetl*) will afterwards require
no title (*grefiat*) for ever. The word *grefiat* implies that the title was
a written one, while *cenetl* points to the recognition of a larger kinship
group than the kindred, with more extensive possessions and possibly
a wider territorial authority. The implications of this entry are however
far from clear. If, as seems likely, *telih* was a personal name then *tir
telih* would have been the land of a person so named. Unfortunately, it
is difficult to identify this land. Seebohm equated *tir telih* with a place
near Rhosili in Gower which was named *telich* in *Liber Landavensis*,
but this same compilation also records another *telich* in south-west
Wales. Apart from these possible locations, and the Bryntelych (Telych
Hill) near Pontlliw some six miles south of Maenor Meddyfnych,
there are three other places of this name much nearer to Llandeilo
Fawr where, it has been suggested, the gospel-book was at one time
kept. One of these places is within Maenor Llys (the Maenor of the
Court) where there was also a *maerdref*. The other is the township
named Telych in the parish of Llandingad near Llanymddyfri (Carm),
a township which again contained a *maerdref* and where a large stone
monolith bearing an inscription was once found.[1] Most intriguing
of all, however, is the name Cefn Telych (Telych Ridge) given to
a hill-slope a mile or so south-west of the gold mines of Dolau Cothi
and within the parish of Caeo.[2] But, whatever the full implications
of *tir telih*, Chad 2 appears to support the evidence of four other
entries in this gospel-book in suggesting that already by the mid-ninth
century settled rights in land were old-established in Wales. Viewed
in terms of these entries, three of the customary tenures recorded in
the lawbooks appear to have ancient roots. These are *tir gwelyog*, *tir
cyfrif*, and *tir corddlan*.

'TIR GWELYOG' (HEREDITARY LAND)

The normal tenure, taken for granted in the lawbooks, was *tir gwelyog*
(hereditary land). The essential features of this kind of land were
that the right to it passed to descendants in equal shares and that the

---

[1] Seebohm, *op. cit.*, p. 183; *Liber Landavensis*, pp. 125, 240, 255; PRO DL/42/120;
Richards, *op. cit.*, p. 214; RCAHM, *Carmarthen*, p. 99.

[2] I am particularly indebted to Professor M. Richards for his comments on the
name Telych and on Welsh toponymy in general. In a private communication
Professor Richards says he is fairly certain that *tir telih* contains a personal name.

rights of the 'owner' (*perchennog*) for the time being were limited to his lifetime, so that he could not defeat his descendants' right to succeed. Continued occupation of land by the members of an agnatic lineage over a period of four generations converted bare possession into legal proprietorship (*priodolder*) and the "fourth man" became a proprietor. By the thirteenth century such a hereditary proprietor's share of his patrimony (*treftadaeth*) would normally have consisted of a personal holding of appropriated land (*tir priod*) and an undivided share of joint land (*cytir*). The appropriated land would have included a homestead (*tyddyn*), some parcels of "scattered land" (*tir gwasgar*) lying in one or more arable sharelands, and parcels of meadowland. The joint land on the other hand would probably have embraced an expanse of wood, pasture, and waste, subject to joint control but within which the proprietor exercised proportional rights calculated in terms of his acreage of appropriated land. In accordance with the rules of partible succession (*cyfran*), rights over appropriated land could be divided equally *per stirpes* among the sons of the proprietor. Correspondingly, rights over the still undivided joint land would be reduced in proportion to the ensuing diminution of personal holdings of appropriated land. On the father's death the youngest son would succeed to the parental homestead. His brothers were expected to remain in the homesteads they had made for themselves on the hereditary land in their father's lifetime, for after attaining the age of fourteen years a scion of free stock was permitted, if he so wished, to settle in a house of his own on some part of the family land. Following a partition between brothers, homesteads could be subject to no further redistribution, but, under certain conditions, the appropriated land could be reallocated. Thus after the brothers had died, their sons, being first cousins, *if they wished*, could revise the sharing of the land, presumably so as to prevent the rise of marked inequalities. Likewise the second cousins, if they wanted it, had a right to a revision of the sharing. Even if only some of the cousins wanted to do so they could, it appears, compel their kinsmen to join in a re-sharing of their common grandfather's holding. Second cousins could likewise compel a re-sharing of their common great-grandfather's holding. Nevertheless there was no general obligation to reopen an arrangement for the sharing of land made in a previous generation; and in any case the rules for re-sharing only extended as far as the second cousins. After this stage, known as the final partition (*gorffenran*), there was to be no more re-sharing, or as one text puts it, no more sharing except for the joint land (*cytir*).[1]

[1] *The Latin Texts of the Welsh Laws*, pp. 132, 227, 387; *The Laws of Hywel Dda*, pp. 77–80; *Llyfr Blegywryd*, p. 75; *Llyfr Iorwerth*, pp. 82–3; *Llyfr Colan*, pp. 58–9.

The adjective *gwelyog*, which qualifies *tir* (land) in the phrase *tir gwelyog*, appears to be a derivative of *gwely*, meaning bed. In terms of social and tenurial organization, however, its primary meaning was a limited group of relatives, so that *tir gwelyog* probably meant, at first, land which passed on death to heirs within this group. Only later did *gwely* come to be used of the holding of appropriated land in the sense of a stake in the soil, a 'resting place' for an agnatic lineage, or, as the late Professor Jones Pierce described it, a 'clanland'.[1] The group of relatives originally designated by this word *gwely* was not necessarily of the same kind in every instance. In the lawbooks *gwely* is used infrequently, and, in connection with land-holding, altogether very rarely. In the main it is associated with payments of *galanas* (*wergild*) in lieu of blood-feud, made by both male and female relatives of the homicide, or with the distribution of the receipts which passed to the agnatic and cognatic relatives of the victim.[2] *Gwely* therefore meant a defined, though variable, narrow group of relatives within the wider circle of kindred. In verse the same word was used in a more general sense, and the English 'stock' seems to be the best equivalent. The word *gwelygordd* (*gwely* group) is used much more frequently, alike in the lawbooks, where the Latin equivalent is *parentela*, and in other writings. In the lawbooks *gwelygordd* is sometimes used in conjunction with hereditary land but also in connection with blood-feud payments, where it appears to be equivalent to *cenedl* (kindred).[3] The use of *gwely*, no less than *gwelygordd*, in the context of the blood-feud, in itself implies that the notion of *gwely* as a social institution was old-established. Since the *gwelygordd* figures in a court poem by Cynddelw Brydydd Mawr in the twelfth century, already by that

[1] T. Jones Pierce, 'Pastoral and Agricultural Settlements in Early Wales', *Geografiska Annaler* XLIII, 1961, pp. 182–9; id., in *Agrarian History of England and Wales* IV, pp. 363–5.

[2] D. Jenkins, 'A Lawyer looks at Welsh Land Law', *Hon. Soc. Cymm.*, 1967, pp. 241–7; *Llyfr Iorwerth*, p. 72; *Llyfr Colan*, p. 16; T. Jones Pierce, 'The Laws of Wales: the Kindred and the Blood Feud', pp. 117–37. At an early stage in the evolution of the institutions associated with the blood feud, kindred to the ninth degree were to make, or receive, payments of *galanas*. These degrees of relationship were defined as follows in a text produced after 1282: "the first degree of the nine is the father and mother of the murderer or of the murdered; the second is a grandfather; the third is a great-grandfather; the fourth is brothers and sisters; the fifth is a cousin; the sixth is a second cousin; the seventh is third cousins; the eighth is fourth cousins; the ninth is fifth cousins." See *The Laws of Hywel Dda*, p. 45. Cf. also *The Latin Texts of the Welsh Laws*, pp. 23, 122, 140, 258. If the murderer could not ensure the necessary payment, his land – given the agreement of his father, brother, cousins, second cousins, and his lord – could be yielded as blood-land to the relatives of the murdered.—*Llyfr Iorwerth*, p. 57.

[3] *The Laws of Hywel Dda*, pp. 33, 76, 118; *The Latin Texts of the Welsh Laws*, pp. 230, 387, 482.

date it must have been a traditional designation.[1] Towards the close of the same century Gerald of Wales, though perhaps exaggerating Welsh failings, conveys a related impression that partible inheritance, the basic idea in the concept of *tir gwelyog*, was no new phenomenon. Thus, *c.* 1190, he wrote: "This nation is, above all others, addicted to the digging up of boundary ditches, removing the limits, transgressing landmarks, and extending their territory by every possible means. So great is their disposition towards this common violence, that they scruple not to claim as their hereditary right those lands which are held under lease, or at will, on condition of planting, or by any other title, even although indemnity has been publicly secured on oath to the tenant by the lord proprietor of the soil. Hence arise suits and contentions, murders and conflagrations, and frequent fratricides, increased, perhaps, by the *ancient national custom of brothers dividing their property amongst each other* [my italics]."[2] Gerald's observations are in keeping with the distributional evidence that in independent North Wales *tir gwelyog* was often located on the best of cultivable lands.[3] In the face of all these pointers to an early beginning for the *gwely*, we must reject, albeit with much regret, the thesis advanced by the late Professor Jones Pierce, that this institution emerged only after a primary settlement by freemen on virgin land in the twelfth century.[4]

The lawbooks themselves point to the antiquity of *tir gwelyog*. Continued occupation of land over four generations, successively by the incomer (*gwr dyfod*), the patrimonial (*treftadog*), the third man, and the fourth man, would ensure that the latter became a proprietor, whose estate was of a higher standing than that of his predecessors.[5] Once rights of proprietorship (*priodolder*) had been thus acquired by

---

[1] *Llawysgrif Hendregadredd*, ed. J. Morris Jones and T. H. Parry Williams, Cardiff, 1933, pp. 163–6; Richards, 'Early Welsh Territorial Suffixes', pp. 206–7.

[2] Giraldus Cambrensis, *The Itinerary through Wales: the Description of Wales*, ed. W. Ll. Williams, London, 1908, pp. 193, 203; *Giraldi Cambrensis Opera*, VI, pp. 211–12, 225.

[3] G. R. J. Jones in *Geography as Human Ecology*, ed. S. R. Eyre and G. R. J. Jones, London, 1966, pp. 214–21; id., 'The Distribution of Bond Settlements in North-West Wales', WHR II, 1964, pp. 22–8.

[4] T. Jones Pierce, 'Medieval Settlement in Anglesey', *Anglesey Antiq. Soc.*, 1951, pp. 7–9, 30–3; id., 'Agrarian Aspects of the Tribal System in Medieval Wales', *Géographie et Histoire Agraires, Annales de l'est*, Mémoire No. 21, Nancy, 1959, pp. 333–5; id., in *Agrarian History of England and Wales* IV, pp. 364–5. Cf. G. R. J. Jones, 'The Distribution of Medieval Settlement in Anglesey', *Anglesey Antiq. Soc.*, 1955, pp. 53–7; id., 'The Tribal System in Wales: A Re-assessment', pp. 122–8; id., 'Professor T. Jones Pierce – An Appreciation', *Caernarvon Hist. Soc.*, 1965, pp. 9–19; D. Jenkins, 'A Lawyer looks at Welsh Land Law', pp. 220–1, 244–7.

[5] *Llyfr Iorwerth*, p. 50; *Llyfr Colan*, p. 30.

the fourth man, subsequent abandonment, for reasons such as absence, did not extinguish these rights until nine further generations had elapsed. During the course of the nine generations a descendant of the last proprietor to have possession of the land could return to claim his right. If no one else had ascended, over four generations of continued occupation, to be a proprietor on the same land, the descendant would have all the land, for a non-proprietor had to yield to a proprietor. But, over a period of prolonged absence, continued occupation of the same land for four generations by the descendants of a second incomer could have created rights of proprietorship for them as well. If this happened the returning descendant could, according to the Book of Iorwerth, raise an outcry to which the law listened. He could then be allotted a share equal to that of the sitting proprietors; such a share obviously would be bigger if he returned in the eighth genera-tion rather than as the "ninth man." There are several passages in the lawbooks which suggest that, in practice by the thirteenth century, the exercise of this right had become limited. The outcry was known as *dyaspat uuch Annuuen*, a phrase tentatively interpreted as "a cry louder than that of the Underworld," but whose very obscurity is in itself a pointer to the antiquity, possibly the remote antiquity, of *tir gwelyog*.[1] In themselves, the contents of these rules imply that a procedure for overcoming problems associated with land settlement had been established for a period of at least thirteen generations, say 300 to 400 years. If, as most authorities agree, Hywel *Dda* (the Good) earned his unique qualification more by re-stating the existing custom of the tenth century than by enacting new legislation, then the obscurely designated outcry procedure was probably a part of that re-statement. In this event, some settlement on land which in due course became *tir gwelyog* must go back at least to the seventh century. Hints of a double *dominium* of the kind which could have arisen under the rules of *priodolder* have been detected by Mr C. E. Stevens in Roman Britain. This raised issues of such importance that recourse was made to the emperor's court in what was likely to have been a test case involving the well-to-do. A general principle contained in an enactment in the Theodosian Code addressed to the Vicar of Britain could have been pleaded in a conflict between Roman and Celtic law which arose, at least in parts of Britain, from such double *dominium*.[2]

[1] *Llyfr Iorwerth*, pp. 55–7, 120. Among the causes for prolonged absence as recorded in a later text were detention as a hostage, absence in another country, and *galanas.—Ancient Laws and Institutes of Wales*, II, pp. 76–7.

[2] C. E. Stevens, 'A Possible Conflict of Laws in Roman Britain', JRS XXXVII, 1947, pp. 132–4; id., in *Rural Settlement in Roman Britain*, ed. C. Thomas, 1966, pp. 108–11.

The parallels between Irish and Welsh institutions suggest that, with the withdrawal of the Roman legions, a resurgence of Celtic tradition occurred in Wales. Hints of an old Celtic customary law are provided by some similarities in the methods adopted in both countries for making a claim upon the land. Under the archaic Irish procedure known as *tellach* a claimant wrongfully deprived of his share could make three 'entries' on land at fixed intervals, on each successive occasion bringing with him an increased number of witnesses and a larger amount of stock. At the third entry they remained on the land overnight and the claimant kindled fire. Then, if the occupier still refused to submit to arbitration, ownership was vested in the claimant.[1] The Welsh lawbooks, on the other hand, describe an action for recovery of patrimony known as *dadannudd*, a name whose very meaning of 'uncovering' conveys a picture of the claimant uncovering the fire of his father's hearth. The three things which preserved a memory of land and homestead, standing in the status of witnesses and thus permitting the hearth to be uncovered, were a fire-back stone, the stones of a kiln, and a mounting stone. All this strongly suggests an archaic and pre-curial origin, for it is reasonable to suppose that at first the claimant actually made his claim by occupying a hearth and kindling a fire. He remained on the land for a period determined by the extent of his claim. If the claimant asserted that his father had occupied the land by tilling and ploughing it, he could stay until after harvesting and stacking the crop; if he claimed that his father had occupied the land by having a wagon and other furniture on it, he could stay there for five days without opposition; and if he asserted that his father had occupied the land by carrying a burden thither and lighting a fire, he could stay there for three days. Under *dadannudd*, which in origin was a possessory action, the successful claimant gained possession of the land but after the period prescribed had elapsed he might have to answer another claimant, presumably in an action based on the latter's hereditary right. This action, known as *ach ac edryf*, meant literally maternity and paternity but it depended on proof of hereditary right in the male line, and preferably over four generations.[2] Appropriately, *tir gwelyog* tenure on the estate of the bishop of St David's at Llanddewibrefi (Card) was known in 1326 as holding "by the ancient tenure, that is by *Ach* and *Edrid*," a statement which provides further evidence for the early origin of the *gwely*.[3]

---

[1] M. Dillon and N. K. Chadwick, *The Celtic Realms*, London, 1967, p. 105.

[2] *Llyfr Blegywryd*, pp. 71–3; *The Laws of Hywel Dda*, pp. 75–6, 134; *Llyfr Colan*, pp. 34–5, 145; *The Latin Texts of the Welsh Laws*, pp. 130–1; *Ancient Laws and Institutes of Wales*, II, pp. 522–3; Jenkins, *op. cit.*, pp. 228–30.

[3] *The Black Book of St Davids*, pp. 200–1.

Alike in Ireland and in Wales the four-generation group was of particular importance in social organization. From a wider orbit, moreover, there are parallels between this group in Irish and Welsh law and, for example, the Hindu *sapinda*, a family group of four generations. All three systems, the Irish, the Hindu, and the Welsh, permitted succession to family property in 'ideal' shares, without recourse to actual division. Such parallels and many others, unlikely to be explained away by polygenesis, could have developed from a common and therefore very ancient *corpus* of custom.[1]

In Wales recourse would be made to ideal shares of land for a variety of reasons, including resistance on the part of a lineage to royal encroachments. Frequently however the reason why heirs should decide not to make a physical division of their inheritance is likely to have been based on the consideration that the inheritance was not worth dividing. This is probably the reason for the joint holdings of freemen recorded during the early fourteenth century in Ceinmeirch, a commote flanking the fertile Vale of Clwyd, where the greater part of the land was held by bondmen.[2]

The use of the word *rhandir* (shareland) in the oldest extant text of the Laws in the twelfth century implies that physical division is likely to have been practised by that date and probably long before. Hence the notional scheme recorded in the thirteenth-century texts of the Book of Iorwerth whereby progressively smaller divisions of the *twnc* pound in lieu of the freemen's *gwestfa* were imposed on progressively smaller subdivisions of the *maenol* until ultimately a farthing was imposed on every *erw* ('acre'). Thus we learn that there are successively: four 'acres' in – or as stated elsewhere in the same text – by a homestead (*tyddyn*); four homesteads and thus sixteen 'acres' in a shareland (*rhandir*); four sharelands (sixty-four 'acres') in a holding (*gafael*); and four holdings (256 'acres') in a township. Elsewhere, in that section of the Book of Iorwerth which deals with partible inheritance, we are told that Bleddyn ap Cynfyn changed the allocation from four 'acres' per homestead to twelve in the case of

---

[1] D. A. Binchy, 'The Linguistic and Historical Value of the Irish Law Tracts', *B. Acad.* XXIX, 1943, pp. 199–200, 214–16, 222; id., 'Linguistic and Legal Archaisms in the Celtic Law-Books', *Philological Soc.*, 1959, pp. 23–4; id., *Celtic and Anglo-Saxon Kingship*, Oxford, 1970, pp. 7 sqq.; id., in *Early Irish Society*, ed. M. Dillon, Dublin, 1954, pp. 52–65; Dillon and Chadwick, *op. cit.*, pp. 10–12.

[2] G. R. J. Jones, 'The Llanynys Quillets: A Measure of Landscape Transformation in North Wales', *Denbighshire Hist. Soc.* XIII, 1964, pp. 146–8; D. H. Owen, *The Lordship of Denbigh, 1282–1425*, unpublished Ph.D. thesis, University of Wales, 1967, p. 14; *Survey of Denbigh*, pp. 1–50; thus for example all the 25 members of the free progeny of Owain Goch held "everywhere" (*ubique*) some 870 statute acres of "land, wood, and waste" in four townships and one hamlet.

a notable (*mab uchelwr*), eight in the case of one kind of bondman (*mab aillt*), and four in the case of the lesser bondman (*godaeog*). Nevertheless we are informed "it is most usual that four *erwau* is the *tyddyn*."[1] These statements probably mean that Bleddyn attempted to modify the assessments imposed on holdings; if this is true, the original assessments, attributed in one text to Hywel Dda, date back at least to the close of our period, for Bleddyn died in 1075.

The whole scheme in the Book of Iorwerth appears to be artificial. Nevertheless it may reflect, at least in a broad sense, actual conditions in North Wales. Thus the Survey of Denbigh, the most detailed of all the post-conquest extents, records that an escheat *erw* in Prys, a township inhabited by the descendants of notables, was assessed for *twnc* at ½d., whereas an *erw* in Hendregyda, a township inhabited by freemen of less distinguished lineage, was assessed for *twnc* at ¼d. Moreover there were in Denbighland some large townships assessed at exactly 240d. and also smaller townships assessed at 60d.[2] Again, along the eastern border there were townships assessed at exactly 60d.[3] Since one lawbook draws a distinction between land used for agriculture and that used for building, it is possible that in these cases the land used for building, though assessed under the Iorwerth scheme, was not liable for payment; thus from every 64d. there would be an exemption of 4d., representing sixteen *erwau*, the notional equivalent of four homesteads, in the sense of buildings.[4] There is, however, some evidence to show that the Iorwerth scheme was applied literally; thus there was one large free kindred in Denbighland holding five whole townships and a fractional share of three others which was assessed at exactly 256d.[5] These examples of course may well represent nothing more than deliberate rearrangements of renders so that these came to accord with the notional ideas of the lawyers; nevertheless to make such rearrangements practicable the schematic constructs of the lawyers cannot have been too far divorced from actual conditions on the ground.

A similar impression is conveyed by the available survey evidence for the *erw*. In the Book of Iorwerth this was 480 Welsh feet (360

---

[1] *Llyfr Iorwerth*, pp. 53, 60; *Llyfr Colan*, p. 39.

[2] *Survey of Denbigh*, pp. lx–lxiii, pp. 96, 102, 234, 245. In the time of the Welsh princes the township of Prys was assessed for *twnc* at 240d. and ½d., the ½d. being for the escheat *erw* mentioned above.

[3] Thus for example in the Lordship of Oswestry four townships out of the ten recorded in an extent of 1393 paid a *twnc* render of 5s. each. See W. J. Slack, *The Lordship of Oswestry, 1393–1607*, Shrewsbury, 1951, pp. 30–5.

[4] *Llyfr Blegywryd*, p. 71.

[5] That is 4 × 64d.; *Survey of Denbigh*, pp. 157, 162–71, 182; cf. however the statement in *The Laws of Hywel Dda*, p. 84, that the chief of a kindred paid the king a pound every year. See also *Llyfr Blegywryd*, p. 83.

statute feet) long by 48 Welsh feet (36 statute feet) broad, so that it contained only 1,440 square yards statute measure.[1] A *tyddyn* in the township of Cegidog contained 3½ roods; by the local measure of the survey, this was 5,373 square yards, an area which is only slightly less than the 5,760 square yards of the legal homestead of four 'acres'. Another entry in the same survey refers to a *tyddyn* which it defines as a messuage with one local acre, that is 6,141 square yards, an area which is only slightly in excess of the legal homestead of four 'acres'.[2]

We may therefore accept the *erw* of the Book of Iorwerth as an actual, and not only an ideal, unit of measure. Accordingly the shareland which was deemed under the Venedotian scheme to contain sixteen 'acres' covered slightly less than five statute acres. This shareland possibly consisted of arable land only, for one Iorwerth text refers to "four acres of tillage in a homestead," but even so the notional area of the shareland is small.[3] A later thirteenth-century revision of the Book of Iorwerth, known as *Llyfr Colan* (the Book of Colan), records that there were four holdings, each of sixteen 'acres', in a shareland, and that it was the latter which contained sixty-four 'acres', that is about nineteen statute acres.[4] Clearly therefore the word shareland might be used in a variety of ways. It could designate an area in which a number of people held a share, or alternatively be used of an individual's share of land within an area which could be small or large.

The lawbooks which reflect conditions in South Wales present a somewhat different picture. The Book of Cyfnerth records that "there are to be four sharelands in the township from which the king's *gwestfa* shall be paid;" and in the shareland (*rhandir*) 312 'acres' "between clear and brake, wood and field, and wet and dry." Since the *erw* in this lawbook was only 243 statute feet long by 27 feet wide this acre contained only 729 square yards, so that the whole shareland contained only 47 statute acres. The Book of Blegywryd records that "there are to be 312 acres in the lawful shareland so that the owner (*perchen*) may have in the 300 acres arable, pasture, and fuel wood, and space for building on the 12 acres." Since the *erw* in this lawbook was only 192 statute feet long and 24 feet broad, it contained but 512 square yards and the shareland as a whole only 33 statute acres.[5]

    [1] *Llyfr Colan*, pp. 10, 69; *Llyfr Iorwerth*, pp. 59–60; T. Jones Pierce, 'A Note on Ancient Welsh Measurements of Land', AC XCVII, 1943, pp. 195–204; C. A. Gresham, 'A Further Note on Ancient Welsh Measurements of Land', AC CI, 1951, pp. 118–22.
    [2] *Survey of Denbigh*, pp. 121, 226.
    [3] *The Chirk Codex*, p. 65, a lacuna filled from BM Add. MS. 14,931.
    [4] *Llyfr Colan*, pp. 39, 161.
    [5] *Welsh Medieval Law*, pp. 54, 204–5; *The Laws of Hywel Dda*, p. 75; *Llyfr Blegywryd*, p. 71.

The oldest Latin text refers to the *rhandir* as the component of the *maenor* whereas other texts and lawbooks describe the *maenor* or *maenol* as consisting of townships.[1] The implication may well be that lawyers therefore envisaged the patrimony as consisting of a wide area, even a *maenor*, which on transmission to heirs could be subdivided into shares of land each consisting of one or more townships. A wider patrimony of this kind is implied by Chad 3 and 4 which, taken together, suggest that Rhys and the kindred of Grethi exercised rights over a wide area from which Trefwyddog could be donated to the Church. Likewise, in Domesday Gwent, Berddig, the king's poet, held no less than three townships, once part of a wider *maenor*. Three other townships, apparently once part of this same *maenor*, were held by individuals in 1086 but, significantly, only one appears to have been shared internally, that held by the sons of Wasuuic. The use of multiples of four in the assessment of Ballingham in Archenfield may reflect a similar internal subdivision in keeping with the kind of schematic subdivision of the township recorded in the Book of Iorwerth. But though first recorded in a lawbook of the thirteenth century, the actual internal partitions of land which prompted lawyers to devise this notional scheme may have taken place before 1086, as the Ballingham example suggests, albeit probably infrequently, if at all, before the introduction of the farthing. Ballingham however is perhaps atypical for it occupies a fertile lowland site on the south-eastern border of Wales.

Away from the border and especially in poorer districts an internal subdivision of townships resulting from the partible inheritance of patrimonies is likely to have occurred at a later date. Internal division bringing about the emergence of a number of *gwelyau*, in the sense of holdings, within the compass of a single township, appears to have become widespread only after about 1150. Earlier subdivision was almost certainly postponed by the Norman onslaught, to say nothing of the victories of Earl Harold which, it was claimed though no doubt with exaggeration, had left scarcely a man alive in Wales so that women had to beg permission of the king to marry Englishmen. Subsequently, as Gerald of Wales reports, the population increased and it was probably this resumed growth which resulted in the phenomenon, noted by the late Professor Jones Pierce, that the eponyms of a great many *gwelyau* were individuals who lived after 1150.[2]

---

[1] *The Latin Texts of the Welsh Laws*, pp. 135, 239; *The Laws of Hywel Dda*, p. 75; *Llyfr Blegywryd*, p. 71; Rees, *op. cit.*, p. 231.

[2] Lloyd, *op. cit.*, pp. 371–2; *The History of Gruffydd ap Cynan*, p. 125; H. C. Darby and I. B. Terrett, *The Domesday Geography of Midland England*, Cambridge, 1954, pp. 54, 95–8, 142–6; *Giraldi Cambrensis Opera*, VI, pp. 217–18; T. Jones Pierce, 'Agrarian Aspects of the Tribal System in Wales', pp. 333–5.

Largely for this reason Jones Pierce argued that the *gwely*, which he termed a 'clanland', emerged only after this date. This late origin for the *gwely*, even in the restricted sense of holding, appears to be unfounded. Nevertheless we have to explain the puzzling feature which commanded the attention of Jones Pierce, namely why it was that the unity of many a *gwely* named in the twelfth century was maintained thereafter without its subdivision into new *gwelyau*. For there can be no question that the names of twelfth-century eponyms continued to be used for designating such 'clanlands' over the succeeding centuries.[1] In the light of the evidence already deployed this cannot be explained on the basis that the holdings which came to be known as *gwelyau* were necessarily new. On the contrary, the most likely explanation is that in earlier centuries the precursor of the *gwely* as a holding, however designated, would have embraced a number of townships and, even in the late eleventh century, at least one township; hence the scale envisaged for a claim of *dadannudd*. This, as we have seen, was an action of archaic origin, yet it is stipulated, albeit in a fifteenth-century text, that the custodian of the land and the claimant were to have the support of the land-borderers from those sharelands of the townships of notables whose boundaries met the boundary of the *tref* wherein the dispute occurred. Appropriately therefore it was assumed that a claimant could acquire through *dadannudd* not only a *rhandir* but possibly a *tref* or even a *maenol*.[2] This no doubt is the reason why the tenure with which we are here concerned was known, even in surveys of the fourteenth century when much fragmentation of holdings had already taken place, as *tref welyog* (*gwely* township) rather than *tir gwelyog* (*gwely* land).[3] The former conveys an impression of a larger area and also carries with it the implication that each township was part of a larger territorial unit. When this larger unit, co-extensive with one or more townships, was subdivided under the continued operation of partible succession, the

[1] A point first emphasized by T. P. Ellis in *Welsh Tribal Law and Custom in the Middle Ages*, I, p. 156, where he refuted Seebohm's erroneous views that the *gwely* was a family group under a common ancestor embracing kindred as far as great-grandchildren, and that this group automatically generated new *gwelyau* on the death of its head (Seebohm, *op. cit.*, 1904, pp. 28 sqq.; id., *Tribal Custom in Anglo-Saxon Law*, London, 1911, pp. 21–30).

[2] *Ancient Laws and Institutes of Wales*, II, pp. 112–13, 738–41. One plaint of kin and descent cited there concerned the lands of a notable in Maenor Llanddeusant (Carm). These lands amounted to 1,000 *erwau* of furrow land, by the measure of the rod of Hywel Dda; and 1,000 *erwau* of wild land, woodland, hayland, and pasture land by the measure of the same rod.—*ibid.*, pp. 450–5.

[3] As Sir Goronwy Edwards emphasized at the Second Colloquium on Welsh Medieval Law, at Gregynog in 1966, the term used in the extents of the fourteenth century was *treweloghe*, i.e. *tref welyog*. Cf. Jenkins, *op. cit.*, p. 235.

name of each incoming heir, usually a patronymic, was applied to the new subdivision or *gwely*. But, given that unusual increase in population which Gerald reports in his time, there were obvious limits to this process, lest the proliferation of new *gwelyau* bearing new names should become unmanageable within the relatively small area of the typical township. Thus the identity of the last new 'clanlands' to emerge, usually in the twelfth century, was normally preserved thereafter. In many instances, it is true, the term *gafael* was used for a subdivision of the *gwely* in the succeeding generation or sometimes generations, but even in these cases there was usually a conservatism in nomenclature which helped to preserve an awareness of the unity of the *gafael*.

Despite the perpetuation of *gwely* or *gafael* names, the custom of partible inheritance remained in force, so that the inheritance of a typical clansman came to be much smaller than that of his forebears. Under these conditions relatively small arable sharelands became the characteristic internal units within the *gwely* or the *gafael*. With growing pressure of population there was probably an enhanced demand for an equiponderance of rights, not only as previously in terms of approximate area, but increasingly in terms of land quality, especially where scarce resources of arable land and meadow were concerned. Thus land was now inherited not in compact blocks but rather in long narrow parcels scattered through a number of sharelands.[1] As an investigation of many townships including Hendregyda (Den) and Llysdulas (Ang) has shown, most heirs displayed a shrewd awareness of the superior quality of the arable land adjoining the primary settlement, the *hendref* (old settlement). This, no doubt reinforced by links of sentiment, led most heirs to retain a share here, at least in early partitions. In the outlying sharelands, on the other hand, a conscious effort seems to have been made to forestall the incidence of fragmentation by permitting the participation of only a few lineages (*gwelygorddau*). Given the delayed incidence of fragmentation in the outlying sharelands, it became convenient for many an heir to establish his home there, away from the old settlement. To economize on good arable land, such homesteads were often sited on the outer edges of the arable sharelands, thus giving rise to girdle patterns of dispersed dwellings.[2] There was therefore much truth in the report on the

[1] As is clearly indicated for example at Abergele (Den) in 1334 (*Survey of Denbigh*, pp. 253–8). Cf. also Jones Pierce in *Agrarian History of England and Wales* IV, pp. 360–1.
[2] G. R. J. Jones, 'Some Medieval Rural Settlements in North Wales', *Institute of British Geographers*, 1953, pp. 62–4; id., 'The Distribution of Medieval Settlement in Anglesey', *op. cit.*, p. 33; id., 'Medieval open fields and associated settlement patterns in North-West Wales', *Géographie et Histoire Agraires, Annales de l'est*, Mémoire No. 21, 1959, pp. 316–17; id., *Geography as Human Ecology*, pp. 203–11.

Welsh made by Archbishop Peckham to Edward I: that "They do not live together but far from each other" (*Il ne habitent pas en semble, eins meint chescun loinz de autre*). Hence, too, the statement in later law-texts that every habitation ought to have a footpath to its church, another to its watering place, and a bye-road to the common waste of the township.[1]

Before 1042 the fragmentation of land is likely to have arisen infrequently, save among sub-tenants. Occasional plagues and recurrent warfare between the minor kingdoms of Wales are likely to have hindered growth of population. The partible succession to the minor kingdoms of Wales, coupled with the practice of entrusting royal children to the care of notables, led often to strife and even fratricide which must have hindered the growth alike of royal and noble families. Under these circumstances we may suppose that the territorial possessions of leading families were literally precarious.[2] Thus only rarely would they have matured, over the period of four generations stipulated under the rules of *priodolder*, into appropriated land (*tir priod*). Moreover there is evidence to suggest that the endowment of an individual with land, which in propitious circumstances would mature into *tir priod*, was frequently an act of conscious royal policy. The lawbooks reveal that the officers who served the ruler's court held their land free, and appropriately therefore the surveys compiled after 1282 show that many a *gwely* was in origin the holding of a royal official or even servant. Such was the case in the commote of Malltraeth, where the ancient court of Aberffraw had long been located. Tref Walchmai, a constituent hamlet of the ancient multiple estate of Dindryfol, was named after Gwalchmai, the noted court poet who flourished at the close of the twelfth century. Tref Walchmai contained three *gwelyau* named after three of the poet's sons, and one of these units, Gwely Meilir ap Walchmai, embraced part of Trefwastrodion (the *Tref* of the Grooms). In the same locality near Aberffraw was Trefddisteiniaid (the *Tref* of the Stewards) which contained, among others, Gwely *Wyrion* Einion ap Walchmai, named not directly after a son of Gwalchmai but rather after the son's descendants. Further afield, however, at Lledwigan Llys near the commote border, there was a *gwely* named after this same son of Gwalchmai, inhabited it would appear only by freemen. The link with Aberffraw implied by the wide-ranging endowments of Gwalchmai or his descendants, and

---

[1] *Registrum Epistolarum Fratris Johannis Peckham*, ed. C. T. Martin, Rolls ser. 77, 1885, III, p. 776; *Ancient Laws and Institutes of Wales*, II, pp. 270–1.

[2] Binchy, *Celtic and Anglo-Saxon Kingship*, pp. 24 sqq. Cf. D. A. Binchy, 'Some Celtic Legal Terms', *Celtica* III, 1956, pp. 225–6; E. John, *Land Tenure in Early England*, Leicester, 1960, pp. 48–58.

by the names of the townships near the court, is further emphasized by the obligations of the heirs of Gwely Meilir ap Walchmai in Trefwastrodion. Like the heirs of five of the six free *gwelyau* in the township, they were responsible for roofing the hall and chamber of the Prince's manor at Aberffraw, whereas the heirs of the remaining free *gwely*, a small unit known as the *Gwely* of the Falconers, did not owe this building service. Appropriately enough, at Aberffraw itself was a *Gwely* Porthorion (the *Gwely* of the Gatekeepers), whose heirs were responsible for constructing and repairing that part of the wall enclosing the court buildings which was on either side of the gate.[1] Genealogists have often demonstrated that the eponyms of the major *gwelygorddau* (clans) of Wales were the kinsmen of kings. Confirmation is provided by the Book of Cyfnerth, which records that a royal offspring who was neither a successor to the throne nor a head of a kindred could take land and assume the status of a notable (*uchelwr*), in which event "however bond his land may be, it becomes as free as the land of an *uchelwr*."[2] At the opening of our period it is possible that such donations of land, whether to kinsmen or officials, were in some sense precarious and were tenable by heirs only at the king's pleasure, or for such time as the recipients continued to perform their courtly duties. If so, this would have been another factor militating against the development of endowments into estates in proprietorship (*priodolder*) and thus in due course into *gwelyau*.

These considerations are of importance not only for the genesis of free estates but also in the development of bond settlement; hence the single bond *gwely* in Trefwastrodion whose heirs, besides paying heavier rents than the heirs of the free *gwelyau*, were also responsible for building services at Aberffraw. The Book of Iorwerth shows that aliens, literally 'other-countrymen' (*alltudion*), could become proprietors in the fourth generation after they had been settled on the king's waste. Similarly the aliens of notables became proprietors "in the fourth man" if they occupied the same land under them "for so long a time." Such aliens of the king, or of the notables, then became tied to the soil (*adscripti glebae*) in bondage. After becoming proprietors they were to have homesteads with adjoining land, and also arable land known as "land of plough-share and coulter."[3] This latter rule meant that aliens, after becoming bondmen, were to inherit homesteads and share arable land in the same way as freemen. In other words, they held *tir gwelyog* (hereditary land), for, as these rules indicate, an estate

[1] *Record of Caernarvon*, pp. 44–50.
[2] A. W. Wade-Evans, 'Peniarth MS. 37', *Y Cymmrodor* xvii, 1904, pp. 138–54; cf. *The Laws of Hywel Dda*, p. 26; *Ancient Laws and Institutes of Wales*, ii, pp. 608–9.
[3] *Llyfr Iorwerth*, pp. 58–9.

in *priodolder* could exist in land of different tenures. Other texts, including the oldest, reveal that not only the king and the notables but even bondmen could have bond under-tenants of alien origin. The Book of Iorwerth reveals that, just as the king exercised lordship (*arglwyddiaeth*) over his aliens, so the notables, by the thirteenth century at least, were to exercise lordship over their own aliens.[1] If such aliens were to depart from their lords before becoming proprietors they were to leave half their goods to these lords. On the other hand, if the notable expelled his aliens against their will before they became proprietors he was not entitled to any of their goods. A later text reveals that, besides the kind of outcry which we have already considered in relation to *priodolder* on free land, there could be two others: one was the very human cry of a wife for her husband; the second, of importance here, the cry of a notable for his aliens when they leave without doing right by him.[2] This suggests that the rules for the settlement of aliens as tenants of the king, or as under-tenants of the notables, were old-established. Supporting testimony is provided for the mid-ninth century by Chad 5 which, as we have seen, shows that a family stock of bondmen could be owned and manumitted by a family stock of notables.

'TIR CYFRIF' (RECKONED LAND)

The second great customary tenure in early Wales was *tir cyfrif* (reckoned land), which was also the most important of the early bond tenures. The primary name of the tenure appears to have been *tir cyllidus* (geldable land), a name which emphasizes the liability of bondmen for the rendering of dues; for *tir cyfrif*, as this tenure came to be known, was the tenure obviously appropriate to villeins. In Wales the villein (*bilaen*, or *mab aillt*, or *taeog*) was in essence the man without pedigree. Although he was bound to the soil, his rights in reckoned land were not heritable at all. Thus according to the Book of Iorwerth: "*Tir cyllidus*, however, it is not right to share according to brothers, but it is right for reeve and chancellor to share it and give to everyone in the township as good as to each other and on that account it is called *tir cyfrif*."[3] Occasionally in the lawbooks, and invariably in the

---

[1] *The Latin Texts of the Welsh Laws*, p. 140; *Llyfr Colan*, pp. 38, 158, suggests that the notable could hold a court on behalf of his aliens, an interpretation which, in the case of the descendants of Ednyfed Fychan, seneschal of Llywelyn the Great, was confirmed after the Edwardian Conquest by proceedings *Quo Warranto.—Record of Caernarvon*, pp. 150–1, 167–9.

[2] W. Wotton, *Leges Wallicae*, London, 1730, p. 318, cited by D. Jenkins in *Llyfr Colan*, p. 147.

[3] *Llyfr Iorwerth*, p. 54; *Llyfr Colan*, p. 36.

surveys, the expression used to designate this tenure was *tref gyfrif*. As we have seen in the case of *tref welyog*, this suggests that the bond township, like the free township, was part of a wider unit. *Tref gyfrif* (reckoned township) moreover is a very appropriate name for a township in which land was re-shared after a counting of adult male heads. This apparently took place when one of the bondmen in the township died or when any, save the youngest, of a bondman's sons came of age at fourteen years. Thus, according to case law: "One son who need not await his father's death for his father's land is the son of a man from *tref gyfrif*, since the father shares his acre with him no more than the furthest man in the township." On the other hand, "law sees that it is proper for the youngest son to await the death of his father, since he sits in his place according to entitlement."[1] Despite the re-sharing which therefore took place in the bond township, a limited right to a particular house plot appears to have been recognized; thus: "It is right to maintain every man of a *tref gyfrif* in his homestead (*tyddyn*) if it can be done without exiling another." The central feature of this tenure was that the right to share in the land of a township did not depend on inheritance. Thus in those thirteenth-century law-books which reflect Venedotian conditions we learn that although hereditary land (*tir gwelyog*) could revert to the lord as escheat there could be no escheat 'acre' (*erw*) in reckoned land. If however an escheat acre should lie within reckoned land then the reeve and chancellor should share it equally "in common" (*yn gyffredin*) among all. This rule thus gives a hint, amply confirmed in other sections of the laws and other sources, that arable land lay in open field.[2]

Tir cyfrif (reckoned land) and *tref gyfrif* (reckoned township) are named as such only in the lawbooks which relate particularly to North Wales. Moreover the lawbooks nowhere specifically identify *tref gyfrif* with the bond township. Nevertheless, as the obligations imposed on bondmen show, it is clearly this reckoned township which is taken for granted in the notional scheme of the *maenol* in North Wales, and in the account of the *maenor* in South Wales. The progresses of dogs and horses, and the *dofraeth* (quarters) which were imposed on the bond *maenol* of the Venedotian scheme, are specifically stated in a late text to be imposed on the reckoned township.[3] The summer foodgift of the bondmen, as recorded alike in the Book of Cyfnerth and the Book of Iorwerth, included, as we have seen, cheese made

[1] *Ancient Laws and Institutes of Wales*, II, pp. 64–5; Jenkins, 'A Lawyer looks at Welsh Land Law', pp. 235–6.

[2] *Llyfr Iorwerth*, p. 54; *Llyfr Colan*, p. 36.

[3] *Llyfr Iorwerth*, pp. 61–2; *Ancient Laws and Institutes of Wales*, II, pp. 48–9, 690–1. Cf. *The Laws of Hywel Dda*, p. 57.

from a pooling of the yield from one milking of all the milk animals in the bond township. But the Latin texts make it clear that cheese was not the only joint obligation of the bondmen. From them we learn that the other renders of the bond township (*villa rusticana*), or *rhandir* as it is sometimes called, were a communal obligation whether the tenants were few or many (*vel unus vel plures*).[1] The same kind of joint liability is said to be "of the nature of reckoned township" (*de natura de trefgevery*) in the Record of Caernarvon in 1352, whereas the heir on hereditary land by this date paid only for his own lands. An entry relating to Maerdref in Aberffraw is more explicit, for it records that this hamlet was "of such a nature that if there were only one tenant he would be charged with the whole rent."[2] It was no doubt in keeping with these arrangements that some of the Latin texts of the laws, including the oldest, refer to a *pastor communis ville*, a neatherd of the common township.[3] The late medieval surveys reveal that, by the thirteenth century, the kind of servitude associated with reckoned-land tenure had disappeared from the greater part of Wales and survived on a significant scale only in Gwynedd. Even here it was by no means the most characteristic bond tenure, for townships held by bondmen on conditions similar to those enjoyed by freemen on hereditary land easily outnumbered the reckoned townships. A fifteenth-century law-text, though late in date, provides a possible explanation. In this it is stated that Hywel Dda permitted every notable to hold his land according to its status and to rule his bondmen according to conditional bondage in South Wales and perpetual bondage in North Wales; and that the king's villeins are to be regulated according to the status and law of the bond township in which they dwell. These conditions need not necessarily be ascribed to the tenth century, but, as we have seen, conditional bondage could have arisen at a similarly early date under the rules whereby exiles were allowed to settle on the land of a king or notable.[4]

---

[1] *The Latin Texts of the Welsh Laws*, pp. 36, 204.   [2] *Record of Caernarvon*, p. 49.
[3] *The Latin Texts of the Welsh Laws*, pp. 124, 216; *The Laws of Hywel Dda*, p. 50; *Llyfr Blegywryd*, p. 39.
[4] *Ancient Laws and Institutes of Wales*, II, pp. 364–5; T. Jones Pierce, 'Medieval Cardiganshire: A Study in Social Origins', *Ceredigion*, 1959, pp. 8–10, 13–15, 17–18. This earlier development of conditional bondage under notables in South Wales may well be the explanation for one of the regional contrasts noted by Gerald of Wales. Thus South Wales was the least desirable part of the country "from the number of noble chiefs, or *Uchelwyr*, men of superior rank, who inhabited it, and were often rebellious to their lords, and impatient of control."—*The Description of Wales*, p. 157; *Giraldi Cambrensis Opera*, VI, p. 166. It may also help to explain why the free *gwelyau* of South Wales were territorially much more circumscribed and less widely ramifying than those of North Wales. See also G. R. J. Jones, 'The Defences of Gwynedd in the Thirteenth Century', *Caernarvon Hist. Soc.*, 1969, pp. 38–41.

These, or similar rules, came to be applied also to reckoned townships held by the king or the Church; for the late medieval surveys show that in the townships of Gest and Pentyrch in Eifionnydd (Caern) bondmen had been allowed to establish *gwelyau* though continuing to hold by *tir cyfrif* tenure.[1] On Church land in Bryngwyn (Flint) bondmen, on payment of increased rents, had been permitted to ascend the social scale even further so as to attain the same conditions as the "proprietors and co-heirs" (*proprietarii et coheredes*) of a free *gwely*.[2] The recorded progressions are always from reckoned-land tenure to hereditary-land tenure and never from the latter to the former. In the later medieval surveys bondmen are occasionally reported as having claimed that they were of the nature of *tref welyog* (hereditary township) rather than of the nature of *tref gyfrif* (reckoned township). Since they were fined for these false claims, it is clear that, in the eyes of officials and tenants alike, *tref gyfrif* was the more servile and – we may note – probably the more ancient of these two bond tenures.[3] Since proprietorship (*priodolder*) could be acquired on land subject to conditional, as distinct from perpetual, bondage it is possible that the outcry procedure already described could have applied to land which, before it became *tref welyog*, was originally of the nature of *tref gyfrif*. That such was the case is suggested by the inheritance customs of the commotal Norman lordship of Coety in the intermediate zone between the low plateau and the upland plateau of Morgannwg. Here copyholds descended to the youngest child, males before females of the same degree, to the ninth degree of kin, after which they escheated to the lord.[4] Despite the nine-generation rule, this was probably not hereditary-land tenure, for under this the land escheated to the lord where there were no heirs within the third degree of kin.[5] Inheritance by the youngest child suggests a modification of reckoned-land tenure whereby the youngest son inherited his father's homestead and share of land in the township. Presumably this custom was fossilized by the superimposition of Norman authority in the early twelfth century

---

[1] Jones, 'The Tribal System in Wales: A Re-assessment', pp. 125–7.

[2] National Library of Wales: Wigfair MS. 8, first cited by Seebohm in *The Tribal System in Wales*, 1895, p. 126, Appendix E.

[3] *Record of Caernarvon*, p. 35.

[4] G. T. Clark, 'Manorial Particulars of the Vale of Glamorgan', AC 4th series, IX, 1878. Cf. however the evidence of *Grith Gablach*, an Irish law-text of the early eighth century. This reveals that a *fuidir* (tenant-at-will) whose ancestors had been settled on a lord's land for nine generations was reduced to the level of a *sen chleithe* (hereditary serf or villein); and he and his descendants became *adscripti glebae*, henceforth unable to renounce their tenancy.—*Crith Gablach*, ed. D. A. Binchy, Dublin, 1941, pp. 13, 93.

[5] *Survey of Denbigh*, pp. 47, 150, 313.

over what came to be known as Coety Anglia. Given the nine-generation rule there is therefore good reason for believing that bond settlement had been effected on the low plateau of Coety at the latest by the eighth century. Nor was this an isolated instance, for inheritance by the youngest son was characteristic of the copyhold and servile tenures within the Englishries of manors in the lowlands of Glamorgan, including Llantwit Major, the site of a celebrated Celtic *clas*, and Newton Nottage.[1] On the other hand, in the Welshries, the areas which remained subject to Welsh tenure, no trace of this custom has been discovered. Instead the universal custom of inheritance among the copyholders appears to have been equal division among the sons and sometimes among the daughters as well. Presumably therefore perpetual bondage had been displaced by conditional bondage on the generally less fertile Welshry lands either before or after the Norman conquest; for it is highly probable that both Welshries and Englishries had once been subject to perpetual bondage. Thus 'boardland', the literal translation of *tir bwrdd*, the term applied to the Welsh king's mensal land at his court, was used of the demesnes in the commote of Meisgyn in the Rhondda valley; similarly 'boardland' has been recorded at Newton Nottage on the coast of Glamorgan.[2] But, in any case, this inference is justified for another part of South Wales on the basis of the evidence of Chad 3 and Chad 4. By showing that the render of Trefwyddog, so resembling the bondmen's foodgift, was a township liability, these entries confirm that *tref gyfrif* tenure was already in existence by the mid-ninth century.

There is also indirect evidence to suggest that *tref gyfrif* tenure was much older than this. The many parallels between the territorial organization of Durham and Wales in the twelfth century, buttressed as these are by some identities in terminology, suggest that *maenor* organization was already a feature of British polity before the overland links between Wales and the North were gradually severed during the course of the seventh century.[3] In this event the reckoned township

[1] H. J. Randall, *The Vale of Glamorgan: Studies in Landscape and History*, Newport, 1961, pp. 64–5, 90–4. This custom of inheritance by the youngest son or, if there were no son, by the youngest daughter, persisted at Nolton until 1521 (*Cartae et Alia Munimenta*, VI, ed. G. T. Clark, Cardiff, 1910, pp. 2,395–6). At Bishopston in Gower, which was allegedly granted to Llandaf in the seventh century, this custom still obtained on customary lands in 1673 (*Surveys of Gower and Kilvey*, ed. C. Baker and G. G. Francis, London, 1870, pp. 151–4; *Liber Landavensis*, pp. 145, 369). At Rohan in central Brittany the youngest son inherited to the exclusion of other sons and daughters.—Coutume de Rohan cited by A. de Courson in the introduction to the *Cartulaire de l'Abbaye de Redon*, Paris, 1863, p. cclxxxviii.

[2] Randall, *op. cit.*, p. 64; Rees, *op. cit.*, p. 139.

[3] J. E. A. Jolliffe, 'Northumbrian Institutions', EHR XLI, 1926, pp. 1–42. Jones, 'Rural Settlement: Wales', p. 342; G. R. J. Jones, 'Basic Patterns of Settlement

of Wales was already in being before the seventh century, for its strictly communal obligations are matched by those of the villein hamlets in twelfth-century Northumbria.

In a Latin text of the mid-thirteenth century giving prominence to Venedotian matters the phrase *id est trefgord* is given as a gloss on the phrase *pastor communis ville*.[1] This word *trefgord* appears to have meant a hamlet, with a communal organization which affected many aspects of life. From occasional references we learn of the bath-hut in which water was heated for special ablutions, a surprisingly civilized provision in the lowliest settlements envisaged in the laws and possibly representing a heritage of Rome. The same was perhaps true of the hamlet kiln for drying corn, a facility very necessary in a moist western climate. Since the bath-hut, like the kiln, was tiled and, in order to prevent the spread of fire, was placed at least seven fathoms from the nearest houses, the *trefgordd* was presumably a nucleated settlement consisting of closely juxtaposed dwellings. Incidental hints of this kind in thirteenth-century law-texts and occasional references in late thirteenth-century surveys to hamlets, each occupied by nine or so tenants, suggest that the complement of the legal *trefgordd*, as given in a fifteenth-century text, was founded on fact. This complement was: nine houses, one plough, one kiln, one churn, one cat, one cock, one bull, and, appropriately, one neatherd.[2] Thus the laws convey a clear impression of small co-operative groups of tenants housed in hamlets. Their scarcity in modern Wales is no argument that they were merely the constructs of a lawyer's imagination. As later records reveal, many hamlets disappeared when their bond inhabitants fled during the later medieval period, whereas the better sited examples which prospered have been buried by subsequent village growth, as at Aberffraw, or by urban development, as at Denbigh. It would be rash however to claim that the *trefgordd* was invariably a nucleated settlement. An adaptation of settlement forms to suit local circumstances is a charac-teristic feature of the Welsh landscape, and there is evidence to suggest that some bond settlements consisted of girdles of homesteads or even of dispersed dwellings. Certainly such dispositions appear to have been characteristic of the single farmsteads, known as 'enclosed homesteads', to be found in north-west Wales, where they are attributed to the Romano-British period.[3]

Distribution in northern England', *Advancement of Science* XVII, 1961, pp. 192–200; id., 'Early Territorial Organization in England and Wales', *Geografiska Annaler* XLIII, 1961, pp. 174–81; Rees in *Angles and Britons*, pp. 159–68.

[1] Redaction B of *The Latin Texts of the Welsh Laws*, pp. 172, 216.

[2] *Ibid.*, p. 123; *Llyfr Iorwerth*, p. 81; *Ancient Laws and Institutes of Wales*, II, pp. 576–7; Jones, 'The Tribal System in Wales: A Re-assessment', pp. 120–1.

[3] Jones, 'Early Settlement in Arfon', pp. 11–13.

'TIR CORDDLAN' (NUCLEAL LAND)

In the lawbooks there are a few references to suggest that a number of other tenures were recognized. Little is known of these apart from the tenure designated in the Book of Iorwerth as *tir corddlan, tir corflan,* or *tir corthlan,* and in the Book of Colan as *tir gorflan.*[1] These variations in nomenclature imply that the name, if not the attributes, of this tenure had become obscure by the thirteenth century. It is reasonable therefore to postulate that *tir corddlan* was an ancient tenure, an assessment which is in accord alike with its inherent nature and with the evidence for its characteristic settings.

According to the Book of Iorwerth, *tir corddlan* was not to be shared as 'homesteads' (*tyddynod*), here probably meaning home crofts or enclosures. Instead it was to be shared as 'gardens' (*gerddi*), a term which in this context probably means 'strips' or quillets rather than simply gardens as in modern Welsh.[2] On *tir gwelyog* (hereditary land), as on *tir cyfrif* (reckoned land), the youngest son inherited his father's homestead. If however there were buildings on *tir corddlan* the youngest son was no more entitled to them than the eldest, but they were to be shared as *ystefyll* (cells or rooms). Immediately after this statement about the inheritance of *tir corddlan* we are told that "no one is to retain gardens (*gerddi*) for more than one year in his possession, on account of having manured them; for they are to be manured every year." There then follow statements, also found in other lawbooks, about what appear to be leases for rent in the form of cultivation or manuring. For different kinds of land different durations of cultivation are stipulated. In the Book of Iorwerth we are told, of fallow land (*brynar*), that "two years it is to be ploughed;" land where stock lie without folding, two years; wild land, two years; land manured by folding, three years; land manured with carted dung, four years; wood-land, four years; manured fallow, four years. The Book of Cyfnerth gives some supplementary information. Thus the man who manures land by folding is to have it for two years with the owner's permission, but in the third year it reverts freely to the owner; likewise, whoever manures land with carted dung is to have it for three years, but in the fourth it reverts to the owner.[3] This supplementary information suggests that for each kind of land the period stipulated was deemed to be the desirable maximum duration of cultivation

---

[1] *Llyfr Iorwerth*, pp. 44, 58; *Llyfr Colan*, pp. 38, 155–6.

[2] A. N. Palmer, *A History of Ancient Tenures of Land in the Marches of North Wales,* Wrexham, 1885, p. 8.

[3] *Llyfr Iorwerth*, pp. 44, 48; *Llyfr Colan*, pp. 38, 155–6; *The Latin Texts of the Welsh Laws,* p. 230; *Welsh Medieval Law,* pp. 62, 211.

before fallowing or manuring was repeated. The periods stipulated vary slightly in different texts, but the overall impression created by these statements is that there already existed in medieval Wales a developed awareness of the differing potentials of different kinds of land. The lands manured with, or without, folds were the equivalent of the Irish or Scottish outfields which were cultivated at intervals. To judge from late medieval and post-medieval surveys, such land in Wales included 'mountain land' (*terra montana* or *wilde grounde*) used at long intervals for the cultivation of oats or rye after paring and burning the sod.[1] Correspondingly, *tir corddlan*, consisting of gardens cultivated year in and year out, constituted the Welsh equivalent of the regularly manured and cultivated *infield* recorded centuries later in many an Irish or Scottish hamlet.[2] As such, *tir corddlan* can perhaps be best described as nucleal land.

The lawbooks do not specify the occupants of *tir corddlan*, but presumably they were under-tenants. They could have descended from serving slaves; for, as we are told in later case-law, one kind of voluntary slave could be "in the house of an *uchelwr*, at spade and fork," and presumably therefore adequately equipped for the cultivation of a garden.[3] The worth of such a slave was twice that of a purchased slave (*caeth*). Nevertheless if a voluntary slave came to the house of an *uchelwr*, accepted land from him, held a house, and paid *twnc* and *gwestfa* to his lord, he attained the worth of an alien tenant (*alltud*). It would appear, therefore, that the occupants of *tir corddlan* were cottagers like the dependants of English manors who had no peasant holding but got a scrap of land from the lord, technically a garden, for which they did service.[4] Appropriately, therefore, at the nucleated settlement which contained the *maerdref* of Aberffraw, there were, in the late thirteenth century, no less than fourteen gardens, some apparently adjoining the court. Similarly, in the ancient *maerdref* of Ystrad in the Vale of Clwyd there were bond cottages with crofts, including *due crofte incluse circa manerium*.[5]

This impression, that *tir corddlan* was to be found at the more important ancient settlements which served as focal points for the

[1] National Library of Wales: Peniarth MS. 231B; Wynnstay MS. 1279; B. E. Howells, 'Pembrokeshire Farming *circa* 1580–1620', *National Library of Wales Jnl* IX, 1956, p. 325.

[2] H. L. Gray, *English Field Systems*, London, 1959, pp. 157–71, 187–94.

[3] *Ancient Laws and Institutes of Wales*, II, pp. 82–3; on the other hand there could be domestic slaves who "went not to spade nor quern." – *ibid.*, pp. 118–19. Cf. also *The Latin Texts of the Welsh Laws*, pp. 139, 220.

[4] N. Neilson in *The Cambridge Economic History of Europe* I, 1st edn., ed. J. H. Clapham and E. Power, Cambridge, 1941, p. 390.

[5] *Record of Caernarvon*, pp. 70–2; *Survey of Denbigh*, p. 2.

community, is reinforced by another statement in the oldest text of the Book of Iorwerth which appears to deal with this kind of tenure. This reveals that "the measure of a *corflan* is a legal *erw* in length with its end to the *mynwent*; and that circling the *mynwent*, its compass." In one Welsh text of the thirteenth century *mynwent* is used of the burial place but in other, earlier and later, texts the graveyard is designated by *corfflan*, meaning literally 'corpse enclosure'. A fifteenth-century text distinguishes between these two words in a reference to a *mynwent corfflan*, a phrase which suggests that the *mynwent*, whose dimension is given as "a legal *erw*...in compass," lay within the *corfflan*.[1] Similarly the Book of Iorwerth, in giving the measure of a *corflan*, implies that it was outside the *mynwent*. It is likely, therefore, as Mr Dafydd Jenkins has suggested, that *corflan* was the primary form, with *corf* meaning some kind of boundary or defence and the suffix *llan* referring to the area within.[2] In other words, *corflan* was originally an enclosed piece of ground which in some cases incorporated, even if it did not literally encircle, a graveyard, hence the confusion with *corfflan*. The alternative form *corddlan* might have arisen from the circumstance that such an enclosure could be held by a *cordd*, a group, of kinsmen. On the other hand, since *cordd* could have referred to any kind of group, *corddlan* could have meant an enclosure used for cattle, hence its development into *corlan* meaning a fold for stock. *Tir corddlan* was presumably land within, or possibly without, such an enclosure. Since gardens of *tir corddlan*, the land most regularly manured, are likely to have been those nearest the settlement, where a church graveyard was often located, the confusion with *corfflan* is understandable. The Book of Iorwerth portrays the very kind of circumstances under which these various meanings could have become confused. The measure of a *corflan* is given in a section of this lawbook dealing with church land (*tir llan*) and the right of sanctuary. The church envisaged in this context is one belonging to a *clas*, a clerical community of canons under an abbot or bishop-abbot. Thus: "Whoever shall take protection is to walk about within the *mynwent and* the *corfflan* without relics upon him; and his cattle are to be with the cattle of the *clas* and the abbots to the furthest limits they go..."[3] Before the Book of Iorwerth had been compiled, Gerald had a similar situation in mind when he wrote of the Welsh: "We observe that they show a greater

[1] *Llyfr Iorwerth*, p. 44; *The Chirk Codex*, ed. J. Gwenogfryn Evans, 1921, p. 51; *The Black Book of Chirk*, p. 60; *Welsh Medieval Law*, p. 51; *Llyfr Blegywryd*, pp. 35, 43, 74; *The Laws of Hywel Dda*, pp. 48, 54, 77; *Ancient Laws and Institutes of Wales*, II, pp. 360–1.
[2] *Llyfr Colan*, p. 156; T. P. Ellis, 'The Catholic Church in the Welsh Laws', *Y Cymmrodor* XLII, 1931, p. 20.
[3] *Llyfr Iorwerth*, p. 44; *The Chirk Codex*, p. 51; *The Black Book of Chirk*, p. 60.

respect than other nations to churches and ecclesiastical persons, to the relics of saints, bells, holy books, and the cross, which they devoutly revere; and hence their churches enjoy more than common tranquillity. For peace is not only preserved towards all animals feeding in church-yards, but at a great distance beyond them, where certain boundaries and ditches have been appointed by bishops, in order to maintain the security of the sanctuary. But the principal churches to which antiquity has annexed the greater reverence extend their protection to the herds as far as they can go to feed in the morning and return at night."[1] Such no doubt were included among "some Welsh churches, with the settlements and graveyards" (*Walensium ecclesias aliquot, cum villis et coemeteriis*) in Powys which, according to Gerald, the English had burnt, to the intense resentment of the Welsh, during an expedition by Henry II. But revered though they might be, these *clas* churches incurred the criticism of Gerald when he wrote: "Their churches have almost as many persons and sharers as there are principal men in the parish. The sons, after the decease of their fathers, succeed to the ecclesiastical benefices, not by election, but by hereditary right possessing and polluting the sanctuary of God."[2] The hereditary occupants of these benefices, sometimes known as abbots, had under-tenants holding *tir gwelyog*, as for example at Gwytherin (Den).[3]

This is precisely the state of affairs which prevailed at Llanynys in the Vale of Clwyd (Fig. 45), an example which merits our detailed consideration, not only for this reason but also because around it there have survived down to the present day some traces of *tir corddlan*, as well as *tir gwelyog*.[4] Llanynys occupies a well-drained site, standing up a little above the floor of the Vale of Clwyd. It was the focal

[1] *The Description of Wales*, p. 186; *Giraldi Cambrensis Opera*, VI, p. 203. Cf. the church estate of Lamphey (Pem) in 1326; here, apparently around the bishop's court, there was one carucate (about 80 acres) of highly valued arable sanctuary land, part of which was held by cottagers, part by bovate holders, and part by the lord.—*The Black Book of St Davids*, ed. J. Willis-Bund, 1902, pp. xiv, 168–95.

[2] *The Itinerary through Wales: the Description of Wales*, pp. 135, 195; *Giraldi Cambrensis Opera*, VI, pp. 43, 214.

[3] *Survey of Denbigh*, pp. 187–92; G. R. J. Jones, 'Die Entwicklung der ländlichen Besiedlung in Wales', *Zeitschrift für Agrargeschichte und Agrarsoziologie* X, 1962, pp. 189–91. If church land (*tir eglwys*) were occupied successively over four generations by the great-grandfather, the grandfather, the father, and the fourth man, the latter – being in possession and paying his *twnc* and *ebediw* (heriot or death-fee) to the abbot, without disturbance such as burning the houses of a rival claimant or killing enemies – became an inheritor of that land. But here, as on secular land, a successful "cry louder than that of the underworld" could modify this progression.—*Ancient Laws and Institutes of Wales*, II, pp. 76–7.

[4] For the later agrarian history of this parish see G. R. J. Jones, 'The Llanynys Quillets', pp. 133–58.

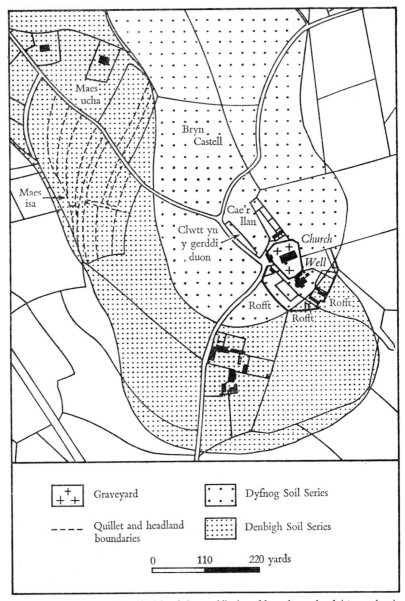

Fig. 45. The setting of nucleal land (*tir corddlan*) and hereditary land (*tir gwelyog*) at Llanynys, Denbighshire.

III. Air-photograph of Llanynys showing traces of nucleal land and quillets of former hereditary land (Ministry of Defence [Air Force Department] Photograph, Crown Copyright Reserved).

point of a large parish extending from the vale to the hills to the south-west. Since the name Ysgeibion, meaning "the territory of the bishop" was applied to one township at the south-western limit of this area it is likely that the *clas* territory was originally coterminous with the parish.[1] Despite the severance of parts of this territory, including Ysgeibion, Llanynys church remained one of the richest in North Wales. A papal mandate of 1402 reveals that the substantial revenues of Llanynys, which for a time had exceeded a hundred marks, were anciently divided into twenty-four portions called *'claswriaethe'*, instituted for the maintenance of twenty-four perpetual portionaries called *abad a chlaswyr* (abbot and *clas* men).[2] To one of these, commonly called the portion of David the priest, was assigned the cure of the souls of the parishioners. Some, if not all, of these portions can be identified with lands held, a century or so earlier, of free inheritance (*de libera hereditate*) in Llanynys and in Gyffylliog, an upland township some four or five miles to the south-west. They included the half carucate of land and two messuages held by David, *decanus de Lannanys*, and Gronw his brother. These two, with three other prominent freemen and the community of the vill (*communitas ville de Lannanys*) also held land in various moors, including that of Trefechan a mile or so to the north.[3]

Trefechan, as its name of 'small *tref*' would suggest, was a subsidiary settlement within Llanynys township, and in later centuries there were numerous holdings "in free tenure by *gavelkind*" containing scattered parcels of land in both Llanynys and Trefechan.[4] The settlements at both places occupied well-drained sandy loams – of the Dyfnog Series – but the soils of the intervening area, though well drained, are slightly heavier silty clay loams – of the Denbigh Series – and were therefore relatively less attractive of early settlement.[5] Here in

---

[1] M. Richards, 'Sgeibion, Llanynys', *Denbigh Hist. Soc.* IX, 1960, p. 187.

[2] W. E. Lunt, *The Valuation of Norwich*, Oxford, 1926, p. 194; *Taxatio Ecclesiastica* p. 294; *Calendar of Papal Letters*, IV, 1902, p. 349; G. Williams, *The Welsh Church from Conquest to Reformation*, Cardiff, 1962, pp. 17–18, 158, 168. The medieval wall-painting of St Christopher recently discovered on the north wall inside the church is attributed to the period 1400–30. Despite the deterioration in the value of the living of Llanynys by this period the painting was executed by an artist of the first rank and the halo around the Christ Child's head was originally covered with gold leaf.—E. Baker, 'A Medieval Painting in Llanynys Church', AC cxviii, 1969, pp. 135–8; L. Parry Jones, *Llanynys Church Past and Present*, 2nd ed., 1969, pp. 26–7.

[3] PRO Wales 15/8; also printed in R. I. Jack, 'The Lordship of Dyffryn Clwyd in 1324', *Denbigh Hist. Soc.* xvii, 1968, pp. 8–53.

[4] National Library of Wales: Lordship of Ruthin MS. 1,593; N.L.W. MS. 86; LR 2/239.

[5] D. F. Ball, *The District around Rhyl and Denbigh*, Memoirs of the Soil Survey of Great Britain, 1960, pp. 39–45. I am particularly indebted to Mr D. F. Ball of the

the fifteenth century were some of the 'lands' lying in the open fields of Llanynys (*seliones in campis de Llanenys*). These, in part at least, were sharelands including hereditary land (*tir gwelyog*) said to lie on either side of the highway from Llanynys to Trefechan.[1] In the same area, on both sides of the road, which even today is little wider than the twelve Welsh feet stipulated for the king's highway in the laws, there survived until 1970–1 a number of quillets in intermingled ownership. Although lying within two enclosures named Maes isa and Maes ucha these quillets were bounded only by turf balks. In general these balks, or "skirts" as the lawbooks described them, were of the width specified in the laws. The quillets themselves differed considerably in size but within the enclosure known as Maes isa there were in 1841 no less that fifteen quillets, one with a headland (*talar*) attached, and since Maes isa contained 8 acres 1 rood 27 perches the average quillet measured 2,716 square yards.[2] These parts of the hereditary lands of Llanynys appear to have come into permanent cultivation as a result of an expansion from more anciently cultivated areas. The latter were the well-drained sandy loams within the girdle of homesteads at Trefechan and the similar loams which encompassed the very small nucleated settlement around the church at Llanynys, which was undoubtedly the primary settlement within the township.

The walled graveyard where the church is located contains about three-quarters of an acre and is itself placed within the northern half of what appears to have once been a larger and roughly circular walled enclosure containing about two acres. In the early nineteenth century these two acres contained the vicarage with its outbuildings and garden, a well, a former smithy, a stable for the use of the parishioners, some glebe land, and also some parcels owned by laymen, including an "old pasture." This larger enclosure was perhaps the original *corflan*, but if so it had come to be flanked on the outside by what appears to have been *tir corddlan*. Among the parcels of scattered glebeland recorded for Llanynys from the seventeenth century onwards was one running north-westwards from the graveyard and disposed in exactly the same way as that implied in the Book of Iorwerth for the legal 'acres' (*erwau*) in a *corflan*. It had its inner narrow end almost abutting on the track flanking the graveyard wall and had earlier clearly been one of a group of radial gardens. Hence its name, Clwtt

Nature Conservancy and Mr E. Roberts of the Ministry of Agriculture for their comments on the soils of the area; and to the Head of the Soil Survey of England and Wales for permission to incorporate some unpublished findings of the Soil Survey in Fig. 45.   [1] SC 2/222/4.

[2] *Welsh Medieval Law*, pp. 55, 210; National Library of Wales: Tithe Apportionment and Map, Llanynys, 1841. Unfortunately most of these quillets of former *tir gwelyog* were ploughed out in 1970–1.

yn y gerddi duon (Piece in the black gardens), which is especially
appropriate, for constant manuring and cultivation has long since
darkened its naturally reddish-brown sandy-loam soil. That there had
once been other radial gardens abutting on to the same track which
flanked the graveyard is revealed by the name of the enclosure
immediately to the east of this piece of glebe land. Although now
known as Cae'r llan (Enclosure of the church), this was formerly
called Gerddi duon (Black gardens). The radial disposition not only
of the Piece but also of two cottage gardens on the eastern boundary
of Cae'r llan suggests that these other black gardens were also disposed
radially in relation to the graveyard wall. Moreover, since each of
the three large fields butting on to the eastern and southern sides of
the larger vicarage enclosure bore the name Rofft (Croft) it is likely
that these also had once contained radial gardens.[1]

The dimensions of the surviving Piece in the black gardens are
especially significant. Some 225 feet long by about 36 feet wide, this
parcel of glebe was only slightly shorter and slightly broader than
the legal 'acre' (erw) in the Book of Cyfnerth. The radius of the
circular vicarage enclosure was of the same length, so that here it was
the corfflan rather than the mynwent (graveyard) within it, as suggested
by the fifteenth-century text, which had a compass of a legal erw.

The northern limit of the enclosure called Gerddi duon is marked
by a sunken roadway which is presumably ancient. Immediately to
the north of this roadway, within the field named Bryn Castell, there
were, in earlier centuries, two other parcels of glebe land. One apparently
parallel to the roadway, and thus roughly at right angles to "the
black gardens" in Cae'r llan, was known as Gardd llidiard y bengam
(Garden at the gate of the crooked head). In itself this name suggests
that access to such gardens was by means of gateways, perhaps through
fences. From this garden at the gate a second parcel of glebe extended
northwards about "119 yards to a stone in the ground within the said
Bryn Castell." Known as Cefn ym mryn y Castell (Ridge or butt in
Castle hill), it was clearly the last of a group of such unenclosed
parcels to have survived consolidation. These Castle hill parcels were
probably first established with the extension of cultivation away from
the older nucleus around the larger circular enclosure of Llanynys.
It was perhaps for this reason that the Ridge in Castle hill was longer
than the Piece in the black gardens; though when recorded in the
glebe terriers only about 10 feet wide, it was 357 feet long and thus

[1] Llanynys Glebe Terriers for 1671, 1697, 1749, 1808, 1811; I am particularly
indebted to the Rev. L. Parry Jones, of Llanynys, and Mrs I. Rogers Jones, formerly
of Plas Llanynys, for facilitating access to these documents, which are still kept in the
parish chest.

only 3 feet shorter than the legal *erw* in the Book of Iorwerth. The surviving quillets in Maes isa were probably the outcome of a still later transition from temporary outfield cultivation to the permanent cropping of a *tir gwelyog* shareland, and here appropriately many of the quillets were of an even greater length.

There is abundant evidence, therefore, to suggest that the land immediately outside the circular enclosure of Llanynys was *tir corddlan*. The three curtilages which were said to be held by a prominent portionary in 1324 were probably the gardens of this freeman's under-tenants within the *tir corddlan*. The messuage of this freeman was probably close at hand, while those of David the deacon and his brother were probably, like the later vicarage, within the larger circular enclosure. In other words, Llanynys proper was then a small nucleated settlement. The name Bryn Castell suggests that at the summit of the hill, where the church stood within this enclosure, there was originally some kind of circular fortification, hence perhaps the ancient obligation on the parishioners to repair the churchyard wall.[1] The typical *clas* was, as Sir John Lloyd suggested, originally a monastic community, so that here, as at Nendrum, it is likely that the various buildings of the community stood within the larger circular enclosure.[2] If, as Rhigyfarch

---

[1] *Mynwent* (graveyard) was derived from *monumenta*; cf. R. E. Latham, *The Revised Medieval Latin Word List*, London, 1965, p. 308, s.v. 1. *munimen*, 'enclosure 6C', '*munimentum arcis*' c. A.D. 793, *burhbote*. The freemen of Rhufoniog Is Aled owed building services which involved the erection and maintenance of a fence around the court of the secular lord but, significantly, the *priodorion* of the *clas* of Nantglyn Sanctorum (Den) were exempt from this obligation.—*Survey of Denbigh*, pp. 94–6, 149.

[2] Cf. Lloyd, *op. cit.*, I, pp. 204–5, 208–9. See also E. R. Norman and J. K. St Joseph, *The Development of Early Irish Society: The Evidence of Aerial Photography*, Cambridge, 1969, pp. 97–8. At Nendrum (Co. Down) an early monastic community was established within the concentric enclosures of a pre-Christian cashel. The twelfth-century church, presumably on the site of the original Christian oratory, was located in the central enclosure. At Kiltiernan (Co. Galway), another early monastery, a circular dry-stone wall, eight to eleven feet thick, encloses an area of four acres. In a roughly square enclosed plot in the centre was a monastic cemetery, later the site of a pre-Romanesque church. The area between this enclosed plot and the encompassing wall was divided by walls into some fifteen *radial* sectors (*ibid.*, pp. 102–3). At the early monastery of Clonard (Co. Meath) the site of the original enclosure is suggested by a circle of trees, banks, and ditches within which the present church and farm buildings are located. Around this nucleus there are faint traces of a large outer enclosing ditch of slightly irregular shape. Outside this outer enclosing ditch there are numerous access ways, square enclosures, and disturbed ground – perhaps marking the site of huts (*ibid.*, pp. 113–14). At a site near Rathangan (Co. Kildare) early field boundaries of irregularly looped and roughly rectangular shapes *radiate* outwards like the petals of a flower from a large rath (*ibid.*, pp. 64–5). I am indebted to Professor A. C. Thomas for information about recent aerial surveys which show that field-encumbered enclosures *around* smaller monastic enclosures of *llan* type – as at Clonard – occur much more frequently in Ireland than hitherto appreciated.

suggests in his Life of St David, Welsh monks tilled with hand and foot, and hauled the plough in place of oxen, gardens of *tir corddlan* would have provided an appropriate setting for their ascetic endeavours.[1] But whatever the merits of these necessarily tentative suggestions, it is highly probable that Llanynys itself was an old-established *clas* to which antiquity had added reverence.

Similar traces of *tir corddlan* have survived elsewhere near important churches, as for example around St Elaeth, the church of the vast parish of Amlwch in Anglesey. In South Wales a radial arrangement partly of gardens and partly of glebe land survived into the nineteenth century around Llanfilo (Bre), an ancient Welsh foundation dedicated to Belyau, one of the legendary daughters of Brychan, and subsequently, as Professor Finberg has shown, to Mildburg, Mercian abbess of Much Wenlock, after she had acquired a property in this part of Brycheiniog in the late seventh century.[2]

THE OVERALL PATTERN OF LAND USE

That *tref welyog* and *tref gyfrif* were characteristic tenures within the territorial frameworks of *cantref* and *maenol* is implied by their township attributions. The same appears to have been true of *tir corddlan* even when this was associated with *clas* churches rather than royal courts. Thus the *clas* of Clynnog Fawr, which figures in the Privileges of Arfon, was in the southern part of the *cantref* of Arfon. The *clas*, and later diocesan seat of Bangor, in the northern part of the same *cantref* where it marched with Arllechwedd, was itself the *caput* of a *maenol*. Again, the territorial endowment of the *clas* church dedicated to St Cadfan at Towyn (Mer) was known as Maenol Gadfan. The *maenor* of Meddyfnych, as its inclusion in the *marginalia* of the Book of St Chad would suggest, no doubt served a similar purpose in relation to either Llandybïe or the ancient *clas* of Llandeilo Fawr (Carm).

In keeping with such dispositions, the compilers of the lawbooks could assert that "no land is to be without a king," whether abbey land held by laymen, or bishop land, or hospice land.[3] Hywel Dda no doubt had strengthened these royal claims through the medium of his codification, but, if Gildas is to be believed, his countrymen in the sixth century were ruled by kings whose forebears had clearly been impressed by the majesty of Roman justice. Resting their authority

[1] Lloyd, *op. cit.*, pp. 155–6.
[2] National Library of Wales: Tithe Apportionment and Map, Llanfilo, 1841; the "*Lanch Milien wallice dicitur*" of BM Add. MS. 34,633 cited by H. P. R. Finberg in *Lucerna*, London, 1964, pp. 70, 74–5.
[3] *The Laws of Hywel Dda*, p. 99; *Llyfr Iorwerth*, pp. 54–5.

on military force, these kings were not only donors to the Church but also appear to have tried and imprisoned criminals in their courts as part of the ordinary business of kingship.[1] Thus, although the lawbooks reflect a royal standpoint, it may not be entirely inappropriate to employ the only pointers to overall land use which we have, namely those which, however notional, the lawbooks alone provide.

According to the Book of Cyfnerth there are four sharelands in the free *tref* from which the *gwestfa* is paid; of these, three are for "occupancy and the fourth pasturage for the three sharelands." In similar vein we are told: "There are three sharelands in the bond township; in each of the two there are three bondmen, and the third pasturage for the two." The impression thus conveyed that there was more pasture within the bond township than in the typical free township may well reflect the true state of affairs, for, unlike the bondman or alien on hereditary land, the bondman on *tir cyfrif* (reckoned land) was not to exercise rights over land in more than one township.[2]

An affectation of even greater precision is conveyed by the Book of Iorwerth, which gives the 'acre' (*erw*) content not only of homestead, holding, shareland, and township, but successively also of the *maenol*, the commote, and the *cantref*. The latter, we are informed, contained 25,000 'acres' (*erwau*), "neither more nor less," that is, in statute measure, 7,617 acres. But the total area of the *cantref* of Arfon, which extended south-eastwards from the Menai Strait to include the highest summit in Snowdonia, was over 110,000 acres; and even in Anglesey each of the three hundreds contained on average some 58,000 acres. The *erw* assessment probably referred only to the arable land, but even with this qualification the discrepancy between the assessed area and the total area is very marked, especially for fertile lowlands like those of Anglesey. Yet Gerald's description of Anglesey in the twelfth century as the granary of Wales is no mere rhetoric, for it is confirmed by the substantial contribution made by Anglesey, as compared with other parts of North Wales, to the Norwich taxation half a century

---

[1] Gildas, *De Excidio Britanniae*, pp. 20–5; Binchy, *Celtic and Anglo-Saxon Kingship*, pp. 20–4. Thus, according to the Welsh lawbooks, Hywel Dda received one-third of the *galanas* or compensation for homicide. In Archenfield at Domesday "If so be that a Welshman shall kill a Welshman, the relatives (*parentes*) of the slain meet together, and plunder the slayer and his kin, and burn their houses until on the morrow at about noon the corpse of the dead man is buried. Of this plunder the king has the third part, but they have all the rest without interference"—DB I, 179a. According to *Crith Gablach*, in Ireland during the early eighth century when a base client was slain his lord was entitled to one-third of the *eraic* (wergild) received by the deceased's kin.—*Crith Gablach*, p. 86.

[2] *Welsh Medieval Law*, pp. 54, 108, 204–5; *Ancient Laws and Institutes of Wales*, II, pp. 690–1.

or so later.[1] Thus we can safely postulate a considerable enlargement of the cultivated area of Anglesey after the initial imposition of the *erw* assessment. Originally in kind, this assessment was probably one of long standing and possibly antedated Bede's favourable comparison of Anglesey with the Isle of Man.

Much of the expansion seems to have been achieved by means of temporary outfield cultivation. In a statement made in the Book of Cyfnerth concerning evidence about a dead person's title to land, a distinction is drawn between the *erwau* ('acres') and the furrows of the land ploughed. The former almost certainly represent continuous cultivation, the latter temporary cultivation. Even in Anglesey this was practised as late as the thirteenth century in the most productive corner of the island. The arable resources of the "best lands" in the ancient *maerdref* of Llanfaes were supplemented by those of the so-called "mountain land" (*terra montana*) on nearby hills which attained a height of just over 300 feet. Similarly during the fourteenth century the occupants of both free and bond *gwelyau* in the Lordship of Denbigh appear to have practised a considerable amount of temporary cultivation on lands exceeding 400 feet in altitude. This is the reason why in the two free *gwelyau* of Hendregyda no less than 70 per cent of the lord's escheat was rented out in 1334 as what was described as arable land. Such a surprisingly high proportion of arable can only be explained in terms of the temporary cultivation of much of this escheat land, and thus of the *gwelyau* of which the escheat was a fractional share. Similarly in Meifod, a township where two of the three *gwelyau* were bond, nearly 50 per cent of the lord's escheat was arable, but, as later records show, much of this land would bear crops for only two or three years out of every ten or twelve. Such land could be valued at as little as 4d. per local acre, whereas in the neighbouring township of Dinorben for example the few acres of land which could be sown every year were valued at 19d. per acre.[2] The *erwau* in regular cultivation, as distinct from land cultivated only at long intervals, covered only a small part of the typical Welsh township, so that it was feasible for the English victors after 1283 to transfer whole *gwelygorddau* from one township to another.

Even Gerald, when he claimed that the greater part of Wales was laid down to pasturage, drew a distinction between the area cultivated and the smaller area which was sown. Temporary outfield cultivation was probably of such significance in the agrarian economy that it may well explain the emphasis placed on co-tillage in the lawbooks. In the

---

[1] *Llyfr Iorwerth*, p. 60; *Giraldi Cambrensis Opera*, VI, p. 127; Lunt, *op. cit.*, pp. 192–3, 195–6; Jones, 'The Distribution of Medieval Settlement in Anglesey', pp. 49–53.

[2] SC 11/767; *Survey of Denbigh*, pp. 27–33, 222–5, 230, 233–9, 278.

Book of Cyfnerth we are informed that "a bond township (*taeog-tref*) is not to begin ploughing until each bondman shall have obtained co-tillage."[1] At first sight it is puzzling that rules for co-tillage should have been laid down for bond townships where its practice appears to have been obligatory. After all, the lawbooks lay it down explicitly that the regulation of tillage in the *maerdref* was in the hands of the lesser reeve and in the *tir cyfrif* townships in the hands of the greater reeve. Rules, however, and the accompanying penalties to the king for breach of co-tillage, are likely to have been more necessary if outfield cultivation was practised in the more distant parts of a township.

Originally co-tillage among freemen was voluntary and, no doubt much less necessary, for many freemen, as in Domesday Archenfield, themselves owned one or more plough-teams. But among freemen contractual co-tillage developed as patrimonies became divided, fewer freemen remained possessed of whole plough-teams and, with increasing population, more outfield land was brought into cultivation. Hence the elaboration of the rules for co-tillage in the thirteenth-century texts of the Book of Iorwerth. Under these rules an ideal partnership of twelve men was envisaged: a ploughman and a caller contributed their labour, another the wooden plough frame, a fourth the coulter and plough-share, and the remaining eight an ox each to draw the plough. The ideal contract applied to twelve 'acres', that is one for each partner, and it is clear that the *erw* envisaged was that also used for the assessment of royal revenue or for the sharing of patrimonies. In the Book of Iorwerth this was the 'acre' of 36 feet in width by 360 feet in length.[2] Care was taken to regulate precisely the order and conditions of ploughing. In the oldest Latin text, which appears to refer to co-tillage in bond townships, the first acre was said to be that of the plough-share (*vomer*) but in the Book of Iorwerth the first *erw* was that of the ploughman so as to ensure the best possible standard of ploughing. Thus it was decreed that "should there be a dispute about bad ploughing, let the ploughman's acre be examined and the depth and the length and the breadth of this tilth, and according to that must everyone's be done." The ploughman was also a craftsman for it was decreed that no one was to undertake the work of ploughing unless he knew how to make a plough from "the first nail to the last." The second acre was that of the "irons," presumably so as to ensure that the plough-share and coulter retained their sharpness throughout the contract. The fifth *erw* was that of the caller, who brought with

[1] *Welsh Medieval Law*, pp. 57, 207–8.
[2] T. P. Ellis, *Welsh Tribal Law and Custom in the Middle Ages*, II, 1926, pp. 57–63; *Llyfr Iorwerth*, pp. 96–8; *Llyfr Colan*, pp. 10–12, 67–76; *The Latin Texts of the Welsh Laws*, p. 151.

him the actual yoking gear apart from the yoke-trees; he was to yoke the oxen carefully and to call them by chanting all the working morning in such a way "as not to break their hearts." The third and fourth 'acres' were respectively those of the owner of the outermost furrow ox and the owner of the outermost land ox, "lest the yoke be broken;" and the remainder belonged to the owners "from best to best" of the oxen. In other words yoke-fellows were carefully graded for age and strength, it being considered that the ox was in his prime as a six-year-old. If an ox should die in the yoke and the owner would swear that it was not his fault, he was permitted his 'acre' and that was known as the *erw* of the black ox. It is likely that the underlying principles were adaptable to all kinds of variations in the numbers of partners or oxen involved. Even the yoking could be line abreast or line ahead.[1]

Under some circumstances, as for example when a patch of outfield was cultivated for the first time, or when a *gwely* was still held jointly, the 'acres' might perhaps be allotted to the partners for the first time after the ploughing. Frequently, however, the rules for co-tillage appear to have applied to 'acres' already in the occupation of the partners. There is no warrant for the statement made by Seebohm and repeated by later writers that the 'acres' were allocated only after the ploughing.[2] This assumption, which is often invoked as a general explanation for the scattering of 'lands' in the open fields of England and elsewhere, appears to be unfounded. Had this been the case a defaulter who sold his ox before the co-tillage ended would merely have been deprived of his *erw*; but the rules envisage a situation in which the defaulter had "obtained his *erw*," which in this context probably means that his *erw* had already been cultivated. Under such circumstances the defaulter was obliged to "support the yoke," that is, provide a worthy substitute. Further confirmation of this interpretation is provided by the rules for settling disputes between two co-tillers, one having wild land to plough and his reluctant partner having land already under cultivation. Similar disputes were envisaged where one co-tiller had distant land and the other had only nearby land. A limit was however stipulated; this was that the oxen, both weak and strong, should be able to journey from their stalls to their work within the limits of the commote.[3]

[1] F. G. Payne, 'The Plough in Ancient Britain', *Arch. J.* CIV, 1947, pp. 82–111; id., in *Studies in Folk Life*, ed. G. Jenkins, London, 1969, pp. 236–42.

[2] F. Seebohm, *The English Village Community*, 1883, pp. 118–25, 191–3; C. S. and C. S. Orwin, *The Open Fields*, 2nd ed., 1954, pp. 5–12; E. Kerridge, *The Agricultural Revolution*, London, 1967, p. 157.

[3] *Llyfr Iorwerth*, p. 98; *Llyfr Colan*, pp. 10–11, 67–8. Cf. F. W. Maitland, *Domesday Book and Beyond*, Cambridge, 1897, p. 346.

The lawbooks mention three kinds of horse, the palfrey, the rouncy or packhorse, and a working horse, but the horse had no place in the plough-team. Nor had the mare or the cow, but if they were so used and as a result should miscarry no compensation was to be paid. The ox found the job of harrowing distressing and so this was a task performed by a horse. Carts were also drawn by horses, and dung was normally carried out in horse panniers. Indeed the attributes of a mare were defined as the ability to draw a cart uphill and downhill, to carry a burden, and to breed colts. There were black cattle, and also those described as white with red ears, now represented by the Dinefwr and other park cattle. If there was a dispute about the milk yield of a cow, she was to be taken on the ninth of May to a luxuriant place, wherein no animal had been before her, and milked by the owner, leaving none for the calf; and if her milk did not fill the measuring vessel twice a day the deficiency was to be compensated from then on until the calends of winter successively by oatmeal, by barleymeal and ryemeal. Animals, on being sold, were to be warranted against various diseases, horses against the staggers, the black strangles, and farcy; cows against "the three disorders" of cattle, and the mange; pigs against quinsey and devouring their young; and sheep against rot, redwater, and scab. The legal, meaning presumably the ideal, herd of swine was 12 animals and a boar; the legal flock of sheep 30 animals and a ram; the legal herd of cattle was 24 kine, and the legal stud 50 mares, but the bull and the stallion were mentioned separately. The worths of the goat, the tame fowl, the duck, and the goose were also specified. Especially important was the herd dog that went before the herd in the morning and followed the cattle home at night, a valiant protector against the wolves of the woodlands and not a penny inferior in legal worth to the best ox in the herd.[1]

A bizarre and probably ancient folk element in the laws is the definition of the *precium* of the cat in various texts, including the oldest; the unfortunate animal was to be held upside-down by its tail and corn poured over it until it was covered to the tip of its tail.[2] This definition may not have been at all humorous to contemporary husbandmen concerned with the problems of preserving corn in their barns. Like many other statements in the laws, it reveals the importance attached to cultivated crops, above all cereals. The spring and autumn were closed seasons in law "because sowing and harrowing are to suffer no interruption in spring nor the corn carriage in harvest" save presumably the kind of delay caused by inclement weather. The corn-

---

[1] *The Latin Texts of the Welsh Laws*, pp. 152–6; *Welsh Medieval Law*, pp. 73, 82–8.
[2] *The Latin Texts of the Welsh Laws*, pp. 87, 157; *The Laws of Hywel Dda*, p. 92; *Ancient Laws and Institutes of Wales*, II, pp. 76–7.

grinding quern was valued at the same sum as a she-calf, that is at 4d., thus adding veracity to Gerald's observation that the Welsh ate thin, but broad, cakes of bread, baked every day, probably on that kind of baking griddle which is also mentioned in the laws. When, as sometimes happened, husband and wife separated and, in accordance with the laws, shared their possessions, the husband retained the upper stone of the quern and the wife the lower. The plough "irons" were likewise shared, the wife keeping the plough-share and the husband the coulter.[1]

Barley and especially oats were cultivated as spring cereals, but spring tilth was considered to be only half the value of winter tilth. Both rye and wheat were cultivated as winter cereals but the latter was the more highly prized. Wheaten flour was not only preferred for the loaves of the bondmen's foodgifts but was also used in porridge for infants. Gerald, who sometimes wrote for effect, affirmed that the Welsh had neither orchards nor gardens.[2] Paradoxically, however, the apple tree was recorded in a contemporary text of the laws, though its value as there stipulated at 60d., the equivalent of ten male calves, may reflect its relative scarcity. Later thirteenth-century texts refer to gardens in which were grown flax, cabbages, and – appropriately – leeks. Nevertheless Gerald was probably not exaggerating when he asserted that the Welsh ate flesh in larger proportions than bread. The important point is that he included bread and mentioned oats along with milk, butter, and cheese, among the products on which the Welsh lived. His observation that they gladly ate the fruit of orchards and gardens when given to them helps to explain the high values attached to cultivated produce in the lawbooks, for these were relatively scarce commodities.[3] Good meadowland, like good arable land, was a scarce factor of production, but whereas livestock could be moved fairly easily on the hoof, harvested crops were difficult to transport in this period of rudimentary landward communications. The permanent settlements were therefore usually placed in the immediate vicinity of good arable land and accordingly were normally sited in the lowlands.

The uplands, though the scene of seasonal outfield cultivation in time of need, were in the main used for summer grazing.[4] According

---

[1] *The Latin Texts of the Welsh Laws*, pp. 143, 151–2; *Welsh Medieval Law*, p. 317; *Llyfr Iorwerth*, pp. 92–5; *Ancient Laws and Institutes of Wales*, pp. 609–11.

[2] *Giraldi Cambrensis Opera*, VI, p. 201; *Llyfr Iorwerth*, p. 95; *The Laws of Hywel Dda*, p. 68.

[3] Redaction A in *The Latin Texts of the Welsh Laws*, pp. 150, 152; *Giraldi Cambrensis Opera*, VI, p. 201; cf. M. Richter, 'Giraldus Cambrensis', *National Library of Wales Jnl* XVI, 1969–70, pp. 194, 201, 300, 311.

[4] M. Richards, '*Hafod* and *Hafoty* in Welsh Place-Names', *Montgomery Coll.*, LVI, 1959, pp. 1–8; id., '*Meifod, Lluest, Cynaeafdy* and *Hendre* in Welsh Place-Names',

to the Book of Iorwerth, the king had one township in every commote
which served as a summer pasture, and this was usually in the uplands.
At the other end of the social scale the bondman was also accustomed
to moving his flocks and herds to summer pastures. The three nets or
sources of profit for a bondman, according to a triad in the Book of
Blegywryd, are: "his cattle; his swine, and his winter residence (*hendref*).
For every beast found among them from the calends of May to the
time of reaping, the bondman receives 4d." This appears to mean that,
from the first of May until September, grazing of the *hendref*, the
permanent residence in the lowlands, was forbidden so as to conserve
resources of pasture for the winter months. There is here too a hint
that the bondman, when he grazed his cattle on the common summer
pastures, often did so independently of his neighbours, from his own
summer dwelling (*hafdy*).[1] In this event the summer dwellings of the
bondmen are normally perhaps likely to have been scattered units, as
the surviving remains of many stone huts in the mountains would
suggest.[2] Likewise, it seems possible that the bondman sought pannage
for his swine in the woodlands in autumn independently of his neighbours, and perhaps operated in this season from the dwelling known
as the autumn house (*cynhaeafdy*).

As compared with the bondman's permanent homestead, which was
valued at 80d., the autumn and summer houses were slight, even
temporary, structures valued at only 4d. and 8d. respectively.[3] They
are probably to be equated with the crude structures described by
Gerald as small huts on the borders of the woods "made of the boughs
of trees twisted together, constructed with little labour and expense,
and sufficient to endure throughout the year." The permanent house
of even the bondman was a much more substantial timber structure;
supported it would appear by three pairs of crucks, it was probably
of a basilical character with side aisles and a nave. In addition the laws
envisage that the bondman could possess a number of penthouses.
Apart from the summer house and the autumn house, these were his
chamber, cow-house, barn, kiln, sheep-cote, and pigsty. Moving up
the social scale, the hall of the notable (*uchelwr*, *breyr*), built on the same

---

Montgomery Coll., LVI, 1960, pp. 177–87; id., 'Ffridd/Ffrith as a Welsh Place-Name',
Studia Celtica II, 1967, pp. 29–90.

[1] *The Laws of Hywel Dda*, p. 101; *Llyfr Blegywryd*, p. 108. In Llyfr Iorwerth the
period was from the first of May until August, but some texts refer to the summer
dwelling rather than the winter dwelling as the bondman's net; cf. *Llyfr Iorwerth*,
p. 22; *The Black Book of Chirk*, p. 50; *The Chirk Codex*, p. 29.

[2] W. J. Hemp and C. A. Gresham, 'Hut Circles in N.W. Wales', *Ant.* XVIII,
1944, pp. 183–4; W. E. Griffiths, 'The Development of Native Homesteads in
N. Wales', *Ant.* XXV, 1951, pp. 174–84; RCAHM, *Caernarvonshire*, III, pp. xc–xcii, cv.

[3] *Llyfr Iorwerth*, p. 91; *The Laws of Hywel Dda*, pp. 92–3.

basilical pattern with crucks, was twice the value of that of the bondman but only half the value of the king's timbered hall. Like the bondman, the notable owned a number of outhouses including a summer house and an autumn house so that he too practised transhumance.[1]

The duration of the period when the community was absent from the *hendref* varied slightly according to different lawbooks. In the Book of Iorwerth this extended from the beginning of May to August, but in the Book of Cyfnerth it lasted to the end of September. From the Book of Blegywryd we learn that no compensation for damage was to be paid for corn left unreaped until the calends of winter (1 November). Later case-law gives the ninth day after the calends as the date, but explains that the owner of the corn was not entitled to impound the animals which had caused the damage on the ground that "the privilege of corn is not to be continued from one year into the other."[2] Both spring and winter cereals should have been reaped and gathered by this date, so that the stubble was thrown open and could be grazed as freely as the common pastures of the *hendref*. If a person had moved his corn from the stubble to the ley and made a rick there which subsequently became damaged, he was not to have redress. The main impression conveyed by these and other statements in the laws is that most of the arable land lay in open fields where the 'acres' were divided from each other only by "skirts" (turf balks), said to be two furrows (18 inches) wide. Where the boundary between two townships lay on cultivable land, a not infrequent occurrence when arable land was scarce, even the boundary could lie open; hence the severe penalties imposed on those who ploughed up township boundaries. The laws also envisage the situation in which corn adjoining a hamlet could be damaged by grazing animals. Seasonal transhumance made possible the alternation, in the lowland settlements, of winter grazing on unenclosed pasture and stubbles with the summer production of spring cereals. To accommodate winter cereals it was probably necessary to adopt flexible arrangements for temporary fencing, hence the references in law to the individual who made a fence about his corn. Such practices appear to be old-established, for Bleddyn ap Cynfyn, who died in 1075, is credited with the modification of the rules concerning compensation for damage caused to either winter tilth or spring tilth.[3]

[1] *Giraldi Cambrensis Opera*, VI, pp. 200–1; *The Latin Texts of the Welsh Laws*, p. 150; I. C. Peate, *The Welsh House*, 2nd ed., Liverpool, 1944, pp. 118–19.

[2] *Ancient Laws and Institutes of Wales*, II, pp. 94–5.

[3] *Ibid.*, pp. 268–9; *The Black Book of Chirk*, p. 47; *Llyfr Iorwerth*, pp. 19, 63, 99–103; *Llyfr Colan*, pp. 12–13, 41; *The Laws of Hywel Dda*, pp. 85–6; *The Latin Texts of the Welsh Laws*, p. 157.

Meadows were at all times to be closed against swine, for, as a late text explains, "they injure the land by turning it up." No one, however, except a lord was to have more than two reserves of grass, a *cae* (fenced field) and a *gweirglodd* (hay close). The latter was defined as land appropriated for hay only and enclosed by a fence. Whoever wished thus to preserve a meadow was to keep it from the feast of St Patrick onwards until the calends of winter, "because it is mowed twice in the year." Gardens on the other hand were to be enclosed so strongly that beasts would not be able to break in.[1] That no compensation should be paid if they did so, suggests that this was always a possibility because, as we have seen in the case of Llanynys, gardens could be adjoined by open-field sharelands.

THE INTEGRATION OF UPLAND AND LOWLAND
FOR DEFENCE

Even in the absence of an elaborate field system on the arable sharelands of the lowlands the kind of agrarian economy portrayed in the lawbooks was nevertheless feasible because of the use made of upland pastures during the summer months. This integration of the uplands and lowlands into one organizational complex is clearly revealed not only in the lawbooks but also in a variety of literary sources, some of which are early. But, not unnaturally, the clearest evidence for this integration comes from later compilations like *Liber Landavensis*.

Among the possessions of Llandaf as listed in two papal bulls of the early twelfth century was the vill of *Caerduicil* in Morgannwg, allegedly granted to the Church in the late ninth century. In the Book of Llandaf the donation was described as "the castle of *dinduicil*, that is *Caer Duicil* with its church and three *modii* of land around the fortress on the mountain and below it."[2] The papal bulls also refer to "the land below *Castell guent, Pen celli guenuc* and *cestill dinan*," with the wood and coastland, and with their tithes, oblations, sepultures, refuges, and free common.[3]

The place known as Cestill Dinan (the Castles of Dinan) also figures in a perambulation accompanying a lengthy record of a grant allegedly made to Llandaf of Llangadwaladr in Gwent Is Coed. It has therefore been identified with the site of Bishton (Bishopston) Castle, some four miles south-east of Caerleon. The perambulation shows that the lands donated extended southwards from a wooded ridge, past Cestill Dinan to the arable lands, the meadow, and *hendref* (old settlement) of the lower slopes, and thence to the marshes on the coastal levels.

---

[1] *Llyfr Iorwerth*, pp. 99–103; *The Laws of Hywel Dda*, pp. 83, 86.
[2] *Liber Landavensis*, pp. 31, 43, 90, 226–7.   [3] *Ibid.*, pp. 32, 44.

According to the Book of Llandaf this land was granted in the early eighth century to Bishop Berthguin of Llandaf by one Guidnerth in atonement for the murder of his brother, Merchion, during a contention for the kingdom. The perambulation is surprisingly detailed, and, to judge from later evidence, quite accurate, but the authenticity of the grant itself is open to question.[1] According to a much briefer memorial of a grant incorporated in the *Vita Sancti Cadoci* of the twelfth century, Llangadwaladr had already been donated to St Cadoc apparently in the sixth century and for the same reason as that given in the Llandaf record. But in this case we are informed that "on account of the fratricide of his own brother, Merchiun," Guoidnerth gave "*Lann Catgualader* to God and St Cadoc, that it might pay him every year a vessel of three *modii* of beer with all things due," and "at length he gave the returns to *Docgwinn* (Llandough)."[2] Whatever the relative merits of these two so-called charters, it does seem clear that in the eyes of one clerical compiler of the twelfth century a small territory donated to the church in an earlier period could have included an elevated refuge, together with a variety of lands, meadow, pasture, and arable, appropriate for a largely self-sufficient local economy.

The significance of the refuge becomes apparent from the Life of St Illtud which dates from about 1140. This Life was doubtless compiled at Llanilltud Fawr (Llantwit Major), the site of the ancient monastery of St Illtud in the vicinity of a former Roman villa and from the ninth century onwards a place of royal burial.[3] The compiler, after recounting Illtud's exploits, ends his narrative with a vivid account of a victory won by the clergy of St Illtud before "the fortress of King Meirchion" in the late eleventh century. A force of some 3,000 horsemen and footsoldiers, led by the men of Gwynedd, came to waste and burn Glamorgan. On account of this hostile attack the clergy of St Illtud "with the inhabitants of their district" (*cum suis parochianis*) fortified themselves by means of a ditch and a hedge firmly made above the sea shore. So fortified they entered, endeavouring to protect their wealth by defence. The incautious foe came by night before the gate, but, thanks to divine intervention, the defenders, aided by unarmed women and weak boys, put the army of Gwynedd to flight. As the compiler explained, "the refuge of God and of the most holy Illtud

[1] *Ibid.*, pp. 180–3, 373–4.

[2] *Vitae Sanctorum Britanniae et Genealogiae*, p. 135; A. W. Wade-Evans, 'The Llancarfan Charters', AC LXXXVIII, 1932, pp. 163–4.

[3] S. Frere, *Britannia*, 1967, pp. 266–7; V. E. Nash-Williams, 'The Roman Villa at Llantwit Major, Glamorgan', AC CII, 1953, pp. 89–163; id., 'The Medieval Settlement at Llantwit Major', BBCS XIV, 1950–2, pp. 313–33; id., *The Early Christian Monuments of Wales*, 1950, pp. 140–5; W. H. Davies, in *Christianity in Britain 300–700*, ed. M. W. Barley and R. P. C. Hanson, 1968, pp. 131–2, 136.

was violated wherefore three thousand were overcome before the fortress by a smaller number." The compiler knew his countryside well and the pre-existing fortress of King Meirchion above the sea shore is evidently the Iron-Age fort known as the Castle Ditches at Colhugh. In other words, as late as the eleventh century an Iron-Age fort in Morgannwg could be deliberately refurbished with a ditch and hedge for the protection of the inhabitants of the surrounding district during a period of strife.[1]

Viewed against this kind of background the obligation on the bondmen of the king to build encampments, as recorded in the lawbooks, becomes real and meaningful. Similar purposeful arrangements may well explain certain curious dispositions as portrayed in the extents of the thirteenth and fourteenth centuries. The *maerdref* of the Anglesey commote of Twrcelyn was at Penrhosllugwy in the vicinity of the Romano-British site at Din Llugwy, and only some three miles distant from the *hendref* of Llysdulas in the same commote. The freemen of the seven *gwelyau* of Llysdulas, in conjunction with the other freemen of the commote, made payment for the maintenance of the commotal court at Penrhosllugwy, and here too the occupants of a small bond *gwely* sited near Hendref Llysdulas performed building services. Curiously however the heirs and tenants of the seven free *gwelyau* of Llysdulas were also responsible for building services at the *maerdref* of Cemais in the neighbouring commote of Talybolion. They were also responsible for transporting the necessary materials for the hall, the chamber, and the chapel to the nearest gate of the court at Cemais.[2] These duties outside the commote may in part be explained on the grounds that both Twrcelyn and Talybolion were once components of the *cantref* of Cemais, but there may be an additional reason. Two of the Llysdulas *gwelyau* contained land in an outlier of Llysdulas township in Talybolion which incorporated the large promontory fort of Dinas Gynfor a mile or so to the north of the *maerdref* at Cemais. It may be suggested, therefore, that the obligations imposed on the Llysdulas *gwelyau* point to the continued use of the Iron-Age fort of Dinas Gynfor as the major strongpoint and place of refuge in the *cantref* of Cemais during our period.

Similarly in Bodeilias, a lowland settlement whose name reveals

---

[1] H. J. Randall, *The Vale of Glamorgan: Studies in Landscape and History*, 1961, pp. 73–4, 76, 90; cf. Asser's statement about the siege in A.D. 878 of the English by the Danes in *arcem Cynuit*, a "fortress altogether unprepared, and without fortification, except such as were erected after our fashion" (Asser's *Life of King Alfred*, ed. W. H. Stevenson, Oxford, 1959, p. 43); cf. also Ethelfleda's *burh* of Worcester "to shelter all the folk" (CS 579); *Vitae Sanctorum Britanniae et Genealogiae*, pp. 232–3.

[2] *Record of Caernarvon*, pp. 63–6, 72. The court of Cemais, like that of Aberffraw, was surrounded by a wall.

that it had once been the dwelling of a chief, the bondmen were responsible for the transport of the king's victuals into the mountains. This duty was known as *Teymynyth* which, literally interpreted as "mountain houses," could well refer to a site on Garn Boduan, a summit within a mile or so of Bodeilias.[1] Within the hill-fort which adjoins the Iron-Age settlement on this summit was constructed the fortified homestead of a powerful though seemingly not very prosperous notable. Projecting stone steps which provide access to the summit of this homestead wall are matched by similar features at Hamsterley Castles, a fortification in upland Durham attributed to the post-Roman period. There is therefore some support for the traditional attribution of the fortified homestead on Garn Boduan to one Buan, allegedly the grandson of the poet Llywarch Hen, who must therefore have lived *c.* A.D. 700.[2]

In the border lordship of Oswestry similar dispositions were characteristic in the twelfth century. In this multiple estate, upland outliers were attached to lowland townships. The occupants of one bond township and one *gwely* were obliged to keep and despatch the lord's hounds. From an inquisition of 1272 we learn that the men of *Soutover* paid a certain custom called *mut* "in time of war for keeping their cattle at Oswestry in peace." Since *mut* is probably from the Welsh *mudo* meaning "to move," this custom, also known elsewhere under the name *treth mud*, was here probably a payment for keeping cattle within the security of the ramparts of the Iron-Age hill-fort known as Hen Dinas or Old Oswestry.[3] The *caput* of the lordship was not at Oswestry originally but instead at Maesbury, some two miles to the south. According to Domesday Book, Maesbury, Whittington, and Chirbury together owed half a night's *ferm* (food-rent) during the reign of Ethelred II (968–1012). All three were places of significance. Chirbury, like Maesbury, appears at Domesday as the *caput* of its hundred, while Whittington was to become the *caput* of the lordship which embraced the hill-fort of Old Oswestry. Maesbury is an Old

---

[1] Jones, 'Early Settlement in Arfon', p. 15; M. Richards, 'Nennius's *Regio Guunnessi*', *Caernarvon Hist. Soc.*, 1963, p. 25; T. Jones Pierce, 'Lleyn Ministers' Accounts', BBCS VI, 1932, p. 262; cf. *Record of Caernarvon*, p. 213; *The Extent of Chirkland*, ed. G. P. Jones, London, 1933, pp. xxvi, 11.

[2] A. H. A. Hogg, 'Garn Boduan and Tre'r Ceiri, excavations at two Caernarvonshire Hill-forts', *Arch. J.* CXVII, 1960, pp. 1–39; RCAHM, *Caernarvonshire*, III, p. cxvii; J. E. Hodgkin, 'The Castles Camp, Hamsterley, Co. Durham', *Archit. and Archaeol. Soc. Durham and Northumberland*, VII, 1934–6, pp. 92–8.

[3] W. J. Slack, *The Lordship of Oswestry, 1393–1607*, 1951, pp. 22–6; R. W. Eyton, *Antiquities of Shropshire* X, London, 1860, pp. 331–2; A. N. Palmer and E. Owen, *A History of Ancient Tenures of Land in North Wales and the Marches*, Wrexham, 1911, p. 90; *The Extent of Chirkland*, pp. xxvii, 9, 20; W. Rees, in *Angles and Britons: O'Donnell Lectures*, p. 161.

English name meaning "the *burh* (or fortification) by the boundary."[1]
If, as seems likely, the fortification implied was the hill-fort of Old
Oswestry, which is nearer to Offa's Dyke than is Maesbury township,
then there is here even in toponymy a link between a hill-fort refuge
and an old-established lowland centre. A hint of the age of this
centre at Maesbury is given by its Welsh name, which is none other
than *Llysveisyr*, "the court of Meisyr."[2]

The name Meisyr was borne by a sister of the hero Cynddylan, and
of Heledd, both of whom figure in *Canu Llywarch Hen*, the remaining
verse elements of two lost sagas which, Sir Ifor Williams guesses, were
composed *c.* A.D. 850. Inspired by patriotic motives when the fortunes
of the kingdom of Powys were at their lowest ebb, these sagas purport
to deal with characters, including Llywarch Hen, who lived in the
sixth and seventh centuries. The saga of Heledd deals with the first
half of the seventh century, the period when Oswald of Northumbria
attacked Mercia and, after driving Penda into Wales, was defeated by
a combined Welsh–Mercian force at Maserfelth (probably Old
Oswestry) in 642. Cynddylan assisted at this battle which is named in
the saga of Heledd as Maes Cogwy, the name which Nennius also
used for Maserfelth.[3] Later, however, Cynddylan was hard pressed
by his enemies, and the saga portrays Heledd on a height overlooking
the court of Pengwern, where she had fled for safety with her maidens.
Cynddylan must have fallen and when night comes the women make
their way to the ruins of the burnt royal court. When the body of
Cynddylan is found they bear it to Eglwysseu Bassa (Baschurch) for
burial, but, because of the English flood, these "churches" – probably
the *llan* associated with the *llys* – have lost their privilege (*braint*). Later
Heledd is pictured, scantily clad, on a mountain side driving her one
remaining cow to safety.

However legendary the battles of Arthur and Vortimer, the account
of them given by Nennius suggests that much of the military activity
in the early part of our period took place in the open as part of mobile
warfare in which cavalry played a part.[4] Nevertheless it would be
rash to think that all military activity at this time was of this kind.
Many actions were fought at strongpoints. Taliesin confirms this
impression by recounting that some battles took place before "fair

[1] DB I, 253b; B. G. Charles in *Angles and Britons: O'Donnell Lectures*, pp. 98–9.
[2] *Ibid.*, p. 106.
[3] I. Williams, 'The Poems of Llywarch Hen', *B. Acad.* XVIII, 1932, pp. 273, 295,
297, 299; *Canu Llywarch Hen*, ed. I. Williams, 1935, pp. xxxvii, lxxii, lxxxi;
I. Williams, *Lectures on Early Welsh Poetry*, Dublin, 1944, pp. 45–8; H. P. R. Finberg,
Lucerna, pp. 79–80; Nennius, *op. cit.*, p. 208.
[4] L. Alcock, 'Some reflections on early Welsh Society and Economy', WHR
II, 1964, p. 2.

forts." He also refers to soldiers sleeping under dykes and embankments, for though they could relax in winter their life in summer was a constant guard day and night against the enemy. A medieval triad reveals that Cefn Digoll (the Long Mountain) in the Chirbury district was the scene of a victory won in the early seventh century by the Welsh, under the leadership of Cadwallon of Gwynedd, over the English, led by Edwin of Northumbria. A poem of the ninth or the tenth century which lists Cadwallon's battles also refers to Cadwallon's camp on the summit of this mountain, where seven battles were fought each day for seven months. Clearly therefore the Welsh poets of the ninth or tenth centuries could envisage the hill-fort of Caer Digoll (Beacon Ring), which stands on the summit of the Long Mountain at 1,336 feet and near a Roman road, as a likely setting for a prolonged series of battles in the seventh century. Similarly, in a poem of the mid-tenth century, a protagonist of Gwynedd prophesies that an army from Gwynedd will be joined by one from Powys and that together they will fight for Llys Llonion in Pembroke, but their enemies will find no refuge in *Din-clud, Din-maerud, Din-daryfon,* and *Din-rhieddon.*[1]

Nor was this simply a poet's fancy, for an entry in the *Annales Cambriae* under A.D. 906 refers to the battle of *Dinmeir* and the damaging of St David's. As Sir Ifor Williams has shown, *din* was the equivalent of *dinas,* used by the poets not so much in the original sense of a stronghold but rather as a refuge. Taliesin in the sixth century refers to the *tut achles,* the refuge of the people. Similarly a perambulation of the boundaries of Llandaf, included in *Liber Landavensis,* refers to a *Castell teirtut,* but here *tut* was used in its later territorial sense, for the three units implied by the word *teirtut* were specified as Cantref Bychan, Cantref Selyf, and Buellt.[2] Such places of protection or succour in the uplands as *Castell teirtut* were much needed during the summer months of upland pasturage and warfare when herds all too frequently became mobile booty. Fortunately there survived, on the upper slopes of the main valleys, the substantial remains of numerous hill-forts of the Iron Age which could be refurbished in time of need.

As we have seen, lowland forts like Castle Ditches were sometimes used for the same purpose, and so too were steep-sided, though relatively low, coastal headlands. Some of these lower strongholds,

[1] *The Poems of Taliesin*, ed. I. Williams (English version by J. E. Caerwyn Williams), Dublin, 1968, pp. xxvii, 7, 8, 13, 76, 82, 89–90; *The Book of Taliesin*, ed. J. Gwenogfryn Evans, Llanbedrog, 1910, p. 73; *Trioedd Ynys Prydein*, ed. R. Bromwich, Cardiff, 1961, pp. 182–3; *Breudwyt Ronabwy*, ed. M. Richards, Cardiff, 1948, pp. 9, 47; RCAHM, *Montgomery*, 1911, pp. 61–2.

[2] *The Poems of Taliesin*, pp. xxvii, 2, 3, 32, 46; *Canu Aneirin*, ed. I. Williams, Cardiff, 1938, pp. 16, 172, 176, 201; *Canu Llywarch Hen*, pp. 6, 13, 87, 120; *Liber Landavensis*, pp. 134, 367.

however, appear to have been permanently occupied. Such was the fortress (*caer*) or stronghold (*dinas*) which is the subject of a poem dated by Sir Ifor Williams to *c.* 875. Entitled *Etmic Dinbych*, which means literally "in praise of *Dinbych*," this poem describes "a mighty stronghold sea-girt" yet standing "on a promontory." As Sir Ifor Williams has cogently argued, this was a fortification on the site of the later Tenby Castle. Despite the apparently Scandinavian form of its name, Tenby is derived, like Denbigh, from Dinbych. Defended, it would appear, by a palisade, this Dinbych was a court containing lodgings for a retinue, and a host besides, as well as rooms for food and drink. Loud therefore was "the revelry of bards over the mead horns" and the wine in the crystal bowls. But more serious purposes were also served at Dinbych, for within the circuit of the stronghold was a room (*cell*) where "The writings of Britain were the chief object of care." Some measure of social stability is thus implied. How this was achieved is indicated by the observation of the poet that "better are the slaves of Dyfed (*kaeth dyfed*)" than the yeomen (*eillon*) of Deudraeth (Caern); and the poet is also aware that he and his friends could be reduced to be mere tillers of the soil or herdsmen by a victorious army. This stability in Dyfed, though perhaps only relative, was seemingly of long standing. Bleiddudd, the lord of Dinbych, can be dated from the genealogies to about the ninth century. As the poet informs us, he was the head of a line named after Erbin who in turn, according to the pedigrees, was the son of Aergol Lawhir, the contemporary of Gildas.[1] Aergol's court at *Liscastell*, described in *Liber Landavensis* as *caput totius demetice regionis*, is traditionally located some three miles south-west of Tenby in the lowland hamlet of Lydstep. A component, at the close of our period, of the parish of Penalun, this district, according to *Liber Landavensis*, was the scene of Aergol's generosity to the monastic movement of his day. It was here that Aergol (Agricola), whose name indicates that he inherited some Roman traditions, gave three vills to St Teilo who was born in this locality. These three vills were on the fertile slopes below the low summits of 200 to 300 feet which flank the Ritec, the stream entering the sea immediately to the south of Tenby. Penalun itself, a mile or so from Tenby to the south of the Ritec, had allegedly been granted to the Church at an earlier date. But whatever the truth of this claim by Llandaf, sherds of imported Mediterranean pottery discovered in a cave in Longbury Bank on the Penalun side of the Ritec point to the existence in this locality of a monastic community during the fifth or sixth centuries.[2]

[1] I. Williams, 'Moliant Dinbych Penfro', *Hon. Soc. Cymm.*, 1940, pp. 66–83.
[2] *Liber Landavensis*, pp. 125–6, 366; B. E. Howells in *The Land of Dyfed in Early Times*, ed. D. Moore, 1964, pp. 37–8; see also p. 293 above.

Like most of the written evidence cited *faute de mieux* in this essay, the poem in praise of Tenby is preserved in a manuscript later than our period. Fortunately however some of the features which this poem portrays figure also in some Welsh verses written down in the first half of the ninth century on the upper margins of the Juvencus metrical version of the Gospels. These verses portray a chieftain in low spirits for he has lost all his retinue save for one foreign mercenary whom he calls his Frank; around their bowl together they drink "clear mead." This strictly contemporary evidence supplements that of the less securely dated *Canu Llywarch Hen* which, as we have seen, refers to the borders of Powys *c.* 850. The similes in *Canu Llywarch Hen* are appropriate for a society which is far from being composed of nomadic pastoralists. In the spring there are free furrows and in the autumn the stubble is yellow. Even in time of war the ploughing continues. Thus the furrows remain but there is no certainty as to who will reap them. Alas, too, there was blood on the straw, and the fallow (*brynar*) was not ploughed. During the sixth century Taliesin could write of "the ploughing of the sea" and, towards the end of the same century, Aneirin envisaged his heroes thrusting through the enemy as would a plough-share through the soil.[1] There must therefore have been many lowland settlements capable of producing that ale (*cwrwf*) of which the poets at times write with enthusiasm.[2] Among them we may certainly include those settlements in Dyfed which, though they bear distinctly English names, contain churches dedicated to Celtic saints. Such were Haroldston East dedicated to Ysfael, Haroldston West and Nolton to Madog, and Steynton to Cywil. All four are sited below 250 feet, yet here we surely must have examples of settlements founded in the pre-Norman period and given new names after the Anglo-Flemish colonization of Rhos (Pem).[3]

[1] I. Williams, 'Tri Englyn y Juvencus', BBCS VI, 1931–3, pp. 101–10; I. Williams, *Lectures on Early Welsh Poetry*, pp. 28–9; *Canu Llywarch Hen*, pp. 9, 40, 44, cited by Payne in *Yr Aradr Gymreig*, p. 51; *Canu Aneirin*, pp. 12, 18, 21, 37, 57.

[2] I. Williams, *Lectures on Early Welsh Poetry*, p. 52; *The Poems of Taliesin*, pp. 4, 57. The ale was probably made from grain produced by the substrate population; cf. the statement by Posidonius about the Celts (in Athenaeus IV) – "The lower classes drink wheaten beer prepared with honey, but most people drink it plain. It is called *corma*." There is evidence for the use of cereals for brewing at an early stage in the occupation of the civilian settlement of the Roman legionary fortress at Caerleon.—H. Helbaek, 'The Isca grain, a Roman plant introduction in Britain', *New Phytologist* LXIII, 1964, pp. 158–64.

[3] B. E. Howells, *op. cit.*, p. 239; A. W. Wade-Evans, '*Parochiale Wallicanum*', *Y Cymmrodor* XXI, 1908, pp. 33, 34.

EARLY PLOUGHING AND THE LAYOUT OF THE 'ACRE'

Thus it is in the light of the probable occurrence of a significant amount of lowland cultivation that we must view the only example of reasonably firmly dated 'rig-and-furrow' of the pre-Norman period hitherto discovered in Wales. This occurs within the framework of the ancient multiple estate of Chirbury, which appears to have extended as far west as the ridge whose northernmost summit was crowned by the Iron-Age hill-fort of Ffridd Faldwyn. Some two miles to the north, the Roman fort of Forden Gaer commanded the Rhyd Chwima crossing of the Severn. Roughly midway between these two fortifications was the motte and bailey castle of Hen Domen, built very shortly after the Norman Conquest, in the border forest which three English thegns had earlier used as a great chase. Assessed at 52½ hides, this estate, now focused on Hen Domen, contained no less than 22 hamlets, of which 5 were still held by Welsh bond tenure as late as 1540.[1] Among them was Thornbury, named no doubt after the scrubby vegetation of the adjacent Roman fort. The neighbouring slopes on which Hen Domen stood were, without question, the scene of early cultivation. In the Boulder Clay beneath the bailey rampart and to the north of the castle there are plough-marks which suggest 'rig-and-furrow' with a width of about 13 feet. This cultivation was presumably therefore of pre-Conquest date, particularly since the land appears to have been abandoned to small bushes before the castle was built. The only finds in the buried soil were two sherds of Roman pottery probably from Forden Gaer but fortunately there are also traces of a rectangular building which antedates the plough-marks. The building is probably a post-Roman structure and therefore a date in the period from the fifth to the seventh or eighth century is suggested for the 'rig-and-furrow'.[2] The lengths of the ridges at Hen Domen cannot be determined and their widths are not in accord with those of the 'acres' already described. Nevertheless they provide clear examples of the kind of 'rig-and-furrow' which could have been produced in our period by the employment of an asymmetrical plough-share of the type found in a late-Roman context at Dinorben. Appropriately the immediate vicinity of Hen Domen, like that of Dinorben, appears to have been a place of some significance alike in the Roman and medieval periods.

The lawbooks reveal that there were two kinds of plough, one

[1] DB I, 253b, 254a, 316a, 318a; RCAHM, *Montgomery*, p. 157; G. R. J. Jones, 'The Pattern of Settlement on the Welsh Border', AHR VIII, 1960, pp. 79–80.

[2] P. A. Barker, 'Excavations at Hen Domen, Montgomery, 1969', *Arch. J.* CXXVI, 1969, pp. 177–8.

with wheels and the other without, but both were of the type found in north-west Europe rather than that in southern Europe. Given the number of oxen suggested for a contract of joint ploughing, we may assume that both kinds of plough were heavy but the wheeled variety was the heavier. The laws of co-tillage reveal that a recognized standard of ploughing was deemed to be feasible with the use of these ploughs. If the number of furrows in a field could not be ascertained, each furrow was assumed to be a Welsh foot, or nine inches, in width. This stipulation, however, does not imply that the ploughing was untidy; rather it suggests that harrowing could follow ploughing without delay. Indeed the ploughs used were of the type which constantly turned the furrow to one side. Hence the references to oxen which were put to the ploughing either in the furrow or on the land; and once a contract had been agreed the oxen were not to be moved from their agreed positions without leave. Thus the mould-board or its equivalent must have been a fixture on the plough of the lawbooks.[1] The plough-share found at Dinorben is not the only pointer to the antiquity of this practice, as is revealed by the manuscript known as *Oxoniensis Posterior* which was written either in Wales, or more probably in Cornwall, in the tenth century. This manuscript contains glosses in Old Welsh on Latin words, among them agricultural terms including not only the Old Welsh versions of coulter, share, and handle, but also the word *ciluin* as a gloss on *buris* which was used for the wooden plough-beam of a Roman plough.[2]

The lengths of the yokes recorded in the lawbooks provide further indirect evidence of the antiquity of cultivation. Yokes of four different lengths are mentioned. There was a yoke of four Welsh feet used for two oxen, a yoke of eight feet for four oxen, a yoke of twelve feet for six oxen, and one of sixteen feet for eight oxen. As Mr Ffransis Payne has shown, the animals would be placed abreast of each other under the three longer yokes. Since Gerald of Wales reports four oxen abreast as being most usual in the twelfth century, it seems likely that the longer yokes had been laid aside by his day and that a team of eight would normally be arranged under two yokes. It is probable, therefore, that the two longest yokes were in the nature of fossils embedded in the lawbooks of the thirteenth century.[3] Yet, according to the Book of Iorwerth, the legal *erw* was laid out with the aid of the long yoke of sixteen feet. Thus: "a rod equal in length to that long yoke in the hand

---

[1] Payne, *op. cit.*, pp. 54, 68–70.
[2] *Ibid.*, p. 52; K. Jackson, *Language and History in Early Britain*, 1953, pp. 55–6; *Early Scholastic Colloquies*, ed. W. H. Stevenson, Oxford, 1929, p. 4; K. D. White, *Agricultural Implements of the Roman World*, Cambridge, 1967, pp. 123–35.
[3] F. G. Payne in *Studies in Folk Life*, ed. G. Jenkins, 1969, p. 241.

of the caller with the middle spike of that long yoke in the other hand of the caller, and as far as he can reach with that rod, stretching out his arm, are the two skirts of the *erw*, that is to say the breadth of a legal *erw*; and thirty of that is the length of the *erw*." The Venedotian *erw* was therefore three yokes broad by thirty yokes in length. In the Book of Blegywryd the *erw* was based on the same unit and measured two yokes broad by sixteen yokes long. In the Book of Cyfnerth the *erw* was based on the rod of Hywel Dda, said to be 18 feet in length. In the Latin texts the yoke is said to be $16\frac{1}{2}$ feet in length and the *erw* based on this unit was either eight or nine times as long as it was broad.[1] Redaction B, a Latin text of the thirteenth century, besides describing the *erw* based on the yoke of $16\frac{1}{2}$ feet, also refers to an *erw* measured on a different basis. The rod used for the latter was as long as the tallest man in the township together with the length of his arm, presumably extended above his head. In length this *erw* was sixty of these rods. Its breadth however was determined by the length of the rod plus the length of the caller's reach, with the caller placing one hand on the mid-point of the plough and reaching out as far as possible with the rod in his other hand. This procedure was then repeated on the other side of the plough to give the overall width of the *erw*. This inconsistency of Redaction B in referring to two distinct methods of laying out an 'acre' is matched by other inconsistencies as well as repetitions and faulty sequences, thus demonstrating that this text of the thirteenth century was derived from a number of earlier sources. Our problem is to determine the relative ages of the *erwau* thus inconsistently defined. In this text the second *erw* is immediately followed by, and associated with, a statement that there are eight such *erwau* in the homestead of a notable and only four in the homestead of a bondman.[2] Accordingly it is reasonable to postulate that the second *erw* is connected with the reforms in assessments introduced by Bleddyn ap Cynfyn. In this event, the second kind of *erw* was already in use before Bleddyn's death in 1075 and therefore the first *erw*, based on the rod of $16\frac{1}{2}$ feet, must be older still.

Indeed it is possible that the various ways of laying out units of land as recorded in the lawbooks represent successive stages in the evolution of the *erw*. In order, these were probably as follows: the first and smallest was the *erw* based on the earlier yoke of 16 feet (12 statute feet), or that of $16\frac{1}{2}$ feet, and eight times as long as broad; the second was the *erw* based on Hywel's rod of 18 feet, and nine times as long as broad; a third stage is possibly represented by the Venedotian

[1] *Llyfr Iorwerth*, pp. 53–4; *Llyfr Colan*, p. 10; A. W. Wade-Evans, *Welsh Medieval Law*, 1909, pp. 54, 204–5; *The Latin Texts of the Welsh Laws*, pp. 136, 383, 476.
[2] *Ibid.*, pp. 22–3, 226, 230.

erw which, though based on the yoke of 16 feet, was ten times as long as broad; and last among these *erwau* was that associated with the reforms of Bleddyn. Although varying in accordance with the height of the tallest man in the township, this *erw* is likely to have been about 480 statute feet long and about 30 statute feet wide, whereas the first *erw* was only 192 feet long by 24 feet broad.[1] The progressive lengthening of the *erw* thus envisaged was possibly bound up with increased efficiency in ploughing, and the relative narrowing of the *erw* probably reflected the progressive subdivision of the parcels within holdings. But, as the lawbooks show, especially in relation to Bleddyn's reforms, the older order was not necessarily displaced and, as was the case at Llanynys, older units would usually survive alongside the new.

The multiplicity of methods of measuring land already considered makes it likely that the *erw* was already old when the oldest extant text of the laws was written in the late twelfth century. Even so, a still older stratum of land measurement can be discerned in the texts of the Book of Iorwerth. These give an account of the measurement of Britain by one Dyfnwal Moelmud who, it is claimed, on becoming king was the first to establish good laws in this island. He also measured Britain so that he might know the tribute (*mal*) as well as distances. This account, though traced to the *Historia Regum* of Geoffrey of Monmouth, was not derived solely from this source, for Geoffrey makes no reference to the measurement of the island. Though legendary the account may have some foundation in fact, for the royal pedigrees in Harleian MS. 3859 refer to a *Dumngual moilmut* as the grandson of Coel Hen, so that there was probably a historical person of this name, a Northern prince, who lived *c.* 500. According to the lawbooks, the laws which Dyfnwal established remained in force until the time of Hywel Dda. From these same sources we learn that before the measure of the legal *erw* was made by the long yoke, Dyfnwal used a measure, like the yoke itself, based on the length of a barleycorn. Thus: "three

---

[1] Cf. the small area of surviving 'rig-and-furrow' at Gwithian (Cornwall). The ridges, which are attributed to the period from A.D. 850 to 1050–1100, are about 180 feet in length and vary in width from 7 to 20 feet. Enduring ridges were built up here by the use of a fixed mould-board plough which turned the furrow to one side only.—P. J. Fowler and A. C. Thomas, 'Arable Fields of the pre-Norman Period at Gwithian', *Cornish Archaeology* 1, 1962, pp. 61–84. I am particularly indebted to Professor A. C. Thomas for the information that, on the opposite side of the same valley at the farm named Nanterrow, a tripartite *gwel*, the complex remnant of some sharelands, survived into the nineteenth century. The suffix in the name Nanterrow is probably the Old Cornish *ereu* which may be compared with the Welsh word *erw*. *Gwel*, like the Welsh *gwely*, means bed. But it is also the most widespread, and probably the oldest, Cornish word for an unenclosed arable field. It is possible therefore that in Wales *gwely* was used to designate arable land before it was adopted as a technical tenurial term for the land of an agnatic lineage.

lengths of a barleycorn in the inch; three inches in the palm breadth; three palm breadths in the foot; three feet in the pace; three paces in the leap; three leaps in a land (the land in new Welsh is called a ridge); and a thousand of the lands is the mile. And that measure we still use here."[1] The Book of Colan gives the gist of these statements apart from the last sentence; but in addition it adds the information that there are three ridges in the *erw*. Since the ridge by this measure was $20\frac{1}{4}$ statute feet the *erw* must have been $60\frac{3}{4}$ feet. The tradition that the width of a ridge is three leaps survived down to the present century in Abergeirw (Mer), but the ridge itself was old.[2] The oldest text of the Book of Iorwerth, which was written *c.* 1200, records that *tir*, the Welsh for land, was displaced by a word in new Welsh, *grwn*, meaning a ridge. Yet this word *grwn* was itself sufficiently old and traditional to have figured in the verse of Llywarch ap Llywelyn in the twelfth century.[3]

The *erw* of three ridges is much narrower than the typical 'Celtic long field' to be found on the downlands of southern Britain; for these long fields, which are ascribed to the Romano-British period, can attain widths of about 160 feet.[4] It is also much narrower than the elongated cultivation terraces associated with Dinas near Cadnant (Ang), for these are about 150 feet in width. Accordingly we cannot be certain when the relatively narrow *erw* of three ridges was introduced. Nevertheless it is possible that this *erw* was an innovation of Dyfnwal's period. No length is specified in the lawbooks for the *erw* of three ridges, and therefore it is possible that the length of this 'acre' bore a fixed relationship to its width. Certainly in *Canu Aneirin*, which is attributed to the sixth century, there is a reference to "the width of one acre" (*let un ero*), thus implying that an *erw* width was already a recognized dimension.[5]

To judge from the variety of yokes recorded in the lawbooks, Welsh ploughmen were well able to adapt their practices to local circumstances. Oxen could be yoked line ahead in pairs, or line abreast in fours, sixes, or eights, and moreover at least two different types of plough were used. It would be unwise therefore to assume that the shape of the 'acre' invariably bore a fixed relationship to the

[1] *The Chirk Codex*, p. 64; *Llyfr Iorwerth*, p. 59; *Llyfr Colan*, pp. 39, 159; Lloyd, *op. cit.*, pp. 318–19, 355; E. Phillimore, 'The *Annales Cambriae* and Old Welsh Genealogies from Harleian MS. 3859', *Y Cymmrodor* IX, 1888, p. 174.

[2] *Llyfr Colan*, pp. 39, 160; M. Richards, 'Some Medieval Township and Hamlet Names', BBCS XX, 1962–4, pp. 52–3.

[3] *The Chirk Codex*, p. 65; F. G. Payne, *Yr Aradr Gymreig*, p. 49.

[4] H. C. Bowen, *Ancient Fields*, London, 1963, pp. 23–4, 44; RCAHM, *Anglesey*, pp. xcii–xciii, 52–4.

[5] *Canu Aneirin*, pp. 38, 296.

type of plough used. Even after the heavy one-side plough had been widely adopted in place of the older light plough or ard, pre-existing 'Celtic fields' are unlikely to have passed out of use. Good cultivable land in Wales was probably much too scarce to be readily abandoned, especially when it lay on the well-drained soils of the lowlands. Ploughing in long narrow lands is likely to have been intruded into the framework of roughly rectangular 'Celtic fields'. As Payne has indicated, the problem of turning the full plough-team of eight oxen used to draw the heavy plough would be minimized when these animals were yoked line abreast. Especially is this likely to have been the case when the 'Celtic fields', though delimited by banks, were not well enclosed. In Cregennan (Mer) at an altitude of about 650 feet there are 'Celtic long fields' about 300 feet long by about 100 feet broad, adjoined by some subrectangular 'Celtic fields' of sides 200–400 feet in length and bounded by boulders. Into the framework provided by the latter are dovetailed large numbers of long narrow 'lands'. Immediately adjacent to the 'Celtic long fields' is the site of a 'platform house' named Llys Bradwen after the Bradwen who was lord of Dolgellau in the early twelfth century. These different kinds of fields, which lie within the largest area of tolerably cultivable land in the core of the township, came to form part of the nucleus of a *gwely*.[1]

At a slightly higher altitude in Clynnog (Caern) strip lynchets about 100 feet wide and as much as 800 feet long were superimposed on, and also added to, an older series of 'Celtic fields' of some 150 feet in length by about 150–300 feet in width. The latter, which were probably connected with nearby 'enclosed homesteads' of the second and third centuries A. D., appear to have been originally enclosed by walls. Elsewhere in North Wales too there are abundant field remains to suggest that many, if not most, 'Celtic fields' were originally enclosed.[2] Even at a l ter date when, as the lawbooks reveal, arable sharelands lay in open field, the homesteads (*tyddynod*) continued to be enclosed, as was also the case with gardens. Nevertheless even within our period it is highly probable that arable *tir cyfrif*, if no other land, lay in open field so as to facilitate periodic re-allocation. Given the communal nature of the renders of the reckoned township, it would be surprising if a primitive form of common-field organization did not already exist on such lands before the ninth century, if not earlier.[3]

[1] F. G. Payne, 'The Plough in Ancient Britain', *Arch. J.* CIV, 1947, pp. 82 sqq.; G. R. J. Jones, 'The Distribution of Bond Settlements in North-West Wales', WHR II, 1964, pp. 24–5.

[2] RCAHM, *Caernarvonshire*, II, pp. 47–51, 106–8.

[3] The 'rig-and-furrow' at Gwithian cited above occurred in an isolated rectangular field about 190 feet north-south by about 300 feet east-west on a gentle southward

The evidence from Brittany, where the agrarian organization of this same period closely resembles that already described for Wales, is especially relevant in this particular context. This evidence is preserved in the *Cartulaire de l'abbaye de Redon*, which, though written in the eleventh century, consists of copies of older documents most of which date from the ninth century. These ninth-century charters reveal that the characteristic share of land (*ran*) was usually delimited on part of its outer periphery by means of a ditch or bank. But within the *ran* there was usually a *campus* or two containing parcels each equivalent to a day's ploughing, and these arable lands were occasionally delimited only by means of boundary stones even where they adjoined pastures.[1] Significantly, such arrangements are sometimes recorded for lands donated to the abbey by prominent persons "without rent, without tribute and *sine cofrit*" to any men save the monks of Redon; and the phrase *sine cofrit* has been interpreted as meaning "without comprehension, without community of possession."[2] Similar field arrangements are recorded for lands granted to Redon and held *dicombit*, that is undivided, without renders and works to any men save the monks. These rights and exemptions imply that there must have been other lands where such favourable conditions did not apply. In Brittany during the ninth century there was certainly some land subject to partible inheritance and, like the *tir gwelyog* of Wales at a later date, subdivided into sharelands.[3] It is clear too that at least some of the

facing slope. This field had nothing more in the way of bounds than headlands at its northern and southern limits and a boundary ditch on its eastern side; its western limits were uncertain.—Fowler and Thomas, *op. cit.*, p. 76.

[1] *Cartulaire de l'abbaye de Redon*, pp. 71, 81, 95, 152. See also the corrections by A. de la Borderie in 'La chronologie du Cartulaire de Redon', *Annales de Bretagne* V, pp. 535 sqq., XII, pp. 473 sqq., and XIII, pp. 11 sqq., 263 sqq., 430 sqq., and 590 sqq. For a discussion of the field patterns portrayed therein see A. Guilcher, 'Le finage des champs dans le Cartulaire de Redon', *Annales de Bretagne* LIII, 1946, pp. 140–4; A. Guilcher, 'Le Mot Ker', *Mémoires Soc. d'Histoire et d'Archéologie de Bretagne* XXVI, pp. 35–48; P. Flatrès, 'Les anciennes structures rurales de Bretagne d'après le Cartulaire de Redon', *Etudes Rurales* (forthcoming).

[2] *Cartulaire de Redon*, pp. 6, 69, 91, 93–4, 112–14, 117–18, 131–2, 137, 178, 214–15; L. Fleuriot, *Dictionnaire des Gloses en Vieux Breton*, Paris, 1964, pp. 111, 112, 138, 185; K. Jackson, *A Historical Phonology of Breton*, Dublin, 1967, p. 788.

[3] *Cartulaire de Redon*, pp. 131–2, 150–1, 178, 214–15. Thus according to the cartulary, Riuualt in A.D. 833 gave to the abbey of Redon a share of land with a house (*tigran Bot Louuernoc*) and what appears to have been a share of a kindred's land (*couuenran que vocatur Rangleumin*), with its under-tenants and their descendants. —*ibid.* pp. 6, 93–4; K. Jackson, *op. cit.*, p. 147. Later in the century the abbey was allegedly given one part of a notable's share of hereditary land, which was held by a serf and his descendants; this share yielded an annual rent which included cereals, pigs, and cash.—*ibid.*, p. 216. Cf. the use of *parentela* in documents of the early tenth and eleventh centuries, *ibid.*, pp. 222, 225, 274, 276.

land in "community of possession" (*cofrit*) was held by a substrate population. Thus, although the Breton *cofrit* and the Welsh *cyfrif* are two distinct words, it is probable that, in ninth-century Brittany, land in community of possession was held on conditions analogous to those recorded at a later date for *tir cyfrif* in Wales.[1]

THE RÔLE OF THE REEVE AS A FACTOR
FAVOURING CONTINUITY

The various strands of evidence presented in these pages are necessarily disparate. They can however be stereoscopically fused when viewed through the medium of the office of the *maer* (reeve). Redaction B of the Latin texts of the laws contains a statement about the *galanas* of some reeves. *Galanas*, the payment made in lieu of the blood-feud, is also recorded as *galnes* among the customs of the Cumbrians and therefore belongs to the pre-Saxon heritage of Britain. The *galanas* of the reeve of Castell Argoel, near Dinefwr, the historic capital of Dyfed, was substantial. As listed it amounted to 189 cows from three places, a sheep and a pig between two cows (*ovis inter duas vaccas, et porcus*), and two *maenorau* of land (*due maynaur de terra*), with two washerwomen. The *galanas* of each of the other four Demetian reeves mentioned was smaller but still substantial. It amounted to one *maenor*, one washerwoman, and 126 cows with a sheep and a pig between every two cows.[2] Not all the four centres with which these four reeves are equated in the law-text can be located with certainty, but they include two centres already mentioned, namely Dinbych (Tenby) and Llonion. To judge from the inclusion of the *maenor* in the *galanas* of the reeve, there appears to be an old-established link between the office of reeve and fortified courts like Tenby. The reference to washerwomen used in payment recalls the slaves mentioned in the ninth-century poem "in praise of Dinbych." Llonion too, later famous throughout Wales for its barley, was the setting of the *llys* (court) which, according to the poetic prophecy of the mid-tenth century already cited, was to be attacked by the forces of Gwynedd and Powys.[3] This site, near the modern Pembroke Dock, was adjoined by a refuge, probably on a headland to the west, for *Liber Landavensis*

---

[1] *Ibid.*, pp. 28–9. I am particularly indebted to the Abbé Ronsin, archivist of the Archevêché de Rennes, for facilitating access to the original manuscript of the *Cartulaire de Redon*; and also to Professeur L. Fleuriot and Professor M. Richards for their comments on the Breton terms cited from this source.

[2] *The Latin Texts of the Welsh Laws*, pp. 248–9. 266: *Acts of the Parliaments of Scotland* 1, 1844, pp. 299–301; K. Jackson in *Angles and Britons: O'Donnell Lectures*, 1963, p. 66; id., 'The Britons in Southern Scotland', *Ant.* XXIX, 1955, pp. 87–8.

[3] *The Book of Taliesin*, pp. 72–3; *Liber Landavensis*, pp. 124, 255.

claims that among the possessions of Llandaf in St Teilo's day, and in that of Bishop Joseph during the early eleventh century, was *Dinguennham in lonnion*.

The *maer* is also mentioned in other early literary sources including *Armes Prydein*, the patriotic poem of the tenth century. In the Juvencus manuscript the plural of *maer* is used as a gloss on the plural of *actor* (overseer), and again in *Oxoniensis Posterior* the singular form is used as a gloss on *praepositus*.[1] In Brittany, according to the ninth-century charters of the *Cartulaire de l'abbaye de Redon*, this same officer was known as the *mair* or *maior*.[2]

The Breton evidence is especially important, for the Redon charters are sufficiently numerous to confirm in graphic local detail the essential validity of our reconstruction of agrarian organization in early Wales. The inhabitants of ninth-century Brittany included 'notables', freemen, bondmen, some of whom were under-tenants, and others, apparently of an intermediate status, often known as *coloni*, *manentes*, or *heredes*. As in Wales, these various groups contributed rents and services for the maintenance of the *lis* (court) of the local ruler.[3] The rents and services of the bondmen included labour services, the duty of providing for officials as well as horses and dogs, and the payment of food-renders which resembled the foodgifts of bondmen in Wales.[4] One charter dated A.D. 876 is particularly worthy of note, for it records that Prince Pascuueten gave to Redon a *ran* (share of land) of the *chef-lieu* Guerranda which was inhabited by a *colonus* and his brothers. Their obligations had hitherto included not only a food-render to the prince but also smaller renders to two officers, one of whom was a *maior* and the other a *decanus*.[5] Moreover there was one multiple estate in southern Brittany which bore the meaningful name Chaer, or the variants thereof, Kaer, Ker, and Caer. A royal estate comprising cottages, lands, meadows, and vineyards, this *plebs* of Caer embraced a number of settlements as well as the offshore island of Crialeis, which was

[1] *Armes Prydein*, ed. I. Williams, Cardiff, 1964, pp. 1, 18; I. Williams, 'Naw Englyn y Juvencus', BBCS VI, 1931–3, pp. 206–7; I. Williams, 'Glosau Rhydychen', BBCS V, 1929–31, pp. 1–8; *Early Scholastic Colloquies, op. cit.*, p. 8.

[2] *Cartulaire de Redon*, pp. 34, 85, 89, 103, 203, 217; Jackson, *op. cit.*, pp. 156, 161.

[3] *Cartulaire de Redon*, pp. 23, 43, 59, 86, 92, 100, 117, 154.

[4] *Ibid.*, pp. 60, 66, 91–2, 193. In A.D. 858 the prince of Auizac allegedly granted the vill of Ursuualt to Redon, with all its tenants *sine censu, sine tributo et sine pastu caballi vel canum, et sine aliquo majore vel judice*—ibid., p. 95.

[5] *Ibid.*, pp. 209–10; Earlier in A.D. 852 Pascuueten had allegedly granted to Redon two vills, one significantly called *Ranlis*, with their tenants *sine censu, sine tributo, et sine cofrito* to any men save the monks. This was presumably a share (*ran*) of the land hitherto used for the maintenance of the court (*lis*). The render of the two vills comprised oats, wheat, rye, loaves, a pig, a piglet, two sheep, two lambs, and some pence,

cultivated. This complex, with its *manentes*, was granted to Redon by Erispoe, son of King Nominoe in the mid-ninth century.[1]

According to the Book of Iorwerth the greater reeve of the Welsh lawbooks, besides being responsible for regulating the bondmen, was also to hand the goods of the king to the lesser reeve (*maer*) of the *maerdref*.[2] In other words the greater reeve appears to have had some duties as a collector of tribute. In a similar fashion the *mairs* of Galloway as late as the twelfth century were responsible for collecting *cain*, a tribute in cattle, pigs, and cheese. Likewise on the Isle of Man there was an officer known as a *maor* who collected tribute. On this island, as Professor Jackson has shown, the evidence of a bilingual inscribed stone of the fifth century suggests that the Goedelic population was not ancient but had recently been established amidst a pre-existing British population. The application of the name *maor* to an officer on the island suggests therefore that his office may go back to the fifth century. Again, according to the *Gododdin* of Aneirin, the court officer responsible for the year-long feast in the court of Mynyddog, which preceded the British defeat at Catraeth (Catterick) *c.* 600, was known as a *maer*.[3] Since this name, like the Old Cornish *mair*, is derived from the Vulgar Latin *maior* (steward), some at least of the administrative functions of this officer, as recorded in the lawbooks, may date from the late-Roman period; if not indeed from much earlier, for there was an officer with not dissimilar functions in early Irish society.[4]

In Britain the latinized name of the reeve reflects the spread of Latin amongst the upper classes, but the reeve himself, by virtue of his rôle as an intermediary, could have served as an agent of cultural transmission. Professor Jackson has compiled a remarkable list of loan-words taken from Latin into British. Many of these are connected with administration or communal life, such as the words for chancellor, prison, fort, church, foreigner, and district. Others are associated with building such as the words for column, window, wall, door, and glass. There are words associated with housekeeping in the sense of a butler's work and the like, such as cheese, kitchen, oven, and wine. Many are connected with agriculture and hint at improvements

---

[1] *Ibid.*, pp. 55–6; the name *Caer* is preserved in the last syllable of Locmariaquer.

[2] *The Chirk Codex*, pp. 24, 67; *Llyfr Iorwerth*, pp. 18–19, 62.

[3] G. W. S. Barrow, 'Northern English Society in the early Middle Ages', *Northern History* IV, 1969, pp. 19–20; *Acts of the Parliaments of Scotland*, p. 378; W. F. Skene, *Celtic Scotland* III, 2nd ed., Edinburgh, 1890, pp. 279–80; *Canu Aneirin*, pp. 9, 34, 135, 274; K. Jackson, *Language and History in Early Britain*, pp. 173, 354; id., *The Gododdin*, pp. 33–4, 102.

[4] *Crith Gablach*, p. 63; D. A. Binchy, *Celtic and Anglo-Saxon Kingship*, pp. 4, 7, 20. I am particularly indebted to Mr T. Charles Edwards for his comments on early Irish social organization.

effected after contact with Rome; such are the words for beans, hay ditch, fruit, pear-tree, and a grain, possibly rye (*secale*). There are also words associated with the equipment for agriculture such as those for coulter, scythe, and fork.[1] If the structural and administrative terms are appropriate for a greater reeve, the housekeeping and agricultural terms are words such as a steward or lesser reeve might use.[2] Latin speech, as Professor Jackson has argued, was never part of the British heritage as a whole but was confined essentially to the upper classes. When these perished in the villas of the Lowland Zone of Britain and its westward extension along the coastal plateaux of South Wales, this Latin speech died with them. But some words passed on into Welsh. These in the main were the words of the former estate owners, for the land and its use endured.[3] Estates tend to last in one form or another, whoever may own them and whatever language the owner may speak. With such estates is likely to have gone their apparatus and some of their products for which the Vulgar Latin words survived, if not in the mouths of the men at least in the vocabulary of the *maior*, the intermediary between the men and the new master. In north-west Wales there were no villas, but here, despite the advent of tyrants, an awareness of a wider Venedotian administrative unit appears to have survived into the fifth or possibly the sixth century.

Nevertheless, if continuity there was from the Roman period onwards in some parts of Wales, then this continuity is much more likely to have been a continuity of estates than of settlements on unchanging sites. The multiple estate with a church focus as well as a secular focus was already present in the Aberffraw district by the seventh century, and in Meddyfnych *maenor* by the ninth. If the *dinas* overlooking Llandybïe was the refuge of the latter, then to judge from the instance of Dinas Gynfor in Anglesey, the promontory fort of the Iron Age at Twyn-y-Parc in Llangadwaladr possibly served a similar purpose in relation to the Aberffraw estate.[4] Even in troubled times an awareness of linkages between the *llys*, the *llan*, and the *dinas*, and a measure

---

[1] K. Jackson, *op. cit.*, pp. 78–80; White, *op. cit.*, pp. 98–103.

[2] As in medieval Wales so in the Ireland of the eighth century the king was provided with a certain amount of mensal land with which to supply his table. This was attached to his office like the Homeric *temenos basileion* and the *wanaketero temeno* of the Linear B inscriptions.—D. A. Binchy, *op. cit.*, pp. 20–1. In the kingdom of Pylos each of the sixteen tributary localities was in the charge of a "district officer." For these and other parallels between Mycenaean Greece and early Celtic societies see L. R. Palmer, *The Interpretation of Mycenaean Greek Texts*, Oxford, 1963, pp. 83–91, 213, 429, 456; and id., *Mycenaeans and Minoans*, London, 1965, pp. 97–108.

[3] Jackson, *op. cit.*, pp. 94–112; I. A. Richmond in *The Civitas Capitals of Roman Britain*, ed. J. S. Wacher, Leicester, 1966, pp. 19–20.

[4] RCAHM, *Anglesey*, pp. 87–8.

of survival in only one of these components, would have been adequate to preserve a knowledge of estate circumscriptions. It is perhaps significant that the Roman fort of Llanio was sited in a township incorporated in the later parish of Llanddewibrefi (Card) whose *llan* was the abode of a *clas* and the reputed setting of an early synod of the Church.[1] Similarly Basaleg (Mon), the only place in Wales named after *basilica*, probably in its ecclesiastical sense of church as used by Gildas, could have been a component of a multiple estate during the sixth century. According to a memorial of a grant in the *Vita Sancti Cadoci*, one Guallunir gave the land (*ager*) of *Pencarnov* to his son Iudnou to the end "that he and his heirs might serve the *familia* of Cadog with the produce of this land in addition to themselves. The *census* of this land is nine *modii* of beer, bread, and flesh with honey. Nay, wherever the clergy of Cadog may choose to eat or drink, to wit in *Basseleg* or in *Pencarnov*, the aforesaid Iudnou will bring to them the food and drink which we have before mentioned." Yet Pencarn, as it is now known, the place where tradition avers that St Gwladus, mother of St Cadog, built her church, is about three miles distant from Basaleg on the fertile coastal plain of South Wales. Appropriately, at the close of our period Basaleg appears as the mother church of most of the land between the Rhymni and the Ebbw, and included among its chapels one named Henllys (Old Court).[2]

The organization of the multiple estate may provide some clues to the fate of Caerwent. Here, in the Roman period, as an inscription reveals, a local government had the responsibility of maintaining the wellbeing of the town and the territory of the Silures.[3] Caerwent was flourishing as a place of refuge in the troubled times which accompanied the collapse of the Empire, but, it has been cogently argued, the site has yielded no evidence to prove that the town continued long into the fifth century. In particular, there appear to be good reasons for doubting the hitherto accepted interpretation of a structure on the site as a church, and for questioning its attribution to the post-Roman

[1] Lloyd, *op. cit.*, pp. 74, 258–9; *The Black Book of St Davids*, pp. 197–203; Wade-Evans, 'Parochiale Wallicanum', p. 61; CBA, *Archaeology in Wales*, 1969, p. 17.

[2] *Vitae Sanctorum Britanniae et Genealogie*, pp. 124–5, 128–9; 'The Llancarfan Charters', pp. 154–5; Wade-Evans, 'Parochiale Wallicanum', p. 74; *Cartae et Alia Munimenta* 1, ed. G. T. Clark, 1910, p. 38; Gildas, *De Excidio Britanniae*, ed. H. Williams, 1899, pp. 30–1; M. Richards, 'Ecclesiastical and Secular in Medieval Welsh Settlement', *Studia Celtica* III, 1968, p. 12; Lloyd, *op. cit.*, p. 278; National Library of Wales: Tithe Apportionment and Map, Basaleg, 1841.

[3] V. E. Nash-Williams, 'The Roman Inscribed and Sculptured Stones found at Caerwent (*Venta Silurum*)', BBCS XV, 1952–4, pp. 81–7; J. M. Reynolds, in *The Civitas Capitals of Roman Britain*, pp. 72–3; H. R. Loyn in *The Cardiff Region*, ed. J. F. Rees, Cardiff, 1960, p. 90.

period. Thus, the foot of earth and rubble which lies between the foundations of this structure and the ruined remains of the colonnade of the Roman baths may represent made ground rather than a slow accumulation of débris.[1] Accordingly, this structure need not be later in date than A.D. 400. Moreover, the deposition of the massive hoards of late-fourth and early-fifth century coins at Caerwent has been interpreted as evidence that disaster befell the town sometime before A.D. 450.[2] Nevertheless Mediterranean *amphorae* found at Caerwent provide clear evidence of a partial occupation of the town after about A.D. 500. Given these finds of pottery the small number of Byzantine coins of the sixth to the eleventh centuries apparently found at Caerwent may be of greater significance than recent interpretations would suggest. If reinterpreted as representing coinage rather than bullion they would point to a survival of life in at least part of the town.[3] Hence the one metal object attributable to the fifth or sixth century which has been found at Caerwent, namely a double-headed iron pin of Irish or, more probably, Saxon origin. Again, according to the Life of St Tathan, which was composed by a Norman writer, it was at Caerwent that Caradog king of Gwent, permitted the Irish immigrant Tathan to establish a collegiate church in the sixth century. This perhaps stood on the site of the present church south-west of the *forum* but within the walls of the Roman town.[4] Caradog allegedly resigned Caerwent to St Tathan and moved to a *palacium* elsewhere in Gwent Is Coed.

[1] L. Alcock in *Prehistoric and Early Wales*, ed. I. Ll. Foster and G. Daniel, 1965, p. 185; L. Alcock, *Dinas Powys*, 1963, pp. 61, 63; cf. V. E. Nash-Williams, 'Further Excavations at Caerwent, Monmouthshire, 1923–5', A LXXX, 1930, p. 235; V. E. Nash-Williams, 'The Forum-and-Basilica and Public Baths of the Roman Town of *Venta Silurum* at Caerwent in Monmouthshire', BBCS xv, 1952–4, pp. 159–67. On the other hand a small pewter bowl with a Chi-Rho monogram on its base, found near the *forum* and *basilica* at Caerwent, may bear witness to the presence of at least a house-church probably at a time of crisis in the fourth or fifth centuries.— G. C. Boon, 'A Christian monogram at Caerwent', BBCS xix, 1960–2, pp. 338–44; Davies, *op. cit.*, pp. 136, 145.

[2] L. Alcock in *Celtic Studies in Wales*, ed. E. Davies, 1963, pp. 38–9.

[3] V. E. Nash-Williams, 'The Coins found at Caerwent and Caerleon', BBCS II, 1923–5, pp. 92–100; id., 'The Coins found at Caerwent', BBCS IV, 1927–9, pp. 99–100; G. C. Boon, 'A note on the Byzantine Æ Coins said to have been found at Caerwent', BBCS xvII, 1956–8, pp. 316–19; R. E. M. Wheeler, *Prehistoric and Roman Wales*, Oxford, 1925, p. 253. I am particularly indebted to Professor A. C. Thomas for drawing my attention to the B-*amphorae* found at Caerwent and for suggesting that the Byzantine coins may need to be reviewed as potentially coinage not bullion.

[4] A. Fox in *A Hundred Years of Welsh Archaeology*, ed. V. E. Nash-Williams, n.d., pp. 107–8; S. S. Frere in *The Civitas Capitals of Roman Britain*, p. 95; Lloyd, *op. cit.*, p. 279; *Lives of the Cambro-British Saints*, ed. W. J. Rees, Llandovery, 1853; K. Meyer, 'A Collation of Rees's Lives of the Cambro-British Saints', *Y Cymmrodor* xiii, 1900, p. 293; E. G. Bowen, *Celtic Seaways and Settlements*, Cardiff, 1969, pp. 61, 201.

Nevertheless his kingdom took its name from Caerwent, *Venta Silurum*, the capital of the city-state of the Silures and the main Roman town in Wales. If the testimony of Asser may be accepted, Caerwent in his day was a populous place and probably the site of an abbey. Later in the tenth century this abbey was no doubt the abode of the abbot (*abbas guentonie urbis*) and the reader (*lector urbis guenti*) who are named as witnesses in *Liber Landavensis*. Significantly the same compilation refers to the clergy of Caerwent as the *presbiteri tathiu*. Better however is the evidence of Domesday Book which, though portraying Caerwent in rather confused terms, nevertheless reveals that it was the centre of an important multiple estate with an outlier some two miles distant at Caldicot.[1]

Nor was Caerwent the only Roman site selected for a church. Thus for example, at Caerleon, the church of St Cadog was placed on the site of the former *praetorium* within the legionary fortress. On the opposite bank of the River Usk, to judge from a detailed perambulation in *Liber Landavensis*, was located the *territorium* of Julius and Aaron, the holy martyrs of the Roman period who are mentioned by Gildas. If we may accept the memorial of yet another grant in the *Vita Sancti Cadoci*, there was, close at hand, "a half part (*partem*) of land near *Civitas Legionis*," given to St Cadog in perpetual right of possession. This allegedly was land which concerned the donor, one Retone, by right of inheritance but which, because at that time it had devolved on another, he bought and gave to the church.[2]

Further west in Dyfed it was perhaps a wish to retain control of the focal township of a multiple estate which explains the exclusion of the significantly named Trelissey from grants which, according to *Liber Landavensis*, had been made to St Teilo in the sixth century. These were grants of "*Lan rath* (Amroth) and *lann cronnguern* (Crunwear) with the three territories of *amrath*." Whatever the fate of the romanized farmstead of Trelissey, the exclusion of the lands which surrounded it from the grants made to St Teilo could have been a deliberate step, for these lands, if only supplemented by Trelissey, would have formed a natural unit on the coastal plateau, well defined by the Cronwern Brook on the eastern side and by the Nant Rath on the western.[3]

[1] Asser's *Life of King Alfred*, ed. W. H. Stevenson, 1904, pp. lxxiii, 65, 313–14; *Liber Landavensis*, pp. 2, 22, 243; DB I, 162a.

[2] Bowen, *op. cit.*, pp. 93, 210; Gildas, *De Excidio Britanniae*, pp. 26–7; *Liber Landavensis*, pp. 225–6, 377; Davies, *op. cit.*, p. 136; W. Rees, *Historical Map of South Wales and the Border in the Fourteenth Century*, Cardiff, 1952; *Vitae Sanctorum Britanniae et Genealogiae*, pp. 128–9; Wade-Evans, 'The Llancarfan Charters', pp. 164–5.

[3] *Liber Landavensis*, pp. 124, 255; Rees, *op. cit.*; W. G. Thomas and R. F. Walker, 'Excavations at Trelissey, Pembrokeshire, 1950–51', BBCS xviii, 1958–60, pp. 295–303.

In the post-Roman period the multiple estate, with its characteristic sharing of functions between different component settlements, appears to have provided a guiding framework for the evolution, or the devolution, of settlement.[1] The countryside was probably divided into territorial units ruled by kings but served by reeves. The survival of the word *maer* (*maior*) hints at the survival of at least some of his functions throughout our period. Moreover the re-use of Iron-Age forts for defensive purposes in times of stress in itself suggests that the dispositions of the main settlements within already established territorial frameworks may have continued with but little change from the early Iron Age onwards. In this event, changes which took place in Roman times and later were to a considerable degree merely dovetailed into pre-existing frameworks. This would explain the arrangement of the main components of the settlement pattern in Castell, a large township on the western flank of the Conway valley. Inhabited during the thirteenth century in the main by freemen, it then still contained a number of bond enclaves alike in the uplands and the lowlands.[2] The *hendref* (old settlement) of Castell lay on the valley floor within a mile of, but some 1,200 feet below, the elaborately defended Iron-Age hill-fort of Pen-y-Gaer. The emphasis on fortification implicit in the name Castell would have been appropriate not only for Iron-Age times but also for later periods. Some two miles to the north-east of the *hendref* the Romans established the fort of *Canovium*,

[1] The division of functions between the court (*llys*) and the church (*llan*) in the typical multiple estate may well explain some puzzling statements in the lawbooks concerning the consecration of churches in bond townships. In a legal triad it is stated that in "a bond settlement in which a church is consecrated with the consent of a king, a person of that settlement who is a bondman in the morning becomes that night a freeman."—*The Laws of Hywel Dda*, p. 105; *Llyfr Blegywryd*, p. 112. Some versions of the laws, including the oldest Latin text, stipulate that, before this privilege was accorded, Mass had to be said in the church, and corpses buried within its precincts.—*The Latin Texts of the Welsh Laws*, p. 132; *Llyfr Colan*, p. 34. These provisions notwithstanding, the medieval extents record the existence of many bond settlements containing churches, though it is true to say that most of these contained bond hereditary land (*tir gwelyog*) rather than reckoned land (*tir cyfrif*), which was held by the most servile of the bond tenures. Accordingly it seems likely that the provisions concerning the consecration of churches relate to an earlier period, as their inclusion among the triads would suggest. They would have been appropriate in a period when the consecration of churches was a rare event because a mother church would normally have served all the component settlements of a multiple estate save the court which had its own chapel. Hence probably the statement in the laws of the court that the priest of the royal bodyguard and the queen's personal priest had the right to conduct an offender under protection (*nawdd*) to the sanctuary of the nearest church.—*The Laws of Hywel Dda*, p. 27; *Llyfr Blegywryd*, pp. 6–7; *Llyfr Iorwerth*, p.16.

[2] T. Jones Pierce, 'The Gafael in Bangor Manuscript 1939', *Hon. Soc. Cymm.*, 1942, pp. 158–88.

later named Caerhun because, tradition avers, Rhun son of Maelgwn Gwynedd had a *llys* (court) here. Many centuries later a medieval motte, now known as Bryn Castell, was sited towards the northern limit of the township at a point commanding an ancient ford over the River Conway.[1] Throughout our period therefore it would appear that Castell was of strategic significance along the line of the Conway; hence the preservation of the administrative unity of the township despite its unwieldy extension from near sea level to an altitude of over 3,000 feet.[2]

With economic development the fission of such units had generally supervened in most localities, including the fertile Vale of Clwyd.[3] Nevertheless the very striking contrasts in the broad pattern of settlement, as between the Vale of Clwyd and the Conway valley alike in the Iron Age and in the medieval period would suggest that the basic territorial framework of settlement was already established before the advent of the Roman legions. Narrow, easily flooded, and with but few fertile islands or terraces of dry soil along its floor, the Conway valley was flanked by few hill-forts in the Iron Age. Correspondingly it contained relatively few important settlements by the thirteenth century and only three or four reeves' settlements. On the other hand the Vale of Clwyd is wide and contains frequent median mounds and extensive terraces with fertile, well-drained soils. Not surprisingly

[1] RCAHM, *Caernarvonshire*, I, 1956, pp. 21, 27–38, 100–3. The parish church of Caerhun stands in the north-eastern corner of the Roman fort and in earlier centuries was adjoined by a small hamlet green.

[2] G. R. J. Jones, 'The Distribution of Bond Settlements in North Wales', WHR, 1964, p. 33; cf. also Talgarth (Mont) where the mensal land of the court consisted of two distinct areas. The larger of the two areas, known as the hamlet of *Tir Bwrdd* the Greater, was at an altitude of about 500 feet and has yielded evidence of Roman occupation; the other, known as the hamlet of *Tir Bwrdd* the Lesser, a mile or so distant, was at an altitude of about 1,000 feet. Significantly it adjoined a hamlet named *Maerdref* (Reeve's Settlement) which embraced on its common pastures a huge hill-fort.—*ibid.*, pp. 34–6.

[3] As Professor M. Richards has demonstrated ('Early Welsh Territorial Suffixes', *Jnl Royal Soc. Antiquaries of Ireland* xcv, 1965, pp. 205–12), territorial suffixes added to personal names form an extremely rich element in a very early stratum of Welsh onomastics. All the persons who can be identified with varying degrees of certainty are men who lived between the fifth and tenth centuries. The territorial units so designated range in size from the kingdom, through the *cantref* and commote, to the township. Professor Richards tentatively suggests that territorial suffixes ceased to become viable not later than the tenth or eleventh centuries. This accords well with the thesis advanced above (pp. 329–30) that partible inheritance among notables at first led to the subdivision of large *maenor* estates into component townships, and only after the eleventh or twelfth centuries brought about the internal subdivision of townships into free *gwelyau*. For the subdivision of the larger territorial units see M. Richards, 'The Significance of *Is* and *Uwch* in Welsh Commote and Cantref Names'—WHR II, 1964, pp. 9–18.

therefore it was flanked during the Iron Age by numerous hill-forts, presumably the refuges of correspondingly numerous settlements on the many favourable sites within the Vale. In the thirteenth century likewise, it contained many reeves' settlements and numerous other important settlements.[1]

In these two valleys and probably throughout Wales the agrarian economy with which we have been concerned appears to have been old-established. As the evidence of pollen stratification in the peat bogs of Central Wales is beginning to show, pastoral farming appears to have predominated in Wales from Neolithic times onwards. But this does not mean that arable farming was of no significance; and fluctuations there must have been from time to time in the relative importance of these two aspects of husbandry. The natural chronicle of the landscape provided by pollen has already revealed that in the Roman period and again after about 1150 arable farming must have been of greater importance than in the intervening period. Nevertheless the evidence of the palynologist confirms that of the archaeologist and the historian in suggesting that, even in Central Wales, cultivation did not disappear during this intervening period. On the contrary, the pollen evidence suggests that, following the regeneration of woodland which accompanied the Roman withdrawal, there ensued a long phase during which cultivation gradually increased in importance.[2] All the evidence available for Wales, whether written or material, points to the existence of a territorial organization far more stable than earlier investigators have hitherto envisaged for the long period between the departure of the legions and the coming of the Normans. Over these centuries the slow agrarian development of Wales was essentially a variation on a well-established theme whose keynote had been struck in a distant past.

[1] *Ordnance Survey Map of Southern Britain in the Iron Age*, 1967; G. R. J. Jones, 'Rural Settlement: Wales', *Advancement of Science* xv, 1959, p. 341.

[2] P. D. Moore, 'Human influence upon vegetational history in North Cardiganshire', *Nature* CCXVII, 1968, pp. 1,000–9; P. D. Moore and E. H. Chater, 'The changing vegetation of west-central Wales in the light of human history', *Jnl of Ecology* LVII, 1969, pp. 361–79; cf. J. Turner, 'The anthropogenic factor in vegetational history', *New Phytologist* LXIII, 1964, pp. 73–90.

ANGLO-SAXON ENGLAND TO 1042

By H. P. R. FINBERG
M.A., D.Litt., F.S.A., F.R.Hist.S.
Professor Emeritus of English Local History
University of Leicester

CHAPTER I*

REVOLUTION OR EVOLUTION?

R EVOLUTIONS IN rural economy are not always concomitant with political revolution. At least nine Germanic kingdoms had established themselves in Britain by the year 600, and the first question we have to face here is what changes, if any, this political revolution, and the obscure century and a half which led up to it, had brought about in the agrarian life of the former Roman province.

It is necessary to distinguish between conquest and settlement. Far back in the time of imperial rule men of Germanic origin had served in units of the Roman army stationed here. Inscriptions record the presence at Housesteads (N'umb) after Caracalla's pacification of the northern frontier (A.D. 212) of Frisian and German troops, and at Burgh-by-Sands (Cumb) of a German cohort, a thousand strong.[1] In 278 the emperor Probus removed Burgundians and Vandals, east Germans living beyond the Oder, to Britain, where they settled and helped the government to quell an incipient revolt.[2] In 306 Constantius Chlorus brought a force of Alamanni under their own king to Britain as auxiliaries, and when he died they took a leading part in promoting the accession of his son Constantine.[3] Pottery found at Birdoswald (Cumb) and believed to come from the Rhineland has been held to indicate that Germanic forces were installed by Count Theodosius when he reorganized the northern defences in 369.[4] Three years later a strong force of Alamanni already stationed in Britain were placed by Valentinian I under the command of one Fraomar, who had previously ruled over a tribe dwelling opposite Mainz.[5]

* I am greatly indebted to the scholars who were good enough to read the following chapters and by their criticisms helped me to improve the first draft. Especial thanks are due to Mr P. J. Fowler, Professor V. H. Galbraith, Professor H. E. Hallam, Dr C. R. Hart, Miss S. Harvey, Professor E. Miller, Dr J. R. Morris, Dr M. Spufford, and Dr J. Thirsk. I am grateful also to Mr H. Fox for his kind help with some of the maps.—H.P.R.F.

[1] R. G. Collingwood and R. P. Wright, *Roman Inscriptions in Britain*, I, Oxford, 1965, nos. 1576, 1594, 1597, 2041.

[2] *Zosimi Historia Nova*, I, 68, ed. L. Mendelssohn, Leipzig, 1887, p. 49.

[3] Sextus Aurelius Victor, *Epitome de Caesaribus*, XLI, 3, ed. F. Pichlmayr, Leipzig, 1911, p. 166.

[4] S. Frere, *Britannia*, 1967, p. 355.

[5] Ammianus Marcellinus, XXIX, 4; cf. H. P. R. Finberg, *Lucerna*, 1964, p. 12 *n.*, and Frere, *op. cit.*, p. 220 *n.* The passage in Ammianus has been misinterpreted by Collingwood and more recently by J. N. L. Myres, *Anglo-Saxon Pottery and the*

It is reasonable to suppose that some of these imported German soldiers married native women and remained in Britain when their term of service expired. A certain Barates is known to have purchased a girl, by birth a Catuvellaunian, set her free, and married her. He called her his queen, Regina, and when she died at the age of thirty he set up a tombstone on which she is portrayed holding a distaff, spindle, and work-basket with balls of wool. Barates was a native of Palmyra, not a German, but he is unlikely to have been a solitary case, except perhaps in the fervour of his conjugal devotion.[1]

The government of the later Empire also bred Germans on Roman soil by the system of *laeti*. *Laetus* is a Germanic word used to describe barbarian settlers either planted in tribal groups under the control of Roman prefects or assigned to individual landowners. In 465 the praetorian prefect decreed that when *laeti* had intermarried with *coloni* or slaves their offspring should go to the landowner, not to the army.[2] They were primarily tillers of the soil, but with a liability for military service. Contemporary orators, in alluding to this dual function, lay particular stress on the agricultural work of the *laeti*.[3] The *Notitia Dignitatum* lists groups of Swabian *laeti* settled around Rheims, Bayeux, Coutances, Senlis, Le Mans, and Clermont-Ferrand, and of Franks near Rennes.[4] One would give much to know whether similar groups of peasant soldiers were planted in Britain also, perhaps behind the forts of the so-called Saxon Shore, but unfortunately the *Notitia* breaks off its list before crossing the Channel. All we can say for certain is that the *laeti* reappear under that name in the continental Germanic law-codes and also in the earliest Anglo-Saxon laws.[5]

The native authorities who assumed control after the collapse of imperial rule in Britain revived the Roman policy of hiring Germanic mercenaries to defend the island. Gildas, writing in the second quarter of the sixth century, states that "a proud tyrant" ruling in Britain found himself faced with a serious threat from behind the northern frontier. To meet this, he introduced a force of Saxons. Three shiploads

Settlement of England, Oxford, 1969, p. 66 *n*. On the same page Dr Myres cites Dio Cassius, LXXI, 16, for the statement that Marcus Aurelius settled Marcomanni in Britain; they were in fact Iazyges, Sarmatian horsemen from the Hungarian plain.

[1] Collingwood and Wright, *op. cit.*, no. 1065. The tombstone was found at South Shields in 1878.

[2] A. H. M. Jones, *The Later Roman Empire*, Oxford, 1964, p. 244. According to J. Grimm, *Deutsche Rechtsalterthümer*, 2nd ed., Göttingen, 1854, p. 307, the word *laetus* implies a condition of bondage.

[3] *XII Panegyrici Latini*, ed. R. Mynors, Oxford, 1964, pp. 189–90, 229.

[4] *Not. Dig.*, pp. 216–17; Donald A. White, *Litus Saxonicum*, Madison, 1961, pp. 61, 62.

[5] See below, p. 431. On the ceramic evidence for early Germanic settlement see Myres, *op. cit.*, p. 67 and *passim*.

of Saxons arrived in answer to his call and "fixed their terrible claws" into the eastern part of the island.[1] Bede, who finished the composition of his History in 731, interprets this passage as meaning that the Saxons were given land to settle in. He follows Gildas in stating that the three shiploads were soon followed by many others, and that the Britons undertook to keep the newcomers supplied with provisions.[2] This arrangement kept them quiet "for a long time" according to Gildas; for little more than a decade if we accept the reckoning which places the original, north-eastern, settlement in 443, and the later, Kentish, settlement of Hengist and his followers about ten years later.[3]

Archaeology helps to fill out the picture. It has brought to light early Anglo-Saxon cemeteries in significant proximity to the gates of such Roman towns as York, Malton, Ancaster, Cambridge, and Leicester. York was the most important military centre in Roman Britain. Less than a mile from the centre of its legionary fortress urn-burials have been found showing in their pottery close affinity with urns from Germanic cemeteries on the continent. Similar urns from Sancton, Broughton, and Elmswell on the Yorkshire Wolds suggest the presence of Germanic auxiliaries who drew their supplies from that rich corn-growing area.[4] On the hillside to the south-east of Caistor-by-Norwich many hundreds of pots have been dug up, betraying by their form and ornament obvious Germanic taste. A few of them would be dated on continental parallels to the later fourth century, and quite a number between 400 and 450. Within the walls of Roman Canterbury there were already some Saxon huts in Hengist's time, for sherds of Saxon or Frisian pottery of this date have been found in hut floors and pits intruded into the remains of Roman buildings. Early Saxon burials at Dorchester-on-Thames, Frilford, and Long Wittenham occur in close proximity to Romano-British settlements. The consensus of archaeological opinion now interprets all these finds as testifying to the presence of Germanic mercenaries installed by Roman-British authority near walled towns and other Roman sites.[5]

---

[1] Gildas, *De Excidio et Conquestu Britanniae*, XXIII, in *Monumenta Germaniae Historica, Auctores Antiquissimi*, XIII, ed. Mommsen, Berlin, 1898, p. 38.

[2] Bede, *Historia Ecclesiastica*, I, 15, ed. C. Plummer, Oxford, 1896, p. 31.

[3] C. F. C. Hawkes, in *Dark-Age Britain*, ed. D. B. Harden, 1956, pp. 92–6. More recently J. Morris has argued that the original three shiploads arrived *c.* 430 and that the northerners they were hired to repel were sea-borne Picts.—*Britain and Rome*, ed. M. G. Jarrett and B. Dobson, Kendal, 1966, pp. 155–7.

[4] P. Hunter Blair, *The Origins of Northumbria*, Newcastle, 1947, pp. 37–43.

[5] Myres, *op. cit.*, pp. 6–8. Here and in other recent archaeological writing certain grave-goods are confidently – perhaps too confidently – assigned to *laeti* rather than *foederati* or some other branch of the military establishment.

Thus by the middle of the fifth century the population of the island in all probability included an appreciable element of Germanic blood and speech, and, as a natural sequel, a hybrid Anglo-British element. The presence in force of German settlers, bound to the native authorities by fragile treaty arrangements, may well have contributed not a little to the subsequent establishment of Anglian kingdoms in Bernicia, Deira, Lindsey, and East Anglia. It was in Kent, if Nennius and the Anglo-Saxon Chronicle can be trusted, that the mercenaries first turned their arms against their employers. Gildas paints a lurid picture of the massacres that followed, but he seems here to be compressing incidents which in fact spread over half a century or more, for he himself makes it clear that after the initial successes of Hengist the Britons put up a prolonged, skilful, and often successful resistance. Meanwhile immigrants in ever increasing numbers poured into the island. No doubt much blood was shed; under the year 491 the Anglo-Saxon Chronicle records that not a single Briton was left alive when Ælle and his South Saxons took the Roman fort Anderida near Pevensey by storm. Forts and towns were in any case the likeliest scenes of such local massacres, and many warriors on both sides would perish on the battlefields, but a wholesale slaughter of the rural population would be difficult to compass even if it had been desired.

We shall find in the earliest West Saxon laws clear evidence of a mixed Anglo-British society in seventh-century Wessex. Cerdic, the traditional founder of the West Saxon royal house, and Caedwalla, who reigned briefly over the kingdom in the 680's, both bear obviously British names. The first element in the name Caedbad, an early king of Lindsey, is also British.[1] Eanfrid, eldest son of Ethelfrith, king of Bernicia, married a daughter of the Pictish royal house, and his brother Oswiu seems to have married into the British family ruling southern Cumbria.[2] These examples of royal intermarriage are very likely to have been followed in the lower ranks of society.

For a period of unknown duration Britons and Anglo-Saxons had to face and surmount difficulties of linguistic intercourse. The personal name Wealhstod, borne by a monk of Lindisfarne c. 685, by a bishop of Hereford c. 730, and by a Mercian or West Saxon priest in 744, means an interpreter of Welsh; it could not have come into use as a baptismal name until it had become familiar as denoting the occupation of a professional interpreter.[3] Several place-names on our maps today

---

[1] F. M. Stenton, *Preparatory to Anglo-Saxon England* (hereafter cited as *Collected Papers*), Oxford, 1970, p. 129.

[2] H. P. R. Finberg, *The Early Charters of the West Midlands*, Leicester, 1961, p. 168.

[3] W. G. Searle, *Onomasticon Anglo-Saxonicum*, Cambridge, 1897, p. 481; J. R. R. Tolkien in *Angles and Britons*, Cardiff, 1963, pp. 23, 24.

must have originated at a time when English settlers formed a minority among a predominantly Celtic-speaking population. Pensax (Worcs) is a Welsh name meaning 'hill of the Saxons', and Englebourne (Devon) is 'the bourne or stream of the English'.[1] Such names point to a bilingual phase in early English history,[2] which may well have been protracted. As natural increase and fresh waves of immigration multiplied the Germanic population this change, coupled with the growing political ascendancy, would tend in time to make English the dominant speech. The English have never been good linguists, and no Englishman will be at pains to learn Welsh if he can help it.

It is always the dominant race which sets the fashion in personal names. Such names, therefore, cannot be taken as a sure proof of ancestry. In the tenth century we find record of two Cornishmen who coupled their indigenous names with names borrowed from their English overlords.[3] A generation or two later the Celtic descent of their families would in all probability be completely masked under Anglo-Saxon names.

As with personal names, so with place-names. Susibre, the British name for a hill in the north Cotswolds, appears in a Mercian charter dated 718;[4] after that – but how soon after we cannot tell – it disappears; it is now called Chastleton Hill. By contrast, Cynibre, the British name for a wooded hill in Staffordshire, recorded in a charter of 736,[5] has survived as Kinver to the present day. A charter issued by Centwine, king of Wessex, in the last quarter of the seventh century, illustrates the process of change: it speaks of a hill "named Cructan in the British tongue, by us Crycbeorh."[6] This is now Creechbarrow. Here *cruc*, the British word for a hill, mound, or barrow, is being consciously absorbed into Old English, but coupled with an English synonym. Behind the modern *combe* or *coomb* lies the Old English *cumb*, and behind that again the British *cumbo*, just as the early British

---

[1] On Pensax see E. Ekwall, *Oxford Dictionary of English Place-Names*, 4th ed., Oxford, 1960, p. 362, and cf. K. Jackson, *Language and History in Early Britain*, Edinburgh, 1953, p. 539. On Englebourne, PN *Devon*, p. 326. Ekwall, *op. cit.*, p. 167, thinks this name points to an Anglian settlement in Saxon territory, but since the place lies in a district covered by an Anglo-Saxon charter of 846, the boundary of which contains clear indications, including a primitive Cornish word for lime-kiln, of a mixed Anglo-Celtic population surviving in the ninth century, the name is far more likely to have originated in the same circumstances as Pensax: see H. P. R. Finberg, *West-Country Historical Studies*, Newton Abbot, 1969, pp. 13–22.

[2] Cf. K. Jackson, *op. cit.*, pp. 241–6.

[3] CS 1197, 1231.

[4] CS 139, perhaps better dated 727.

[5] CS 154.

[6] CS 62, dated 672, but more probably ascribed to 682.

duno, later *din*, meaning a hill or fort, underlies the Old English *dun*, now *down*.[1]

Occasionally the Anglo-Saxons invented a name of their own for some natural feature, as when they called a Gloucestershire stream the Tillath or Tillnoth; but after a while the Celtic or pre-Celtic name reasserted itself, and the river has ever since been known by its older name, the Coln.[2] British river-names have indeed survived in every part of England.[3] So have the names of Roman towns. Canterbury, it is true, is *Cantwaraburg*, the town of the Germanic settlers in Kent, but its British name, *Dorovernia*, far from being forgotten, was stamped on an English coin of the early seventh century, and was still being used by its archbishops in formal documents as late as 1042.[4] And when a village or a hamlet passed from British into English hands, its name would naturally reflect the change of ownership. Thus Withington (Glos), in the post-Roman period doubtless the estate of a British landowner, became *Widiandun*, that is, Widia's hill pasture, as a matter of course when appropriated by an Anglo-Saxon of that name.[5] Where the Anglo-Saxons created entirely new settlements on land previously unoccupied, these naturally received English names from the start, but in the innumerable cases where an Old English personal name is coupled with a habitative element like –*ham* or –*tun*, the place-name does not by itself provide certain evidence that an Englishman founded the settlement; he may conceivably have taken the place of a dispossessed Briton.

When we turn from the names of places to the places themselves, we are brought up short by Maitland's contention that agrarian history becomes more catastrophic as we trace it backwards, and that it is doubtful whether any village in England has not been once, or more than once, a deserted village.[6] And it is true that we cannot prove the continuous existence of an English village which is named for the first time in an eighth-century charter, reappears in Domesday Book 300 years later, and is then again lost to view until the thirteenth century. The best we can hope to do is to establish a weight of probability sufficient to persuade anyone who approaches the subject with an open mind.

In almost every period village communities have moved from their

[1] A. H. Smith, *English Place-Name Elements*, Cambridge, 1956, I, pp. 119, 139.

[2] It is *Tillath* in CS 156 (*c.* 736), *Tillnoth* in CS 217 (774), *Tilnoth* in CS 299, an undated perambulation of Withington.

[3] See the distribution-map, no. 2, in A. H. Smith, *op. cit.*

[4] C. H. V. Sutherland, *Coinage and Currency in Roman Britain*, Oxford, 1937, p. 109; K 1332.

[5] Finberg, *Lucerna*, pp. 42, 58.

[6] F. W. Maitland, *Domesday Book and Beyond*, Cambridge, 1897, pp. 364, 365.

original site, impelled by the need for a better water supply, by the superior opportunities for buying and selling on a main road, or even by a landowner's caprice. It need not surprise us, therefore, that the thirty-three Saxon houses excavated by E. T. Leeds, and long regarded as a typical early Saxon village, were found on a deserted site between Drayton and Sutton Courtenay, or that an ancient village site covering at least 250 acres is situated in the middle of the now enclosed north field of Long Wittenham (Berks), and this in an area which provides abundant evidence of continuous occupation.[1] Discontinuity of site may in certain cases imply, but does not by itself prove, discontinuity of settlement.

At this point we may permit ourselves a glance at one or two places where the balance appears to come down strongly in favour of continuity.[2]

Under the parish church and in the churchyard at Lyminge, near Folkestone (Kent), abundant traces of Roman building have been found, but unfortunately not dated. If the archaeologists are right in believing it to have been a private dwelling, it may well have had, like the Roman villa at Lullingstone in the same county, its Christian chapel. Two pagan cemeteries, one a quarter of a mile south-east of the church, the other about half a mile across the valley, show that groups of Germanic origin settled here early in the sixth century. Most of the grave-goods appear to have been buried during the middle and latter part of that century. By 600 Christianity had become the official faith of Kent, and Augustine, encouraged by King Ethelbert, not only built new churches but also repaired those of the Roman and post-Roman period. There are indications that Lyminge was one of those built or restored at this time, for Roman building material is embedded in the walls of the church, which is one of a small group now recognized as the work of architects and masons who accompanied Augustine to Kent, or followed shortly after. Lyminge was now the centre of a royal estate. Its name is a hybrid, the Germanic *ge*, meaning district, having been tacked on to Limen, the British name of the East Rother. In 633 King Eadbald gave it to his sister Ethelburg for the founding of a minster. A series of charters from 697 onwards show the community being enriched by royal grants of pastures, fisheries, and ploughlands. Like other such establishments, it subsequently devolved upon the local bishop, in this case the archbishop of Canterbury, who kept it until the sixteenth century. In the face of such

[1] *Archaeologia* XCII, 1947, p. 79; VCH *Berkshire*, I, pp. 220–2, 229–32.

[2] Excavations, not yet completed, point to continuous occupation of the Roman site at Portchester (Hants) from the late third century through and beyond the Anglo-Saxon period.—B. Cunliffe in *Ant. J.* L, 1970, p. 67.

a record it is difficult to believe that Lyminge was at any time a deserted village.[1]

In the third quarter of the eighth century King Ethelbald of Mercia granted to the bishop of Worcester an estate at "Baecceshora," the modern Batsford (see Fig. 46).[2] This parish extends from the 400-feet contour line on the level ground near Moreton-in-Marsh up the slope of a hill which rises to 800 feet, commanding, at the summit, a fine view over Blockley and the country to the north. In the last 200 feet the ground rises steeply, and it falls away just as abruptly on the northern side. The ridge thus formed is part of the watershed between the Thames and Severn. It is the *ora* (= brink of a hill) which forms the second element in the name Baecceshora. King Ethelbald's grant names no habitation-site, but the bounds were drawn in such a way as to include at the south-east corner, on the Roman Fosse Way, a hamlet named Dorn. This has long been known as a Roman site. Haverfield saw nearly 200 Roman coins at the present farm. In a large arable field lying between the farm and the Fosse Way traces of stone foundations have been observed, with many fragments of Roman pottery. West of this, in the railway cutting, two sculptured stones were found.[3] Dorn now figures on the Ordnance Survey map of Roman Britain as a "major settlement." Its name is derived from the British *duro–*, signifying a gate, a town with gateways, a walled town.[4] Since no town is strictly self-supporting, we must suppose that it formed the market centre for an agricultural or pastoral hinterland. And if so there can be no doubt that the hinterland of Dorn lay not on the marshy, water-logged ground east of the Fosse Way, but on the *ora* of the Saxon place-name, the high ground between Dorn and Blockley, and beyond it the valley of the Blockley Brook, which forms the western boundary of Ethelbald's grant. In the course of the following century the bishop of Worcester laid successful claim to an estate on the other side of the valley, named Upton because it lay high up on the wold.[5] This was in all probability a Roman site. Coins from the reign of Constantine were being found there a hundred years ago, and other Roman objects have come to light in the course of recent

---

[1] VCH *Kent*, III, p. 121; *A. Cant.* LXIX, 1955, pp. 38, 39; Bede ("ecclesias fabricandi uel restaurandi licentiam"), *Hist. Eccl.*, I, 26, ed. Plummer, I, p. 47; *Arch. J.* LVIII, 1901, pp. 403, 406, 419, 431; *Medieval Archaeology* IX, 1965, p. 24; Thomas of Elmham, *Historia Mon. S. Augustini*, Rolls ser. VIII, p. 228; CS 97, 98, 148, 160, 289.

[2] CS 163.

[3] VCH *Worcestershire*, I, p. 221; JRS LI, 1961, p. 133 and Plate XI.

[4] A. H. Smith, PN *Glos.*, I, p. 235; IV, pp. 20, 24, 28.

[5] Finberg, *Early Charters of the West Midlands*, nos. 63, 78, 86. On the meaning of *up–* as a place with a lofty situation, cf. A. H. Smith, *English Place-Name Elements*, II, p. 227.

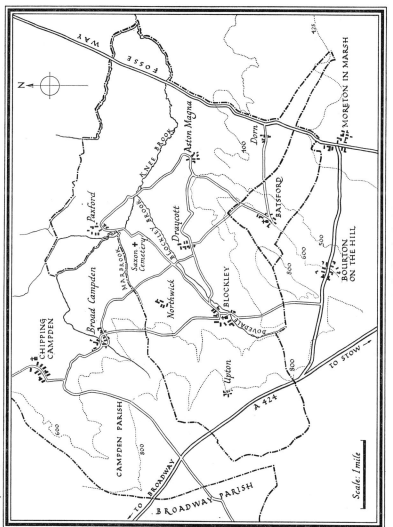

Fig. 46. Batsford and Blockley.

excavation.[1] Before its acquisition by the bishop, Upton belonged to the Mercian royal house. To meet the spiritual needs of his now extensive manor, the bishop built a church down in the central valley at the *leah* or woodland clearing named after one Blocca. This church became the mother-church of the whole district. The bishop's manor-house too was built here, and the estate as a whole was henceforth known as *Bloccan-leah*, or Blockley.[2] Now, if we looked only at Blockley itself, its purely Anglo-Saxon name, and its history from the ninth century onwards, we might be excused for taking it as just another instance of the "unanswered protest" with which the names of our English villages, according to Maitland, refute any notion of a link between their inhabitants and the Roman past.[3] In reality, as we have seen, Blockley comes into existence to serve the needs of two earlier settlements, one probably, the other certainly, Roman. At Dorn, a place of some importance on the Fosse Way which had retained its pre-English name in living use at a time when the neighbouring settlements, Bourton, Daylesford, and Evenlode, had already received English names, the survival of a Welsh-speaking community under Saxon lordship seems clearly indicated.

The Mercian settlers in Shropshire took over Welsh names of villages and hamlets such as Ercall, Hodnet, Lizard, Prees; and, as Professor Kenneth Jackson has remarked, while names of hills and rivers might have been picked up from a few survivors, the adoption of British settlement-names implies the continued existence of British rural communities.[4] Parallels could be cited from Cumberland, Gloucester-shire, and the south-western shires.[5] And what are we to make of the Waltons, "Welshmen's villages," with which the map of England is plentifully besprinkled?

There is a Walton Head in the large West Riding parish of Kirkby Overblow. At another hamlet in the same parish called *Tiddanufri* in the Life of St Wilfrid, later Tidover or Tetherfield, Wilfrid baptized or confirmed a British woman and raised her dead child to life. The mother promised to give the boy to the Church when he should reach the age of seven, but her husband persuaded her to break her promise. They left home and took refuge with another community of Britons. The story is good contemporary evidence of Welsh survival in

[1] A. J. Soden, *History of Blockley*, Coventry, 1875, p. 103; BGAS LXXXV, 1966, pp. 99, 100, 136.
[2] The name is first recorded in 855 as "the minster called Bloccanleeh."—CS 489.
[3] Maitland, *Domesday Book and Beyond*, p. 222.
[4] On Welsh place-names in Shropshire see B. G. Charles in *Angles and Britons*, p. 86; and on the significance of such survivals, K. Jackson, *ibid.*, p. 74.
[5] Cumberland, *ibid.*; Gloucestershire, PN *Glos.*, IV, pp. 23–7; Devon, Somerset, Dorset, PN *Devon*, I, p. xix.

Wharfedale towards the close of the seventh century; it confirms the inference to be drawn from the place-name Walton.[1]

Attempts have been made to minimize the significance of this place-name, on two grounds. In the first place, it is not always possible to distinguish the element *wealh* or *walh* = Welsh from topographical elements like *wald* = woodland, *wall* = wall, and *walu* = ridge. Zachrisson, who published his *Romans, Kelts, and Saxons in Ancient Britain* in 1927, recognized barely a dozen instances where the meaning is certainly Welsh.[2] More recently Ekwall has recognized at least a score, distributed over fourteen counties; he adds that Wales, in the West Riding of Yorkshire, indicates the survival of Britons in the district south-east of Rotherham.[3] No one disputes that Walworth in south London takes its name from a British settlement. It is argued, again, that *wahl, wealh* bears a secondary meaning of slave or serf, and that Waltons can therefore have been villages inhabited mainly by people of servile condition, whatever their racial origin. A. H. Smith, indeed, opines that this is the meaning in the majority of cases.[4] Certainly Ælfric, in his Glossary, uses *weal* and *theow* indifferently for the Latin *mancipium* = slave.[5] Ælfric was a West Saxon, and the same use of *weal* alternately with *theow* occurs in the West Saxon translation of St Matthew's gospel.[6] On the other hand, *servus*, which occurs fifty-five times in the Vespasian Psalter, invariably becomes *theow* in the interlinear translation; *weal* does not occur. This ninth-century Psalter may be either Mercian or Kentish; it is certainly not West Saxon.[7] The Northumbrian version in the Lindisfarne Gospels has *thegn* in Matt. 24, vv. 45, 46, *thrael* in vv. 48, 50. The Rushworth Gospels, also Northumbrian, have *esne* throughout;[8] this is also the

---

[1] *The Life of Bishop Wilfrid by Eddius Stephanus*, c. 18, ed. B. Colgrave, Cambridge, 1927, pp. 38–40; A. H. Smith, *The Place-Names of the West Riding*, Cambridge, 1961–3, V, p. 43, and VII, pp. 31, 32; Glanville Jones in *Trans. Yorkshire Philosophical Soc.*, 1966, pp. 49–53.

[2] *Skrifter utgivna av Kungl. Humanistika Vetenskaps-Samfundet*, Uppsala, XXIV, pp. 41–70.

[3] E. Ekwall, 'Tribal Names in English Place-Names', *Namn och Bygd* XLI, 1953, pp. 160–3, and *Dictionary of English Place-Names*, s.vv. Walbrook, Walburn, Walden, Walford, Walla Brook, Wallington, Walpole, Walton.

[4] *English Place-Name Elements*, II, p. 242.

[5] *Ælfric's Grammatik und Glossar*, ed. J. Zupitza, Berlin, 1880, pp. 18, 19, 101, 102.

[6] *Servus* in Matt. 24, vv. 45–9 is *theow*; in v. 50 *weal*.—*The Gospel according to St Matthew*, ed. J. W. Bright, Boston, 1904, pp. 119, 120.

[7] *The Vespasian Psalter*, ed. Sherman S. Kuhn, Michigan, 1965. Kuhn thinks (p. vi) the interlinear gloss was written at Lichfield in standard literary Mercian. R. M. Wilson thinks it might equally well be Kentish.—*The Anglo-Saxons*, ed. P. Clemoes, 1959, pp. 292–310.

[8] *The Four Gospels in Anglo-Saxon, Northumbrian, and Old Mercian Versions*, ed. W. W. Skeat, 1871–87.

usual rendering of *servus* in the Mercian translation of Bede. It would seem, therefore, that *wealh* in the servile sense is a distinctively West Saxon usage; and if so, it cannot be securely predicated of the many Waltons in other parts of the country.[1]

In assessing the linguistic evidence, the question we ought to ask, then, is not whether the native population of Britain learnt to speak English, but how soon they did so. As J. C. Wedgwood pointed out, "the isolated coloured race that inhabits St Helena, and the almost equally isolated Cape Boys of Cape Colony, speak English or Dutch and have forgotten their original tongue in less than two centuries."[2] How long did it take the Britons to forget theirs? In the seventh century the great Hilda of Whitby employed a neatherd with an obviously British name, Cædmon,[3] yet Cædmon spoke English, and is indeed accounted the earliest English Christian poet. In remote areas the older speech may have been handed down for generations. Down to the nineteenth century shepherds in Cumberland and the Yorkshire Dales used Welsh numerals, in more or less corrupt forms, for counting their sheep, and this has been reasonably interpreted as an inheritance from the Britons of Cumbria.[4]

Our picture of Anglo-Saxon settlement is easily over-simplified if we take insufficient account of political bargaining and treaty arrangements. In his classic *History of Wales*, Lloyd says: "No record has been preserved of the English conquest of Cheshire, Shropshire, or Herefordshire."[5] There is, in fact, little reason to suppose that any such conquest ever took place, and we have good grounds for believing that the original Anglian settlement in Shropshire and Herefordshire was effected by agreement between the Mercian war-lord Penda and his Welsh allies, for in 641 a Northumbrian attempt to split this dangerous coalition was defeated at the battle of Maserfelth, better

---

[1] The tenth-century regulations of the Cambridge Thegns' Guild fix the compensation for the slaying of a *wylisc* (= Welsh) man at half the rate for an English husbandman. This need not mean a slave; it could be a Welshman of any rank or any other foreigner. Cf. EHD I, p. 557, and C. Fox, *The Archaeology of the Cambridge Region*, Cambridge, 1923, p. 283.

[2] *Collections for a History of Staffordshire*, William Salt Archaeological Soc., 1916, p. 146.

[3] This was emphatically the opinion of Henry Bradley, seconded by York Powell: cf. J. C. Atkinson, *Memorials of Old Whitby*, 1894, p. 33.

[4] Michael Barry, 'Traditional Enumeration in the North Country', *Folk Life* VII, 1969, pp. 75–91. This article includes a comprehensive survey of the earlier literature. Professor Kenneth Jackson, in a personal communication, says he has little doubt that the numerals are a genuine survival from the time when Cumbric was still commonly spoken.

[5] J. Lloyd, *History of Wales from the Earliest Times to the Edwardian Conquest*, 1911, I, p. 195.

known as Oswestry, and shortly afterwards we find a son of Penda reigning, with the title of king, over the predominantly Welsh-speaking territory between the Wrekin and the Wye. For two generations this Anglian principality co-existed peacefully with its Welsh neighbours, long enough to establish a minster at Wenlock and to found a cathedral church at Hereford. After the dynasty became extinct, the province was administered by ealdormen who owed their appointment to the Mercian king. The Anglians who settled under such conditions are altogether unlikely to have remodelled the system of husbandry and the pattern of fields and villages they found in this border country.[1]

The Germanic mercenaries whom the Roman and post-Roman authorities installed in the island obviously depended for their provisions on the existing rural economy. If some of them were *laeti*, their husbandry must have conformed to the pattern established by their masters. Down to the time of Hengist they could have had no opportunity, even had they been able, to introduce modifications of agrarian practice. It was only when their increasing numbers made it impossible for the Britons to fulfil their part of the bargain and keep the newcomers supplied with provisions that the process of land-grabbing began. Then the most natural course of action was to drive out the native land-owners and step into their place. Maitland admitted, somewhat grudgingly, that "from the time of the Teutonic conquest of England onwards there may have been servile villages, Roman villas with slaves and *coloni* cultivating the owner's demesne, which had passed bodily to a new master," and Vinogradoff says roundly: "It would be preposterous to suppose that Roman landmarks and arrangements were wilfully destroyed and no advantage taken of the existing stock and labour arrangements."[2] The human tendency to follow the line of least resistance must have operated here as in other fields.

What of agricultural technique? The coulter, which enables the ploughman to slice through heavy soil, had already made its appearance in Roman Britain. To turn over the slices so that they could be drained by exposure to sun and air was a problem solved by fixing a plank, the so-called mould-board, to the side of the plough; and this too was in use in the late Romano-British period.[3] Down to the end of that period Germanic plough-irons show no improvement on those of

[1] Finberg, *Lucerna*, pp. 66–82, and references there cited. Wenlock is a wholly Welsh name = white monastery.

[2] Maitland, *op. cit.*, p. 321; P. Vinogradoff, *The Growth of the Manor*, 1904, p. 221. For a detailed examination of a Roman villa-estate in Gloucestershire which shows no sign of having undergone any significant modification, other than a change of name, under Saxon rule, see *Lucerna*, pp. 21–65.

[3] F. G. Payne, 'The British Plough', AHR v, 1957, pp. 74–84; W. H. Manning, 'The Plough in Roman Britain', JRS LIV, 1954, pp. 63–5.

Britain. There is no evidence whatsoever that the Anglo-Saxon immigrants brought with them better ploughs or a more advanced agricultural technique than those they found when they arrived.[1]

Seebohm, whose book *The English Village Community* was rightly described by Maitland, its chief critic, as making an epoch in agrarian history,[2] put the common-field system of arable husbandry in the foreground of the picture, and hinted that some features of that system might have originated in the Roman world. At the same time, he thoroughly endorsed the conclusion previously reached by Georg Hanssen, that the Anglians, Frisians, Jutes, and Saxons who migrated to Britain could not have brought the system with them because they did not use it themselves in their homelands.[3] And Maitland agreed that it would be extremely rash to assume that the system was commonly used in seventh-century England.[4] Yet other historians of repute have been willing to entertain the notion. Stenton, for instance, was prepared to believe that in eastern Yorkshire, Lincolnshire, the east midlands, and Wessex, arable common fields may date from the beginning of permanent English settlement.[5] And as recently as 1962 H. R. Loyn could write: "One of the basic and still unsolved problems of the whole period lies in deciding if the open-field system of agriculture was brought, virtually lock, stock, and barrel, from the Continent by the invading Germanic peoples; or if, with the germ of it certainly in being in their native institutions, the Anglo-Saxons followed a similar path of agrarian evolution to that practised on the Continent."[6]

Few German or Danish scholars today regard this as an open question. In 1960 A. Krenzlin showed by geographical analysis that big fields with long plough-strips are not a primary phase in the evolution of field patterns; in Germany they supervened upon an earlier layout of *blockfluren*, fields of the approximately square shape which suited the lighter ploughs: in short, what until lately were miscalled Celtic fields.[7] In 1964 G. Mertins examined Frankish settlements in the

[1] F. G. Payne, 'The Plough in Ancient Britain', *Arch. J.* CIV, 1948, pp. 102–9. See also E. M. Jope in *History of Technology* II, 1956, p. 93; P. J. Fowler and A. C. Thomas, 'Arable Fields of the pre-Norman Period at Gwithian', *Corn. Arch.* I, 1962, pp. 61–84.

[2] F. W. Maitland to E. Ashworth, 12 Nov. 1900, printed in his *Letters*, ed. C. H. S. Fifoot, 1965, p. 220.

[3] G. Hanssen, *Agrarhistorische Abhandlungen*, I, Leipzig, 1880, p. 496; F. Seebohm, *The English Village Community*, 4th ed., 1890, pp. 373, 410.

[4] *Domesday Book and Beyond*, p. 365.

[5] Stenton, *Anglo-Saxon England*, 3rd ed., 1971, p. 280.

[6] H. R. Loyn, *Anglo-Saxon England and the Norman Conquest*, 1962, p. 148.

[7] A. Krenzlin, 'Zur Genese der Gewannflur in Deutschland', a paper read to the Vadstena symposium, 1960, printed in *Morphogenesis of the Agrarian Cultural Landscape* (*Geografiska Annaler* XLIII, 1961), pp. 190–203. Cf. D. J. Davis, reviewing the papers of a symposium at Göttingen, AHR XII, 1964, p. 59: "It appears now that the long

Rhineland and the Ruhr dating from the sixth century and found similar fields, comprising only four or five hectares, adjoining the oldest farms.[1] Even more decisive were the excavations conducted between 1960 and 1962 by D. Zoller at Gristede in the north of Oldenburg. Zoller uncovered a settlement on sandy soil begun about the beginning of our era and abandoned at the end of the fourth or the beginning of the fifth century, just when the Saxons were migrating to Britain. The settlement consisted of a number of farmhouses standing on either side of a street, and, adjoining each house, fenced arable fields of some 50 × 50 or 50 × 100 metres, considerably smaller than the later Frankish fields examined by Mertins. The present village of Gristede, founded in the ninth century near and partly overlying the older settlement, ploughed its arable in long ridges and manured it by applying an artificial topsoil of *plaggen*, dung-laden sods pared from the heath and stored under cover during the winter season. The pattern of long plough-strips and intermixed holdings belongs entirely to the later settlement.[2]

An excavation, not yet published, has revealed a similar pattern of square fields at Store Vildmose in northern Jutland; they date from the fourth or fifth century.[3] At Vallhagar in Gotland a settlement of the migration period consisted of dwellings and outbuildings arranged within fields, roughly square, bounded by stone walls.[4]

Evidence is thus accumulating from the coastlands of northern Europe to prove that up to the time of their migration to Britain the field pattern familiar to the English settlers was of exactly the same type as that prevailing at the time in Wessex, widespread traces of which have been revealed by air-photography. If here and there they came upon large fields with the long furrows produced by the heavy plough, they were encountering an appreciably more advanced system than they had known in their homelands.[5]

When they tried to seize political control, they were opposed by British kings – tyrants, Gildas calls them – who had taken up the reins

cherished idea that the 'three-field system' was established at the time of the original settlement has now no supporters.''

[1] W. Abel, *Geschichte der deutchen Landwirtschaft*, 2nd ed., Stuttgart, 1967, p. 15. On the size of continental fields in this period see H. Jankuhn, *Vor- und Frühgeschichte vom Neolithikum bis zur Völkerwanderungszeit*, Stuttgart, 1969, pp. 149–56.

[2] D. Zoller, 'Die Ergebnisse der Grabung Gristede', in *Nachtrichten aus Niedersächsens Urgeschichte*, no. 31, pp. 31–57, and no. 33, pp. 3–23, printed in *Niedersächsisches Jahrbuch für Landesgeschichte*, XXXIV, Hildesheim, 1962; and XXXVI, 1964.

[3] Information kindly supplied by Professor Axel Steensberg.

[4] *Medieval Archaeology* IX, 1965, p. 6.

[5] Cf. J. Thirsk, 'The Common Fields', *Past and Present*, no. 29, 1964, pp. 3–25. In a discussion, remarkable for its acerbity, of this important article, G. C. Homans resolutely turns a blind eye to all recent work.—*Ibid.*, no. 42, 1969, pp. 32, 33.

of government during the fifth century and must have maintained more than the rudiments of political and fiscal organization, else they could not have put armies into the field and countered the Saxon peril, as they did, with a resistance more obstinate than was seen anywhere else in the western empire. Gildas implies that they and their subjects were all Christians, however unworthy of the name. They were faced by Anglo-Saxon war-lords who also styled themselves kings. Many of them claimed descent from the god Woden, and for a while their followers continued to worship their old gods, long enough to leave traces of Anglo-Saxon heathenism in such place-names as Woodnes-borough and Wednesbury;[1] but by the seventh century they too, impelled perhaps as much by policy as by conviction, had accepted Christian baptism, and their conversion involved a deliberate acceptance of things Roman. In 627, when Edwin of Northumbria, the king who used to have Roman ensigns borne aloft before him, caused himself to be baptized by a Roman missionary in the Roman city of York, the language of the Church he entered was the language of the Empire, and the head of that Church was the bishop of Rome, upon whom something of the imperial majesty had devolved. Thus, in becoming Christians, they also became, and meant to become, in more than one sense, Romans.

For revenue the British kings no doubt continued to levy *tributum*, the land-tax of the later Empire. From the time of Diocletian onwards this tax had been paid partly in money, partly in produce. Since the Britons struck no coinage of their own, it may well be that payments in cash were altogether superseded by the system of food-rents we encounter in later Welsh custom. Food-rents, a form of *tributum* which the English called *feorm*, outlived both the Saxon and the Norman conquests, and, as Vinogradoff says, there is hardly any room for doubt that this ancient form of tribute ran in an uninterrupted sequence from the period of British rule.[2] In the third quarter of the eighth century, when an English king granted an estate at Islingham (Kent) to the bishop of Rochester, "with all the *tributum* which it paid to the kings," he at once bore witness to this form of administrative continuity and set an example which would often be followed later.[3]

The structure of rural society in Roman Britain has been examined earlier in this volume. Here it suffices to recall that at its base stood the *coloni*, or dependent cultivators of the soil, and below them the slaves. Both classes will be found reappearing under Anglo-Saxon rule. Thus, when the curtain goes up again at the close of the dark centuries, it

[1] Margaret Gelling, 'Place-Names and Anglo-Saxon Paganism', *University of Birmingham Historical Journal* VIII, 1961, pp. 7–25.
[2] *The Growth of the Manor*, p. 223.   [3] CS 194.

reveals a social structure which both at the top and bottom shows marked resemblances to that of the Roman and post-Roman world.

In the light of the foregoing considerations it will be prudent to think of the anglicization of Britain's rural economy as a long-drawn evolutionary process rather than a sudden and complete revolution.

The great pioneers of our agrarian history, Seebohm, Maitland, and Vinogradoff, worked backwards from the known to the unknown. It is an entirely legitimate method, one which in the hands of the masters yielded admirable results, but it also has its dangers, and it will only occasionally be followed here. Our task is to clear our mind of preconceptions, to work forwards from the beginning, and to examine the admittedly inadequate evidence as it comes, without reading into the laws and charters inferences which derive their justification, if at all, only from later sources. This chronological approach will be far from easy to maintain. It demands a resolute rejection of hindsight where most scholars find themselves almost unconsciously bringing to Anglo-Saxon history preconceptions based not on contemporary evidence but on Domesday Book. This is as anachronistic as it would be to look at the restoration of Charles II in the light of Queen Victoria's jubilee. In the end, history must be written forwards, not backwards. In this difficult field to begin at the beginning and move forward step by step is perhaps the most hopeful way now to establish the truth. At all events, it is time the attempt was made.

CHAPTER II

THE AGRARIAN LANDSCAPE IN
THE SEVENTH AND EIGHTH CENTURIES

NO ESTIMATE of population in the seventh century can be
anything but hypothetical. What is certain is that Britain
was then a land through which the wild creatures of the
wood roamed all the more freely because men were few. St Guthlac
in his solitude at Crowland thought he knew what a bear looked like.[1]
Place-names like Wolvey (Wark), Woolley (Berks), Woolmer (Hants),
Wolborough (Devon), Wolsty (Cumb) testify to the ubiquity of the
wolf, and the boundary clauses of Anglo-Saxon charters are full of
compounds like *wulfpyt*, signifying either a wolf's lair or an artificial
excavation where the creature was trapped.[2]

THE FORESTS

Wolves, boars, deer, and wild cats found ample cover in the still
uncleared natural forests. It is difficult for us to appreciate how much
of England remained densely wooded at the beginning of the Anglo-
Saxon period. Between the Tees and the Tyne lay a region almost
uninhabited except by wild beasts.[3] In Bede's time the site of Beverley
was still known as Inderauuda, "in the wood of the Deirans," a forest
which covered the greater part of Holderness.[4] Similarly Wychwood
in north-west Oxfordshire represents the wood of the Hwicce. In the
west midlands the forests of Dean, Wyre, Morfe, and Kinver, and
in the east those of Rockingham and Sherwood covered scores of
miles. As late as 958 Sherwood touched the boundary of Sutton,
three miles north-west of Retford and well beyond the limit of its
thirteenth-century perambulation.[5] The Boulder-Clay of East Anglia
and the east midlands, much of it heavy impermeable soil, must have

[1] *Felix's Life of St Guthlac*, c. 36, ed. B. Colgrave, Cambridge, 1953, p. 114.

[2] See the examples collected by A. S. Napier and W. H. Stevenson, *Crawford
Charters*, Oxford, 1895, p. 53. *Wulf-pyt* survives today as Woolpit (Suff).

[3] *Symeonis Monachi Opera Omnia*, ed. T. Arnold (Rolls ser. 75), I, p. 339. The
authority is the twelfth-century biographer of King Oswald, but, as Colgrave
remarks (*Two Lives of St Cuthbert*, p. 314), the rarity of early Anglian burials bears
out his description of what is now the county of Durham.

[4] *Hist. Eccl.*, v, 2; p. 283 in Plummer's edition.

[5] CS 1044, 1349.

borne dense forests of oak and ash.[1] The names of Newton Bromswold (N'hants) and Leighton Bromswold (Hunts) commemorate the now vanished Bruneswald. Oak, hornbeam, ash, and thorn dominated the greater part of Essex. The northern edge of this forest sloped away from near the Suffolk border towards the thickly wooded Chilterns. In the south-east the great forest of Andred (Andredsweald) was described by an annalist, writing in the year 892, as 30 miles wide and stretching 120 miles from east to west.[2] In Wessex the forest of Selwood, known to the Britons as Coit Maur, the great wood, ran north and south from the western edge of Salisbury Plain and for a century or more presented a natural obstacle to the westward expansion of the kingdom.

Timber, in Old English, meant building material of any kind, but its more restricted sense points to the general predominance of wood in house-building and fencing. For these purposes, and for their supply of fuel, the Anglo-Saxons naturally drew upon the woodlands. There too they could gather the wild honey from which they brewed the mead that enlivened their festive gatherings. Some of them certainly kept bees at home, but the almost total disappearance of mead from modern life is due as much to the progressive denudation of the forests as to any other single cause.

The woods also served as feeding-grounds for the Anglo-Saxon pig. As such they played a vitally important part in rural economy. In 706, when an under-king of the Hwicce sold Ombersley (Worcs) to Bishop Ecgwine for his newly-founded monastery at Evesham, his charter included a proviso that if the island belonging to the estate should produce an unusually large crop of acorns, beechmast sufficient for one herd of swine should be reserved to the king.[3] So active was the king's interest in swine-pastures that more than a century later a dispute about encroachments by his swine-reeve at Sinton, in Leigh (Worcs), was brought before the great council of the realm. The bishop and clergy of Worcester successfully claimed two-thirds of the wood and mast, and refused to give up mast for more than 300 swine, declaring on oath that such had been the arrangement under King Ethelbald (716–57).[4]

We have already come across the "wood of the Deirans" and the "wood of the Hwicce." The names appear to hint at woodland tracts in which a whole people had once enjoyed rights of pasture. A Kentish charter dated 724 refers to "Limenweara wald" and "Weowera weald," wealds belonging to the settlers in the districts of Lyminge and Wye,[5] and the *Tenetwara*, men of Thanet, originally had their *denn* or swine-

[1] A. G. Tansley, *The British Islands and their Vegetation*, Cambridge, 1949, pp. 173, 174.
[2] EHD I, p. 185.   [3] CS 116.   [4] CS 386.
[5] CS 141. There is another reference to "Limenwero weald" in CS 248, dated 786.

pasture thirty miles away at *Tenetwara denn*, now Tenterden.[1] A grant
of Islingham, north of the Medway, includes four swine pastures
"in commune saltu," more than twenty miles away in the western
Weald.[2] The Weald might be "common," but evidently the kings
of Kent could assign portions of it to particular estates in private hands.[3]

Despite the manifold uses of the forests they were being steadily
eroded throughout the Anglo-Saxon period, so much so that a poet
could speak of the ploughman as "the old enemy of the wood."[4]
King Ine's code (43, 44) imposes a fine of 60 shillings upon the man
who cuts down a tree big enough to shelter thirty swine. If he fells
a large number of trees in a wood, he must pay 30 shillings for each
of the first three, but nothing for the rest, "because the axe is an
informer, not a thief," but if he secretly destroys a tree by fire he
must pay the full fine "because fire is a thief." Nevertheless many
place-names – Brentwood is the most obvious example – indicate
that burning was a commonly practised method of clearance. The
traveller in the western Cotswolds who comes upon a place called
St Chloe may well wonder what the nymph so named was doing
there and how she acquired her sainthood, but the place appears first
in an eighth-century charter as "sengedleag."[5] This word, which in
the neighbouring county of Worcester has become Syntley, is compounded of the Old English *senged*, meaning singed or burnt, and
leah, which from its primary meaning of an open glade in a wood
early developed the secondary sense of a woodland clearing. As *leigh*
or *–ley* it is now one of the commonest elements in our place-names,
its very prevalence bearing witness to the energy with which "the
old enemy" went to work on the woods.

MARSHES AND FENS

Almost equally with the forests, marshland formed a striking feature
of the Anglo-Saxon landscape. The coast on both sides of the Thames
estuary, Romney marsh, and the Pevensey levels offered excellent
pasturage for sheep, but until they were drained they could not house
large numbers of men. Nor could the saltmarsh north of Bristol and
the mosslands of Lancashire. The Somerset levels west of Mendip lay

[1] Ekwall, *Oxford Dictionary of English Place-Names*, s.v. Tenterden.

[2] CS 194, granted between 761 and 765; on the place-names see J. K. Wallenberg,
Kentish Place-Names (Uppsala Universitets Arsskrift), 1931, pp. 47–9.

[3] Cf. CS 260, a grant to the bishop of Rochester of Halling on the Medway, with
appurtenant swine-pastures "in commune saltu" at Speldhurst, Marden, Rusthall,
and elsewhere.

[4] *The Exeter Book, Part II*, Early English Text Soc., 194, 1934, no. 21, line 3.

[5] CS 164, on which see PN *Glos.*, I, p. 98.

under water most of the year, only a few islands of higher ground and the long dry ridge of the Poldens offering sites for early settlement.[1] "Glastingai," the oldest English name of Glastonbury, means the island of Glast's people.[2] King Alfred's biographer describes Athelney as surrounded on all sides by vast swampy and impassable marshes, to be approached only by boat until the king had a causeway built at a great expenditure of toil.[3] Early West Saxon settlers established themselves on the uplands, and year by year waited to move their flocks and herds down to the levels until those rich pastures had been dried out by the summer sun. Hence the name Somerset, originally *Sumorsaete*, the summer dwellers.[4]

"There is in the midland district of Britain," says the biographer of St Guthlac, writing shortly before 730, "a most dismal fen of immense size, which begins at the banks of the river Granta not far from the camp which is called Cambridge, and stretches from the south as far north as the sea. It is a very long tract, now consisting of marshes, now of bogs, sometimes of black waters overhung by fog, sometimes studded with wooded islands and traversed by the windings of tortuous streams."[5] The fens extended beyond the Wash and up the coast of Lindsey. Another belt of marshland stretched for more than thirty miles north and south of the Ouse.

Guthlac's biographer dwells much on the horrors of the wilderness in which his hero contended with the powers of evil. At the same time he makes it clear that a constant stream of visitors made their way to the saint's hermitage at Crowland. The fens, in fact, were neither uninhabited nor unproductive. They naturally abounded in fish and wildfowl. Bede says, rightly, that Ely derives its name from the plentiful supply of eels that were taken there.[6] Unlike their modern descendants, the Anglo-Saxons knew better than to neglect an article of diet as palatable as it is nutritious.

In 697 the king of Kent granted to the church of Lyminge pasture for three hundred sheep in the district of the "Rumining seta," south of the river Lympne.[7] Evidently Romney Marsh, then as now, was highly valued as a feeding-ground for sheep. In 774 King Offa granted Lydd to the archbishop of Canterbury, and his charter alludes to a royal property in Denge Marsh.[8]

---

[1] M. Williams, *The Draining of the Somerset Levels*, Cambridge, 1970, pp. 17–21.
[2] For the early forms of the name see H. P. R. Finberg, *Lucerna*, p. 92 *n.*
[3] *Asser's Life of King Alfred*, ed. Stevenson, pp. 79, 80.
[4] W. G. Hoskins, *The Westward Expansion of Wessex*, Leicester, 1960, p. 6.
[5] *Felix's Life of St Guthlac*, c. 24, p. 87.
[6] *Hist. Eccl.*, IV, 19, ed. Plummer, p. 246.
[7] CS 98.
[8] CS 214. Nothing is known of the King "Adwi" named in this charter.

THE PASTURES

After the woods and marshes, the third most important feature of the agrarian landscape was the *feld*, land free from wood, lying on the downs and moors, or sometimes in the open spaces of the forest. The *feld* provided common pasture for the sheep and cattle. Every village needed such ground, and sometimes two or more villages would share one and the same area of rough grassland. The farther back we trace the usage of intercommoning, the larger the areas over which it was practised. Even after the Norman Conquest men will speak of pastures used in common by all the townships of a hundred. Kentis Moor in Devon, for example, belonged to the whole Hundred of Hayridge; and the Domesday of Suffolk records a pasture common to all the men of the Hundred of Colneis.[1] Every landowner in Devon, except the inhabitants of Barnstaple and Totnes, had the right to depasture his cattle without payment on the purlieus or outer fringe of Dartmoor, and upon the central portion of the moor on payment of $1\frac{1}{2}$d. per head a year for horned cattle, and 2d. per head for horses and colts.[2] Where the commons were large, as in Devon, portions might be ploughed up and sown from time to time: a practice of which more will be said presently; but it was not until the areas of *feld* had been very generally reduced by the advance of tillage that the word acquired the sense of unenclosed land held in common for the purposes of cultivation; and the modern sense of field as an enclosed plot is later still.[3]

THE MEADOWS

Portions of the *feld* could be, and often were, assigned to estates in royal or private hands, without necessarily thereby depriving the villagers of their rights of common. On the other hand, a law of Ine (49) decrees that a man who finds swine intruding in his private mast pasture may take security from their owner against a repetition of the trespass. "Pascua," pastures, figure among the appurtenances of the estate in Thanet which King Hlothhere in 679 granted to Abbot Bercuald. "Pascua" are always distinguished from "prata," meadows. In the same document Hlothhere associates "prata" with his grant of Sturry, and here, as elsewhere, the term signifies meadowland lying along the bank of a river, in this case the Stour.[4] A century later, when King Egbert of Kent granted Bromhey *alias* Broomy in Cooling to the bishop of Rochester, he included four meadows adjoining

---

[1] *Trans. Devonshire Assocn.* XXXII, 1900, p. 546; DB II, p. 339 *b*.
[2] *Publications of the Dartmoor Preservation Assocn.*, Plymouth, 1890, I, p. xxv.
[3] A. H. Smith, *English Place-Name Elements*, I, p. 167.   [4] CS 45.

Cliffe, ranging in size from six to seventeen acres.[1] The meadows were mown for hay, and the aftermath provided grazing for the cattle. As a source of winter fodder meadowland was very highly valued, and in an age which knew no systematic cultivation of grassland as such there was never enough of it to provide all the hay that was needed.

PIG-KEEPING

Numerous place-names compounded from *swin-* and *swine-* prove how generally pigs were kept in Anglo-Saxon England, and evidence already cited shows that the kings of Mercia engaged in it on a big scale. The pigs themselves must have been of the long-legged, long-haired, razor-backed type that survived in Britain until the sixteenth century or later.[2] Lean as they were, they were valued for their meat. Ine's law (49 §3) says that if pasture is paid for in kind, every third pig shall be given when the bacon is three fingers thick, every fourth with it two fingers thick, and every fifth when it is the thickness of a thumb.

The oak and the beech, yielding acorns and mast, kept the pigs well fed throughout the autumn. In winter they fed chiefly on the roots of fern; in spring, on fresh grasses; in summer, on berries and seeds. Nearly every wood included some patches of open ground which could provide such nutriment. There are no references in this early period to swine-pasture on the *feld*.

In order to shelter the pigs from beasts of prey and to collect them for slaughter, enclosures of some kind must have been provided. Loose, a village two and a half miles south of Maidstone, takes its name from the Old English word for a pig-sty, *hlose*, which also enters into compounds such as Loseley (Surr) and Luscombe (Devon).

Anyone who has ever tried to drive a pig will wonder how a herd of several hundred could be controlled. William Gilpin, writing towards the end of the eighteenth century from personal observation in the New Forest, describes a method which may well have been practised there and elsewhere from time immemorial. The swineherd wattles a slight circular fence around some spreading tree, covers it roughly with boughs and sods, and fills it plentifully with straw or fern. When the pigs have eaten their fill of acorns or beechmast to the music of his horn he turns them into the litter. There, "after a long journey and a hearty meal, they sleep deliciously. The next morning he lets them look a little round them, shows them the pool or stream where they may occasionally drink, leaves them to pick up the offal

[1] CS 227.
[2] R. Trow-Smith, *A History of British Livestock Husbandry to 1700*, 1957, pp. 50–4.

of the last night's meal, and, as evening draws on, gives them another plentiful repast under the neighbouring trees, which rain acorns upon them for an hour together, at the sound of his horn. He then sends them again to sleep." After another day of this routine he throws his sty open and leaves them to cater for themselves. "In general they need little attention, returning regularly home at night, though they often wander in the day two or three miles from their sty...The hog, if he be properly managed, is an orderly docile animal. The only difficulty is to make your meanings, when they are fair and friendly, intelligible to him. Effect this, and you may lead him with a straw."[1]

The swine-pastures in the Weald of Kent, often many miles distant from the parent village, must have been looked after by resident swineherds. Such places would in course of time develop an independent life of their own, as did Speldhurst near Tunbridge Wells, in the eighth century a swine-pasture belonging to Halling on the Medway.[2]

SHEEP

The pig is much more prominent in the husbandry of this early period than the sheep, although the sheep is an animal of more varied uses, providing milk and wool as well as meat, and contributing much to the fertility of the soil by its droppings. Ine's laws value a ewe with its lamb at a shilling until a fortnight before Easter (55), and provide that twopence shall be deducted from the price of a sheep if it is shorn before midsummer. Late as it seems to us, this was evidently the normal time for shearing (69). A food-rent specified in the early Wessex laws of Ine equates ten wethers with two full-grown cows.[3] The food-rent reserved to the king in the last years of the eighth century when Offa granted Westbury-on-Trym (Glos) to the church of Worcester included six wethers, the other items being seven oxen, 40 cheeses, 30 measures of unground corn, four measures of meal, two tuns

[1] W. Gilpin, *Remarks on Forest Scenery*, 1791, II, pp. 113–16. (I am indebted to Professor A. M. Everitt for this reference.)

[2] CS 260. Prof. Everitt has drawn my attention to a settlement called Meopham Bank, two miles north-west of Tonbridge, and suggests that it was originally a wealden swine-pasture belonging to Meopham. The distance between them is about thirteen miles, and is covered partly by bridleways and footpaths, partly by roads still in use. He points out that hundreds of ancient Kentish roads run across the grain of the county, leading from downland settlements in a southerly or south-westerly direction into the Weald, and he thinks it probable that many of them began as drove-roads.

[3] F. L. Attenborough (ed.), *The Laws of the Earliest English Kings*, Cambridge, 1922: Laws of Ine, 70 §1.

full of clear ale, a coomb full of mild ale, and a coomb full of Welsh ale.[1] The cheeses may well have been made then as in later centuries from ewe's milk.

A charter of King Wihtred, confirmed in 716, refers to a minster at Sheppey, which evidently engaged in sheep-farming since the name means island of sheep.[2] Across the water at Canvey a community of shepherds living in crude temporary shelters guarded large flocks of sheep from the recurrent dangers of the spring tides which flooded the open marsh pastures.[3]

A charter with some doubtful features records the purchase by the bishop of Worcester of an estate by the river Stour "at the ford called Sheepwash."[4] This is now Shipston-on-Stour, one of the many place-names recorded later which point to systematic sheep-farming in many parts of England, but especially on the Cotswolds, where it seems to have flourished during and beyond the Roman period. The early importance of Winchcombe, a royal manor lying at the base of the Cotswold scarp, is best explained by the fact that it controlled the northern approaches to the wold pastures. Upton, later annexed to the episcopal manor of Blockley, was originally a royal estate administered from Winchcombe.[5] Early in the eighth century the abbess of Gloucester acquired Pinswell, between Coberley and Withing-ton, expressly for a sheep-walk, and in the same period the abbess of Withington added to her property a tract of land east of the Coln, sloping gently from the river-bank up to a "common lea" adjoining another settlement, significantly named Shipton.[6] Finally, a letter written in 796 by Charlemagne to Offa, asking the king to ensure that the *saga* – woollen cloaks or blankets – exported from his realm shall be of the same size as they used to be, points to a long-established commerce in the products of Mercian sheep-flocks.[7]

OXEN AND OTHER LIVESTOCK

The English of Alfred's day heard with surprise that the Norwegians used horses to draw their ploughs.[8] There can be little doubt that the ox was the normal plough-beast in England before and for some time after the Norman Conquest. Manuscript illustrations, none earlier than the tenth century, show ploughs drawn, sometimes by two,

[1] CS 273; EHD I, p. 467.   [2] CS 91.
[3] Basil E. Cracknell, *Canvey Island: the History of a Marshland Community*, Leicester, 1959, p. 10.   [4] CS 205.
[5] CS 575; H. P. R. Finberg, *The Early Charters of the West Midlands*, p. 51.
[6] *Gloucestershire Studies*, ed. H. P. R. Finberg, Leicester, 1957, pp. 11–14.
[7] EHD I, p. 782.
[8] *King Alfred's Orosius*, ed. H. Sweet, Early English Text Soc., 79, 1883, p. 18.

sometimes by four oxen.[1] One manuscript of Ine's laws shows that the "yoke" a husbandman may hire from another is a yoke of oxen, but it is not clear whether he needs them because he has none of his own or because his own are not strong enough for the work.

At the end of his working life the ox would provide some lean and sinewy joints for the table. That he was valued for meat as well as for traction is clear from Ine's law (57) that the wife of a man who steals a beast and takes it home may retain her third share of the household property if she can declare on oath that she has not tasted the stolen meat. Another law declares that an orphan child must have for its keep a cow in summer and an ox in winter (38).

Ine's legislation includes the first of a long series of enactments, running through the whole of the Anglo-Saxon period, which impose heavy penalties on cattle thieves (46). It does not state the price of the whole beast, but values the parts as follows (58, 59).

	OX	SHEEP
Tail	1 shilling	5 pence
Horn	10 pence	2 pence
Eye	5 pence	1 shilling

The equation in the same code of two full-grown cows with ten wethers hints, but does not prove, that the average sheep was more valuable than the average cow.[2] It is probable that cows were kept mainly to breed replacements for the plough-team, and after they had suckled their calves had little milk left for the dairy; hence the Anglo-Saxons looked to ewes and she-goats as their principal source of milk and cheese. We may note, however, that Archbishop Wulfred paid a high price for a tract of marshland between Faversham Creek and Graveney which was known as "the king's cow-land."[3] Earlier the archbishop had purchased an estate enjoying the right of common pasture in the neighbouring wood "according to ancient custom." The land was known in Latin as "campus armentorum" and in English as "hrithra leah."[4] This word for cattle or oxen, *hrither*, appears on the map today in such names as Rotherfield and Rotherhithe.

The goat, by nature a denizen of the woods, provided milk, hides, and the flesh of its kid for meat. There is no doubt that it was widely kept, but mention of it is rare in early records. The only instance I have noted is a charter by which King Ceolwulf granted an estate on the River Darent to the archbishop of Canterbury, with pasturage in Andred for swine and cattle or goats.[5]

[1] F. G. Payne, 'The Plough in Ancient Britain', *Arch. J.* CIV, 1948, pp. 103–8.
[2] R. Trow-Smith, *op. cit.*, p. 60.
[3] CS 348.   [4] CS 322.   [5] CS 370.

Documentary evidence of an interest in horses does not become plentiful until the tenth century, but the element *stod*, meaning a herd or stud of horses, occurs frequently in place-names, the earliest example being Stodmarsh, on the south bank of the Great Stour, which is mentioned in two seventh-century Kentish charters.[1]

The food-rent which Ine of Wessex expected to receive from every ten hides of land included ten geese and twenty hens (70 § 1). We hear nothing of ducks, and the rabbit did not appear in Britain until the second half of the twelfth century.[2]

Enough has been said to show that pastoral husbandry loomed large in the rural economy of early England, larger than it would do when more of the forest had been cleared and more of the marshes drained. But there was never a time when men would go without bread and beer if they could help it. We must turn to the land on which they raised their crops.

UNITS OF ASSESSMENT

For a starting-point we may take a law of Ine. "If a man takes a yard of land, or more, at a fixed rent, and ploughs it, and the lord requires service as well as rent, the tenant need not take the land if the lord does not give him a dwelling; but in that case he must forfeit the crops" (67). This law needs to be read in the context of an expanding West Saxon kingdom. Its purpose is evidently to encourage new gains for the plough. The husbandman is not to be deterred from enlarging his ploughland by the fear that he will thereby incur a heavier liability for service on his lord's demesne. So the king attaches the liability for labour service to the house, the messuage, rather than to the arable holding. We have no reason to believe that the enactment was generally observed or lasting in its effects, but it may well have encouraged the colonizing movement which had already drawn men like the father of St Boniface to take up land in Devon, land forfeited or left vacant by the defeated enemies whom they called the West-Welsh.

In this law we hear for the first time of the "yard of land." For centuries to come this unit, latinized sometimes as *pertica* (perch), more often as *virgata* (virgate), will stand out as the normal holding of the typical husbandman. It is essentially an arable holding: the king takes it for granted that when a man applies to his lord for a new yardland his object is to plough it, with the tacit corollary that he will graze his livestock on the common pasture. The *gyrde*, the yard

[1] CS 36 (A.D. 675), 67 (686).   [2] AHR v, 1957, pp. 85–90.

from which it takes its name, is not a length of thirty-six inches nor an area of nine square feet: these are not dimensions in which a plough can move. It is a measuring-rod laid across the furrows to determine their width and along them to determine the length. There is unlikely to have been a standard rod in Ine's day; there were certainly number-less local variations even a hundred years ago, despite the thirteenth-century ordinance of weights and measures which appointed a standard rod, pole, or perch of sixteen and a half feet or five and a half yards. By that time the ideal yardland is taken to be a parcel of thirty acres, each acre being 4,840 square yards, or forty statute rods in length and four in width. The acre is of that length because forty rods make a furlong ('furrow-long'), in theory the length of the furrow which oxen will plough if they are not turned round before they have gone as far as they can without undue effort.[1]

The yardland meets us in a code which also speaks of hides. It tells us of the Welshman holding half a hide, a whole hide, or five hides, and of others, presumably but not certainly English, who have as many as ten. Here we cannot avoid what Maitland called "that dreary old question," what was the hide? From every ten hides the king expects a stated food-rent. Here the hide appears as a unit of assessment enabling the king to collect his dues. The same meaning stands out by clear implication in the document known as the Tribal Hidage. This is a list of peoples, beginning with the inhabitants of eighth-century Mercia, to whom it attributes 30,000 hides. Then follow the names of twenty-eight smaller peoples, with assessments ranging from 300 to 7,000 hides apiece. Between them they account for 55,100 hides. Finally come the men of five whole kingdoms: East Anglia, Essex, Kent, Sussex, and Wessex, bringing the total up to 244,100 hides.[2] All the figures are round figures: x hundreds, y thousands. Hence it does not pretend to be an enumeration of men or families or estates. It is a tribute-list, of transparently Mercian origin but not, as it stands, limited to the peoples immediately subject to the Mercian king, for it includes five other kingdoms which in the eighth century had to recognize, however briefly, the Mercian king as their lord paramount. In short, it is the tribute-list of a Mercian *bretwalda*, probably Offa (757–96), the most powerful of them all.[3]

There are indications of a more ancient origin. Before the Mercian supremacy there has been a Northumbrian supremacy. Under neither is the *bretwalda*-ship a merely titular distinction. The paramount king,

---

[1] Maitland, *Domesday Book and Beyond*, pp. 371–80.

[2] CS 297. The total given above is the sum of the thirty-four items; in the origina it is given incorrectly as 242,700 hides.

[3] C. R. Hart, 'The Tribal Hidage', TRHS 5th ser., XXI, 1971, pp. 133–57.

whether Northumbrian Oswald or Mercian Offa, can not only exact
tribute from less powerful kings; he can interfere to protect Christianity
when they show signs of backsliding into heathenism;[1] he can join
with them in granting land in their own territory;[2] a time will come
when Offa will disallow land-grants made by them without his
consent.[3] The *bretwalda* has indeed no civil service competent to
carry out a systematic cadastral survey such as had been made from
time to time under Roman rule, but he is quite equal to demanding
from Sussex a tribute of 7,000 pence, or a multiple thereof, leaving
the king of Sussex and his advisers to determine how it shall be raised
from the occupants of Sussex land. That the system goes back to the
age of Northumbrian overlordship is shown by the fact that in the
pages of Bede as in the Tribal Hidage Sussex accounts for 7,000 hides.[4]
Bede also knows the hidation of Anglesey and Man.[5] Neither appears
in the Mercian list, but both had been subjugated by the Northumbrian
King Edwin.

Bede, an accomplished writer of Latin, is not going to sully his
pen with an uncouth Old English word like *hid*. So he invents
a cumbrous paraphrase, all his own, for it does not occur in continental
texts. He calls it "terra *x* familiarum," the land of so many households,
"according to the English reckoning." The clerks who drafted the
land-charters were equally reluctant to use the English word. The
two earliest Hampshire charters which have any claim to respect
were drawn up for King Cuthred by men who had evidently read
their Bede, for they speak of lands at Highclere and elsewhere in
terms of so many *familiae*.[6] But the usage never took root; with one
doubtful exception it does not recur in the land-books.[7] Outside Kent
the draftsmen employ a variety of expressions. They speak of "manses"
(*mansae, mansiones, mansiunculae*), or the land of *x tributarii*, meaning
no doubt *gafolgeldas*, or of so many *manentes* (settled occupants) or
cassati (cottagers), and sometimes two of these terms are used inter-
changeably in one and the same text. They may even omit the reference
to land and speak as if ten, twenty, or more human beings are to
be conveyed into new ownership. Or again, they will show that the
hidation is an estimate of potentialities: thus, in the last decade of
the seventh century Ethelred of Mercia describes Fladbury as an
estate "with a capacity of 44 *cassati*."[8]

The hide, then, is a unit of assessment, applied to the land. Since it

[1] Cf. Wulfhere's intervention in Essex.—Bede, *Hist. Eccl.*, III, 30.
[2] *Ibid.*, III, 7: Oswald is associated with Cynegils of Wessex in the grant of
Dorchester to Birinus. Cf. CS 181, a grant by Ethelbald of land in Wiltshire.
[3] CS 332.   [4] *Hist. Eccl.*, IV, 13.   [5] *Ibid.*, II, 9.
[6] CS 179, 180.   [7] CS 696.   [8] CS 76.

is used initially for assessing whole peoples, the numbers are large and round. When it comes to the assessment of particular estates granted to ecclesiastical or lay magnates – the humbler folk do not receive royal charters – it naturally appears in smaller numbers ranging from five to twenty hides or more. It is laid on the estate as a whole, with behind it some rough and ready notion of actual or potential value, without enquiring whether the value is derived mainly from pasture or ploughland. In the undeveloped state of the country at this early time there must have been many estates where pastoral husbandry was far more profitable than tillage. Bede's description of that watery tract the Isle of Ely calls up a picture of wildfowl and eels rather than shining cornfields, yet Bede knows it as a region of 600 hides more or less.[1] Arable or pasture, it is all one to the king and his overlord so long as they get their tribute. We have seen reason to believe that the yardland was from the start essentially an arable holding. There is no evidence and no likelihood that this was originally true of the hide.[2]

King Ine's reference to the Welsh occupant of half a hide proves that smaller properties were known, and we need not believe that they were held only by Welshmen. A time will come, later in Anglo-Saxon history, when the system will be radically altered, and of the resulting changes we shall have to take account in due course. Meanwhile it is futile to ask what was the acreage of the normal hide – if there was such a thing as the normal hide.

Some assessments had a remarkably long life. For instance, in 781 the bishop of Worcester had twelve "manentes" at Hampton Lucy (Wark); his successor still had twelve hides there when the Domesday record was compiled three centuries later.[3] Other examples could be cited.[4] In nearly every case our information comes from an ecclesiastical source and the land belongs to an ecclesiastical corporation. The Church has a long memory and is tenacious of her rights; laymen on the whole are less successful in resisting increased assessments. Now it might be possible to select two or three properties distinguished by continuity of ownership, persistence of rating, and unaltered boundaries, to ascertain their present acreage, and thus to discover how many acres went to the hide at the earliest recorded date in each case. It could be an interesting exercise if performed circumspectly, but the chances are heavily against its leading to anything like a uniform result.

---

[1] *Hist. Eccl.*, IV, 19, ed. Plummer, p. 246.

[2] Cf. Vinogradoff, *Growth of the Manor*, p. 162. Kemble, on the other hand, believed that the hide had consisted only of arable.—*The Saxons in England*, 1849, I, pp. 101, 118.   [3] CS 239, DB I, p. 238 bi.

[4] Aust: CS 269, DB I, p. 164b2; Sedgeberrow: CS 223, DB I, p. 173b2; Standish: CS 535, DB I, p. 164bi; Pyrton ("Readanora"): CS 216, DB I, p. 157b; Tidenham: CS 927, DB I, p. 164ai.

Much ink has been wasted in arguing from Bede's phrase, the "land of one household," that the hide was at one time the "typical tenement." Yet the Wessex of Ine's day knew Welshmen occupying half a hide, and there is no reason to think they were exceptional. A Mercian-Kentish charter of 805 speaks of half a "mansiuncula."[1] And if half-hides, why not also quarter-hides? At the end of the seventh century 600 monks at Wearmouth and Jarrow, with their servants and tenants, were supported by the "land of 150 families."[2] In other words, a quarter-hide sufficed for each. We know that Wessex landlords had yardlanders among their tenants, and by the eleventh century the equation 4 yardlands = 1 hide will be well established. So the landlord will have no difficulty in reckoning how much *gafol* to collect from each of four yardlanders. On Bede's notional "land of one household," therefore, there may easily be four actual households or more. Bede is thinking of taxation and tribute; he is not asserting nor even implying that only one household is occupying each hide. When the time comes for detailed manorial surveys, the obligations of tenants will be stated in terms of hides even when it is perfectly clear that the services are performed by yardlanders.[3]

In this matter of assessment Kent takes a different road from that of other kingdoms. Some few early Kentish charters deal in hides, "manentes,"[4] but in the great majority the unit is the ploughland, in Latin "terra unius aratri," in English *sulung*.[5] It is the land a team of oxen can be expected to plough in a year. Judging from a bequest which leaves four oxen with half a *sulung*, the full team is an eight-ox team.[6] As oxen are yoked in pairs, the normal subdivision of the ploughland for purposes of assessment is a "jugum," a 'yoke' of two oxen, and four yokes make a *sulung*. The two charters which give this equation are both issued by the king of Mercia, Coenwulf, who for the benefit of his Kentish subjects condescends to use the terms familiar to them, but at the same time makes it clear to the rest of England that a Kentish *sulung* is the equivalent to two hides.[7] By the tenth century the equation has been altered, and the *sulung* is now one hide.[8] This may reflect an attempt by the now unified monarchy to bring

---

[1] CS 321.   [2] Life of Ceolfrid, c. 33: p. 400 in Plummer's edition of Bede.
[3] H. P. R. Finberg, *Lucerna*, p. 63, and instances there cited; also R. Lennard, *Rural England*, Oxford, 1957, p. 367 *n.* 4.   [4] CS 35, 40, 42, 96.
[5] CS 214: "aliquam partem terrae trium aratrorum, quod Cantianice dicitur *threora sulunga.*"
[6] CS 412; the date is between 833 and 839.   [7] CS 321, 341.
[8] CS 791 (A.D. 944), 12 *mansae* "which the Kentishmen call *twelf sulunga;*" CS 869 (A.D. 948), 6 *mansae* "which the Kentishmen call *syx sulunga;*" CS 880 (A.D. 949), 26 *cassati* = 25 + 1 *sulungs* in the boundary; CS 1295 (? A.D. 973), 10 *mansae* "which the Kentishmen call 10 *sulunga.*"

Kent into line with the rest of England, but if so it did not succeed in ousting the *sulung*, which even in Domesday Book stands as the normal unit of Kentish assessment.[1] Since it denotes a ploughland, the charters express its fractions in terms of the acre, ideally one day's work for the plough-team.[2]

THE ARABLE

From these arid topics of assessment and measurement we turn with a sigh of relief to the fields themselves. Here, too, we have to consider one of Ine's laws. As the text is of fundamental importance for English agrarian history, it will be advisable to give it in full (42). —

"If husbandmen have a common meadow or other share-land to enclose, and some have enclosed their share while others have not, and if cattle eat up their common crops or grass, then let those to whom the gap is due go and make amends to the others who have enclosed their share. The latter shall demand such reparation as is proper. If, however, any beast breaks fences and wanders at large therein, and its owner will not or cannot control it, he who finds it on his cornland shall take it and kill it. The owner shall take its hide and its flesh and suffer the loss of the rest."

The first thing to be noticed about this enactment is that it is conditional. It does not take for granted that arable share-land or a common meadow is attributable to all husbandmen. The man who applies to his lord for a yardland and ploughs it may well want it for his own sole use. Just such a one, in all probability, is the husbandman who is told he must keep his farm, his *worthig*, fenced both summer and winter, else he will have no claim to a beast that strays in (40). His farm is not just a dwelling-place and its yard; the arable, and probably some pasture too, is enclosed within the ring-fence. Patient research based on local knowledge has identified many single farms which appear as statistical units but are not named individually in the Domesday record. In the broken country of the south-west, a landscape of innumerable little valleys nestling between steep hills and watered by springs and a plentiful rainfall, the isolated farmstead must have been very common indeed, a form of settlement perhaps already in existence long before the Saxon conquest.[3]

Ine's famous reference to common meadows and arable share-lands is often quoted as proving that an 'open-field' system of agriculture existed in seventh-century Wessex. With certain necessary qualifications

[1] H. C. Darby and E. M. J. Campbell, *The Domesday Geography of South-East England*, Cambridge, 1962, p. 502.

[2] CS 344, 373, 380, 411, 426, 449, 460, 486, 502.

[3] W. G. Hoskins, *Provincial England*, 1963, pp. 15–52.

the statement can be accepted as true. In the first place, the term 'open' field is misleading. Every field in which crops were grown would need to be surrounded by a fence or wall or hedgebank or deep ditch if cattle were not to come and trample or eat the growing corn. The small prehistoric *blockfluren* had been thus protected, and Ine's law proves, if proof is needed, that the arable share-land of Wessex was also enclosed. The field is 'open' only in the sense that no obstacle separates one man's ploughland from his neighbour's. But there is no hint of communal ownership. The shares are clearly regarded as held by individuals, each of whom must be compensated for damage caused by his neighbour's default. We must think of these individuals as forming what has been aptly termed "a community of shareholders."[1]

That one shareholder's ploughland lay in parcels intermixed with those of his neighbours – perhaps the most striking feature of the open-field system when we meet it in later centuries – cannot safely be deduced from Ine's law. The law rather implies the contrary, that each man's holding extended to the edge of the field, so that he could be held responsible for the adjacent part of the enclosing fence. Intermixture of parcels may come later from one cause or another. We may also guess that the furrows all lay in one direction. The pattern of a common field divided into smaller plots, with groups of furrows at right angles to one another, is familiar to all who have studied old field-maps, but in all probability it was not an original feature. In England as in Germany it seems to represent a later, more sophisticated plan.[2]

In a comparatively large estate there may have been two or more open fields, each cultivated by a separate group of partners.[3] That the partners turned their cattle out to graze the field or fields in common after harvest cannot be taken for granted. Thus while Ine's law is good evidence that common meadows and ploughlands were already present in seventh-century Wessex, it does not entitle us to assume the complicated, fully matured system with which the textbooks have made us familiar. Nor does it tell us whether the system was new or old. We may guess, but we cannot prove, that it was known much earlier and in other parts of the country. Not until the tenth century will the charters furnish us with local details.

Nor, unfortunately, has archaeology so far done much to fill the

---

[1] Vinogradoff, *Growth of the Manor*, p. 176.

[2] B. H. Slicher van Bath, *The Agrarian History of Western Europe*, tr. O. Ordish, 1963, p. 56, states that this development is believed to have taken place in Germany after 1350.

[3] As suggested by J. Thirsk, *Past and Present*, no. 29, 1964, p. 5.

FAH

gaps in our knowledge. This is disappointing, especially when we recall how much has been revealed about the fields and crops of earlier periods.[1] By contrast with the five centuries or so before and after the beginning of our era, little evidence from the ensuing half millennium has survived on the ground – or has been recognized as surviving. It may be that prehistoric and Roman fields spread far over what subsequently became marginal land, so that traces of them still remain, or remained until recently. It may also be that in the early centuries of English settlement the arable was more narrowly confined to land which has been much cultivated since, with the result that later agriculture has blotted out its traces. This line of argument assumes that some of the pre-Saxon fields went out of use, and that those which did not were of a pattern sufficiently distinctive to have left recognizable marks on the landscape had they not been obliterated by subsequent ploughing. In any case, it is on marginal land, particularly in the west, that traces of early post-Roman arable are most likely to survive, but even when found they will not necessarily reflect what was happening in the main areas of Saxon settlement.[2]

Claims have been made for the high antiquity of some existing field patterns in Wales and the south-west.[3] Although some have been demonstrated to represent piecemeal enclosure made well after Domesday, it does seem probable that here and there in the west small enclosed arable fields and pastures existed in our period, and that a few of them may have survived intact, to the present or to the recent past, incapsulated perhaps in later systems. In only two cases, however, can surviving ridge-and-furrow be cited from before the Norman Conquest, and both probably belong to the tenth or eleventh centuries rather than earlier. The first was recorded at Gwithian in west Cornwall, where narrow, parallel undulations were observed in part of a field bounded by a headland, a ditch, and a marsh. They were dated by pottery similar to that from the appropriate occupation-layer in an adjacent settlement.[4] The second, very similar, example has lately been recorded beneath and outside the bailey bank and ditch of the small castle at Hen Domen (Mont), known from documents to have been built in 1070.[5] It is obvious that little can be deduced

---

[1] Above, pp. 83–121.

[2] In this and the next three paragraphs I am heavily indebted to the assistance of Mr P. J. Fowler.

[3] W. G. Hoskins, *The Making of the English Landscape*, 1955, pp. 20–4; W. G. V. Balchin, *Cornwall*, 1954, pp. 31–3; G. R. J. Jones, 'The Pattern of Settlement on the Welsh Border', AHR VIII, 1960, pp. 66–81, especially pp. 71–8.

[4] P. J. Fowler and A. C. Thomas, 'Arable Fields of the Pre-Norman Period at Gwithian', *Corn. Arch.* I, 1962, pp. 61–84.

[5] P. A. Barker in *Medieval Archaeology* XV, 1971.

from only two examples, but their similarity could imply something of wider import. It suggests that in two areas of western Britain towards the end of the Anglo-Saxon period a plough capable of turning a furrow was in use, that it was being used deliberately to create the form of seed-bed known to us as ridge-and-furrow, and that the process was repeated sufficiently often to leave permanent marks on the land-surface. The very slenderness of the evidence, however, shows how easily such traces could be destroyed by later activity. Moreover, the evidence from Gwithian and Hen Domen bears primarily on the technique of cultivation, and carries with it no implication of 'open' or any other type of field system.

Two other types of evidence produced by excavation are relevant but – again – not particularly helpful for this period. The first consists of plough-marks, the second of ploughs or parts of ploughs. In the study of early agriculture plough-marks are a well-known phenomenon. They consist of grooves or lines made perhaps by accident in the process of cultivation, sometimes etched into the subsoil, sometimes represented only by changes in the consistency or colour of the soil. Again there are only two instances directly relevant to this period, and again both are in the Celtic west. The clearest example, this time from a date between the sixth and ninth centuries and therefore earlier than the ridge-and-furrow already discussed, is once more at Gwithian.[1] Here the unusual circumstance of a plough-soil lying immediately on and sealed by wind-blown sand, made it possible to see that the plough-marks retained traces of the sod which had been inverted by the plough. The clear implication is that the implement employed a share, a coulter, and probably a mouldboard. If this interpretation is correct, the possibility that such a plough was known in the remote south-west before the Saxon conquest of that area is of considerable interest. The same point is made by the other, probably later, example, recorded beneath a Viking barrow at Cronk Moar in the Isle of Man. Here the plough-marks lay parallel not only to one another, as at Gwithian, but also to a probably contemporary boundary ditch and to the existing alignment of field boundaries.[2]

In both these cases, the plough-marks or furrow-tips lay parallel to one another in one direction only, forming a pattern much less complicated than the criss-cross pattern of earlier plough-marks. The implication is that cross-ploughing had ceased, presumably because an improved type of plough made it unnecessary. Unfortunately, this

---

[1] Fowler and Thomas, op. cit., pp. 63–8.
[2] G. Bersu and D. M. Wilson, Three Viking Graves in the Isle of Man, Soc. for Medieval Archaeology, Monograph 1, 1966.

scanty evidence is not yet supplemented by parts of ploughs from post-Roman pre-Viking contexts in Britain. In the present state of knowledge, therefore, we can only speculate on the origin and development of such a plough in the west. The same is in effect true of the implements used in the seventh and eighth centuries by Saxon farmers further east. Relevant evidence on the continent being equally scarce, it is tempting to look back to Roman Britain, but until archaeologists produce parts of a plough from a context indisputably belonging to the four centuries after A.D. 400 little or no progress can be made. Our ignorance is emphasized by uncertainty about an Old English riddle, possibly composed in the eighth century, which appears to describe a plough with a coulter, share, and share-beam.[1] In short, the evidence could hardly be more defective; hence the tendency in the past to project backwards concepts, techniques, and descriptions based on later sources.

We are equally in the dark about the common meadows. Was it customary to divide the meadow into strips and allocate one or more strip annually by the drawing of lots? In some villages this usage, accompanied by picturesque formalities, persisted into modern times, but it would be unsafe to assume that it goes back as far as the seventh century.[2]

THE CROPS

After the harvest and its attendant revelry the ploughman went to work, sowing wheat and rye. Barley and oats waited for the spring sowing. These four were the standard cereals of Anglo-Saxon England, but not all four were cultivated everywhere. Saint Cuthbert tried to grow wheat on the rocky island of Farne, but although he waited till midsummer it failed to germinate. Then he tried barley, with much better success, for, leaving miracles aside, barley will ripen farther north than any other grain. In his hermitage at Crowland Guthlac lived – naturally to no great age – on barley-bread and water.[3]

The carbonized grains recovered from Anglo-Saxon dwellings and examined under the microscope by palaeobotanists are still too few to provide useful statistics. A little more has been achieved by studying the rough domestic pottery which was made without help of the

---

[1] Riddle 21 in *The Exeter Book, Part II*, ed. W. S. Mackie, Early English Text Soc., 194, 1934, p. 111.

[2] See the description of the still existing lot meadows at Yarnton (Oxon) in Stapleton, *Three Oxfordshire Parishes*, Oxford Hist. Soc. XXIV, 1893, pp. 307–11.

[3] Bede's *Life of St Cuthbert*, c. 19, ed. Colgrave, p. 220; *Felix's Life of St Guthlac*, cc. 28, 30, ed. Colgrave, pp. 94, 100.

wheel by shaping lumps of clay on the floor and then baking them on the hearth. Such pots occasionally picked up grain and seeds from the floor and took impressions which remained after firing had destroyed the grain itself. By means of plastic material positive impressions can be taken from the small cavities left on the surface of the pots, and the seeds which made them can then be identified. When Danish palaeobotanists applied this method to pots from some eighteen Anglo-Saxon cemeteries, mostly around Oxford and Cambridge, they found impressions of barley, oats, flax, and woad in the following proportions: 3 of naked barley; 80 of hulled barley; 14 of oat (*Avena sativa*); 1 of wild oat (*Avena fatua*); 2 of flax; 1 of woad.[1] No traces were found of wheat and rye, as they would certainly have been in a larger sample. The importance of rye in the early English period is shown in the preamble to King Wihtred's laws which declares that they were drawn up by the Kentish royal council in an assembly held on the sixth day of *Rugern*, that is, in the month of the rye harvest, in 695.[2] Ryarsh, the name of a village seven miles north-west of Maidstone, signifies 'rye field'. English "country folks" did not have to wait till Shakespeare's time to lie "between the acres of the rye."

At the end of the eighth century an earldorman named Oswulf bequeathed twenty ploughlands at Stanstead to Christ Church, Canterbury, and requested the monks to commemorate his anniversary and that of his wife with masses and almsgiving. A few years later Archbishop Wulfred prescribed the quantities of food and drink to be distributed on these anniversaries. The list begins with 120 wheaten loaves and 30 "clean" loaves, the former presumably wholemeal, the latter fine white bread made from carefully sifted flour.[3] Churchmen needed such bread for use at the altar. The widespread cultivation of wheat gave rise to many place-names, none recorded earlier than the tenth century, yet at the very beginning of that century we shall meet with husbandmen in a Hampshire village whose obligations to their lord included the payment of a quantity of *hlaf-hwete*, wheat for bread. At about the same time the bishop of Worcester granted a lease of Elmstone (Glos), reserving three measures of wheat as an annual payment of church-scot to Bishop's Cleeve.[4]

Oats were fed to the calves and foals, and also provided porridge for human consumption. Barley, ground into meal for bread-making

---

[1] K. Jessen and H. Helbaek, *Cereals in Great Britain and Ireland in Prehistoric and Early Historic Times*, Copenhagen (Kongelige Danske Videnskabernes Selskat, Biologiske Skrifter, III, no. 2), 1944, pp. 23, 27.

[2] Attenborough, *Laws of the Earliest English Kings*, p. 24.   [3] CS 330.

[4] A. J. Robertson, *Anglo-Saxon Charters*, Cambridge, 1956, no. CX, p. 206 (on which see p. 457 below); no. XVI, p. 30.

or converted into malt for brewing, easily eclipsed all other cereals; in this respect the sample of grain cited above, small as it is, may well give a true reflection of its preponderance. The Anglo-Saxons consumed beer on an oceanic scale. This will not surprise us when we remember how much of their meat had to be salted. The original meaning of *beretun* and *berewic* is 'barley-farm' in each case, but barley was so clearly taken to be the principal Anglo-Saxon grain that both words came to be used of establishments where corn of any kind was stored; hence the numerous Bartons and Berwicks to be found on the map today.[1]

Beans, always an important article in the diet of the poor, were perhaps grown in the fields as well as in garden plots. *Bene-stede*, a place where beans grew, occurs in charter boundaries and in such place-names as Banstead and Binstead. Flax (*lin*), cultivated to provide linen fibres and lamp-wicks, has left its mark on several Linacres and Lintons;[2] and pollen analysis has traced the cultivation of flax and hemp in East Anglia back to the Anglo-Saxon period.[3] That woad (*wad*) was widely cultivated in that period for use as a dye is proved by numerous place-names, Waddon, Wadborough, and the like.[4]

It can only be an assumption, though a reasonable one, that the Anglo-Saxons continued to harvest the wild and cultivated fruits which had been known in the Roman period, including apples, medlars, cherries, mulberries, plums, bullaces, and damsons.[5]

MINES

Under Roman rule gold had been mined in Wales, lead chiefly in the Mendips and Derbyshire, tin in Cornwall, coal in Somerset and the north, iron in the Forest of Dean and the Kentish Weald. There is no reason to believe that all this activity ceased with the advent of the Anglo-Saxons. In 689 the king of Kent grants one ploughland containing an iron-mine to the monks of Canterbury. His charter states that it had belonged to the hereditary royal estate administered from Lyminge, but gives no exact indication of its whereabouts.[6] In 835 an abbess, presumably of Repton, grants Wirksworth (Derb) to an ealdorman, subject to an annual rent-charge of 300 shillings-worth of lead to Archbishop Ceolnoth for Christ Church, Canterbury.[7] Some years later Lupus of Ferrières in Gaul wrote to King Æthelwulf asking

---

[1] A. H. Smith, *op. cit.*, I, p. 31.   [2] *Ibid.*, I, p. 21; II, p. 24.
[3] H. Godwin, 'The Ancient Cultivation of Hemp', *Antiquity* XLI, 1967, pp. 42 sqq.
[4] PN *Worcestershire*, p. 221.
[5] S. Applebaum, 'Agriculture in Roman Britain', AHR VI, 1958, p. 71.
[6] CS 73.   [7] CS 414.

him to send lead for the roofing of his church.[1] A lead-mine figures in the boundary of Stoke Bishop near Bristol.[2] Scattered references like these are all the evidence we have for mining operations in the Old English period.

FORMS OF SETTLEMENT

A landscape so varied as that of England naturally produced a wide variety of practice, with arable husbandry predominating in one region and pastoral in another. It also exerted a direct influence on the pattern of settlement. Maitland reproduced on facing pages two portions of the original one-inch Ordnance map to point a dramatic contrast between the land of villages in Oxfordshire and Berkshire and the land of hamlets in Somerset and Devon. In the purest form of village, he says, "there is one and only one cluster of houses. It is a fairly large cluster; it stands in the midst of its fields, of its territory, and until lately a considerable part of its territory will probably have consisted of spacious 'common fields'." In the land of hamlets, on the other hand, "the houses which lie within the boundary of the parish are scattered about in small clusters; here two or three, there three or four. These clusters often have names of their own, and it seems mere chance that the name borne by one of them should be also the name of the whole parish."[3] Maitland goes on to point out that we may easily fall into the error of making the early village too populous. Originally the difference must have been one of spacing rather than size. The midland settlement which on nineteenth-century maps appears as a large village may well have started life as a nucleus of one or two hardy pioneers, indistinguishable in point of numbers from the population of a south-western hamlet.

It is idle, therefore, to expect that the Old English nomenclature of settlement will clearly express characteristics which only become well-defined much later. The name Roding, now shared by eight parishes in Essex covering between them some twenty square miles, referred originally not to villages but to the followers of one Hroða. Many scholars have drawn attention to other place-names in which the ending –ingas is coupled with a personal name. It used to be held that such names belong to the earliest phase of English settlement, but recent study of their correlation with early Saxon cemeteries points to a different conclusion. It suggests that the burials record the first immigrations into coastal lands or districts already opened up by the

[1] A. W. Haddan and W. Stubbs, *Councils and Ecclesiastical Documents*, III, Oxford, 1871, pp. 648, 649.
[2] CS 551, dated 883.   [3] *Domesday Book and Beyond*, pp. 15–17.

Romans, and that the *–ingas* belong to the second colonizing impetus, beginning in the sixth century.[1]

The *vicus*, the smallest unit which the imperial authorities had recognized for purposes of administration, might be a small town or a civil settlement outside a Roman fort. The Anglo-Saxons, when they found one, knew it for what it was. They borrowed the Latin word and turned it into *wic*. In the laws of Kent London itself appears as *Lundenwic*, and the king has a reeve there called a *wic-gerefa*. The word *wic-ham*, a compound of *wic* and the Germanic element *ham*, seems to have been applied by early English settlers to places close to Roman roads and usually near Roman-British *vici*; hence a number of Wick-hams and Wycombs.[2] In the very common place-name Wick or Wyke, *wic* has its more general sense and means no more than a collection of buildings. In course of time it was associated with buildings used for special purposes, especially those connected with livestock and dairy produce: Shapwick (= sheep-farm), Butterwick, Chiswick, and the like.[3]

Ham, from its primary sense of home or dwelling, comes to mean a group of dwellings, a village, and finally an estate or manor. In 743 we hear of a *cyne-ham*, a Mercian royal residence.[4] When *hams* and *tuns* occur in genuine charters of the seventh century, the former outnumber the latter by two to one.[5] Thus both are ancient, but *ham* is relatively uncommon in the midlands and the west, and this suggests that its use in place-names was becoming obsolete as the tide of English conquest surged westward. By contrast, *tun* was used in name-forming throughout the Old English period and for some time after the Norman Conquest. In primitive German it seems to have denoted a fence or hedge. This leads naturally to the successive Old English meanings: an enclosed piece of ground; an enclosure containing a house; a farmstead. Then, as a *tun* expands from its original nucleus, it comes to mean, first, a hamlet or village, later a whole estate. The laws of Ethelbert (5, 13) show that a king and a nobleman might each have his *tun*; those of Hlothhere and Eadric (5) imply a village, for they rule that a freeman charged with theft shall bring at least one witness from the *tun* to which he himself belongs. The current meaning of *town* as an urban area was not developed until after the close of the Old English period.

[1] J. M. Dodgson, 'The Significance of the Distribution of the English Place-Name in *-ingas, -inga*, in South-East England', *Medieval Archaeology* x, 1966, pp. 1–29; K. Cameron in *Nottingham and its Region*, ed. K. C. Edwards, Nottingham, 1966, p. 214.

[2] Margaret Gelling, 'English Place-Names derived from the compound *wic-ham*', *Medieval Archaeology* x, 1967, pp. 87–104.

[3] A. H. Smith, *op. cit.*, II, pp. 257–63.

[4] CS 165.   [5] CS 41, 72, 78, 81, 97, 98.

Sometimes an ancient *ham* gave birth to a secondary settlement called a *tun*: thus, Briningham and Brinton (Norf), Corringham and Carrington (Lincs), Ovingham and Ovington (N'umb), Nottingham and Sneinton (Notts), Wintringham and Winterton (Lincs). Or again a *tun* may itself produce a daughter settlement. When Saint Cuthbert as a young man was travelling in stormy weather through what is now the county of Durham he took shelter in some thatched dwellings used only in spring and summer. In the north such huts, called shielings, were built chiefly on the moors and mountains. There is mention of such "pastoral dwellings" on the moors of the North Riding.[1] In the south the herdsmen of the parent village drove their cattle in summer to a low-lying and well-watered standing-place which they called a *stoc*. This in time developed an independent life of its own. Calstock (Corn), for example, begins as the *stoc* of Callington, Plymstock (Devon) as the *stoc* of Plympton, and Basingstoke (Hants) as the *stoc* of Basing.[2]

We have already met the husbandman who is bidden by Ine's law (40) to keep his *worthig* fenced both winter and summer. This is clearly a farm surrounded by a stockade. *Worð*, a simpler form of *worthig*, is common in the midlands, and the variant *worðign* especially so in the west midlands. All three are frequently compounded with personal names, suggesting that they begin as individual possessions; and all may end as substantial villages: Bayworth, Holsworthy, Bedwardine. Even the humblest form of dwelling, the *cot* or *cote*, can become a nucleus of settlement. Some two dozen *cotes* will figure as manors in the Devonshire Domesday, four of them named after their occupants in 1066.[3]

Villages are of all shapes and sizes. Modern industry and mining have given rise to settlements where the dwellings are dotted about at random by a stream or crowded on hillside terraces without any coherent plan. Setting these aside, three main types can be distinguished. Some villages are built around an open space, such as a green, as at Bledington (Glos), or a pond, as at Finchingfield (Ess). Others are grouped round a central building, usually the church, as at Bringhurst (Leics). In others again the houses are strung out along both sides of a roadway.[4] On one occasion Saint Cuthbert was staying in a place called Hruringaham, apparently somewhere near Melrose, when a

[1] *Two Lives*, ed. Colgrave, pp. 70, 126.

[2] E. Ekwall, *Studies on English Place-Names*, Stockholm, 1936, pp. 11–43; A. H. Smith, *op. cit.*, I, pp. 226–9; II, pp. 188–98.

[3] A. H. Smith, *op. cit.*, I, pp. 108–10; II, pp. 273–7; H. P. R. Finberg, *Tavistock Abbey*, Cambridge, 1951, p. 37.

[4] W. G. Hoskins, *The Making of the English Landscape*, 1955, pp. 48–54; Joscelyne Finberg, *Exploring Villages*, 1958, pp. 6–15.

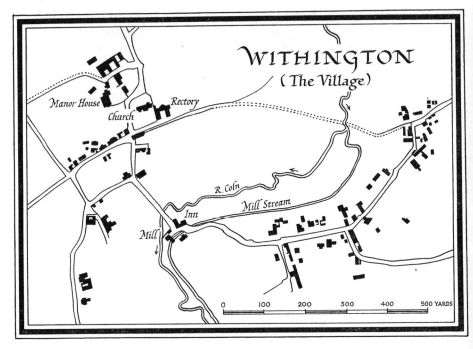

Fig. 47. Withington.

house at the east end caught fire, and as the wind was blowing strongly
from that quarter it looked as if the whole village would be destroyed;
but the saint by his prayers brought about a change of wind and
saved the situation.[1] This sounds like a village built along a single
street. The type is certainly ancient.

The core of Withington (Glos), a villa-estate under Roman rule
and from the close of the seventh century the site of an Anglo-Saxon
minster, is a compact rectangular nucleus of lanes and buildings,
including the church, rectory, and manor house, with a street leading
westward out of it and up to an ancient trackway from Corinium, the
Roman Cirencester (see Fig. 47). But at some date before 774 the abbess
of Withington acquired a tract of land on the other side of the little
River Coln, and a new settlement grew up, of an entirely different
pattern. Here the buildings, instead of forming a rectangular group,
are strung out for more than a quarter of a mile along the road to
Compton Abdale. The result is that side by side in what today forms
one village are two different patterns, the one shown by documentary
evidence to be appreciably older than the other.[2] The example warns

[1] *Two Lives*, p. 90.   [2] H. P. R. Finberg, *Lucerna*, pp. 32–6.

us that it is unsafe to construe the aspect of a mature village seen on the map or on the ground today as evidence of its original shape. Documents of early date are needed to help us dissect it into its component parts, and such documents are rare. But intelligent fieldwork combined with documentary research has lately succeeded in isolating the original pattern of Linton in the West Riding, where two fields immediately adjoining the village on the east and west, of 72 and 70 acres respectively, are certainly older than Domesday Book and antedate the outer fields created by an extension of tillage in the twelfth and thirteenth centuries.[1] There is room for much more work of this kind.

HUTS, FARMS, AND PALACES

We are a little better informed about early Anglo-Saxon dwellings. Thirty-three buildings, occupied from about the end of the fifth century, were uncovered by E. T. Leeds on a deserted site between Drayton and Sutton Courtenay (Berks). On a floor about two feet below ground level a tent-like superstructure had been erected, supported by slanting posts secured to a central ridge-pole. The roof must have come down to the edge of the excavation. Two of the buildings appear to have been used as weaving sheds, and one as a potter's workshop.[2]

The sunken hut, usually quite small, little more than 3 × 2 metres, and built over pits which vary in depth from 0·2 to 1 metre or more, was by far the most common type of Anglo-Saxon building. It is also found over large areas of continental Europe. Wijster, in north-east Holland, a settlement abandoned at the time of the migration to Britain, contained 80 sunken huts, apparently used as outbuildings by the occupants of large farmsteads. Of the latter, 72 out of 86 were long-houses, in which human beings and livestock were sheltered under one roof. The interior, with a length of more than twice the width, was divided by roof-posts into a wide gangway and two side aisles, one of which was used as a byre and the other as a dwelling by the farmer and his family.[3]

Wijster is not the only European site where the sunken huts were associated with larger structures at ground level, and it has been suggested that at Sutton Courtenay and elsewhere in this country

---

[1] A. Raistrick, *West Riding of Yorkshire*, 1970, pp. 68–71. See also Lord Rennell of Rodd, *Valley on the March*, 1958, pp. 92–118.

[2] *Archaelogia* LXXIII, 1923, pp. 147–92; LXXVI, 1926–7, pp. 59–80; XCII, 1947, pp. 79–93.

[3] W. A. Van Es, 'Wijster, a Native Village beyond the Imperial Frontier', *Palaeohistoria* XI, Groningen, 1967, pp. 49–77, 565, 566.

these larger buildings have simply been overlooked in the course of excavation. It is a possibility which must always be borne in mind, and if substantiated it may justify us in concluding that the sunken huts were used mainly as workshops, not dwellings. On the other hand, 101 sites in this country, ranging in date from *c.* 400 to *c.* 850, have yielded traces of only 13 buildings at ground level as against 24 sunken huts.[1] An excavation still in progress at the time of writing has brought to light 68 such huts at Mucking (Ess) bearing signs of continuous occupation from the late Roman period to the first half of the sixth century, but so far there is no trace of other houses.[2] At West Stow (Suff) 34 sunken huts have been excavated, many of them used for weaving and other processes connected with wool, but only 3 buildings at ground level have been located as yet.[3] In the present state of archaeological knowledge, therefore, it appears that in this early period comparatively few Anglo-Saxon countrymen occupied houses of any size; the majority lived rather squalid lives in sunken huts.

Since long-houses on the continent go back to the Bronze Age, and were known to the Anglo-Saxons at Wijster and elsewhere in their continental homelands, it is reasonable to suppose that they were also built on this side of the North Sea. They have in fact been found at Mawgan Porth in Cornwall and at Jarlshof in Shetland, but in the greater part of England they have yet to be proved older than the twelfth century.[4]

Until quite late in the Old English period the use of stone as a building material was confined to churches and some fortified strongholds. With a few exceptions, every dwelling-house was built of wood, turf, or some form of unbaked earth. This is true not only of farmhouses but of manors and even royal palaces. When the royal manor of Cheddar (Som) was excavated, a farmhouse-like wooden structure, 78 feet long and 20 feet wide in the middle, dating from the eighth or ninth century, was the earliest recognizable feature of a site destined to be much enlarged in the reign of Alfred or somewhat later.[5] Early in the seventh century a massive timber hall was built at Yeavering in Glendale (N'umb), with lesser halls set about it, probably dwellings for the king's companions in arms. One structure of more primitive type may have housed the native servants. There was also a grand-stand for open-air assemblies. Later the grand-stand was enlarged; additional small dwellings were built, and a hall of more ambitious design took the place of the original great hall. This phase

---

[1] M. Beresford and J. G. Hurst, *Deserted Medieval Villages*, 1971, p. 148.

[2] *Medieval Archaeology* XI, 1967, p. 265; *Antiquaries Journal* XLVIII, 1968, pp. 210–30.

[3] Beresford and Hurst, *op. cit.*, p. 101.

[4] *Ibid.*, p. 104.   [5] P. Rahtz, in *Medieval Archaeology* VI–VII, 1962–3, p. 57.

is believed to have begun in the period when King Edwin held court there and entertained the Roman missionary Paulinus, who spent thirty-six days at Yeavering baptizing converts in the River Glen.[1] After a devastating fire buildings of lighter construction were put up, some of them with annexes or porches at the gable ends, and a Christian church was added. A second fire made it necessary to rebuild the great hall, the church, and two smaller halls. The place was occupied until 670 at latest, then finally abandoned.[2] Today silence reigns over Yeavering except when the wind rages through the valley where a *bretwalda* feasted his warriors and the mead-horn passed from hand to hand.

[1] Bede, *Hist. Eccl.*, II, 14; p. 115 in Plummer's edition.
[2] *Medieval Archaeology* I, 1957, p. 149.

CHAPTER III

ENGLISH SOCIETY IN THE
SEVENTH CENTURY

BEDE SAYS that among the other benefits King Ethelbert conferred on the people of Kent, he established for them with the advice of his councillors judicial decrees after the example of the Romans. He did indeed follow Roman example in committing his laws to writing, but they were written in English, not in Latin, and in substance they are a statement of Germanic custom rather than an echo of the imperial jurisprudence. Even the acceptance of Christianity appears only in the first clause, which recognizes the hierarchical gradation of bishop, priest, deacon, and clerk, and fixes penalties for wrong done to them in proportion to the rank of the aggrieved. Composed at some date between the arrival of St Augustine in 597 and Ethelbert's death in 616, and still in force when Bede wrote more than a century later, the laws are our earliest source of information on the social structure of an English kingdom.[1]

THE SLAVE

They reveal an elaborately graded society. In Kent, as throughout the western world, the lowest rank was filled by slaves. Some of the female slaves were employed as domestic servants. Here the word used is *birele*, meaning cup-bearer, and penalties for raping her are appointed in proportion not to her feelings but to her master's rank: 12 shillings, or 240 pence, for a nobleman's; 6 shillings or 120 pence for a commoner's; 50 and 30 pence for women of still lower grades.[2] Higher values are set on the honour of other slave-women, presumably employed not in the household but on the farm: 50 shillings for one belonging to the king, 25 and 12 shillings for women of the second and third class. The second-class or 25-shilling woman is described as a "grinding slave:" evidently in seventh-century Kent, as in the Palestine of the New

[1] Five charters (CS 3, 4, 5, 6, 8) purport to be grants by Ethelbert of land to the churches of Canterbury, Rochester, and London, but none of them stands up to critical scrutiny.

[2] *The Laws of the Earliest English Kings*, ed. F. L. Attenborough, Cambridge, 1922: Laws of Ethelbert, 14, 16.

Testament, women were employed to grind corn.[1] To distinguish slaves from freeborn women, their hair was cropped.[2]

The *theow*, or male slave, figures under that name only as the perpetrator or victim of robbery.[3] If he steals, he is supposed to have means to pay twice the value of the stolen goods as compensation. More is said about the *esne*. In other texts this is the word used to translate the Latin *servus*,[4] and no doubt a taint of servility clings to the *esne*. At best he is only half-free. He may be a married man, for one clause (85) refers to his wife. Presumably he has a household of his own, not a mere lodging in the outbuildings of his master's farm. At a guess we may identify him with the *servus casatus* of the continent, a slave whose master has provided him with a hut to live in but reserves the right to call upon him for agricultural services. If so, he will probably spend much of his time working on his master's land, receiving food or perhaps money in return, and when not so engaged will be tilling his garden-plot or hiring himself out to his more prosperous neighbours.

THE 'LAET'

More difficult questions arise concerning the *laet*, who makes his first and only appearance under that name in Ethelbert's laws. It is natural to connect him with the *laetus* of the Roman Empire and the *litus*, *latus*, *lazzus* of the continental codes, where he is a member of a subject people settled on the land in a position intermediate between freemen and slaves. The law of the Ripuarian Franks, somewhat later in date than Ethelbert's, speaks of a slave whose master makes him a *litus*; his life, like that of a slave, is valued at 36 shillings, while the Frankish freeman's life is valued at 200 shillings.[5] Ethelbert, however, distinguishes three classes of *laet*, and fixes the compensation payable for killing them at 80, 60, and 40 shillings respectively.[6] Since the normal (*medume*) compensation for homicide was 100 shillings,[7] it seems clear that some Kentish *laets* occupied a far higher position than their continental counterparts. This tells against Lappenberg's hypothesis that the *laet* was one of a small number of kindred race brought over by the conquerors. Later scholars have seen him as a survivor of the Roman-British population, somewhat reduced in status under

[1] *Ibid.*, 10, 11; cf. Matt. 24, 41.
[2] *Ibid.*, 73 (the freeborn woman has long hair).
[3] *Ibid.*, 89, 90.
[4] See above, p. 395.
[5] *Monumenta Germaniae Historica, Leges*, III, Part 2, *Lex Ribuaria*, ed. F. Beyerle and R. Buchner, Hanover, 1951, pp. 9–51, 77 (tit. 7), 117 (tit. 65).
[6] Laws of Ethelbert, 26.   [7] *Ibid.*, 21.

Germanic rule.[1] May he not equally well have been a descendant of Germanic *laeti* installed in Kent while Britain was still a Roman province? His three grades may represent, like the threefold grades of slaves and cup-bearers, a classification according to the rank of their masters, in which case a *laet* of the first class might be settled on the king's land, of the second on that of a nobleman, of the third on that of a commoner. Alternatively, as Seebohm conjectured on the analogy of later Norse custom, the three grades may represent stages in a slow progress from outright slavery to full freedom.[2] These are questions which admit of no certain answer.

THE 'CEORL'

The next person to be considered is the *ceorl*. Much has been written about the Kentish *ceorl*, much more indeed than the evidence warrants. The word means, first of all, a husband, 'man' as correlative to 'wife'.[3] Then, by extension, it comes to mean the head of a rustic household. Ethelbert (25) speaks of the *ceorl's* "loaf-eaters," the children, domestic servants, and farm-hands who look to him for food. The exact equivalent of his designation in modern English is not 'churl', its lineal descendant, but 'husbandman'. The word tells us nothing about his racial origin, nor, whatever the lexicographers may say, does it carry with it any connotation of either freedom or unfreedom. He is certainly a commoner, as distinguished from the *eorl* or nobleman. The clearest indication of his social status is his *mundbyrd*, the fine payable for an offence against one of his dependants. This is fixed at 6 shillings, that of the nobleman being 12 shillings, and the king's 50 shillings.[4]

---

[1] J. M. Lappenberg, *History of England under the Anglo-Saxon Kings*, tr. B. Thorpe, 1881, II, p. 393; P. Vinogradoff, *The Growth of the Manor*, p. 124; Stenton, *Anglo-Saxon England*, p. 315.

[2] F. Seebohm, *Tribal Custom in Anglo-Saxon Law*, 1902, pp. 260-7, 502.

[3] Laws of Ethelbert, 80, 85. Is this why a Mercian thegn, hoping to disguise his true status, pretended to be a married man as well as a *ceorl* ("rusticum...atque uxoreo uinculo conligatum")? See below, p. 442.

[4] *Ibid.*, 8, 13, 15, 25. On the nobleman's *mundbyrd* see H. M. Chadwick, *Studies on Anglo-Saxon Institutions*, p. 105. Compensation for homicide, which in Ethelbert's laws is called *leodgeld*, a Frankish word (7, 21), but in later codes *wergeld*, is specified for the three classes of *laet* and for the husbandman's "loaf-eater." Clause 21 gives 100 shillings as the "normal" *leodgeld*, but does not make it clear to which class it is applicable. Whether *medume* here is taken to mean normal, ordinary, or average, the implication is that some payments may be higher and some lower. Cf. Vinogradoff, *op. cit.*, pp. 123, 237, who takes it as referring to different grades of *ceorl*, not elsewhere specified.

THE FREEMAN

Ethelbert speaks also of a class of freemen, seemingly distinct from the *ceorls*, but perhaps including some of them.[1] In several clauses the freeman appears to stand in some kind of special relationship with the king. If he robs the king, he must pay ninefold compensation (4); if he is killed, the murderer must pay 50 shillings to the king (6); if he robs another freeman, the king takes the fine (9). A penalty of 20 shillings is laid on any one who attempts to deprive him of his freedom (24). For the rest, he is liable to penalties if he breaks and enters another man's enclosure (27, 29), and if he commits adultery, he must provide the injured husband with a new wife at his own expense (31).

Four classes of widow are distinguished by the gradations of their *mundbyrd* (75). These gradations are presumably determined by the standing of their late husbands. The lowest, 6 shillings, is identical with the *mundbyrd* of the *ceorl*; the highest, 50 shillings, with that of the king. The first-class widow is said to be nobly born, perhaps a lady of the royal house. If so, the 20-shilling widow may be a non-royal noblewoman and the 12-shilling one the widow either of a lesser gentleman or of a freeman.

THE NOBLEMAN

Twelve shillings is the penalty for slaying a man on the premises of a nobleman and for seducing his domestic slave-woman (13, 14). This is all that Ethelbert's laws have to say about the *eorl*: enough to show that he stands twice as high in social estimation as the *ceorl*.

At the apex of society the king wielded considerable power. Ethelbert was not only king of Kent but also *bretwalda*, or overlord of all England south of the Humber. This position entitled him to collect tribute from the other English kingdoms; and it enabled him to provide Augustine with a safe-conduct for a meeting with the British bishops on the frontier of the Hwicce and the West Saxons.[2] His position doubtless owed something to his marriage with a daughter of the Merovingian king reigning in Paris. The marriage also paved the way for his ready acceptance of Christianity. Bede says that while Ethelbert compelled no man to become a Christian, his favour was a powerful factor in the conversion of Kent. As a landowner and a receiver of tribute he had much to give. The conversion introduced a new element into Anglo-Saxon society, making it necessary to endow the clergy and to secure

---

[1] It is not clear on what grounds Stenton, *op. cit.*, p. 304, takes freeman here to be a synonym for *ceorl*.

[2] On the right of the *bretwalda* to collect tribute from other kingdoms, cf. Stenton, *op. cit.*, p. 36. The Hwicce were the people of Worcestershire and Gloucestershire.

them in the possession of their property. As we have seen, the first clause in Ethelbert's code deals with this subject, fixing penalties for wrong done to them in accordance with the hierarchical gradation of bishop, priest, deacon, and clerk.

THE LAWS OF HLOTHHERE AND EADRIC

In 679 Ethelbert's great-grandson Hlothhere, by the earliest English royal charter which has survived in its original form, granted land in Thanet and at Sturry, two and a half miles north-east of Canterbury, to an abbot named Bercuald and his minster, which was probably the one at Reculver.[1] This same Hlothhere, reigning jointly with his nephew Eadric, issued a code of laws by way of supplement to those already in force. The code adds little to our knowledge of the social system. It speaks of the *esne* and his owner, who must surrender the *esne* if the latter has killed a man, and must in addition pay a *wergeld* or compensation for homicide proportionate to the rank of the victim. If the victim is a nobleman with a *wergeld* of 300 shillings, the additional payment will be the value of three men: that is, no doubt, three slaves. But if the victim is a freeman with a *wergeld* of 100 shillings, the additional payment is limited to the value of one slave.[2] It will be remembered that 100 shillings was the amount prescribed by Ethelbert as the ordinary, normal, or average (*medume*) *wergeld*, implying that the amount might be more or less. In view of frequent statements to the contrary by historians of repute, it is necessary to emphasize that neither code gives any specific information on the *wergeld* of the *ceorl*.

For the rest, the freeman's home is in a village, a *tun*. If accused of stealing a man, he must bring at least one witness from the village to which he himself belongs (*hyre*).[3] Does this mean that some villages were populated by freemen who acknowledged no superior but the king? It may appear so when we remember that several of Ethelbert's laws imply, or seem to imply, a particularly close relationship between some freemen and the king. On the other hand, Ethelbert makes it perfectly clear that the nobleman has a *tun* of his own (13). The verb *hyran*, implying some degree of subjection, may therefore point not to the king of Kent but to the noble lord of the village where the accused freeman lives.

[1] CS 45.
[2] Laws of Hlothhere and Eadric in Attenborough, *op. cit.*, 1 and 3.
[3] *Ibid.*, 5.

THE CHURCH AND SLAVERY

King Hlothhere's Reculver charter was issued with the consent of Theodore, archbishop of Canterbury, of whom Bede says that he was the first archbishop whom the whole Church of the English agreed to obey. From Theodore's *Penitential* we learn more than the contemporary secular laws tell us about Anglo-Saxon slavery. A father driven by poverty may sell his son as a slave, but if the boy is above the age of seven his consent is required. An invading army leads its prisoners away and enslaves them. If your wife is carried off by the enemy and you cannot buy her back, you may take another wife; and the wife may also remarry if she loses her husband in this way. If a free woman is sold into slavery when she is with child, the child goes free. If you allow a couple of your slaves to marry, and one of them is later bought into freedom, he or she may either buy out the other or contract a new marriage with a free partner; but the marriage of a freeman with a slave, if both parties were willing, cannot be dissolved. If you seduce your slave-girl you must set her free, but her child remains your slave. Theft, fornication, and the act of enticing a monk from his cloister may be punished by slavery. It is lawful for bishops and abbots to own men penally enslaved.[1]

Perhaps the most important provision is one that relates either to the slave or to the servile *esne*, the man whose master has provided him with a dwelling and the means to support himself, but retains possessionary rights over his person and property. The Church protects him by decreeing that his master may not lawfully deprive him of his *pecunia*, money or livestock which he has earned by his own toil.[2]

SOCIAL GRADES IN THE LAWS OF WIHTRED

Manumission is now treated by the Church as a religious act, one which may take place at the altar. This makes it necessary for the secular power to safeguard the position of the lord by decreeing that he who raises his man from slavery to serfdom under the Church's auspices shall not lose any of the rights over him which he retained under the older system. Accordingly the code issued in 695 by Wihtred, king of Kent, provides that although a man freed at the altar shall be "folk-free," that is, free as against all men except his lord, the lord shall be the guardian of his household even if he is settled elsewhere than on the

[1] A. W. Haddan and W. Stubbs, *Councils and Ecclesiastical Documents*, III, Oxford, 1871, pp. 179, 188, 199, 200–2: Book I, 3, 1; *ibid.*, 14, 12; Book II, 2, 5; *ibid.*, 12, 8, 20–4; *ibid.*, 13, 1–7.

[2] *Ibid.*, p. 202, Book II, 13, 3.

lord's estate, and when he dies his property and *wergeld* will belong to his lord.[1] The reference to his household proves that he is now a *servus casatus*, one whom we have tentatively identified with the *esne* of the laws. He is found on royal, episcopal, and monastic estates,[2] and doubtless also on those of lesser men. If he works on Sunday, he must pay a fine to his lord, unless he can plead the lord's command, and if he rides abroad on an errand of his own on that day, he must pay a heavier fine or be whipped if he cannot find the money. For the serf is still so far a slave that he remains liable to the flogging which in England as in classical antiquity is the slave's distinctive punishment.[3]

By contrast, the fully free man who works in the forbidden time only pays a fine (11). But if he is caught stealing, the king will decide whether he shall be put to death, or sold into slavery beyond the sea, or held to ransom for the price of his life (26).

In Wihtred's laws the nobleman, or *eorlcundman* of the earlier codes, is styled a *gesithcundman*. He owes his standing partly to his birth, no doubt, but the emphasis henceforth is on his position as a *gesith* or companion to the king. One clause (26) refers to him as a "king's thegn." Between him and the slave stands the *ceorlisc man*, or commoner, a broadly inclusive term embracing small freemen, husbandmen, *laets*, perhaps also the "folk-free" *esne*. If a nobleman enters into an illicit union, he must pay 100 shillings to the king, twice as much as a commoner guilty of the same offence (5). A king's thegn may clear himself of an accusation by his own oath, but a commoner requires three oathtakers of his own class (20, 21).

SLAVERY IN SUSSEX

Shortly before Wihtred began to reign in Kent, St Wilfrid spent five years preaching the gospel in the neighbouring and still heathen kingdom of Sussex. His biographer records that King Æthelwalh gave him an estate in Selsey where the king himself resided, to be the seat of a bishopric, and subsequently endowed it with 87 hides of land.[4] From a later document we gather that the 87 hides consisted of a group of villages in the promontory of Selsey, with seven more round Chichester, and three between Arundel and Petworth.[5] We may take it for granted that these villages were inhabited by all sorts and conditions of men,

[1] Laws of Wihtred, 8, in Attenborough, *op. cit.*, p. 27.   [2] *Ibid.*, 22, 23.
[3] *Ibid.*, 9, 10; cf. 13, 15.
[4] *The Life of Bishop Wilfrid by Eddius Stephanus*, c. 41, ed. B. Colgrave, Cambridge, 1927, p. 82.
[5] CS 64. This charter is of questionable authenticity, but there is no reason to doubt its topographical details. Cf. CS 997.

but Bede states that they included 250 male and female slaves, all of whom Wilfrid baptized and set free. Bede also says that Sussex at that time contained 7,000 hides.[1] If the Selsey endowment was a representative cross-section of South Saxon society, this would give more than 20,000 slaves in Sussex as a whole. When we remember that in neighbouring Kent even a husbandman kept a slave or two, this large figure cannot be ruled out, but then the king was doubtless better off in that respect than most of his subjects.

SLAVERY IN WESSEX

We meet the slave again in the laws of Ine, king of Wessex, issued at some date between 688 and 694.[2] The slave may be either Welsh (23 § 3) or English (24), for the time has not yet come when "Welshman" on West Saxon lips will have become synonymous with "slave."[3] If his master makes him work on Sunday, he is to be set free; but if he works of his own accord he must be whipped or pay a fine. The freeman who works on that day, however, may be reduced to slavery unless he can pay a heavy fine or plead his lord's command (3). It seems, then, that a Wessex freeman may have a lord set over him. If a freeman is found guilty of theft and sentenced to slavery, the accuser will have the right to flog him (47). The slave's evidence is not admissible as warranty for chattels alleged to be stolen (47). To steal a slave is an offence of which the law takes cognizance (53). It is a crime to sell one of your own countrymen, whether slave or freeman, beyond the sea (11). This is the first of many enactments intended to discourage the export of slaves into foreign markets, an action which the Kentish law of Wihtred (26) allowed in certain cases.

In 694 Ine appears to have led a campaign against the men of Kent. It would be usual on such occasions for a number of prisoners to be taken and enslaved. An interesting sidelight is thrown on this feature of Anglo-Saxon life by a letter from the archbishop of Canterbury asking the bishop of Sherborne to bring pressure to bear on the abbot of Glastonbury for the release of a captive Kentish girl. The archbishop had already intervened on her behalf without success. We are not told why the abbot was unwilling to let her go; she may have been a particularly skilled embroideress. At all events, her family were offering a ransom of 300 shillings, the *wergeld* of a Kentish nobleman, and the archbishop requests his colleague to obtain the abbot's acceptance of this offer so that the girl's brother, the bearer of the letter, may bring her back to home and freedom.[4]

[1] Bede, *Hist. Eccl.*, IV, 13: pp. 230, 232 in Plummer's edition.
[2] Attenborough, *op. cit.*, pp. 36–61.   [3] See above, p. 395.   [4] EHD I, p. 731.

An earlier Anglo-Saxon captive, Baldhild or Bathildis, was more fortunate. After being sold as a slave to a Frankish magnate, she married Clovis II, king of Neustria, and bore him three sons, for one of whom she later acted as regent.

The *esne*, or *servus casatus*, appears only once by name in Ine's code, where penalties are appointed for any one who actively helps him to abscond (29).

BRITONS IN WESSEX

As might be expected in a kingdom that was still expanding westward into British territory, Ine's laws provide a definite place for Britons in the social scheme. The tariff of *wergelds* payable in compensation for taking a Welshman's life is arranged in a sevenfold gradation:

A Welsh slave 60 or in some cases	50 shillings	(23 §3)
A landless Welshman	60 shillings	(32)
A landed Welshman with half a hide	80 shillings	(32)
The son of a Welsh rent-payer	100 shillings	(23 §3)
A Welsh rent-payer ⎫	120 shillings	(23 §3)
A landed Welshman with one hide ⎭		(32)
A Welsh horseman in the king's service	200 shillings	(33)
A landed Welshman with five hides	600 shillings	(24 §2)

The word for rent-payer is *gafolgelda*. We shall meet it again: it is the equivalent of the Latin *tributarius*. *Gafol* is the rent paid to the king or to a lesser landlord, but when it is paid to the king it is not easily distinguishable to our eyes from a tax. As the *wergeld* of a Welsh *gafolgelda* is identical with that of a Welshman occupying one hide of land, it may well be that these clauses relate to one and the same indigenous class.

The hide, which makes its first appearance here in the documents, is obviously a unit of assessment for calculating the payments in money or kind due to the king or other landlord. It has a long history before it: a history which has yet to be written. All that can be said here is that Ine's laws throw no light on the method by which the assessment was imposed or the extent of land which lies behind it. One clause (70 §1) specifies the substantial food-rent due from ten hides as 10 vats of honey, 300 loaves, 12 measures of Welsh ale, 30 measures of clear ale, 2 full-grown cows or 10 wethers, 10 geese, 20 hens, 10 cheeses, a full measure of butter, 5 salmon, 20 pounds of fodder, and 100 eels.

The Welshman with five hides of land is clearly a man of substance, but other men, probably English, held as much as 10 or 20 hides (64, 65). For Ine's English subjects no comparably detailed tariff of *wergelds* is provided. Sums of 200, 600, and 1,200 shillings are mentioned, with corresponding amounts of 30, 80 and 120 shillings payable to the lord if you kill a man in one of these three classes (70). We suspect that neither classification is exhaustive: if the son of a rent-paying Welshman is to be paid for at five-sixths of his father's *wergeld*, why should the same proportion not apply to an English family? We have seen that 600 shillings is the amount payable for killing a 5-hide Welshman, but we are not told whether the same or a higher compensation is exacted for killing a 5-hide Saxon. As for the 200-shilling man, he is clearly a commoner, since in 34 §1 he is contrasted with a man of noble birth, and according to 70 you must pay his lord 30 shillings if you slay him. His *wergeld* puts him on a par with the king's Welsh horseman and above the one-hide landed Welshman.

THE 'GENEAT'

Clause 19 speaks of a king's *geneat* whose *wergeld* may be as much as 1,200 shillings. In 45 and in Wihtred 20 we hear of a king's thegn. *Geneat* means companion or retainer and *thegn* originally meant servant. In poetry the two words are interchangeable, and they may be synonymous in Ine's code, or one class may have been a subdivision of the other, with the thegn always ranking as a 1,200-shilling man, and the king's *geneat* sometimes less.[1] A *geneat* might have a master other than the king (22). In the later Saxon period he will figure as the most dignified of rustics, and it is reasonable to conjecture that he owes that position to a gift of land made by an early lord to one of his retainers.[2]

THE WESSEX NOBLEMAN

In Ine's code, as in Wihtred's, the nobleman is styled a *gesithcundman*, and is contrasted with the *ceorlisc man* or commoner. Normally, but not always, he is a landholder. He forfeits his land by neglecting military service and has to pay a fine of 120 shillings, twice as much as that paid by a landless man of his own class, and four times as much as a commoner for the same offence (51). Any one who breaks into his residence is fined 35 shillings, compared with 60 shillings for that of a king's thegn, 80 shillings for that of an ealdorman, and 120 shillings for that of a bishop or the king (45). If a foreigner is killed on a *gesith*'s land, the foreigner's *wergeld* is divided equally between the king and the *gesith* (23 §1).

The recent West Saxon conquest of Devon and Cornwall provided the more enterprising *gesithcundmen* with opportunities for taking up forfeited or vacant lands in the newly-won territory, and Ine shows himself anxious that their original estates in the heartland of Wessex

[1] Chadwick, *op. cit.*, p. 138.   [2] Stenton, *op. cit.*, p. 473.

shall not be left to run down in consequence; if they were, the king would lose his food-rent. So a departing nobleman may take with him only his reeve, his smith, and his children's nurse (63), but if he has twenty hides, he must show twelve hides of *gesettland*, land occupied by husbandmen; if ten, then six; and if three, then one and a half, before he leaves.[1]

THE 'CEORL'

We have already seen that the *ceorlisc man* is liable for military service (51), and in a Mercian context we shall learn more presently about the nature of that service. He has a *wergeld*, the amount of which is not stated (30). If he is convicted of theft, his hand or foot is to be struck off (18, 37).

The *ceorl* or husbandman who gives his name to this class appears as occupying a farm which he is bound to keep fenced both summer and winter; if he fails to do this he has no claim on his neighbour's beast when it strays in and does damage (40). He may share ploughland or meadow-land with others of his kind (42), and he may have occasion to hire a yoke of oxen from a neighbour (60). As a householder he is entitled to protection against brawling in his premises (6 § 3). In this clause he is described not as a *ceorl* but as either a rent-payer (*gafolgelda*) or a *gebur*. This last word seems to denote a man of servile antecedents whose master has set him up on a farm and provided him with a house. In this connection we should note Ine's ruling that if the lord does not give him a dwelling the man who rents land and ploughs it may give up his tenancy should the lord try to exact service as well as rent. It seems to follow that given both land and house, he is tied to the land and owes labour-service to his lord. But if he surrenders the tenancy he cannot claim the value of the standing crops.[2] This strongly suggests that the land had originally been sown with seed provided by the lord, a charac-teristic of the *gebur* as we shall find him more fully described in later texts.

When a lord turns a group of his slaves into serfs with domiciles of their own to which plots of land are attached, they are described in Latin texts as *coliberti*. We shall find Domesday Book treating *colibertus* as a synonym for *gebur*. A record from St Peter's abbey at Gloucester throws a vivid light on his condition. Early in the eighth century a certain Cynemær, son of a *colibertus* named Wulfmær, "oppressed

---

[1] Ine, 64–6. On the interpretation of *gesett land* in these clauses, see T. H. Aston, 'The Origins of the Manor', TRHS 5th ser., VIII, 1958, p. 65, and authorities there cited; also John F. McGovern, *Speculum* XLVI, 1971, pp. 589–96.

[2] Ine, 67. On this clause see Stenton, *op. cit.*, p.313, and Professor Whitelock, EHD I, p. 371 *n*.

by the work and the name," gave the abbey a fishery at Framilode in return for full emancipation.[1] Thus three terms are used in different contexts to designate the freedman. As one of a half-free community he is a *colibertus*; as a cottager with little or no land he is still sometimes called an *esne* (a word which henceforth occurs very rarely in the laws); and as a householder farming a substantial acreage he is commonly called a *gebur*.

THE POSITION OF THE LORD

We may surmise that the *gafolgelda*, like the *gebur*, is 'folk-free', free too in the eyes of the Church. But there is hardly any room for doubt that most if not all men of the *ceorlisc* class had a lord set over them, a lord who was by no means always the king. The king will share with the lord the *wergeld* of an illegitimate child whose father has disowned him (27). Compensation is payable to the lord whose man is slain (76). If a Welsh slave kills an Englishman, his owner must hand him over to the dead man's lord and kinsmen (74). It is not unknown for a freeman to be compelled by his lord to work on Sunday (3 §2). Any man who moves into another district stealthily without his lord's permission must come back when discovered and pay 60 shillings to the lord (39).

Perhaps the most significant clause of all is one decreeing that a *gesithcundman* who intercedes with the king, the ealdorman, or his own lord, on behalf of his free or unfree dependants shall have no portion of the fine they have incurred, because he has not taken care to restrain his men from evil-doing (50). Few, if any, lords will not be *gesithcund*, but it seems that one *gesith* may be under another's lordship. Moreover it is clear that the state imposes on every lord some responsibility for his men's good behaviour. Much as we should like to know how systematically and through what agents the West Saxon lord exercised his coercive power, Ine's code does not enlighten us on that important subject; but the lord's right of jurisdiction, with the concomitant right in normal circumstances to take a portion of the misdoer's fine, is plainly visible here at least in germ. It was no novelty, for it had existed, however unofficially, in the later Roman empire.[2] In England, of course, a long future lay before it.

The service which Ine forbids a landlord to exact unless he provides his tenant with a dwelling will obviously be performed on the lord's own land. It follows that some lords, if not all, keep at least a portion of

---

[1] DB I, pp. 38b2, 174b2; *Historia et Cartularium Mon. S. Petri Gloucestriae*, ed. W. H. Hart, Rolls ser. 33, 1863–7, I, pp. 77, 124; III, p. 274.

[2] J. Percival, 'Seigneurial aspects of late Roman estate management', EHR LXXXIV, 1969, pp. 468–73.

their estate in hand as a demesne or home-farm, and do not rely exclusively on slave labour for its cultivation, but may require agricultural service from their tenant farmers.

SOCIAL GRADES IN MERCIA

We have lingered in the south of England because the laws of Kent and Wessex are our earliest and fullest sources of information on Anglo-Saxon society. Mercia, too, had laws of its own: Alfred the Great says he had studied those enacted by King Offa (757–96), and deemed them worthy to be ranked with the laws of Ethelbert and Ine. But neither Offa's nor any other Mercian code has survived.

We turn for light to a compilation put together in the first quarter of the eleventh century. The compiler, who has been plausibly identified with Wulfstan, archbishop of York, based his work on careful antiquarian research. He reproduces accurately Ine's laws on the *wergelds* of one-hide and half-hide Welshmen. Probably, therefore, we may safely take his word for it that under Mercian law a husbandman's *wergeld* was 200 shillings and a thegn's 1,200 shillings.[1] Thus a Mercian nobleman's life was six times as valuable as the life of a husbandman, and perhaps the same proportion held good in Wessex.

An incident related by Bede throws a welcome light on the military obligations of these two classes. In 679, when a great battle was fought between the armies of Northumbria and Mercia, a young Northumbrian thegn named Imma was left for dead upon the field. Attached at one time to the household of Queen Etheldreda and more recently to that of the Northumbrian prince Ælfwine, he was evidently of high social standing. On the following day he began to revive and tried to make his escape, but was soon captured by Mercian soldiers and brought to their lord, a *gesith* of the Mercian king. Fearing to invite the customary vengeance if he disclosed his rank, he declared that he was a *ceorl* ("rusticum") who had come on that campaign with others of his class to bring provisions to the troops. His face, bearing, and speech gave the lie to this pretence, and his captor questioned him again, promising to spare him if he would frankly declare the truth. When Imma did so, the Mercian kept his promise not to kill him, but sold him in London to a Frisian slave-trader, from whom Imma presently managed to buy back his freedom.[2]

Throughout Anglo-Saxon history the typical warrior is the man of noble birth. The *ceorl* was indeed liable for military service, and in Ine's Wessex had to pay a substantial fine if he disregarded the summons, but

[1] EHD I, p. 433.
[2] Bede, *Hist. Eccl.*, IV, 20: p. 249 in Plummer's edition.

the story of Imma shows conclusively that the husbandman's place was in the commissariat, not in the fighting line.[1]

The Book of Llandaff records that a Welshman named Riataf gave a precious sword, a horse, and a Saxon woman as the price of some land in Archenfield which he subsequently made over to the local bishop.[2] We may take it that what we have learnt about the slave-class from Theodore's *Penitential* holds good of Mercia and the other kingdoms, since Theodore was the first archbishop whom the whole Church of the English obeyed. The biographer of St Werburg, a daughter of the Mercian royal house, tells of a neatherd employed on her estate at Weedon, Ælfnoth by name, a man "of holy life so far as might be for a man under the yoke of human slavery." This unfortunate somehow incurred the displeasure of the reeve, who gave him a cruel whipping, and would have flogged him to death if the saint had not worked a miracle to stay his hand.[3]

NORTHUMBRIAN SOCIETY

It is well known that Gregory the Great, not yet pope, encountered some fair-haired Anglian youths on sale in the Roman market, and indulged in some word-play on Deira, the name of the Northumbrian kingdom whence they had been exported. Later, as pope, he directed that some of the surplus revenue from the papal estates in Gaul should be spent in purchasing English youths aged seventeen or more so that they might be placed in monasteries and trained as Christians.[4] When Aidan, the saintly bishop of Lindisfarne, received gifts of money from the rich, he either gave the money to the poor or spent it on ransoming those who had been wrongfully sold.[5] After King Egfrith's disastrous incursion into Pictland (A.D. 685) slavery awaited those Anglian survivors who did not succeed in making their escape.[6]

Of the Northumbrian husbandman we learn from the eleventh-century compilation already cited that the price of his life was equivalent to that of his Mercian counterpart, 200 shillings. The life of a thegn was rather more than seven times as valuable. Higher values, in ascending order, are set on a nobleman and a king's high-reeve, a bishop and an

---

[1] H. M. Chadwick, *The Origin of the English Nation*, Cambridge, 1907, p. 160; E. John, *Orbis Britanniae*, Leicester, 1966, pp. 134–9.

[2] *The Text of the Book of Llan Dâv*, ed. J. G. Evans and J. Rhys, Oxford, 1893, p. 185.

[3] *Acta Sanctorum*, February I, p. 393. She caused the reeve's head to be turned back to front until he desisted.

[4] Plummer's Bede, I, p. 79; II, p. 390; Haddan and Stubbs, *op. cit.*, III, p. 5.

[5] Bede, *Hist. Eccl.*, III, 5.

[6] *Ibid.*, IV, 24.

ealdorman, an archbishop and a royal prince, each of these couples being paired for the purposes of *wergeld*.[1]

The Northumbrian nobleman of this period, like his counterpart in the southern kingdoms, is called a *gesith*, in Latin *comes*, a companion of the king. Excavations at Yeavering have revealed a wedge-form structure resembling the seating accommodation of a Roman theatre, seemingly designed for occasions when King Edwin held parley with his *gesiths*.[2] A number of texts depict the Northumbrian *gesith* as landlord of a village. On one occasion St Cuthbert goes to a village near the Tweed by invitation of its lord, a *gesith* of King Egfrith (A.D. 670–85) named Sibba. In the following reign a preaching tour brings Cuthbert to the village of a *gesith* named Hemma.[3] St John of Beverley heals the wife of a *gesith* named Puch who had invited him to dedicate a church on his estate at Bishop Burton. This same nobleman is said to have given the neighbouring manor of Walkington to Beverley Minster when his daughter became a nun there. The bishop also dedicated a church at Cherry Burton at the request of a *gesith* named Addi. The parish of Cherry Burton originally included Leconfield and Scorbrough, an aggregate of more than 8,000 acres, and if it was co-extensive with Addi's manor, this nobleman was indeed handsomely endowed.[4]

The lord of Bishop Burton could give a portion of his estate to the minster where his daughter became a nun. Does this mean that he was free to divide the rest among his other children, or transmit Burton itself to one of them? By no means. All that is known of early England suggests that the church of Beverley would have been extremely ill-advised to accept his gift without confirmation by a royal charter. For the magnate owed his position to the king's favour and had only a life interest in the estate. Even when the lands passed from father to son, as no doubt they often did, they did so as a mark of favour from the king.[5] A younger son might take holy orders: the captive warrior Imma had a brother named Tunna who had become a priest and abbot. Or he might serve in personal attendance on the king, hoping to be rewarded with a grant of land that would enable him to marry and support a family. If disappointed of this hope, he might retire into a monastery, as Benedict Biscop's cousin Eosterwine did at Wearmouth

---

[1] EHD I, p. 432. It should be noted, however, that according to Chadwick, *Studies on Anglo-Saxon Institutions*, p. 76, the code from which this tariff is derived can hardly be earlier than the tenth century.

[2] *Medieval Archaeology* I, 1957, p. 149.

[3] Anonymous Life of St Cuthbert, cc. 3, 7, in *Two Lives*, ed. B. Colgrave, Cambridge, 1940, pp. 114, 120.

[4] Bede, *Hist. Eccl.*, V, 4 and 5; W. Dugdale, *Monasticon Anglicanum*, 1817–30, II, pp. 128, 129.

[5] Chadwick, *Origin of the English Nation*, p. 169.

after spending some time in the service of King Egfrith.[1] If the worst came to the worst he would leave the kingdom and seek his fortune elsewhere. Guthlac, a scion of the highest Mercian nobility, spent nine weary years in foreign service, part of the time among the Welsh.[2] It was the need of the Church for permanent endowments carrying full possessionary rights and not limited to the life of one beneficiary which led Anglo-Saxon rulers to grant land by 'book', that is, by charter solemnly attested by the magnates of Church and state. Hence the long series of charters which, next to the laws, provide the most illuminating evidence on Old English history. The 'book-right' they conferred was at first known as *jus ecclesiasticum* or *jus monasteriale*. For a long time after the introduction of book-right it was confined to the churches; if a layman received a land-charter, as occasionally happened, it was always subject to the express or implied condition that the recipient would use it to found or endow a minster. Not until the last quarter of the eighth century do we begin to find kings granting land to laymen in hereditary possession.[3] Long before that Bede was in his grave. Almost with his last breath he complained in strong terms that scores of Northumbrian ealdormen, *gesiths*, and royal servants had been procuring land-charters by having themselves tonsured and calling their establishments monasteries, which they staffed with clerics of dubious character, so that there was not enough land left to provide for the class on whom the safety of the realm depended, and young warriors, unable to marry and settle down, either left the country or stayed at home and amused themselves by seducing nuns.[4]

THE OTHER KINGDOMS

On the social systems of Lindsey, East Anglia, and Essex the sources fail us, but there is no reason to suppose that they differed in any significant respect from the kingdoms already studied. The loose association of tribes collectively known as the Middle Angles may originally have been governed by ealdormen, for there is no record or tradition of a royal house. In the course of the seventh century they fell under Mercian domination, and their earlier social system, if in any way distinctive, must then have been assimilated to that of Mercia.

[1] Bede, *Historia Abbatum*, I, 8, p. 371 in Plummer's *Bede*.
[2] *Felix's Life of Saint Guthlac*, cc. 18, 34, ed. B. Colgrave, Cambridge, 1953, pp. 80, 110.
[3] CS 225, a Wessex charter dated 778. The earliest Mercian example is CS 230, of the following year.
[4] *Epistola ad Ecgbertum Episcopum*, in Plummer's Bede, pp. 414–16; EHD I, p. 741.

The impression left upon us by this survey is one of a highly class-conscious society ruled by powerful monarchs. Around the king stands a retinue of nobles whose main function is to fight his battles. If their service merits it, he will in time reward them with grants of land, and they will form a territorial aristocracy supported by the rents and services of the tillers of the soil, whom they are bound to protect and keep in order.

The modern study of place-names has reinforced this impression. The map is studded with names of which a high proportion are compounded of a personal name followed by the suffix *-ingas*: hence Tooting, Havering, Ealing, Hickling, and the like. They constitute, if not perhaps the earliest, certainly a very early stratum of English place-names, and they signify the kinsmen or followers of the leader whose name they perpetuate. The expeditions which effected the conquest and colonization of Britain, led by men like Hengist, would seem to have involved an organization in which each detachment had its captain and was known by his name. If this organization was kept up after landing, the name would be transferred to the settlement when the leader received his share of the conquered land. We can only guess at such details: what is clear is that Tota, Hæfer, and Hicel who gave their names to Tooting, Havering, and Hickling led bands of settlers over whom they wielded at least the kind of authority which leadership normally bestows.[1]

At the other end of the social scale we find both predial and domestic slaves in considerable numbers. Some of them were Britons now serving new masters, but the English did not scruple to enslave men and women of their own blood. The class was constantly recruited from prisoners of war, convicts, and hungry freemen who sold themselves for bread. At the same time, in England as on the continent the transition has begun from downright slavery to serfdom. It is cheaper to give your slave a plot of land and allow him some spare time in which to earn money than to bear the whole cost of his maintenance. It is also meritorious in the eyes of the Church. But he remains your man, and in strict law his belongings are all yours. The road is still a long one that will lead him uphill to full freedom.

What of the intermediate class, the ordinary Anglo-Saxon farmer? For a century or more he has loomed large in our historical literature. Maitland, for instance, pictures the Anglo-Saxon countryside as peopled in the seventh century by "large masses of free peasants." He refers continually to "a large class of peasant proprietors," "free men who with their own labour tilled their own soil."[2] The picture is filled

[1] For the fullest discussion, see E. Ekwall, *English Place-Names in -ing*, 2nd ed., Lund, 1962. Cf. also p. 423, above.

[2] *Domesday Book and Beyond*, pp. 221, 223, 323, 326.

in by scholars who have adopted Maitland's conception of the typical Anglo-Saxon husbandman, free by birth and condition, accustomed to speaking his mind on public affairs in popular assemblies, and acknowledging no superior but the king. We are even assured that the free peasant community forms the true starting-point of English social history.[1]

Others who have studied the subject say roundly that the free village community has never been more than a figment of the romantic imagination.[2] And its proponents cannot but admit that the existence of such a community is a matter of inference – inference more or less plausible – than of actual historical record. What in fact is the sum-total of the knowledge we have gleaned from the sources examined thus far? We may leave out of account the *geneat*, for his lord may not yet have settled him on a farm. Ine's code recognizes the Welsh *gafolgelda*, and there is no reason to doubt that this man had his Anglo-Saxon counterpart. The distinctive mark of the *gafolgelda*, Welsh or English, is that he pays rent for his land, with little or no labour-service. The same code also mentions the *gebur*, without giving any details of his condition; he seems to be a man of servile origin whose master has helped him to start life on a holding of his own. To these we may perhaps add the Kentish *laet*. All of them, being commoners, will be included under the generic term *ceorl*, but we have no means of knowing which of them is typical of the class as a whole, nor is there any proof that, taken all together, they will outnumber the slaves. Place-names in this early period tell us little about the social condition of those who bestowed them, but the implications of the *–ingas* names show how right Stenton was in foreseeing that the most notable result of a thorough investigation of English place-names would be a recognition of the seignorial idea as a primitive force in the organization of rural society.[3] No one has studied Anglo-Saxon law more intensively than Liebermann, and his judgement is even more emphatic: "From the earliest Anglo-Saxon times the peasant's obligation to pay rent, and by the same token the village on the soil of a landlord, must have been the rule."[4]

We do indeed hear of Kentish freemen living in a village. We also hear of the West Saxon *ceorl* who shares arable and meadow with some of his fellows.[5] The agricultural implications of this communal husbandry have been discussed in the preceding chapter. Here we need only observe that it must have involved a certain amount of discussion among rustic neighbours, for not every unforeseen problem of sowing

---

[1] Stenton, *Anglo-Saxon England*, p. 314.
[2] C. Stephenson, *Mediaeval Institutions*, Cornell University Press, 1954, p. 244.
[3] F. M. Stenton, *The Place-Names of Berkshire*, Reading, 1911, p. 25.
[4] F. Liebermann, *Die Gesetze der Angelsachsen*, Halle, 1903–16, II, p. 298 ('Bauer', 5).
[5] Hlothhere and Eadric, 5; Ine, 42.

and harvesting could be met by invoking customary practice. The discussions could, and probably did, take place in informal meetings at the village ale-house. Much has been made of the fact that the law makes no mention in this context of any supervision by the lord.[1] But any one who has lived in a closely knit agricultural community will testify that the wilful nonconformist stands little chance against the massed force of public opinion. Besides, it is ludicrous to suppose that a dispute about the fencing of a field at, say, Tichborne or Wootton Bassett will have to be referred to the king. The landlord may be in the background, but he is there, and when the law has enunciated a general principle he probably has means to enforce it if need be. We have to wait another century for any mention of a popular assembly, a *folcgemot*, and the context in which we shall find it then is one of fiscal administration and the punishment of serious crime; it is not concerned with petty agrarian disputes.[2]

Legal freedom is one thing, economic independence another, and without economic independence freedom will be no very sturdy growth. The husbandman who must hire a yoke of oxen from his neighbour before he can plough his corn-plot is obviously a man of slender resources. A succession of bad harvests, an enemy raid, a cattle plague could soon reduce him to such poverty that he would sell himself and his offspring for bread. The law allows him to bargain with his lord, but it will be a very unequal bargain, for if he throws up his holding where is he to go? Against the lord who can fetch him back and fine him heavily if he absconds and seeks a change of masters, what is his legal freedom worth?

That the ranks of the Anglo-Saxons who migrated to Britain included a certain number of adventurers who could not boast of noble birth; that some of them secured substantial holdings in the former Roman province: these are reasonable surmises. The followers of Hengist, who settled in the south-east not at first as conquerors but under treaty, may have numbered such men in their ranks. If they and their descendants prospered, they would form an upper layer of the rural population, in course of time creating their own circle of dependants; if they failed, they would lose their freedom and become satellites of more powerful men. But all this is conjecture, incapable of proof. Evidence which cannot be gainsaid obliges us to think of the English countryside in the seventh century as largely dominated by an aristocratic, slave-owning class, with demesnes cultivated for them partly by slaves, partly by tenants with servile antecedents. For positive evidence of independent and self-governing rural communities we search in vain.

---

[1] Liebermann, *loc. cit.*, followed by Stenton, *Anglo-Saxon England*, p. 280.
[2] CS 201, undated endorsement of *c.* 800.

CHAPTER IV

KING ALFRED'S ENGLAND

ALFRED THE GREAT (871–99) inherited a kingdom much larger and more powerful than the Wessex of Ine's day. His grandfather Egbert had absorbed the once independent kingdoms of Sussex, Kent, and Essex. Devon had long since been organized as a West Saxon shire with an ealdorman of its own. In Cornwall a shadow of British royalty still lingered, and did not finally disappear until the reign of Athelstan (924–39), but Egbert had completed its military subjugation and bequeathed to his descendants large estates in Cornwall.[1] Alfred's father Æthelwulf (839–55) had recovered Berkshire from the Mercian kings, and successfully initiated a policy of creating for his successors a permanent royal demesne not automatically divisible among coheirs.[2] By a particularly interesting charter dated 26 December 846 Æthelwulf assumed direct lordship over a large territory in the south of Devon, comprising some 65,000 acres between the Erme and the Dart. Judging from the subsequent history of the area, his object was not so much to enrich himself and his heirs, for only two estates within its bounds were annexed to the royal demesne, as to encourage the development of a sparsely populated but potentially fertile district by granting portions of it piecemeal to his thegns and increasing the assessment to make it keep pace with the expansion of settlement.[3]

The really formidable challenge to West Saxon power came from the Vikings, who from 865 onwards threatened the whole fabric of English society. They extinguished the kingdom of East Anglia, and established English puppets on the thrones of Mercia and Northumbria. After years of desperate fighting Alfred managed to save Wessex and to make himself overlord of western Mercia, which was governed under him by his son-in-law Ethelred with the title of ealdorman, for the last of the Mercian kings had now disappeared; but he had to leave the Danes in possession of East Anglia, and it remained for his son and successor Edward the Elder (899–924) to impose West Saxon authority over the whole of England.

The Danish inroads took a heavy toll in slaughter, plunder, and devastation. In 872 the bishop of Worcester found it necessary to

[1] H. P. R. Finberg, *Lucerna*, pp. 103–11.
[2] E. John, *Orbis Britanniae*, pp. 37–44.
[3] CS 451; for a detailed exposition of this charter see H. P. R. Finberg, *West-Country Historical Studies*, pp. 11–28.

raise money by selling a four-life lease of land in Warwickshire to a king's thegn "on account of the immense tribute taken by the heathen when they occupied London."[1] The church of Winchester, "unable to raise the huge tribute which the whole of our people used to pay the heathen," had to borrow the money from King Alfred.[2] In a letter to Edward the Elder Bishop Denewulf states that when he took in hand an estate of seventy hides at Beddington (Surr) he found it destitute of livestock and stripped bare by the heathen army.[3] It says much for the inherent strength of the realm which Egbert, Æthelwulf, and their predecessors had built up that Wessex managed to survive the drain on its resources in men and money, and in doing so to lay the foundation of a united England. It says even more for Alfred himself that while devising an effective system of national defence he also found time to foster education, publish books, and promulgate a new code of laws.

ALFRED'S LAWS

In the preamble to his code Alfred states that he has collected and reproduced what seemed to him the best enactments of Ethelbert of Kent, Ine of Wessex, and Offa of Mercia, and has added a few of his own.[4] The oldest manuscript, written, according to Liebermann, about 925, includes the laws of Ine as an appendix to those of Alfred; it looks as if he meant the earlier code to remain in force. He does not reproduce the scale of *wergelds*, ranging from 50 to 600 shillings, which Ine had appointed as compensation for murdered Welshmen of various grades. The only *wergelds* specified by Alfred are 200, 600, and 1,200 shillings, and we are not told in so many words to what classes these belong, but fines equivalent to a fortieth of the *wergeld* are prescribed for breaking into a man's premises, and the detailed tariff shows that the 1,200-shilling man was a noble inferior in status to a bishop or an ealdorman, and the 200-shilling man a *ceorl* or husbandman (40). A twelfth-century gloss on the Latin translation of the laws identifies the intermediate 600-shilling man with the *radcniht* of Domesday Book, a free tenant who gave occasional service to his lord in the capacity of a mounted retainer.[5] But under Ine 600 shillings had been the *wergeld* of a Welshman with five hides of land, and we cannot be sure that it was anything else in Alfred's time.

The laws add little to our knowledge of the lowest class. It appears that the ordinary husbandman might employ a slave-woman as his domestic servant (25). Slaves and unfree labourers (*esnewyrhtan*) are

---

[1] CS 533. [2] CS 565, on which see *Lucerna*, p. 135.
[3] CS 619. [4] Attenborough, *Laws of the Earliest English Kings*, p. 62.
[5] Liebermann, *Gesetze der Angelsachsen*, I, p. 73; id., TRHS N.S. VII, 1893, p. 103.

placed on a level where holidays are concerned; they are not granted the full thirty-seven days in a year allowed to all freemen, but the four Ember Wednesdays are reserved for slaves who may wish to sell anything they have received in alms or earned by working in their free time (43).

THE 'CEORL'

All tillers of the soil other than slaves are comprehended under the generic word *ceorl*, husbandman, whatever their legal or economic status. Thus, in the context where Ine had spoken of the *gafolgelda* and the *gebur* (6 §3), Alfred speaks only of the husbandman (*cierlisc mon*, 39). For Alfred the typical *ceorl*, though not a slave, was a tiller of the soil who like the *esne* and the *gebur* of the earlier laws had still some way to go before he could be accounted fully free. This is clear from the translation of the Latin historian Orosius which Alfred published. Orosius relates that the Volscians freed their slaves indiscriminately; then the former slaves, now freedmen (*libertini*), conspired to gain full freedom, and even mastery. The Alfredian translator writes: "They had freed some of their slaves, and also became too mild and forgiving to them all. Then their *ceorls* resented the fact that they had freed their slaves and would not free *them*" (i.e. the *ceorls*).[1] He has misunderstood the original here, not seeing that Orosius is speaking of only one group, the former slaves, now freedmen. But this misunderstanding does not affect the conclusion we must draw from his use of *ceorl* as equivalent to *libertinus*. It proves that in the mind of Alfred and his contemporaries the *ceorl* or ordinary husbandman, like the villein of later centuries, was a man still only half-free, free perhaps against other men than his lord, but needing a further act of emancipation before he could enjoy the full and undisputed status of a freeman.

The laws imply that both husbandmen and men of noble birth live under lordship (4 §2, *ge georle ge eorle*). A man may not fight against his lord, even to defend a kinsman, but he may defend his lord from attack without incurring the reprisal of the blood-feud (42 §§5, 6). He may leave one lord and seek another, but if so he must do it with the cognizance of the ealdorman (37). It is highly improbable that this freedom to change lords was enjoyed by any but gentlemen: it could hardly extend to the rustic whose master was empowered by the still unrepealed law of Ine to seize him and fine him heavily if he took himself off without permission.

---

[1] "For þaem þe hie sune heora þeowas gefreoden, 7 eac him eallum wurdon to milde 7 to forgiefene. þa ofþute heora ceorlum þaet mon þa þeowas freode, 7 hi nolde."—*King Alfred's Orosius*, ed. H. Sweet, Early Eng. Text Soc., 79, 1883, p. 162. The decisive words are "7 hi nolde."

THE 'CEORLS' OF HURSTBOURNE

The chequered history of an estate in Hampshire tells us something of what subjection to a landlord meant in practice. In the last quarter of the eighth century an ealdorman named Hemele gave Hurstbourne Priors to the church of Abingdon. Presently King Egbert, by an exchange of land with Abingdon, acquired Hurstbourne and left it to his son Æthelwulf. Æthelwulf in turn bequeathed it by will to Alfred for his lifetime with remainder to the church of Winchester. When Alfred succeeded to the kingdom another exchange was effected; the Winchester clergy gave up 100 hides at Cholsey to the king in return for Chisledon and Hurstbourne, which by this time was assessed at 60 hides. But presently, finding themselves unable to pay the heavy sum required to buy peace from the Vikings, they asked Alfred to pay it for them and to take back Chisledon and Hurstbourne: which he did. While Hurstbourne was in Alfred's hands he detached a portion of the estate and entrusted it as a "sundorfeoh," a separate holding, to a certain Ecgulf, a thegn, perhaps, or a royal reeve. This "sundorfeoh," assessed at ten hides, lay at Stoke, four miles north-west of Hurstbourne itself, the assessment of which was thus reduced to fifty hides. When the time came for Alfred to make his will, he left both Hurstbourne and the "sundorfeoh" to the church of Winchester in accordance with his father's injunction. Less than twelve months after his death his son and successor, Edward the Elder, executed two charters, one for Hurstbourne and one for Stoke, assigning both to Winchester and thus restoring the integrity of the original sixty-hide estate.[1]

Such frequent changes of ownership are apt to unsettle people's minds. Now that Winchester had regained possession, it was important that the economy of the demesne should not be injured by subtraction of dues or clandestine withdrawals of man-power. The Stoke charter therefore provides expressly that the land shall come to the minster with all the men who were there both at Stoke and at Hurstbourne when the great Alfred went the way of all flesh; and to close any possible loophole the obligations of these men are recorded in detail. The custumal included in the Stoke charter is the earliest surviving statement of the dues which English kings and churchmen claimed from the

---

[1] CS 592, 594. For a full discussion of these and other relevant texts, and an answer to Maitland's attack on them (*Domesday Book and Beyond*, pp. 330, 331), see *Lucerna*, pp. 131–43. The harmful effects of Maitland's polemic have been far-reaching. Stenton treats the Hurstbourne custumal as almost contemporary with the eleventh-century *Rectitudines* (*Anglo-Saxon England*, p. 476) and the editors of EHD print it in the wrong volume (II, p. 816), where it is dated "? *circa* 1050" without any indication that it is taken from a charter of 900. So also G. Duby, *L'économie rurale et la vie des campagnes dans l'Occident médiéval*, Paris, 1962, II, p. 676.

tillers of the soil. A document of such importance for agrarian history must be given in full.—

"Here are written the dues which the husbandmen (*ceorlas*) ought to render at Hurstbourne. First, from each hide (*hiwisce*) they should pay 40 pence at the autumnal equinox, and 6 church-measures of ale, and 3 sesters of wheat for bread; and they should plough 3 acres in their own time and sow them with their own seed and bring it to the barn in their own time; and give 3 pounds of barley as rent; and mow half an acre of meadow as rent in their own time, and make it into a rick; and supply 4 fothers of split wood as rent, made into a stack in their own time; and supply 16 poles of fencing as rent, likewise in their own time; and at Easter they should give two ewes with two lambs, reckoning two young sheep to one full-grown; and they should wash the sheep and shear them in their own time; and work as they are bidden every week but three – one at midwinter, the second at Easter, the third on the Rogation Days."

Stenton saw that the *ceorls* of Hurstbourne were closely involved in an agricultural routine organized in relation to the lord's demesne and hall. Nevertheless he held that they were, "in origin, unquestionably free," farming inherited land with stock and implements that were their own property, since the custumal gives no hint that the lord has provided them with an outfit, or that he will take any of their substance when they die.[1] This is to press the argument from silence rather too far. Behind it lies the tacit but false assumption that the freedom of the *ceorl* is implicit in his very name. But we have seen that for Alfred and his contemporaries the reverse was true. Moreover the number of holidays allowed to the *ceorls* of Hurstbourne is appreciably fewer than the thirty-seven days which Alfred's law provides for every free man. These husbandmen, ancestors of the *villani* and *bordarii* whom the emissaries of Norman William will find at Hurstbourne, may well be descended from slaves or *coliberti*. Nor can it be assumed that each of them occupies a hide of land. The word *hiwisc* can mean household as well as hide. If it means hide in this context, "forty pence from each hide" is only another way of saying "tenpence from each yardland," which is exactly what we shall find the eleventh-century *Rectitudines* demanding from the half-free *gebur*.

THE PLACE-NAME CHARLTON

The ten hides which Alfred detached from Hurstbourne to form a separate holding for Ecgulf did not last long as a "sundorfeoh," and therefore left no trace in local nomenclature, but often enough the village thus detached took its name from the new owner; thus the place

[1] Stenton, *op. cit.*, p. 476.

in Rutland granted by King Edward to a thegn called Æthelstan became *Æthelstanestun*, now Ayston.[1] Once begun, the process of erosion may be carried very far indeed. Provision has to be made for the king's younger sons; great noblemen demand favours; old companions in arms expect their reward; and there are churches to be endowed. In the end nothing may be left of the original estate except the king's *tun* itself and one neighbouring village which is not granted away because the rents and services of its inhabitants are vital to the economy of the capital manor. This village, geographically distinct from the king's *tun* but close to it, and tenurially distinct from the alienated *tuns* which now pay dues to other lords, becomes known as Charlton, *Ceorlatun*, because it is where the king's own husbandmen live, tilling the soil partly on their own account, but partly also, and perhaps chiefly, for the king. Where conditions are similar the name and the thing may equally well occur on private estates. Thus the episcopal manor of Cropthorne (Worcs) had its Charlton about a mile away. The Charltons are not confined to any one part of England (see Fig. 48), and the place-name illustrates a well-marked phase of social development. It denotes a village on an estate which includes more than one unit of settlement. It is not the principal unit, being situated a mile or more away from the seat of lordship, but it is subject to the same lord, and the dues and services of its husbandmen are indispensable to the economy of the estate as a whole.[2]

LABOUR SERVICES

It is important, in reading the Hurstbourne and later custumals, to bear in mind that the enumeration of labour services must always be understood as a formal statement of total liability. If every husbandman at Hurstbourne really spent an unlimited time each week at work on his lord's demesne, he could scarcely have wrung a livelihood from his own holding, even with the help of such able-bodied men and women as could be mustered from his own household. But there may never have been a time when the available services did not outrun the demand. Every well-organized estate would aim at providing a margin over current needs. These husbandmen do week-work "as they are bidden," a pregnant phrase which may mean only that they do it if required, but it can also mean that they must undertake any task of husbandry which may be demanded of them at the discretion of the lord's reeve or bailiff. The essence of serfdom is not labour service but subjection to the

---

[1] K 784; C. R. Hart, *The Early Charters of Eastern England*, no. 161.
[2] For a full discussion of the historical and topographical evidence see H. P. R. Finberg, *Lucerna*, pp. 144–60.

Fig. 48. Charltons and Carltons.

will of the lord. It will be noticed that apart from renders in kind, of
ale, barley, wheat, hay, timber, and sheep, each quarter-hide pays
tenpence a year. This is the only rent paid in cash, but we cannot be
sure that some small additional payment was not required in lieu of
service if the labour was not needed in a particular year. Such temporary
commutation, or "sale of works" as it is called in later manorial
accounts, may well be as old as the system of labour services itself.

Alfred's laws provide only occasional glimpses of husbandry in practice. A reference to the theft of bees implies the private ownership of bee-hives (9 §2). Trees may be either felled or burnt (12); the case is envisaged of accidental manslaughter caused by a falling tree when a band of men are at work in a privately owned wood (13). Here we may picture a landlord employing servile dependants to clear part of his woodland, perhaps with the intention of settling them as *coliberti* on the soil thus cleared.

CHARGES UPON THE LAND

Besides the dues they paid to the lord of the soil, the occupants of land were liable to various charges which may be classified under three main headings: purveyance, public labour, and justiciary duties. Purveyance might be exacted in many forms. Examples have been given in previous chapters of the food-rents demanded from a ten-hide estate in Wessex and from a sixty-hide estate in Mercia. These were regular charges; but on occasions when the king, or a prince of the royal house, or an ealdorman, or a king's reeve, or one of a class of personage called *fæstingmen* – apparently royal emissaries – came upon an estate in the course of his travels, he was entitled to demand food, drink, and lodging. To this list of uninvited but expensive guests one charter adds bishops. Again, the king might quarter his horses, hounds, hawks, and falcons wherever he pleased. From a charter dated 904 it appears that Taunton was liable to provide one night's hospitality for the king and nine nights for his falconers, to maintain eight hounds and their keeper, to escort travellers on their way to the nearest royal residence, and with horses and carts to transport anything the king needed either to Curry or to Williton.[1]

Escort duty might include the supplying of travellers with additional post-horses. This, with cartage and work on royal buildings, fell into the category of public labour. So did the obligations which it is convenient to epitomize as the three common dues: the construction and repair of bridges, the construction and repair of fortifications, and the duty of sending a certain number of armed men when the king or the ealdorman called out the host.

Finally every occupant of land was expected to help in the pursuit and arrest of thieves. There were other "poenales causae," or *witeræden* as they were called in the mother tongue, arising from offences committed within the estate. Here too the responsibility for bringing the offender to justice rested squarely upon the landholder and his men. Justice would normally be done at the nearest *cyninges tun* – we shall

[1] CS 612. Note the interesting implication that at Taunton carts were normally drawn by horses, not oxen.

hardly be coining a word if we call it a kingston – one of those domains which the king owned in every shire. The kingston, managed for him by a reeve, was a fundamental unit in the Old English organization of justice and finance. From Alfred's laws we learn that it included a prison in which the king's reeve would keep wrong-doers until they could be brought before a folk-moot, a public court over which the same reeve would preside (1 §§2, 3). And to the kingston the tillers of the soil would deliver the produce which made up the monarch's food-rent.

CHURCH DUES

When he had satisfied the claims of the lord of the soil, the husbandman had still to meet those of the Church. Bishops and minsters owned considerable tracts of land. Even a parish church would own a yardland or two of glebe, making the priest a partner in the husbandry of his flock. But the income from land was supplemented by regular payments of tithe and church-scot. All Christians were expected to set aside, as a matter of religious duty, a tenth of their income not only for the maintenance of the clergy but also, and even principally, for the relief of pilgrims and the poor. To Archbishop Theodore tithe was part of the revenue of the Church as a whole rather than a means of supporting the parish priest. He expressly decreed that the poor must suffer no wrong in the customary payment of tribute to the Church.[1] In 786 a council presided over by papal legates enjoined the payment of tithe on all men, preferably in the form of private almsgiving.[2] Not until the tenth century would the obligation be enforced by secular law.

In this respect tithe differed from church-scot. This too was a payment in kind, usually of grain or poultry, the amount being calculated in proportion to the payer's holding. The laws of Ine decree that it shall be paid at Martinmas (11 November), and that a defaulter shall pay twelve times the amount due, besides a fine of sixty shillings to the king (4, 61). The amount varied from place to place, but every tiller of the soil other than a slave was bound to pay it.

These were local payments. England also sent offerings to the central government of the Church. Offa of Mercia seems to have promised a yearly gift of 365 mancuses to Rome for the relief of the poor and the maintenance of lights, and Æthelwulf of Wessex by his testament bade his successors pay 300 mancuses a year to Rome, two-thirds of the sum to provide oil for lighting the basilicas of St Peter and St Paul, and one-third as a personal offering to the pope.[3] This bequest was certainly

[1] Haddan and Stubbs, *Councils and Ecclesiastical Documents*, III, p. 203.
[2] *Ibid.*, pp. 456, 457.
[3] CS 288; *Asser's Life of King Alfred*, p. 15. A mancus was equivalent to thirty pence.

carried out, for the Chronicle records that in 887 the ealdorman of Wiltshire "took to Rome the alms of King Alfred and the West Saxons."[1] The wording of the annal implies that the people were associated with their ruler in this liability, and in fact several later kings issued laws enforcing payment of 'Rome-scot' or Peter's Pence upon their subjects.

Unlike the regular payments which have been described, soul-scot arose as a voluntary offering, made by a dead man's heirs. It consisted of a portion of his goods offered to the parish priest. The amount varied in proportion to the wealth of the deceased, and its purpose was to secure prayers for his soul.

Altogether the demands of Church and State bore heavily upon the tillers of the soil. We must not draw too dark a picture, nor minimize the rough sense of equity with which the demands would be enforced – if indeed they were enforced at all, for English monarchs had not yet learnt to refrain from enacting regulations that were as likely as not to remain dead letters. King Ine might threaten the defaulter who failed to pay his church-scot with a swingeing twelvefold penalty, but the priest knew as well as his flock if a succession of bad harvests had left the barns empty. The poets lauded generosity as the prime virtue of a nobleman, and public opinion required him to protect those on whose labours he depended for support. Moreover, at a time when man-power was never abundant, it was not to a landlord's interest to drive his tenants away or to let them die of hunger. Even so, for the Anglo-Saxon husbandman life must often have been a grim struggle, and at best would leave him only a meagre margin over current needs.

LAND TENURE

Land in this period is classified under two comprehensive headings, folkland and bookland. Folkland is land under customary law which the king may turn into either loanland or bookland. Loanland was a precarious tenure, in the sense clearly expressed in a passage which Alfred inserted into his translation of St Augustine's *Soliloquies*. "Every man," says the king, "when he has built himself a home on land lent to him by his lord, with his help, likes to stay in it sometimes, and to go hunting and fowling and fishing, and to support himself in every way on that loanland, both by sea and land, until the time when through his lord's favour he may acquire bookland and a perpetual inheritance."[2] In other words, the thegn, though he has the full beneficial enjoyment

---

[1] EHD I, p. 183.

[2] *König Alfreds des Grossen Bearbeitung der Soliloquien des Augustinus*, ed. W. Endter, Bibl. der Angelsächsischen Prosa, XI, Hamburg, 1922, p. 2.

of the estate so long as he lives, cannot alienate it or leave it to his children without the king's permission, and if he dies without issue it will revert to the king. Only a 'book', a royal charter, can give him full power to sell, exchange, or bequeath it as he may think fit. Such a 'book' was granted by King Offa to a Kentish thegn named Ealdberht and his sister Selethryth. Their father had held lands in Ickham, Palmstead, and Ruckinge, evidently as a 'loan', for his death brought the property back into the king's hand. He now granted it to them as fully as their father had it, but this time with the added right to bequeath it to whomsoever they might choose. The loanland was thus transformed into bookland.[1]

Originally introduced for the benefit of the churches, bookland was at one time held exempt from all secular charges. Early kings of Kent and Wessex legislated to that effect,[2] and there is evidence that the same principle held good in Mercia and Northumbria. The first blow at ecclesiastical privilege was struck in Mercia. In 749 King Ethelbald, to the great scandal of churchmen, proclaimed that their lands would henceforth be liable to provide man-power for bridge-building and the defence of fortified places. He added that kings and ealdormen would require purveyance only as a free-will offering.[3] It was no doubt as obvious to Ethelbald as to his audience that favours asked by a strong ruler are not easily refused. His successor, Offa, added a third liability, extending to church lands the obligation of military service.[4] The kings of Wessex followed suit. As early as 739 they had exacted military service.[5] By 801 they were demanding bridge-work, and by 842 fortress-work.[6] Henceforth whenever an Anglo-Saxon king granted land by book to churchman or layman, he regularly reserved these three common dues.[7]

It is not surprising that landowners, whenever they could, took steps to secure exemption from the other liabilities. In 844 or 848 the minster at Breedon-on-the-Hill (Leics) gave the king of Mercia 180 mancuses of gold and lands rated at 15 hides to be discharged from the obligations of cartage and hospitality to travellers; at the same time the local ealdorman for his part was presented with a costly drinking-cup in return for the waiver of his rights. Even so the king reserved hospitality for ambassadors coming from Wessex and Northumbria, or from beyond the sea.[8] As Mercian power declined, and the king's need for

---

[1] CS 248, dated 786.　　[2] Kent: CS 99 (A.D. 699); Wessex: CS 108 (A.D. 704).
[3] CS 178.　　　　[4] E. John, *Land Tenure in Early England*, pp. 64–79.
[5] *Crawford Charters*, ed. Napier and Stevenson, p. 2, on which see Finberg, *West-Country Historical Studies*, p. 62.
[6] CS 282, 438.
[7] Except possibly between 928 and 934: see Finberg, *op. cit.*, p. 37.
[8] CS 454, on which see Stenton, *Latin Charters of the Anglo-Saxon Period*, p. 54 *n.*

ready money became more pressing, exemptions multiplied, but even then they did not extend to the three common dues.[1] The movement naturally spread to Wessex. In 844 King Æthelwulf proclaimed his intention of releasing one in every ten hides of bookland from all public burdens except the inevitable three. Ten years later he announced a gift to the churches of a tenth of his own demesne, at the same time converting the tenure of those thegns whom he or his predecessors had settled there from loanland to bookland.[2]

In 904 the bishop of Winchester gave the king three estates, assessed altogether at 50 hides, in exchange for the endowments of the minster at Taunton, and he surrendered another 20 hides in Wiltshire to have Taunton released from cartage and purveyance.[3] By this time laymen as well as churchmen could receive lands granted by charter of perpetual inheritance. Until the last quarter of the eighth century a landbook had been given to a lay recipient only on the express or implied condition that it should be used to endow a church. Without such a 'book' the layman held his land merely on 'loan'. It could be lent him for his lifetime, in which case it needed an act of royal grace before it could pass to his heir. The earliest English lease on record was granted by the bishop of Worcester to a lay magnate for his lifetime and that of the magnate's daughter. No premium is mentioned, nor any other inducement but that of friendship.[4] But towards the close of the eighth century the abbot of Medeshamstede (Peterborough) received from a Mercian ealdorman a premium of 1,000 shillings and an undertaking to provide the minster with a day's food-supply or its equivalent in money every year, in return for a lease of ten hides at Swineshead (Lincs) during the ealdorman's life and the lives of such heirs as he might choose to name.[5] A later abbot of the same monastery granted a lease for two lives of Sempringham (Lincs) without premium but reserving an annual rent of 30 shillings, with one day's food-rent and stated quantities of faggots, timber, and brushwood.[6] Some scholars have conjectured that the man who in Ine's laws takes a yardland and pays rent for it to the lord of the soil is in fact a leaseholder; if so, the situation in which he may decide to give up the holding if the lord demands labour service as well as rent can only arise when the lease comes up for renewal.[7]

In the passage already cited Alfred speaks of the man who dwells on land lent to him by his lord. The context shows that the lord in this

[1] Finberg, *Early Charters of the West Midlands*, nos. 54, 57, 59, 66, 76, 77, 80, 82, 236, 242, 243, 247, 249.

[2] For a full discussion of Æthelwulf's two 'decimations' and a critical edition of the texts see Finberg, *Early Charters of Wessex*, pp. 187–213.

[3] CS 611, 612; *Early Charters of Wessex*, pp. 221–3, 229, 234.

[4] CS 166; the date is between 718 and 745.   [5] CS 271, between 787 and 796.

[6] CS 464.   [7] EHD I, p. 371, n 3.

case is the king, for it is the same lord who will eventually give him the 'book' that transforms loan tenure into a heritable possession, and only the king can grant such a book. In the early days of book-right, when it was still regarded as *jus ecclesiasticum*, the lay recipient could found a minster and bequeath it to his descendants, who if male would have to take holy orders or if female take the veil. But any testator who made a will in these terms inevitably faced the likelihood that a time would come when these conditions could not be fulfilled: the founder's kin would die out, or refuse to give up the lay state.[1] To provide for such contingencies, and to prevent the estate from being secularized, he often arranged that the ultimate heir should be the local bishop. In course of time many properties by this means went to swell the episcopal endowments, and, not surprisingly, the appetite of laymen for un-shackled freedom of testamentary disposition became too strong to resist.

One of Alfred's laws forbids the holder of inherited bookland to alienate it if his forebears have entailed it in the family (41). In general, however, the recipient of a book could give, sell, or bequeath the land to whomsoever he pleased. This freedom was the essence of book-right, but it was not the only power book-right conferred. If the king or other previous owner had reserved part of the land for exploitation as his demesne, that demesne passed to the book-holder as his *inland* or home-farm, to be cultivated for him by his servile dependants. This is clearly what happened when the king of Sussex endowed Wilfrid with Selsey and fifteen other villages. Bede says he gave Wilfrid the lands, the men, and "omnes facultates," that is, all the powers inherent in book-right.[2] These powers Wilfrid used to set free 250 male and female slaves, some at least of whom must have been employed previously on the royal *inland*: what other reason could there be for their existence?[3] Book-right, therefore, included the power to manumit slaves, as well as the direct ownership of such land as had been reserved for seignorial demesne.

Bede's language, however, implies that the slaves were only one element in the population of the sixteen villages. There must also have

[1] *Select English Historical Documents*, ed. F. E. Harmer, 1914, no. 15, pp. 25, 57, where every member of the family says he would rather forfeit the property than take holy orders.

[2] E. John, *Orbis Britanniae*, pp. 265–71, conclusively establishes this meaning of "facultas" in the context. Among numerous quotations with which the *Thesaurus Linguae Latinae* illustrates "facultas" in the sense of legal right the following are especially noteworthy: f. testamenti faciendi; f. servum libertate donare; priori coniugi f. dabitur...omnem dotem posterioris uxoris ad semet ipsam transferre; f. nostram adire maiestatem et tarditatem iudicis in querellam deducere.

[3] H. M. Chadwick, *Studies on Anglo-Saxon Institutions*, p. 373.

been free and half-free husbandmen, who had formerly helped to support the king and would henceforth support the bishop and his clergy. Wilfrid and the companions who had accompanied him into exile were not going to farm the land themselves, any more than the king had done. In giving him book-right, the king had not only empowered him to free slaves: he had also invested him with what Maitland calls a 'superiority' over the other tillers of the soil. Their numbers were henceforth swollen by the former slaves, who by Wilfrid's action probably became *coliberti*, half-free husbandmen still bound to give rent and service to their lord.

Something has already been said of the rights which kings reserved to themselves when granting land by charter to a subject. Of the rights they made over to their beneficiary the most ancient and universal was the *tributum*, rent in money or in kind. Thus in the seventh century when the king of Kent granted Islingham to the bishop of Rochester, he gave it "with all the *tributum* which was paid thence to the king."[1] This might be a substantial food-rent: Alfred's law refers to minsters which are entitled to receive the king's food-rent (2). Examples of such rents have already been cited in these pages. From their estate at Tichborne (Hants) the clergy of Winchester expected to receive each year 12 sesters of beer, 12 of Welsh ale, 20 vessels of clear ale, 200 large loaves, 100 small loaves, 2 oxen – one salt, the other fresh – 6 wethers, 4 swine, 4 flitches of bacon, and 20 cheeses.[2]

JUSTICIARY RIGHTS

There can be little doubt that book-right, once fully developed, conferred on its holder not only heritable tenure and economic benefits, but also justiciary powers.[3] We must ask how these were fitted into the prevailing system of law-enforcement. Normally the king did not do justice in person, but particularly serious and difficult cases might be referred to him for decision: we hear of one instance when litigants who appealed to King Alfred found him washing his hands in his room at Wardour and had to wait for his pronouncement until he had finished.[4] Alfred's code speaks of folk-moots held under the presidency of ealdormen and royal reeves (22, 34, 38), and two centuries earlier King Ine had contemplated the possibility that a nobleman might intercede with the king or the ealdorman on behalf of his dependant (50).

[1] CS 194; cf. CS 254, a Kentish grant by Offa with the same clause.
[2] *Anglo-Saxon Charters*, ed. A. J. Robertson, Cambridge, 1956, p. 39. The capacity of the sester in this period is uncertain: see Harmer, *op. cit.*, p. 79.
[3] The classic discussion is Maitland's, *op. cit.*, pp. 258–92.
[4] *Select English Historical Documents*, ed. Harmer, pp. 31, 61.

The ealdorman governed a shire; therefore in the public moot over which he presided we catch a glimpse of the shire-court, in which the landed gentry of the shire gave judgement and the ealdorman passed sentence. At a lower level offenders would be haled before a royal reeve. Two Mercian landbooks of the early ninth century stipulate that if a malefactor is thrice caught red-handed he must be handed over to a kingston, a "regalem vicum."[1] In the kingston, a royal estate provided with a jail and managed by the king's reeve, we find the precursor of the hundred-court, and we can understand why Domesday Book will speak of such ancient royal manors as Bensington, Headington, and Bampton as possessing 'soke' or jurisdiction over two or more hundreds.[2] But if the evil-doer is to be taken to a kingston only at the third offence, the implication is that up to that point his own lord will have dealt with him. We have seen that already in Ine's reign the state was imposing upon each lord a general responsibility for the behaviour of his men. Alfred, in the introduction to his laws, declares that from the time of the conversion to Christianity secular lords have been allowed to take from first offenders the fine prescribed for almost every misdeed.[3]

It was in full accordance with these ideas that in 801 a *gesith* named Pilheard paid 200 shillings to the king of Mercia and undertook to pay 30 shillings a year thereafter to have his Middlesex estate freed from most of the usual public burdens, including penalties imposed in folk-moots ("popularia concilia").[4] This does not mean that transgressors were to go unpunished. As Maitland remarks, "no lord would wish his territory to be a place where men might murder and steal with impunity."[5] It means that when wrong is done Pilheard himself will do justice on the offender. It may be added that since he is a layman the estate is not to be exempt from the three common dues, but the charter provides that when military service is required, only one man shall be sent from every six hides. And in case of theft, nothing more than the simple value of the stolen property need be paid to the owner; if a fine is imposed on the thief, the fine will go into Pilheard's pocket.

As Pilheard already holds the land with its earlier charters and has to pay the king in order to enjoy the profits of justice, it is clear that the fiscal aspect of seignorial jurisdiction is not yet automatically inherent in book-right. Some thirty years earlier an under-king of the Hwicce

---

[1] CS 357, 364.

[2] Maitland, *op. cit.*, p. 287; H. M. Cam, *Liberties and Communities in Medieval England*, Cambridge, 1944, pp. 75–90.

[3] EHD I, p. 373.   [4] CS 201.

[5] *Domesday Book and Beyond*, p. 274.

had granted a small estate at Aston in Stoke Prior (Worcs) to a thegn with the same clause providing that no fine should be paid to outsiders; compensation to an outside owner of stolen property would be paid at the boundary of the estate.[1] Here, although the grantee is a layman, book-right is still thought of as *jus ecclesiasticum*, and in fact the recipient gets another charter three years later on the same terms but limiting his tenure of Aston to three lives, with remainder to the church of Worcester.[2] During the first half of the ninth century a number of charters confer the profits of justice on high-ranking churchmen,[3] but by now the concept of book-right as *jus ecclesiasticum* is already obsolescent, and in 842 Æthelwulf of Wessex grants lands in Somerset to a lay magnate subject to the three common dues but free of all other secular burdens, including penal causes and the arrest of thieves.[4] Seven years later the king of Mercia, having obtained from the church of Worcester a lease of some of its land, proceeds to assign it to one of his thegns, free of all secular dues except the obligation to have claims by outsiders dealt with on the boundary of the estate.[5]

By the end of the ninth century clauses with this tenor have disappeared from the landbooks. We must suppose that freedom from outside interference in dealing with offenders, and the concomitant right to take the profits of justice, are henceforth covered by the normal exemption from all public burdens but the inevitable three. What the charters of the period do not tell us in so many words is whether the owner of bookland was entitled to hold a court of his own. We shall have to wait until the middle of the tenth century for an explicit mention of the right to hold a private court.[6] But from the earliest time it must have been convenient, if not necessary, to hold periodical assemblies under the presidency of the lord or his reeve in order to settle disputes between the lord's unfree and half-free tenants, and to regulate the husbandry of the demesne. Such an assembly could deal, at least as a court of first instance, with the offences of delinquent serfs, and it could easily attract within its orbit any free husbandmen whose original dues to the king had been made over to the landlord by including their farmsteads within the area of his bookland. The details of the process remain hidden from us; it is at any rate clear that by Alfred's time the state has given many landlords a vested interest in the misdeeds of their tenants. It has done so because this is the easiest way to extend local government and to provide increased facilities for law-enforcement. The process would in time lead naturally to the creation of private 'hall-moots' side by side with the public moots of shire and hundred.

[1] CS 202.   [2] CS 203.   [3] CS 351, 368, 370, 400, 487.
[4] CS 438.   [5] CS 455.
[6] CS 1029; Stenton, *Anglo-Saxon England*, p. 495.

BOOKLAND OR MANOR

The Anglo-Saxon name for a chartered estate was *boc-land*. In the shires which made up Alfred's kingdom it occurs frequently on modern maps as the place-name Buckland. More than a century after the Norman Conquest the men of Devon, that conservative shire, would still speak of "jurors from four neighbouring booklands."[1] This was long after the Normans had introduced their own word *manerium*, our manor. Some historians, having convinced themselves that what they call manorialism did not make its appearance until towards the end of the Anglo-Saxon period, have been shy of calling the ninth-century bookland a manor.[2] Yet the mosaic of evidence pieced together in these pages has shown men called lords reserving part of their estate for exploitation as a private demesne. It has shown the demesne being cultivated for them by slaves and also by half-free husbandmen who owe labour services like those due to their lord from the husbandmen of Stoke and Hurstbourne. So far the bookland figures as an economic unit organized to yield a livelihood for the lord and his tenants. But it is also a unit of local government, with a part of its own to play in policing the land. Held responsible from the first for the good behaviour of his men, the lord has begun to take their fines and will soon hold a court, if he has not already begun to do so, in which the fines will be imposed. This dual function, economic and judiciary, is characteristic of the manor properly so called. The institution will become more widespread and more highly organized as time goes on, but already in the ninth century it is firmly established over a vast area of continental Europe.[3] In view of what the documents have revealed, it is only pedantry that can inhibit us from speaking of the manor as already rooted in the soil of Alfred's England.[4]

[1] EHR LXII, 1947, p. 363; Stenton, *Latin Charters*, p. 64.

[2] Vinogradoff, *Growth of the Manor*, p. 235.

[3] *The Cambridge Economic History of Europe*, 2nd ed., Cambridge, 1966, pp. 235–8.

[4] Stenton saw that the evidence of place-names points in the same direction. "If Wonston means the *tun* of Wynsige the fact is a very definite obstacle to the assumption that this *tun* was at the beginning a community of free and equal settlers... In countless villages the germ of the manor will appear at once if we hold a measure of lordship to be implied by the personal element in local nomenclature."—*Collected Papers*, p. 20.

OLD ENGLISH DESIGNATIONS OF
SOCIAL CLASSES

NOTE. The categories in the following table are not mutually exclusive: e.g., a *gebur* might also be a *gafolgelda*, and every *ealdorman* would also be a *thegn*. Those marked * were probably all included in the genus *ceorl*.

	Early Saxon c. 500–c. 650	Middle Saxon c. 650–c. 850
Slave	*theow*	*theow*
Unfree or half-free cottager	*ʔesne*★	*ʔesnewyrhta*★
Freedman occupying a farm		*gebur*★ *ʔtwyhynde*★
Rent-paying tenant	*gafolgelda*★	*gafolgelda*★
Free farmer	*frigman*	*geneat* *ʔsyxhynde*
Landed nobleman	*gesith*	*gesith* *thegn* *ʔtwelfhynde*
Governor of a shire	*ealdorman*	*ealdorman*

CHAPTER V

THE SCANDINAVIAN IMPACT

THREE ANNALS in the Anglo-Saxon Chronicle record all too concisely the main events of the Scandinavian settlement in the east of England.—

"876. Healfdene shared out the land of the Northumbrians, and they proceeded to plough and support themselves." The area they occupied was approximately that of modern Yorkshire.

"877. The Danish army went away into Mercia, and shared out some of it, and gave some to Ceolwulf." The last legitimate king of Mercia had given up the struggle and retired to Rome. In his place the Danes set up an English thegn, Ceolwulf, to rule the western half of the kingdom, themselves annexing what are now the shires of Lincoln, Nottingham, Derby, and Leicester.

"880. The army went from Cirencester into East Anglia and settled there and shared out the land."[1] The boundary line of the territory then occupied was defined in the treaty Alfred made with the Viking leader Guthrum as running from the mouth of the Thames, then up the River Lea to its source, thence in a straight line to Bedford, and then up the Ouse to Watling Street.[2] This gave Guthrum and his men the modern shires of Huntingdon, Cambridge, Norfolk, Suffolk, and Essex, the north-eastern portions of those of Hertford, Bedford, and Buckingham, and all but the south-west quarter of Northamptonshire.

Not all the Viking settlers came from Denmark. Some of their neighbours from the north of Frisia accompanied or followed them, leaving traces of their advent in the place-names Frisby and Firsby. There are two Frisbys in Leicestershire, one Firsby in the West Riding of Yorkshire, and two in Lincolnshire. Other adventurers came from Norway. Four Normanbys in Lincolnshire and three in the North Riding, as well as two Normantons in Derbyshire, two in Leicestershire, four in Nottinghamshire, and one each in Lincolnshire, Rutland, and the West Riding, show that the Danes recognized the presence in their midst of men who came from a homeland north of their own.

A year or two after Alfred's death a company of Scandinavians, mainly Norwegians but with a sprinkling of Danes and Irish, sailed from a base in Ireland and settled in the peninsula of Wirral, where the place-name Thingwall, five miles south-west of Birkenhead, denotes

---

[1] EHD I, pp. 179, 181.   [2] Attenborough, *op. cit.*, p. 99.

the meeting-place of their *thing*, or public assembly. Another Thing-wall, north of the Mersey, shows that Norwegians established themselves in south Lancashire, where Old Norse place-names occur chiefly along the coast in a region which may have been only sparsely inhabited before the Scandinavian influx. Compared with the Danish occupation of eastern England, the Norse infiltration into the north-west finds very little reflection in written sources. Only the modern analysis of place-names has provided clear evidence that the strangers from the north spread far and wide over Lancashire north of the Ribble, over Cumberland and Westmorland, and across the Pennines into Yorkshire.[1] They seem to have come as boatloads of wandering immigrants, among whom there was little or no military cohesion, and who were content to occupy unwanted, relatively unattractive, lands, or to settle down quietly side by side with the English.

At some date between 912 and 915 a Viking named Raegnald| descended on the coast of Northumbria, won a great battle at Corbridge, and divided a large territory among his followers. In 919 he captured York and established himself there as king.

This Raegnald, after the battle of Corbridge, seized the estates of St Cuthbert's old bishopric. He gave all the lands between Billingham and Castle Eden (Dur) – approximately eleven miles in a straight line – to one "mighty warrior," and a slightly larger share between Castle Eden and the River Wear to another.[2] School Aycliffe in Heighington (Dur) is believed to derive the first part of its name from Scula, the warrior who received the southern portion. This method of sharing out the spoils is very likely to have been employed in the three great land-divisions recorded in the Chronicle. The leader of a victorious expedition would assume control of a large region – in the case of East Anglia a whole kingdom – and assign handsome shares to his chief lieutenants, who in turn would deal out smaller portions to the rank and file.

Unlike the Norsemen who settled in Cumbria, the Danes, even while settling down as farmers, kept up their military organization. A code of laws issued by King Edgar in or about 962 refers to "all the army" living in Northumbria.[3] In the east midlands the Danes grouped themselves around fortified centres which provided convenient places of assembly in time of peace and defensible posts against attack by English or Norwegians. Hence the largest and most populous division of the Danelaw derived its name from the five principal strongholds, the boroughs of Lincoln, Stamford, Nottingham, Leicester, and Derby.

[1] F. T. Wainwright, *Scandinavian England* (forthcoming).
[2] Symeon of Durham, *Opera Omnia*, ed. T. Arnold, Rolls ser. 75, 1882–5, I, p. 209.　　　　[3] IV Edgar, 15, in EHD I, p. 400.

All five were subdued by King Edmund in 942, but they retained a large measure of autonomy under the English crown. Each borough had its own moot: a record from the late tenth century shows an English ealdorman purchasing an estate "at a meeting of the whole army at Northampton," and in the same period the Five Boroughs were still holding a common assembly.[1]

It is arguable that the invaders who took part in the original great land-divisions were numbered in hundreds rather than thousands, but later, and especially after the Danish conquest of all England, they are very likely to have been reinforced by waves of immigrants arriving from their homeland in considerable numbers and settling down behind the shield of the armies.[2] How else explain the hundreds of place-names made up of Scandinavian elements (see Fig. 49), and the deep impress the invaders made on language, law, and agrarian custom?

The two commonest Scandinavian elements in place-names are –by and –thorp. By is believed to have originated in Sweden and to have meant at first a secondary settlement formed by colonization from a parent village. As population grew, –by came to mean simply 'village'. In Denmark it had already acquired that sense in the early Viking age. In England it could be applied to older English settlements taken over by the Danes, as when *Northworthig* became Derby, *Streonæshalch* became first Prestby, then Whitby, and Badbury (N'hants) became Badby. In Scandinavia –by is most often combined with elements relating to natural features or to the parent village. The English picture is different: here approximately two-thirds of the –bys are combined with personal names, in many cases probably the names of the first Danish occupants.[3]

The greatest concentration of –by names in the north-east midlands is found on the Lincolnshire wolds. The older English villages are situated near the coast, on the light soil of the Chalky Boulder-Clay, easily cleared and cultivated. With one exception, all the settlements with Danish names lie to the west, on a belt of Glacial Gravel, where the soil is less fertile, much of it rough pasture and heathland. The Danes clearly liked the slopes of river valleys. Where these had already been occupied, they settled along the banks of tributaries and minor streams. The pattern is repeated in south-east Kesteven, Nottinghamshire, and Leicestershire. In Leicestershire Danish colonists spread out, not along the Soar, which had already been substantially settled by the English, but on less

[1] R xl, p. 76; EHD I, p. 403.
[2] P. H. Sawyer, *The Age of the Vikings*, 2nd ed., 1971, pp 120–31; K. Cameron, *Scandinavian Settlement in the Territory of the Five Boroughs*, Nottingham, 1965, p. 3.
[3] A. H. Smith, *English Place-Name Elements*, I, pp. 66–72.

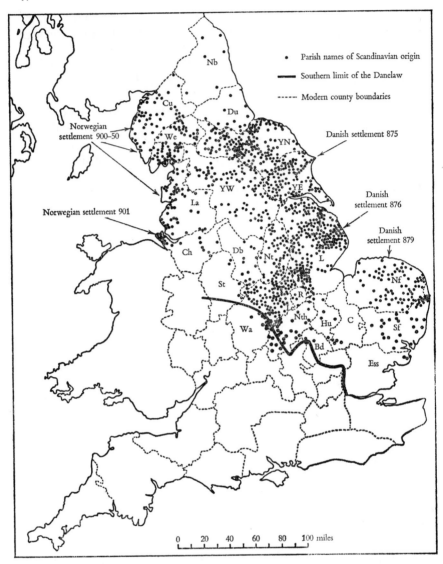

Fig. 49. The Scandinavian settlement.

attractive sites along the Wreak and its tributaries. They seem in general
to have preferred sandy and gravelly soils, which perhaps resembled
those of their homeland.[1]

Thorp, used either alone or in combination, denotes an outlying,
dependent settlement colonized from an older and larger one. Thus

[1] K. Cameron, *op. cit.*, pp. 11-20.

Barkby (Leics) has its Barkby Thorpe, Ewerby (Lincs) its Ewerby
Thorpe, and Ixworth (Suff) its Ixworth Thorpe. In compounds,
personal names form a high proportion of first elements, high enough
to suggest that many of them were new settlements made by individual
pioneers.[1] Some *thorpes* may have come into being when the original
settler died and his land was divided among his heirs.

The application of a Scandinavian element to an older English
village stands out very clearly in the common place-name Charlton.
A glance at Fig. 48 on p. 455 will show that in regions exposed to
Danish or Norse influence the Scandinavian *karl* has been substituted
for the Old English *ceorl* and the name is transformed into Carlton.
A corresponding sound-change alters church to kirk.

As with place-names, so with personal names. These too bear witness
to Anglo-Scandinavian interpenetration. As late as the twelfth century
large numbers of countrymen in East Anglia bore Scandinavian names.
So did those of the Lincolnshire fens and the Yorkshire wolds. Feminine
names like Thora, Tola, and Gunhild survived for centuries, and have
been taken by some scholars to suggest that the armies sent for their
womenkind when they turned from war to agriculture.[2] But we ought
not to overlook the influence of fashion. From 1013 to 1042 all England
was ruled by Danish kings, and it was not unusual for English families
to mingle Scandinavian names with those of native origin. Archbishop
Oda, a Dane by birth, had a nephew named Oswald.[3] The records of
Ely tell of a priest called Æthelstan, of whose two brothers one bore
the Scandinavian name Bondo, the other the Old English Ælfstan.[4]
Stigand, the future archbishop, whose name was Danish, had a brother
called Æthelmær. The example of these bilingual mixtures is very
likely to have been followed in the humbler ranks of society. Presently
the Norman Conquest brought about another change of fashion. At the
end of the tenth century the tenants of Bury St Edmunds bore either
English or Scandinavian names, but a century later between one half
and three-quarters of their descendants bore names which had been
introduced by the Normans: William, Robert, Henry, and the like.[5]
Personal names, therefore, cannot safely be accepted as proof of ancestry
or national origin, any more than a Danish or Norse village name,
taken by itself, proves that the village was founded by Scandinavian

[1] A. H. Smith, *op. cit.*, II, pp. 205–12.

[2] F. M. Stenton, 'The Danes in England', *Collected Papers*, p. 155.

[3] *The Historians of the Church of York*, ed. J. Raine, Rolls ser. 71, 1879–94, I, p. 404.
For other examples of bilingual family nomenclature see E. Ekwall, *Selected Papers*,
Lund, 1963, p. 95.

[4] *Liber Eliensis*, ed. E. O. Blake, Camden 3rd ser., XCII, 1962, pp. 107, 108.

[5] R. H. C. Davis, 'East Anglia and the Danelaw', TRHS, 5th ser., V, 1955,
p. 29.

immigrants. Not without reason did Maitland warn us that "we must be careful how we use our Dane."[1]

Nevertheless, when all due qualifications have been made, we are left with massive evidence that the invasion opened a new chapter in English agrarian history. In all likelihood the topmost layer of society was at first the one most adversely affected. We have seen how in Durham a Viking leader dispossessed the bishop, and the bishop was doubtless not the only sufferer. But the Viking chieftain who stepped into the place of an English landowning churchman or layman would need the services of the native tenants to make the most of his acquisition. Stenton points out that in the very heart of the Danelaw there can have been no extermination of the English peasantry. Even where Scandinavian settlement was most intense, and Scandinavian place-names are most numerous, much of the older Anglian nomenclature survived.[2]

In East Anglia the Norfolk Broadland shows a heavy concentration of villages with names of the purest Scandinavian type, as well as a large number of Scandinavian field-names. Except at Caister and Yarmouth there is no archaeological evidence of older settlement. With its great extent of marsh, the region can hardly have attracted the earliest settlers. All its –by names except Stokesby are compounded with Scandinavian personal names. It looks, therefore, as if these villages were appropriated and colonized by Danish owners after whom they are named; but the Danes may well have employed English freedmen and slaves to do the work.[3]

The village of Wigston Magna, four miles to the south of Leicester, stands on an important traffic-route (A50), the principal of the two main roads between Leicester and Northampton. An Anglian cemetery provides evidence of occupation from the sixth century onwards. We shall never know whose *tun* it was originally, but from the time of the Domesday survey, and almost certainly as a result of the Scandinavian invasion, it has been called *Wichingestone*, that is, Viking's *tun*. The Domesday entry has been plausibly interpreted as pointing to the superimposition of a Scandinavian settlement on the existing English village, with the result that as late as 1086 two distinct communities are found living side by side, each in its own quarter of the village, and with its own place of worship. A similar dual pattern has been detected in four or five other Leicestershire villages.[4]

At the close of the ninth century England north of the Thames was still a half empty land. There was room to spare for vigorous, land-hungry immigrants. When studied in detail, the evidence of place-

[1] *Domesday Book and Beyond*, p. 139.   [2] Stenton, *op. cit.*, p. 141.
[3] R. H. C. Davis, *op. cit.*, pp. 30–2.
[4] W. G. Hoskins, *The Midland Peasant*, 1957, pp. 7–10.

names and archaeology shows that the strangers made full use of their opportunities, founding scores of new villages and settling down in more or less peaceful co-existence with their English neighbours. Their language could be understood by any Englishman who would take a little trouble. Indeed, they contributed greatly to the enrichment of the native tongue. Many of our commonest words, such as anger, fellow, husband, root, skill, skin, sky, and wing, are borrowed from the Scandinavian. It has been remarked that in any conversation on the thousand nothings of everyday life or on the five or six things of paramount importance to high and low alike such borrowings are bound to occur. An Englishman cannot *thrive* or be *ill* or *die* without involving the use of Scandinavian words.[1]

No doubt the arrival of the Danes caused a certain amount of disruption, particularly during the troubles which preceded and followed the seizure of the throne by Danish kings in the early eleventh century; and of this we shall have to take account. But the social system with which they had been familiar at home was not totally dissimilar from the one they found in England.

In Scandinavia, as in England, the lowest rank was filled by slaves. One of the two Norwegians who began the colonization of Iceland took with him ten thralls whom he had seized in Ireland; they murdered him when they got there.[2] The Frostathing Law of mid-tenth-century Norway takes three slaves to be the proper complement of a farm stocked with twelve cows and two horses; a lordly estate might well require thirty or more.[3] The Old English word for slave, *theow*, has left no representative in our vocabulary, but we still speak of thralls and thraldom. Here and there the Scandinavian *thræll* is to be found in place-names; Threlfall (Lancs) denotes a clearing in which the trees have been felled by slaves.[4] All over England the temptation for a slave to desert his old master and take service with a new one in the hope of better conditions must have been strong indeed, and the Scandinavian invasion offered him many chances. In an attempt to block the process, a clause in the treaty between Alfred and Guthrum binds both parties on oath not to let either slaves or freemen pass over to the other side without permission.[5]

Between slaves and freemen stood an intermediate class in process of emancipation. The process was a lengthy one, for the *leysing*, or freedman, remained subject in many respects to his former master and could

---

[1] O. Jespersen, *Growth and Structure of the English Language*, 9th ed., Oxford, 1948, pp. 69, 74.
[2] *Origines Islandicae*, tr. G. Vigfusson and F. York Powell, Oxford, 1905, pp. 20–2.
[3] Gwyn Jones, *A History of the Vikings*, 1968, p. 148.
[4] A. H. Smith, *op. cit.*, II, p. 212.   [5] Attenborough, *op. cit.*, p. 100.

not bring legal proceedings against him. Generations might come and go before his posterity attained full freedom.[1] The Scandinavian *leysing*, as might be expected, has left more visible traces of his presence than the thrall. It is not certain whether Lazenby, near Kirkoswald (Cumb), Lazenby near Wilton (Lincs), and another Lazenby in the North Riding, represent settlements founded by individuals or by groups of freedmen planted there by their lords. If the latter, they would correspond in some sort to the English Charltons. It may be significant that Lazenby in the North Riding stands as close to the obviously Danish village of Danby Wiske as any Charlton to its capital manor; and the form Laysingthorpe (a lost place in the east of Lindsey, formerly too the name of a place in the West Riding which has changed to Lazencroft) supports the idea of a dependent settlement. But the Scandinavian *leysing* was more numerous than can be gathered from surviving place-names. A note in the sacrist's register of Bury St Edmunds records a bequest to the abbey on the eve of the Norman Conquest of Wereham (Norf) with its *leysings* and slaves.[2] They were evidently a ubiquitous and important class.

The treaty between Alfred and Guthrum appoints the same *wergeld* for the Danish *leysing* as for the English *ceorl*: 200 shillings in each case. This will not surprise us when we recall that for Alfred and his public the typical *ceorl* was a half-free husbandman, on a par with the Roman *libertinus*.[3] The treaty refers to him as a *ceorl* settled on *gafol-land*: in other words, a half-free *gebur* who pays rent, like those *geburs* at Chinnock (Som) whom the lady Wynflæd describes in her will as settled on *gafol-land* and whom she bequeaths to the nuns of Shaftesbury.[4] If this is taken to imply that there were some English husbandmen not paying rent, they are most likely to have been still lower in the social scale: cottagers, perhaps, with little more than a garden plot or an acre or two in the fields, and owing service but little or no rent.

Concerning the upper classes, the treaty simply provides that the same value, namely eight half-marks of pure gold, shall be placed on the life of a man who is slain, whether he is an Englishman or a Dane.[5] Stenton considered that this clause "included not only English and Danish nobles but also Danish settlers of peasant rank and English *ceorls* farming their own land."[6] Against this it has been convincingly objected that "it is hard to see why in the case of the English, no less than in that of the Danes, the peasant-farmer should on a sudden have been given the same *wergeld* as a nobleman; and it is still harder to see why an East Anglian

---

[1] F. Seebohm. *Tribal Custom in Anglo-Saxon Law*, pp. 259–66.
[2] W XXXVI, p. 92.
[3] See above, p. 451.
[4] W III, p. 12.
[5] Attenborough, *op. cit.*, p. 98.
[6] *Anglo-Saxon England*, p. 261.

ceorl should have been rated six times as high as his equal in Wessex."
A much more likely explanation is that the treaty reproduces, at least
approximately, the classification of 200-shilling men, or commoners,
and 1,200-shilling men, or nobles, in Alfred's laws.[1]

The Yorkshire place-names Dringhoe and Dringhouses attest the
former presence of the Scandinavian *dreng*, who has been described as
a petty squire burdened with agricultural and personal services of
a rather humble kind. In many respects the *dreng* resembled the Anglo-
Saxon *geneat*. He received a holding from the king or other magnate,
and was expected to attend his lord in hunting, ride on his errands, and
send reapers to cut his crops. He is perhaps best described as a yeoman
farmer. In the north of England, and particularly in Lancashire between
the Ribble and the Mersey, he survived the Norman Conquest.[2]

The Danish aristocracy comprised a first rank of men distinguished
by the title *jarl* or earl, equivalent to the Anglo-Saxon ealdorman, and
a second rank of *holds*. Two *jarls* and five *holds* are named in the
Chronicle as having fallen in battle against Edward the Elder in 910.
The district of Holderness in the East Riding is believed to derive the
first part of its name from a noble of the second class, and if the derivation
is correct it shows how large an allotment might fall to a *hold* who
survived to reap the fruit of victory.

Between the *hold* and the *leysing* stood the free Danish farmer, the
bondi, owner of land and stock on almost every scale from a smallholder to a rich franklin. A society in which men of this class flourished
must have been accustomed to a looser system of lordship than prevailed
in England. In law and politics the *bondi* enjoyed an appreciably higher
status than his English counterpart. He could pronounce verdicts in the
courts and speak his mind on even the weightiest matters of state in the
general assembly. Not for centuries, if indeed at any time in the past,
had Wessex or Mercia known anything like him. A fictitious resemblance to him colours much that has been written about the early
English *ceorl*.[3] There are no unmistakable traces of him in Alfred's
treaty with Guthrum, and it is possible that he played no conspicuous
part in the first Danish settlement. Our sources are not abundant enough
to furnish anything like an exact chronology, but it is clear that the

[1] R. H. C. Davis, *op. cit.*, p. 34.
[2] P. Vinogradoff, *English Society in the Eleventh Century*, Oxford, 1908, pp. 62–6, 409.
[3] "We are certainly not entitled to assume that the social consequences of the
English settlement of the fifth century must have corresponded with any nearness
to those which followed from the Danish settlement of the ninth. That the greater
number of the men of eastern Lincolnshire were free in 1086 does not imply the
original independence of the men of Berkshire."—Stenton, *Collected Papers*, p. 21,
and *Types of Manorial Structure in the Northern Danelaw*, Oxford, 1910, p. 91.

situation in which Alfred had confronted a by no means overwhelming number of Danes who were prepared to make peace and settle down as landowning farmers, differed radically from the crisis of 1013, when Swein of Denmark, intent on the conquest of all England, brought the whole force of Scandinavia to bear on a country fatally weakened by the ravages of the previous twenty years.

It is unquestionable that the upheaval of the Danish conquest involved widespread chaos. In a celebrated jeremiad delivered in 1014, Wulfstan, archbishop of York, painted a lurid picture of disruption. Widows, according to him, are wrongfully forced into marriage; poor men are cruelly defrauded and sold out of the country into the power of foreigners; the rights of freemen are withdrawn and those of slaves restricted. "Often a slave binds very fast the thegn who previously was his master, and makes him into a slave." At the same time, "free men are not allowed to keep their independence, nor go where they wish, nor deal with their own property as they wish; and slaves are not allowed to keep what they have gained by toil in their own free time."[1]

Making all due allowance for what a great French historian has called "the natural pessimism of sacred oratory," it is entirely credible that so massive an intrusion of foreigners should have gravely disturbed the social fabric. Many an English thegn, and perhaps his son too if of age to bear arms, must have perished in battle, leaving no one to inherit his land. In a region where the English king's writ did not run there was nothing to prevent a Dane from stepping into his place. In these conditions numbers of countrymen would seize the opportunity to emancipate themselves, by purchase or mere usurpation, from the demands of lordship, especially on those great discontinuous estates which had wielded authority over villages miles away from the capital manor. The degree of emancipation would vary from village to village, and even between one tiller of the soil and his neighbour, with results that were still being felt when the Normans came and did their best to reimpose seignorial control.

A class of freemen (liberi homines) formed a distinctive element in East Anglian society as recorded in Domesday Book. There were nearly 8,000 of them in Suffolk, over 5,000 in Norfolk, and some 425 in Essex. They also appear sporadically and much more sparsely in the counties of Stafford, Leicester, Northampton, Hertford, and Kent. Another class, denominated sokemen, was even more numerous, with over 10,000 in Lincolnshire, over 5,000 in Norfolk, nearly 2,000 in Leicestershire, and numbers ranging from 830 to 52 in the counties of Northampton, Rutland, Suffolk, Essex, Cambridge, Huntingdon,

[1] EHD I, pp. 854–9.

Bedford, Hertford, Buckingham, and Kent.[1] Contemporary documents sometimes use freeman and sokeman as interchangeable terms;[2] and it is practically impossible to distinguish their tenure and economic standing. Each of them was the man of some lord, though not necessarily of any lord but the king; the sokeman was so called because of his obligation to 'seek' the lord's court. His presence in Kent should perhaps discourage belief in his Danish ancestry, and it could be wished that more of those who have written about him had paid heed to Maitland's warning that "we should be rash to find anything characteristically Scandinavian in the sokemen."[3] The fallacy of arguing from personal names has already been pointed out. Nevertheless, the geographical distribution of these two classes, and their absence from the rest of England, tells in favour of their descent from the rank and file of the Danish armies. In the two or three generations which elapsed between their original settlement and the compilation of Domesday Book there was plenty of time for their status to be modified in one direction or another, often for the worse.

When the lineaments of an ordered society begin to emerge after the Danish conquest they display strongly marked Scandinavian characteristics. The Danes had ideas of their own on currency, law, and administration, so much so that men could speak of the area governed by those ideas as the Danelaw.[4] Already in Alfred's treaty with Guthrum we encounter the mark, a novel unit of reckoning which denotes eight 'ores' of sixteen silver pence each. The Danes produced a long-lasting and highly individual body of customary law, with distinctive forms of procedure.[5] In the reign of Ethelred II we begin to hear of an institution unknown to Old English law, the sworn jury, consisting of twelve leading thegns in each district.[6] Domesday Book will record the presence of twelve "judges" at Chester and twelve "lawmen" at Lincoln and Stamford, personages whose specialized knowledge gave them a leading part in the framing of judgements. Later still a kind of public prosecutor called a sacrabar, the Old Norse *sakaráberi*, will appear spasmodically in legal records.[7]

Under Scandinavian direction Yorkshire and Lindsey were each divided into three Ridings. This too is a disguised Norse word meaning

---

[1] H. C. Darby et al., *The Domesday Geography of Eastern England*, Cambridge, 1952, p. 379; *The Domesday Geography of Midland England*, Cambridge, 1954, p. 453; *The Domesday Geography of South-East England*, Cambridge, 1962, p. 617.

[2] R. Welldon Finn, *An Introduction to Domesday Book*, 1963, p. 137.

[3] *Domesday Book and Beyond*, p. 67.

[4] On the geography of the Danelaw see H. M. Chadwick, *Studies on Anglo-Saxon Institutions*, pp. 198–201.

[5] Stenton, *Anglo-Saxon England*, pp. 507–13.

[6] III Ethelred, 3, in EHD I, p. 403.

[7] Stenton, *Collected Papers*, p. 157.

a third part. The Ridings and the territory of the Five Boroughs were divided into wapentakes, the Old Norse *vápnatak*, or 'weapon-taking'. The extension of the term to cover both the local assembly and the district from which its members came is peculiar to the Danish colonies in England.[1]

Land transactions in the Danelaw were authenticated not so much by charters and leases as by the testimony of the wapentake. When an English ealdorman purchased an estate from one Frena at a meeting of the army of Northampton, "the whole host was security on his behalf" that the vendor's title was sound.[2] The comparative ease with which land could be bought and sold encouraged the multiplication of freeholds, and helped to undermine in the Scandinavian east of England the manorial structure which remained intact in areas under the direct control of the English crown.

The Scandinavian wapentake has its counterpart in the English hundred. As late as the eleventh century the same district could be described indifferently as a hundred or a wapentake, the choice being determined in the end by the relative strength of the Danish and English strains in the local population.[3] The archaic system under which a district was appended for administrative and judiciary purposes to a kingston was being transformed into the hundredal system. An area comprising in theory one hundred hides, though in practice it might be a good deal less, now constituted the regular unit of judicial, fiscal, and military organization. It may well be that the military aspect predominated at first. In Scandinavia the 'weapon-taking' seems to have been purely symbolic, a brandishing of spears or battle-axes to signify approval of a decision proposed to the assembly, but when the armies of the Five Boroughs responded to a call to arms their weapon-taking would be more literal than symbolic. And the hundred, like the wapentake, had its military function. The Anglo-Saxon Chronicle records an incursion into Wiltshire by the ealdorman of the Hwicce at the beginning of the ninth century, and its defeat by the men of Wiltshire under the command of Weohstan, their own ealdorman; but the chronicler Æthelweard, writing two centuries after the event, and using the language of his own time, says that Weohstan met the invaders "with the hundreds of Wiltshire."[4]

Just as the Danish armies of Lincoln, Nottingham, Derby, and the rest grouped themselves each around a fortified borough and took their

---

[1] Stenton, *Anglo-Saxon England*, p. 504, mentions that the word is first recorded in 962.

[2] R XL, p. 76.   [3] Stenton, *op. cit.*, p. 505.

[4] *Monumenta Historica Britannica*, ed. H. Petrie, 1848, pp. 509, 510. On the military aspect of the hundred see further E. John, *Orbis Britanniae*, Leicester, 1966, pp. 142–6.

name from it, so in English Mercia the local militia, called up by the ealdorman, assembled at a borough such as Hereford, Worcester, or Warwick. Hence the Worcester scribe who at some time before 1016 set himself to copy out the charters of the bishopric, and decided to arrange them topographically under what we should call counties, headed the five main sections of his cartulary with the names of Worcester, Winchcombe, Oxford, Warwick, and Gloucester. But to three of these names another hand, or the same hand at a somewhat later date, has added "shire." This confirms the inference which C. S. Taylor drew from the fact that whereas not one of the Mercian shires appears by name in contemporary chronicles before 1000, thirteen of them are mentioned as such within sixteen years thereafter. It is clear that the English plan of reconquest had involved the creation early in the tenth century of a system based on towns, each the military and administrative capital of the surrounding district, and that later in the century the nomenclature was revised in view of the fact that these Mercian districts performed the same functions as already pertained to the ancient shires of Wessex. Some of the latter had once been kingdoms, and some, like Kent, had natural boundaries, but the new Mercian shires were artificial creations cutting across the older political and religious demarcations, the work, evidently, of a strong central power which mapped out the region between Thames and Humber into shires on the principle that each one should contain as nearly as possible either 1,200 hides or twice that number.[1]

All this may seem to be matter of political rather than agrarian history, but it compels us to ask: What was now the hide? And the answer to this question will reveal that under Scandinavian influence the unit of assessment has assumed an entirely new complexion.

It will be remembered that the hide, when first encountered, appeared as a unit imposed in round numbers upon a whole people for the purpose of levying tribute to the paramount king. Local rulers imposed it on the lands within their jurisdiction as a convenient method of apportioning the renders payable in money or in kind to themselves or their beneficiaries. Hence an estate is granted as a land of so many hides. Behind this assessment lay a rough estimate of total resources, actual or potential, rather than an exact calculation of arable or pastoral capacity, either of which might predominate in a given case. But the Scandinavian settlement introduced an all-important modification. The Danes, in

---

[1] C. S. Taylor, 'The Origin of the Mercian Shires', in H. P. R. Finberg (ed.), *Gloucestershire Studies*, Leicester, 1957, pp. 17–51. For the geography of the short-lived shire of Winchcombe, see H. P. R. Finberg, *The Early Charters of the West Midlands*, pp. 228–35. On the tenth-century hidation of the Danelaw see the valuable discussion by C. R. Hart, *The Hidation of Northamptonshire*, Leicester, 1970.

particular, put arable cultivation in the forefront of their husbandry, and treated all other branches as appendant to it. All their calculations revolved consistently around the ox-drawn plough.

An estate at Wittering (N'hants) is described in a tenth-century document as consisting of one hide less an ox-gang.[1] About 1030 another document refers to ox-gangs and ploughlands in Yorkshire.[2] Both terms are rooted in the conception of an eight-ox team and the amount of land it can plough in the course of the agricultural year. Divided by eight, the amount becomes an ox-gang. It is not known whether the Danes had used these measurements in their homeland, but in the duchy of Normandy, founded by their kinsmen in 911, grants of land were frequently expressed in terms of the ploughland, latinized as *terra aratri* or *terra caruce*, the later *carucata*. The Normans were also acquainted with the ox-gang or *bovata*.[3]

The ploughland, *terra unius aratri*, in English *sulung*, and its fraction the *jugum* or yoke of two oxen, will be recalled as having been the usual terms of assessment in early Kent. Outside Kent it seems to have been unknown. The Tribal Hidage assesses the whole of England in hides. Bede and other writers of his age refer to hides in Northumberland and Yorkshire, and successive charters from the seventh to the ninth century apply the term to estates in Lincolnshire.[4] It was not immediately ousted in the Danelaw. In one of the texts already cited hides, ploughlands, and ox-gangs figure side by side.[5] But in the shires where Danish influence had predominated – those of York, Lincoln, Derby, Nottingham, and Leicester – and occasionally in other shires, the carucate rather than the hide will be the normal Domesday unit of assessment.[6]

This emphasis on the plough and its work reflected the realities of agrarian life in a country where more and more land had been deforested or drained and brought under tillage. The Old English word for plough, *sulh*, has left no descendant in our vocabulary. *Ploh* is found only with the meaning of 'a measure of land'; our modern "plough" is more nearly affiliated to the Danish name of the implement itself.[7]

It made little difference in practice whether local usage dictated that land should be assessed in hides or carucates, for both were now, theoretically at least, on the same level. The hide could still be divided into four yardlands of 30 acres more or less, but its fractions could also be expressed as ox-gangs. The ideal extent of the ox-gang was 15 acres,

[1] R XI, p. 78.   [2] R LXXXIV.

[3] EHR XXVII, 1912, p. 23, and references there cited.

[4] Bede, *Hist. Eccl.*, ed. Plummer, I, pp. 179, 325; C. R. Hart, *The Early Charters of Eastern England*, nos. 143, 144, 145, 147, 149.   [5] R LXXXIV.

[6] R. Welldon Finn, *op. cit.*, p. 245.   [7] O. Jespersen, *op. cit.*, p. 65.

and eight ox-gangs made a hide.[1] Both the hide and the carucate therefore end by being held to consist of 120 arable acres, the average stint
of an eight-ox team. In an agricultural routine which begins in October,
continues until Christmas, is resumed on Plough Monday, and carried
on until the fallow receives a light stirring between May and July, there
will be time enough, even allowing for Sundays and spells of bad
weather, for 120 acres to be ploughed by the slave who in Ælfric's
Colloquy states that he is expected to plough daily "a whole acre or
more."[2] So a mid-tenth-century will refers to "a hide of 120 acres,"[3]
and in the last quarter of that century, when a dispute arises over the
purchase of three hides in the Cambridgeshire village of Chippenham,
a party of men go round the land and measure it, expecting to find
360 acres, but find only 226, or 2 hides less 14 acres.[4]

The change from a system based on arbitrary assessment imposed
from above, and bearing only a distant relationship to the facts of
husbandry, to one based on arable acreage measurable on the ground,
was nothing short of a revolution in the life of rural England.[5] It
provided the working countryman with an intelligible framework for
the apportionment of the services he owed to his lord and the adjustment
of rights he enjoyed in common with his neighbours. Naturally it
could not and did not supersede at a stroke the older conception of the
hide as an assessment of pasture and woodland as well as arable. In 1086
the Domesday commissioners will find that at Abbots Langley (Herts)
one hide consists of "wood and field," and at Chedworth (Glos)
"wood, field, and meadow" together account for 15 hides.[6] They will
also find that "in this hide there are only 64 acres when it is ploughed"
at Hambrook (Glos), a cryptic statement which may perhaps be explained by the proximity of Hambrook to the Kingswood ironfield.[7]
In Kent the Domesday *sulung* seems to have varied between 180 and 200
acres.[8] All sorts of local variations, a small acre here, a larger there, will
help to complicate the system, even within the Scandinavian third of
England. In Lincolnshire the average ox-gang comprised not 15 but
20 acres.[9] But when money was needed for the defence of the realm,

[1] In R LXXXIV (p. 166, Ilkley) 6 ox-gangs do not make a whole ploughland. At
Ripon (*ibid.*) the priests' lands consist of 4+4+1 hides and 3+3+2 ox-gangs,
making, on the standard reckoning, 10 hides in all.
[2] *Ælfric's Colloquy*, ed. G. N. Garmonsway, 1939, p. 20.   [3] W II, p. 8.
[4] *Liber Eliensis*, ed. Blake, pp. 89–91. The same source mentions double hides of
240 acres at Fordham, Horningsea, and Snailwell, pp. 104, 106, 108.
[5] Stenton, *Collected Papers*, p. 160.   [6] DB I, pp. 135d, 164a.
[7] DB I, p. 165.
[8] Darby, *The Domesday Geography of South-East England*, p. 503.
[9] F. M. Stenton, *Documents Illustrative of the Social and Economic History of the
Danelaw*, 1920, pp. xxviii, xxix, citing twelfth-century charters.

a uniform assessment provided a rational basis for taxation, and the monarchy, whether under a Danish, an English, or a Norman king, would struggle against all odds to impose it. Hence the Conqueror will instruct his commissioners to find out not only the existing assessment of each manor but how many ploughs are in fact at work there; and more than a century later Richard I will levy a 'carucage' of two shillings on each ploughland of 120 acres.[1]

[1] Roger of Howden in *Select Charters*, ed. W. Stubbs, 9th ed., Oxford, 1913, p. 247. The chronicler here identifies the carucate with the ancient *tenmantale*, or *tenmanlot*, of 120 acres: cf. Vinogradoff, *op. cit.*, p. 103 *n.*

CHAPTER VI

THE LATER AGRARIAN LANDSCAPE

REASONS HAVE been given on an earlier page for holding that it
is not often practicable to uncover the original pattern of settlement in a village which has taken hundreds of years to mature.
Instances of complete replanning can be quoted, of much earlier date
than the well-known case of Milton Abbas (Dors), where the lord of the
manor in the last quarter of the eighteenth century rebuilt the entire
village on a new site in order to improve the prospect from his mansion.
At Eaton Socon (Beds) a castle was built in the twelfth century where
a late Saxon village had stood, with its church and churchyard; the
village was then rebuilt on quite a different site, and provided with
a new church.[1]

Every allowance, therefore, must be made for the possibility of
radical but unrecorded changes. Nevertheless, the evidence of tenth-
and eleventh-century documents, read in the light of fieldwork, sometimes helps to pierce the veil. It may be worth while here to look
briefly at two villages, one in Hertfordshire, the other in the Gloucestershire Cotswolds, where the lineaments of early history seem tolerably
well defined.

BYGRAVE

For more than a century Bygrave in the remote north-east of Hertfordshire engaged the attention of important personages. Before 973 it
belonged for a while to the great Ethelwold, bishop of Winchester, who
sold it to one Leofsige; it was then assessed at six hides. Then Athelstan,
son of King Ethelred II, took it from Leofmær, perhaps a son of
Leofsige, but left it back to him by will in or about 1015.[2] Some time
later it fell into the hands of Archbishop Stigand, under whom it
was occupied by another Leofmær. In 1086 it belonged to Robert de
Limesey, bishop of Chester, being then assessed at five hides, of which
two were in Robert's demesne.

The village stands four-fifths of a mile north of the Icknield Way and
nearly two miles east of the Roman road (A 1) leading through Baldock
to Biggleswade. Around it stretches the manor and parish, comprising
some 1,800 acres. The church stands at a height of 314 feet on a hill
the crest of which, unlike the chalk hillsides and surrounding land, is

---

[1] Beresford and Hurst, *Deserted Medieval Villages*, p. 128.
[2] CS 1297; C. R. Hart, *Early Charters of Eastern England*, pp. 168, 177; W xx (p. 60).

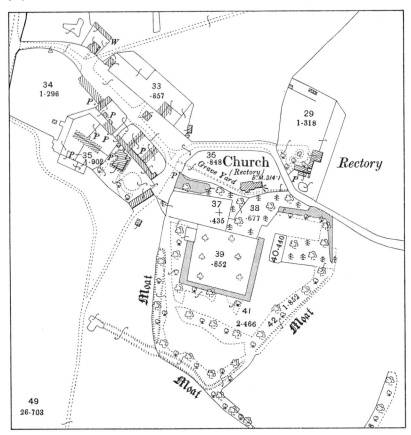

Fig. 50. Bygrave.

capped with clay and capable of retaining water. Beside the church
stood the original manor house, defended by concentric moats.

In 1845 the manor contained 14 acres of woodland, 80 acres of
meadow and pasture, and 1,418 a. 3r. 18p. of arable land, much of
which lay in unfenced strips.[1] The large-scale Ordnance map printed
in 1898 shows that the north side of the inner moat had been filled in,
but there remained three sides of a square about 200 feet across. The
outer moat, an irregular quadrilateral, was and still is wet at the north-
west and north-east corners. The area enclosed by these defences is about
17 acres. Outside them were traces, not now visible, of an even larger
and possibly later entrenchment (Fig. 50).[2]

[1] Herts County Record Office, 26293.
[2] RCHM *Hertfordshire*, 1910, pp. 75, 76; E. Herts Arch. Soc., *Transactions* IV,
1911, pp. 279–99.

In 1912 Bygrave contained some 31 houses and two outlying farms. At that date the village was described as "immediately surrounded by its enclosed pasture lands," beyond which common arable fields, occupying nearly 1,000 acres, stretched over the surrounding slopes with only grass balks to divide the furlongs. The cottagers had lost such rights of common as they had ever had, but any occupant of arable strips could graze his livestock over the whole field after harvest.[1]

In 1920 the land between the village and Baldock was purchased by the Hertfordshire County Council. It was still being ploughed in strips, but was known as Bygrave Common because the occupant of the demesne farm was entitled to run sheep over the whole common annually between the harvest and the winter ploughing. By 1922 the Council had abolished the strips, levelled some 36,500 yards of grass balks, and let the land in small holdings of some fifty acres apiece.[2]

From this record, from the maps, and from the present aspect of the place, what can we glean?

There is no evidence of human occupation before the Anglo-Saxon period. The oldest feature of the Bygrave palimpsest is the moats, one or more of them already there, it seems, in 973, when the name is first recorded. *Bygrafan* means the place "by the entrenchment" or "entrenchments," for the noun can be either singular or plural. To the eye they do not obviously differ from the moats which surround so many fifteenth-century manor houses, but the recorded name establishes at least one of them firmly in the tenth century. A contemporary parallel can be cited from a lease of Aston Magna (Glos) granted in 904, which states that "all the demesne land is surrounded by a dyke."[3] Since the pastures immediately adjoined the village, as they did also in Ashwell, the neighbouring settlement, we may surmise that pastoral husbandry at first predominated in Bygrave; the moats, possibly supplemented by stockades, may have been designed to secure flocks and herds against nocturnal marauders, though with the advance of tillage they might also serve to pen the livestock and prevent them from trampling the crops. In any case, the plough had certainly been set to work over much of the area well before Domesday. In 1086 the lord of the manor had three ploughs on his demesne. Two sokemen, two husbandmen, nine small-holders, and a priest had nine ploughs between them; there were also six cottagers and seven slaves. The priest would seem to imply

[1] VCH *Herts*, III, 1912, pp. 211–15.

[2] Information kindly supplied by the Clerk of the Herts County Council.

[3] PN *Herts*, p. 155; Ekwall, *Oxford Dictionary of English Place-Names*, s.v. Bygrave, takes it to be singular. For the lease of Aston Magna see *Early Charters of the W. Midlands*, p. 52.

a church, and his plough-oxen certainly imply some glebe. There was also a mill, doubtless driven by the water of the Ivel at the western edge of the manor.[1]

There is some likelihood that before long the inner moat may be bull-dozed out of existence. But even today there are still very few hedges between Bygrave and Baldock, so that the eye of historical imagination finds it easier here than in most places to conjure up the classic picture of the open fields.

HAWLING

In the last decade of the eleventh century, when the monks of Worcester set themselves to copy out their early charters, an impulse to modernize an archaic text of which they misunderstood the place-names led them to attach a survey of Hawling, in the western Cotswolds, to a charter of 816 which really belongs to Hallow, twenty-five miles away in Worcestershire. A charter for Hawling apparently still lay in their archives though the manor was no longer theirs, but only the survey has come down to us, perpetuated by their fortunate blunder. Hence it cannot be securely dated. But it shares one peculiarity with certain other Worcester charters in that it distinguishes the woodland of Hawling from its *feld* and gives a separate perambulation of each. The texts which make similar distinctions belong to the last quarter of the tenth century, and it seems likely that the double survey gives us a picture of Hawling at about that time.[2]

The woodland, when its landmarks are plotted, is seen to comprise a very large area north of Hawling which includes most of Sudeley and the whole of the former parish of Roel. The *feld* or open pasture occupies the south of the parish. Halfway between the two stands the village of Hawling, not touched by any landmark. There was no need of further definition: anyone who had followed both perambulations would know that the village and its adjacent arable lay between the two blocks of territory they delimit.

A map of the manor drawn in 1748 shows that the arable then lay in three common fields. One of them, the East Field, thrusts the jagged edges of its furlongs into the shrunken remnant called "Halling Downs" in the south-east corner, all that remains of the ancient *feld*. (Here, as throughout England, the evolution of the word *feld* into field with its modern sense betokens the triumph of the plough over what had once been open pasture.) On the other side of "Halling Downs" the West Field stretches to the parish boundary, where the strips and furlongs

[1] DB I, p. 135a.
[2] This and the next three paragraphs are based on the full discussion in my *Early Charters of the W. Midlands*, pp. 184–96.

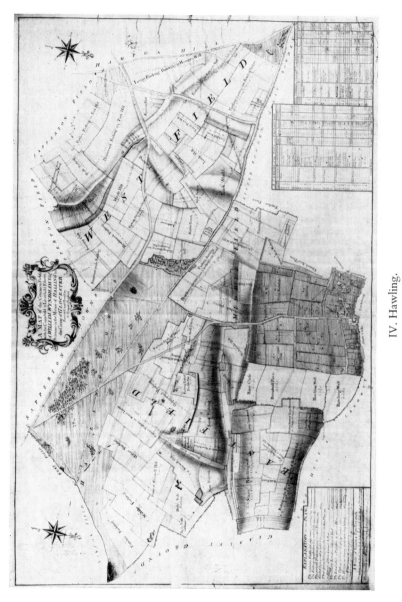

IV. Hawling.

interlock with those of Salperton. There remain some old enclosures immediately adjoining the village on the south, taking up about 85 acres between them, and the Middle Field of some 75 acres. This was clearly the original nucleus of cultivation, for it lies within the area which the Anglo-Saxon survey excluded from the *feld* and woodland. Before 1086 much of the woodland had been cleared and annexed to the manors of Sudeley and Roel. All that remained to Hawling was some 86 acres of detached woodland in three parcels isolated in Roel, one of which is still called Hawling Grove.

We may thus picture the original settlers establishing themselves high up on the wold, which here rises to 830 feet, on a site between two brooks which provided them with water. The very large area of woodland to the north, and the importance they evidently attached to it and to the open pasture on the south, point to pastoral husbandry as their main pursuit.[1] For bread-corn they tilled the ground nearest to their village, but we have no means of knowing what method of cultivation they pursued. It may be that they began at the stage described by William Marshall, who as late as 1789 observed in the neighbourhood of Gloucester some common fields "cropped year after year, during a century, or perhaps centuries, without one intervening whole year's fallow. Hence they are called 'Every Year's Land'. On these lands no regular succession of crops is observed."[2] However that may have been, the men of Hawling had evidently made considerable advances by the end of the Old English period, for in 1086 twelve plough-teams were at work in Hawling, besides ten in Roel and seventeen in Sudeley.

THE OPEN FIELDS

In the boundary surveys of tenth-century land-charters we frequently come across terms which indicate that the square or nearly square *blockflur* of primitive agriculture is now a thing of the past. We hear, for instance, of the headland (*heafod-land*), a margin left at the top and bottom of the field so that the plough-team may have room to turn.[3] When the rest of the field has been worked over, the headland in its turn is ploughed, at right angles to the rest, and it is then sometimes called the fore-earth (*forirth*).[4] If the field is not perfectly rectangular, it may be necessary to plough a 'gore' consisting of one or more 'gore-

---

[1] See above, p. 409, on the importance of the Cotswold sheep-flocks in the Anglo-Saxon period.

[2] W. Marshall, *The Rural Economy of Gloucestershire*, 1789, I, pp. 17, 65–6.

[3] CS 945 (Cuddesdon, Oxon); R LVI (Himbleton, Worcs).

[4] CS 601 (Hardwell, Berks); CS 752 (Christian Malford, Wilts); CS 775 (Cheselbourne, Dorset). But *forirth* can also mean a part of the arable which juts forward.

acres' tapering at one end, so that the sides of the gore are not parallel like those of the ordinary plough-strip.[1] Gores and headlands are familiar features of the open fields as delineated in the field-maps of later centuries.

In the early Kentish charters the word for plough is *aratrum*; in the tenth-century Danelaw it is *caruca*. Strictly speaking, the *aratrum* was a light implement which made no very deep incision and was chiefly suitable for ploughing well-drained soils, in contrast with the heavy wheeled *caruca* which produced deep furrows and plough-strips about ten times as long as they were broad. But it would be rash to construe the charters as implying a real distinction between the types of plough in use at the time. And the old idea that the use of the *caruca* is related to the shape of long-strip fields as cause and effect has been discarded in the light of evidence that in several parts of the world, and notably in Sweden, strip fields were produced by the *aratrum*, and the *caruca* properly so called was unknown.[2] It is now widely held that social and tenurial conditions exert as much influence on field-shape as any single technical factor.

The tantalizing reference in Ine's laws to arable share-land (*gedal-land*) must be recalled here, a reference which provoked more curiosity than it satisfied. The term meets us again, a little more instructively, in the third quarter of the tenth century. An estate at Maxey (Northants) is described as consisting of 29 "*gedale.*"[3] Charters refer to "*gedal land*" at Ardington (Berks), Clifford Chambers (Wark), and Cudley (Worcs).[4] At Ardington the land is described as "*gemang* [sic] *othran gedal lande,*" lying in common with other share-land, indicating that *gemæne* and *gedal* in this context are nearly synonymous. There is mention of "*gemæne land*" at Curridge (Berks) and Winterbourne (Wilts).[5] Draftsmen who wrote in Latin used "*communis terra*" for *gemæne land*[6] and sometimes gave this as a reason for not including a perambulation of the bounds.[7] In other cases the difficulty of describing a grant of common land was met by giving the bounds of a whole manor and adding that the grant refers to only a portion of it.[8]

[1] CS 814 (Weston, Som); CS 967 (Tadmarton, Oxon); K 687 (Fovant, Wilts).
[2] M. Bloch, *Les caractères originaux de l'histoire rurale française*, I, 1952, pp. 51–7; II, 1956, pp. 46–9.
[3] R XL, p. 80. In this document the 60 "sticca" of land amounting to 30 acres at Oxney (N'hants) sound like half-acre strips in open field.
[4] CS 1079 (A.D. 961), 1181 (A.D. 966), 1298 (A.D. 974).
[5] CS 900 (A.D. 953), CS 1145 (963×975).
[6] Charlton (Berks), K 1278 (A.D. 982); Drayton and Sutton Courtenay (Berks), K 1280 (A.D. 983); Dumbleton (Glos), K 692 (A.D. 995) and K 1295 (A.D. 1002); Westwood (Wilts), K 658 (A.D. 987).
[7] So at Charlton (Berks), CS 925 (A.D. 956) and K 1278 (A.D. 982).
[8] CS 1099, Stanton Prior (Som).

The Ardington charter goes out of its way to explain what it means by common share-land: it states that the open pasture is common, the meadow is common, and the arable is common ("feld læs gemane and mæda gemane and yrthland gemæne"). These terms correspond to the Latin *pascua*, *prata*, and *terra*. In reference to an enclosed common meadow Ine had used the word *gærston*, which also appears in a tenth-century Sussex charter, as well as in a number of place-names.[1] Where arable alone is in question, another way of expressing that it is held in common is to declare that the hides consist of mixed acres ("segetibus mixtis"), as at Harwell (Berks),[2] or that the land lies always acre between acre ("æcer under æcer"), as at Drayton, Hendred, and Kingston Bagpuize.[3] In such cases a proportionate share in the common pastures and meadows is almost certainly taken for granted.

We may ask: why should any man share ploughland with others? The answer surely is that he can seldom afford not to do so. Man-power is scarce, and capital resources in the form of oxen even scarcer. We have already met in Ine's laws the husbandman who finds it necessary to hire oxen from his neighbour. The lord who sets up a group of *coliberti* on plots of their own is unlikely to provide them with more than two oxen apiece, and on heavy soil a stronger team may well be required. Men will huddle together on sites recommended by a natural water-supply, and will till the land lying as near to the settlement as possible. All their working hours will be taken up in tending their livestock and raising their none too abundant crops. They will have no time for walking to distant fields or for making and maintaining more hedges than are absolutely necessary.

INTERMIXED HOLDINGS

Although Ine's law proves that some form of arable share-land was known in seventh-century Wessex, it tells us nothing of its earlier history. Moreover, while the law makes it clear that two or more husbandmen might plough together in one field, the regulations about fencing suggest that each man's share lay undivided in one block. But now in the tenth century charters provide unquestionable evidence of intermixed acres: what a later age will call the "mingle-mangle" of the open fields. In 956 King Eadwig grants to his thegn Wulfric five hides at Charlton by Wantage (Berks). The charter states that the land is separated by no fixed bounds, for the acres adjoin other

[1] CS 669: "pratum...quod Saxonice Garstone appellatur"; A. H. Smith, *English Place-Name Elements*, I, p. 191.
[2] K 648 (A.D. 985). For "segetes" in the sense of acres cf. CS 380, 864, 1027.
[3] CS 1032, 1095; K 1276.

acres.[1] A later grant of the same five hides declares that they are "in common land" and "are not demarcated on all sides by clear bounds because to left and right lie acres in combination one with another."[2] Still more explicitly, three hides at Avon (Wilts) are described as consisting of "single acres dispersed in a mixture here and there in common land."[3]

CAUSES OF INTERMIXTURE

It is natural to wonder how this intermixture had come about. We shall be well advised not to postulate a single governing factor, but to consider more than one possible explanation.

First, have we here an effect of partible inheritance? A man dies leaving what he has to leave to his three sons, A, B, and C, in equal shares. The most equitable way to apportion the arable will be to give A, B, and C three or four acres apiece, in that order, and then to repeat the process until the whole is allotted. This may have been what was done by the four kinsmen to whom Thurketel of Palgrave left 20 acres in the open fields of Roydon (Norf) after giving "the middle furlong" to the parish church.[4]

We know too little about customs of inheritance in the humbler ranks of Anglo-Saxon society to speak with any assurance on the subject. We do know that landlords occasionally framed their leases on these lines. For example, Oswald, bishop of Worcester, grants a lease of one and a half hides at Alveston (Wark) with "every other acre in the divided hide at Upper Stratford"; and the same Oswald, leasing Moreton in Bredon (Worcs) to two brothers, arranges that "the elder shall always have three acres and the younger the fourth, both central and outlying."[5]

Oswald's language confronts us with a third possibility: that the intermixture of parcels may have been imposed on the tillers of the soil by the combined powers of church and state in order that dues and services might be justly and efficiently apportioned. This is the period when the king is beginning to take a hand in enforcing payment of tithe. King Edmund says that "every Christian man" who refuses to pay tithes must be excommunicated. King Edgar does not leave it to the Church; he orders his reeves to accompany the bishop's reeve and the local priest and seize what is due from a recalcitrant payer; and

---

[1] CS 925: "Praefatum rus nullis certis terminis dirimitur set jugera adjacent jugeribus."

[2] K 1278: "Rus namque praetaxatum manifestis undique terminis minus dividitur, quia jugera altrinsecus copulata adjacent."

[3] CS 1120: "...singulis jugeribus mixtum [? mixtim] in communi rure huc illacque dispersis."

[4] W xxiv.   [5] R xliii, lxiv.

Ethelred II, re-enacting this law, defines tithe as "the produce of every tenth acre as traversed by the plough."[1] This method could be applied anywhere, even on demesne land, but it would obviously be the simplest and most effective way of collecting tithe-corn from a community of husbandmen whose arable lay in open fields.

SCANDINAVIAN INFLUENCE

One of the most influential churchmen of the age, Oswald, two of whose leases have been cited, held the see of Worcester from 961 and with it that of York from 972 until his death in 992. Himself of Danish or partly Danish parentage, he was well placed for observing the usages of the Danelaw. His predecessor at York, the Danish-named Oscytel, had received a grant of 20 hides at Southwell (Notts) with jurisdiction over a number of other villages. One of these was Normanton, where the church was given "every third acre."[2] Oscytel figures among the witnesses to a royal charter granting Newbald in the East Riding to a nobleman with a Scandinavian name; the grant includes "every other acre at Hotham."[3] In the same period we find another nobleman with a Scandinavian name selling "every eighth acre" at Brandon (Suff).[4] Transactions in these terms could obviously generate an intermixture of arable parcels even if it was not already present.

In all these cases the grants are made either to thegns or to great churchmen. Maitland could not believe that the system was invented by such people. He granted that they might think fit to maintain it where they found it already established, but he held that it must have been originally the work of free and equal peasants who "could not be prevented from sacrificing every interest of their lords at the shrine of equality."[5] Now if we look in the England of the tenth century – not of the seventh, as Maitland did – for a class of men strongly imbued with the idea of equality, and free enough to act upon it, we have not far to seek. We have already met the *bondi*, the free Danish warrior-farmer who attended the wapentake and enjoyed an appreciably higher

---

[1] I Edmund, 2; II Edgar, 3 §1; VII Ethelred, 5; VIII Ethelred, 7 (A. J. Robertson, *The Laws of the Kings of England from Edmund to Henry I*, Cambridge, 1925, pp. 6, 20, 110, 120, 164).

[2] CS 1029, 1348, dated 958 by mistake for 956: cf. EHD I, p. 513.

[3] CS 1113, 1353.

[4] *Liber Eliensis*, II, c. 36 (ed. Blake, p. 111). Cf. the grant of the third tree in a grove at Wylye (Wilts), CS 757 (A.D. 940), and references to "every third tree" at Farcet (Hunts), Hart, *Early Charters of Eastern England*, p. 160 (A.D. 956), and at Oxney (N'hants), R XL, p. 80. There are similar references in two writs of the Confessor, H 77 (doubtful), 93 (spurious).

[5] *Domesday Book and Beyond*, p. 338.

status than English countrymen of the same economic standing.[1] It would certainly be unsafe to interpret *gedælde*, the word used in the Anglo-Saxon Chronicle to describe the main Scandinavian land-divisions, as implying a division into small and equal plots of *gedal land*; but the Norse word 'man's-lot', applied to holdings of no great size, pretty clearly implies an allotment of standard shares. The charter of 956 assigns to Southwell two man's-lots at Farnsfield, at Halam every sixth acre and three man's-lots, at Fiskerton two-thirds of the whole estate and four man's-lots;[2] and a record from Bury St Edmunds enumerates seven groups of man's-lots belonging to the abbey.[3]

When a community of free and equal Danish farmers colonized virgin soil in England and founded a new *–by*, it might well occur to them to lay out their man's-lots in regular sequence over the arable field or fields, with the strips of B, C, and D consistently lying between those of A. This would be the simplest method of allotting to each a fair share of good and bad soil alike, and confining no man to a part of the field which might often become water-logged. Documents from the thirteenth century onwards will bear witness to the persistence of this remarkably regular pattern in the areas of Scandinavian settlement.[4] The method could equally well be applied when an established English or Danish community, under pressure of growing population, took in land from the common pasture and put it under plough.

The Danish emphasis on arable husbandry, and its far-reaching effects on fiscal assessments, were noticed in the last chapter. It may now be suggested, very tentatively, that the effects were far-reaching enough to bring about a reorganization of the arable fields in many villages of older settlement. Dramatic changes are rare in agriculture, but from time to time a rural community did reorganize its fields: Vinogradoff cites a remarkable instance from Bedfordshire in the twelfth century.[5] There are indications that agrarian and fiscal concepts were being radically modified in the reign of Eadred. In 949 that king issued a charter from which we learn that the Kentish *sulung* was now equated with one hide, not with two as of old.[6] A couple of years before this Eadred had granted one of his thegns five hides in Denchworth (Berks). The charter includes a perambulation of the five hides in the usual form, proceeding clockwise back to the starting-point, but it then adds a statement – so far as I know unique – that in the north of Denchworth

[1] See above, p. 475.   [2] CS 1029, 1348.
[3] R CIV.
[4] G. C. Homans, 'Terroirs ordonnés et champs orientés', *Annales d'histoire économique et sociale*, VIII, 1936, pp. 438–48; S. Göransson, 'Regular Open-Field Pattern in England and Scandinavian Solskifte', *Geografiska Annaler* XLIII, 1961, pp. 80–101.
[5] *Growth of the Manor*, p. 178.
[6] CS 880; the same equation is made in CS 1295. Cf. p. 415 above.

three of the five hides are "*undælede*," not divided into shares.[1] This may mean only that the thegn will receive the northern part of Denchworth as his demesne, to be held in severalty, like the thegn to whom Eadred granted five hides in Curridge (Berks), an estate which included 65 acres apparently lying outside the bounds "in the common land."[2] But other constructions are possible. The statement may mean that the Denchworth arable is being remodelled as intermixed parcels of shareland, but that the process has not yet been fully carried out. Or again, the pattern of intermixture may have been so much the rule in tenth-century Berkshire that its absence in this one case was felt to demand special notice.

Some historians have held that the open-field system goes back to the earliest days of Anglo-Saxon settlement. We cannot prove the contrary, but we have seen good reason for doubting that it is as old as that.[3] It has certainly left no traces in charters earlier than the tenth century. Can it be mere coincidence that we begin to find clear documentary evidence of intermixed arable holdings shortly after the Scandinavian occupation?

GEOGRAPHY OF THE OPEN FIELD

Charters already cited from Curridge, Charlton, Ardington, Hendred, Harwell, Sutton Courtenay, and Kingston Bagpuize indicate that open-field husbandry was very much at home in tenth-century Berkshire. The bounds of Cuddesdon in Oxfordshire include a headland and at three points run along furrows.[4] At Sandford in the same county we find references to "communis terra."[5] A clear mention of intermixed parcels of arable at Avon in Wiltshire has already been noted,[6] and the bounds of Alton Priors (Wilts) include a "common gore."[7] Of ten hides at Winterbourne Bassett (Wilts) divided into halves by the Kennet, the five hides west of the river are held in severalty, while the five on the east bank are common land on Hackpen Hill.[8] Ten hides at Wheathampstead (Herts) are described as situated "in communi terra."[9]

While the charters vouch for the existence in the Thames valley and the eastern counties of arable tilled in common, and frequently speak of it as common land, they leave it uncertain whether the fields were grazed by the stock of all the commoners after harvest and in fallow seasons. Nor do they provide any clue to the rotation of crops. If we subscribe to the austere doctrine that these are essential features of the developed system, we may have to wait until the twelfth or thirteenth

---

[1] CS 833. [2] CS 900 (A.D. 953). [3] See above, p. 398.
[4] CS 945. [5] K 793, 800. [6] CS 1120.
[7] R XVII. [8] CS 1145.
[9] F. Barlow, *Edward the Confessor*, 1970, p. 334.

century for evidence to justify us in speaking of common fields thus strictly defined in any part of England.[1] There is at any rate no difficulty in believing that the system took a long time to mature.

INFIELD AND OUTFIELD

South-west England took a different course. Here the ploughland consisted of an area close to the farmstead or hamlet, called the infield or in-ground, which was permanently cultivated, like the Every-Year Lands which Marshall came across in Gloucestershire, while the outfield or out-ground was an area taken in from the common pasture, ploughed and cropped for a year or two, and then allowed to revert to its former state, after which the process might be repeated on another part of the common. This intermittent cultivation of the outfield was particularly suitable for regions where great tracts of moor and heath provided a superabundance of rough pasture. It was practised in Cornwall and Scotland down to the eighteenth century. Traces of it have been found in Devon and elsewhere in the highland zone.[2] As Clapham says, "there can be little doubt that if we knew medieval England completely, we should meet plenty of it."[3]

A solitary reference to outfield cultivation occurs in a charter dated 958 by which King Eadwig granted two and a half hides and 25 acres at Ayshford and Boehill in east Devon to a certain Eadheah. The document includes a perambulation of the twin properties in the usual form. Then a laconic postscript adds: "There are many hills there that one may plough."[4]

Boehill, as its name implies, was itself a hill. By 1066 it had become two small manors with 55 acres of pasture between them. Their assessment, combined with that of Ayshford, amounted to the two and a half hides of Eadwig's charter, all but one-eighth of a yardland.[5] We may hazard a surmise that in 958 Boehill was being cultivated intermittently as outfield of Ayshford, and that the 25 acres mentioned in the charter lay there. A century later it had been developed as an independent settlement divided between two holders. However that may be, the almost casual reference to the many hills in the vicinity that could be ploughed takes for granted a well-established practice.

Fortified by Clapham's dictum, we may look for possible hints of the

---

[1] J. Thirsk, 'The Common Fields', *Past and Present*, no. 29, 1964, pp. 1–25, and no. 33, 1966, pp. 142–4; A. R. H. Baker, 'The Terminology of British Field Systems', AHR XVII, 1969, pp. 136–40.

[2] H. P. R. Finberg, *West-Country Historical Studies*, pp. 147–51.

[3] J. Clapham, *A Concise Economic History of Britain*, Cambridge, 1949, p. 48.

[4] CS 1027.   [5] DB IV, p. 368 (Biheda [*sic*], Aiseforda).

practice in other documents. Had the three yardlands in common land at Farleigh Hungerford, described in 987 as appendant to Westwood on the Wiltshire side of the Frome, begun as outfield cultivation?[1] Farleigh means a clearing of fern-covered land. The common land on Hackpen Hill appurtenant to Winterbourne Bassett may have been used chiefly for grazing, but its five-hide assessment hints that it was not always left under grass. The bounds of Buckland Newton (Dors) go "up on Duntish."[2] The second element in this name, according to Ekwall, is cognate with the Low German *esch*, so that here we have an unenclosed cornfield on a down or hill pasture.[3] The bounds of Upton-on-Severn (Worcs) run "to the *feld*, always beside the wood as plough and scythe may go there," which seems to imply that the *feld* was occasionally ploughed;[4] and a grant of "every third acre of *feldland*" near Alveston (Wark) would be meaningless if it referred only to common pasture.[5] A large estate at Dumbleton (Glos) consisted in 1002 of 17 hides round Dumbleton itself, five hides of woodland at Flyford Flavell twelve miles away to the north, and two hides described as common by popular allotment ("sorte communes populari") at Aston Somerville on the other side of the Isbourne from Dumbleton.[6] Again we wonder: is this outfield? Finally, an eleventh-century transcript of an early charter relating to land in the far north of Worcestershire includes a boundary which at one point goes "up by the common land to the middle of Heath Hill."[7] This may be just common pasture, but "land" in Old English, like the Latin *terra*, usually means cultivated land in contrast to the uncultivated *feld* and *læs*.

THE WEST MIDLANDS

Here in the west midlands we might for a moment imagine ourselves back in open-field country. In 904 the bishop of Worcester grants a lease of Barbourne with 60 acres of arable to the north and 60 acres to the south.[8] Barbourne, however, is a stream-name, so the bishop may be merely giving a geographical description of a single holding. Another episcopal lease refers to 30 acres in the two fields of share-land outside the bounds of Cudley.[9] Barbourne and Cudley are both in the suburbs of Worcester, and it sounds as if the pattern at Cudley was the classic pattern of the two-field system, with a rotation of crop and

---

[1] K 658.   [2] CS 768.
[3] E. Ekwall, *Selected Studies*, Lund, 1963, p. 157.
[4] CS 1088 (A.D. 962).   [5] R XLIII (A.D. 966).
[6] K 1295. Seven years previously 2½ hides at Dumbleton had been described as situated in common land (K 692).
[7] CS 455, dated 849.   [8] R XIX.   [9] CS 1298, dated 974.

fallow alternating either between the two fields or within the area of each.

But we must beware of reading too much into the evidence. Rotation seems to be ruled out in places where we find patches of arable assigned more or less permanently to particular crops. The bounds of Himbleton (Worcs) run "along the hedge to the rye-growing croft, along the headland of the croft to the other headland, from that headland to the barley-growing croft."[1] Similarly "the third acre of beanland" is included in a lease of Bishopton (Wark), where the bounds also mention "barley-land."[2] We hear of "the bishop's oat-land" at Bredons Norton (Worcs),[3] and of a road to the flax-fields (*Linaceran wege*) where there is now a farm called Linacres.[4] In granting a lease of two hides at Wolverton (Worcs) Archbishop Oswald excepted 60 acres which he had attached as wheat-growing land to his manor of Kempsey.[5] The archbishop was a business-like prelate who carried out far-reaching tenurial changes on his lands, and the Wolverton lease shows him in the act, here at least, of reorganizing the agricultural pattern. On the evidence of other leases it has already been suggested hypothetically that his experience in the Danelaw may have prompted him in some cases to create intermixed arable holdings on the lands of his west-midland see.

REGIONAL VARIETIES

A charter for Bromley shows that in 987 Kent remained faithful to the custom of providing a manor with appurtenances in the shape of distant swine-pastures: Bromley had five such *denns* miles away in the Weald.[6] No contemporary evidence informs us how Kentish arable was managed.

For the rest of England the sources fail us. Thus the accidents of survival oblige us to make what we can of information from sources which are unevenly distributed and far from sufficiently detailed. Those which have been examined in these pages allow us to draw conclusions that will come as no surprise to students of H. L. Gray's pioneer work.[7] They point to four distinct varieties of practice. In the Thames valley and the eastern counties we find what Gray called the midland system, based on farming by village communities who held their pasture and

---

[1] R LVI, c. 977.

[2] K 724, dated 1016. Cf. the "bean-furlong" in the bounds of Sparsholt (Berks), CS 1121, dated 963.

[3] J. Earle, *A Hand-Book to the Land-Charters, and other Saxonic Documents*, Oxford, 1888, p. 208.

[4] Earle, *op. cit.*, p. 239; PN *Worcs*, p. 111.   [5] R LV, dated 977.

[6] K 657.

[7] H. L. Gray, *English Field Systems*, Cambridge, Mass., 1915, reprinted 1959.

meadow in common and their arable in scattered strips. In Kent, and probably also in Sussex and parts of Hampshire, the economy is based largely on stock-raising and therefore lays great stress on the use of distant forest pastures. In the south-west and possibly elsewhere the intermittent cultivation of the outfield supplements a more intensive crop-raising nearer home. Finally, in the west midlands the arable appears to be so managed as to preclude crop-rotation, with no pre-ponderance of tillage over pastoral husbandry; but the picture is indistinct, for here and there we find intrusions of the midland system.

Later evidence will no doubt fill in these outlines, and may well multiply the number of regional variations.

LIVESTOCK

The interest of kings and magnates in stock-raising, and especially in pig-keeping, has been mentioned in an earlier chapter. That the nutritive value of bracken as well as of mast was recognized is shown by a charter from the king of Mercia exempting Bentley (Worcs) from the obligation to supply "fern-pasture" for the royal swine.[1] A late ninth-century ealdorman's will leaves 2,000 swine on his estates in Kent and Surrey to his wife, and 400 swine to other kinsmen.[2] Thorney Abbey, founded in 972, was given eighty swine valued at one and a half pounds and a swineherd valued at half a pound; at the same time thirty full-grown swine were moved from Hatfield (Herts) to Thorney or one of its estates. Hatfield belonged to Ely, and the same document, which is illegible in places, gives an inventory of stock on several of the Ely manors in Cambridgeshire:

Ely	47 full-grown swine	197 young pigs
Stretham	20 sows	
Horningsea	18 full-grown swine	40 hogs
?		44 hogs
Hauxton	30 full-grown swine	99 hogs
Melbourn	23 sows	

At Hatfield Ely at one time possessed 40 oxen, 250 sheep, 47 goats, 15 calves, 190 swine, and 40 flitches of bacon.[3] This inventory may be compared with that of the stock on a Peterborough estate at about the same time. At Yaxley (Hunts) the abbey possessed 13 "work-worthy" men, 5 women, 8 young men, 16 oxen, a stalled ox, 305 sheep, 30 swine, and 100 flitches of bacon.[4] A contemporary testatrix, Æthelgifu, who

[1] CS 487.
[2] CS 558.
[3] R App. II, IX.
[4] R xxxix, p. 74.

possessed lands in three shires, Bedford, Huntingdon, and Northampton, left 130 head of cattle and some 600 sheep.[1]

Occasionally the documents allow us glimpses of individual estates and their livestock. For example:

> Beddington (Surr): 9 full-grown oxen, 114 full-grown pigs, 50 wethers, besides the sheep and the pigs to which the herdsmen are entitled, 20 of which are full-grown; 110 full-grown sheep, 7 slave-men, 20 flitches of bacon.[2]
> Luddington (Wark): 12 slave-men, 2 teams of oxen, 100 sheep, 50 fothers of corn.[3]
> Norton (Worcs): 1 man, 6 oxen, 20 sheep, 20 acres of corn sown.[4]
> Egmere (Norf): 7 oxen, 8 cows, 4 grazing bullocks, 2 inferior horses, 115 sheep and lambs, 160 acres sown, 1 flitch of bacon, 1 pig, 24 cheeses.[5]

If the horse was ever used for ploughing or harrowing, the fact is not mentioned in our sources. It is known, however, that Anglo-Saxon magnates maintained stud farms. There was one at Ongar (Ess) belonging to a lord named Thurstan.[6] Ælfhelm leaves half his stud at Troston (Suff) to his wife and half to his companions.[7] The lady Wynflæd speaks of horses some of which are unbroken, others tame.[8] The founder of Burton Abbey, Wulfric, gives the monastery 100 wild horses and 16 tame geldings, with other livestock. Another will speaks of a white horse and two stallions, one black, the other pied.[9]

MILLS

One important feature of the agrarian landscape, the water-mill, found no place in our earlier survey. The laws of Ethelbert show that the kings of Kent employed slave-women to grind corn for them, and doubtless their subjects did the same. But when slaves grow scarce or costly, the expedient suggests itself of applying water-power instead of human muscles. The water-driven mill, no novelty in the Mediterranean world, took centuries to supersede the hand-quern in northern Europe. The capital outlay and the cost of repairs would be unprofitable unless there were a large enough quantity of grain to be ground. Only kings and magnates could face the expense, and only they could successfully

---

[1] *The Will of Æthelgifu*, transl. and examined by D. Whitelock, Roxburghe Club, 1968, pp. 64, 76, 77.

[2] CS 619 (A.D. 899 × 908).

[3] R LXXIX (early 11th cent.).

[4] R LXXXI (early 11th cent.).

[5] R CIV, p. 196.

[6] W XXXI, p. 82.

[7] W XIII, p. 32.

[8] W III, p. 14.

[9] W XVII, p. 50. See also W II, XII, XX.

assert a legal right to draw off the necessary water. A law of the Alamanni says that if a man owns both banks of a stream he may construct a mill, but if only one bank is his he must make terms with the landowner on the other side.[1]

A village in Saxony on the River Unstrut, founded by Frankish warriors in 775, is significantly named Mühlhausen. The English equivalent of this name is *Mylentun*, borne by an estate at or near Otford which the archbishop of Canterbury purchased from King Ceolwulf in 822.[2] But if a record from St Augustine's, Canterbury, can be trusted, the abbey had preceded the archbishop as a mill-owner. It possessed one at Chart, and in 762 made over half the miller's rent to King Ethelbert II in order that their tenant might have pasture in the Weald for one herd of swine.[3] The same or another mill at Chart is recorded in 814.[4] From this time onwards mills appear fairly often among the appurtenances of Kentish estates.[5] It is not surprising that the water-mill should make its earliest appearance in Kent, which from its proximity to the European mainland was naturally receptive of continental ideas, but once introduced it would not for long be confined to the south-east. We hear of a mill-brook at Woolland (Dors), a mill-ditch at Hardenhuish (Wilts), mill-burns at Taunton and Creech (Som), a mill-pool at Stoke Bishop (Glos), and mill-stalls at Easton and Stonham (Hants).[6] In 943 we find King Edmund granting ten hides at Leckhampstead (Berks) to one of his thegns, and adding "in augmentation of this gift" a mill on the River Lambourn.[7] Thirteen years later the bounds of an estate in Tadmarton (Oxon) begin and end at "Edward's mill."[8] About this time a mill-leat nearly three-quarters of a mile long, with a flat bottom over twenty feet wide and a depth at its maximum of about twelve feet, was dug across a loop of the Thames at Old Windsor to drive a large mill equipped with three water-wheels.[9] Of windmills we shall hear nothing until the twelfth century is nearly over, but at the close of the Old English period water-mills in this country would be numbered in thousands.

[1] *Monumenta Germaniae Historica*, Leges v, Part i, *Lex Alamannorum*, ed. K. Lehmann, Hanover, 1888, LXXX, p. 145.

[2] CS 370.   [3] CS 191.   [4] CS 343.

[5] CS 418 (A.D. 838), 442 (A.D. 843), 496 (A.D. 858).

[6] CS 410 (A.D. 833), 469 (A.D. 854), 476 (A.D. 854), 550 (A.D. 882), 551 (A.D. 883), 543 (A.D. 871), 692 (A.D. 932). The Mylenburnan in the south-west, a manor which Alfred the Great disposed of by will, was probably Silverton in Devon.—H. P. R. Finberg, *The Early Charters of Devon and Cornwall*, p. 9, no. 15.

[7] CS 789.   [8] CS 965.   [9] *Medieval Archaeology* II, 1958, pp. 183–5.

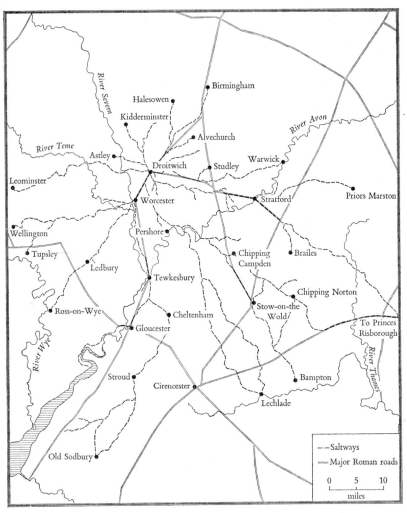

Fig. 51. Map of saltways and Roman roads from Droitwich.

SALTERNS AND SALTWAYS

All round the coast and in the estuaries lay salterns where sea-water was boiled to extract the salt by evaporation, consuming large quantities of fuel in the process. In 732 Ethelbert II of Kent granted to an abbot named Dun a quarter of a ploughland by the River Lympne for salt-making, with a yearly allowance of a hundred and twenty cartloads of firewood.[1] Somewhat later Cynewulf of Wessex gave the church of

[1] CS 148.

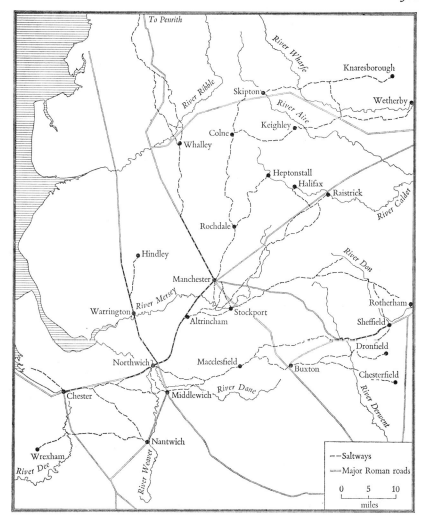

Fig. 52. Map of saltways and Roman roads in Cheshire.

Sherborne a saltern on the west bank of the River Lyme, explaining that salt was needed both as a condiment and for sacramental use.[1] Inland the main sources of supply were the brine springs of Droitwich in Worcestershire (see Fig. 51) and Nantwich in Cheshire (see Fig. 52). Early in his reign Ethelbald of Mercia gave the church of Worcester a plot of ground on the south bank of the River Salwarp for the construction of three salt-houses and six furnaces, in exchange for six other

[1] CS 224. The custom of placing a grain or two of salt in the mouth of a neophyte as a symbol of wisdom was retained in the Latin rite of baptism until 1969.

furnaces and two salt-houses on the north bank.[1] He and his successors drew a steady revenue from the tolls they levied on the trade in salt.

From the main inland centres tracks called saltways radiated in all directions to be travelled by distributors of this indispensable commodity. Place-names and documentary references enable the routes of many saltways to be traced and mapped. They must have played nearly as important a part in the Anglo-Saxon road system as the prehistoric ridgeways. These, following high ground in order to avoid river crossings, remained in use, as also did the great Roman roads. The Anglo-Saxons turned the Latin word *strata* into *stræt*, our 'street', to denote a paved road, usually but not invariably Roman. A road used primarily for military purposes or leading to a well-known battle site was called a *here-pæth*, or army path. *Weg*, the commonest of all words for a road, covered a wide variety of tracks, from a Roman road like the Fosse Way to the innumerable unnamed country lanes which figure in charter boundaries.

A charter by which King Ethelbald exempted two ships belonging to the bishop of Worcester from payment of tolls in the port of London is only one of many evidences for the regular use of water transport.[2]

MINSTERS

Churches, like mills, required an outlay of capital for their construction and, like mills again, were expected to provide an income for their founders. If only because the burden of their support fell ultimately on the tillers of the soil, they must be accounted a feature of the agrarian landscape.

Eccles, a fairly common element in place-names, represents the Latin *ecclesia*, and may often indicate the site of a Roman-British church or even its surviving fabric. When Augustine arrived in Kent he found one such church in Canterbury, dedicated to St Martin, still in use, and others which needed only to be repaired. After the conversion of the English new church-building went on apace. No account of Anglo-Saxon architecture will be given here, but the different grades of church must be briefly described. The cathedral, where the bishop had his seat, was called a minster, *monasterium*, because his clergy were monks or at least shared a communal life. From this central power-house priests went out to preach and offer mass at rural spots marked at first only by a standing cross. Presently noblemen built churches on their estates for the convenience of their tenants and for their own temporal profit. They appointed the priest and bargained with him for a share in the offerings and tithes. With the growth of population and settle-

[1] CS 137.   [2] R I.

ment such churches multiplied, giving rise to conflicts of pecuniary interest. King Edgar laid down a rule that the old minsters should keep their tithes, but that a thegn who had a church and graveyard on his bookland might pay that church a third of his own tithe; if there was no graveyard he could pay his priest what he liked out of the nine remaining parts. Church-scot from all free hearths was still reserved to the old minster.[1] The legislation of Ethelred II and his Danish successor classifies churches as 'head minsters' or cathedrals, 'ordinary minsters', the original mother-churches of a district, lesser parochial churches possessing graveyards, and 'field churches' built for recently established communities and not yet possessing the graveyard which entitled them to the burial-fee called soul-scot.[2]

Most Anglo-Saxon churches were small, those in rural parishes often log-built and roofed with thatch, but at Brixworth (N'hants) we can still admire the ancient minster with its nave 60 feet long; and Wilfrid built churches at Hexham and Ripon on a still more impressive scale.

BOROUGHS AND PORTS

Where men congregated for worship they would remain to buy and sell. The dairy-woman with a cheese to spare, the farmer desirous of selling a sheep or cow, the reeve buying seed-corn for his master's land, would find an informal market ready-made outside the church on Sunday. Athelstan tried to prohibit Sunday trading, but later repealed the prohibition.[3] Ethelred II made more persistent efforts in the same direction, as also did Cnut after him, seemingly to no avail.[4] The law frowned on transactions not conducted under the eye of responsible officials who would see to it that tolls were paid. It demanded regular markets, and the best place for a regular market was in a town.

It is not now believed that urban life became totally extinct after the collapse of Roman administration. Canterbury, London, Dorchester-on-Thames, and York, to name no other Roman towns, have provided convincing archaeological evidence of continued habitation, and the establishment of bishoprics there after the conversion of the English must have strengthened their chances of survival. But the policy of Alfred the Great and his successors gave a new impetus to the growth of urban life and institutions. For military reasons Alfred devised a plan,

[1] II Edgar I, 2 (Robertson, p. 20).

[2] VIII Ethelred, 5 §1; I Cnut, 3 §2 (*ibid.*, pp. 118, 156).

[3] II Athelstan, 24 §1; IV Athelstan, 2; VI Athelstan, 10 (Robertson, pp. 140, 146, 166).

[4] V Ethelred, 13 §1; VI Eth., 22 §1, 44; VIII Eth., 17; I Cnut, 15 (*ibid.*, pp. 82, 96, 104, 122, 166).

which his son Edward and his daughter Æthelflæd brought to completion, of protecting the main lines of communication by covering England with a strategic network of *burhs*, garrisoned strongpoints in which the country people could take refuge when the Vikings were on the warpath.

At a time when the military significance of the *burh* was uppermost in the public mind, legislators employed another word, *port*, borrowed from the administrative terminology of the Carolingians, to denote not a sea-port but a market centre, whether inland or on the coast. Edward the Elder prohibited all buying and selling except in *ports*.[1] Athelstan, re-enacting this law, at first limited its application to goods worth more than twenty pence, and finally repealed it altogether.[2] At the same time he took steps to bring the coinage under control, for without a steady supply of money trade would languish and die. He decreed that no man should coin money except in a *port*. He goes on to give a list of mints, with the number of moneyers in each. In Canterbury there should be 4 moneyers for the king, 2 for the archbishop, 1 for the abbot of St Augustine's; in Rochester 2 for the king, 1 for the bishop; in London 8; in Winchester 6; in Lewes 2; in Hastings 1; in Chichester 1; in Southampton 2; in Wareham 2; in Dorchester 1; in Exeter 2; in Shaftesbury 2; in each of the other boroughs 1.[3] These, then, are all *ports*, but in the last item the word is *burgum*. Not every *port* is a *burh*, but the words are beginning to be interchangeable, and will remain so for centuries. The officer who collects the tolls and rents for the lord of a *port* and by his presence authenticates commercial transactions is styled the portreeve. A road leading to a town is called a Portway or Port-street. Oxford still has its Port Meadow. The English spoke of *portmen* where the Normans would speak of burgesses, *burgenses*.

Not until Domesday will our information be full enough to provide a complete list of boroughs and ports. Most villagers would find one or the other within easy reach. The inhabitants of Bygrave, for instance, could take their goods to market at Ashwell only two miles away, and a journey of four miles along "the northern-most portway" would bring those of Hawling to the royal borough of Winchcombe. Stone walls defended some of the boroughs, but the houses were built of more combustible materials. Thetford (Norf), burnt down by the Danes in 1004, was rebuilt only to be burnt again in 1016.

---

[1] 1 Edward, 1 (Attenborough, p. 114).
[2] II Athelstan, 12; IV Athelstan, 2; VI Athelstan, 10 (*ibid.*, pp. 134, 146, 166).
[3] II Athelstan ,14 (*ibid.*, p. 134).

HOUSES

Once destroyed by fire, the wooden foundations and walls of Anglo-Saxon houses are hard to detect. Often nothing survives but marks, visible in the subsoil, of the holes into which the builders fitted posts, beams, and planks. These leave a pattern which requires to be interpreted by the excavator, and he is always exposed to the temptation of finding just what he is looking for. Many archaeologists believe that the sunken huts described in an earlier chapter co-existed with larger timber buildings at ground level. This belief has been to some extent confirmed by recent research on the same sites.

At St Neots (Hunts) an excavation reported in 1933 revealed eight huts which the excavator assumed to date from the tenth and eleventh centuries. The inhabitants, according to him, "lived in almost as primitive a condition as can be imagined. They had no regard for cleanliness, and were content to throw the remains of a meal into the furthest corner of the hut and leave it there. They were not nervous about ghosts, since they did not mind having a skeleton sticking out of the wall of one of their huts...It is almost certain that they were wretchedly poor serfs."[1] This gloomy picture has been somewhat modified by the more recent discovery of substantial timber buildings at St Neots, one of them over 60 feet long.[2] Similarly at Maxey (N'hants) an excavation undertaken in the hope of finding larger buildings between the sunken huts already known there brought to light seven rectangular structures built of timber, wattle, clay, and thatch. They varied in length between 30 and 50 feet, and in width between 16 and 20 feet.[3] These findings accord very well with the documentary evidence of a social system which included, side by side in the same village, cottagers of the lowest grade and more substantial farmers with an appreciably higher standard of living.

What of the landlord? At Sulgrave (N'hants), best known as the ancestral seat of George Washington's family, excavation has brought to light an Anglo-Saxon manor house which seems to have been built early in the eleventh century. On the ground floor a cobbled porch led into a single-bay room screened by a cross-partition from the main body of an aisleless hall, 75 by 20 feet, which had a central hearth, side benches against the south wall, and a dais at the east end. The eastern-most bay was carried on stone footings four feet high. Beyond it stood a two-storied block, L-shaped or possibly T-shaped, containing two or three rooms on the ground floor and on the upper floor a chamber which

[1] C. F. Tebbutt in *Proc. Cambridge Antiquarian Society* XXXIII, 1933, p. 149.
[2] *Medieval Archaeology* VI–VII, 1962–3, p. 308.
[3] *Medieval Archaeology* VIII, 1964, pp. 20, 44.

extended over the end bay of the hall. Associated with this complex was a free-standing tower or bell-house, a composite structure of stone and timber. It is clear from this example that by the late Saxon period, if not earlier, the dwelling of a rural thegn could exhibit a noteworthy degree of sophistication.[1]

In the second quarter of the tenth century a new hall, 60 feet long and 28 or 30 feet wide, was built in the royal manor of Cheddar (Som), superseding the hall which had been used in Alfred's reign. Massive posts, up to two feet square, were set at eight-foot intervals and presumably connected by plank walling. A chapel and what may have been a corn-mill were added to the site. Later still, perhaps in the reign of Ethelred II, the nave of a new and larger chapel was built round the older one.[2]

Tapestried wall-hangings helped to mitigate the discomfort of noble and royal dwellings, but Alfred's biographer makes it clear how easily and often the wind found its way through the chinks. To prevent his candles from being extinguished by the draughts Alfred had them encased in finely planed translucent horn.[3] For anything as effective as the central heating which had protected the inhabitant of the Roman villa from the rigours of our northern winter Englishmen had to wait another thousand years.

[1] *Current Archaeology*, no. 12, Jan. 1969, pp. 19–22.
[2] *Medieval Archaeology* VI–VII, 1962–3, pp. 53–6.
[3] W. H. Stevenson, *Asser's Life of King Alfred*, pp. 91, 340.

CHAPTER VII

THE SOCIAL STRUCTURE IN THE
LATE OLD ENGLISH PERIOD

ONE RESULT of the unification of England under a single crown
was to make it practically impossible for a Northumbrian
warrior to be sold into slavery by his Mercian captors, or
a Kentish woman to be carried off and held as a slave in Wessex. Warfare
between the smaller kingdoms had ceased to provide a constant supply
of slaves. But the class was still recruited from above. A free man might
fall into penal servitude, either directly as a punishment for law-breaking
or because he had incurred a heavy fine which he found himself unable
to pay. Poverty, again, and fear of starvation might drive an innocent
man to sell himself and all his family. When he does this he must put
his head between his master's hands and be given a bill-hook or an ox-
goad in token of his new condition.[1] This was the ceremony to which
a Northumbrian lady referred when she set free "all those people whose
heads she took in return for their food in the evil days."[2]

SLAVES AND THE ECONOMICS OF SLAVERY

It was still not uncommon for slaves to be bought and sold. We hear of
such transactions taking place at the church door in Bodmin, where the
portreeve collected toll on the sale.[3] In calculating the price, a woman
was sometimes valued at half a pound, and a man at a whole pound, or
eight times as much as an ox.[4] When a personage named Ælfric tried to
enslave one Putrael, a well-to-do Cornishman, on what ground is not
recorded, Putrael by a fee of 60 pence to Ælfric's brother induced him
to intercede with Ælfric and persuade him to accept eight oxen as the
price of freedom for himself and all his family.[5] Five other Cornishmen
with their sons and grandsons obtained King Edgar's leave to defend
themselves by oath against an evil-doer who had asserted that their
fathers had been serfs of the king.[6]

[1] *Leges Henrici Primi*, LXXVIII §2 (Liebermann, *Gesetze*, I, p. 594).
[2] EHD I, p. 563.
[3] Earle, *Hand-Book to the Land Charters*, p. 273.
[4] Earle, *op. cit.*, pp. 268, 269; Liebermann, *Gesetze*, I, p. 378, §7.
[5] EHD I, p. 562, no. 147.
[6] *Ibid.*, no. 144. The word for serf here is *colonus*. A doctored passage in a Winchester
charter uses the same word to distinguish the lord's demesne ("quod episcopo

Periods of social upheaval offered many chances of escape from thraldom. We have Archbishop Wulfstan's word for it that the Viking incursions enabled many a slave to change places with his master.[1] Less violent in their operation, economic forces also pressed upon the slave-owner. "In twelve months," one writer told him, "thou shalt give thy slave men 720 loaves, besides morning meals and noon meals."[2] This, if really provided, was no meagre ration, no negligible item in the household expenses. No wonder many masters found it worth while to set their slaves up as self-supporting or partly self-supporting tillers of the soil. The Church encouraged them to do so, not only from religious motives – to free men from a recognized evil like slavery was a charitable action, and the emancipator would expect the emancipated to pray for him – but also because the serf with a plot of ground and a dwelling of his own became liable for Peter's Pence and other ecclesiastical dues. Already in 816 the Council of Chelsea had decreed that on the death of a bishop a tenth of his livestock should be distributed in alms and every Englishman reduced to slavery in his time should be freed.[3]

OLD ENGLISH DESIGNATIONS OF SOCIAL CLASSES

NOTE. The categories in the following table are not mutually exclusive, e.g., a *gebur* might also be a *gafolgelda*, and every *ealdorman* would also be a *thegn*. Those marked ★ are probably all included in the genus *ceorl*.

	Middle Saxon c. 650–c. 850	Late Saxon c. 850–c. 1066
Slave	*theow*	*theow* *thraell*
Unfree or half-free cottager	? *esnewyrhta*★	*cotsetla*★
Freedman occupying a farm	*gebur*★	*gebur*★ *leysing*★ (Latin) *colibertus*★
Rent-paying tenant	*gafolgelda*★	*gafolgelda*★
Free farmer	*geneat* ? *syxhynde*	*geneat* *dreng* *radcniht*
Landed nobleman	*gesith* *thegn* ?*twelfhynde*	*thegn* *landrica*
Governor of one or more shires	*ealdorman*	*ealdorman* *eorl*

aratur") from the land of his tenants ("quod coloni inhabitant").—*Early Charters of Wessex*, p. 246.   [1] EHD I, p. 858.

[2] J. M. Kemble, *The Poetry of the Codex Vercellensis*, 1843, p. 193.

[3] Haddan and Stubbs, *Councils and Ecclesiastical Documents*, III, p. 583.

'COLIBERTI'

From the middle of the tenth century onwards testators frequently provide by will that all their *witetheow men*, their penal slaves, shall be set free.[1] On the face of it this clause would release even those who had incurred the penalty only a month or two before the testator's death; if so, they were lucky to escape so lightly. Other wills make no distinction between penal and born or purchased slaves; they merely direct that "half the men" on a given manor[2] or "all my men"[3] shall be free. It is usually held that the "men" in these cases were slaves. And when an East Anglian lady desires that all her men shall be set free, both "in the household and on the estate,"[4] we may reasonably assume that the first-named group are domestic slaves; but what of those on the land? The men to whom another East Anglian testatrix bequeaths their homesteads (*toftes*) are certainly settled on the land, for she calls them *landsethlan*.[5] Another testator desires that the men to whom he grants freedom shall have all things which are in their possession "except the land."[6]

The truth is that men "freed" in batches like these, *coliberti* as they are called in Latin documents, may be settled on the land, but they are still only half free. Sometimes the ceremony of manumission was performed at a cross-roads, implying that the freedman might go wherever he would and choose a new master,[7] but more often he remained, perhaps by choice, on his master's land, subject to more or less burdensome dues and services. As late as the sixteenth century Englishmen who are certainly not slaves, who are often substantial farmers, will pay handsomely to rid themselves of a residual bondage to which the law still holds them liable.[8]

About the middle of the tenth century a rich and highly connected widow named Wynflæd made a will disposing of her unfree dependants, her livestock, and lands of which some belonged to her in her own right and some were leased from the minster at Shaftesbury, where she appears to have taken the veil. One of the slave women, exceptionally, is given freedom to choose her own mistress; others, including a seamstress and a weaver, are left to various members of her family. She also owned a number of penal slaves, some of them with wives and children. She frees two dozen or more of them by name and expresses the hope that

[1] W III (p. 12), IV (p. 16), VIII (p. 20), IX (p. 24), XVIII (p. 54), XX (p. 56), *Crawford Charters*, X (p. 23). [2] W I (p. 4), XIV (p. 36), XXXII (p. 84).
[3] W I (p. 4), XXIV (p. 68), XXVII (p. 74), XXIX (p. 78), XXXI (p. 80), XXXIII (p. 86), XXXIV (p. 88), XXXVIII (p. 94).
[4] W XXIX (p. 76). [5] W XXXVIII (p. 94). [6] W XXXIV (p. 88).
[7] *Chronicon Rameseienis*, ed. W. D. Macray, Rolls ser. 83, p. 59 (East Anglia, A.D. 986); Earle, *op. cit.*, pp. 254–6 (Devon, *c.* 1050).
[8] *Agrarian History of England and Wales*, IV, p. 267.

for the good of her soul her children will release any others there may be. Two of her Somerset estates, Chinnock and Charlton Horethorne, appear to have been leaseholds, for at neither does she make a bequest of land, and she expressly states that Chinnock will belong to the nuns of Shaftesbury after her death, but she adds that she herself owns the stock and the men. The slaves and livestock she leaves to her daughter-in-law, but the occupants of the rented land (*gebura the on tham gafollande sittath*) are to go with the estate to the minster. Similarly at Charlton she frees two men and one woman but leaves the rest of the men and stock to her daughter, "except the freedmen."[1] The implication is that she had stocked these estates with men and oxen, and that both alike remained her property. The men are clearly of servile status, and those who have not been freed may presently be sold off by her heirs or removed to some other estate like the half-dozen serfs on the royal manor of Bensington (Oxon) who were uprooted by the ealdorman of Mercia and transferred bodily, with their offspring, to an estate under other ownership five miles away.[2] The freedmen, however, pass with the land, either to the next leaseholder or to the owners of the estate. In practice they have security of tenure, but the fact that they have it by express stipulation, and not as of right, shows how much their lot depends on grace and favour.[3]

Wynflæd's will is a most instructive document. Taken in conjunction with the two East Anglian wills already cited, it proves that the "men" disposed of by testators were not all slaves, but included farmers of servile antecedents who by law, if not always in practice, were tied to their master rather than to the estate. They owned him rent for their holdings. To such "men" Wulfgeat of Donington bequeaths a year's rent as a gift.[4]

THE 'COTSETLA' AND THE 'GEBUR'

The lord who meant to turn his slave into a freedman had to decide what he wanted from him: rent, service, or some of each. If the continued need for service was uppermost in his thoughts he might call the man "work-worthy" and describe his holding as "work-land" or "earning-land."[5] He could stipulate for unpaid labour on the demesne one day a week throughout the year. In such cases he might allow the

[1] W III; cf. T. H. Aston in TRHS, 5th ser., VIII, 1958, p. 71.
[2] CS 547 (A.D. 880).
[3] For other bequests of freedmen in considerable numbers see W XIX (p. 54), XXI (p. 64).   [4] W XIX.
[5] We hear of "work-worthy" men at Farcet and Yaxley (Hunts), also at Bury St Edmunds (R XXXIX, pp. 72, 74; App. III, p. 248); of "earningland" at Worcester (K 679), Harling (Norf) (W XXXIV, p. 88), Bury St Edmunds (R CIV, p. 194), and perhaps Weston Colville (Camb) (W XXXI, p. 80).

freedman enough timber to build himself a cabin, and with it a few acres of land. If this proved insufficient for his support, the cottager might hire himself out for wages on one or more of his free days. This freed-man of the lowest class is called in the mother tongue a *cotsetla*. We meet him first under this designation in 956, when King Eadwig makes a grant of 15 hides at Milton (Berks) and throws in six *cotsetlan*.[1]

For a number of reasons – pressure of growing population, the consequent drive to expand tillage, a desire to reward good service, a greater need for money than for labour – the lord may see fit to create larger holdings, of perhaps a yardland or more, and let them to rent-paying farmers. The rent-payer is a *gafolgelda*, and we remember here that where King Ine had spoken of the *gafolgelda* and the *gebur*, Alfred the Great classed both together as *ceorlisc* men.[2] We remember, too, that Alfred's treaty with Guthrum had equated the English *ceorl* settled on *gafol-land* with the Danish freedman. But the vaguely generic *ceorl* is being displaced in this context by the more specific *gebur*. The *gebur* is not a boor, any more than the *ceorl* is a churl as we understand the words, though we may well believe that he has much to make him boorish and churlish. Wynflæd calls her rent-payers at Chinnock "*geburas* settled on *gafol-land*." There is a shorter way of expressing this. The bounds of twenty hides at Hinksey, Seacourt, and Wytham (Oxon) granted to Abingdon Abbey *c.* 956 are described as the bounds of the *geburland*, and in 963 the *gebura londe* appears in the bounds of Laughern (Worcs).[3] Two persons at Bedwyn (Wilts) pay 300 pence each to be "done out of the *geburland*," given freedom, in other words, to go wherever they please.[4] The monks of Ely kept an extremely precise record of the *geburas* on their Hatfield estate (Herts) and of the marriages which took their children off to other villages, sometimes more than a dozen miles away. It is reasonable to guess that their offspring, like the couple at Bedwyn, had paid or were liable to pay for being "done out of the *geburland*."[5]

THE CUSTUMAL OF TIDENHAM

At some date between 956, when King Eadwig granted Tidenham (Glos) to the monks of Bath, and 1065, when they gave a lease of the manor to Archbishop Stigand, a custumal was drawn up, recording the

[1] CS 935.   [2] Above, p. 451.   [3] CS 1002, 1108.
[4] WAM LII, 1947–8, p. 364. The word survives in field-names in Wiltshire and elsewhere.—PN *Wilts*, p. 424.
[5] Earle, *op. cit.*, p. 275. This record seems to me to underline the lord's right over the person of the *gebur* rather than the bond which ties the *gebur* to the estate, as Seebohm and others have maintained.—*English Village Community*, p. 139 *n*; T. H. Aston, *op. cit.*, p. 72.

dues and services of the tenants.[1] Tidenham was a multiple estate at the confluence of the Rivers Wye and Severn. It included dependent settlements at Stroat, Milton, Kingston, Bishton, and Lancaut. It also had 95 fish-wears on the Wye and Severn, the great majority of them basket traps of the kind still in use today.[2] The lord of the manor claimed every alternate fish caught, and while in residence had to be informed when any fish were to be sold. Sturgeon, porpoises, herrings, and sea-fish were at all times reserved to him. The services of the *geneat* – of whom more presently – are stated in very vague and general terms, but the more servile *gebur* was bound to supply wooden rods for making fish-traps and fencing for the manorial demesne. The rent for each yardland, of which there were 27 at Stroat, 14 at Milton, and 13 at Kingston (now Sedbury), was twelve pence, besides fourpence as 'alms' to the church.

The principal agricultural service of the Tidenham *gebur* takes the form of 'week-work', labour performed on an unspecified number of days every week throughout the year. In each week he must plough half an acre, the seed for which he will fetch from his lord's barn, and a whole acre for church-scot for which he supplies the seed himself. He must reap an acre and a half, mow half an acre, and do work of any other kind that may be demanded of him. Besides the rent of his yardland, he must give sixpence and half a sester of honey after Easter, six sesters of malt at Lammas, and a ball of good net yarn at Martinmas. If he keeps pigs he must pay for mast and give three pigs out of the first seven and thereafter always the tenth. There is no need to labour the interesting points of resemblance and contrast between these services and those claimed in Alfred's day from the *ceorls* of Hurstbourne.[3]

THE 'RECTITUDINES'

To fill out the picture of manorial economy in the eleventh century we have the illuminating tract entitled *Rectitudines Singularum Personarum*, a text which has no surviving parallel before the Norman Conquest. It reads as if it had been prepared by Wulfstan, bishop of Worcester and archbishop of York, from memoranda left by Oswald, his predecessor in both sees.[4] It shows clear signs of drawing on experience of a large estate in the west midlands, but the writer insists that no two manors are exactly alike, that services are heavy on some, lighter on others.

---

[1] CS 927; R CIX, CXVII.
[2] Seebohm, *English Village Community*, pp. 151–3.   [3] See above, p. 453.
[4] For the text, see Liebermann, *Gesetze*, I, pp. 444–53; translation, EHD II, pp. 813–16. On the authorship, D. Bethurum in *Studies in Old English Literature in Honor of Arthur G. Brodeur*, Oregon, 1963, p. 165.

Since the obligations of the slave are limited only by what is feasible, they are not enumerated in detail, but the writer declares that a slave woman ought to have eight pounds of bread-corn, one sheep or three pence for winter food, one sester of beans for lenten food, and whey in summer or one penny. The male slave should have twelve pounds of good corn, the carcases of two sheep and a good cow for meat, and the right of cutting wood for fuel or building. The allowance of corn, if annual as Liebermann believed, seems small, but perhaps it is seed-corn, intended to be sown on the plough-acre which the writer says every bondman on the estate ought to have, and it will no doubt be supplemented by the meals which the lord will give his slaves while they are working for him. They are also entitled to a "harvest-handful" and to be feasted at Christmas and Easter.

We hear also of slaves employed as swineherds, bee-keepers, and herdsmen, each of whom is entitled to his perquisites. When they die, all their belongings go to the lord.

In the writer's opinion the *cotsetla* ought to have five acres or more; anything less will be inadequate. This humble tenant pays no rent, but is burdened with heavy services. On some estates he must work for his lord every Monday in the year, and on three days a week in August. As a day's work he is expected to reap an acre of oats and half an acre of other corn, after which the lord's reeve or bailiff should give him a sheaf as his perquisite. He may be called upon to keep watch on the sea-coast and to perform services incidental to the king's hunting. He pays church-scot at Martinmas and Peter's Pence on Ascension Day "as every free man ought to do." This last phrase should not be construed as implying that he is anything but a serf; it is put in only to remind him, rather pointedly, that being now so far emancipated as to occupy a cottage and a small holding, he incurs the normal obligations of a householder to the Church, obligations from which the slave is exempt.

The lord who sets his man up as a *gebur* should provide him with two oxen, one cow, six sheep, and seven acres already sown on his yardland, besides all necessary tools for his work and utensils for his house.[1] Both land and outfit remain the property of the lord, and will revert to him when the man dies. For the first year no rent is payable; thereafter the *gebur* must pay ten pence a year at Michaelmas, equivalent, we may note

---

[1] If we may assume a standard yardland of some thirty acres, half of which will lie fallow in any given year, the seven acres will be that half of the remainder which has to be sown with either winter or spring corn, according to the time of year. This seems a simpler and more likely explanation than Seebohm's. He assumes a threefold division of the yardland and accounts for the three acres out of ten left unsown by supposing them to be 'gafol-earth', not sown because no *gafol* is due in the first year. —*English Village Community*, p. 141.

FAH

in passing, to the rent that Alfred's *ceorls* had paid at Hurstbourne. He must perform week-work as ordered: on some manors for two days in each week of the year, and for three days a week at harvest and from Candlemas to Easter. At Martinmas he must pay two hens and 23 sesters of barley, presumably for church-scot, and at Easter a lamb or two pence. From the time when ploughing is begun until Martinmas he must plough an acre a week and fetch the seed for its sowing from the lord's barn. He must also plough three acres a year as 'boon-work' at the lord's request, two acres a year for his pasture-rights, and three acres a year as part of the rent for his holding: for these last he must provide the necessary seed-corn. Between Martinmas and Easter he takes his turn to watch at the lord's fold. He too, like the *cotsetla*, is liable for Peter's Pence. He must give six pence to the swineherd when he drives the village herd to the woods, and must join with another man of his own condition to maintain one of his lord's hounds. The writer adds that on some estates the *gebur* pays rent in honey, on some in meat, on some in ale. It all depends on the custom of the manor.

The *gebur* of the *Rectitudines* has been described as a man "trembling on the verge of serfdom."[1] To most of us he will seem well over the verge. He may have started life as a slave or fallen into slavery for one reason or another. If so, he has certainly gone up in the world, but his lord retains all the rights he had over him while enslaved, except the right of punishing him by the lash. If he is the younger son of a free husbandman too poor to keep him, he may be able to implead other free men in the hundred court, but he himself is in all probability justiciable in the court of his lord. These are matters of surmise; what is certain is that economically he is an utterly dependent being, possessing nothing that he can really call his own, and the only recognizable mark of his freedom is his obligation to pay a householder's dues to the Church.

THE 'GENEAT'

Well above him in rural society stands the *geneat*. There is nothing servile in his condition. On some manors he pays his lord a rent and gives him a swine a year in return for pasture-rights. He is expected to reap and mow on the demesne, to join with others in maintaining the hedge around the manor-house and in cutting and erecting the fences required when the lord goes hunting, to provide cartage service, to escort visitors, to entertain his lord, to keep guard over his person and his stables, and to ride on errands far or near wherever he may be directed. The Tidenham custumal says in much the same words that the *geneat* must work on or off the estate, whichever he is bidden, and ride

[1] Stenton, *Anglo-Saxon England*, p. 475.

and furnish cartage service and supply transport and drive herds "and
do many other things." For agricultural service he probably sends his
servants to lend a hand in the busy season or goes himself to superintend
the labours of the humbler tenants. A law of Edgar couples *geneatland*
with the lord's demesne as land from which tithe is due.[1] In a later law
the same king says that if a *geneatman* does not pay his rent by the
appointed day the lord should be forbearing and not exact any penalty;
if, however, the *geneat* resorts to violence he may lose his life as well as
his land.[2] The sensational picture of a recalcitrant *geneat* barricading
himself in his farmhouse and holding out there to the death does credit
to the lawgiver's imagination, but can seldom indeed have been realized
in practice. Normally the *geneat* is most in evidence when his lord
requires the services of a horseman. Thus when the bishop of Worcester
complains of encroachments on his woodland, the defendant orders his
geneat named Ecglaf to ride round with one of the bishop's clergy and
identify all the landmarks which the priest will read out from the old
charters of the estate.[3] We may safely identify the *geneat* with the
countryman of superior status who will figure in the Domesday account
of many manors, particularly in the west midlands, as a *radcniht* or
mounted retainer.

The author of the *Rectitudines* goes on to detail the customary perquisites of the manorial servants. The sower may have a basketful of
every kind of seed he sows; the oxherd may pasture his cow and two or
more oxen with the lord's oxen on the common; the cowherd is to have
the milk of a grown cow for seven days after she has calved, and that of
a young cow for a fortnight; the goatherd ought to have a year-old kid,
the milk of the herd after Martinmas, and before that his portion of
whey. The shepherd is entitled to have twelve nights' dung at Christmas,
one lamb, one bell-wether's fleece, the milk of his flock for a week
after the equinox, and a bowlful of whey or buttermilk all through the
summer. Any remaining buttermilk is for the cheese-maker, who – if
the text at this point has not been misunderstood – can keep a hundred
cheeses for herself. The overseer of the granary takes all the corn spilt
at the door of the barn. Every tree blown down in the wood belongs to
the woodward.

The *Rectitudines* ends with a cheerful allusion to feasting at Christmas,
at Easter, at reaping, ploughing, mowing, at the making of hay-ricks,
the gathering of wood, the making of corn-ricks, and on other occasions
of rustic revelry.

[1] II Edgar, I, in A. J. Robertson, *The Laws of the Kings of England from Edmund to
Henry I*, Cambridge, 1925, p. 20.
[2] IV Edgar, I, §§1, 2, *ibid.*, p. 28.   [3] CS 574.

THE 'GEREFA'

In the same manuscript as the *Rectitudines*, and probably by the same author, is a tract called *Gerefa*.[1] It deals with the functions of the reeve, whom it depicts as literally a man for all seasons, a walking encyclopaedia of country lore. The list of tools he is expected to provide runs to fifty items, followed by a further list of sixty-three necessaries, including beehives, beer-barrels, and candlesticks. "He ought never to neglect anything that may prove useful, not even a mousetrap." The most interesting part of the tract is its picture of the agricultural routine, which is given with the caveat that in many districts the work of the farm begins earlier than in others. In May, June, and July men must harrow, spread manure, set up hurdles, shear the sheep, make good the fences and buildings, cut wood, clear the ground of weeds, make sheep-pens, construct fish-weirs and mills. During the next three months they reap, mow, set woad with the dibble, thatch and cover the crops, clean out the folds, prepare the sheep-pens and pig-sties and ploughs. During the winter they plough, in frosty weather split timber, prepare orchards, put the cattle in stalls and the pigs in sties, set up a drying oven on the threshing floor, and provide a hen-roost. Finally in spring they graft, sow beans, set a vineyard, make ditches, hew wood to keep out the wild deer, set madder, sow flax and woad, and plant the vegetable garden. "I have spoken about what I know," says the writer in conclusion; "he who knows better, let him say more."

AELFRIC'S 'COLLOQUY'

More had in fact been said earlier, and more imaginatively, by Ælfric, monk and schoolmaster at Cerne Abbey in Dorset. Nearly all abbeys at the time housed a number of oblates, boys whose not over-fond parents had placed them at a tender age in a monastery to be trained as monks. To help his oblates with their Latin, Ælfric composed a charming *Colloquy* in which each pupil in turn impersonates a labouring man and answers questions about his occupation.[2]

First the ploughman describes himself as rising at daybreak in all weathers. After yoking the oxen and fastening the share and coulter, he must plough daily a full acre and more. He is accompanied by a boy who applies the goad to the oxen and is hoarse from cold and shouting. He fills the cattle-stalls with hay, carries out the dung, and waters the oxen. "It is heavy toil, because I am not free."

[1] Liebermann, *Gesetze*, I, pp. 453–5; translated by W. W. Skeat in W. Cunningham, *The Growth of English Industry and Commerce*, 5th ed., Cambridge, 1915, pp. 573–6.
[2] *Ælfric's Colloquy*, ed. G. N. Garmonsway, 1939.

At the end of the day the oxherd leads the oxen to the pasture and watches over them all night to guard against thieves. In the morning he hands them over, well fed and watered, to the ploughman.

The shepherd leads his flock to pasture, with dogs to protect them from wolves. He shifts their folds, milks the ewes twice daily, and makes butter and cheese. (In fact this would usually be done by his wife.)

The king's huntsman cuts the throats of the prey his dogs have driven into nets. With hounds he pursues the stag, the boar, the roedeer, the she-goat, and sometimes the hare. The king feeds and clothes him, and occasionally gives him a horse or a bracelet for his trouble.

The fisherman uses fish-hooks and baskets. He takes eels, pike, minnows, trout, lampreys, and generally all freshwater fish. Sometimes he fishes the sea for herrings, salmon, dolphins, sturgeon, oysters, mussels, cockles, plaice, flounders, sole, crabs, and lobsters. He does not join the fishing-fleets which go out whaling; lucrative as that is, he thinks it too dangerous. He could always sell more fish if the catch were larger.

The fowler uses nets, traps, lime, whistling, and hawks. He likes full-grown hawks because in winter they feed themselves and him. In summer he lets them fly to the woodland and fend for themselves; they would eat too much at home. In the autumn he takes and tames their young.

The merchant imports purple and other dyes, gold and precious stones, wine, oil, silk, ivory, bronze; at times also tin, sulphur, and glass.

Questioned about the value of his calling, the cook retorts, in strikingly twentieth-century terms: "If you try to do without me, you will all be cooks yourselves, and none of you will be a lord."

This leads in conclusion to the oblate's own diet. It includes meat, eggs, fish, butter, cheese, and beans. His drink is beer, or failing beer water. Wine is not for the young, but for the old and wise.

SOCIAL MOBILITY

Enough has been said to show how wrong it would be to think of Anglo-Saxon society in terms of caste. Hungry men might enslave themselves for food in the evil days, but particular and collective acts of manumission provided frequent ways of escape from downright slavery into the mitigated bondage we call serfdom. At a given moment in any period some men are prospering while others less fortunate or less industrious are sinking in the social scale. Difficult as it might be for a half-free cottager to thrive, the more substantial *gebur* could some-times find means to get himself "done out of the *geburland*." "It often happens," wrote Archbishop Wulfstan, "that a miserable slave earns freedom from a *ceorl*, and a *ceorl* becomes worthy of a thegn's rights through an earl's gift."[1] A compilation put together by the same prelate or in his circle shows more explicitly how the *ceorl* might become a gentleman. "If a *ceorl* prospered so that he had fully five hides of his own land, church and kitchen, bell-house and fortified dwelling, a seat and special office in the king's hall, then was he thenceforth entitled to the rights of a thegn."[2]

How could a *ceorl* acquire the five hides of property in land which qualified him to rank as a thegn? The patronage of an earl or other magnate was not the only way. In their study of Laxton the Orwins dwelt upon the opportunities arising more particularly from the organization of farming in open fields. A lad would seek employment away from home and save a few pounds from his wages. When a cottage fell vacant he would apply for it and continue to work for wages while cultivating his plot in his free time, if necessary hiring plough-beasts from his neighbours. In six months he could buy a few sheep with the proceeds of his first harvest and use his right to graze them at no expense to himself on the common and the fallow field. In due time he might sell them at a profit. In this way he could build up some capital by the profit on his crops and stock till he felt strong enough to apply for a larger holding and become a full-time farmer. He might move again, or even more than once, each time to a larger holding until he reached the top of the agricultural ladder.[3] We have no means of knowing how often this happened in the Old English period, but that it did happen sometimes is proved by a reference, in a charter issued by Ethelred II in 984, to eight hides of land formerly held by a *ceorl* ("rusticus") named Ætheric.[4] The bounds identify this property with Leverton in the valley of the Kennet, and it is pertinent to recall that Berkshire is a county in which numerous charters vouch for the presence of open fields.

THE FREEDOM OF THE TOWN

Towns, as well as open fields, held out prospects of wealth and freedom. The security of boroughs and 'ports' naturally tended to attract a settled population. It also led in time to the establishment of borough courts distinct from the courts of rural manors and hundreds. The laws of Edgar require the borough-moot to meet three times a year, the hundred-moot every four weeks, and the shire-moot twice a

[1] Quoted by Stenton, *Collected Papers*, p. 388.
[2] Liebermann, *Gesetze*, I, p. 456.
[3] C. S. and C. S. Orwin, *The Open Fields*, pp. 171, 172.
[4] K 1282. E. John, *Orbis Britanniae*, p. 138, plausibly suggests that the simple *ceorl* who played a heroic part in the battle of Maldon was a man of this type.

year.[1] The burgesses or portmen would live chiefly by trade and handi-craft, not agriculture. In some boroughs, it is true, an obligation to render agricultural service on the lord's demesne would linger on, and in others the burgesses would continue to cultivate the soil outside the walls on their own account. But their hallmark is the payment of a uniform money-rent for their houses. They are not serfs of the manor, and nobody will be so misguided as to call them *ceorls*. Their status is nearer to that of the *geneat*; it even approximates to that of the thegn.[2]

THE THEGN

The word thegn has by this time ousted the older *gesith*. The *gesith* had been or had hoped to become a landed proprietor with men on his estate for whose good behaviour he was responsible, but he himself might well be the man of a higher lord.[3] The same is true of a thegn who has acquired his position by gift of an earl or bishop, like that Eadric to whom Archbishop Oswald granted three hides at Tiddington (Wark), increased to five hides eight years later.[4]

To the author of the *Rectitudines* the thegn was one who held his land by charter, subject to the three common dues of military service, the repair of fortresses, and work on bridges. Other obligations might be laid on him by royal edict, such as service connected with the deer-fence at the king's residence, equipping a vessel for coastguard duty, acting as a personal bodyguard, paying church-scot and Peter's Pence, "and other things, many and various."

When a lady named Wulfwaru made her will, she divided her estate at Butcombe (Som) between her eldest son and her younger daughter in equal shares, and enjoined them also to share the mansion-house "as evenly as they can."[5] If a five-hide thegn used his power of testamentary disposition to divide his property in this way between two sons, they would inherit his rank but their economic position would be little better than that of a *geneat*. In the late Old English period the rural population included numberless petty thegns distinguishable only in title from the neighbouring farmers. At the other end of the scale were rich men like Wulfric, the founder of Burton Abbey, whose will disposed of more than seventy villages in Staffordshire, Derbyshire, and six other counties.[6] To run this complex he must have employed a small army of reeves and other officials.

---

[1] I Edgar, 1; III Edgar, 5 (Robertson, *op. cit.*, pp. 16, 26). In 1018 a mortgage of land in Devon is formally communicated to the borough courts (*burhwiton*) of Exeter, Totnes, Lydford, and Barnstaple.—*Crawford Charters*, IV, p. 9.

[2] Cf. J. Tait, *The Medieval English Borough*, Manchester, 1936, pp. 82–5.

[3] See above, p. 441. [4] K 617, 651. [5] W XXI. [6] W XVII.

EALDORMEN AND EARLS

In authority and influence even such wealthy nobles as Wulfric took second place after the ealdorman. From the time of Edgar, if not before, the ealdorman shared with the diocesan bishop the presidency of the shire-court.[1] In time of war he called up the militia and commanded them in the field. References in charter boundaries to "the ealdorman's land" imply that certain estates were earmarked for his maintenance. He was also entitled to a share of the fines levied to the king's use in boroughs, hundreds, and the shire. In process of time he was appointed to govern not one shire as of old, but two or more. Towards the close of the Old English period his enlarged sphere of office found expression in a change of title. By analogy with the Norse *jarl*, the English *eorl* came to mean, not as originally any nobleman, but, at first in Northumbria and finally over the rest of England, the governor of a province which might be co-extensive with a former kingdom, a Wessex or a Mercia. At the same time it became normal for a son to succeed a father in his earldom, though his appointment still had to be confirmed, and could on occasion be revoked, by the king,

CHURCHMEN WITH SECULAR POWER

Thus by the end of the tenth century England was largely dominated by rich and formidably powerful lay magnates. If the king was to keep his supremacy intact, he needed a counterpoise on which he could rely. The problem was not peculiar to this country. In Germany and Italy Edgar's contemporary and uncle by marriage, the emperor Otto, solved it by granting secular power to bishops and abbots. In England Edgar did the same by giving them large powers over the hundreds in which their estates lay. The most conspicuous beneficiaries of this policy were the two leaders of the current monastic reformation, Ethelwold, bishop of Winchester, and Oswald, bishop of Worcester. Ethelwold received the hundreds of Chilcomb (Hants), Downton (Wilts), and Taunton (Som). According to a statement later made by Edgar's widow concerning the large manor of Taunton, the king "commanded every one of his thegns who held any land on the estate that they should hold it in conformity with the bishop's will, or else give it up." All the inhabitants, including those of the highest rank, became as fully subject to the bishop's lordship as the inhabitants of royal manors were to the king's. Amercements and forfeitures, all the profits of justice, henceforth went to the bishop. He also took the market tolls and burgage rents from Taunton itself, the earliest known example in England of a mediatized

[1] III Edgar, 5, §2 (Robertson, p. 26).

or seignorial borough.[1] Similarly in Worcestershire Bishop Oswald acquired full secular jurisdiction over the triple hundred of Oswaldslow, to the complete exclusion of the ealdorman of Mercia and his deputies. The bishops responded to these handsome concessions by habitually magnifying in the strongest possible terms the authority of the anointed and crowned monarch.

OSWALD'S LEASES

Thanks to the careful preservation of the Worcester records it is possible to make out some of the uses to which Oswald put his viceregal powers. The texts of seventy-two leases granted by him between 962 and 980 are extant. Fifty-six of them deal with properties of less than five hides, and only five with lands of higher assessment. Eight of the recipients are churchmen, four are the bishop's kinsmen, one is a "matron," and two are artificers, but the great majority are thegns, *ministri*, occasionally styled *milites*, *cnihtas*, or *fideles*, the last probably implying men who had taken an oath of fealty to the bishop. They must have been petty thegns indeed, unless they possessed other lands of their own, as presumably did the king's thegn to whom Oswald granted three hides.[2] Nineteen leases impose the three common dues; thirteen require the payment of church-scot; thirty state no conditions at all.

Strictly speaking, land held on lease should have been described as loan-land, but Oswald did his best to give his leases the form and semblance of royal charters creating bookland. In three cases, indeed, he states that the recipient of his 'book' already holds the land as loan-land.[3] He even goes so far as to speak of perpetual inheritance, but the inheritance is not really meant to be perpetual; it is limited to a term of lives, normally three lives, after which the land must revert to the church of Worcester. It becomes clear on closer study that the main object of these so-called 'books' is to put on record the reversionary title of the bishop and his church, a very necessary precaution, for experience showed that it would be anything but a matter of course to regain possession of an estate held on lease by one family over three lifetimes.

The terms on which Oswald granted his leases, then, are not fully revealed in these texts. For fuller information we turn to the solemn letter by which Oswald informs King Edgar how he has been granting to his faithful men for the term of three lives the lands committed to his charge. He does so to the end that "succeeding bishops may know what to exact from these men according to the covenant they have made

[1] For a discussion of the early history of Taunton and a criticism of the sources, see H. P. R. Finberg, *The Early Charters of Wessex*, pp. 221–3, 229–30.
[2] CS 1091.   [3] K 617, 651, 679.

with me." The men must "fulfil the whole law of riding which belongs to riding men." They must pay church-scot, toll, and pannage; lend their horses and ride on errands themselves; be ready to build bridges and to burn lime for church-building; erect a hedge for the bishop's hunt and lend their own hunting-spears if required. In consideration of the fief ("beneficium") which they hold on loan, they must swear to obey with all humility and subjection the bishop as their lord and *archiductor*, their commander in chief. When the term of the lease expires, the bishop shall be free to keep the lands for his own use or to let them out for a further term, always provided that these services are duly rendered in accordance with the quantity of the land.[1]

The emphasis Oswald lays on riding service recalls what the *Rectitudines* had to say about the services of the *geneat* and points forward to his descendant the Domesday *radcniht*. Historians preoccupied with the abstraction they call feudalism have argued at length about Oswald's famous letter. Some find and others fail to find in those riding tenants the precursors of the Norman knights. The bishop's leases, it is true, contain no specific demand for services of a military character, but we must not ignore the significance of the fact that Oswald styles himself *archiductor*. This undoubtedly means that in time of war the bishop will either command the levies in person, as a later bishop, Ealdred, did in 1049, when he took the field against the Welsh, or delegate the work to a lay captain, such as that Edric who in the Confessor's reign led the bishop's "army" into battle, and was also helmsman of the bishop's warship.[2] It is hard to improve on Maitland's summing up. "Dependent tenure is here and, we may say, feudal tenure, and even tenure by knight's service, for though the English *cniht* of the tenth century differs much from the knight of the twelfth, still it is a change in military tactics rather than a change in legal ideas that is required to convert the one into the other...The day for heavy cavalry and professional militancy was fast approaching when Oswald subjected his tenants to the *lex equitandi*."[3]

FUNCTIONS OF LORDSHIP

In its latest phase Anglo-Saxon society was permeated from top to bottom by the concept of lordship. Not that there was anything new in this. Lords had been there from the beginning, and we have seen that

---

[1] CS 1136.

[2] "Edricus, qui fuit, tempore regis Edwardi, stermannus navis episcopi, et ductor exercitus ejusdem episcopi ad servitium regis."—*Hemingi Chartularium Ecclesiae Wigorniensis*, ed. T. Hearne, Oxford, 1723, I, p. 81. For the events of 1049 see *The Anglo-Saxon Chronicle*, tr. D. Whitelock, p. 114.

[3] *Domesday Book and Beyond*, p. 309.

from the end of the seventh century, if not earlier, kings were holding them responsible for the good behaviour of their men. At first they shared this responsibility with groups of kindred. The fact of kinship loomed large in primitive minds, and for centuries the kindred occupied a place in the foreground of law-enforcement as well as in personal relations. As late as Athelstan's reign (924–39) the citizens of London contemplated the possibility that a group of kinsmen might be powerful enough to frustrate them in the exercise of their legal rights.[1] But much had occurred to loosen old ties, and three-quarters of a century later we find Archbishop Wulfstan complaining that a kinsman does not now protect a kinsman any more than a stranger.[2] More and more the duty of supervision and protection was devolving upon the lord. It is a mere accident that the charter of 956 by which King Eadwig gave the arch-bishop of York rights of secular jurisdiction ("sake and soke") over Southwell and the discontinuous group of villages appendant to South-well has survived to give the first unequivocal evidence for the existence of private courts of justice in England.[3] There is no reason to believe that Southwell was in fact the earliest manor to hold a court of its own, and we know that in the following reign not single manors but whole hundreds with their courts were handed over to ecclesiastical magnates.

Protection was the obverse of the loyalty a lord required from his men. To him they looked for support when in trouble with their neighbours or the public courts. Cnut complains that some lords represent their free men as slaves and their slaves as free, whichever makes it easier to defend their cause.[4]

The troubles of the ninth and tenth centuries gravely disturbed the social fabric and left behind a number of lordless men. Such men were an anomaly on which legislators cast a decidedly unfriendly eye. Athelstan commanded the relatives of a lordless man to settle him in a fixed abode and find him a lord at an assembly of the folk. He also penalized any lord who should provoke an appeal to the king by failing to redress a wrong done by one of his men. Every lord must stand surety for his men. To remain lordless, or to plot against one's lord, is to risk outlawry and death.[5]

Where earlier laws had spoken of the landlord (*landhlaford*), the codes of Ethelred II and Cnut speak of the *landrica*, the land-ruler, or lord of the manor, and entrust him with multifarious rights and duties. He shares with the wapentake the money lodged as security by men under

---

[1] VI Athelstan, 8 §2 (*Attenborough*, p. 162).   [2] EHD I, p. 856.
[3] CS 1029. See also CS 1052, with its list of eight villages over which the lord of Howden has sake and soke.
[4] II Cnut, 20 §1 (Robertson, p. 184).
[5] II Athelstan, 2, 3, 4 (Attenborough, pp. 128, 130).

arrest, and with the king's portreeve the security deposited by any one who seeks to clear a thief.[1] It is for him to see that a man charged with theft goes to the ordeal, and if the accused evades the ordeal, half the fine he incurs goes to the owner of the goods, half to the *landrica*.[2] The *landrica* may impound livestock acquired without surety.[3] He sends his own reeve with the bishop's to collect a defaulter's tithe.[4] It is his duty to suppress heathen sanctuaries. If a villager fails to pay Peter's Pence, the *landrica* must pay it for him and impound the villager's ox.[5] We may think it highly unlikely that a government which employs the lord of the manor to collect a tax due to the pope will not also employ him to collect taxes due to the king.

These enactments assume that the whole country is parcelled out into manors, each under the jurisdiction of a *landrica*. They also take it for granted that every lordless man has by now complied with Athelstan's injunction to find himself a lord, and that as a rule the lord is the local holder of book-right. Over much of England this was true enough, but it was not so in the eastern counties. Here many a land-book had been practically nullified when its holder fell in battle, leaving no legitimate heir. Many charters no doubt went up in flames when the Vikings burnt down the monasteries where they had been deposited for safe keeping. Moreover, land had changed hands often and easily, not by charter or lease, but by the testimony of the wapentake. Under such disruptive impacts the fabric of English landlordship had collapsed. Where the manor survived, its lord might well be too poor and insignificant to give his men the security they needed. Athelstan's decree obliged the lordless man to put himself under somebody possessing 'sake and soke', to become what a later generation would call a sokeman of that personage, but – and this was its fatal weakness – it did not oblige him to seek a patron in or near his own village, nor did it tell him what to do if no one in the village possessed rights of sake and soke. It left him free to go far afield and make what terms he could with some magnate – any magnate – powerful enough to lend effective support if he got into a scrape, but too remote to interfere with the daily business of his life. And if his neighbour had done homage to the earl, he might well think it a clever move to place himself under the still more exalted patronage of the archbishop. It was a situation which might have been expressly designed to produce tenurial chaos, just such a tangled network of personal and manorial relationships as would confront the Domesday

---

[1] III Ethelred, 3 §§2, 3; 7 (Robertson, pp. 66, 68).
[2] III Ethelred, 4 §§1, 2 (Robertson, p. 66).
[3] III Ethelred, 5 (Robertson, p. 66).
[4] VIII Ethelred, 8; I Cnut, 8 §2 (Robertson, pp. 120, 164).
[5] EHD I, p. 438, nos. 54, 59.

commissioners in the eastern shires and perplex them by its marked contrast with the more orderly, old-established society of the south and west.

Alfred the Great had remarked that a king required three classes of men with which to fashion a well-wrought kingdom. He needed men who work, men who pray, and men who fight.[1] These three components of a well-ordered society all awaited Edward, the only surviving son of Ethelred II, when he returned to his native land. The tillers of the soil, from the slave to the comparatively free man who cultivated his farm and occasionally served his lord as a mounted retainer, were organized in clearly distinguished grades to support the landowners who administered the courts of manor, hundred, and shire, and manned the army in wartime. The men of prayer, in a hierarchy of their own, gave the society which maintained them all that it knew of art, scholarship, and religious faith. All looked up to the monarch as the tie which bound the edifice together. Edward, who in 1042 succeeded to the throne of his forefathers, had spent the whole of his early manhood in Normandy. His accession marks the end of Danish rule and the true beginning of the Norman period. To his Norman successors he bequeathed a rich and well cultivated land and a social structure which despite certain weaknesses was more complex, more advanced, than they had known how to build for themselves at home.

[1] EHD I, p. 846.

SELECT BIBLIOGRAPHY

Alcock, L. 'Celtic Archaeology and Art', *Celtic Studies in Wales*, ed. Davies, 1963.
   Dinas Powys: An Iron Age, Dark Age and Early Medieval Settlement in Glamorgan. Cardiff, 1963.
   'Excavations at Degannwy Castle, Caernarvonshire, 1961–6', *Arch. J.* CXXIV, 1967.
   'Hill Forts in Wales and the Marches', *Ant.* XXXIX, 1965.
   'Pottery and Settlements in Wales and the March A.D. 400–700', *Culture and Environment*, ed. Foster and Alcock, 1963.
   'Settlement Patterns in Celtic Britain', *Ant.* XXXVI, 1962.
   'Some reflections on Early Welsh Society and Economy', WHR II, 1964.
   'Wales in the Fifth to Seventh Centuries A.D.: Archaeological Evidence', *Prehistoric and Early Wales*, ed. Foster and Daniel, 1965.
Ancient Laws and Institutes of Wales. Record Commission, London, 1841.
Angles and Britons: O'Donnell Lectures. Cardiff, 1963.
Anglo-Saxon Chronicle, The, a revised translation ed. by D. Whitelock. London, 1961.
Asser's Life of King Alfred, ed. W. H. Stevenson. Oxford, 1904.
Attenborough, F. L. (ed.). *The Laws of the Earliest English Kings.* Cambridge, 1922; reprinted New York, 1963.
Ball, D. F. *The District around Rhyl and Denbigh*, Memoirs of the Soil Survey of Great Britain, 1960.
Ballard, A. *The Domesday Inquest*, London, 1906.
Barker, P. A. 'Excavations at Hen Domen, Montgomery, 1969', *Arch. J.* CXXVI, 1969.
Barlow, M. W. and Hanson, R. P. C. (eds.). *Christianity in Britain, 300–700*, 1968.
Bede. *Venerabilis Baedae Opera Historica*, ed. C. Plummer. Oxford, 1896.
Beresford, M. and Hurst, J. G. (eds.). *Deserted Medieval Villages.* London, 1971.
Binchy, D. A. *Celtic and Anglo-Saxon Kingship.* Oxford, 1970.
   'The Linguistic and Historical Value of the Irish Law Tracts', *Brit. Acad.* XXIX, 1943.
   'Linguistic and Legal Archaisms in the Celtic Law-Books', *Philological Soc.*, 1959.
   'Some Celtic Legal Terms', *Celtica* III, 1956.
   (ed.). *Crith Gablach.* Dublin, 1941.
Birch, W. de G. (ed.). *Cartularium Saxonicum.* London, 1885–93.
Birley, E. B. *Britain and the Roman Army.* Kendal, 1953.
Bloch, M. *Les caractères originaux de l'histoire rurale française.* 1st ed. Paris, 1931: 2nd ed. vol. I, Paris 1952; vol. II, Paris, 1956.
Boon, G. C. 'A Christian Monogram at Caerwent', BBCS XIX, 1960–2.
   'A note on the Byzantine Coins said to have been found at Caerwent', BBCS XVII, 1956–8.
Bowen, E. G. *Celtic Seaways and Settlements.* Cardiff, 1969.
Bowen, H. C. *Ancient Fields.* London, N.D. [1962].
Chadwick, H. M. *The Origin of the English Nation.* Cambridge, 1907.
   Studies on Anglo-Saxon Institutions. Cambridge, 1905; reprinted New York, 1963.
Chadwick, N. K. *Celtic Britain.* London, 1964.
Charles, B. G. *Old Norse relations with Wales.* Cardiff, 1934.
   'The Welsh, their language and Place-names in Archenfield and Oswestry', *Angles and Britons: O'Donnell Lectures.* Cardiff, 1963.
Clark, G. T. (ed.). *Cartae et Alia Munimenta*, VI. Cardiff, 1910.
Clark, G. T. 'Manorial Particulars of the Vale of Glamorgan', *Arch. Camb.*, 4th ser., IX, 1878.

Collingwood, R. G. and Myres, J. N. L. *Roman Britain and the English Settlements.* 2nd ed., Oxford, 1937.

Collingwood, R. G. and Wright, R. P. *Roman Inscriptions in Britain*, I. Oxford, 1965.

Columella, Lucius Iunius Moderatus. *De re rustica.* Loeb edn, ed. H. B. Ash. London, 1941–55.

Crawford, O. G. S. *Air Survey and Archaeology.* Ordnance Survey Professional Papers, N.S.7. 2nd ed. Southampton, 1924.

Crawford, O. G. S. and Keiller, A. *Wessex from the Air.* Oxford, 1928.

Darby, H. C. and Terrett, I. B. *The Domesday Geography of Midland England.* Cambridge, 1954.

Davies, E. (ed.). *Celtic Studies in Wales.* Cardiff, 1963.

De Courson, A. (ed.). *Cartulaire de l'Abbaye de Redon.* Paris, 1863.

Dickson, A. *The Husbandry of the Ancients.* Edinburgh, 1798.

Dillon, M. and Chadwick, N. K. *The Celtic Realms.* London, 1967.

Dimock, J. F. (ed.). *Giraldi Cambrensis Opera*, VI, Rolls ser. 21, 1868.

Dolley, A. H. M. *The Hiberno-Norse Coins in the British Museum.* London, 1966.

Dopsch, A. *The Economic and Social Foundations of European Civilization.* London, 1937.

Dugdale, W. *Monasticon Anglicanum*, ed. J. Caley, H. Ellis, and B. Bandinel. London, 1817–30.

Earle, J. *A Hand-Book to the Land-Charters and other Saxonic Documents.* Oxford, 1888.

Eddius Stephanus, *Life of Bishop Wilfrid*, ed. B. Colgrave. Cambridge, 1927.

Edwards, J. G. 'The Historical Study of the Welsh Law Books', TRHS, 5th series, XII, 1962.

'Studies in the Welsh Laws since 1928', WHR, *Special Number, The Welsh Laws*, 1963.

Ekwall, E. *The Concise Oxford Dictionary of English Place-Names.* 4th ed. Oxford, 1960.

Studies in English Place-Names. Stockholm, 1936.

Ellis, H. (ed.). *The Record of Caernarvon.* Record Commission, London, 1838.

Ellis, T. P. 'The Catholic Church in the Welsh Laws', *Y Cymmrodor* XLII, 1931.

Welsh Tribal Law and Custom in the Middle Ages, 2 vols. Oxford, 1926.

Emanuel, H. D. *The Latin Texts of the Welsh Laws.* Cardiff, 1967.

Emery, F. 'The Farming Regions of Wales', *The Agrarian History of England and Wales*, IV, ed. Thirsk. Cambridge, 1967.

English Historical Documents, I, c. 500–1014, ed. D. Whitelock. London, 1955.

Evans, J. Gwenogfryn (ed.). *Facsimile of the Chirk Codex of the Welsh Laws.* Llanbedrog, 1909.

Eyre, S. R. and Jones, G. R. J. (eds.). *Geography as Human Ecology.* London, 1966.

Felix's Life of St Guthlac, ed. B. Colgrave. Cambridge, 1956.

Finberg, H. P. R. *The Early Charters of Wessex.* Leicester, 1964.

The Early Charters of the West Midlands. Leicester, 1961.

Lucerna. Studies of some Problems in the Early History of England. London, 1964.

Tavistock Abbey: A Study in the Social and Economic History of Devon. Cambridge, 1951; 2nd. ed. Newton Abbot, 1969.

West-Country Historical Studies. Newton Abbot, 1969.

(ed.) *Gloucestershire Studies.* Leicester, 1957.

Fleuriot, L. *Dictionnaire des Gloses en Vieux Breton.* Paris, 1964.

Foster, I. Ll. 'Wales and North Britain', *Arch. Camb.* CXVIII, 1969.

Foster, I. Ll. and Alcock, L. (eds.). *Culture and Environment.* London, 1963.

Foster, I. Ll. and Daniel, G. (eds.). *Prehistoric and Early Wales.* London, 1965.

Fowler, P. J. and Thomas, A. C. 'Arable Fields of the Pre-Norman Period at Gwithian', *Corn. Arch.* I, 1962.

Fox, A. 'Early Christian Period: Settlement Sites and Other Remains', *A Hundred Years of Welsh Archaeology, Centenary Volume 1846–1946*, ed. Nash-Williams, N.D.

Fox, Sir Cyril. *The Archaeology of the Cambridge Region.* Cambridge, 1923.

The Personality of Britain. 4th ed. Cardiff, 1943.

Offa's Dyke. London, 1955.

Frank, T. (ed.). *An Economic Survey of Ancient Rome.* Baltimore, 1933-40.

Fremersdorf, F. *Der römische Gutshof Köln-Müngersdorf.* Berlin, 1933.

Frere, S. *Britannia.* London, 1967.

Galbraith, V. H. and Tait, J. (eds.). *Herefordshire Domesday c. 1160–1170.* London, 1950.

Gardner, W. and Savory, H. N. *Dinorben, A hill fort occupied in the Early Iron Age and Roman times.* Cardiff, 1964.

Godwin, H. *The History of the British Flora.* Cambridge, 1956.

Gray, H. L. *English Field Systems.* Cambridge (Mass.), 1915; reprinted London, 1959.

Grenier, A. *Manuel d'archéologie préhistorique, celtique, et gallo-romaine*, VI, ii. Paris, 1934.

Gresham, C. A. 'A Further Note on Ancient Welsh Measurements of Land', *Arch. Camb.* CI, 1951.

Guilcher, A. 'Le finage des champs dans le Cartulaire de Redon', *Annales de Bretagne* LIII, 1946.

Haddan, A. W. and Stubbs, W. *Councils and Ecclesiastical Documents Relating to Great Britain and Ireland.* Oxford, 1869–71, reprinted 1965.

Hall, A. D. *The Soil: an Introduction to the Scientific Study of the Growth of Crops.* 4th ed. London, 1945.

Hart, C. R. *The Early Charters of Eastern England.* Leicester, 1966.

Haverfield, F. *The Romanization of Roman Britain.* 4th ed. Oxford, 1923.

Hogg, A. H. A. 'Excavations at Pen Llystyn', *Arch. J.* CXXV, 1968.

'Garn Boduan and Tre'r Ceiri, excavations at two Caernarvonshire Hill-forts', *Arch. J.* CXVII, 1960.

Hoskins, W. G. *The Making of the English Landscape.* London, 1955.

The Westward Expansion of Wessex. Leicester, 1960.

Howells, B. E. 'Medieval Settlement in Dyfed', *The Land of Dyfed in Early Times*, ed. D. Moore, Cardiff, 1964.

Hughes, K. *The Church in Early Irish Society.* London, 1966.

Jack, R. I. 'The Lordship of Dyffryn Clwyd in 1324', *Denbigh Hist. Soc.* XVII.

Jackson, K. 'The Britons in Southern Scotland', *Ant.* XXIX, 1955.

The Gododdin. Edinburgh, 1969.

A Historical Phonology of Breton. Dublin, 1967.

Language and History in Early Britain. Edinburgh, 1953.

Jarrett, M. G. and Dobson, B. (eds.). *Britain and Rome: essays presented to E. Birley.* Kendal, 1966.

Jenkins, D. *Cyfraith Hywel.* Llandysul, 1970.

'A Lawyer looks at Welsh Land Law', *Hon. Soc. Cymm.*, 1967.

'Legal and Comparative Aspects of the Welsh Laws', WHR, *Special Number, The Welsh Laws*, 1963.

(ed.). *Llyfr Colan.* Cardiff, 1963.

Jenkins, G. (ed.). *Studies in Folk Life.* London, 1969.

John, E. *Land Tenure in Early England.* Leicester, 1960, 1964.

Orbis Britanniae, and other studies. Leicester, 1966.

Jolliffe, J. E. A. 'Northumbrian Institutions', *EHR* XLI, 1926.

Jones, A. H. M. *The Later Roman Empire.* Oxford, 1964.

Jones, E. D. 'The Book of Llandaff', *National Library of Wales Jnl* IV, 1945–6.

Jones, G. D. B. 'The Dolaucothi Gold Mines I: The Surface Evidence', *Ant. J.* XLIX, 1964.
Jones, G. D. B., Blakey, I. J. and Macpherson, E. C. F. 'Dolaucothi: The Roman Aqueduct', BBCS XIX, 1960–2.
Jones, G. R. J. 'Die Entwicklung der ländlichen Besiedlung in Wales', *Zeitschrift für Agrargeschichte und Agrarsoziologie* X, 1962.
'The Distribution of Bond Settlements in North-West Wales', WHR II, 1964.
'The Distribution of Medieval Settlement in Anglesey', *Anglesey Antiq. Soc.*, 1955.
'Early Settlement in Arfon; the setting of Tre'r Ceiri', *Caernarvon Hist. Soc.*, 1963.
'Early Territorial Organization in England and Wales', *Geografiska Annaler* XLIII, 1961.
'The Llanynys Quillets: A Measure of Landscape Transformation in North Wales', *Denbighshire Hist. Soc.* XIII, 1964.
'Medieval open fields and associated settlement patterns in North-West Wales', *Géographie et Histoire Agraires, Annales de l'est*, Mémoire no. 21, 1959.
'The Pattern of Settlement on the Welsh Border', AHR VIII, 1960.
'Rural Settlement in Anglesey', *Geography as Human Ecology*, ed. Eyre and Jones, 1966.
'Some Medieval Rural Settlements in North Wales', *Institute of British Geographers*, 1953.
'The Tribal System in Wales: A Re-assessment in the light of Settlement Studies', WHR I, 1961.
Jones, T. 'The Black Book of Carmarthen: "Stanzas of the Graves"', *B. Acad.* LIII.
Kemble, J. M. (ed.). *Codex Diplomaticus Aevi Saxonici*. London, 1839–48.
Kendrick, T. and Hawkes, C. F. C. *The Archaeology of England and Wales, 1914–31*. London, 1932.
Kirby, D. P. *The Making of Early England*. London, 1967.
Latham, R. E. *The Revised Medieval Latin Word List*. London, 1965.
Lewis, T. (ed.). 'Copy of *The Black Book of Chirk, Peniarth MS. 29*, National Library of Wales, Aberystwyth', *Zeitschrift für Celtische Philologie* XX, 1936.
Liber Eliensis, ed. E. O. Blake. London, 1962.
Liebermann, F. *Die Gesetze der Angelsachsen*. Halle, 1903–16.
Liversidge, J. *Britain in the Roman Empire*. London, 1968.
Roman Villas in Britain. Cambridge M.Sc. thesis, 1949.
Lloyd, J. E. *A History of Wales*, 2 vols., 3rd ed. London, 1948.
'Welsh Place Names'. *Y Cymmrodor* XII, 1890.
Loyn, H. R. *Anglo-Saxon England and the Norman Conquest*. London, 1962.
Maeyer, R. de. *De Romeinsche Villa's in Belgie*. Antwerp, 1937.
Maitland, F. W. *Domesday Book and Beyond*. Cambridge, 1897; reprinted 1907.
Moore, D. (ed.). *The Land of Dyfed in Early Times*. Cardiff, 1964.
Moore, P. D. 'Human Influence upon Vegetational History in North Cardiganshire', *Nature* CCXVII, 1968.
Moore, P. D. and Chater, E. H. 'The Changing Vegetation of West-Central Wales in the Light of Human History', *Jnl of Ecology* LVII, 1969.
Morris Jones, J. 'The *Surexit* Memorandum', *Y Cymmrodor* XXVIII, 1918.
Myres, J. N. L. *Anglo-Saxon Pottery and the Settlement of England*. Oxford, 1969.
Napier, A. S. and Stevenson, W. H. *The Crawford Collection of Early Charters and Documents*. Oxford, 1895.
Nash-Williams, V. E. 'The Coins found at Caerwent', BBCS IV, 1927–9.
'The Coins found at Caerwent and Caerleon', BBCS II, 1923–5.
The Early Christian Monuments of Wales. Cardiff, 1950.
'The Forum and Basilica and Public Baths of the Roman Town of *Venta Silurum* at Caerwent in Monmouthshire', BBCS XV, 1952–4.

'The Medieval Settlement at Llantwit Major', BBCS xiv, 1950–2.
'The Roman Inscribed and Sculptured Stones found at Caerwent (*Venta Silurum*)', BBCS xv, 1952–4.
'The Roman Villa at Llantwit Major, Glamorgan', *Arch. Camb.* cii, 1953.
(ed.). *A Hundred Years of Welsh Archaeology, Centenary Volume 1846–1946.* Gloucester, N.D.
Norman, E. R. and St Joseph, J. K. *The Development of Early Irish Society: The Evidence of Aerial Photography.* Cambridge, 1969.
Ordnance Survey Map of Roman Britain. 3rd ed. Chessington, 1956.
Orwin, C. S. and C. S. *The Open Fields.* 3rd ed. Oxford, 1967.
Owen, A. (ed.). *Ancient Laws and Institutes of Wales.* 2 vols. London, 1841.
Palmer, A. N. *A History of Ancient Tenures of Land in the Marches of North Wales.* Wrexham, 1885.
Palmer, A. N. and Owen, E. *A History of Ancient Tenures of Land in North Wales and the Marches.* Wrexham, 1911.
Palmer, L. R. *The Interpretation of Mycenaean Greek Texts.* Oxford, 1963.
Mycenaeans and Minoans. London, 1965.
Payne, F. G. 'The Plough in Ancient Britain', *Arch. J.* civ, 1948.
'The Welsh Plough Team to 1600', *Studies in Folk Life*, ed. Jenkins, 1969.
Yr Aradr Gymreig. Cardiff, 1954.
Peate, I. C. *The Welsh House*, 2nd ed. Liverpool, 1944.
Phillimore, E. 'The *Annales Cambriae* and Old-Welsh Genealogies from *Harleian MS* 3859', *Y Cymmrodor* ix, 1888.
Phillips, C. W. 'The Excavation of a Hut-Group at Pant-y-Saer in the Parish of Llanfair-Mathafarn-Eithaf, Anglesey', *Arch. Camb.* lxxxix, 1934.
Pierce, T. Jones, 'Agrarian Aspects of the Tribal System in Medieval Wales', *Géographie et Histoire Agraires, Annales de l'est*, Mémoire no. 21, Nancy, 1959.
'The Gafael in Bangor Manuscript 1939', *Hon. Soc. Cymm.*, 1942.
'Landlords in Wales – The Nobility and Gentry', *The Agrarian History of England and Wales*, iv, ed. Thirsk, 1967.
'The Laws of Wales: the Kindred and the Blood Feud', *University of Birmingham Historical Jnl* ii, 1952.
'Lleyn Ministers' Accounts', BBCS vi 1932.
'Medieval Cardiganshire: A Study in Social Origins', *Ceredigion*, 1959.
'Medieval Settlement in Anglesey', *Anglesey Antiq. Soc.*, 1951.
'A Note on Ancient Welsh Measurements of Land', *Arch. Camb.* xcvii, 1943.
'Pastoral and Agricultural Settlements in Early Wales', *Geografiska Annaler* xliii, 1961.
'Social and Historical Aspects of the Welsh Laws', WHR, *Special Number, The Welsh Laws*, 1963.
Pitt-Rivers, A. L. *Excavations in Cranborne Chase.* London, 1887–1905.
Ralegh Radford, C. A. 'The Early Church in Dyfed', *The Land of Dyfed in Early Times*, ed. Moore, 1964.
Randall, H. J. *The Vale of Glamorgan: Studies in Landscape and History.* Newport, 1961.
Rees, W. *Historical Map of South Wales and the Border in the Fourteenth Century.* Cardiff, 1932.
South Wales and the March 1284–1415. London, 1934.
Richards, M. 'Early Welsh Territorial Suffixes', *Jnl Royal Soc. Antiquaries of Ireland* xcv, 1965.
'Ecclesiastical and Secular in Medieval Welsh Settlement', *Studia Celtica* iii, 1968.
'*Ffridd/Ffrith* as a Welsh Place-Name', *Studia Celtica* ii, 1967.
'*Hafod* and *Hafoty* in Welsh Place-Names', *Montgomery Coll.* lvi, 1959.

'The Irish Settlements in South-West Wales', *Jnl Royal Soc. Antiquaries of Ireland* XC, 1960.

'*Meifod, Lluest, Cynaeafdy* and *Hendre* in Welsh Place Names', *Montgomery Coll.* LVI, 1960.

'Nennius's *Regio Guunnessi*', *Caernarvon Hist. Soc.*, 1963.

'The Significance of *Is* and *Uwch* in Welsh Commote and Cantref Names,' WHR II, 1964.

Welsh Administrative and Territorial Units. Cardiff, 1969.

(ed.). *The Laws of Hywel Dda (The Book of Blegywryd).* Liverpool, 1954.

Richmond, I. A. 'Industry in Roman Britain', *The Civitas Capitals of Roman Britain*, ed. Wacher, 1966.

Roman Britain, 2nd ed. Harmondsworth, 1963.

'Roman Wales', *Prehistoric and Early Wales*, ed. Foster and Daniel, 1965.

(ed.). *Roman and Native in North Britain.* Edinburgh, 1958.

Richter, M. 'Giraldus Cambrensis', *National Library of Wales Jnl* XVI, 1969–70.

Rivet, A. L. F. *Town and Country in Roman Britain.* London, 1958.

(ed.). *The Roman Villa in Britain.* London, 1969.

Roberts, G. M. *Hanes Plwyf Llandybïe.* Cardiff, 1939.

Robertson, A. J. *Anglo-Saxon Charters.* 2nd ed. Cambridge, 1956.

The Laws of the Kings of England from Edmund to Henry I. Cambridge, 1925.

Rostovtzeff, M. *A Social and Economic History of the Roman Empire.* 2nd ed. revised by P. M. Fraser. Oxford, 1957.

Royal Commission on Ancient and Historical Monuments in Wales and Monmouthshire, *Anglesey Inventory*, London, 1937.

Royal Commission on Ancient and Historical Monuments in Wales and Monmouthshire, *Caernarvonshire Inventory*, 3 vols. London, 1956–64.

Royal Commission on Historical Monuments. *A Matter of Time: the Archaeological Survey of the River Gravels.* London, 1960.

Salway, P. *The Frontier People of Roman Britain.* Cambridge, 1965.

Savory, H. N. 'Excavations at Dinas Emrys, Beddgelert (Caern), 1954–6', *Arch. Camb.* CIX, 1960.

'Excavations at Dinorben Hill Fort, Abergele (Denbs.), 1956–7', BBCS XVII, 1958.

Seddon, B. 'Report on the Organic Deposits in the Pool at Dinas Emrys', *Arch. Camb.* CIX, 1960.

Seebohm, F. *Customary Acres and their Historical Importance.* London, 1914.

The English Village Community, 4th ed. London, 1890.

Tribal Custom in Anglo-Saxon Law. London, 1902, 1911.

The Tribal System in Wales, 1st ed., London, 1895; 2nd ed. London, 1904.

Slack, W. J. *The Lordship of Oswestry, 1393–1607.* Shrewsbury, 1951.

Smith, A. H. *English Place-Name Elements.* Cambridge, 1956.

Stamp, L. Dudley (ed.). *The Land of Britain: the Report of the Land Utilisation Survey of Great Britain.* London, 1937.

Stenton, F. M. *Anglo-Saxon England.* Oxford, 1943. Third (posthumous, inadequately revised) ed., 1971.

The Latin Charters of the Anglo-Saxon Period. Oxford, 1955.

Preparatory to Anglo-Saxon England. Collected Papers, ed. D. M. Stenton. Oxford, 1970.

Stevens, C. E. 'Agriculture and Rural Life in the Later Empire', pp. 92–124 in *The Cambridge Economic History of Europe*, I, 2nd ed. Cambridge, 1966.

'A Possible Conflict of Laws in Roman Britain', JRS XXXVII, 1947.

Stevenson, W. H. (ed.) *Early Scholastic Colloquies*, Oxford, 1929.

Sutherland, V. *Coinage and Currency in Roman Britain*. Oxford, 1937.

Tait, J. 'Flintshire in Domesday Book', *Flint Hist. Soc.* XI, 1925.

Thirsk, J. (ed.). *The Agrarian History of England and Wales*, IV, Cambridge, 1967.

Thomas, A. C. (ed.). *Rural Settlement in Roman Britain*. Council for British Archaeology Research Report 7. London, 1966.

Thomas, W. G. and Walker, R. F. 'Excavations at Trelissey, Pembrokeshire, 1950–1', BBCS XVIII, 1958–60.

Two Lives of St Cuthbert, ed. B. Colgrave. Cambridge, 1940.

Varro, M. Terentius. *Res Rusticae*, ed. W. D. Hooper and H. B. Ash. Loeb ed. London, 1960.

Vinogradoff, P. *English Society in the Eleventh Century*. Oxford, 1908.

    The Growth of the Manor. London, 1904; 2nd ed. 1911.

Vinogradoff, P. and Morgan, F. (eds.). *Survey of the Honour of Denbigh, 1334*, B. Acad. Records of Social and Economic History, I, London, 1914.

Wacher, J. S. (ed.). *The Civitas Capitals of Roman Britain*. Leicester, 1966.

Wade-Evans, A. W. 'The Llancarfan Charters', *Arch. Camb.* LXXXVII, 1932.

    'Parochiale Wallicanum', *Y Cymmrodor* XXI, 1908.

    'Peniarth MS 37', *Y Cymmrodor* XVII, 1904.

Wade-Evans, A. W. (ed.). *Vitae Sanctorum Britanniae et Genealogiae*. Cardiff, 1944.

Wade-Evans, A. W. (ed.). *Welsh Medieval Law*. Oxford, 1909.

Ward, J. *The Roman Era in Britain*. London, 1911.

White, K. D. *Agricultural Implements of the Roman World*. Cambridge, 1967.

Whitelock, D. (ed.). *Anglo-Saxon Wills*. Cambridge, 1930.

Wiliam, A. R. (ed.). *Llyfr Iorwerth*. Cardiff, 1960.

Williams, G. *The Welsh Church from Conquest to Reformation*. Cardiff, 1962.

    (ed.). WHR, *Special Number, The Welsh Laws*, 1963.

Williams, H. (ed.). *Gildas De Excidio Britanniae*, Cymmrodorion Record Series, III, London, 1899.

Williams, I. 'Glosau Rhydychen', BBCS V, 1929–31.

    Lectures on Early Welsh Poetry. Dublin, 1944.

    'Moliant Dinbych Penfro', *Hon. Soc. Cymm.*, 1940.

    'The Poems of Llywarch Hen', *B. Acad.* XVIII, 1932.

    'Tri Englyn y Juvencus', BBCS VI, 1931–3.

    (ed.). *Canu Llywarch Hen*. Cardiff, 1955.

Williams, J. E. Caerwyn (ed.). *The Poems of Taliesin*. Dublin, 1968.

Williams, S. J. and Powell, J. E. (eds.). *Llyfr Blegywryd*. Cardiff, 1961.

INDEX

A-S = Anglo-Saxon   EIA = Early Iron Age   IA = Iron Age
R-B = Romano-British   R-S = Romano-Saxon
The alphabetical order of entries is on the 'letter by letter' system.